БУХАЦЫ

р. ЕИКЪ

КАМЫ ꙗ

КГУҐ КѠБЫ

ꙊРꙖЛЮГ КОБЫ

Р. ВОЛГА

БАШКИРЦЫ

р. ТОБО

Р. ТЕ ЧА

мїꙗ

Р. СИНАРА

р. Рѡ ЮХ ц

БѸА

Адама

мꙗ тѡ

Р. КАМА

Р. ИСГ ТЬ

Г. КАЗА

покровъ

Г. ТЮМЕНЬ Р. ИРѢ

КАМꙖ

ЗАПА

Р. тꙋра

ка мское

ГРА ТОБОЛЕСКЪ

Р тавда

Г. ВЕРХО ТꙊРЬꙖ

ПЕРМЬ

СꙊРГꙊТъ

деманко

ТꙊСКꙊ КАМЕНЬ

Р. СѠБА

Р. ДВИ на

Г. КОМО горь

ам самаꙗ росꙗнꙟ

таваꙟ

Р Река

пелымъ

Г. АРХАН

ꙗскѡ

БИСКАꙗ ПОВЕХО

ИРТЫШЬ

м коре ре ꙗ скꙟ

косꙗой

Р. ѠБЬ

БЕРЕЗОВъ

м. СОЛОВЕЦ коꙟ

МОРЕ

печеркꙟ

ПОМО РѢЕ

р. колскоꙟ

ЛОПАРИ

ꙗ ЗЕМЛꙗ Галав ꙟ

RUSSIA'S CONQUEST OF SIBERIA

Тогда Московсшии людие и казацы, Божиею милостию . . . богатства себе приобретають множества, оть торгу мягкия рухляди, и пребывающе вь радости и вь веселии, благодаряще всемогущаго Бога, что дарова Богь Государю такую благодатную землю.

Летопись Строганова

Then through God's grace the Muscovites and the cossacks . . . became very wealthy from trading in furs, and they lived in joy and happiness, thanking Almighty God for having given the Sovereign such rich land.

Stroganov Chronicle

RUSSIA·S

TO SIBERIA AND

CONQUEST

RUSSIAN AMERICA

OF SIBERIA

THREE CENTURIES OF
RUSSIAN EASTWARD EXPANSION

1558 - 1700

VOLUME ONE
A DOCUMENTARY RECORD

EDITED AND TRANSLATED BY
BASIL DMYTRYSHYN
E.A.P. CROWNHART-VAUGHAN
THOMAS VAUGHAN

WESTERN IMPRINTS
THE PRESS OF THE OREGON
HISTORICAL SOCIETY
1985

Endpapers: Remezov's 1667 manuscript map of Siberia. Contrary to modern rendering, north and south are reversed on this map.

The preparation of this volume was made possible in part by a grant from the Translations Program of the National Endowment for the Humanities, an independent federal agency.

This volume was designed and produced by Western Imprints, The Press of the Oregon Historical Society.

The paper used in this publication meets the minimum requirements of American National Standard for Information Sciences—Permanence of Paper for Printed Library Materials, ANSI Z39.48-1984.

Library of Congress Cataloging in Publication Data
Main entry under title:
Russia's conquest of Siberia, 1558–1700.
  (To Siberia and Russian America; v. 1) (North Pacific studies series; no. 9)
  Translated from Russian.
  Bibliography: p.
  1. Siberia (R.S.F.S.R. and Kazakh S.S.R.)—Discovery and exploration—Sources. 2. Soviet Union—Territorial expansion— Sources. I. Dmytryshyn, Basil, 1925– . II. Crownhart-Vaughan, E.A.P. 1929– . III. Vaughan, Thomas. 1924– . IV. Series. V. Series: North Pacific studies; no. 9.
DK43.T6 vol. 1 [DK753]   947 s [957'.07]   84-29080
ISBN 0-87595-148-1 (Alk. paper)

Main entry under title:
To Siberia and Russian America.
  (North Pacific studies series; no. 9–11)
  Translated from Russian.
  Bibliography: v. 1, p.
  Contents: v. 1. Russia's conquest of Siberia, 1558–1700.
  1. Soviet Union—Territorial expansion—Sources. 2. Siberia (R.S.F.S.R. and Kazakh S.S.R.)— Discovery and exploration—Russian—Sources. 3. America—Discovery and exploration—Russian—Sources. I. Dmytryshyn, Basil. 1925– . II. Crownhart-Vaughan, E.A.P. 1929– III. Vaughan, Thomas. 1924– . IV. Series: North Pacific studies; no. 9, etc.
DK43.T6   947   84-29079
ISBN 0-87595-147-3 (set) (Alk. paper)

Printed in the United States of America.

NORTH PACIFIC STUDIES SERIES

CONTENTS

vitors in Iakutsk and Okhotsk ostrogs for defense against natives and the Chinese.

ILLUSTRATIONS

FOREWORD

The Oregon Historical Society's far-seeing members, in their small nineteenth century congregation, early perceived our on-going association with the Russian Far East Maritime Provinces as well as with Korea, Japan, and China. Some, in fact, traded there, as, for example, suppliers of huge bridge timbers to the Trans-Siberian Railroad then under construction, of new iron work, lumber, food, and other necessities.

It was obvious too that these Siberian undertakings and commercial relationships were often episodic and sometimes eccentric. Few persons knew the Russian Maritime Provinces firsthand let alone the limitless interior fanning west toward Moscow and Europe. The collection of materials relating to the Pacific voyages gathered in the Oregon Historical Society by Messrs. Charles Fenton, Charles Carey, Charles Holman, Burt Barker, Elliott Ruggles Corbett, Henry Corbett, and George Himes defined our early interests; but even here there was no real knowledge of exploration of Siberia nor of its immensity as an emotional as well as a physical fact.

Details of the swift and emphatic conquest of the vast reaches of Siberia were then and are now scarce. There was little awareness of extensive Russian colonial designs for the long west coast of North America, including the Columbia River area. Scholars as well as the public have been deprived of this fundamental information, facts necessary to understand European Russian as well as Siberian affairs. This also holds for Chinese history, especially the early Russian contact phases. This world-wide information gap poses serious problems to ranks of new countries and their leaders. A better knowledge of historical developments is imperative to our daily considerations of this immense international theater. The great and basic Russian thrust has long been entwined with our own regional preoccupations and designs, with American dreams and notions about the North Pacific arena, its countless embayments, islands, and strategic continental shores.

While the Oregon Historical Society's collections of a generation ago were estimable, they were in no way as rich as the vast treasures held today. Then, as now, one could savor the books and pamphlets, the broadsides, the charts, and the drawings. One could sometimes see what our earliest collectors and preservationists were striving for as they approached the twentieth century. Only now, in reflection, one can appreciate the true value of their endeavors to our own generation.

Among their rare gifts I first encountered the earliest English-language publications concerning Russian expansion east out of Europe, across the Urals and the Siberian vastness—east toward the rising sun and the "quiet ocean," our Pacific. As obscure Russian documentary materials came to hand, English translation of such definitive sources became an immensely challenging, even an imperative, objective of our learned society. We believe this major three-volume publication, in the North Pacific Study Series, so tenaciously and tirelessly unraveled by our editors, has substantially narrowed this knowledge gap with a fascinating mass of documentation and interpretation gathered to illuminate the Siberian-North Pacific story.

These publications follow, while greatly expanding upon, the wishes of our Society leaders of a century ago who stated that we must gather and diffuse knowledge concerning the Pacific Rim, that we might know and better understand the obscure events of the North Pacific and the real story of our neighbors there.

Thomas Vaughan
General Editor
North Pacific Studies Series

PREFACE

Four hundred years ago a raiding band of Russian cossacks led by Ermak Timofeev and provisioned by the ambitious Stroganov merchant family crossed the Urals into Siberia. In 1581 they defeated the tribesmen of Kuchum, the Tatar khan of Siberia, imposed tribute on the natives and laid Russian claim to these lands. By the middle of the seventeenth century smaller bands of pillagers had overrun all of northern Asia, navigated the vast riverine systems of the east, sailed through the Bering Straits and traced the shores of the Arctic and the Siberian coast of the Pacific Ocean.

This great feat, which succeeding generations of Russians glorified in songs, tales, paintings, films, literature and scholarly works, resulted in three far-reaching developments. First, it brought under Moscow's control boundless lands rich in natural resources, inhabited by scattered tribes of diverse cultures. Second, this addition transformed the hitherto East European, predominantly Orthodox Slavic realm of Muscovy into the powerful multinational and multicultural Eurasian colonial empire of Russia. Centuries of clash and campaign impregnated and fused the rich Russian and Asian cultures. Finally, from the beginning to our own time, the Russians used each outpost won as a base from which to launch new explorations, make new contacts, and undertake new penetrations and conquests.

In the seventeenth century the Muscovites established a fitful dialogue with the Chinese in remote Peking. On the far Pacific shore in the eighteenth and early nineteenth centuries, they explored and laid claim to the fogbound Kurils, the coastal waters of northern Japan, the Aleutians and parts of Alaska, the Pacific Northwest, northern California and Hawaii. They accomplished

xxix

all this while seemingly preoccupied with age-old European, Black Sea and Baltic affairs. In the second half of the nineteenth century they conquered Central Asia, the huge Amur basin and Sakhalin Island. In the twentieth century the increasingly disciplined military troops fought to dominate Korea, Manchuria and Mongolia. The Russian drive to the Pacific frontier was a momentous event of historic, economic, political, cultural and geopolitical consequences, so vast the implications are as yet not fully perceived. This is in part, of course, because the drama continues.

Our purpose in this volume is first to assess rare and fugitive source materials which together reveal Russia's empire-building process from the Urals to the Pacific, 1558–1700. Second, to make most of these obscure sources available to the English-speaking world for the first time. And third, to intensify Western scholarly interest and understanding in this little known and dynamic imperative of Russian history. It is brilliant and epochal in the making, cruel and colorful, not always humane and not always successful.

Knowledge and understanding of this purposeful sweep and the fashioning of countless procedures now lodged in the Russian psyche, and these several well-practiced, centuries-old gambits and systems are basic to our real perception of twentieth century designs and intentions. These documents should be fully absorbed by leaders of Western thought and geopolitical action and by third-world leaders who must better estimate, as well, present-day Chinese thinking, so long entwined with Russian expansionist dreams and political procedures.

This study is Volume I in a three-volume series entitled *To Siberia and Russian America: Three Centuries of Russian Eastward Expansion, 1558–1867*. The second volume, *Russian Penetration of the North Pacific Ocean, 1700–1799*, will cover Russian exploration in the North Pacific and will include the conquest of Kamchatka, the incredibly ambitious projects of the two Bering expeditions, and accounts, both official and private, of many of the fur and exploring expeditions to the Aleutians and to Alaska in the second half of the century. The third volume, *The Russian American Colonies, 1799–1867*, concentrates on Russian America and embraces wide-ranging correspondence, reports, official documents and private memoirs. Hitherto imperfectly perceived Russian activities in Alaska, the Pacific Northwest, California and Hawaii are included.

In this present collection we have used materials from many sources: annals; chronicles; government decrees; instructions from the Tsar to special envoys and administrators of conquered regions; reports from these officials to Moscow; instructions and directives from colonial administrators to their subordinates; reports from those subordinates; travel accounts; inventories of tribute collections; descriptions of routes and regions; resources of newly won areas; accounts of bloody encounters between Russians and indigenous populations; harrowing accounts of the plight of Russian personnel in isolated outposts; petitions from low-ranking Russian officials to colonial administrators or to authorities in Moscow; grievances from Russians against the brutality of their superiors or the corruption of their own comrades; piteous complaints from natives about heinous crimes, ruinous assessments of tribute and extortion; compacts between Russian colonial officials and native chieftains; texts of the oaths of allegiance to the Tsar taken by native leaders; accounts of Russo-Chinese military and diplomatic encounters; and perceptive observations on life in the newly conquered region.

The originals of these and most other sources concerning Russian expansion to the Pacific frontier are currently held in widely dispersed archives in the USSR, difficult of access even to Soviet scholars. Fortunately, since the middle of the eighteenth century a number of documents pertaining to Siberia have been published, but in limited and rare Russian editions. These include: *Polnoe sobranie zakonov rossiiskoi imperii s 1649 goda* (First Series, 1649–1825), 44 volumes, St. Petersburg, 1830; *Akty istoricheskie sobrannye i izdannye arkheograficheskoiu kommissieiu*, 5 volumes, St. Petersburg, 1841–42; *Dopolneniia k aktam istoricheskim*, 12 volumes, St. Petersburg, 1846–72; A. A. Titov, ed., *Sibir v XVII veke: Sbornik starinnykh statei o Sibiri i prilezhashchikh k nei zemliam*, Moscow, 1890; I. P. Kuznetsov-Krasnoiarskii ed., *Istoricheskie akty XVII stoletiia, 1633–1699: Materialy dlia istorii Sibiri*, 2 volumes, Tomsk, 1890–97; G. I. Spaskii, ed., *Letopis sibirskaia*, St. Petersburg, 1821; G. F. Müller, *Istoriia Sibiri*, 2 volumes, Moscow, 1937; N. S. Orlova, ed., *Otkrytiia russkikh zemleprokhodtsev i poliarnykh morekhodov XVII veka: Sbornik documentov*, Moscow,

1951; G. N. Rumiantsev and S. B. Okun, eds., *Sbornik dokumentov po istorii Buriati: XVII vek*, Ulan Ude, 1960; N. S. Demidova and Ia. P. Miasnikov, eds., *Pervye russkie diplomaty v Kitae*, Moscow, 1966; *Russko-kitaiskie otnosheniia v XVII veke: Dokumenty i materialy (1608–1691)*, 2 volumes, Moscow, 1969–72; S. A. Tokarev, ed., *Materialy po istorii Iakutii XVII veka (Dokumenty iasachnogo sbora)*, 3 volumes, Moscow, 1970; M. I. Golman and G. I. Slesarchuk, eds., *Materialy po istorii russko-mongolskikh otnoshenii, 1636–1654*, Moscow, 1974; and V. A. Divin, eds., *Russkaia tikhookeanskaia epopeia*, Khabarovsk, 1979.

A number of persons in this country and abroad have generously aided us in obtaining materials or have been helpful in providing definitions for words and terms no longer used. We particularly wish to thank: Robert V. Allen of the Library of Congress; the Right Reverend Gregory, Bishop of Sitka and Alaska; the Honorable Victor Atiyeh, Governor of Oregon; Colonel M. J. Poniatowski-d'Ermengard and the late Ivan L. Best, Portland, Oregon; George Sabo, Elberon, New Jersey; Raymond H. Fisher, Los Angeles; James R. Gibson, York University, Toronto; Patricia Polansky, Honolulu; Elisabeth Tokoi, National Library, Helsinki; Helen Wallis, Keeper of the Maps, British Library; Dr. Susan Mango, Washington, D.C.; John D. Taylor, St. Paul, Minnesota; Acad. Iu. V. Bromley and Nikolai N. Bolkhovitinov, Moscow. We are grateful to many institutions in the Soviet Union: the Library of the Academy of Sciences, Leningrad; Saltykov-Shchedrin State Public Library, Leningrad; Lenin Library, Moscow; State Public Scientific Library of the Academy of Sciences, Siberian Section, Novosibirsk; Institute of Ethnography of the Academy of Sciences, Moscow and Leningrad; the Geographical Society of the USSR; and Zhdanov State University Library, Irkutsk.

None of this work would have been possible without the foresight and work of the Oregon Historical Society, which in 1968 established the Irkutsk Archival Research Group and has since supported research in the important field of Russian eastward expansion to the Pacific frontier and Russian-American North Pacific relations. The extensive collections of the Society are the backbone of this and the succeeding two volumes. This important research group was first headed by John Youell; Samuel S. Johnson succeeded him; the present chairman is Jane West Youell. James B. Thayer is chairman of the OHS Publications Committee.

The design and production of this series is the work of Bruce Taylor Hamilton, OHS Assistant Director—Publications, and the Western Imprints staff: Krisell M. Buxton, Colleen Compton-Campbell and Stephanie A. Smith.

To all, we extend our warmest thanks and gratitude.

Basil Dmytryshyn
E. A. P. Crownhart-Vaughan
Thomas Vaughan

Top left: Mounted cossack trooper. Top right: Tungus hunter.
Lower left: Kirgiz warrior. Lower right: Kalmyk warrior. All late
eighteenth-century engravings.

INTRODUCTION

Between 1580 and 1650 small bands of cossacks and other adventurers driven by wanderlust, desperation, ambition, restlessness and greed penetrated Siberia and brought under Moscow's control all of northern Asia from the Ural Mountains to the Pacific Ocean. This great exploit was accomplished by the skillful utilization of the vast navigable river systems which became interior highways; the invaders' stamina, drive and determination to survive; their lust for riches—gold, silver, hardstones, ivory and most of all "soft gold" or furs; their technical knowledge and weapons, which gave them great superiority over the natives they encountered; their canny use of natives as guides, interpreters and providers of transport; the scarcity of significant organized native resistance, and the existence of disunity and often intertribal enmity among the indigenous natives.

Russia's conquest of northern Asia was an event of momentous historic, economic, political, cultural and geopolitical consequence. It brought under Muscovite control a vast territory rich in resources inhabited by primitive tribes of diverse cultures. The conquest transformed the hitherto East European, Orthodox, Slavic, Muscovite state into a powerful multinational and multicultural Eurasian colonial empire belonging to Russia. The process cross fertilized Russian and Asian culture. From the initial trans-Ural foray to the present time, the conquest has provided the Russians bases from which to launch new explorations, new conquests and new contacts.

Ironically, while this colonial adventure produced many far reaching developments, continues to exert powerful influence, and has obvious implications for the future, Russian expansion to the Pacific frontier has to date generated only marginal interest among western scholars, not to mention Russian historians generally. The Russians have been more apt to commemorate this adventure in song, legend, art and folk history, with a far from exhaustive scholarly literature of diverse interpretations. Some Russian scholars view the expansion process as a "civilizing and christianizing enterprise." Others consider it "the gathering of the Russian lands." Still others see it as "the urge to the sea." A few view it as pure colonialism and imperialism not unlike that experienced by other contemporary European powers. And finally, some Soviet scholars regard it either as "a rapprochement (*sblizhenie*) between Russian and non-Russian peoples of northern Asia" or as "a complex process of annexation (*prisoedinenie*) and assimilation (*osvoenie*)." This interpretive literature grows as new source materials are slowly made available.

Each of these views holds interest, but none is entirely satisfactory. Russian expansion across northern Asia to the Pacific frontier cannot be reduced to a single formula. It would be misleading and inappropriate to try. It was not a meticulously planned undertaking, carefully carried out. It did not operate in accordance with a grand design or specific timetable. Like contemporary Spanish, Portuguese, English, French and Dutch expansions, the Russian drive was a convulsive process propelled by many pressures and forces that varied in purpose, skill, intensity and duration. Heroes and villains, triumphs and disasters were produced, as well as successes and bitter failures and some startling and wholly unforeseen results. Some persons rose from rags to reputation, while others faded into ignominious beggary and oblivion. It was a massive and complex process whose infinite ramifications are not yet fully comprehended because they remain unfinished.

MOTIVES, DIRECTION AND PARTICIPANTS IN RUSSIAN EXPANSION TO THE PACIFIC FRONTIER

Russia began her eastward expansion across northern Asia to the Pacific frontier in the sixteenth century. One body of scholarly opinion contends that this expansion began in the Kievan period of Russian history, ca. 900 to 1200 A.D. We find no concrete evidence to substantiate this. There was at that time no political entity called "Russia." Kievan Rus was composed of a loose confederation of self-governing eastern Slavic principalities. The economic and cultural activity of these principalities hugged the Varangian road ranging from Scandinavia south to Byzantium along the Volkhov, Dnieper and Don rivers and their tributaries. This was the lifeline of Kievan Rus. The few written records from the Kievan period contain some references to sporadic clashes between the principalities of Riazan and Suzdal and their non-Slavic neighbors to the east, the nomadic Khazars, the Volga Bulgars and the Mordva.

These references, however, provide insufficient evidence that there was a planned eastward expansion with the purpose of securing permanent control of land inhabited by others or to reduce border tensions. Recorded eastward drives that occurred in Kievan times had no such intent. Temporary incursions and forays for the manly purposes of plunder or retaliation, these drives were few and localized. Neither of themselves nor considered together do they reveal any clear pattern or design. Finally, all of these eastward forays came to a dramatic end about 1240 when the thundering Mongol horsemen enslaved most of Eastern Europe.

The succeeding two centuries under the Mongol yoke limited eastward movement of the survivors to three activities: frequent homage trips by secular and ecclesiastical leaders to various power centers of the Mongol Empire; regular dispatch of Rus recruits to serve in Mongol armies; and temporary or permanent assignment of Rus craftsmen and artisans in the Mongol Empire. The only exceptions to Mongol control of eastward movement were the northerly trade contacts merchants from the republic of Great Novgorod developed with various tribes of the sub-polar region between the Gulf of Finland and the Ural Mountains. These influential contacts, however, never developed the characteristics of a permanent or conscious territorial expansion or aggrandizement.

The Mongol conquest was a bitter, crushing experience for all peoples in the Rus principalities, but it was not sterile. Many Rus leaders, particularly the Grand Dukes of Moscow who were initially subservient to Mongol authority, found opportunities to acquire knowledge about the Mongol Empire—its strength, weakness, customs, habits and varied cultural practices. Around 1330 they implemented this valuable knowledge as they consolidated a position of their own and increased their military capability. At the same time they exploited enmities among quarreling factions of the rapidly disintegrating Golden Horde, the once powerful western wing of the Mongol Empire. And eventually they lured prominent Mongol and Tatar leaders and their followers into Muscovite service as the Horde had once used their talents and energies. With Mongol aid, Moscow's will, in the person of Grand Duke Ivan Kalita (subsequently Ivan I, "Moneybags," a former tribute collector for the Mongols), was now imposed on many Rus principalities including Novgorod.

As these principalities were slowly absorbed by this grand dukedom, Muscovy emerged as a major force in eastern Europe, cautious but determined to thwart Mongol rule. The process was faltering and laborious. Even then any one of the seven principal khanates of the Horde could rampage, and havoc was frequent. The seven declining but still rapacious khanates were: Kazan, at the junction of the Volga and Kama rivers; the Crimea; the Great Horde, on the lower Volga, with headquarters in Astrakhan; the Nogai on the lower Ural River; Sibir, at the confluence of the Irtysh and Tobol rivers; Kazakh, north of the Aral Sea; and Uzbek, near Lake Balkash. But in spite of their strategic locations and warring dispositions, or because of this, the Horde could not unite. With the breakup of the khanates, a powerful Muscovy, now strategically placed in the geographical process, came to the fore. In 1480 the unstable equilibrium shifted irretrievably in Moscow's favor, terminating the Mongol conquest.

Breaking the Mongol grip was a decisive move, but Moscow lacked power to drive toward the Urals still screened by remnants of the Horde. Moscow leaders continued to respect and fear certain khanates of the once supreme Mongols, but for the next three generations they were engaged with equally rapacious European neighbors, Sweden, Poland, Lithuania (for an outlet to the Baltic), and southerly the Ottoman Empire (for access to the Black Sea). In the middle of the sixteenth century certain pressures lessened and Tsar Ivan IV (the Terrible) was able to redirect Moscow's priorities. He conquered in succession the khanate of Kazan in 1552 and the town of Astrakhan in 1556. These demanding campaigns were supported by defensive considerations, religious ardor, Moscow's military self-assurance, the Tsar's search for new revenues to support the government, and by pressures from new private entrepreneurial interests. Each contributed to the base which maintained Muscovy's eastward expansion.

The new conquests exploited the power vacuum created along Muscovy's indeterminate eastern and southeastern frontiers. Opportunities opened the rich basins of the Kama and Volga rivers to Muscovite colonizations. This afforded Muscovy direct access to the virgin markets of Siberia, Central Asia and the Caucasus. Moreover, the conquest of Kazan and Astrakhan made a deep impression on Muscovy's non-Slavic eastern neighbors, the less powerful of whom soon expressed readiness, if not eagerness, to become Muscovite subjects. So Muscovy became the principal heir to the legacy of the Mongol Empire. Further, Muscovy's swift occupation of the Volga River route provided a shortcut and better access to sources of desirable Oriental goods. This commercial breakthrough soon attracted European traders and adventurers who, eager to gain favors from the Tsar and his immediate advisors, resorted to bribery, deceit, fraud and every other possible device. A few Western Europeans shocked Moscow authorities when in their effort to find the northeast passage to the Orient they sailed along the Arctic coast beyond the Urals.

But the immediate beneficiaries of Muscovy's acquisition of the Volga and Kama rivers basins were Russian merchants, the family of Anika Stroganov. In 1558 the Stroganovs secured a long term tax-free lease from the government on an immense region in Perm and later along the Kama River and some of its tributaries. Their economic operations combined with their exploitation of the indigenous natives brought them into conflict with a descendent of Genghis Khan—Kuchum Khan of Siberia. His claim of overlordship was threatened by the boldness of the audacious cossacks attracted to the Stroganovs' schemes. In 1581 this hardened band of cossacks under the leadership of the *ataman* Ermak Timofeev crossed the Urals. They defeated the forces of Kuchum Khan and imposed tribute obligations on the natives. The cossacks suffered heavy losses, including their leader Ermak, but Muscovy's claim was laid to these territories. The Stroganov ventures were profitable beyond wildest expectations, and the government was immediately responsive. Strong links were forged between successful private enterprises and national interests. These interests were sometimes at odds, but for the most part they meshed not only in the long Russian drive across northern Asia but also along the North Pacific islands and into the North American littoral. This cooperation was forged by the incessant demands of conquest and survival far beyond the horizon; and it was mandated too by the strictures of the socio-political system of the Russian state.

From beginning to end, Moscovy's drive to the Urals, then across Siberia to the Pacific frontier, was essentially water-borne along the great rivers. Between 1585 and 1605 the Russians moved through the lower systems of the north-flowing Ob and Irtysh. By 1628 they had explored the snaking Enisei and its main tributaries, the Lower, Stony and Upper Tunguska rivers. In the 1630s they navigated the length of the Lena and its principal tributaries. In the 1640s they sailed and poled the length of the swift Amur, the Indigirka, Kolyma and Anadyr rivers. Between 1638 and 1650 they penetrated the broken maze of the Baikal taiga.

As they plied the rivers and blazed across portages, the conquerors built *ostrozheks* (small forts) and *ostrogs* (large forts) at strategic locations: Tiumen in 1586, Tobolsk in 1587, Berezovo and Pelym in 1593, Surgut and Tara in 1594, Obdorsk and Narym in 1595, Verkhotur'e in 1598. They reached Mangazeia in 1601, Tomsk in 1604, Kuznetsk in 1618, Eniseisk in 1619, Krasnoiarsk in 1627, Bratsk in 1631, Iakutsk in 1632, Okhotsk in 1649, Irkutsk in 1652 and Nerchinsk in 1653. As the routes lengthened and the legends in Moscow grew, they supplemented these and other forts, which served as headquarters and district control centers, with a network of *zimov'es* (winter shelters) erected at key points for localized observations and *iasak* collection, the basic fur tribute which motivated the entire venture.

Russian conquest of northern Asia and the subjugation of its diverse indigenous peoples was the effort of several distinct groups of explorer-conquerors whom Russian scholars refer to as *zemleprokhodtsy* (land travelers). In order of their importance these included: (1) state employees such as colonial officials, *streltsy* (musketeers) and the cossacks who spearheaded the conquest and protected state personnages (Contemporary sources identify some of these men as *sluzhashchie liudi*. We have translated this term throughout as *servitors*.); (2) *promyshlenniks*, or private trappers and traders who came to the region in search of fortunes but also assisted state employees to gain control over the natives through trade, threats, extortion, theft and tribute; (3) state peasants, craftsmen and ecclesiastical personnel whom the government sent to various outposts to assist Russian colonial officials; (4) *guliashchie liudi* (wanderers), classless runaway serfs and footloose social outcasts and unfortunates who sought escape in the virgin lands and were willing to join in on any assignment; (5) prisoners from the European wars, referred to under the general heading of

Litva, which included Poles, Lithuanians, Ukrainians, Swedes, Belorussians and Europeans, all of whom might be sent to the distant regions by Muscovite authorities to get them out of the way; (6) petty merchants and persons serving as agents of influential Moscow merchants, who went east for their own purposes to seek fortunes or on temporary assignments for their employers; (7) increasing numbers of Russian political exiles and religious dissenters whom colonial officials routinely utilized in every phase of conquest and defense; and (8) displaced natives who served voluntarily or otherwise as guides and interpreters, or who joined the Russians in their conquest to gain group protection or other basic advantages. Whatever the background or future of all these groups, if they did survive the march to the harsh and remote regions, newcomers often became greedy for wealth and adventure. Some became heroes, some beasts, some both; but seldom for long.

Strong leaders emerged from these small diverse groups. In 1581 Ermak Timofeev initiated Russia's march across the Urals toward the Pacific; Fedor Diakov founded Mangazeia in 1601, later the base from which Russians subdued the Samoeds, Ostiaks and Tungus; Petr Beketov founded Iakutsk in 1632, helped conquer the fierce Iakut natives and sent expeditions prowling into the distant Amur basin; in 1638 Posnik Ivanov reached the Indigirka River and subdued the Iukagirs; Ivan Moskvitin became the first Russian to reach the shores of the Sea of Okhotsk in 1643; Vasilii Poiarkov navigated the 2,700 miles of the mighty Amur in 1643; Erofei Khabarov led two expeditions into the potentially productive Amur basin between 1649 and 1653; Semen Dezhnev was the first recorded person to sail from the Kolyma River mouth in the Arctic around the Chukhotsk Peninsula to the Pacific Ocean; Vladimir Atlasov is remembered as the conqueror of spiny Kamchatka.

Most of the explorer-conquerors were illiterate and unschooled. Some were low criminals and cruel by any standard. But all were audacious men, driven by ambition, sheer nerve and energy more than political design. They were the first Europeans to navigate all the major rivers of northern Asia and to reach the Arctic Ocean. They were the first to encounter unknown species of animals, fish and plants in which these regions abounded; the first to observe the indigenous natives and to provide first-contact ethnographic descriptions of their appearance, customs and habits. So also did they reduce many species of fur-bearing animals to near extinction, while equally depleting numerous native tribes who refused to trap for them. And they established, through calculated terrorism, slavery, exploitation and cunning, a recognized European colonial empire even today comprising a huge part of the Asian content.

Among the truly impressive aspects of Russia's conquest of that physical immensity is the speed with which this handful of willful men accomplished it. Their astonishing feats may be explained by the existence of large riverine systems that once discovered aided coverage of great distances in a relatively short time; the absence of any significant organized native resistance on a sustained basis; disunity among the natives, weakened by their primitive methods as opposed to the knowledge and technological superiority of the Russians; a network of strong, simple fortifications which withstood native attack; cunning utilization of native guides and interpreters who were familiar with local and regional geography, tribes, languages and customs; the momentum of constant success; and their ambition, guile, cruelty, greed, resourcefulness and manly determination. These factors were augmented by a series of natural leaders.

A significant circumstance in the Russian drive to the Pacific frontier was the creation of a group of power vacuums in the entire region, born of sparse populations—a vexatious problem perhaps exacerbated today. The Russians moved through the Siberian wilderness with fitful opposition because the area was sparsely inhabited by scattered groups of technologically and politically primitive people who could devise few obstacles to their sinuous advance. The constant drive was an insatiable and newly rich European market demanding the abundance of Siberia's luxuriant fur-bearing animals whose alluring pelts equalled gold in value—"soft gold." Some adventurers were drawn by age old rumors of rich deposits of gold, silver, precious stones, tusk ivory, even copper, iron and salt. A few were tempted by the availability of mastodon ivory! Each nursed that natural hope to quickly gain princely fortune, to reap bountiful riches worth any exertion. And always, a surprising number fled deep into the taiga to escape serfdom and oppression in Russia. Some moved to the frontier edge to slip the boring and monotonous life they had lived in the primitive ostrogs left behind. Others, in favor or disfavor, went east by order of the Tsar or his officials. Some went in search of food supplies while others hoped to slake their craving for women by pillaging the tribes. Finally, a primal force motivating some Russian conquerors bringing European light into the Siberian depths was imperialism, a desire to bring the region and its peoples forever under Moscow's control. Those who harbored this dream believed that their deeds and actions enhanced the power and wealth of the Tsar and thus their own, while preventing other merchants and powers from acquiring access to the rich virgin regions. There is no hard evidence as yet that any Russian entered the new lands to improve life or conditions for the natives.

Russian acquisition of an enormous, albeit cold and foreboding, colony in Northern Asia, was similar in many ways to the process through which Portugal, Spain, England, Holland and France built their colonial empires at about the same time at various points along the coasts of West Africa, India and China, in the Western Hemisphere and in the Philippines. In the Russian and in all West European instances the empire-building effort was the work of a handful of determined opportunists. As a rule they appeared like a thunderbolt from the blue, seized native hostages, imposed the payment of tribute on the startled indigenous population, and, in the name of their respective sovereigns, laid claims to territories. All sovereigns approved these actions and immediately sent fresh military reinforcements to the newly acquired region. In due time they also dispatched administrators, clergy and other support personnel (including even some undesirables) to help transform "the accidental discovery" into a permanent possession. And all colonial powers of Europe, whether Spain or Russia, exploited the resources of the newly gained area and, because they had superior weapons, know-how and technology, they crushed all native attempts to dislodge them.

But while there were many similarities between Russian and West European colonial ventures, there also were several fundamental differences. The most obvious was the direction. West European nations built their colonial empires by sailing either south or west across the Atlantic. The Russians, in contrast, went overland across the Ural Mountains to the east. Immediately and in the long run this meant that West European powers had to rely on naval strength to protect and maintain their colonies; the Russians relied primarily on land forces, which they stationed at strategically built forts. Another difference centered in the products and resources each colony provided its new master. West European countries, for example, received from their colonies gold, silver, precious stones, herbs, spices and various subtropical and tropical products. Siberia supplied the Russians primarily furs and later walrus tusks, gold and silver.

The final and, in many ways, the principal difference between West European and Russian colonial ventures was the fact that the Russians enjoyed a total monopoly in their march across Siberia. They had no rivals or competitors. The only opposition they encountered in their drive to the Pacific and to their hegemony in Asia was from the Chinese. The absence of formidable opposition or competition, therefore, made Russian conquest permanent. In contrast, West European colonial ventures were characterized by prolonged, costly and bitter struggles for supremacy between Spain and Portugal, Spain and England, England and Holland, and England and France. These struggles produced three significant long-term results. First, they prevented any single West European nation from maintaining monopoly power in any given area for a very long time. Second, they weakened each colonial power and eventually contributed to their demise as a colonial power. And, finally, these struggles enabled former colonies, often with the aid of the competing colonial powers, to establish an independent existence. Because it enjoyed the sole monopoly, the Russian colonial empire was immune to this process.

THE ADMINISTRATIVE STRUCTURE

In theory the Tsar of Russia was lord and master of the Siberian colony stretching from the Urals to the Pacific. The entire conquest, with the exception of Ermak's initial foray, was undertaken in the Tsar's name or on his orders. The conquered areas were administered by his appointees, and the indigenous survivors were forced to take the oath of allegiance to him. Tribute which colonial officials collected from the natives and the tithe which Russian merchants and hunters paid was sent directly to the Tsar's Treasury. All contemporary official documents refer to the Siberian colony as the Tsar's patrimony (*votchina*). No major policy, event or action developed there without his personal approval or authorization. Those who disobeyed his orders, Russians or natives, were harshly punished, and those who obeyed often received generous rewards.

In actuality, of course, the development, control and administration of Russia's colony across northern Asia was supervised by two entwined bureaucracies. One was seated in Moscow, the other was dispersed throughout the colony. From 1637 to 1763 the Moscow agency was the *Sibirskii Prikaz*, the Department of Siberian Affairs. Prior to 1637 colonial affairs were handled by the *Posolskii* or Ambassadorial Prikaz, and the Novgorod, *Meshcherskii* and Kazan prikazes. Each prikaz was headed by a *boiar* (an influential landed Moscow aristocrat), assisted by two *diaks* (secretaries). The Tsar made these appointments and the appointees formulated all policies in his name. The boiar supervised the activity of lesser officials and gave rewards and punishments. Occasionally the *boiarskaia duma* (the Tsar's advisory council of boiars) was involved in the formulation of official policy or action in the new colony. The three appointed officials were aided by several *poddiachiis* or *poddiaks* (clerks) who actually composed all official policy pronouncements, statements and instructions and handled correspondence. As the reports reveal, their writing was neither even nor of a standard style.

Subsidiary to these upper echelon administrators were lesser officials in charge of various farflung desks or offices. Some handled geographic areas such as Tobolsk or Eniseisk. Others dealt with specific assignments such as the sable treasury of the Tsar's Treasury. These tasks were supervised by *golovas* (heads) or *tselovalniks* (sworn men). These men and their subordinates performed countless duties receiving, appraising and sorting furs and other objects of tribute. They also kept the official records of the prikaz for annual review and evaluation.

There were two additional Moscow-based groups connected with the affairs of the new colony. The first consisted of special investigators activated for delicate internal assignments, who inquired into matters of abuse by colonial officials, discontent or rebellion among the natives, special problems faced by Russian agricultural settlers and complaints from persons beneath formal notice. The investigators conducted their inquiries on site in the colony and submitted their findings and recommendations to the Tsar or top officials of the Sibirskii Prikaz. The second group comprised officials from other prikazes such as the *Razriadnyi* Prikaz (Department of Military Affairs), who supplied the Sibirskii Prikaz with military personnel, or the Posolskii Prikaz, who were involved in endless diplomatic negotiations with tribes strung along the ill-defined frontiers.

The Moscow-based bureaucracy was supported by colonial officials of several large administrative units, *voevodstvos*, into which the colony was divided. The highest official in each voevodstvo was the *voevoda*, generally a member of a distinguished Moscow noble family. Because he was required to deal with military and civilian affairs, some previous experience in these matters was necessary. The Razriadnyi Prikaz recommended these voevodas for the Tsar's approval, but the Sibirskii Prikaz actually made the formal announcement of the appointment. Until 1695, in order to prevent graft, corruption and sedition, Moscow limited the length of service of each voevoda to two years. In some key outposts two voevodas were appointed and monitored one another's activities. After 1695 service was expanded to six years.

The all powerful voevoda performed many functions, most of which were carefully prescribed and checked by Moscow; however there were always areas in which the far off voevoda used his own judgment and discretion. He was responsible for both the internal and external security of the voevodstvo, and accordingly was the commanding officer of all the military units under his jurisdiction. He was the chief of police and the principal judge as well. He controlled the mobility of each Russian, while also supervising every activity of the indigenous population. He controlled supplies, sent out the reconnaissance units to bring new areas under Russian control, interrogated the leaders of his expeditions, heard all petitions and complaints from Russians and natives, and kept his Muscovite superiors as well as the other voevodas informed of rumors and developments in the region under his jurisdiction. In effect he was tactically absolute.

The voevoda was assisted by many officials and formal groups. The closest were the two or three diaks who often accompanied the voevoda to his new assignment. Immediately below these men was the *pismennaia golova*, literally the "writing chief", who kept records and correspondence and was sent out on special assignments. Together with the voevoda these men formed the elite of Moscow's Siberian administration. They performed their official functions in a wood structure within the ostrog or ostrozhek called the *prikaznaia* or *sezzhaia izba*, the prikàz or assembly office. By contemporary standards they received handsome salaries. The annual income of a voevoda averaged about 250 rubles; a diak received about 130 and a golova, 80. They also received provisions and many other perquisites. These lucrative positions never lacked for applicants. We must remember that at that period 100 rubles would buy and stock a small farm and build a dwelling.

The voevoda and his associates were aided by two divisions of minor officials, the poddiaks or clerks mentioned above and the *prikaznye liudi* or prikaz agents. The voevoda selected these persons from among literate militia, townspeople or clergy. Their number and responsibilities varied from town to town. In general they performed routine work and some even served as leaders of isolated tribute collection centers. They were paid with provisions and clothing plus a few rubles per year.

Colonial officials relied on several military and paramilitary units to carry out Moscow's orders, directives and instructions, and to enforce their own policies. This was not unusual. From 1581 until 1700 Russia's new colony was a vast military network and most Siberian administrators were military men. The most important were the *deti* or *syny boiarskie*, impoverished Russian nobles who flourished as a military elite in the colonial environment. Though from mixed backgrounds, they rose to their status by virtue of exceptional service as they discharged special orders, explored new regions and brought them under Moscow's control, collected tribute from the natives and performed other valuable services. For this they received a good salary and other material rewards.

Under these colonial military officers were six distinct units of armed men. The top rank was occupied by the *streltsy*, Russian regular soldiers, both foot and mounted. They served for life and were armed with muskets, swords, pikes and battle axes. They were assigned to reconnoiter new territories, suppress native discontent, defend Russian centers of control against attacks by the indigenous population, collect tribute and convoy the tribute as well as important officials across hostile territory. Next were the *cossacks*, a term applied to a great variety of men: vagabonds, homeless men, itinerant and hired workers, adventurers, restless misfits and outcasts, all of whom served, either on horse or on foot, to supplement the streltsy. They were also used extensively to defend the Russian agricultural colonists. Below the cossacks were the *guliashchie liudi*, persons not assigned into any tax category, a group that included runaway serfs, itinerant workers, and various unfortunates who sought refuge. They usually accompanied the streltsy and cossacks, but because there was a constant shortage of manpower, colonial officials employed them for other tasks as well.

The next three units differed from those just described in both composition and purpose. One was the *Litva*, prisoners of war and other detained foreigners such as Lithuanians, Ukrainians, Poles, Germans, Swedes, Belorussians and other Europeans, whom Moscow sent for security to various outposts in Siberia. Because many of these persons were well educated and skillful, colonial officials used them in many ways. There were some cases of insubordination, but most of the Litva military fought alongside the streltsy and cossacks to establish and maintain the Russian colony in northern Asia. Some rose to intermediate positions of authority.

Below the Litva were the *sluzhilye liudi iurtovskie*, auxiliary servitors recruited from among Tatars who lived in settlements known as *iurts*. Some of these men formed their own special units that assisted the streltsy and cossacks. Natives who were converted to Russian Orthodox Christianity were somewhat integrated with the streltsy and the cossacks, whom they served as guides and interpreters. The final group were Russian *promyshlenniks*, who were hunters, trappers and petty traders, either self-employed or in the hire of wealthy merchants. They were sometimes recruited by colonial officials to collect tribute, reconnoiter new territory, put down native discontent, and for other difficult assignments. Administratively these six units functioned as independent entities; however men from all the groups might take part on any given mission or assignment.

Great distances separated colonial officials from final authorities in Moscow, but there were several leverages which ensured the Tsar's firm grip over his region. The most effective was the careful selection of all top colonial administrators. And as we have noted, the assignments were short to prevent them from entrenching themselves. Armed with lengthy, detailed instructions, voevodas were warned to act only within prescribed limits, but to use their judgment on how best to increase the Tsar's power and wealth. Colonial officials were enjoined to report to Moscow everything of importance they saw, heard or encountered. Periodically, authorities in Moscow sent inspectors to investigate matters, and retiring voevodas were required to give their replacements detailed accounts of their stewardship. Finally, Moscow kept a firm hold on the Asian colony through the dispatch of supplies and military, and agricultural and other personnel. To some degree these restrictive measures were unnecessary, for regardless of background or purpose, once a Russian or other European found himself east of the Urals he was on hostile ground. To survive, all had to cooperate and defend the Russian colonial principle to the death. Russian military units occasionally rebelled against the brutality of commanding officers, but these outbreaks never reached dangerous proportions; in fact such rebels were often pardoned and returned to service to alleviate the constant problem, a shortage of manpower in Siberia.

Although relatively few in number, the priests, monks and nuns of the Russian Orthodox Church played a prominent part in administering Siberia. This was not unusual. Throughout Russian history there have been close ties between church and state officials. The Tsar was the nominal head of the church, and his chapels were built early in every ostrog and town. The government supplied these churches with furnishings, vestments, religious books, the great church bells and icons, and with land and peasants to farm it. Food was provided for the clergy, as well as salaries as high as 40 rubles per year. Monasteries and convents received similar consideration. In return, the ecclesiastical personnel were expected to care for the old, the infirm and crippled and veterans. They were to supply spiritual guidance for Russian colonial personnel and provide for their religious needs; they sometimes administered the oath of allegiance to natives and baptized those who wished to become converts to Christianity. In the forbidding lands the church rituals provided rich pageantry and color and in the remotest outposts, moments of splendor to be found nowhere else in the early colonial period.

Colonial and ecclesiastical officials cooperated when their interests coincided, but there were numerous disagreements between them because authorities in Moscow failed to delineate clearly the functions of colonial and church officials. Further, like their colonial civilian and military counterparts, church personnel were sometimes corrupt and susceptible to bribery and extortion, and known for alcoholism and loose morals. Some monks and nuns shocked even the lusty frontiersmen by cohabiting in their cramped cells. In spite of these faults by some, the Orthodox Church was a most important institution in the Russian colonial administration of the lands beyond the Urals.

Regardless of rank or status, life was harsh for every Russian in the conquered territories of Siberia. The northerly location of the colony meant that summers were brief, hot, humid and visited by clouds of insects. Winters were bitter cold, dark, endless and imprisoning. Climatic extremes affected all supplies, especially food for men and animals. Provisions had to be hauled or dragged the great distances from European Russia. It sometimes took years to transport heavy equipment, and the cost was enormous. Failure to secure adequate supplies of food, fuel and weaponry meant certain death for an entire garrison through starvation, scurvy, freezing or epidemics. Attacks by natives were a constant threat. Native hostility grew in direct proportions to their exploitation, reduction and mistreatment by the Russians. If they were not too few, natives vented their rage by ambushing small Russian units, burning out defenseless or poorly guarded Russian civilians, murdering isolated travelers and waging open anti-Russian rebellions.

Native discontent was soon repressed because Russians had better weapons, but tribesmen usually outnumbered them. The Russians were forced to confine much of their life to their fortified outposts which were guarded around the clock, leaving these strongholds only in well armed groups. In these drastic conditions the Russians soon devised two routines in their Siberian colony: one in the permanent settlements within the *ostrozhek* or *ostrog*, the other in their constant travel through and across the endless wilderness.

The ostrozhek was the earliest and most familiar Russian fortification. For defensive purposes it was usually located on a bluff overlooking a river route or at some other strategic location, perhaps a portage site. Surrounded by a high timbered stockade with sharpened tops, entry to the ostrozhek was through a main gate overlooked by two or three log towers twenty or more feet high. Small cannon were placed above the gate and in the towers, and along the walls were embrasures for sharpshooters. To afford greater security, the wall of every ostrozhek was surrounded if possible by a deep wide moat filled with water, perhaps from a smaller stream joining the river. Thus the walls of the ostrozhek formed a citadel or *kreml* which protected the official residence of the commanding officer and his associates, a small chapel, a supply depot, and a few structures to house a garrison of several dozen men. Looking back one sees that Kiev, Novgorod, Moscow and other early towns began in a similar way.

When an ostrozhek was enlarged for various reasons, it became an ostrog. The original defense perimeter was then enclosed by a new wall with new towers and embrasures. The enlarged fortress accommodated additional buildings and a larger garrison. In order to withstand a prolonged siege, every ostrozhek and ostrog had to have a supply of water and some direct means of escape, preferably toward a river, to enable the garrison to communicate with other outposts in a crisis. Since ostrogs were safer than ostrozheks they attracted more Russian settlers. The first to come were merchants from Russia and later Bokhara who set up their shops just below the ostrog walls. Other newcomers were clergy, nuns as well as monks and priests, who established monasteries and convents. The third group were peasants, sent to the new region by authorities in Moscow to produce food supplies for the large ostrog garrison. The diverse newcomers soon transformed the settlement into a small Russian colonial town.

Most ostrozheks and ostrogs were surrounded by hostile natives, and were located a considerable distance from other Russian outposts and from Russia proper. Life within the palisade was routine and spartan, monotonous and grim. The primary purpose of the ostrog was to serve as the administrative center of a given territory, as the collection center for iasak, and as a secure base. From it armed Russian units could be sent out to bring new lands and new natives under Russian control, or to put down native discontent. Protected by walls high enough to repel natives, and patrolled by a twenty-four hour vigil, ostrogs afforded relative security to persons who made up the garrison, to the voevoda and his associates, various military units, supporting personnel, and the sick and wounded. With the exception of hostages who were kept in special stockades or cells, the Russians never allowed native men to enter the ostrog lest they observe defenses.

To prevent monotony and boredom from reaching dangerous levels, the voevoda and his staff kept the garrison busy. The aged and infirm were often assigned to sentry duty. Others prepared food and cut wood for fuel. Parties were sent out on routine reconnaissance patrols or to investigate suspicious activities of the natives distant from the fort. Specialists repaired and readied equipment, weapons and sleds for long journeys to far points to conquer, collect iasak and convoy iasak furs or other taxes and reports back along the hazardous trail to Moscow.

Although officials of the ostrog forced every member of the garrison to perform some daily chore, most managed to make time to gamble and drink. From time to time these robust activities were interrupted by the arrival of a winter convoy or messengers from European Russia or other ostrogs, by the return of surviving members of an expedition from distant journeys, or by sudden alarm because of hostile natives, or news of the impending arrival of an exotic embassy from Mongolia or Central Asia. On such occasions life in the ostrog pulsated and the atmosphere hummed with rumor and speculation, gossip and reminiscences. Dangerous developments brought increased tension and apprehension, but other events stimulated singing, drinking, carousing, recounting of adventures, preparation of reports or perhaps trial and punishment.

Life in the wilderness was neither idyllic nor tranquil and men always traveled together. Sometimes they moved in boats, built as opportunity arose, or they went by foot or ski, or with dog or reindeer sleds. Since journeys through these trackless lands lasted months and sometimes years, they carried basic provisions, weapons and equipment with them. Impassable natural barriers were often encountered, as well as fierce swarms of natives. Superior Russian equipment, weapons and technology usually overcame these natural and human obstacles. In the process some Russian units won legendary greatness, while others perpetrated dreadful acts or reprisals that threatened whole tribes. In every campaign there were Russian casualties, and sometimes these occurred when rival Russian units fought over a prized area of wilderness.

To survive the icebound winters, wandering explorers built *zimov'es*, large one-room log cabins. These provided basic shelter and served as iasak collection points. Although zimov'es provided elemental shelter, hardpressed men died of disease and malnutrition. Those who survived the winters were prey to vengeful natives, or they returned to their original ostrogs in bad health, broken by scurvy and an endless list of diseases. Debts were also incurred through endless gambling or forced purchase of supplies. Their written appeals for compensation or assistance are now informative to us and were then probably a far too familiar theme to the administration.

Perhaps the group of Russians who suffered most in the new colonial lands, while receiving the least for their efforts, were the state peasants. Authorities settled these unfortunate and impoverished men, women and children near various ostrogs to grow food for the garrison. There were also volunteer peasants known as *okhochie liudi*. Authorities provided seeds, equipment, livestock and land for the peasants' own use. In return each peasant was obligated to cultivate a certain amount of government land and deliver the harvest to the local garrison. Unarmed and unskilled peasants were predictably harassed by natives and were often the last to be brought within the walls. Peasant families were inevitably killed, their few possessions destroyed, their horses and cattle scattered and stolen by the attackers. To enable them to cultivate crops in safety, authorities eventually assigned aged cossacks to guard the peasant settlements, but this late measure was inadequate. Peasants tried to move on, or simply ran off to the growing town complexes. Others drifted to portages where they carried heavy loads overland from one river landing to another. Still others became part of the unattached guliashchie liudi and would sign on with various expeditions short of labor. Russian political and religious exiles suffered similar fates and were found along the same avenues of escape. Our scrutiny of the several Russian groups in their northern Asian colonies in this period reveals the human price paid for each colonial enterprise. But compared to exploitive undertakings in other times and places, the Russians paid a surprisingly small price for their vast colonial empire in northern Asia, for Siberia was never heavily populated, even along the old Chinese frontiers.

Ostrogs that attracted Russian and Central Asian merchants to their vicinity grew fastest. Merchant success generally lured members of other professions, trades and crafts. Individually and collectively these people offered useful information, goods and services to the ostrog garrison, which transformed the ostrog into a town. But simply speaking, Russian towns in Siberia were always more enlarged ostrogs than true towns, and in tradition and in fact they were dominated, controlled and exploited by ostrog officials. They were small, crowded and dirty, with few streets or essential services, and little sanitation. Primarily built of logs, few towns had a sound defense plan, and they suffered extensive damage when under attack; they were vulnerable to fires, either arson or accidental.

The townsmen were a colorful mix made up of promyshlenniks, agents of Russian merchants, carpenters, smiths, boatmen, miners, craftsmen, sled drivers, couriers, entertainers, harlots, criminals, petty merchants from Russia and Central Asia, government officials, peasants and desperate runaways. These were joined by old, infirm and wounded streltsy and cossacks, the clergy, exiles and vagabonds whose activities are always outside normal classification. Where possible in the short summers, town dwellers prepared food and fuel for the long winters, and in all seasons they consumed vast quantities of alcohol, wild tobacco, and with luck, imported Circassian or Chinese leaf. Men helped themselves to any available women. The constant threats, insecurity, official regimentation, overcrowding, fear and the dull monotony of life led many town inhabitants, like some in the adjacent ostrog, to solicit local administrators for permission to go into the tundra or taiga to carve out new Russian lands. To return west was impossible, and to experience a wilderness life of excitement and adventure at least was a gamble for fortune which others had won.

THE INDIGENOUS PEOPLES OF RUSSIA'S SIBERIAN COLONY

The Russians eventually subjugated every indigenous Siberian tribe they encountered. Between the Urals and the Enisei River the principal tribes included the Voguls, Ostiaks, Samoeds, Tatars and Tungus. Between the Enisei and the Pacific Ocean the major peoples were the Buriats, Iakuts, Mongols, Tungus, Daurs, Duchers, Giliaks, Koriaks, Chukchi, Itelmen and Kamchadals. Linguistically these belonged to major language groups such as the Ugric, Finno-Ugric, Turkic, Mongol and Tungus-Manchu. Technologically all were primitive cultures; some were Neolithic. Most were nomadic. Their tools were stone axes and adzes and fishhooks, their weapons the bow and arrow. In the inhospitable climate most lived on game and fish, roots and berries. There was little settled life and populations were small.

Because of these factors the peoples of Russia's trans-Ural colony had no elaborate political or social system. Some groups were indeed so small that they were actually large family units guided by elders. Other tribes were governed by chiefs. Contemporary Russian sources refer to these as *kniazhtsy* or princelings. Iakuts called their chieftains *toions*; a Tatar tribal leader was a *murza*; a *taisha* or *taidzha* was a Mongol chieftain who could trace his lineage back to Genghis Khan; and Mongol rulers were called *khans*, but were sometimes referred to as "tsars" in contemporary Russian sources. Few tribes possessed a military force, a situation that enabled the numerically small but well-armed Russian units to move at will through Siberia with only minimal casualties. The tribes fought over favored hunting or fishing grounds, past kidnappings, murders and vendettas; all of which eased initial Russian conquests and subsequent control of the endless landscape.

Russian leaders gradually developed a system to subdue tribes. A small group of streltsy or cossacks or some other well armed unit, on orders from Moscow or from colonial officials, or sometimes on their own initiative, would invade desirable tribal lands. If no resistance were offered, the Russians would simply seize some tribal leaders as hostages and imprison them in a rapidly built stronghold. Fellow tribesmen might ransom them through the payment of tribute and by taking an oath to become loyal iasak-paying subjects of the Russian Tsar forever. But most tribes resisted the invaders. Then, "invoking God's help," the Russians used gunpowder. As the survivors rushed into the wilds, the victors seized as many as possible. Their ransom was furs, wherever they might find them, plus eternal loyalty to the Tsar and an annual assessment of more furs. To ensure payment and obedience the victorious Russians kept their hostages imprisoned in the ostrog for months or years. But whether the natives resisted these forays or not, the Russians always helped themselves to two things: women and food.

Whatever the approach, once they were cowed the broken natives usually remained Russian subjects, a burdensome and oppressive relationship. Native men between the ages of 18 and 50, except for the crippled, blind and Orthodox converts, were required to pay the Tsar of Russia annual iasak tribute in prime sable furs. The amount of payment varied from one area to another, and from one year to another, depending on availability. Early in the seventeenth century when sables were abundant, some tribesmen had to produce as many as 22 sables per man per year! By the middle of the century, with the depletion of the animal, the quota dropped to five. Whenever and wherever sables were not available, the Russians accepted larger numbers of fox, marten, ermine, lynx, otter, beaver, wolf or squirrel pelts. Natives who lived close to a Russian fort brought their iasak to that outpost. Those who lived far off handed it over to the roving Russian iasak collectors. Both methods were onerous. In addition to the regular assessment, Russian officials naturally expected to receive generous side gifts, *pominki*, from the natives—also furs. To meet these demands native hunters traveled long distances with great hardship to the subsequent neglect of their family responsibilities. Iasak destroyed many natives. To free themselves from this oppressive shakedown some found means to appeal to the far off Tsar for mercy, others rebelled and killed, still others fled to distant lands. Some died of exhaustion in the wilds and others killed themselves.

Nor was iasak the only burden imposed on the conquered natives. Russians recruited them as guides and as cheap labor to row boats and haul carts. They compelled them to fish and gather berries, prepare firewood, cut logs for building, cultivate the land, and they used them as beasts of burden. Almost all colonial officials, including the lowest ranks, robbed the native men of their women whom they used, abused and sold or bartered. Russians relieved the natives of their horses and cattle, destroyed their dwellings, stole winter clothing, took scarce hunting and fishing equipment along with entire food supplies. They tortured and mutilated natives and starved many to death. Finally, to make room for Russian agricultural settlers, colonial officials often expelled natives from their traditional grazing, hunting and fishing grounds.

The response to Russian exploitation and mistreatment naturally varied. Those who sought redress through petitions addressed to the Tsar found the process vexing and slow. First, someone must be found willing to compose the letter of grievance. There were few literate persons, and most were reluctant to become involved. Second, petitions that were written seldom reached the Tsar because alert and self-serving colonial officials intercepted them. Finally, those petitions that did somehow come to the attention of the Tsar or of authorities in the Sibirskii Prikaz often produced no result because the Tsar commanded his colonial officials, the perpetrators of the abuses, to correct the problems. And time and distance were the officials' allies. As was said, "God is high up in heaven and the Tsar is far off in Moscow."

Because the appeal route was slow and ineffective, natives resorted to violence. They ambushed likely Russian units and killed agricultural colonists. They burned their homes, destroyed harvests and drove off livestock. In concert with other forlorn tribes, native leaders planned combined attacks against Russian ostrogs. Many of these attacks failed because authorities were alerted by native informers. But there were some native uprisings that engulfed large Russian holdings for a considerable time. When the natives failed to repel Russian invaders or were goaded beyond endurance, they sometimes fled to the steppe, inhabited by the populous and warlike Kirgiz and Kalmyks. Others sought protection from the Mongols and Chinese. Russian efforts to regain control of these refugees produced more conflict and added larger dimensions to Russian expansion to the Pacific frontier.

Russian conquest of the Siberian lands brought a few advantages to the indigenous peoples. The Russians taught some natives how to cultivate land. Some were "allowed" to enter the Tsar's service where they learned useful skills. The Russians took basic steps—largely unsuccessful, since the precept of example was strained—to prevent natives from smoking and gambling and drinking to excess. Occasionally authorities in Moscow lowered a iasak assessment or even approved a temporary halt to tax collections in some areas. Periodically the Tsar instructed colonial officials, who in turn instructed their subordinates, to show mercy to the natives and protect them against injustice and violence. The officials exempted cooperative chieftains from iasak, and made gifts to natives who became Christians. Albeit commendable in concept, these measures were inconsequential, random in number, and beneficial to very few individuals. The overwhelming mass of the conquered was unaffected by these imperial gestures and in general paid a dear price for their new status.

RUSSIAN ENCOUNTERS WITH
THE KIRGIZ, KALMYKS,
MONGOLS, MANCHUS AND CHINESE

The Russian drive across northern Asia was essentially north of the 55th parallel. There were three basic reasons. First, north of that line they encountered mostly small tribes with primitive technology who presented little opposition to the Russian eastward advance. Second, the cold climate above that latitude produced finer furs. And finally, in warmer areas south of the 55th parallel lived the populous and advanced Kirgiz, Kalmyks, Mongols, Manchus and Chinese. They boasted elaborate political systems, good armies and effective weapons. Common sense and prudence dictated that the Russians maintain either peaceful relations or minimal hostile contacts with these people.

Two factors made it difficult to achieve these goals. First, there were no clearly defined frontiers among those peoples or between them and the encroaching Russians, a hurly-burly situation which led to frequent and often violent clashes. And second, though each of these nations was populous, none was homogenous. Each was comprised of numerous independent units, bands and fiefdoms with natural jealousies over rights and prerogatives. This situation again provided Russian opportunity to divide, conquer, isolate, exploit and rule.

The Kirgiz were the first nation to take military notice of the Russians as they later came down out of the Urals. The pastoral Kirgiz were a Turkic people under strong cultural influence of the Mongols. Their homeland lay between the Ob and the upper basin of the Enisei river, where they subsisted by raising livestock and by hunting and fishing. In theory the Kirgiz were under the authority of one *kniaz* (prince), but in practice the Kirgiz consisted of four principal tribes, each governed by a *kniazhets* (princeling). Each tribe was divided into several smaller units called an *ulus* led by chieftains whom the Russians referred to as *lutshie liudi*. This loose organizational structure enabled each Kirgiz unit to adopt and pursue a policy or action that brought it maximum benefits. With such a division of authority some Kirgiz groups assisted the Mongols, while others, in return for gifts and bribes, cooperated with the Russians. And there were those men who dependably joined anti-Russian revolts against Russian ostrogs, towns and agricultural settlements. The Russians at last dealt effectively with the Kirgiz only in the eighteenth century when they neutralized them with an overwhelming number of settlers and military reinforcements.

The Kalmyks presented the same problems as the Kirgiz, except that they were even more populous and more dangerous. The Kalmyks were a Mongol people, and according to a Chinese classification they belonged to the Western or Oirat group of Mongols. Before the seventeenth century the Kalmyks inhabited Dzhungaria (presently the Altai and northwestern Sinkiang), so the Chinese considered them subjects. Early in the seventeenth century some of the Kalmyks moved west from Dzhungaria and occupied the upper Irtysh and Tobol river basins, and a few nomads strayed westward across the Urals. When the Russians encountered them early in the seventeenth century they were divided into two groups, the Black and the White Kalmyks. In 1623 the Russians tried and failed to bring a small Kalmyk group under their suzerainty. They were more successful in 1655 when they persuaded a band of Kalmyks to take the oath of allegiance to the Tsar. But the Kalmyks adhered to the oath only when it benefited their immediate interests, which led to disagreements and clashes between them and the Russians. These set-tos were complicated by the efforts of the Chinese to return the Kalmyks to their suzerainty, and by the elevation of one Kalmyk leader to the status of khan, brought about by the Tibetan Dalai Lama in the 1670s. Because they were able to offer the Kalmyk leaders substantial material bribes, however, the Russians managed to reduce the threat they posed. Early in the eighteenth century many Kalmyks joined Russian service and became unreliable "loyal subjects" of the Tsar.

In contrast to their varying problems with the Kirgiz and the Kalmyks, the Russians were more successful with the tribes of Eastern Mongols under the leadership of the Altyn-khan. They made contact early in the seventeenth century. In return for Russian gifts of gold, silver, woolens, armor and the like, and for special considerations, the Altyn-khan agreed to assist the Russians in their attempts to reach China, to defend Russian interests when requested, and to inform them of any developments which might endanger Russian security. To coordinate and improve their special relationship, high-ranking Russian and Eastern Mongol delegations occasionally met in their respective capitals. These meetings were usually formal and solemn ceremonies which produced results for the Russians. The Mongols also sent emissaries to the new Russian towns in Siberia where they were housed and fed, sometimes for months on end. A few Kirgiz and Kalmyk units also adopted this form of diplomacy in order to indulge in Russian hospitality. Their hosts found this form of entertainment relatively undemanding, and it provided Russian leaders with valuable information and further opportunities to divide and conquer.

While the Kirgiz, Kalmyks and Mongols caused the Russians occasional concern, they were never a sinister threat to the Russian aim to establish themselves solidly on the Pacific frontier. That distinction went to the Chinese. Toward them the Russians pursued a two-pronged policy, both before and after the rise of the Manchu dynasty in 1644. One aim was to establish diplomatic ties in order to develop profitable commercial relations. The other was to bring as many Chinese subjects as possible, together with their lands (particularly in the Amur basin), under Russian control.

The Russians initiated diplomatic and commercial ties with China early in the seventeenth century. Between 1608 and 1675 they sent ten embassies on the months-long journey to Peking. Three of the early missions never reached their destination. Of the remaining seven, three deserve our attention because each introduced a new element into Sino-Russian relations.

First is the embassy headed by Ivan Petlin (1618–19). This was the earliest Russian group to reach Peking, the first to be well received by the Chinese, the first and only one to obtain a formal written invitation to trade with China (which labyrinthine statement took the Russians 56 years to translate because of language barriers), and the first to provide a description, forever fascinating, of the journey to Peking.

The second is the embassy led by Fedor Baikov (1653–57). Its purpose was to place Russo-Chinese trade on a firm and permanent foundation and to establish formal diplomatic relations with the Chinese Empire. To achieve these goals Baikov brought with him desirable gifts and two illuminating documents: a letter from the Tsar (which purported to trace his ancestry directly to Caesar Augustus!) and lengthy instructions on precisely how Baikov was to behave in Peking. He was ordered to negotiate only with the Emperor of China, to bow only to him, to express the Tsar's desire to live in friendship and amity with the Chinese, and to invite Chinese diplomats, merchants and skilled craftsmen to come to Russia. In addition, while in Peking Baikov was secretly to amass information on many questions: Chinese intentions toward Russia; trade routes; goods abundant or scarce in China; Chinese attitudes toward Russian goods; court ceremonials; China's strengths, weaknesses, neighbors, religion, demographic make up and other major problems the Russians needed to understand.

In spite of painstaking plans, the mission was a diplomatic failure. Baikov himself was largely to blame. In order to make his entry into China elaborate and impressive he sent a Bokhara merchant named Setkul Ablin to Peking to announce the impending arrival of his embassy. Manchu officials mistook merchant Ablin for Baikov, accepted his gifts, forced him to kowtow, then dismissed him and made no preparations to receive Baikov either at the frontier or in Peking. Baikov's subsequent unwillingness to comply with Peking court ceremonial demands or to compromise on any issue angered the Manchu officials. They treated him with scant courtesy and on one occasion even threatened him with death. Ultimately he was sent away without accomplishing the objective of his mission.

But Baikov's embassy was not a total failure. His six months' stay in Peking gave him an opportunity to observe the Manchu-Chinese way of life which he carefully recorded. His descriptions of Peking, the Manchu and Chinese people, their food, goods, shops, prices and other details are extremely interesting. His information gave Muscovite officials their first detailed picture of conditions in Peking and enabled them to plan more carefully for future ambassadors. Among these was Nikolai G. Milescu, a Moldavian noble in Russian service, generally referred to in Russian documents as Nikolai G. Spafarii because of his rank in his guards unit.

Spafarii's mission (1675-78) was the last important seventeenth century attempt to establish commercial and diplomatic dialogue with China. Like Baikov, Spafarii carried gifts, a letter from the Tsar to the Emperor of China, and an intricate and lengthy set of instructions. Spafarii failed to achieve his objectives because he too refused to comply with Chinese court ceremonial and etiquette, first at the border and later in Peking. Spafarii's arrogance, cunning, unscrupulous behavior and overconfidence alienated the Manchu-Chinese officials, as did concurrent devastating raids by the Russians against northern Chinese subjects in the Amur basin. To force the Russians to comply with their demands, the Manchu-Chinese officials restricted the mobility of Russian personnel, threatened their lives, refused commerce and forced proud Spafarii to kowtow, thus acknowledging Russia's inferiority to China. Early in September 1676 Spafarii's embassy was dismissed and finally reached Moscow on January 1, 1678. Although it failed to secure diplomatic and commercial relations with China, during its long residence in Peking Spafarii's mission, even more than Baikov's, secured valuable information on the Chinese Empire which no other European nation then possessed.

One of the major reasons for the failure of Russian diplomatic missions to Peking in the seventeenth century was the fact that together with these undertakings Russian bands were making destructive raids against various tribute paying peoples in the Lake Baikal and Amur River basins. The earliest major recorded raid occurred between 1643 and 1646, and was led by Vasilii Poiarkov, the first Russian to navigate the length of the Amur. The second and even more destructive raiding period took place from 1649 to 1653 under the command of the redoubtable Erofei P. Khabarov. His men established the first Russian settlement at the confluence of the Shilka and Argun rivers and perpetrated brutal acts against the natives they encountered. They also inflicted heavy losses on a Manchu force that came to the defense of the natives. Khabarov's replacement, Onufrii Stepanov, continued his predecessor's predations until he was killed by the Manchus in 1658, the same year in which the Manchu forces razed the new Russian settlement. To counter their setbacks and strengthen their position in the Trans-Baikal region, the Russians built two important ostrogs, Nerchinsk in 1653 and Selenginsk in 1666. Three years later a rampaging cossack group rebuilt the razed ostrog which they named Albazin, brought the surrounding territories and inhabitants under control and in 1672 returned this area to the jurisdiction of Russian colonial administrators.

Russian desire to dominate the Amur watershed and the Manchu-Chinese inability to dislodge them blocked establishment of peaceable relations between the two empires. In the 1680s conditions deteriorated rapidly with each military confrontation. To defuse the explosive situation, representatives of the two empires came to Nerchinsk, and there on August 27, 1689, signed a critical treaty, drawn with the aid of the Chinese advisors—two Portuguese Jesuits. Under the terms of the treaty the Russians renounced "for eternity" their claim to the Amur watershed, and accordingly razed the rebuilt Albazin ostrog. They also pledged to halt all raids against Chinese territory and subjects. The treaty set the principle of extraterritoriality and laid broad rules governing commerce between the two countries and the handling of fugitives and criminals. The Treaty of Nerchinsk thus placed the first limits on Russian expansion to the Pacific frontier. The Russians amended economic provisions of the "eternal treaty" in their favor in 1727, in 1768, and in 1858 when they finally eliminated territorial restrictions.

Scholarly interest in Russian expansion to the Pacific frontier began around 1740. In spite of its erratic nature, an interesting body of monographic and periodical literature has been produced. The first great scholar, justly called "the father of Siberian history," was Gerhard F. Müller (1705–83). Born and educated in Germany, Müller came to Russia in 1725. He mastered the Russian language and in 1733 the newly established Academy of Sciences designated him to represent its interests on Bering's celebrated Second Kamchatka Expedition (1733–43). During those ten years Müller examined, copied and gathered thousands of documents on historical, geographic, legal, ethnographic, linguistic and other problems. These rich files, known subsequently as "the Müller portfolios," exist today in Soviet archives. Over the years a number of scholars have tapped this rich source, but it would appear that none has yet been allowed complete and unrestricted access.

Müller himself was the first to use the materials he had retrieved from dozens of remote outposts in Russia's colonial empire. These were the foundation of his first comprehensive history of Siberia and of Russia's expansion to the Pacific frontier in his landmark work, *Opisanie Sibirskogo tsarstva i vsekh proisshedshikh v nem del ot nachala, a osoblivo ot pokoreniia ego Rossiskoi derzhave po sie vremena* (An Analysis of the Tsardom of Siberia and of All the Events That Have Transpired There from the Beginning, but Especially from Its Conquest by the Russian State to the Present). Müller finished twenty-three chapters of his projected three-volume work, of which five chapters, supplemented by many pertinent documents, were published as the first volume in 1750. The Academy censors approved other chapters for publication, but these did not appear in book form. Pressed by other commitments, Müller discontinued this work. Between 1755 and 1764, however, he published selected passages along with other material in a journal of which he was the industrious editor, *Ezhemesiachnye sochineniia* (Monthly Works) and in his *Sammlung Russischer Geschichte* (A Collection of Russian History), volumes 7 and 8.

Early in 1753 on orders from officials of the Academy, Müller gave 23 chapters of his manuscript to Johann E. Fischer (1697–1771), a German compatriot and previously his unwelcome companion in Siberia. The Academy chose Fischer to complete Müller's work. Fischer condensed, rearranged and updated Müller's material and published it in 1768 in a two-volume German edition entitled *Sibirische Geschichte von der Entdeckung Sibiriens bis auf Eroberung dieses Landes durch die russische Waffen* (A History of Siberia from the Discovery of Siberia to the Conquest of this Land by Russian Forces). A Russian translation of this work appeared in 1774. According to A. N. Pypin, an eminent nineteenth-century Russian scholar, Fischer simply paraphrased ten of Müller's chapters for three-quarters of his work, and appropriated the rest of his information from Müller's unpublished material.

The most extensive, but still incomplete results of Müller's scholarly endeavors appeared in 1937. Under the direction of Sergei V. Bakhrushin (1882–1950), a leading Soviet scholar of Russian expansion, the Academy of Sciences published two of the projected three volumes of Müller's original work. The third volume has yet to appear. Entitled *Istoriia Sibiri* (The History of Siberia), each volume consists of four parts: a lengthy introduction by the editors, Müller's narrative account, pertinent documents and extensive notes. Even with the final volume missing Müller's work is a classic. Its value is in its scope, methodology, faithful reliance on sources, incorporation of Russian and native folklore, attention to archaeology, linguistics and ethnology, and its rejection of speculation and doubtful hypotheses. Because of its comprehensive and modern scholarship, Müller's work has set standards for research on all aspects of Russian expansion to the Pacific frontier and has remained an indispensable guide for all scholars interested in this great field. We eagerly await its completion.

Scholarly interest in Russian expansion to the Pacific frontier increased in the nineteenth century, thanks to the publication of many pertinent sources on various aspects of the problem and the emergence of many qualified scholars, of whom three are particularly noteworthy: P. A. Slovtsov (1767–1843), P. N. Butsinskii (1853–1916), and N. N. Ogloblin (1852–?). Educated in St. Petersburg, Slovtsov became interested in Siberian history when he was exiled to Siberia for life. During his exile in Tobolsk he was permitted some travel to gather information. At first he published his articles on various topics in a number of newspapers. Then in 1838 appeared the first volume of his principal work, *Istoricheskoe obozrenie Sibiri s 1585 do 1742* (Historical Survey of Siberia from 1585 to 1742). The second volume, covering the years 1742 to

1823, was published in 1844, and both volumes were republished in 1886. His work is complex: the style is ponderous, the arguments weak, and documentation inadequate by present standards. Moreover he salted his account with moral and religious precepts as well as personal observations. But despite these shortcomings and flaws, Slovtsov's work is important for two reasons: first, it was the first major study after Müller to explore certain issues which spurred Russian scholarly interest in Siberia; and second, Slovtsov was the first to emphasize the positive aspects of church and government in Russian expansion and colonization.

Butsinskii, a graduate of the University of Kharkov and later a professor there, sought to explain the process of Russian expansion first through the activity of Russian settlers and then through an exhaustive study of the administrative regions. The first approach resulted in a well documented work entitled *Zaselenie Sibiri i byt ee pervykh eia naselnikov* (The Settlement of Siberia and the Life of Its First Settlers). Butsinskii advanced three novel ideas. First, he insisted that the Russian conquest of Siberia had been peaceful, injuring only a few natives. Second, he praised tsarist colonial policy and attributed most mistakes and failures to Russian officials in Moscow and in the colony for their lack of understanding of the problems of the newly conquered region. And third, he argued that since the government had built the towns and villages and had organized the entire colonial administrative apparatus, the government and not private enterprise deserved credit for subduing Siberia for Russia. Butsinskii's interest in the administrative apparatus resulted in two other major works: *Mangazeia i mangazeiskii uezd, 1601–1645* (Mangazeia and the Mangazeia uezd, 1601–1645), and *Istorii Sibiri: Surgut, Narym i Ketsk do 1645* (The History of Siberia: Surgut, Narym and Ketsk Before 1645). Careful reading of Butsinskii's works reveals that he examined many sources but, perhaps because of the enormity of the problems, he appears to have sometimes read the difficult script hastily or carelessly.

The last true groundbreaker in nineteenth century scholarship was Ogloblin, who graduated from the Archaeological Institute in St. Petersburg but achieved his reputation as an archivist and historian. For many years he was the chief archivist of the Ministry of Justice, which was then the prime repository for materials from the Sibirskii and Razriadnyi prikazes. Through his long familiarity with these hitherto untapped resources, Ogloblin analyzed their content and wrote numerous articles that detailed little known episodes about persons who had subdued the enormous wilderness of northern Asia for Russia. Like Müller, he had rich and unworked sources materials at his disposal; but he was critical of Müller's methods of research and use of sources. His own monumental work, for which he is greatly esteemed, is *Obozrenie stolbtsov i knig sibirskogo prikaza, 1592–1768* (A Survey of the Rolls and Books of the Sibirian Prikaz, 1592–1768). This richly informative study, for which the Academy of Sciences presented him an award, consists of four parts: the administration of the voevodstvos; customs collections; relations between Muscovite officials and their subordinates in Siberia; and the nature and operations of the central administration in Moscow. Because Ogloblin's *Obozerenie* for the first time revealed the existence of such rich material, it immediately became the basic guide for all scholars interested in this area of study.

The quantity of twentieth century Russian research is impressive, but the same cannot be said of its quality. Since 1917 Soviet scholars have been pressured to adhere in their works not only to Marxist ideas but also to the current interpretations of those ideas held by men in power. Under Lenin (who had been exiled to Siberia) and for a few years after his death, in accordance with his criticism of imperialism, it was fashionable to condemn tsarist colonial policies, expose their negative aspects, and sympathize with the plight of the indigenous Siberian population. Under Stalin, on the other hand, it was mandatory to emphasize the positive role the Russians had played and to be silent about or to minimize their excesses. Since Stalin's death the official line has stressed common interests between Russian and non-Russian peoples of northern Asia and the voluntary mergers between them. Such politically mandated shifts affect not only the direction but the substance and quality of research. Faced with these limitations, Soviet scholars have produced a number of valuable studies.

The leading Soviet scholar to date has been Sergei V. Bakhrushin (1882–1950). During his long association with Moscow University and with the Academy of Sciences, Bakhrushin wrote more than 40 scholarly and popular items on Siberia that deal with sources, historiography, the indigenous peoples and Russian colonial policy. His best known work is *Ocherki po istorii kolonizatsii Sibiri v XVI i XVII vekakh* (Essays on the History of the Colonization of Siberia in the Sixteenth and Seventeenth Centuries), which argues that Russian promyshlenniks played the critical role in the acquisition of Siberia for Russia. Bakhrushin intended to develop this skeletal outline into a comprehensive work and in pursuit of that goal he wrote numerous articles, a number of which became classics. For unknown reasons he never finished his project. He did, however, train many Soviet Sibirologists, and for his work he was elected a Corresponding Member of the Academy of Sciences in 1939 and later received several medals.

The second leading Soviet scholar was the prolific writer Aleksandr I. Andreev (1887–1959). During the 45 years he was associated with the Academy of Sciences in various capacities, Andreev wrote more than 150 studies. He is best remembered for the two volume work, *Ocherki po istochnikovedeniiu Sibiri, XVII–XVIII v.* (Essays on Source Guides on Siberia in the Seventeenth and Eighteenth Centuries) and *Russkie otkrytiia v Tikhom Okeane-Severnoi Amerike v XVIII v.* (Russian Discoveries in the Pacific Ocean and North America in the Eighteenth Century). Most interestingly, Andreev is reported to have left several completed manuscripts, including the missing third volume of Müller's *History of Siberia*. In 1937 he had collaborated with Bakhrushin on the first two volumes.

The third influential Soviet scholar was Viktor I. Shunkov (1900–68). A graduate of Moscow University, Shunkov was associated with the Academy of Sciences for more than 30 years. He authored and edited many items, but is best remembered for two works: *Ocherki po istorii kolonizatsii Sibiri v XVII–nachale VIII v.* (Essays on the History of the Colonization of Siberia, Seventeenth–Early Eighteenth Century) and *Ocherki po istorii zemlevladeniia v Sibiri, XVII v.* (Essays on the History of Landownership in Siberia in the Seventeenth Century). In these closely related works Shunkov argued that credit for the conquest and subjugation of the region east of the Urals belonged neither to the promyshlenniks nor the cossacks nor the government, but to the hard and peaceful work of Russian peasants. This interpretation was in full accord with the then prevailing Soviet official emphasis on the people's work.

In 1968–69 the Academy of Sciences sponsored and published a five-volume study, *Istoriia Sibiri*, with Shunkov and A. P. Okladnikov as joint editors, and a number of scholars involved in the research and writing of the history. It is important because it provides the first overall review of Siberia as we recognize it today, from early times to the mid-twentieth century. For our purposes, unfortunately, the early chapters contain little material useful to our survey.

In addition to Bakhrushin, Andreev and Shunkov, a number of other Soviet scholars should be mentioned. In alphabetical order these include: V. A. Aleksandrov, *Russkoe naselenie Sibiri XVII–nachala XVIII v.* (Russian Population of Siberia, Seventeenth–Early Eighteenth Century); M. I. Belov, *Podvig Semena Dezhneva* (The Exploits of Semen Dezhnev); B. O. Dolgikh, *Rodovoi i plemennoi sostav narodov Sibiri v XVII veke* (Clan and Tribal Composition of the Peoples of Siberia in the Seventeenth Century); A. V. Efimov, *Iz istorii velikikh russkikh geograficheskikh otkrytii v severnom ledovitom i tikhom okeanakh, XVII–pervaia polovina XVIII v.* (A History of Great Russian Geographical Discoveries in the Northern Arctic and Pacific Oceans, Seventeenth to the First Half of the Eighteenth Century); V. I. Ogorodnikov, *Ocherki istorii Sibiri do nachala XIX st. Zavoevanie russkikh Sibiri* (Essays on the History of Siberia to the Beginning of the Nineteenth Century: The Conquest of Siberia by the Russians); and A. P. Okladnikov, *Ocherki iz istorii zapadnykh buriat-mongolov, XVII–XVIII vv.* (Essays on the History of the Western Buriat-Mongols, in the Seventeenth and Eighteenth Centuries). All these works are based on extensive archival research.

Foreign scholars (German, French, Japanese, Chinese, Canadian, British and American) have at various times studied different aspects of Russian expansion to the Pacific. In the twentieth century the most productive among these have been English-speaking scholars. Early in the century interest was kept alive by two persons: Frank A. Golder (1877–1929) in the United States and John F. Baddeley (1854–1940) in Great Britain, who were attracted to this study for different reasons. In Golder's case it was the impact the expansion produced on Alaska, while Baddeley was fascinated by the hitherto unexplored problem of Russo-Chinese encounters in the seventeenth century. Because both men had influential connections, Russian imperial authorities allowed them access to certain archival materials.

Golder focused his attention not on the trans-Siberian but rather the trans-Pacific aspect of Russian expansion. In that area he produced three major studies: *Russian Expansion on the Pacific, 1641–1850* (Cleveland, 1914); *A Guide to the Materials for American History in Russian Archives* (Washington, 1917); and *Bering's Voyages:*

An Account of the Efforts of the Russians to Determine the Relation of Asia and America 2 vols. (New York, 1922–25). Because he expressed reservations about Russian achievements, some Soviet scholars have accused Golder of an anti-Russian bias. He has also recently been criticized for hasty reading of sources, which we have to say, under the conditions described is somewhat understandable. Baddley has fared better. His two-volume study is *Russia, Mongolia and China, Being Some Record of the Relations Between Them from the Beginning of the XVIIth Century to the Death of the Tsar Alekei Mikhailovich A.D. 1602–1672* (London, 1919; reprint, New York, 1973). The value of Baddeley's work lies in its judicious use of Russian sources (many of which are reproduced), the detailed analysis of Russian missions to China; a balanced review of Russian geographic and cartographic efforts in the seventeenth century, a useful summary of the tribes in Russia's new colony in Asia, plus copious notes and the inclusion of certain documents. Unfortunately his translation of original materials is sometimes awkward and inaccurate.

Between 1930 and 1956 Robert J. Kerner (1887–1956) was the most forceful proponent of the study of Russian eastward expansion. A graduate of the University of Chicago and Harvard, Kerner joined the faculty of the University of California at Berkeley in 1928 and later organized the Northeast Asia Seminar. That experiment, called by some "the California school," encountered many problems and setbacks, but was nonetheless a success. It produced three works by Kerner himself: "Russian Expansion to America: Its Bibliographical Foundations," in *The Papers of the Bibliographical Society of America*, vol. 25 (1931), pp. 111–29; *Northeast Asia: A Selected Bibliography. Contributions to the Bibliography of the Relations of China, Russia and Japan, with Special Reference to Korea, Manchuria, Mongolia and Eastern Siberia, in Oriental and European Languages*, 2 vols. (Berkeley, 1939); and *The Urge to the Sea: The Course of Russian History. The Role of Rivers, Portages, Ostrogs, Monasteries and Furs* (Berkeley, 1946). In 1943 two additional products of the seminar appeared and received immediate acclaim: Raymond H. Fisher's *The Russian Fur Trade, 1550–1700* (Berkeley, 1943), which argues that furs served as the principal propelling force behind Russia's eastward expansion; and George V. Lantzeff's *Siberia in the Seventeenth Century: A Study of Colonial Administration* (Berkeley, 1943), which offers the best analysis in English of the working of the Russian colonial administration and policies. Subsequently Fisher wrote several articles on various aspects of Russian expansion, a major study concerning Bering's two voyages, *Bering's Voyages: Whither and Why?* (Seattle, 1978) and *The Voyages of Semen Dezhnev in 1648* (London, 1981). Lantzeff's promising career was cut short by his death in 1955, but in 1973 Richard A. Pierce, one of his students, completed and brought out Lantzeff's survey of Russian expansion, *Eastward to Empire: Exploration and Conquest on the Russian Open Frontier to 1750* (Montreal, 1973).

The pioneering efforts of the California school attracted new students to the study of Russia's march across northern Asia. But we need many more scholars to interpret the complexities of that modern-day giant for our present strategic needs and understanding. Yet we are pleased to note that during the past 20 years several works have been published in English on this vital problem. In alphabetical order these include: Terence E. Armstrong, ed., *Yermak's Campaign in Siberia* (London, 1975); James R. Gibson, *Feeding the Russian Fur Trade: Provisionment of the Okhotsk Seaboard and the Kamchatka Peninsula, 1639–1856* (Madison, 1969); George A. Lensen, *The Russian Push toward Japan: Russo-Japanese Relations, 1697–1875* (Princeton, 1959); and Mark Mancall, *Russia and China: Their Diplomatic Relations to 1728* (Cambridge, Mass., 1971).

Although modest in quantity, the quality of these studies is solid. But the work has just begun. We hope that the appearance of this volume of sources, the first of three volumes, will direct other scholars toward studies in Russian expansion into the Pacific, and to bring their research and insights to bear on this herculean colonial venture.

EDITORIAL
PRINCIPLES

E xcept for two unusually long entries, all the documents in this collection appear in their original form. The task of selecting pertinent documents which would illuminate and provide understanding and appreciation of the nature and progress of Russian expansion to the Pacific frontier has been difficult. Our selection has been guided by our wish to offer examples which reveal the major aspects of each situation presented, while holding the reports to a reasonable length.

Most of these original documents which we have selected and translated for this volume were written in Old Slavonic. The bureaucratic sentences are often tortuous mazes which have made the translation process very trying. Some were surely as fearfully taxing to write as they have been to translate. They were often inscribed by unskilled, uneducated persons using primitive writing tools and at best inferior papers and parchments. The problems of uncertain light, subzero weather and the clouds of summer insects are a few other factors, not to mention the hazards of travel, water damage, et cetera. Moreover, because of the considerable differences in syntax and style, each translation has presented individual technical problems. Therefore we have worked to retain original flavor while striving above all for accuracy and clear, modern English translation, breaking endless labyrinthine passages into sentences and paragraphs with standardized punctuation and spelling.

We have standardized the spelling of the names of known persons, rivers and sites which are inconsistently spelled in the various documents. Where we were unable to establish standardized spelling we have paralleled the original variations in the translations. Reports and dispatches from Siberia to Moscow frequently refer to servitors, promyshlenniks and other persons of lower rank by the diminutive forms of their given names: Fedka, Petka. For clarity we have used the formal form of each name: Fedor, Petr. Where material is illegible [missing], or where the editors have decided to omit repetitive or unclear information, it is so noted in brackets within the text: e.g. [names follow].

In transliterating Russian words into English we have used the Library of Congress system, slightly modified; we have omitted ligatures and terminal soft signs, but retained certain internal soft signs: zimov'e, Verkhotur'e. We have anglicized plurals of words which defy exact translation: *voevodas*, *promyshlenniks*, not *voevody*, *promyshlenniki*. We have capitalized *Treasury* (*kazna*) when the word refers to the government institution, and have used the lower case, *treasury*, when the word refers to the iasak furs or other specific items. *Kniaz* is capitalized as *Prince*; *kniazets* we use in lower case *prince*. The word *tsar* is capitalized when it refers to the head of state; lower case is used when a tribal leader is indicated. The Glossary gives details.

After much analysis and reflection we believe that we have restored to knowledge a most important list of obscure and arcane words and phrases. Since most of these "found" terms are so important to the text, we have placed the Glossary in the front of this volume.

Dates are given in accordance with the Julian calendar, which was in official use in Russia from 1700 to 1918. In the seventeenth century that calendar was eleven days behind the Gregorian calendar. Prior to 1700 all the principalities of Rus including Moscow used the Byzantine system, under which Ermak crossed the Urals in 7090 rather than 1581.

Wherever possible we have given the present archival location of documents so that interested scholars may use the original document in their research rather than published versions. However, because of the massive reorganization of the entire Soviet archival system in recent years, and because published Soviet finding guides to these archives are still far from complete, this has not always been possible. We have therefore also referred the reader to a Russian publication of the document.

Archival initials used in this text:

Arkhiv LO II AN SSSR: Arkhiv Leningradskoe otdelenie Instituta Istorii Akademiia Nauk SSSR.

LOA AN SSSR: Leningradskoe otdelenie arkhiva Akademiia Nauk SSSR.

ROGPB: Rukopisnoe otdelenie. Gosudarstvennaia publichnaia biblioteka imeni M. E. Saltykova-Shchedrina.

TsGADA: Tsentralnyi gosudarstvennyi arkhiv drevnikh aktov.

Archival abbreviations:

Ch.: *chernovik*, draft version.

D.: *delo*, item or unit.

F.: *fond*, basic unit group of archival records.

L., ll.: *list*, folio, leaf.

Ob.: *oborotnaia storona*, verso.

Op.: *opis*, inventory.

Stolb.: *stolbets*, roll or register.

The editors of *To Siberia and Russian America* have taken the liberty to place on the following pages the Glossary for this volume. Normally, glossaries are positioned in the backmatter of scholarly books. However, in the editors' opinion this particular compilation is a painstaking restoration of long lost terms, and the Glossary is so vitally important to the full understanding of this volume that it should precede the translated documents.

The Glossary's placement will aid all who use the vast amount of translated material. Because so many Russian terms cannot be given adequate meaning with a single English word, the editors have chosen to retain many transliterated but untranslated terms throughout the documents. The Glossary, therefore, gives the reader quick reference to the full meaning for each of these special words, and it has been placed in its unique position for that very reason.

GLOSSARY

Aleksandriskaia bumaga. Large size, heavy paper used for important official documents.

Altyn. A Tatar word for six, which between the fourteenth and eighteenth century was used in Russia to designate a monetary unit equal to six *dengi* or three *kopecks.*

Altyn, Altyn-khan. The "Golden" khan, ruler of the Khalkha Mongols.

Amanat. A Muscovite term for a hostage (male or female) seized by the promyshlenniks or government agents from native Siberian and later, Aleut and North American tribes to guarantee tribal payment of iasak, and obedience and loyalty to the Tsar.

Antimins. An altar piece containing sacred relics, necessary for celebration of the Eucharist in Russian Orthodox Church.

Arkhimandrit. The administrative head of two or more monasteries in the Russian Orthodox Church.

Archpriest. A senior parish priest in the Russian Orthodox Church.

Arshin. A linear measure used in Russia from the sixteenth century on, equal to 28 inches or 71.1 cm. An arshin was divided into 4 *chetverts* and 16 *vershoks.* Three arshins comprised one *sazhen.*

Ataman. A word of Ukrainian origin (*otaman*) applied to various ranks of elected and self-appointed cossack military commanders. From the Ukraine the term spread among the Don and Volga cossacks, and later among the Siberian cossacks.

Badian. Anise, star anise; a medicinal herb.

Basurman, bisurman. A pejorative term used in the Ukraine and in Russia from the sixteenth to the eighteenth century to describe Tatars, Turks and other followers of Islam.

Bogdoi, bogdoiskie liudi. A seventeenth century Russia term for the Manchus, also used to refer to the Chinese.

Bogdokhan, Bugdykhan. A seventeenth century Russian term for the title of the Manchu and later the Chinese emperor. Some Russian sources refer to the emperor as "the Bogdoi tsar," or "the Bogdoi khan."

Boiar, boiarin. A term denoting a very few wealthy and influential members of Kievan, and later Muscovite, landed and service aristocracy. The Tsar selected certain boiars to serve as members of the *boiarskaia duma* and appointed others to the highest positions in the armed forces and in the civil administration.

Boiarskaia duma. An advisory boiar council to Kievan princes and later to Moscow's tsars. Although its influence and membership fluctuated, the boiarskaia duma participated in formulating many of Muscovy's administrative, legal, military, economic, social and foreign policy matters.

Briatskie liudi, Bratskie liudi. A seventeenth century Russian term for the Buriats, a Mongol tribe whom the Russians encountered and conquered near Lake Baikal.

Bukhartsy. A term used by seventeenth century Russians to describe merchants from Central Asia (mostly Bokhara) who had settled near Russian outposts in Siberia and often served as commercial intermediaries between Russian officials and various natives of Asia.

Cossack. A word of Tatar origin which denotes a free frontiersman. In Europe the most famous were the Ukrainian cossacks along the Dnieper River and the Russian cossacks along the Don and Volga rivers. In the period of Russian expansion to the Pacific, the term cossack was applied to a military man or a hired worker.

Chelobitnaia. A term meaning a written or oral petition or request submitted to the Tsar or to any of his officials by either Russian or non-Russian subjects.

Chet, chetvert. An old Russian unit of measure; in linear measurement it was equal to seven inches, or one-quarter of an arshin; as a unit of dry measure, it varied according to what was being measured. For example, in the seventeenth century in Tobolsk a chet of rye weighed 4 puds, 23 funts, whereas a chet of oats weighed 2 puds, 11.5 funts.

Dan. A slavic term meaning tribute paid by the conquered to the conqueror. In fifteenth century Muscovy it came to mean a regular direct tax paid by the population to the government.

Denga (pl. *dengi*). A Mongol as well as a Russian term for money; in seventeenth century Russia one denga equalled one-half kopeck.

Desiatina. A unit used to measure land; 2.7 acres. Also used to mean one-tenth, or a tithe.

Desiatilnik (also *desiatinnik*). A term that in Muscovy had a two-fold meaning: an official of the Orthodox Church who collected the tithe; and an official in the church courts.

Desiatnik. A Russian term for a low-ranking leader of ten cossacks, streltsy or other units of men in Muscovy and Siberia prior to 1700.

Deti boiarskie, syny boiarskie. A term used to describe a rather large group of impoverished nobles in Muscovy in the sixteenth and seventeenth century. They played a prominent role in Siberia as middle-ranking military commanders and civil administrators.

Diak. A secretary, clerk, an assistant or an associate of the heads of central and regional departments of Russian administrative, financial, judicial and diplomatic institutions. Sometimes they headed these institutions. In the Russian Orthodox Church, the diak was a reader and assistant to the priest.

Dnishche. A term used to describe the distance covered in one day's travel. This varied greatly according to the terrain and means of travel and weather conditions.

Doshchanik. A flat-bottomed boat used by seventeenth century Russians on Siberian rivers and along the sea coast. The doshchanik was built of wooden boards, was about 50 feet long, was often equipped with both oars and sails and was capable of carrying 50 men and their provisions and equipment.

Dovodchik. An executive agent of local authorities in Muscovy (*namestniks* and *volostels*); a prosecutor; a bailiff.

Dumnyi diak. A diak who had served or was serving in the Boiarskaia duma.

Efimok (pl. *efimki*). A Muscovite term for a large silver coin, the Joachimsthaler, minted in Bohemia. The Muscovites obtained efimki through foreign trade and circulated them as their own currency in the sixteenth and seventeenth centuries.

Esaul. A word of Tatar origin which, among the Ukrainian,

Don and later cossacks in Siberia, meant close assistants to the atamans and other officers.

Funt.   A measure of weight used in Russia from the sixteenth century on. The funt was equal to 96 *zolotniki*, or 409 grams, or 0.903 pounds.

Golova.   The literal meaning is "head." In Muscovy it carried several meanings: a military commander, a civil administrative official, a tax collector, a police officer, an assistant to the voevoda, a secretary (*pismennaia golova*), the head of a custom house, and the like.

Gorodok.   A small fortified settlement.

Gost (pl. *gosti*).   A term used to describe a member of a group of some 30 wealthy merchant families in Moscow. The Tsar appointed each gost to that status and granted him numerous rights, privileges and exemptions. In return each gost served the Tsar in various capacities such as custom house administrator, financial advisor and the like.

Gosudar.   A Russian term for lord, master, sovereign. In sixteenth and seventeenth century Russia the term was reserved almost exclusively for the Tsar who, in official documents, was identified as *velikii gosudar*, the great sovereign, or *gosudar vseia Rusi*, the sovereign of all Rus.

Gramota.   A word of Greek origin which in medieval Rus principalities and later in the tsardom of Muscovy meant a letter, deed, will, charter or any written document, official or private.

Grivna.   The term grivna had a double meaning. It was a unit of weight equal to 410 grams, and it also was a monetary unit. The value of the latter varied at times from place to place. From fifteenth through seventeenth century Muscovy the value of a grivna was 20 dengas; 10 grivnas equalled one ruble.

Guliashchie liudi.   A Muscovite term used in Siberia to describe people not assigned to any tax (*tiaglo*), hence mobile. These included runaway serfs, tramps, itinerant workers and other social misfits and unfortunates. They played a vital role in the Russian conquest of Siberia.

Hieromonk.   In the Russian Orthodox Church, a monk who has been ordained as a priest.

Iasachnye liudi.   A term used to describe the iasak-paying non-Russian natives of the Ural region and of Siberia who, as a sign of submission, paid the government in Moscow an annual tribute in furs or other valuable products of their land.

Iasak. A Mongol-Tatar term meaning tribute paid by the conquered to the conqueror. The Mongols spread the iasak system throughout their domains in Asia and Eastern Europe, while the Russians introduced it in the Aleutians.

Iasyr. A word of Turkish-Tatar origin meaning captive or prisoner of war. In seventeenth century Siberia it referred to any non-Russian native captured by Russian forces in a military skirmish.

Iazyk. A term that in seventeenth century Russia had the following meanings: language, people, foreigner, interpreter, prisoner of war, witness.

Igumen. Head of a Russian Orthodox monastery, an abbot.

Inorodtsy. A Russian term for the natives of Siberia and later of Central Asia, Alaska and the Caucasus, who led a nomadic or semi-nomadic life. In the nineteenth century the term also included Jews.

Iurt. A Turkic word for settlement, camp, dwelling; also a territory inhabited by a tribe.

Izba. In modern Russia a term for cottage, hut, peasant dwelling. In sixteenth and seventeenth century Muscovy it meant a structure housing an office, or the office itself, i.e., *prikaznaia izba* or *sezzhaia izba*, the office of the local voevoda.

Kaiuk. A river barge used by Russian conquerors and explorers in Siberia. It had two gables, a rounded bow and a cabin at the stern.

Kalmyks. A Mongol people who in the seventeenth century inhabited an area stretching from the headwaters of the Enisei River to the Urals. The Kalmyks consisted of several tribes, the most prominent of whom were the White Kalmyks or Telenguts who camped near the headwaters of the Ob, and the Black Kalmyks or Dzhungars, who occupied the upper reaches of the Irtysh River.

Kamka. A Russian term for an oriental silk textile with various decorative designs. There were several types of kamka based on the quality of the fabric and its origin.

Kamlei. The upper garment worn by native men of northeastern Asia.

Kazna. A term that had several meanings in Muscovy and Siberia: a warehouse, a depot; money, furs or precious goods belonging to the government; the government financial office; the state's financial apparatus (which we designate with the upper case: Treasury); the iasak collection (for which we use the lower case: treasury).

Khleb.   A modern Russian word for bread. In sixteenth and seventeenth century Muscovy it also meant grain, food provisions, even a tax-in-kind which the government collected from peasants of northern regions to supply its garrisons in Siberia.

Kholop.   A Russian term for a male slave or bondman. In pre-1700 Russia there were various categories of kholops depending on whether they were inherited, bought, or fell into their status through some other circumstance.

Kholop tvoi.   Literally "your slave." All officials in Muscovy in their correspondence, especially with the Tsar, referred to themselves by this term. We have translated this throughout the present work as "your humble servant."

Kniazhestvo.   A Russian term for principality. In seventeenth century Siberia it referred to a tribal territory.

Kniazhets.   Literally "little prince" or "princeling." A term used by the Russians to refer to certain Siberian tribal leaders. We have translated it as "prince" (lower case), as opposed to Prince (*kniaz*), which is used to designate either a Russian prince or the ruler of a large domain.

Kitaika.   A Russian term for a Chinese cotton fabric.

Koch.   A small flat-bottomed sailing vessel used by seventeenth century Russians on Siberian rivers and along the sea coast. Generally the koch had a small deck and could carry a crew of about ten men as well as their equipment and provisions.

Kontaisha (also *Khuntaidzha*).   A title in feudal Mongolia.

Kopek (also *kopeika*).   Kopeck, a term for a small silver coin in sixteenth and seventeenth century Muscovy which equalled two dengas. In the eighteenth century copper replaced silver in the minting of the kopeck.

Krestianin (pl. *krestiane*).   A Russian term for peasant. In Russian history there were numerous categories of peasants depending on their obligations, location and association. In Siberia the three basic groups of peasants were the *iasachnye krestiane* (peasants who paid tribute in furs); *pashennye krestiane* (state peasants whom the government sent to Siberia to cultivate arable lands in order to feed the local servitors and military garrisons); and *beglye krestiane* (runaway peasants), who in Siberia were often included in the category of guliashchie liudi.

Kufter.   A superior silk fabric of Italian manufacture, brocaded with gold or silver.

Kuiak.   Armor of hammered metallic plates sewn on cloth; used by Manchu and Chinese warriors and by some cossacks in Siberia.

Kumach.   A dark red cotton fabric.

Kutukhta (also *khutukhta*).   An official title of a high Buddhist monk; the term means holy or divine.

Laba (also *lama*).   A Russian term for a Buddhist monk in Mongolia and later in Tibet. *Lama* was also used to refer to a large body of water such as Lake Baikal and the Sea of Okhotsk.

Lan.   A seventeenth century Chinese silver coin.

Levk.   A measure of distance; 17,200 feet.

Lisitsa.   Fox. *Krasnaia lisitsa*, red fox; *sivodushka lisitsa*, cross fox; *chernoburaia lisitsa*, black-brown fox; *belaia lisitsa*, arctic or polar fox.

Litva.   A Muscovite term to designate prisoners of war and other foreigners sent to Siberia as punishment (Poles, Lithuanians, Ukrainians, Belorussians, Germans and Swedes). Russian officials in Siberia utilized the superior knowledge and skills of the Litva men by sending them on various assignments. The Litva played a vital role in the conquest of Siberia.

Lutchie liudi.   The Russian designation for native leaders in Siberia who were preferred as hostages.

Murza.   A Tatar term for persons of Tatar nobility; also a tribal leader.

Muzhik.   A Russian term for a peasant, commoner.

Nadolby.   Vertically placed sharpened logs, used as obstacles against mounted troops.

Nakaz, nakaznaia pamiat.   A Russian term for an instruction or order issued by the government in Moscow to its agents in the provinces, including Siberia.

Namestnik.   A tsar-appointed administrator (usually a boiar) of an important town or a large administrative unit called a *namestnichestvo* in the fourteenth through the sixteenth centuries.

Nemets (pl. *nemtsy*).   A term used in Muscovy in the sixteenth and seventeenth centuries to denote West Europeans (Germans, Dutch, English, Swedes, Italians and others).

Nikan.   A term for the Chinese, used by some Russians during the first half of the seventeenth century.

Obrok. A term that originally meant a fixed payment of obligations, including taxes, payment for services and rent for leased properties. After the reforms of the 1550's, obrok was a quitrent in cash paid to the treasury by Muscovy's population for the use of state lands, forests, fishing and hunting grounds and the like.

Odnoriadka. A singlebreasted long kaftan without a collar.

Okhochie liudi. A term used in seventeenth century Siberia to refer to peasants who volunteered for assignments.

Okolnichii. A high ranking court official in the Tsar's service who was immediately below the members of the boiarskaia duma in order of social importance. The Tsar entrusted many okolnichiis with military, civil and diplomatic assignments.

Opolniki. In seventeenth century Russia, a term used to refer to drafted soldiers who were members of the *opolchenie.*

Orda. A Mongol term for horde, designating a camp or a tribe of nomads. The most famous horde was the "Golden Horde," also known as the Kipchak Khanate, established by Batu Khan following his successful conquest in 1236–1241 of Central Asia and Eastern Europe. Early in the fifteenth century the Golden Horde broke up into seven independent hordes or khanates: Kazan, at the junction of the Volga and Kama rivers; Crimean, on the northern shores of the Black and Azov seas; the Great Horde, on the lower Volga; Nogai, on the lower Ural River; Siberian, at the confluence of the Irtysh and Tobol rivers; Kazakh, north of the Aral Sea; and Uzbek, around Lake Balkhash.

Osmina. A Russian term for two units of measure: 1) a dry measure equal to three bushels; and 2) a measure of land equal to approximately 0.7 acres.

Ostrog. A Russian term with several meanings: fort, fortification, blockhouse, settlement, town.

Ostrozhek. A small ostrog, blockhouse.

Pamiat. In modern Russian, a term for memory and recollection. In sixteenth and seventeenth century Muscovy the word referred to official documents, memoranda, notices, records, certificates, vouchers and instructions, both written and oral. Frequently such instructions were called *nakaznaia pamiat.*

Pishchal. A seventeenth century Russian term for muskets; also small fortress guns.

Pismennaia golova. Literally, "writing chief." An official under the voevoda's command in seventeenth century Russia and in the towns of Siberia. Sent out from Moscow with the voevoda, he might subsequently be sent out by the voevoda on special assignments.

Plastina. A group of furs sewed together.

Poddiak. A Russian term for a minor clerk.

Poltina. A seventeenth century Russian coin equal in value to one-half ruble or 50 kopecks or 100 dengi.

Pominki. A modern Russian term for a funeral repast. In pre-1700 Russia and especially in Siberia, pominki had two principal meanings: 1) A "gift" Russian officials exacted, often by force, from Siberian natives; and 2) A bribe Russian officials received from Siberian natives.

Portishche. A length of fabric sufficient for a garment; a set of furs sufficient to make a shuba.

Posada. A seventeenth century Russian term referring to a settlement whose inhabitants enjoyed certain rights but who had numerous obligations to the state.

Posadskie liudi. The inhabitants of a posada, usually merchants, craftsmen, or trader-promyshlenniks.

Pravedchik. An appointed agent of central or local authorities in Muscovy, who carried out court orders and sentences.

Prikashchik (also *prikazchik*). A low-ranking official or agent of the prikaz; also a town or village administrator; a steward; a manager of an estate; a special agent of the government, the church, or a private enterprise.

Prikaz. A department of the central government in sixteenth and seventeenth century Muscovy. There were 63 prikazes in Muscovy between 1500 and 1700 to deal with finances, military, administration, courts, conquered territories, foreign affairs, church and other matters. The *Posolskii prikaz* dealt with foreign affairs and the *Sibirskii prikaz* was in charge of the administration of Siberia. Every prikaz was formed or dissolved on the Tsar's order, and each was headed by a boiar assisted by diaks and prikashchiks in Moscow and throughout the country.

Pristav. A term used in seventeenth century Russia for an official assigned to escort foreign envoys.

Promyshlennik. In modern Russia the term means a manufacturer, an industrialist, or a self-employed person. During the period of Russian expansion across northern Asia and later across the North Pacific, it referred to a footloose Russian hunter, trader or trapper who worked for himself or in a group of other promyshlenniks, or who was employed by a wealthy merchant or by government officials on such assignments as exploration, conquest and pacification of the natives.

Pud.   A unit of Russian weight measure equal to 36 pounds or 16.38 kg.

Razriad.   Office, department, category, register, military district.

Right bank, left bank.   In Russian use, looking upriver; opposite of English usage.

Rovduga.   Sueded reindeer hide.

Ruka.   A contemporary Russian term for arm and hand. In sixteenth and seventeenth century Muscovy it also meant power, authority, protection, guarantee and pledge. In Siberian sources the expression *byt pod rukoi* is often used; it meant to bring or to be under Russian authority or protection.

Sazhen.   A unit of linear measure; one sazhen = seven feet or 2.134 meters.

Sezzhaia izba.   See *izba.*

Shaitan.   Tatar word for devil, demon, Satan.

Shert.   A term used in the seventeenth century by Russian conquerors throughout Siberia to refer to the oath of allegiance or submission to the Russian Tsar taken by any native Siberian tribe.

Shniak.   A fishing boat four to five sazhens long and one sazhen wide.

Shuba.   A coat or cloak made of furs.

Shulenga.   A Buriat (Briatsk) or Evenk prince (kniazhets).

Sirota.   A modern Russian term for orphan. In sixteenth and seventeenth century Muscovy and Siberia, Russian peasants and non-Russian natives applied this term to themselves in their petitions to the Tsar.

Sloboda.   A term used to designate a settlement of low-ranking servitors in Muscovy, or petty merchants and artisans, or state peasants living on government, church or private lands, who were exempt for a specific number of years or permanently from certain taxes and obligations.

Sluzhiashchie liudi.   Literally, "serving people." We have translated this throughout as "servitor." Servitors were persons in government service who performed their many various kinds of services instead of paying tax. The term included many categories of persons in seventeenth century Siberia; indeed at various times almost any man below top official rank might be a servitor on some special assignment. Cossacks and promyshlenniks often joined the ranks of government servitors on expeditions, and on occasions even natives might be admitted into service, particularly if they had been baptized and taken the oath of loyalty to the Tsar. A low-ranking Russian government employee, military or civilian.

Sobol. Sable. Unless otherwise stated, "sable" as used in this work refers to a mature sable pelt in prime condition. Damaged or immature pelts or summer furs were especially designated.

Sorok. Literally, forty. A bundle of precious furs. Sables and certain other furs were packed and transported in bundles of forty for convenience in handling and counting. Iasak collectors and others often refer to a "forty" of sables.

Sotnik. A Russian term for a commander of a military unit of 100 men, cossacks or streltsy.

Stolnik. A high ranking official in the Tsar's service who was immediately below the members of the *boiarskaia duma* in order of social importance. The Tsar entrusted certain stolniks with military, civil and diplomatic assignments; they also served as voevodas and assistants to important boiars. A category of feudal aristocracy; an important boiar who had the right to be present at the table (*stol*) of the Tsar.

Streltsy. Literally, shooters, musketeers. The streltsy were Muscovy's first permanent regular military units from 1550 to 1698. Some units were cavalry, but most were infantry. Their participation was crucial in Ivan IV's defeat of Kazan in 1552, and in subsequent Russian conquest of northern Asia from the Urals to the Pacific.

Striapchii. A high ranking courtier in the Tsar's court as well as in military and civil service.

Syn boiarskii. An impoverished member of Muscovite nobility in the sixteenth and seventeenth centuries. These persons played a prominent role in Siberia as middle ranking military commanders and civil administrators. Also, a military rank immediately above that of sotnik.

Taisha (also *taidzha*). An official title used by Mongol chieftains who could trace their lineage to Genghis Khan.

Tatars. A Turkic people who formed the bulk of the population of the Golden Horde. In the fifteenth century four principal

Tatar political entities emerged: Crimea, Kazan, Nogai and Siberia. Seventeenth century Siberian sources speak of two Tatar groups: the *sluzhilye Tatary* (Tatars in Russian service who lived near Tobolsk), and the *iurtovskie Tatary* (leaders of various independent Siberian Tatars who were either friendly or hostile to Russian conquerors).

Tiaglie liudi. *Tiaglo* is a modern Russian word for tax and for draught animals. In pre-1700 Russia, tiaglo was a system of obligations in money, kind or labor which the government collected from state peasants and town inhabitants. Officially these people were known as the tiaglie liudi, as distinguished from sluzhiashchie liudi, who performed state service instead of having other kinds of obligations to the government.

Tiun. An appointed agent of the Tsar or of a prince, boiar or high church official, who performed various economic, administrative or even judicial functions. He often assisted namestniks and volostels.

Toion. A Russian term for the elder or leader of a native tribe in Siberia; later also in Russian America.

Tsar. A Russian term for sovereign Emperor. Historically this term was used only for the Byzantine emperors, the Khans of the Golden Horde, the Sultan of the Ottoman Empire, and Khans of Siberia, Kazan, Astrakhan and Crimea, the emperor of China, and Muscovy's rulers beginning with Ivan III (1462–1505). Throughout the present work we have capitalized the word when it refers to the Russian ruler.

Tsarevich. The Tsar's son or brother who was the legal heir to the throne of Russia.

Tselovalnik. Literally, one who kisses. An elected or appointed official in Muscovy who kissed the cross or the Bible upon taking his oath of office. Tselovalniks were government agents active in financial, administrative and judicial affairs, usually as assistants to judges, starostas and voevodas. In Siberia they assisted the tax and iasak collectors and customs officials.

Uezd. A Russian term for a district, country or administrative-judicial territorial unit that included not only a town but the surrounding rural area as well. Smaller rural units, *volosts*, were included in its jurisdiction.

Ukaz. A Russian term for a decree, edict or order issued by the Tsar.

Ulan.   A Tartar word for "son." A young man, a mounted soldier carrying a lance, also an official of a khan.

Ulus.   A Mongol term that had several meanings: a settlement; an area inhabited by a native Siberian tribe; a domain or realm belonging to a Tatar, Mongol, Kalmyk or Uzbek ruler.

Vatashchik.   A Russian term for a member of a *vataga* or cooperative group formed to fish or hunt.

Versta.   Verst, a Russian linear measure equal to 0.663 miles or 1.067 kilometers.

Voevoda.   An old Slavic term meaning military commander. In seventeenth century Muscovy it meant a Tsar-appointed administrator, usually a boiar, holding military, civil and judicial powers over a region. The center of the voevoda's administration was the prikaznaia izba or sezzhaia izba, and was managed by a diak.

Volost.   A rural administrative unit.

Volostel.   An appointed supervisor (usually a petty nobleman) over a volost.

Zakhrebetnik.   A category of Russian persons in Siberia; such persons were free, but had neither land nor household. They were not legally "the tiaglye," taxpayers. Were frequently hired as seasonal workers.

Zemskii starosta.   A local official in towns and rural settlements of Muscovy, either elected by the community or appointed by the Tsar's voevoda, to whom they were accountable. Such officials were responsible for the collection of taxes and the maintenance of public order and safety.

Zender.   Eastern cotton fabric.

Zimov'e.   A Russian term used in Siberia in the seventeenth century which had two meanings: a small Russian winter outpost in the newly conquered region; and a place or area used by Siberian nomads during the winter.

Zhalovanie.   A modern Russian term for salary. In sixteenth and seventeenth century Muscovy it referred to a grant, reward, mercy, grace, favor, salary, and subsidy in money or in goods.

Zolotnik.   A seventeenth century Russian measure of weight equal to $\frac{1}{96}$ of a pound.

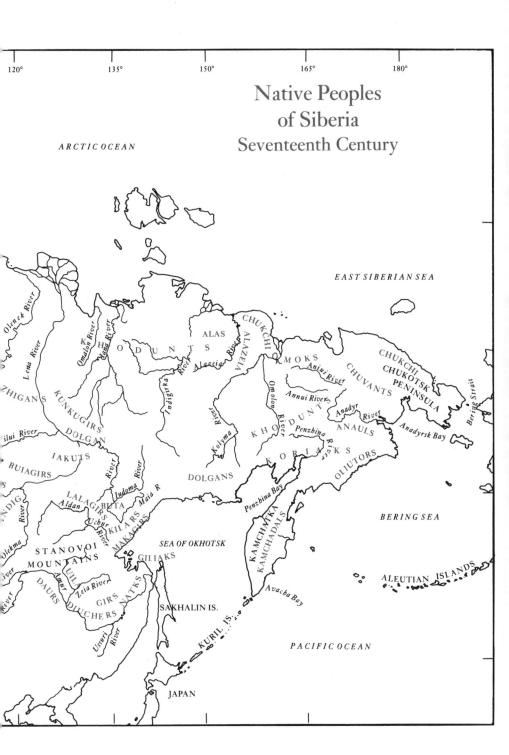

Native Peoples
of Siberia
Seventeenth Century

ARCTIC OCEAN

EAST SIBERIAN SEA

Olenek River

Lena River

Omolon River

Viliui River

ZHIGANS

KUNKUGIRS

DOLGAN

IAKUTS

BUIAGIRS

NDIG

Olekma

LALAGIRS

Aldan

BUTA

KILARS

Ucbur

MAKAGIRS

Maia R

Ludoma River

STANOVOI
MOUNTAINS

UIL

Amur

Zeia River

DAURS

DUCHERS

GIRS

NATKS

Usuri River

O D U N T S

Indigirka River

Alazeia

Kolyma

ALAS

ALAZEIA

CHUKCHI

MOKS

Aniui River

Annui River

Omolon River

KHODUNTS

KORIAKS

DOLGANS

Penzbina Bay

KAMCHATKA
KAMCHADALS

SEA OF OKHOTSK

GILIAKS

SAKHALIN IS.

KURIL IS.

Avacba Bay

JAPAN

CHUKCHI
CHUKOTSK
PENINSULA

Bering Strait

CHUVANTS

Anadyr

River

ANAULS

Anadyrsk Bay

OLIUTORS

BERING SEA

ALEUTIAN ISLANDS

PACIFIC OCEAN

120°   135°   150°   165°   180°

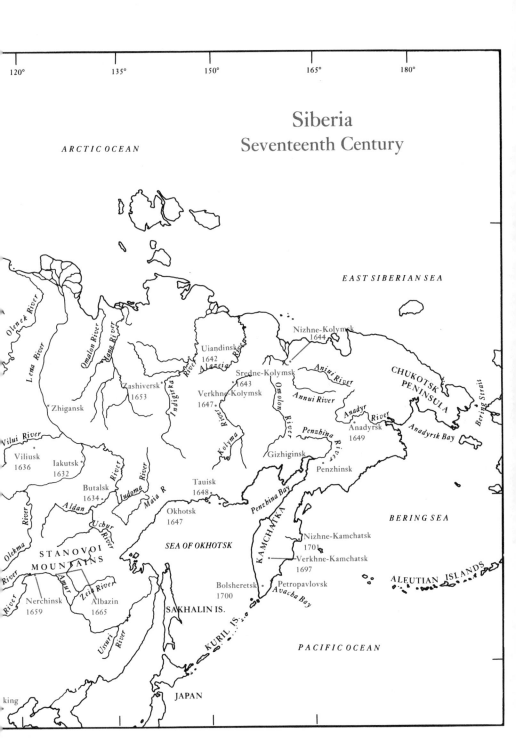

Siberia
Seventeenth Century

ARCTIC OCEAN

EAST SIBERIAN SEA

Olenek River

Lena River

Omolon River

Iana River

Uiandinsk
1642
Alazeia River

Zashiversk
1653

Zhigansk

Indigirka River

Iana River

Kolyma River

Nizhne-Kolymsk
1644

Sredne-Kolymsk
1643

Verkhne-Kolymsk
1647

Aniui River

Annui River

Omolon River

CHUKOTSK
PENINSULA

Bering Strait

Vilui River

Viliusk
1636

Iakutsk
1632

Aldan River

Butalsk
1634

Maia R

Iudoma

Anadyr River

Anadyrsk
1649

Anadyrsk Bay

Penzhina River

Gizhiginsk

Penzhinsk

Tauisk
1648

Okhotsk
1647

SEA OF OKHOTSK

Penzhina Bay

BERING SEA

Olekma River

STANOVOI
MOUNTAINS

Amur River

Uchur River

Zeia River

Nerchinsk
1659

Albazin
1665

Ussuri River

SAKHALIN IS.

KAMCHATKA

Nizhne-Kamchatsk
1701

Verkhne-Kamchatsk
1697

Bolsheretsk
1700

Petropavlovsk

Avacha Bay

KURIL IS.

ALEUTIAN ISLANDS

PACIFIC OCEAN

king

JAPAN

xci

RUSSIA'S
CONQUEST
OF SIBERIA

1

A LETTER PATENT [*ZHALOVANNAIA GRAMOTA*] FROM TSAR IVAN
VASILEVICH TO GRIGORII STROGANOV GRANTING FINANCIAL, JUDI-
CIAL AND TRADE PRIVILEGES ON UNINHABITED LANDS ALONG THE
KAMA RIVER

I, the Tsar and Grand Prince Ivan Vasilevich of all Russia, have
been asked to grant to Grigorii Anikievich Stroganov that for
which he has petitioned, namely: the uninhabited lands, black
[coniferous] forests, wild rivers and lakes and uninhabited islands
and marshlands in our patrimony which extend for some 88 versts
[one verst = 3500 feet], along the right bank* of the Kama from
the mouth of the Lysvaia, and along the left bank of the Kama
opposite Pyznovskaia backwaters, and along both banks of the
Kama to the Chusovaia River. These uninhabited lands extend for
146 versts. To the present time no one [no Russian] has worked
this land nor established homesteads here. To date no tax revenue
has been received from this area into the Treasury I hold as Tsar
and Grand Prince. At present the land has not been granted to
anyone, nor has it been entered in the census books, nor in the
books of purchase, nor in legal records.

In his petition Grigorii Stroganov has also asked permission to
build a small town there where he will place cannon and defense
guns; he will station cannoneers and gunners, and post guards at
the gates to protect the town from the Nogai people and from
other hordes. He will cut timber along the rivers up to their headwaters and around the lakes, put the land into fields, and establish
farmsteads. He will invite persons to settle who are unregistered
elsewhere and do not pay taxes. He will search for salt deposits,
and wherever he finds these, he will set up saltworks and evaporate salt.

Here in Moscow our Treasury officials have inquired about
this area from a man from Perm named Kodaul, who has come
from Perm to bring *dan* [tribute] from all the Perm people. This
man from Perm, Kodaul, has told our Treasury officials that the
region for which Grigorii petitions us has been uninhabited from
time immemorial, that it has brought no revenues into our Trea-

---

*Russians look upriver when designating left or right bank.—Eds.

sury, and that the Perm people have no enterprises of their own in that region.

If it is true, as Grigorii has stated in his petition, and as Kodaul from Perm has affirmed, that these uninhabited lands have hitherto paid us no tribute and presently pay none, that the Perm people pay no taxes from this region nor do they pay any *iasak* [tribute in furs] from it to Kazan, nor have they done so in the past; and if this patent will present no hardship either to the Perm people or to travelers, then I, the Tsar and Grand Prince Ivan Vasilevich of all Russia do grant this petition of Grigorii Anikievich Stroganov, and authorize him to build a small town in the uninhabited lands some 88 versts below Great Perm, along the Kama River, on the right bank of the Kama from the Lysvaia River and on the left bank of the Kama opposite Pyznovskaia backwaters, and down both banks of the Kama to the Chusovaia. He may build a small town in the black forest, in a secure and well protected location, and emplace cannon and defense guns in that town, and I authorize him, at his own expense, to station cannoneers and gunners and gate guards there to protect the town against the Nogai people and other hordes. He may cut timber around that small town along the rivers and lakes and up to the headwaters, and plough arable lands, and establish farmsteads, and invite unregistered, non-tax-paying persons to settle in that small town.

But Grigorii is neither to invite nor accept registered taxpayers from Perm or from other towns into our Empire, nor is he to accept lawbreakers or persons who have run off from *boiars* with their possessions. If taxpayers from other towns within our Empire should come to Grigorii with their wives and children, and the *namestniks* [administrators] or *volostels* [supervisors] or the elected officials object to this, then Grigorii is to send such taxpayers and their wives and children back to the towns from which written objections have come. He is not to accept or hold such persons.

Persons who come to this town from our Empire or from other lands with money or with goods who wish to purchase salt or fish or other things are free to sell their goods and to purchase other items without paying duty.

Grigorii may accept persons who move from Perm to settle in his town, provided they are unregistered and have no tax obligations.

Wherever he may find salt deposits he is to build saltworks and evaporate salt. He may fish in the rivers and lakes without paying *obrok* [quitrent]. Grigorii is to report to our Treasury officials immediately if he should find silver, copper or lead ores, but he is not to mine these deposits for himself without our consent. He is not to intrude into the Perm bee-keeping and fishing concessions.

I have granted him these patents for a period of 20 years, from the Feast of the Annunciation in 1558 to the Feast of the Annunciation in 1578. For the duration of this 20-year patent period, Grigorii is not obliged to pay dan to me, the Tsar and Grand Prince, on behalf of any unregistered non-tax-paying persons who may come to his town or settlement, or to the farms near the town, or to the villages. He is likewise not obliged to perform postal or town service, nor pay either duty or obrok for his saltworks and fisheries in those places. He is not to collect duties of any sort from persons from our Empire or from other lands, who travel through that town, with or without goods, regardless of whether or not they are engaging in trade. But if he takes out or sends out his salt and fish through other towns, he must pay all the taxes on the salt and fish, just as our taxes would be collected from other traders.

Our Perm namestniks and their *tiuns* [agents] will have no judicial authority over Grigorii Stroganov, nor over the farming or non-farming persons who may settle in his town and villages. The *pravedchiks* [court officials] and *dovodchiks* [bailiffs] and their subordinates are not to come to Grigorii Stroganov or to the people in his town and villages. They may not set bail nor impose fines. Grigorii has complete judicial authority over his settlers. If any person in another town has a complaint against Grigorii, such person is to secure an official warrant, on the basis of which both plaintiff and defendent will appear before our Treasury officials in Moscow by the Feast of the Annunciation in the same year.

When the fixed period has expired, Grigorii Stroganov will be required to bring to our Treasury in Moscow on that same date, the Feast of the Annunciation, whatever settlement our officials call for.

I also grant the following to Grigorii Anikievich Stroganov: for the duration of the 20-year privilege, Grigorii and his settlers are not obligated to provide transport, guides or provisions for any of our envoys who go through his town en route from Moscow to

Siberia or from Siberia to Moscow, or for our envoys who go from Kazan to Perm or from Perm to Kazan. Merchants in the town should have bread, salt and other provisions available, and sell these to envoys and emissaries and travelers at the same price at which they would sell such things to one another. Travelers may hire whatever carts, sailing vessels or rowboats they wish, as well as porters, from whatever person asks the lowest price.

I also grant a further privilege to Grigorii Anikievich Stroganov: he is not obligated to collect taxes from the people of Perm nor extend them credit for the duration of the 20-year period. The people of Perm are not to intrude into any of Grigorii's new forests or arable lands from the Lysvaia River along the Kama, along its tributaries, or around lakes, up as far as the upper reaches of the Chusovaia River.

The Perm people may keep their established enterprises which they have held from ancient times, and Grigorii will possess his new lands, from which no taxes are being paid into our Treasury and no iasak has been collected for our Treasury by our boiars and *voevodas*, nor had previously been paid to Kazan.

But if Grigorii has deceived us in making his petition, or if he does not abide by the terms of this letter patent, or if he acts illegally, then this patent will be invalid.

Issued in Moscow, April 4, 1558.

See: G. F. Muller, *Istoriia Sibiri* (Moscow-Leningrad: 1937), I, 332–335.

2

A GRAMOTA FROM TSAR IVAN VASILEVICH TO IAKOV AND GRIGORII
STROGANOV CONCERNING REINFORCEMENTS TO SUBDUE THE CHER-
EMIS AND OTHER NATIVES PLUNDERING ALONG THE KAMA RIVER.

From the Tsar and Grand Prince Ivan Vasilevich of all Russia to Iakov and Grigorii, sons of Anika Stroganov, in their settlement on the Kama River. Our voevoda, Prince Ivan Iurevich Bulgakov, has written to us from Perm this year, 1572, about how the Cheremis are attacking merchant vessels on the Kama. Prince Ivan has also written to us that your man, Tretiak, sent word to him on July 15 from the mouth of the river that 40 insurgent Cheremis had come to the Kama, and had Ostiaks, Bashkirs and Buints with them, and in an attack they killed 87 merchants and *vatashchiks* [entrepreneurs] from Perm. When this our gramota reaches you, you are to act with extreme caution. You are to choose a reliable *golova* [headman] and as many cossack volunteers as you can call upon, all well armed with every manner of weapon from guns to bows and arrows. You are also to take Ostiaks and Voguls who are loyal to us, and cossack volunteers who have not turned against us. Equip them, and order their wives and children to remain in the ostrog.

When you select the golova and the volunteer *streltsy* [musketeers] and cossacks, make a list of their names and include the names also of the Ostiaks and the Voguls and the volunteers. List them according to the weapons they have. Write down how many Ostiaks and Voguls and volunteers will be massed to fight our rebellious subjects, and how many you will keep with you. Forward this list of names, under your seal, by any available courier. Send it to us in Moscow, to the Prikaz of the Kazan Dvorets [Office], to our *diaks* [secretaries] Andrei Shchelkalov and Kirei Gorin, so that we will be informed of this muster.

You are to send this force made up of the golova, the volunteers, the streltsy, cossacks, Ostiaks and Voguls to fight our rebellious subjects, the Cheremis, Ostiaks, Votiaks and Nogai, who have committed treason by turning against us. Volunteers are to be sent to put down the insurgent Cheremis who attack the settlements, but they must be constantly on guard and act with great caution. They are also to put down the insurgent Cheremis, Ostiaks, Votiaks and Nogai who have turned against us; but if there are any loyal Cheremis or Ostiaks who wish to join their comrades [who are with us], you are not to kill them if they will break away from the outlaws and join us. Offer them protection. We will reward them.

In regard to those who have been disloyal but now wish to be loyal to us again, and want to prove this: talk to them; tell them of our mercy; assure them that we will look kindly on them and pardon them and ease their burdens. But in order to prove themselves to us they must assemble with their leaders and join the volunteers in fighting our insurgent subjects, conquer them, and kill them. They may claim the goods of any person they conquer, and take his wife and children [as slaves] for work. You are to order that no one is to take away the captured booty from Cheremis who are genuinely loyal to us and have fought against our insurgent subjects and have taken their wives, horses, livestock clothing, or any other belongings.

Written in Moscow August 6, 1572.

See: G. F. Müller, *Istoriia Sibiri* (Moscow-Leningrad: 1937), I, 338–339.

3

A LETTER PATENT FROM TSAR IVAN VASILEVICH TO IAKOV AND
GRIGORII STROGANOV GRANTING TWENTY YEARS' EXEMPTION FROM
TAXES AND OTHER OBLIGATIONS FOR THEIR LANDS AND THEIR SET-
TLERS ON THOSE LANDS IN TAKHCHEIA AND ALONG THE TOBOL RIVER

I, the Tsar and Grand Prince Ivan Vasilevich of all Russia, have
been petitioned to grant privileges to Iakov and Grigorii, sons
of Anika Stroganov. They have informed me that in our patrimony beyond the Iugra Mountains, in the Siberian borderlands
between Siberia and the Nogai, in Takhcheia and along the Tobol
River and its tributaries and lakes, up to its headwaters, the Siberian sultan [Kuchum, also called Tsar or Khan] is assembling
troops to do battle. In 1573 on St. Elijah's day, the Siberian sultan's
brother Mametkul came from the Tobol River with troops to explore routes which he could use to lead his army to attack Perm.
He killed many of our dan-paying Ostiaks and took their wives
and children into captivity. The Siberian killed our envoy Tretiak
Chebukov and Tatars in his service who were on a mission to the
Kazakh horde. The Siberian came within five versts of the ostrog
where [the Stroganovs] are now carrying on their enterprises under
our patent. By the terms of our patent Iakov and Grigorii were
not to deploy hired cossacks from their ostrog against the Siberian
warriors without our instructions.

In the past the Siberian sultan killed our dan-paying Ostiaks,
Chagir and his men, in these same areas where Iakov and Grigorii
are carrying on their enterprises. The Siberian also took some of
our dan-paying subjects prisoner, and killed others. He will not
allow our Ostiaks, Voguls and Iugras to pay our dan into our
Treasury. He is forcing the Iugras to go in boats to fight these
Ostiaks and Voguls. And when the Cheremis turned against us,
the Siberian sent them to the Takhcheia people and won them
over to his side. Prior to this the Takhcheia people did not pay dan
to us nor iasak to Kazan, but instead, they paid iasak to the Nogai.
The Ostiaks who live near Takhcheia are being informed that
they are to pay dan to us, as our other Ostiak subjects do, that
they are not to pay dan and iasak to the Siberian, and that they
are to band together in order to defend themselves against the
Siberian.

Thus we grant the following patents to Iakov and Grigorii: they may build forts at strategic locations in Takhcheia and along the Tobol River and on its tributaries up to its headwaters; they may hire guards and arm them; they may smelt iron, engage in agriculture, and hold the land.

Any Ostiaks who will turn against the Siberian and pay dan to us are to be protected against the Siberian.

Therefore let it be as Iakov and Grigorii have petitioned. I, the Tsar and Grand Prince Ivan Vasilevich have granted their request to Iakov and Grigorii, sons of Anika Stroganov. They may build strongholds in Takhcheia and along the Tobol River, and fortify them, and keep cannoneers and gunners and maintain garrisons as protection against the Siberian and the Nogai people. Near the forts they may build iron works, engage in fishing and farming along both sides of the Tobol and along its tributary streams and lakes up to its headwaters, cut trees, and cultivate and hold the land. They may take unregistered non-tax-paying people, but they are not to accept brigands, outlaws or any persons who have run off from boiars with their possessions, and they are to be on guard against any evil influences.

Wherever they may discover iron ore in these lands they may mine it. If they find copper, tin or lead ores or sulphur deposits, they are to take test samples. Any other persons who wish to engage in these enterprises may do so, but must pay obrok, so our Treasury will benefit. Anyone who wishes to take part in this undertaking may do so, and is to inform us in writing as to which mining activity he is engaging in, how many *puds* of ore he produces, what the amount of obrok is and which persons are paying it. We will then issue an appropriate *ukaz*.

We are granting the patents in Takhcheia and along the Tobol River and its tributaries up to its headwaters, along with agricultural rights, for a period of 20 years, from Trinity Sunday 1574 to Trinity Sunday 1594.

Unregistered, non-tax-paying people who come to Iakov and Grigorii to live in the forts and to establish settlements and enterprises, and work at cultivating the land, will have no obligation for the duration of these patents to pay the dan due me as Tsar and Grand Prince. Neither need they fulfill postal obligations, nor pay postal assessments, nor perform obligatory road work or town service, nor pay any other assessments or obrok from their enterprises and profits. However, Iakov and Grigorii are not to interfere in any areas which have prior established villages or settlements, or in enterprises in which these inhabitants may be engaged. Such areas are to be taxed and fulfill our other obligations as formerly. Also, Iakov and Grigorii and persons who come to settle in the new lands must pay duties on goods which they take out or send out to other towns, as other merchants do, in accordance with our ukaz.

Any Ostiaks, Voguls and Iugras who will turn away from the Siberian, and begin to pay dan to us, should be sent to our Treasury officials in person with their dan. If they will not bring the dan in person, then Iakov and Grigorii are to choose trustworthy persons and send them with our dan to our Treasury, and deliver it into our Treasury. Iakov and Grigorii are to offer protection in their forts to these dan-paying Ostiaks, Voguls and Iugras and their wives and children, against attacks by the Siberian. Iakov and Grigorii are to gather together volunteers from the Ostiaks and Voguls and Iugras and Samoeds, and together with their hired cossacks and armed detail, send them all into battle against the Siberian, take his men into captivity, and force them to pay dan to us.

I have granted a further privilege to Iakov and Grigorii: if merchants come to them in these new areas from Bukhara or from the Kazakh horde or from other lands, to sell horses and other goods, and these merchants are not continuing on to Moscow, then they may carry on trade in all goods at will, without paying duty. Further, our Perm namestniks and their tiuns will not have jurisdiction over Iakov and Grigorii and their *sloboda* [tax-free settlement] people, nor over any who come to live in their forts whether or not they are agricultural people. Further, neither pravedchiks nor dovodchiks nor their subordinates are to come to Iakov and Grigorii and their sloboda people for any reason; they may not impose bail or exile. Iakov and Grigorii are to rule and judge their sloboda people personally, in all matters, or select someone to do so.

Any persons from other towns who have any complaints against Iakov and Grigorii are to obtain legal warrants from our boiars or diaks, and in accordance with such warrants, both plaintiff and defendant will come, without harassment, to appear before us in Moscow on Trinity Sunday of that year.

On Trinity Sunday of the year in which the patent expires, Iakov and Grigorii are to bring to us in Moscow all the assessments which our officials may impose, according to the record books.

I have granted a further privilege to Iakov and Grigorii, sons of Anika Stroganov: if they or their people or their sloboda peasants travel from Vychegodskaia Sol via Perm to the Takhcheia sloboda, or from the sloboda to Vychegodskaia Sol, our Perm namestniks and their tiuns and dovodchiks and other Prikaz officials in Perm may not impose assessments on Iakov and Grigorii and their people and sloboda peasants, nor will they have judicial authority over them in any matters.

I have granted a further privilege to Iakov and Grigorii: when our envoys or emissaries travel from Moscow to Siberia or to the Kazakh horde, or from Siberia or the Kazakh horde to Moscow, by way of their fort, for the duration of the 20 years of their patent, Iakov and Grigorii and their sloboda people will not be obligated to provide guides, transport or provisions to our Siberian and Kazakh envoys and emissaries. Envoys and couriers and travelers may purchase bread and salt and all provisions at whatever price such provisions are being bought and sold locally. Travelers may hire wagons and sailing vessels and rowboats and guides at the rate then in effect locally.

Finally, I have granted Iakov and Grigorii this privilege: on the Irtysh and Ob and other rivers they may build forts wherever necessary for defense and to provide halting places for volunteers. They are to hold the forts with garrisons of armed men. From the forts they may fish and hunt without paying obrok for the duration of the years of the patent.

This letter patent given in [Aleksandrovskaia] Sloboda, May 30, 1574.

See: G. F. Müller, *Istoriia Sibiri* (Moscow-Leningrad: 1937), I, 339–341.

4

A GRAMOTA FROM TSAR IVAN VASILEVICH TO NIKITA STROGANOV,
CONCERNING SENDING HIS MEN AGAINST THE PELYM PRINCE AND
THE VOGULS, TO ASSIST SEMEN AND MAKSIM STROGANOV

From the Tsar and Grand Prince Ivan Vasilevich of all Russia to Nikita Grigorevich Stroganov. Semen and Maksim Stroganov have reported to us that the Pelym prince and his Voguls have attacked their slobodas and have set fire to many settlements and have taken peasants into captivity and that the Pelym prince and his Voguls are now encamped near Chusovsk ostrog. They ask us to assist them by ordering troops from Great Perm to support them, and say that you are not helping them repel the Voguls. When you receive this our gramota, you are to send as many of your people as possible to aid Semen and Maksim against the Voguls, and your men are to join forces with theirs in order to stand together to offer a strong defense. We have also ordered that the *zemskii starosta* [town official] from Perm assemble a support force of as many men as possible, and we have instructed him that when the Vogul warriors attack, he is to make a stand with Semen's and Maksim's men against the Pelym prince. You, too, are to order your people to aid the people of Perm, and Semen's and Maksim's men, to stand against the Pelym prince and not allow him to wage battle, so that you all will avoid war.

Written in Moscow November 6, 1581.

See: Russia. Arkheograficheskaia kommissiia. *Dopolneniia k aktam istoricheskim* (St. Petersburg: 1846), I, 183.

5

1582

THE CONQUEST OF SIBERIA BY ERMAK TIMOFEEV AND HIS BAND OF
COSSACKS, AS REPORTED IN THE *STROGANOV CHRONICLE* (EXCERPTS)

On September 1, 1582, on the feast day of our Holy Father
Simeon Stylite, Semen, Maksim and Nikita Stroganov sent
out the Volga *atamans* [cossack military commanders] and cossacks, Ermak Timofeev and his men, from their town, against the
Siberian sultan. With these men they sent 300 of their own troops
mustered from the towns and *Litva* [foreigners], Tatars and Russians, all bold and brave. They set forth as one, together with the
Volga atamans and cossacks. In all the total was 840 bold and
brave men. They sang prayers to the all merciful God of the Holy
Trinity and to the Virgin Mother and all the heavenly powers and
saints. [The Stroganovs] recompensed the men handsomely and
outfitted them with fine clothing and cannon, volley guns, seven-
barreled muskets, and provisions in abundance. They also provided guides for the Siberian journey and interpreters of the
Busurman languages*, and sent them all out in peace into the Siberian territory.

The atamans and cossacks and the hired troops organized
themselves into military units and went exuberantly into the Siberian land against the Siberian sultan to scour the land, and after
having taken it, to drive out the godless barbarian.

The atamans and cossacks traveled for four days along the
Chusovaia River to the mouth of the Serebriannaia River, then for
two days along the Serebriannaia until they reached the Siberian
track, where they built an earthen fortress which Ermak called
Kokui. From there they traveled 25 *poprishch* [about 300 miles] and
crossed a portage to a river called the Zharavlia, and went down
that river to the Tura. Here the land of Siberia commenced.

*The Volga atamans and cossacks led by Ermak reach the Tavda River in the
land of Siberia.*

On September 9 of the year 1582, of the feast day of the Holy
Father Ioachim and of Anna, the intrepid warriors reached the

---

*Languages spoken by Siberian natives who had been converted to Islam.
—Eds.

land of Siberia and attacked many Tatar settlements and *uluses* [native settlements] down the Tura River. They valiantly made their way to the Tavda River and captured Tatar prisoners at its mouth. One of them, named Tauzak, was a member of the court of the [Siberian] tsar; he told them all about the Siberian tsars and princes and *murzas* [tribal leaders] and *ulans* [lancers] and about Tsar Kuchum. When they had learned everything from Tauzak, they set him free to inform Sultan Kuchum about their arrival and their strength and bravery. Thus Tsar Kuchum learned from Tauzak of the arrival of the Russian warriors, and of their strength and bravery. Tauzak also informed him, "These Russian warriors are so strong that when they shoot from their bows, a flame bursts forth and a great belch of smoke issues and there is a loud roar like the thunder in the heavens. The arrows shot from these bows are not visible, but they wound and kill, and there is no way to protect oneself against them with any battle defenses. They pierce right through our shields, armor and mail."

Tsar Kuchum was outraged at this news, and much troubled. He sent orders to towns and uluses throughout his realm that men were to come to reinforce him in his city against the mighty Russian warriors. Soon a great multitude of his troops, princes, murzas, ulans, Tatars, Ostiaks and Voguls and other tribes, all under his command, came to him. . . .

Tsar Kuchum sends his son Mametkul to battle the Russian warriors.

The evil Tsar Kuchum sent his son Mametkul with a great multitude of his warriors and ordered them to stand bravely against the invading Russians. Kuchum ordered them to fell trees to build an abatis on the Irtysh River at Chuvash, and to reinforce it with earth, and fortify it with defense weapons. This was to be a substantial fortification.

Mametkul and his multitudinous warriors reached the place called Babasan. The Russian warriors, atamans and cossacks, were considerably alarmed to see such a great assemblage of the heathens, but they put their trust in God and set forth from their ostrogs and fell upon the heathens. The heathens attacked the invading forces mercilessly from horseback and wounded the cossacks with their lances and sharp arrows. The Russian warriors fired back with their muskets, small volley guns, fowling pieces, small calibre fortress cannon, Spanish guns and harquebuses, and killed a vast multitude of the heathen. There was a fierce struggle with the Tatar warriors, and both sides suffered a great number of casualties.

The heathens, seeing so many of their warriors fall before the Russians, took flight. The Russian cossacks followed them along the Tobol River until they came to a hill. The heathens fired on them from the high ground. Their arrows fell like rain on the Russian boats as they passed through the area but no harm was suffered.

The Russian troops reach the ulus of Karacha, a councillor of the Siberian Tsar.

When the cossacks reached Karacha's ulus, a second battle took place against this councillor of Tsar [Kuchum]. They captured his ulus and plundered his honey and other property and loaded it into their boats. The heathens, on horseback and foot, pursued them to the Irtysh River. The atamans and cossacks advanced bravely against the heathens massed on the river bank, and both sides lost many men killed in this great battle. Then the heathens, seeing so many of their men killed by the Russian warriors, took final flight. In that battle Ermak's army lost only a few men, but almost everyone was wounded.

When Tsar Kuchum saw his warriors overwhelmed, he retired with some survivors and camped on the top of a hill called Chuvash. His son Mametkul remained at the abatis with a large rearguard, while the cossacks proceeded up the Irtysh River.

The capture of the settlement of Atik-murza.

When the Russian forces came upon a small settlement which belonged to Atik-murza, they took it and set up their camp there, because night had already fallen and it was dark. The cossacks saw the immense gathering of the heathen at the abatis and were in great consternation. They said to one another, "How can we stand against such a multitude?" They pondered this, then formed a circle and took counsel together. They debated. "Should we retreat, or stand together as one?" Some brooded and were of the opinion, "It would be best for us to retreat." But others were firm and resolute and proclaimed, "Oh, brother comrades in arms, how can we retreat? Autumn has already set in. Ice is freezing in the rivers. We cannot take to flight and bring reproach and disgrace upon ourselves. Rather let us place our trust in God, for victory does not come from having a great mass of warriors, but from the help of God on high. It is possible that God will help even the helpless. Brothers, have we ourselves not heard what evil this godless and cursed heathen of the Siberian land, Sultan Kuchum, has brought on our Russian land of Perm, how he has laid waste the towns of our Sovereign, and murdered and enslaved Orthodox Christians? Do we not know of the number of the Stroganovs' *ostrozheks* [small forts] he has destroyed? Almighty God will punish the cursed one for shedding Christian blood. Brothers, let us recall our oath, which we swore before God in the presence of honest men. We gave our word and promised, kissing the cross, that if Almighty God helped us, we would not retreat, even though we might die to the last man. We cannot turn back. We cannot dishonor ourselves and break the oath we have sworn. If the Almighty Glorious God of the Trinity will help us, then even if we fall, our memory will not die in these lands, and our glory will be eternal!"

Hearing this, the atamans and cossacks were emboldened in spirit, and their courage was renewed. They all shouted an oath in one voice. "We are ready to die for the holy church of God. We will suffer for the true Orthodox faith. We will serve the devout Sovereign Tsar and Grand Prince Ivan Vasilevich of all Russia. We will stand firm against the heathens to the last drop of our blood, unto death itself. Brothers, we will not violate our oath, we will stand as one, steadfast!" And all favored this exhortation.

After the night was spent the new day dawned, and the sun shone forth and pierced the clouds with radiant light. Ermak was deeply troubled, and with tears in his eyes he addressed his men.

"Oh, friends and brothers! Let us pray to God and to His Virgin Mother, and to all the heavenly powers, and to His saints, that they will protect us against invasion by the vile and cursed enemy!"

They set out from the camp to go into battle on October 23, the feast day of the Holy Apostle James, brother of our Lord. All together, in one voice, they gave tongue, shouting, "God be with us! Lord, help us, your humble servants!"

They advanced on the abatis bravely and fearlessly, and there was a fierce battle with the heathens. The heathens fired countless arrows from the top of the abatis and from embrasures. They

17

wounded many of Ermak's brave men and killed others. And when they saw these brave men fall, the heathens rushed out in sorties through the abatis in three places, hoping to force the cossacks into flight. During these they fought ferociously, in hand to hand combat.

The cossacks advanced against the heathens as one man and proved their bravery and ferocity before the dishonored and godless heathen. At length the heathens' strength weakened, and God gave the cossacks victory over them. The cossacks gained ground, overpowered the heathens, and killed a multitude. They forced them back from the abatis and placed their own battle standards on it. They wounded [Kuchum's son] Mametkul, and his warriors carried him off in a small boat across the Irtysh River.

Tsar Kuchum, who was encamped on the hill, saw the defeat of his Tatars and the wounding and flight of his son Mametkul. He ordered his mullahs to call out their wretched Busurman [Muslim] prayer. He called on his foul gods to aid him, but received not the slightest assistance. At the same time the Ostiak princes fell back with their men, however they could.

Tsar Kuchum saw his own downfall and the loss of his tsardom and his wealth. He wept bitterly and cried out to all his people, "Oh murzas and ulans, let us take to flight without delay. We see with our own eyes that we have lost our tsardom. Our strong warriors have been overwhelmed, our brave men killed. Oh, what dread fate is mine? What am I to do? Where can I flee? Let shame cover my face! And who are these who have defeated me and deprived me of my tsardom? The Stroganovs have sent common men from their ostrozheks against me to take revenge on me for my evil deeds. They have sent atamans and cossacks, Ermak and his men, with their own men, and they have been victorious over us. What harm they have caused us! They have defeated my army and wounded my son, who has been rescued barely alive. They have shamed me and driven me from my tsardom. My evil has fallen back upon my own head, and my own injustice has overtaken me. I was joyous when I attacked the Russian lands, Great Perm and the Stroganov ostrozheks, but now I have lost all that was mine, and I have been conquered. There is no joy in the land which does not end in grief!"

The wretched Tsar galloped off to his town of Sibir, taking a small part of his wealth, and then continued in his flight, leaving the town of Sibir deserted. Brave Ermak and his men came to

Sibir, later called Tobolsk, on October 26, the feast day of the Holy Martyr Demetrius of Salonika. They gave thanks to God for having given them victory over the godless and cursed heathens, and rejoiced mightily. They seized a great amount of gold and silver, cloth of gold, precious stones, sables, martens and valuable foxes, and divided these among themselves.

This is splendid to relate, and truly it glorified the Almighty God of the Trinity who had given the small but strong Russian warriors victory over the heathens, and defeat of the boastful Tsar Kuchum. Tsar Kuchum had assembled an army that outnumbered the cossacks by ten or twenty or even thirty to one. The cursed one lamented the great number of his warriors who had fallen. Thus God brings down the haughty and favors the humble Christians.

On the fourth day an Ostiak prince named Boiar [sic] came with many Ostiaks to Ermak in the city and brought many gifts and provisions with him. Then many of the Tatars returned with their women and children and again took up life in their *iurts* [settlements].

The cossacks are killed while fishing at Iabolak.

On December 5 in that same winter the Volga cossacks, Ermak's men, went off fishing, without any foreboding, to a place called Iabolak. The cossacks had just set up camp when the *tsarevich* [prince] Mametkul fell upon them without warning and killed them all. News of their death reached the town. Ermak was enraged and his heart was full of fury. He ordered his men to take up arms and led them off to battle. He rushed after the heathens and found them near Iabolak. Ermak's warriors obeyed his commands and valiantly attacked the heathens, engaging them in battle. Both sides fought fiercely and mercilessly, and the deadly struggle caused many mortalities on both sides. When the dark of night fell the struggle ended. The heathens fled and Ermak and his men returned to the town.

The tsarevich Mametkul, son of Kuchum, is taken alive.

That spring, when the waters were rising, a Tatar named Seibokhta came to town and reported that the tsarevich Mametkul was encamped on the Vogai River. Some of Ermak's men went

19

to the Vogai, and when they reached their destination, they attacked the tsarevich's camp in the night and killed many of the heathens. They took the tsarevich Mametkul alive and brought him to their town. Tsar Kuchum remained on the Ishim River for a long time waiting for his son Mametkul. Then couriers came to him and told him in detail how the cossacks had captured his son Mametkul. Tsar Kuchum was greatly sick at heart over this, and was overwhelmed with grief for his son Mametkul. . . .

Cossacks are sent to the Sovereign in Moscow to report and to offer their service to the Sovereign Tsar.

Ermak Timofeev and the Volga atamans and cossacks went to Moscow from Siberia, to the Sovereign Tsar and Grand Prince Ivan Vasilevich of all Russia, to report the capture of the town of Sibir, the defeat of Tsar Kuchum, the capture of the tsarevich Mametkul, and the subjugation of the Siberian lands. When the Sovereign heard of God's grace in giving him the conquest of the Siberian lands, and that the tsarevich Mametkul had been taken alive, the Sovereign rewarded the cossacks who had brought him this news. He rewarded them generously with money, woolens and cottons. The Sovereign also rewarded the atamans and cossacks still in Siberia by ordering that his generous largesse be sent to them also. He likewise decreed that *voevodas* [military leaders] and servitors should be sent to the Siberian towns which God had entrusted to the Sovereign. The Sovereign also gave instructions that the tsarevich Mametkul be brought to Moscow. . . .

Famine strikes the people in Siberia.

That winter when reinforcements from Moscow came to the cossacks in Siberia, they brought provisions with them, but used them all. The cossacks had prepared enough supplies for their own men, but did not realize the size of the Muscovite force that was coming to them. Consequently there was a great shortage of all provisions. Many died of starvation, both Muscovites and cossacks. The voevoda Prince Semen Bolkhovskii also died and was buried in Siberia. When winter came to an end and the frost and cold yielded to the warmth of the sun, the snows began to melt.

Then they were able to hunt elk and reindeer, and the situation improved for those starving people.

In spring the warm air melted the snow, and all living creatures began to grow sleek again. The trees leafed out and the grasses sprouted and the ice in the rivers began to break. All creatures rejoiced. Birds came to multiply, fish spawned in the rivers, and there was an abundance of fish and game. People could hunt again and no longer had to suffer famine. The natives who lived in the area, who were under the Sovereign's suzerainty, came from far and near. Tatars, Ostiaks and Voguls brought wild game, birds, fish and livestock, all in large amounts. They also brought precious goods and many kinds of furs. Then, with God's grace, the Muscovites and the cossacks had plenty of provisions. They became very wealthy from trading in furs, and they lived in joy and happiness, thanking Almighty God for having given the Sovereign such rich land. . . .

The brave ataman Ermak and his Russian warriors are killed.

That summer, on the fifth of August, the eve of the Transfiguration, and the feast day of the Holy Martyr Eusignius, couriers came from the Bukhara merchants to Ermak and his atamans and cossacks. They reported that Tsar Kuchum would not allow them to pass. Ermak took a few men and went to meet them on the Irtysh River. He reached the Vogai but did not find the Bukhara men. He went on to a place called Atbash, but then turned back because daylight was fading, the dark of night was coming, and the cossacks were much exhausted by their long journey. When they reached a channel [connecting two parts of the river] they set up camp for the night.

Tsar Kuchum espied them and gathered many Tatars and ordered them to keep a close watch. There was a great downpour that night, and the heathens came creeping up like venomous snakes on Ermak and his men. They unsheathed their swords, ready for vengeance, hoping to regain their patrimony and to carry out their plan.

Ermak and his men, thinking themselves secure, were asleep in their camp. Close on midnight the heathens, with vengeance in their blood, prepared for a massacre. They knew the time had come to carry out their plot. They swiftly drew their weapons and attacked the camp, and with their unsheathed swords they killed all but one, who escaped. All the rest were slain. That wise and brave spokesman, Ermak, was killed.* . . .

The voevoda Danilo Chulkov arrives from Moscow.

Shortly after that the noble Sovereign Tsar and Grand Prince Fedor Ivanovich of all Russia sent the voevoda Danilo Chulkov from Moscow to the town of Sibir with many troops and fire-arms. They reached Siberia. When the Busurman natives learned that this strong reinforcement of Russian warriors had come to Siberia, the Tatars were so alarmed that they fled from their town. Prior to this the Tatar capital in Siberia had been Sibir, at the con-fluence of the Tobol and Irtysh rivers. This was the town they abandoned. When the Russian warriors came they took the town and fortified it strongly. Now the town that God saved is called Tobolsk. . . .

Towns and ostrogs are built in the Siberian lands.

In accordance with the decree of the Sovereign Tsar and Grand Prince Ivan Vasilevich of all Russia, and after him, the decree of his son the Tsar and Grand Prince Fedor Ivanovich of all Russia, construction of towns and ostrogs in the Siberian lands began. Likewise the Orthodox Christian faith spread through the Sibe-rian lands. God's churches were built, Gospel teachings spread to all corners of the Siberian lands, and the prayers of the psalmists were heard in many parts. By decree of the Sovereign, Christian towns and ostrogs were built, and God's churches and monas-teries were erected to glorify the Father, Son and Holy Spirit. Seeing such holy edifices spread through their land, and observ-ing the protection the Sovereign extended over them, many hea-thens submitted to the Sovereign's rule, abandoned their godless faith, and were baptized. Those who were baptized lived in the Orthodox faith. God's blessings spread everywhere in abundance throughout the Siberian lands.

---

* Some reports say that Ermak drowned in the river from the weight of his suit of armor, a gift from Tsar Ivan Vasilevich.—Eds.

The collection of iasak.

Those honorable men, Semen, Maksim and Nikita Stroganov, captured and subjugated all the Siberian land. They pacified Busurman natives such as the Siberian Tatars, the Ostiaks and the Voguls. And they accomplished this through trade and with the assistance of the brave and valorous, good and noble warriors, Ermak Timofeev and his Volga atamans and cossacks. These honorable men also succeeded in winning over the Busurman people who live near the Stroganovs' towns and ostrozheks along the Kama, Chusovaia, Usva, Sylva, Iaiva, Obva, Inva, Kosva and other rivers. They brought all of these Busurman people to swear an oath to serve the Sovereign Tsar and Grand Prince Ivan Vasilevich of all Russia, to commit no treasonable acts, to obey the Sovereign in all ways, to keep his interests foremost, and to pay him iasak.

After that Semen, Maksim and Nikita sent their own men out from their towns and ostrozheks to collect iasak along the rivers in Tatar, Ostiak and Vogul uluses. They collected iasak from the Busurman people, and sent it to the Novgorod Chetvert* in Moscow. Subsequently, by decree of the Sovereign Tsar and Grand Prince Fedor Ivanovich of all Russia, iasak was collected from these Busurman people by the voevodas in towns near the natives, such as Cherdyn, Ufa, Verkhotur'e, and others.

See: G. I. Spaskii, ed., *Letopis sibirskaia* . . . (St. Petersburg: 1821). This, one of three versions of the Stroganov Chronicle, was written some time between 1621 and 1673.

*The Novgorod *Chetvert*, also known as *Prikaz*, was one of the departments of the central government in Moscow in charge of the newly conquered region. Others included the Kazan and the Mezhcherskii Dvorets. In 1637 a special department, the Sibirskii Prikaz, was created to administer the area.—Eds.

6

A GRAMOTA FROM TSAR IVAN VASILEVICH TO MAKSIM AND NIKITA
STROGANOV CONCERNING SENDING THE VOLGA COSSACKS UNDER
ERMAK TIMOFEEV TO CHERDYN

From the Tsar and Grand Prince Ivan Vasilevich of all Russia
to the Chusovaia [River], to Maksim Iakovlevich and Nikita
Grigorevich Stroganov. Vasilii Pelepelitsyn has written to us from
Perm that on September 1 you sent out from your ostrogs the Volga
ataman and cossacks, Ermak and his men, to fight the Votiaks and
the Voguls in Pelym and other Siberian places. That same day the
Pelym prince assembled Siberians and Voguls and attacked our
holdings at Perm and came to the town and ostrog of Cherdyn
and killed our people and caused many losses to our subjects. This
happened because of your treason. You turned the Voguls and the
Votiaks and the Pelyms against us; you provoked them and fought
them, and because you aroused the sultan of Siberia, you brought
about quarrels between us. You invited Volga atamans into your
service and hired brigands for your ostrogs without our ukaz.
These atamans and cossacks have previously embroiled us in quarrels with the Nogai horde. They killed Nogai envoys in their boats
on the Volga, robbed and killed merchants from the horde, and also
robbed many of our own people and caused them many losses.
Then they attempted to conceal their guilt by pretending that they
were defending our lands in Perm. They did this with you, just as
they used to rob and pillage on the Volga.

On September 1, the same day that the Voguls came to Cherdyn in Perm, Ermak and his men went out from your ostrogs to
fight the Voguls, but they did not assist Perm in any way. All of
this happened because of your disloyalty and treason. You should
have been serving only us, and you should not have sent those
cossacks out on a military foray at that time. You should have sent
your men out from your ostrogs to defend our lands in Perm.

We have sent Voin Onichkov to Perm, and have given orders
that these cossacks, Ermak and his men, are to be transferred to
Solikamsk in Perm. We have ordered that they remain there, and
divide into smaller groups. From there they are to go out in the
winter, using sleds, to attack the Pelym prince. We have ordered
that all these cossacks and Perm people, as well as those from

Viatka and their emissaries, unite under the command of Voin Onichkov and Ivan Glukhov, so that in the future these warriors from Pelym—the Ostiaks, Voguls and Siberians—will not attack our lands nor lay waste our possessions. We have ordered that these cossacks remain in Perm until spring. They are to go with Voin to attack the Ostiaks and Voguls in an effort to bring them back under our authority, in accordance with our ukaz. In Cherdyn you are to establish contact with Vasilii Pelepelitsyn and Voin Onichkov and send your forces to fight the Voguls and Ostiaks.

At the same time, in accordance with this our gramota, you are immediately to send to Cherdyn all the cossacks who have returned from the military campaign. Do not detain them. If it is impossible for you to remain in the ostrog until they arrive, then you are to leave a few men, up to 100, with an ataman in charge, and send all the rest to Cherdyn immediately.

If you do not send these Volga cossacks, the ataman Ermak Timofeev and his men, out from your ostrogs to Perm; but if instead you keep them in your ostrogs, and do not defend our lands in Perm, and if because of your disobedience at some time in the future the Voguls and the Pelyms and the Siberian sultan inflict some disaster on Perm, then our fearful wrath will be visited upon you because of this, and we will order that all the atamans and cossacks who obeyed and served you, and thereby deserted our lands, be hanged.

You are to send these cossacks to Perm immediately. They are to fight the Pelyms, Voguls and Ostiaks in accordance with our ukaz. They are to join in this effort with Vasilii Pelepelitsyn and Voin Onichkov, so that with God's aid they will conquer [these natives] and bring them under our authority, and defend the lands of Perm as well as your ostrogs.

Written in Moscow, November 16, 1582.

See: Russia. Arkheograficheskaia kommissiia. *Dopolneniia k aktam istoricheskim* (St. Petersburg: 1846), I, 184–185.

7

JANUARY 7, 1584

A GRAMOTA FROM TSAR IVAN VASILEVICH TO SEMEN, MAKSIM AND
NIKITA STROGANOV CONCERNING OUTFITTING FIFTEEN BOATS TO BE
SENT TO SIBERIA

From the Tsar and Grand Prince Ivan Vasilevich of all Russia to the Stroganovs, Semen Anikievich, Maksim Iakovlevich and Nikita Grigorevich. In accordance with our ukaz, Prince Semen Dmitreevich Bolkhovskii has been authorized to requisition 50 mounted men from your ostrogs for our service in Siberia for the winter campaign. We have now received word that it is impossible to travel to Siberia by horse in the winter, and so we have ordered Prince Semen not to go from Perm to Siberia during winter, but to wait until spring when the waters are open. We have also instructed him not to take the 50 mounted men from you, as set forth in our earlier ukaz, but rather to requisition fifteen fully equipped boats from you for our troops and their provisions. Each boat is to accommodate twenty men and their supplies. We have not authorized him to requisition from you either foot soldiers or supply carts or guides or food. We have also given orders that while he is en route to Siberia he is not to mistreat any of your people or peasants.

When you receive this our gramota, you are immediately to prepare the fifteen sound, fully equipped boats for our troops, each boat to accommodate twenty men and their supplies. These are to be ready by spring for the arrival of Prince Semen Bolkhovskii. When Prince Semen Bolkhovskii, or the *golovas* [head men] Ivan Kireev and Ivan Glukhov reach Siberia in the spring with our troops, you are immediately to give these boats to Prince Semen Bolkhovskii or to the golovas Ivan Kireev and Ivan Glukhov, so they will not waste any time having to wait in your ostrogs until the boats are ready.

If you do not have these boats completely outfitted and ready for our troops, and if our interests suffer as a result of this, you will be in grave disfavor with us.

Written in Moscow January 7, 1584.

See: G. F. Müller, *Istoriia Sibiri* (Moscow-Leningrad: 1937), I, 343–344.

8

JUNE 26, 1595

A GRAMOTA FROM TSAR FEDOR IVANOVICH TO THE VOEVODA OF
TARA, PRINCE FEDOR ELETSKII, CONCERNING THE DISTRIBUTION OF
REWARDS TO SERVITORS FOR CAPTURING CHERNYI

From the Tsar and Grand Prince Fedor Ivanovich of all Russia
to Siberia, to the new town of Tara, to our voevoda Prince
Fedor Borisovich Eletskii and his men. Prince Andrei Eletskii and
his men have written to us that they sent Grigorii Iasyr with
Tobolsk cossacks, Tiumen Litva and cossacks, and with Tobolsk
iurt Tatars to gather information about Tsar Kuchum and to take
prisoners near the great lake and in the upper reaches of the
Irtysh River. The entire force of Tobolsk cossacks, Tiumen Litva,
Pelym cossacks and Tobolsk Tatars consisted of 90 men. On December 30, Grigorii Iasyr and his men returned to the new town
of Tara and brought 23 Ialymsk Tatar men with him, none of
whom had ever been to the new town, or had taken the oath [of
allegiance to the Russian Tsar]. They had fled to Tsar Kuchum
when the voevodas came to Ialym to build a town.

During questioning Grigorii Iasyr and his men reported that
they had gone out from the new town of Tara to the Malogoro-
dskaia *volost* [administrative unit], to the village of Vuziuk,
on Lake Vuziuk, where all these Tatars catch fish for Tsar Kuchum, and they captured them there. They put these Tatars on
the rack and interrogated them. During that interrogation under
torture they said that when Tsar Kuchum heard that our voevodas
were advancing with troops up the Irtysh to build a town in the
Ialymsk region, he, Tsar Kuchum, sent his son, the tsarevich
Alei, to the Tatars, and ordered them to bring all their people to
him. Alei assembled 150 Tatars from Ialymsk volost and led them
up the Irtysh to Chernaia Island where they built a small settlement and spent the winter. There were 50 men with them in the
settlement, and the leaders are the *esauls* [lieutenants] Malyk and
Setkul, and the princes Siuiunduk and Ilgului. They fish on Lake
Vuziuk for the Tsar [Kuchum] and send their catch to him. Every
day men come to them from the Tsar while Kuchum is encamped
in the upper reaches of the Irtysh between two small rivers, putting his wagons in order. It takes 22 days of foot travel to reach

Tsar Kuchum beyond the Om River, and five or six days to reach him from the small settlement on Chernaia Island.

Using this information, Prince Andrei sent Boris Domozhirov to the settlement, and with him he sent a force of 276 men consisting of two streltsy *sotniks* [leaders of 100] and 100 streltsy, 60 Tobolsk Litva, 40 Tobolsk cossacks, 15 Perm foot soldiers, and 7 Tobolsk iurt Tatars. When they reached the settlement on Chernaia Island, by the grace of God, they took it. They captured the following Ialym people: the esaul Malyk, the esaul Setkul, prince Ilgului, the son of prince Temsen Kolkildeev, and also 60 Ialym Tatars and their wives and children. During interrogation they said that there had been 200 men in the settlement, and that 20 of Kuchum's men had been with them, but that 90 men had run off from the town, along with 50 townsmen and their wives and children, and Kuchum's 20 warriors.

Boris Domozhirov sent out 70 Litva, cossacks and streltsy after Kuchum's men. They decisively defeated Kuchum's Tatars and took prisoners, including six of Kuchum's Tatars. Boris Domozhirov burned the settlement and then returned safely with all of his men to the new town of Tara. An official list of the names of all the men who served us there, prisoners who fought with distinction, and men who were wounded, has been compiled and forwarded to us.

We are rewarding Prince Andrei Eletskii and Boris Domozhirov and the streltsy and their sotniks who served us. They are to receive the gold coins which we have sent with the cossack ataman, Kazarin Volnin. The wounded and the prisoners who fought with distinction are also to receive rewards from us for their service. We have sent the original list along with this gramota, and also a memorandum for our diak, Vasilii Shchelkalov. If Kazarin should meet the voevoda Prince Andrei Eletskii anywhere along the way, Kazarin is to give Prince Andrei this gramota then and there. As soon as you receive this our gramota, when the ataman Kazarin Volnin reaches you without reward, you are to distribute the gold coins, in accordance with the list, to Boris Domozhirov, the streltsy sotniks, the Litva, cossacks and streltsy for their service. This list is appended to our gramota with the signature of our diak, Vasilii Shchelkalov.

You are also to inform all our servitors that in the future we will reward them with great largesse, and that they are to serve us even better than in the past. You are to live in the new town with

A Siberian cossack. Early nineteenth-century engraving.

great caution, so that your townspeople will be on guard against Tsar Kuchum and the Nogai horde and people of the nearby volosts. You are also to secure information about the intentions of Tsar Kuchum and the Nogai, so that they will not be able to make a surprise attack on the town and cause trouble.

All information you obtain, such as the present whereabouts of Tsar Kuchum's encampment, his intentions, whether he is in contact with the Nogai, which volosts have been brought under our Tsarist control, which pay iasak—all this you are to send, in detail, to Moscow. Send it to the Posolskii Prikaz and the Chetvert Prikaz, to our diak Vasilii Shchelkalov, so that we will be fully informed about all local matters.

Written in Moscow, June 26, 1595.

See: G. F. Müller, *Istoriia Sibiri* (Moscow-Leningrad: 1937), I, 366–368.

9

DECEMBER 15, 1597

A GRAMOTA FROM TSAR FEDOR IVANOVICH TO VASILII GOLOVIN AND IVAN VOEIKOV IN VERKHOTUR'E CONCERNING BUILDING A TOWN AND AN OSTROG ON THE TURA RIVER

From the Tsar and Grand Prince Fedor Ivanovich of all Russia to the Tura River, to Verkhotur'e, to Vasilii Petrovich Golovin and Ivan Vasilevich Voiekov. On December 10, 1597, you wrote to us from Perm that you had been ordered to go on our service along the new Verkhotur'e route in Siberia to build a town at the site of the former settlement of Chiutsk. You further wrote that in order to build this town and an ostrog you were authorized to obtain 300 rubles from Sarych Shestakov in Great Perm, money which had been sent to Perm from Moscow. With that money you were to hire tax-paying people, both on foot and on horse, and carpenters with all their building tools. You were to conclude an agreement with them as to the amount of pay they would receive, and obtain firm written commitments from them that they would build the town and ostrog and not desert before these were completed. And if 300 rubles were not enough, then you were authorized to obtain 100 rubles more, or as much as you needed, from Sarych Shestakov in the local land treasury office. You were to send a written report of this to us in Moscow.

You reached Great Perm on November 11 and that same day you ordered the town herald to make an announcement in Perm, Cherdyn, Sol Kamskaia and in settlements throughout the uezd that volunteers who wished to work to build our town should present themselves for hire. You obtained a plan for the town and ostrog from Sarych Shestakov, which showed how much lumber was needed for the town and for the towers, and it also showed how many towers there were to be. You hired taxpaying people, both on foot and on horse, as well as carpenters, to build the town and ostrog as quickly as possible. According to your estimate, it would take 50 men, both on foot and on horse, and carpenters, to fall the trees, haul the lumber and construct the town and ostrog. Those on foot agreed to wages of one and one-half rubles per month, and asked to be paid for three months in advance. They would not accept this pay for only two months because they insisted the place is so remote and barren that they could not travel there without provisions. The men with horses agreed to 2 rubles 26 altyns 4 dengas per month. The carpenters wanted 2 rubles per month, with a three-month advance. The town and ostrog were to be built as quickly as possible, and the money was to be issued for three months.

According to your estimate, the 360 men without horses will require an outlay of 1,620 rubles. 150 men with horses will require 1,260 rubles. The 40 carpenters will require 240 rubles. The total amount necessary for three months' wages for the 550 men who are to build and town and ostrog is 3,120 rubles. Only 300 rubles were sent from Moscow to Perm, so you have been authorized to obtain 100 rubles more from Sarych Shestakov, or as much as you think you will need. You asked Sarych and the *zemskie* [local] people for the money, but they refused, saying they did not have any tax money; and Sarych said he was not authorized to draw that amount of money from the zemskie people.

Your instructions were to hire 100 men on foot, 50 with horses, and 10 carpenters, and to build the town and the ostrog. Monthly wages were to be one and one-half rubles for the men on foot, 2 rubles 26 altyns and 4 dengas for men with horses; and 2 rubles for carpenters. You were to pay the men three months' wages in advance, but no more than that. They said they needed this in order to go on our service in the new barren distant location, that if they had to go there without provisions they would starve. If you reduced the number of men to 160 it would still cost at least 930 rubles. You were to obtain 630 rubles from Sarych in Great Perm, over and above the 300 rubles which were sent for you from Moscow. Sarych refused to give you the money when you requested it, saying he would ask for the money from the Cherdyn *starosta* [elder] Ivan Klementev and his men. They agreed, but they did not say when they would give you the money.

You stayed in Perm from November 11 to 18. You remained there because the Perm people and Sarych would not give you any money, and without funds you could not arrange for tax-paying people and provisions.

Now you are asking that you be allowed to issue your own order concerning these people and the carpenters and their wages. You have made a mistake by promising too much to these people on foot, with horses, and to the carpenters.

When this our gramota reaches you, if no one has yet gone out from Perm and Verkhotur'e to build our town, and if the Perm people still have not given you any money, you are immediately to obtain money from them, and pay the workers their three months' wages on the following basis: 50 men with horses are to receive 40 altyns per month each; carpenters, 1 ruble; people on foot, 30 altyns. If all these people, those on foot, those with horses, and the carpenters, will not agree to these terms, then you must immediately secure other people, on foot, with horses, and carpenters, from Sarych and from throughout the whole Perm region. These people are to be paid as follows: 50 men with horses, 40 altyns per month; carpenters, 1 ruble; people on foot, 30 altyns per month each. They are to go to Verkhotur'e, according to our previous ukaz. The people of Perm are to send replacements for these people and for the carpenters to Verkhotur'e.

If you have already obtained money from Perm to pay all these people, at the rate of 2 rubles, 26 altyns and 4 dengas for those with horses; one and one-half rubles to those on foot; and 2 rubles to carpenters, then you are to return any extra money to Perm.

We hold you personally responsible for seeing to it that our town and ostrog at Verkhotur'e are completed by spring.

See: G. F. Müller, *Istoriia Sibiri* (Moscow-Leningrad: 1937), I, 375–377.

10

A PETITION TO TSAR FEDOR IVANOVICH FROM TABARINSK TATARS AND
VOGULS REQUESTING AN END TO OBLIGATORY AGRICULTURAL IASAK,
THE RETURN OF RUNAWAYS TO THEIR FORMER SETTLEMENTS, AND
PERMISSION TO PURCHASE AXES AND KNIVES FROM THE RUSSIANS

To the Sovereign Tsar and Grand Prince Fedor Ivanovich of all Russia, a petition from your humble slaves, the Tabarinsk Tatars, Voguls, murzas and sotniks, numbering 50 men in all, on behalf of all their tribesmen in this place. Bagai Kochurentevich and Shelmesk Shevoevich also petition.

In accordance with your Sovereign order, we, your Sovereign's orphans, have been ordered to perform your Sovereign agricultural labor in Tabarinsk to fulfill your Sovereign iasak. We, your Sovereign's orphans, have cultivated your Sovereign lands in past years, 1594, 1595, 1596, 1597 and in 1598. We grew rye in all those years. In order to perform this agricultural labor for you, Sovereign, we had to buy horses, and we have exhausted our resources in attending to your Sovereign agriculture.

We have worn out our clothing; our wives and children have to go begging; and now, Sovereign, we are starving to death. Sire, we your orphans have no money to buy clothing. Sire, we, your orphans are dying of starvation and we have to drag ourselves about barefoot and naked. Sire, in the fall we, your orphans, haul grain to the threshing floor and we have to thresh it by hand. Sire, in summer and winter your voevodas and *detie boiarskie* [petty nobles] and cossacks travel to and from Siberia on your business, and, Sire, they use us to transport them by cart or boat in summer and by sled and horse in winter. We have to take them from Tobolsk to Pelym, and also when they go from Moscow to Pelym and to Kashukov in the uezd of Tobolsk.

Sire, when we provide this transport, on foot and with horses, we starve and our poor horses drop of exhaustion on the portages. Sire, the iurt Tatars and Voguls who used to live along this track ran off so they would not have to provide this transport. Now they are living in forests and hidden places. But we, Sire, your orphans—nine leaders of the Tabarinsk Tatars, murzas and sotniks—we and our poor horses die on these pack trips. Sire, people who do not take part in transport work do not suffer the same losses in horses and in men's lives that we do. They do not suffer because they run off into the forests, away from your Sovereign envoys.

Moreover, Sire, your voevodas in Pelym will not allow us, your orphans, to buy axes or knives. Sire, we, your orphans, are going to die in vain as a result of this. Sire, we do not have among our fellow Busurman [Muslim] worshippers either master craftsmen or woodcutters. Sire, we have no tools with which to cut down trees. Sire, without an axe it is not possible to build traps to catch animals. Moreover, Sire, one cannot make boots without a knife. And therefore, Sire, we your orphans are dying from cold and from lack of food and clothing. Sire, it has become impossible for us, your orphans, to live, and we will soon perish. Sire, some of us, your orphans in Tabarinsk, are old and disabled.

Merciful Sovereign Tsar, spare us, your orphans. Show us your mercy. Do not let your orphans die uselessly. Lighten our burden of work on your Sovereign lands. Be merciful to us, Sire. Permit us to substitute sable iasak for agricultural iasak. Sire, grant us, your orphans, this favor.

In the year 1598 we, your orphans, produced 45 *chetverts* of rye. In the future, Sire, we, your orphans will not be able to work your fields because we have exhausted all our resources, Sire. Our wives and children go hungry and we die of starvation.

Merciful Sovereign Tsar, order our fellow tribesmen to return to their former settlements along the trace where they used to live, so that we nine, your Sovereign's orphans, will not be the only ones forced to carry your envoys, voevodas, detie boiarskie, couriers and cossacks on your Sovereign's affairs; and so that in the future we, your orphans, can survive and pay your iasak, Sire.

Merciful Sovereign Tsar, permit us, your orphans, to trade as previously with the Russians for axes and knives and pots, so that we, your Sovereign's orphans, will not die barefoot from cold, and so that in the future we will not lack the means which which to pay your iasak.

Merciful Sovereign Tsar, have mercy on your orphans, excuse us from field work, relieve us of agricultural obligations. Decree, Sire, that we may pay your iasak by giving sables, or impose some other obligation on us, Sire, so that we, your orphans, will

Ermak Timofeev accepting homage for opening Siberia. From
Shunkov, ed., *Istoriia Sibiri*, Vol. 2.

not starve to death, Sire. And, Sovereign, decree that axes and
knives may be sold to us, your orphans.

Tsar, Sovereign, have mercy!

See: G. F. Müller, *Istoriia Sibiri* (Moscow-Leningrad: 1937), II, 151–153.

11

A GRAMOTA FROM TSAR BORIS FEDOROVICH GODUNOV TO THE PELYM
GOLOVA DEMENTII IUSHKOV, ORDERING THAT THE VOGULS NOT BE
FORCED TO PAY IASAK FOR OLD AND INFIRM MALE MEMBERS AND
GRANTING PERMISSION FOR VOGULS TO PURCHASE AXES AND KNIVES

From the Tsar and Grand Prince Boris Fedorovich of all Russia, to the town of Pelym, to the golova Dementii Grigorievich Iushkov. We have received a petition from the Siberian town of Pelym, from the iasak-paying Voguls Kom Chandin and Tuman Sandin. On behalf of all their fellow iasak-paying Voguls there, they have stated that they pay iasak to us in Pelym for themselves, but that some of the aged Voguls are ill and cannot trap sables. You have ordered that the ablebodied Voguls must pay iasak for the aged ones. This is causing great hardship for them.

They also state that you will not allow them to buy the axes and knives they need from our Russian people and that this also causes them great hardships. Accordingly they have asked us to grant them the following: that we order that our iasak not be collected from them for the old and the sick and the disabled, and that we also order that they may purchase the axes and knives they need from our Russian people.

When you receive this our gramota, you are henceforth to collect our iasak from these Pelym iasak-paying Tatars according to the iasak books, but only from those who are in good health. In the case of Tatars who are old or ill or disabled, who cannot pay our iasak, you are to make a thorough investigation and order that our iasak not be collected from ablebodied Tatars for the old and sick and disabled. But when a Tatar who has been ill recovers, then you are to order him to pay our iasak again, as previously.

When a Tatar comes to you with iasak, you are to be considerate and kind to him. Give him food and drink, and allow him to return without detaining him. Allow such people to purchase a few axes and knives from traders, enough for their own needs.

You are to report to us in Moscow, through our diak Ivan Vakhrameev, so that we will be informed as to how many aged, disabled and sick Tatars there are, and how much iasak they pre-

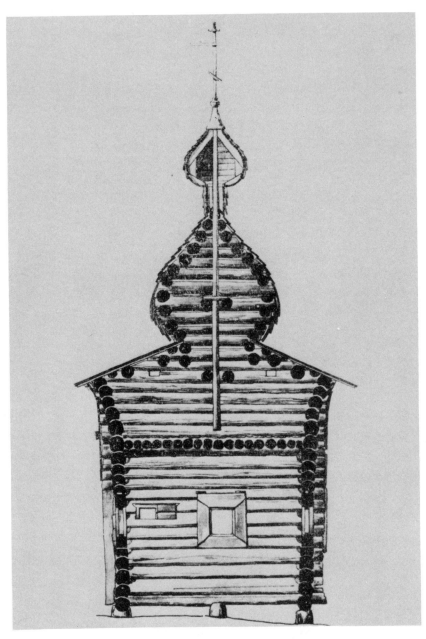

Example of an ostrog chapel. Ilimsk, ca. 1630. From Makovetskii, *Byt i iskusstovo russkogo naseleniia vostochnoi Sibiri*, Vol. 1.

viously paid. You are to make a thorough investigation of the sick and disabled, so that they will not be lost sight of.

See: G. F. Müller, *Istoriia Sibiri* (Moscow-Leningrad: 1937), II, 153–154.

12

JUNE 25, 1599

A GRAMOTA FROM TSAR BORIS FEDOROVICH RELEASING SIBERIAN IASAK-PAYING NATIVES FROM PAYMENT OF IASAK FOR THE YEAR 1600, IN HONOR OF HIS CORONATION

From the Tsar and Grand Prince Boris Fedorovich of all Russia, to the new town of Verkhotur'e, to our voevoda Prince Ivan Mikhailovich Viazemskii, and to the golova Gavril Samoilovich Salmanov. In honor of our coronation as Tsar, and our long life and good health, and that of our son, the Tsarevich Prince Fedor Borisovich of all Russia, and of the long life and good health of all Siberian peoples, we are granting a privilege: for the year 1600 no iasak is to be collected from them, neither sable, marten, fox, beaver, nor squirrel pelts.

When you receive this our gramota, you are to summon as many as possible of the leading Vogul and Ostiak volost men to come to you in Verkhotur'e. You are to await them in the Prikaz office, in full dress uniform, and the detie boiarskie and Litva and cossacks and streltsy are also to be in uniform. You will then inform the people of our Tsarist favor: that with our Tsarist regard for our Tsarist crown and long life and good health, as well as that of our son, the Tsarevich Prince Fedor Borisovich of all Russia, we have granted this privilege to all our subjects in our realm. For all the Siberian lands, for princes, murzas, Tatars, Ostiaks, Voguls, and for all iasak-paying people, our Tsarist privilege is that we have ordered that pelts of sable, marten, squirrel, ermine and other animals are not to be taken from them as iasak; and we have ordered that they are to have this privilege so that these Siberian people will not suffer any deprivation. Thus, because of our Tsarist favor, these Siberian princes, murzas, Tatars, Ostiaks, Voguls and all others will live more easily, in peace and quiet, without any doubts, and may hunt whatever they wish, trade freely, and serve us, the great Sovereign Tsar and Grand Prince Boris Fedorovich, Autocrat of all Russia, and our son, the Tsarevich Prince Fedor Borisovich of all Russia. They are to be loyal in all ways, as they promised in their oath of allegiance to us, the Great Sovereign. They are not to fall into lawless ways or succumb to brigandry or evil ways. They are to gather their children, brothers, uncles and all other relatives, and inform them of our Tsarist privilege, which we have bestowed upon them. This privilege is that we have decreed that iasak is not to be collected from them; they will not have to pay taxes; and they may live in peace in their iurts, towns, uezds and volosts.

But any persons who plot mutiny and insurrection are not to be concealed or hidden. Rather, as a demonstration of loyalty, the people are to inform us of any lawless disloyal rebels. These persons are to be apprehended and brought before you. Anyone who informs on such lawless traitors, who are subsequently proven guilty, will be rewarded with our Tsarist favor. We will decree that the goods and the land [of the guilty] be given to the person who informed us of their treason and lawlessness.

After you have told the people of our gracious intent, you are to give them generous amounts of food and drink from our provisions which have been sent to supply the Tatars.

You are not to collect any iasak in any volost for the year 1600. When iasak is again imposed on them in the future, you are to review the matter and report to us how iasak should be imposed on the Siberian volosts in the future, whether in the same amounts as before, or whether it should be decreased for some and increased for others. Consider who will be able to pay in the future without undue hardship, so that a consistent and firm policy can be established.

You are to conduct yourselves with the utmost consideration for our affairs. Depending on local circumstances you are to seek our advantage in all ways. In all of this, we are entrusting our affairs to you. Any persons you may send out to small towns and volosts are to be ordered to adhere firmly to the policy of not collecting any bribes or *pominki* [gifts] from the Ostiaks and Voguls, not trading anything, and not perpetrating any violence. Anyone who takes bribes or pominki is to be apprehended and punished if he is found guilty. Anything he has taken is to be returned.

Wherever possible you are to send out this gramota through small towns and volosts to whatever local princes you may deem appropriate, depending on the local situation.

See: G. F. Müller, *Istoriia Sibiri* (Moscow-Leningrad: 1937), I, 381–382.

13

A GRAMOTA FROM TSAR BORIS FEDOROVICH TO THE TURINSK GOLOVA
FEDOR FOFANOV, CONCERNING CONSTRUCTION OF A CHURCH IN THE
NEW OSTROG

From the Tsar and Grand Prince Boris Fedorovich of all Russia to Siberia, to the new ostrog at Iapanchin iurt, to golova Fedor Osipovich Fofanov. You have written to us that servitors and agricultural workers have asked that we grant them the privilege of erecting a church, which they wish to name for the Holy Martyrs Boris and Gleb, and that we send them a priest, since they are in great need of one. You report that lumber has already been cut for the church and the altar and refectory, but ask that we issue an ukaz as to how it is to be completed and decorated.

We hereby authorize the construction of the place of worship in the new ostrog in honor of the Holy Martyrs of Christ, Boris and Gleb. The supplies for the consecration of the church and the chrysm and the oil have been sent from Moscow with Avraam, a monk from Tobolsk. The church furnishings have all been sent with Vasilii Tyrkov and the ataman Groza Ivanov. We have ordered a priest to be sent to the church from Verkhotur'e, and a deacon will come out from Perm for the consecration. A list of all the church furnishings, icons and books is being sent to you with our gramota.

When you receive this our gramota, you are to order that the church be completed. When the *antimins* [altar piece containing sacred relics] and church furnishings are delivered, and the priest from Verkhotur'e and the deacon from Perm have arrived, you are to arrange that the church and its furnishings be consecrated. When the ceremony has taken place, you are to send the deacon back to Perm. However, you are to keep the priest at the church and provide him with a place to live. For the year 1601 you are authorized to give him a salary from Verkhotur'e in the amount of eight rubles. Also give him five chetverts of rye, one of groats, and one of oats. Enter this in the expense books, and in the future give him the same amounts of food and money each year.

You are to write a description of the consecration of the church, and send it to us in Moscow, along with your account of

The Remezov manuscript drawing is filled with details of iasak gathering in the Siberian ostrog of Tiumen, ca. 1586. From Shunkov, ed., *Istoriia Sibiri*, Vol. 2.

other matters. This report is to be sent to the *Kazanskii* and the *Mezhcherskii Dvorets*,* to our diaks Afanasii Vlasev and Nechai Fedorov.

See: G. F. Müller, *Istoriia Sibiri* (Moscow-Leningrad: 1937), I, 388–389.

*Until 1637, when the Sibirskii Prikaz was established, most administrative matters were handled by the Novgorod Chetvert and by the Kazanskii and Mezhcherskii Dvorets.—Eds.

14

APRIL 9, 1601

A REPORT FROM THE VOEVODA OF TOBOLSK, FEDOR SHEREMETEV, TO
THE TURINSK GOLOVA FEDOR FOFANOV, CONCERNING PROHIBITING
SIBERIAN SERVITORS FROM TRADING IN FURS

To Gospodin Fedor Konstantinovich [Fofanov] from Fedor Sheremetev. On April 9 of this year, 1601, a gramota from the Sovereign Tsar and Grand Prince Boris Fedorovich of all Russia to the *okolnichi* [court official] and voevoda Semen Fedorovich Saburov and his men states that servitors from Siberian towns are traveling through Siberian towns and carrying on trade in furs without paying taxes. Siberian servitors are not permitted to trade in furs. A strict prohibition has been issued to that effect, and in the future only merchants may trade in furs.

If any servitor should trade in furs, his possessions are to be confiscated and turned over to the Sovereign. Violators are to be beaten and imprisoned. You, Gospodin, are not to allow the servitors of Turinsk ostrog to trade in furs. You are to issue a strict order concerning this, so that henceforth no one but merchants will trade in furs. If any servitor trades in furs, his goods are to be confiscated for the Sovereign, and he is to be punished by being beaten and imprisoned.

See: G. F. Müller, *Istoriia Sibiri* (Moscow-Leningrad: 1937), II, 168.

15

A GRAMOTA FROM TSAR BORIS FEDOROVICH TO THE VOEVODA OF
BEREZOVO, PRINCE IVAN BARIATINSKII, CONCERNING LEGAL ACTION
AGAINST STEPAN PURTIEV AND THE BEREZOVO OSTIAK, SHATROV
LUGUEV, FOR SELLING WOMEN SLAVES

From the Tsar and Grand Prince Boris Fedorovich of all Russia to Siberia, to the town of Berezovo, to our voevoda Prince Ivan Mikhailovich Bariatinskii and the golova Grigorii Potapeevich Vekentev. We have received a petition from a newly baptized man, Stepan Purtiev, against a Berezovo Ostiak named Shatrov Luguev, in which it is stated that in 1595 three women slaves Purtiev had bought ran off to this Shatrov. One woman was a slave from Nerym, another was from Tymsk, and the third was from Voikarsk. They ran away because they had learned of Shatrov Luguev's treasonous attack on the town of Berezovo. After Shatrov Luguev's treason, Stepan went to Shatrov to reclaim his runaway women, but Shatrov would not return these women to him. He is keeping them by force. Stepan petitions us to order that Shatrov be brought to justice.

It is decreed that this be done, as the newly baptized Stepan Purtiev has petitioned us. When you receive this our gramota, you are to hold court for the Berezovo Ostiak Shatrov Luguev and the newly baptized Stepan Purtiev. You are to investigate this matter thoroughly. On the basis of your judgment and the finding of the investigation, you are to pass sentence, in accordance with our ukaz, without any delay.

Done in Moscow April 28, 1601. Without seal.

See: G. F. Müller, *Istoriia Sibiri* (Moscow-Leningrad: 1937), I, 395.

16

AUGUST 30, 1601

A GRAMOTA FROM TSAR BORIS FEDOROVICH TO THE TURINSK GOLOVA,
FEDOR FOFANOV, CONCERNING THE NEED TO PROTECT THE LOCAL
RUSSIAN POPULATION DURING IASAK COLLECTION

From the Tsar and Grand Prince Boris Fedorovich of all Russia to Siberia, to the new ostrog at Tura, to the golova Fedor Konstantinovich Fofanov. According to our ukaz, voevodas and golovas in all Siberian towns have been firmly instructed that there be no violence involving the Siberian iasak-paying people, that these people are not to suffer losses, that they are not to be sold, that no extra iasak be collected from them, that there are to be no additional impositions for bribes, and that their burden be lightened where possible. We have ordered him to collect a reasonable amount of iasak for us, an amount they are able to pay, depending on where they live and how the hunt is.

You are to investigate the case of anyone upon whom a heavy iasak payment has been levied who is unable to meet this obligation. If the amount of iasak is unreasonable and is too burdensome, then in such a case the amount of iasak should be lowered. No iasak is to be taken from poor persons who are unable to pay any iasak, so that none of the Siberian people will suffer and be in deprivation. The inhabitants of Siberia are to live in our Tsarist favor, not be oppressed, and are to be allowed to live in peace and tranquility without fear. They may engage in all kinds of activities, and call upon their children, brothers, uncles, nephews, and friends to enjoy our Tsarist benevolence. They are to fulfill their iurt obligations in the towns, and their volost obligations in the uezds.

We have recently been informed that when previous voevodas were in Siberian towns they were lawless and violent in their dealings with the Siberian iasak people, using criminal methods to collect extra iasak from them. They also collected more than their just share of the voevoda's pominki, so that now many iasak natives owe them both iasak and pominki. They also competed with one another to collect more iasak and pominki than other voevodas. They did not consider the fact that the profit must be stable and constant in the future. When they returned to Moscow they reported to us that while they were stationed in towns in Siberia they made great profit for us in iasak. They also reported that the iasak people brought the pominki furs to them for us, the Tsar, at the same time when they brought their iasak to town, and that the pominki furs were not taken from them by force. The voevodas rewarded the iasak people for bringing in their pominki by giving them food and drink from their own supply of provisions.

Because we believed these false reports, we gave some of the voevodas rewards, and we gave pominki furs to others. But now, because of their criminal profit and false reports, many volosts under the administration of Siberian towns have been depopulated.

Voevodas were also instructed to issue our provisions to our servitors, gunners and obrok-paying people. These supplies were sent to them from Kazan, and consisted of two *verkhs* of rye and equal amounts of groats and oats. But they disobeyed and did not give the servitors and gunners and obrok people as much flour and groats as we had ordered in our ukaz; they gave only a small amount, and kept the rest for themselves, which amounted to twelve chetverts. They also oppressed the servitors and others. Many servitors have families and were not given enough food for them.

When you receive this our gramota, beginning in the year 1602, you are to collect iasak from the Tura uezd villages and volosts. Collect it from princes and murzas, and from Ostiaks and Voguls and iasak-paying people according to our ukaz. Do not collect any extra iasak from them. Do not add any extra for bribes. Do not collect pominki for yourselves.

If anyone brings in extra iasak and asks you to accept it, you are to take it and deposit it in our warehouse. If no one brings in any extra, you are not to ask for any. You are to see to it that the iasak people suffer no violence, no losses, and that they are not sold. If any of the iasak people are poor or ill or disabled and have no way to pay our iasak, but may offer as iasak their inferior *shubas* [fur coats or cloaks] made of immature pelts, or from the pelts of squirrels and poor quality small beavers, you are not to accept these; however you are not to impose additional iasak on them, nor enter this in the iasak books as an unfulfilled obligation.

You are to make detailed itemized entries in the iasak books for the amount of iasak and pominki you collect for the year 1602

Of the early industries, Siberian ironworks were among the most highly prized. Prior to conquest, the technology of the natives was essentially neolithic, except for those groups with Chinese contacts. From Shunkov, ed., *Istoriia Sibiri*, Vol. 2.

from Ostiaks and Voguls, and also the amount which was previously collected. Gunners and obrok people are to receive their food rations in full, in accordance with our previous ukaz, without cheating. An ukaz regarding this has already been issued. Our provisions are being sent from Kazan to the Siberian towns, so they will not be in need.

See: G. F. Müller, *Istoriia Sibiri* (Moscow-Leningrad: 1937), II, 169–170.

17

A GRAMOTA FROM TSAR BORIS FEDOROVICH TO THE VOEVODA OF
PELYM, TIKHON TRAKHANIOTOV, REINSTITUTING COLLECTION OF
IASAK IN SIBERIA

From the Tsar and Grand Prince Boris Fedorovich of all Russia, to the town of Pelym, to our voevoda Tikhon Ivanovich Trakhaniotov, and to the golova Petr Grigorievich Vederevskii. Last year, in recognition of our coronation as Tsar, and our long life and good health, and that of our son, the Tsarevich Prince Fedor Borisovich of all Russia, we decreed that for the year 1600 no iasak was to be collected throughout Siberia. But for the year 1601, and in future years, we decree that iasak is again to be collected for us, as previously, throughout Siberia.

However, from aged iasak people, or those who are disabled, blind or ill and cannot hunt in the forests, we order that no iasak be collected for us, if it is not possible to take any.

When you receive this our gramota you are immediately to select as many men as you need to collect iasak. Choose from among the servitors, deti boiarskie, Litva, cossacks and streltsy. Choose good men, and bring them to swear on the cross that they will collect our iasak in full according to the iasak books from the Pelym uezd, from the iasak princes, from Ostiaks and Voguls, for the year 1601. The iasak is to be made up of pelts of sable, fox, marten, beaver, squirrel and ermine, but they are not to accept any poor quality pelts of sable, marten, beaver or squirrel. They are not to make any personal profit. They are not to take any trade goods to these small towns and volosts. They are not to trade anything with the iasak people. They are not to exchange our iasak by taking the best furs for themselves, whether sable, marten, fox, beaver, squirrel or ermine, and substituting their own lesser quality sable or beaver or other pelts.

They are to bring all the iasak they collect from the iasak people to you, to our warehouse in Pelym. Once you have had them swear on the cross, you are immediately to send these iasak collectors out into the Pelym uezd to collect our iasak. After they have collected it, they are to bring it in to Pelym. You are to order that when the collectors bring in their iasak reports, they are also to bring with them one or two native leaders from each volost.

These leaders are to be questioned as to the iasak collected from them, and they are to be asked whether they were harassed by the collectors. If they lodge a complaint against any collector, you are immediately to order an investigation and punish the guilty according to our ukaz.

If any of the iasak leaders, princes, murzas, Tatars, Ostiaks or Voguls come to you from the small towns and volosts, to petition you not to send iasak collectors to them to collect our iasak, but rather to allow them to bring our iasak to Pelym personally, you are to agree. Do not send iasak collectors to those small settlements and volosts to collect our iasak. Instead, allow some trustworthy person to bring in our iasak, at a specific time which you will set, without delay and without excuses. You are to order them to deliver our iasak on time, and not to seek any personal gain nor try to conceal anything.

If the iasak people come and petition you that they cannot pay our iasak on time this year, then depending on the circumstances you may allow them more time to pay, but enter any deficiency into the iasak books.

When princes and Ostiaks and Voguls come to you in Pelym bringing our iasak, you are to have a *tselovalnik* [sworn appraiser] present at the time of delivery. You are to deposit the iasak in our warehouse and hold it there under seal. If any of the princes, murzas and leaders come to you after they have paid their iasak, and bring pominki for our Tsarist Majesty, or for our son the Tsarevich Prince Fedor Borisovich of all Russia, you are to accept these gifts from them and deposit them in our warehouse and order them to be entered in detail into the iasak books. But do not confuse these gifts with the iasak collection. You are not to distribute the pominki from the iasak people as bribes. You are to take all that is brought and deposit it in our warehouse. In regard to persons who do not bring pominki, you are not to ask them for any. There is to be no transaction in this matter.

When you send the iasak collectors out for our iasak, you are to send trustworthy detie boiarskie out to intercept them after they have met with the iasak people. You are to authorize them to search through all of the collectors' bags and furs. If they find any unauthorized goods or furs, you are to order that these be confiscated and deposited in our warehouse. Guilty collectors are to be knouted or whipped. After they have been punished they are to be imprisoned, the term to depend on their guilt.

If there are any old or ill or infirm persons among the iasak people who have nothing with which to pay our iasak, you are to verify the facts and then do not collect our iasak from these persons, so they will not suffer need and hunger. However, when in the future some of those persons recover, and their situation improves, then you are to order that our iasak be collected from them as previously.

You are to issue strict orders that iasak collectors take only prime pelts of sable, fox, marten, beaver, squirrel and ermine as iasak. They are not to accept furs of poor or indifferent quality. Furthermore they are not to accept any bribes or pominki for themselves from princes, Ostiaks and Voguls. They are not to accept bribes in place of iasak, nor are they to take any goods with them into the towns and volosts. They are not to trade with iasak people. They are not to make any exchanges, substituting their own poorer quality furs for our iasak of prime pelts. They are to deliver all the iasak they collect from the iasak people to you in Pelym, into our warehouse.

You are to order that all Siberian iasak people are to be protected and treated with kindness and courtesy. You are not to be cruel to them in any way. Russians are not to insult them nor sell them into slavery nor treat them with violence.

All iasak which is deposited in our warehouse during the year, and all pominki brought to you for Our Tsarist Majesty or for our son the Tsarevich Prince Fedor Borisovich of all Russia, is to be sent to us in Moscow. You are to send as many deti boiarskie, cossacks and streltsy as possible to guard our Treasury and the inventory. Send them immediately, together in a group, so we will not lose any of our treasure. But do not oppress the peasants, as happened earlier when you frequently sent ten men from one town to another, and our Treasury suffered losses because of this, and there was much trouble.

See: G. F. Müller, *Istoriia Sibiri* (Moscow-Leningrad: 1937), I, 390–392.

18

MARCH 21, 1604

A GRAMOTA FROM TSAR BORIS FEDOROVICH TO THE TIUMEN GOLOVA, ALEKSEI BEZOBRAZOV, CONCERNING SUPPLIES AND PROVISIONS FOR THE DETACHMENT WHICH IS BUILDING TOMSK

From the Tsar and Grand Prince Boris Fedorovich of all Russia to the golova Aleksei Ivanovich Bezobrazov in the town of Tiumen in Siberia. In accordance with our ukaz, authorization has been given to build a town in Surgut uezd, Tomsk volost, on the Tom River above [the confluence of] the Ob. For this purpose we have ordered Gavriil Pisemskii to be sent from Surgut, and Vasilii Tyrkov from Tobolsk. With them, to augment the numbers of the Bogolsk, Surgut, and Berezovo servitors, we have sent 50 servitors from Tiumen, streltsy and cossacks, and two cannoneers, under the command of ataman Druzhin Iurev. These Tiumen servitors have been instructed to remain in the town of Tomsk for one year. We have ordered a detachment to be sent to them from Tiumen, with a volley gun and 200 iron balls and 200 lead balls, as well as 10 puds of powder and 10 puds of shot.

When you receive this our gramota, you are immediately to send this selected group of 50 of the best streltsy and cossacks and two cannoneers from Tiumen to Tobolsk with ataman Druzhin Iurev. In Tiumen they are to be issued provisions and salary for the present year, 1604, in full. And you are to send with them from Tiumen the volley gun, the 200 iron balls and 200 lead balls and 10 puds of powder and 10 puds of lead. You are also immediately to send a detail of servitors with powder and lead from Tiumen to Tobolsk, so that the Tobolsk servitors will have no shortages.

We have sent our ukaz concerning this to Tomsk.

When you send this detail of servitors and the powder and shot from Tiumen to Tobolsk, you are also to send us a report in Moscow. Send it to our diak Nechai Fedorov in the Kazan and Meshcherskii dvorets.

See: G. F. Müller, *Istoriia Sibiri* (Moscow-Leningrad: 1937), I, 411.

19

BETWEEN JULY 7 AND AUGUST 31, 1605

A REPORT FROM THE VOEVODA OF KETSK, POSTNIK BELSKII, TO THE VOEVODA OF TOMSK, GAVRIIL PISEMSKII, CONCERNING A NATIVE UPRISING

Postnik Belskii humbly reports to Gospodin Gavriil Ivanovich [Pisemskii]. On July 3 of the present year, 1605, a woman named Kinotu, wife of a Mogulin man named Maigin, came to Ketsk ostrog and said she had information. I ordered her to be brought to me and I questioned her. She reported that Mogul, Mast, Pit and all the other leaders and young men from the Upper Ketsk and other volosts are plotting an uprising against Ketsk ostrog. They plan to come to Ketsk ostrog and hunt animals in the vicinity, and in the course of the hunt they are planning to seize the ostrog and kill the servitors as they are sent out.

I immediately sent servitors into the native settlements to take the leaders Mogul, Mast, Pit and Girget. With God's help these leaders were apprehended just as they were about to go out in a group. When Mogul and the other leaders were brought in, I interrogated them. They denied everything and insisted they were not plotting against the ostrog or against the government servitors. I handed them over to guards and interrogated them intensely for three days; then on July 7 I interrogated them under torture. Prince Mogul confessed that during the winter prince Basandai of Tomsk and the Kirgiz prince Nomza of Chiulymsk had sent prince Laga to them. The Obsk prince had sent Baibakhta. The rest of the Ob people had sent Legleev's nephew Kachek and Niankul's son Kicheg. All of these urged them to make every effort during the winter and spring to capture Ketsk ostrog and kill the Sovereign's servitors, even if they had to set fire to the ostrog.

All the Ketsk natives as well as those from other areas who pay iasak into the Sovereign's Treasury in Ketsk ostrog were plotting against the ostrog, and planned to kill the Sovereign's servitors when they were sent out. Furthermore, the Tomsk natives, the Kirgiz, those near the Ob and those from other areas who pay the Sovereign's iasak in the town of Tomsk, were plotting against the town of Tomsk and the Sovereign's servitors. They plan to come to the town of Tomsk during the busy season when the populace goes out to farm and to fish. They are making plans as to how to take the town of Tomsk, and how to kill the people who have been sent to farm and to fish. Wherever servitors are sent, they will kill them.

I ordered that Mast and Pit and Girget be brought before me individually. I interrogated them, and each told the same story. They said that the Tomsk prince Basandai and the Kirgiz prince Nomza of Chiulymsk, had sent prince Laga. The Ob prince and his people had sent Meglik's nephew Kachek, and Niankul's son Kicheg, to plot against the town of Tomsk and against the Sovereign's men in Tomsk. The princes ordered [Mast, Pit and Girget] to conspire against Ketsk ostrog, and threatened that if they did not do so, and if [Laga, Kachek and Kicheg] did manage to take the town of Tomsk, that the latter would kill the former and go on to take Ketsk ostrog themselves.

I then questioned all the Ketsk leaders as well as the lesser men, but neither the leaders nor the others knew anything of what was being said. But the woman who came reported that there is a conspiracy against the town of Tomsk by people who pay the Sovereign's iasak in Tomsk.

Gospodin, you need to be vigilant. Act in accordance with the Sovereign's ukaz, and make a very careful investigation into this conspiracy and treason. I am sending this gramota with the strelets Grigorii Butrov, who is accompanied by two Ostiaks. Gospodin, send him back immediately, without detaining him, because the situation here is not peaceful, and we have only a few men.

See: G. F. Müller, *Istoriia Sibiri* (Moscow-Leningrad: 1937), I, 414–415.

20

A REPORT FROM THE VOEVODA OF TOBOLSK, PRINCE ROMAN TROEKU-
ROV, TO THE VOEVODA OF PELYM, IVAN GODUNOV, CONCERNING
DANGEROUS UNREST AMONG THE NATIVES

Roman Troekurov reports to Ivan Mikhailovich [Godunov] and Petr Danilovich. Gospodin, on June 21, 1606, word reached us that the Ostiak prince Okseit Boiarov has joined forces with the iasak people from the Pelym volost of Kondinsk and the iasak Ostiak, Amalyk Grigorev, from Niazymsk volost. They are assembling a large force and plan to attack Prince Ivan and Prince Mikhail, the sons of Igicheev Alachev. They now have some 300 men. In Tobolsk we questioned the Ostiak prince Okseit about this in detail. Under questioning he told us he had not been plotting with the Kondin people and that there is no unrest in his volost, but that there is great unrest among the iasak people of Pelym uezd in the Kondin volost. They are gathering, and plan to attack Prince Ivan and Prince Mikhail in force. When they reach the settlement of Ketsk, they plan to kill these men because they are the ones who collect iasak from them. At the present time Prince Ivan and Prince Mikhail are under siege from these Pelym iasak people in the settlement.

Gospodin, if there is unrest among the iasak people in the Kondin volost, and you learn of it but do not inform us of it, this will be a serious matter. Gospodin, upon receipt of this gramota, you are to send a detailed written report about this by rapid courier to us in Tobolsk. If you do not know anything of this, Gospodin, then you are immediately to send all available servitors from Pelym to the Kondinsk volost, and order that five or six of the Kondinsk volost leaders be brought to you in Pelym immediately so that you can interrogate them about this.

They have given their oath to the Sovereign not to commit treason, nor to assemble warriors, nor to launch an attack. If they know of any rebels, they are to bring them to you in Pelym. You are to find out from them why there is unrest among the iasak people of the Kondinsk volost, why they plan to attack Prince Ivan and Prince Mikhail, the sons of Igicheev, and what oppressions and hardships they have suffered because of them. They may send a petition to the Sovereign about these problems, but they are not to assemble for the purpose of an attack. If there are insurgents, they must be apprehended and brought to you. The Sovereign will give generous rewards to any persons who hand over traitors. And if the plotters personally plead their guilt to the Sovereign, he will pardon them.

Gospodin, whatever you learn from these persons during the questioning, why there is unrest and who is responsible for it, you are to write down all the details immediately, and send the report to us post haste, without losing a minute. Send the report with the first available courier and order him to travel day and night to Tobolsk.

If the unrest in Kondinsk volost becomes any worse, you are not to release any of these suspects from Pelym until you have an ukaz from the Sovereign. Give them as much food as they need. Send to Kondinsk volost two or three iasak-paying people who are well known and well regarded in that volost. Also send Pelym servitors with them and three or four interpreters. Instruct them to speak firmly with the iasak people of Kondinsk volost so that they will disperse back to their settlements, and will not come together to make an unwarranted attack on anyone. They are not to assemble for any reason. They are not to cause any unrest or disturbance. If their dwellings or hunting grounds have been violated, or if they have suffered any other oppression or harm, they are to go to Pelym to file a complaint with you.

The Sovereign Tsar and Grand Prince Dmitrii Ivanovich [The False Dmitrii] of all Russia will issue his Tsarist ukaz against any persons guilty of violence and of inflicting injury.

In addition to investigating unrest in the Kondinsk volost, you are also to make inquiries into other matters there and in other volosts which pay iasak to Pelym. You are immediately to report to Tobolsk any information you may secure from these iasak people and from the servitors you send to them.

See: G. F. Müller, *Istoriia Sibiri* (Moscow-Leningrad: 1937), II, 193–194.

21

OCTOBER 28, 1607

A GRAMOTA FROM TSAR VASILII IVANOVICH SHUISKII TO THE VOEVODA
OF BEREZOVO, PRINCE PETR CHERKASKII, CONCERNING AN UPRISING
OF OSTIAKS, VOGULS AND SAMOEDS

From the Tsar and Grand Prince Vasilii Ivanovich of all Russia to Siberia, to the town of Berezovo, to our voevoda Prince Petr Akhamashukovich Cherkaskii and to the golova Ivan Ignatevich Zubov. On September 5, 1607, you wrote to us that a captive from Narym named Osdonia, the wife of the Ostiak servitor Vaiusk, came to you from a settlement outside of Berezovo. She appeared before you in the Prikaz office and informed you of treason among the Ostiaks in the Berezovo uezd. She said that last year, 1606, a newly baptized man named Petr Kulanov and his son Anton met with Vaiusk in the settlement. They talked with Vaiusk and Atkatk and many other Ostiaks, and told them they were planning to pillage our warehouse and steal provisions and kill the servitors and traders. They did not carry out this treason, however, because Onzha and Mamruk, from the town of Obdorsk, were in Moscow at that time.

That same year, 1606, Petr Kulanov and his son Anton and Vaiusk and Aktatk and the other Ostiaks declared that they knew nothing about burning the town, or pillaging the warehouse of provisions, or killing servitors. During the interrogation Petr Kulanov and his son Anton refused to tell you anything; but Ostiaks from nearby areas, Atkatk and Uchkutk and the Kazym Ostiak, Elgoz, all confessed to treason, implicating themselves and all their fellow Ostiaks from the Berezovo uezd. They implicated Petr and his son Anton as well as the newly baptized man Lev, Shatrov Luguev, Prince Vasilii Obdorskoi, the Toboldinsk *shaitan* [sorcerer] and the Ostiaks from Ketsk, Tugubask and Deruik. They said that these Ostiak and Samoed leaders are plotting serious treason and that all the Berezovo Ostiaks and the Voguls trust them.

Under torture Petr Kulanov and his son Anton confessed to treason. They confessed their own guilt and admitted that they had led the Ostiaks to plot treason, including pillaging the warehouse and provisions and burning the town, just as Vaiusk's wife had said. All the leading men of the area were implicated in the

treason: Prince Vasilii Obdorskoi and his son Mamruk; the Lia-
pinskii Ostiaks Anton and Lelman; the Lominsk Ostiaks Bogdan
Tsyngopov and Enochk; the Sosvensk Ostiaks; the Toboldinsk
shaitan, Talyshk; the Ketsk Ostiak princes Onzha, Chumen,
Tugunas, and Chaul's son, Derun; the Belogorsk Ostiaks Laut
and Tair; the Ostiaks Vaiusk and Atkatk, from near Berezovo; and
the newly baptized man, Lev. The Surgut iasak people and the
Pelym Voguls did not take part, but they had the same intention
and had organized themselves.

In all, there were 2,000 Ostiaks and Samoeds involved. All of
these people had planned to assemble a week before Sv. Petr's
Day in Iziapal, about 15 versts above Berezovo in the Ob valley.
From that place they planned to sack the government warehouses
and attack the town.

The Ostiak Vaiusk was captured and confessed to treason
during the interrogation. He said that the Ostiaks had come to
him with this plan of treason.

Prince Petr, once you have apprehended the traitors, immediately order that the vile criminals Anton Kulanov and Vaiusk
and the newly baptized Lev be hanged for their treason; and also
Petr Kulanov's wife, so that others who witness this will be deterred from such crimes.

According to a report of the Berezovo Ostiaks, Atkatk, Uchkutk, Nerym and their comrades, 60 men were apprehended and
brought to Berezovo to you. These included the Sosvensk Ostiaks, Konzhik Nikitin, Talym, and two shaitans from Lialikarsk
and Toboldinsk. Also included in this group were Zarnesh, Kor-
som, Chevnezh, and the Kazym Ostiaks Enok, Monsin, Abys,
Kokhrom, Gagachen, Tuian and Noivid. All of these Ostiaks confessed to treason, and they implicated all the other Ostiaks of the
Berezovo uezd.

Prince Onzha Iuriev captured the traitorous Kunovatsk Ostiaks, Shatrov Luguev, his brother Vokchim, and Malengin, and
turned them all over to you. You interrogated them, and under
questioning they all confessed their own guilt and implicated
their comrades in the treason.

On June 2 Prince Mamruk Obdorskoi was brought to Berezovo
with eight Ostiak men. Under questioning they confessed their
guilt and implicated Mamruk's father, Prince Vasilii, and all the
Berezovo Ostiaks. [Prince Mamruk] stated that the entire region
was involved in the treason. He confessed his treason against us,

and said the reason he had not informed on his father and all the other Ostiaks was that he was afraid his father and the Ostiaks would kill him. His father, Prince Vasilii, did not go to Berezovo as you had ordered. But on June 9 Prince Vasilii Obdorskoi and the Liapinsk Ostiak named Alyk were apprehended and brought to you there. During interrogation Prince Vasilii Obdorskoi and Lechman acknowledged their part in the treason and confessed their guilt in urging Ostiaks and Samoeds to take part. They confessed that they had plotted to destroy the government warehouses and to attack the town. Prince Vasilii had sent messengers to the leading men in Surgut to persuade them to take part in the conspiracy. All the Berezovo and Surgut Ostiaks were involved in the plot to raid the warehouses, attack the town and ostrog, and kill the servitors.

On June 12 the Belogorsk Ostiaks, Tair Samirov, Mochei and Eran and 20 of their men were brought to Berezovo and confessed their guilt to us and implicated their comrades in the treason. Prince Vasilii Obdorskoi confessed that previously the Samoeds had also turned against us and had destroyed government warehouses and provisions and killed the voevoda of Mangazeia, Prince Miron Shakhovskii, and his servitors. Prince Vasilii was also involved in plotting that conspiracy, and at the time he had told the Samoeds not to reveal their plans to his son Mamruk, because Mamruk was loyal to us and would not follow Prince Vasilii.

When you have investigated the unrest among the Ostiaks, and have apprehended the traitorous criminals Shatrov Luguev, the Toboldinsk shaitan, and the Ketsk Ostiaks, Tugupas and Verun, you are to order that they be hanged, so that by witnessing this, other potential criminals will be dissuaded from committing like crimes. Other traitors are to be knouted. The principals in this treason, Prince Vasilii Obdorskoi and the Liapinsk Ostiak, Lechman, and Bogdan Tsyngopov, are to be imprisoned until we have issued an ukaz concerning them. Prince Mamruk Obdorskoi and Prince Onzha are to receive rewards.

At the present time many Ostiaks and Voguls from all over the Berezovo uezd have confessed their guilt and have petitioned us for pardon. They now pay iasak and wish to summon the Samoeds to do likewise. They told you that they rebelled because excessive iasak had been imposed on them, and they could only pay this iasak by buying furs, and to do this they had to sell their kettles and axes and thus they became indebted to the Russians.

This has impoverished them and put them so deep in debt that they have to sell their wives and children to pay the iasak. Many have starved to death.

Ostiaks from the entire Berezovo uezd under the leadership of Atkatk, Ulkut, Nerym, Naum, Alym, Kushkil and their men, have reported to us about the traitors Prince Vasilii Obdorskoi and Lechman and Bogdan Tsyngopov. This whole conspiracy was brought about by these traitors, who led the Ostiaks and Samoeds into it by threatening to kill them. These Ostiaks are no longer associated with the traitors. All they want is to be allowed to live as before. There will be traitors who will conspire in the future, and you are to issue an ukaz to deal with such traitors. You are to inflict harsh punishment on them. After you have investigated their treason, you are to order that the worst of the criminals be executed. Guard your own person, the town, our warehouse, the provisions and the servitors against traitors.

God willing, you will have an audience with us for your successful service and we will reward you generously. When you receive this our gramota, you are to order that Ostiaks and Voguls from the entire Berezovo uezd assemble. Tell them that Prince Vasilii Obdorskoi and his men have committed treason against us, and that they have confessed. They have caused great discord and suffering, and they have led all the Ostiaks into this treason. Also tell them that Ostiaks from the entire Berezovo uezd have petitioned us that they cannot live any longer with Prince Vasilii Obdorskoi and his followers. Tell them they may anticipate further treason from these men in the future. Tell them that we have pardoned these Ostiaks [who petitioned us] because they were instigated by those vile traitors and criminals, Prince Vasilii Obdorskoi and his men. After you have informed them of this, you are to give the order that Prince Vasilii and his men be hanged, and that all his goods and properties be inventoried and given to his son, Prince Mamruk. Seeing this, in the future others will be disinclined to turn to such criminal acts. Any traitors who, after your investigation, have not been sentenced to capital punishment are to take an oath of allegiance and put up substantial security with an official signature so that in the future they will not be tempted to commit lawlessness and treason.

As for those princes, Ostiaks and Voguls, who confessed but have petitioned us for pardon, and have informed on their traitorous comrades, you are to thank them for us. Tell them that we have pardoned them and that they are no longer in disgrace with us. They are not to behave in this manner in the future; they are not to betray us nor heed criminals; and in the future they are to inform on traitors. They are not to harbor criminals; they must inform the voevoda and the golova about such persons. Then they may live in our Tsarist favor and mercy, as formerly, without fear. You are to allow the woman who informed you about the Ostiak treason to live in the Berezovo settlement. Assign quarters for her, and free her from all taxes and obligatory work. She is to be allowed to engage in her work and trade without paying any taxes on her possessions. In addition, as a demonstration of our favor, you are to give her two good bales of cloth from our warehouse, and ten rubles in cash, and order that she receive protection.

In the future you must conduct yourself with extreme caution. Investigate the Ostiak lawlessness carefully, and examine their treason, so that in the future you will be able to prevent this.

In regard to iasak people who have become impoverished because of having to pay our iasak, and who are unable to pay, and who want to come to Moscow to petition us because their iasak is so excessive that they have to sell their wives and children to pay it—allow two or three of these persons to come to us in Moscow. Also, prepare a detailed list of the iasak people and the volosts, indicating how many iasak persons there are in each volost, and how much iasak they pay. Send this to us, and do not collect any iasak from them until we have issued an ukaz about this. You are to send this information to us in Moscow, to the Kazan and Meshchersk dvorets.

See: G. F. Müller, *Istoriia Sibiri* (Moscow-Leningrad: 1937), II, 202–204.

22

NOT BEFORE FEBRUARY 11, 1609

A REPORT FROM THE VOEVODAS OF TOMSK, VASILII VOLYNSKII AND
MIKHAIL NOVOSILTSOV, TO TSAR VASILII IVANOVICH, CONCERNING
NATIVE UPRISINGS IN THE KUZNETSK VOLOST

To the Sovereign Tsar and Grand Prince Vasilii Ivanovich [Shuiskii] of all Russia, your humble servants Vasilii Volynskii and Mikhail Novosiltsov report. Sire, on November 20, 1608 we your humble servants, Sire, sent the Tomsk servitors, the mounted cossacks Bogdan Kostiantinov, Lev Olpatov and Ivan Shokurov and their men, to collect your Sovereign's iasak in Kuznetsk volost. Sire, on February 11 they returned from Kuznetsk volost and reported to us, your humble servants, that the natives in Kuznetsk volost would not pay iasak and tried to kill them. Sire, all the goods they had taken with them belonging to you, Sovereign, were stolen when the natives tried to kill them. Sire, they were saved from death by a few Kuznetsk people who are loyal to you, Sire, prince Bazaiak and his people in Obinsk volost.

Sire, these people sent messengers to the Kuznetsk people of other volosts to tell them not to kill and rob your men who are assigned throughout the volost. Sire, the men responsible for robbing the servitors in the Kuznetsk volosts were Badachak, Kubasak, Basarak and their men. They did not pay your iasak in full, Sire. They paid in poor sables, Sire, which were not worth putting into your Sovereign warehouse. Sire, in the past the Kuznetsk people have not paid their iasak in full, either, and they have paid in poor, immature sables, which were not worth putting into your Sovereign warehouse.

Sire, we have summoned the Kuznetsk prince Bazaiak to the town of Tomsk to receive your Tsarist reward because he served you loyally, Sovereign, and prevented your Sovereign people from being killed. But, Sire, he has replied that he cannot come to the town of Tomsk, because if he did the Kuznetsk people would rob him and kill his wife and children while he was gone, and because of that it is impossible for him to come, Sire.

Sire, we cannot attack the Kuznetsk people because we have so few men in Tomsk. Sire, the servitors are sent to Tobolsk in the summer to convoy your shipment of money and provisions, which reaches here in the fall. Sire, it is impossible to attack the Kuznetsk people in fall and winter because they live in well fortified places surrounded by marshes and swamps and bogs. The snow is very deep there in winter. Sire, the only time we can attack is in summer when the weather is warm, but at that time, Sire, the servitors are out on assignments. In that season there are only a very few persons left in Tomsk, Sire, and these are posted as guards to protect those who are sent out. They are only a few persons on full time guard duty in the town and the ostrog.

See: G. F. Müller, *Istoriia Sibiri* (Moscow-Leningrad: 1937), I, 421.

23

A REPORT FROM THE VOEVODA OF TOMSK, VASILII VOLYNSKII, TO THE PRIKAZ OF THE KAZAN DVORETS CONCERNING THE FAILURE OF THE MISSION OF TOMSK MOUNTED COSSACKS TO THE MONGOL ALTYN-KHAN, AND TO THE CHINESE EMPIRE

To the Sovereign Tsar and Grand Prince Vasilii Ivanovich of all Russia, your humble servants Vasilii Volynskii and Mikhail Novosiltsov report.

Sovereign, on October 10, 1608, in accordance with your ukaz, Sovereign Tsar and Grand Prince Vasilii Ivanovich of all Russia, we your humble servants, Sovereign, sent Tomsk mounted cossacks, Ivan Belogolov, Matvei Kutin and Fedor Khodekin, and the interpreter Grigorii Mikhailov Litvin, to the Altyn-tsar and to the Chinese Empire. Sire, the Kirgiz princes Nomza and Kochebai wanted to guide your Sovereign servitors to the Altyn-tsar and to the Mongol *kontaisha** and to the Chinese Empire. Sire, they told us, your humble servants, that they had been in the land of the Altyn-tsar, and that the Altyn's people go to the Chinese people.

Sire, we your humble servants questioned Nomza and Kochebai about the Altyn-tsar and about the Chinese Empire. Sire, during the discussion they said that the Altyn-tsar is a Mongol, and that traveling on foot it takes a month to travel to him from the land of the Kirgiz. His people inhabit the entire area between the Matsy and his dwelling place. The [Altyn-] tsar is nomadic, and uses both horses and camel for travel purposes. He rules some 200,000 people, and his main weapons are bows and arrows. It takes three months traveling on foot to go from the Altyn-tsar's land to the Chinese Empire.

Sire, the Chinese Emperor lives in a city built of stone, and the courtyards in the city are similar in design to those of the Russians. The houses facing the courtyards are built of stone. The people there are more powerful than those of the Altyn-tsar, and they are wealthier. The Chinese Emperor has palaces built of stone. Inside the city there are temples that have great bells, but

---

* *Kontaisha* (also *taisha*, *taidzha*). An official title used by Mongol chieftains who could trace their lineage to Genghis Khan.—Eds.

no crosses. We do not know what faith they profess, but they live in a fashion similar to the Russians. They use firearms as weapons. People come from many lands to trade with them. They wear brocaded clothing, and the Emperor receives all manner of richly patterned fabrics from many lands.

Sire, we your humble servants allowed Nomza and Kochebai to go with your Sovereign servitors to the land of the Kirgiz, and we had them take the oath to serve you, Sire, and to be loyal to you, and to live steadfast under your Tsarist might. As hostages for themselves they left Nomza's wife and Kochebai's son in Tomsk.

Sire, we instructed Nomza to take your Sovereign servitors to the Altyn-tsar and to the Chinese Empire. And, Sire, we instructed Kochebai to bring the Kirgiz princes Noian and Koshkai and Obrai under your Tsarist mighty protection so that they will serve you and be loyal to you, Sovereign Tsar and Grand Prince Vasilii Ivanovich of all Russia, and pay you iasak at the same time Nomza and Kochebai do, delivering it in winter when your Sovereign servitors come from Tomsk to collect your Sovereign iasak.

Sire, on March 18 Ivan Belogolov and his men came from the Kirgiz, and when they were questioned, Sire, they said that Nomza did not guide them to the Altyn-tsar and to the Chinese Empire, because he was afraid that your Sovereign servitors might suffer casualties since the Black Kalmyks were warring against the Altyn-tsar and had driven him far from his winter encampment where he had previously stayed, and that the Altyn's iasak people had deserted him and were fighting against him. These are the people who live along the route between the Kirgiz and the Altyn-tsar. This is the reason [your mission] could not proceed to the Altyn-tsar.

Sire, in the future when the Altyn's people come to the Kirgiz, this news should be made known in Tomsk so that your Sovereign servitors can plan to be guided to the Altyn-tsar and to the Chinese Empire by the Altyn's people.

Reference: LOA AN SSSR, f. Portfeli Millera, op. 4, kn. 17, No. 8, 11. 12 ob.–13 ob.
See: *Russko-kitaiskie otnosheniia v XVII veke: Dokumenty i materialy (1608–1691)* (Moscow: 1969), I, 39–40.

24

A REPORT FROM THE VOEVODA OF KETSK, GRIGORII ELIZAROV, TO THE VOEVODA OF TOBOLSK, PRINCE IVAN KATYREV-ROSTOVSKII, CONCERNING A TUNGUS UPRISING AND THE SHORTAGE OF PROVISIONS

Grigorii Elizarov reports to Gospodin Prince Ivan Mikhailovich and to Boris Ivanovich and to Nechai Fedorovich, diak of the Sovereign Tsar and Grand Prince. Gospoda, on December 25, prince Urnuch and the interpreter Olka, iasak Ostiaks of the upper volost, came to Ketsk ostrog with the Sovereign's iasak. Olka went to new lands for the Sovereign's iasak as an interpreter. He went to prince Namak and reported that he had learned in that volost that prince Danul and his Tungus people had attacked the Sovereign's iasak people from Kuznetsk volost, prince Tumet and his people. They went by boat and wounded two men. The rest of the iasak people fled. These Tungus did not pay iasak.

Olka also reported that he had heard in the same volost that these Tungus were plotting to kill the iasak collectors and servitors who came to collect their iasak, sparing only one cossack to serve as an interpreter and guide. They were plotting to attack the iasak people along the Ket River up as far as Ketsk ostrog, so that they would not pay their iasak to the Sovereign, but would hand it over to them instead. Gospoda, on May 6 of this year, acting on that information, I sent government servitors to attack these Tungus. I sent the Surgut streltsy and cossacks led by the desiatnik Ivan Kaidalov, and I also sent the Zyrians who were in the ostrog, and the Ketsk iasak-paying Ostiaks, as well as princes Urnuk, Nomak and Kirgei and their men.

With the grace of God and the luck of the Sovereign they attacked the Tungus and wounded some of them; they also took some prisoners who died of their wounds while in captivity. At the same time that the Sovereign's men were fighting the Tungus, prince Kobyt, son of Tulkin, who lived in the new lands, feared war with the Sovereign's men and sent two forties of sables as iasak to the Sovereign's iasak collectors in the new territory in Veslov volost. Prior to this, prince Kobyt the son of Tulkin, had not paid any iasak to the Sovereign. Gospoda, when the Sovereign's servitors left the land of the Tungus, the Tungus joined together and

Left: A Tatar merchant wearing a fur-lined shuba at Tomsk. Early nineteenth-century aquatint (Le Conte). Right: Samoed hunter. Late eighteenth-century engraving.

attacked the Sovereign's iasak people in the Sym volost, prince Kaiaget and his men.

Gospoda, last year, 1608, the Sovereign's provisions were sent to Ketsk ostrog from Verkhotur'e and from Tobolsk, but they did not arrive in full. They were short ten chetverts of flour and five of groats and five of oats, which were intended for Ostiak expenses. For the current Tungus service, the Sovereign's provisions have been given to the Ostiak princes who were in the Sovereign's service. The natives have received flour, groats and oats. As of July 6 there are on hand in the Sovereign's warehouses 20¼ chetverts of flour and groats and 26 chetverts of oats. This is designated for expenses for the Ostiaks and others. When the Ostiaks bring in the Sovereign's iasak in winter there will be shortages.

See: G. F. Müller, *Istoriia Sibiri* (Moscow-Leningrad: 1937), II, 211–212.

25

AFTER JULY 9, 1609

A REPORT FROM THE VOEVODA OF TOBOLSK, PRINCE IVAN KATYREV-
ROSTOVSKII, TO THE VOEVODAS OF TOMSK, VASILII VOLYNSKII AND
MIKHAIL NOVOSILTSOV, CONCERNING A KIRGIZ UPRISING AND AN AT-
TACK BY THE BLACK KALMYKS

Ivan Katyrev-Rostovskii reports to Gospoda Vasilii Vasilevich
and Mikhail Ignatevich. On January 4, you wrote to Tobolsk
that you had sent a Tomsk cossack named Burnash Nikonov and
his men to collect the Sovereign's iasak from the Kirgiz. Burnash
and his men returned to Tomsk on June 8 and reported to you
that the Kirgiz prince Nomza had paid part of his iasak obligation, sending his wife with it and asking for more time to pay the
rest. You reported that Kochebai and Noian and Koshkai did not
pay iasak, but beat and starved the iasak collectors. You also reported that Nomza's wife said that Kochebai and his men are not
loyal to the Sovereign and that they do not follow her husband,
Nomza. You also reported that a Chiulymsk prince and his iasak
people came to petition you, saying that these Kirgiz princes
Kochebai and his men had attacked and robbed them, stolen their
furs, and caused them great suffering. They asked that you protect them from the violence of the Kirgiz people.

On June 25 you sent 300 Tomsk servitors and Tatars against
the Kirgiz with orders to engage them in battle. There are only
some 150 Kirgiz servitors. On July 4 the Tomsk servitors and
Tatars returned from the Kirgiz expedition and reported that they
had reached the land of the Kirgiz at night, and that the Kirgiz
people had run away beyond the Enisei River, leaving all their
possessions behind. [The Tomsk group] killed all who were left
behind and took their wives and children and all their belongings.
They drove off all the livestock, some 3,000 head. But as they
were returning with their prisoners and plunder from the land of
the Kirgiz, the latter met them en route and attacked them in
great numbers from the forest. [The Russians] fled, but the Kirgiz
pursued them, killing many and wounding twenty or more, and
succeeded in recovering their goods.

On the night of July 4 several Black Kalmyks attacked the
outposts and wounded some of the Tomsk Tatar sentries. They

took prisoners and drove off the livestock which belonged to the Tomsk Tatars. At that time the Tomsk servitors were on service in the land of the Kirgiz, and they returned to Tomsk that same day. You then sent the servitors out after those Black Kalmyks, but they returned without having found them. The White Kalmyk murza, Borzakai, who had remained in the ulus of prince Abakai, stopped them and told them that Abakai had gone out after the Black Kalmyks when he heard how they had murdered the Tomsk Tatar sentries. When he found them, he planned to free the prisoners and send them and the livestock to Tomsk.

On July 9 prince Abakai sent his murzas Izedei and Urzubai to you in Tomsk, with the prisoners and the horses which the Kalmyks had taken. They told you they had defeated the Kalmyks and had wounded some of them and taken prisoners. But they did not bring back all of the horses belonging to the dead Tomsk Tatars because the Black Kalmyks had killed or wounded some of the horses. You told them to bring in the horses, and that the Sovereign would reward them for their service.

In the future you must be on the lookout for an attack against the town of Tomsk by the Black Kalmyks and the Kirgiz.

There are very few servitors and Tatars in the town of Tomsk, and only 100 cossacks. They stand guard in the town and in the ostrog, and there are no relief guards. There is no one to guard the gates or to serve as sentry for those who go out to work in the fields and tend the livestock. We must have reinforcements in Tomsk in order to prevent the Kirgiz from joining with the Black Kalmyks to attack Tomsk.

Gospoda, you are to give orders that prince Abakai be given two kaftans made of fine cloth as a reward; one is to have long sleeves and the other not. The murza Borzakai is to have one with long sleeves. You are to send these to them in their ulus with anyone available. Tell them that if they will serve the Sovereign in the future, and be loyal in all ways, that the Sovereign will reward them.

You have reported a shortage of men, but the fact is that you have brought this about by your own poorly planned actions in Tomsk. You have dismissed many servitors from Tomsk to idle in other Siberian towns, and these people have not returned to you. We have very few servitors in Tobolsk, and we cannot send any of them to you in Tomsk. All of our servitors are on duty.

Early settlement on the Ob River. Late seventeenth-century engraving.

Some are in Mangazeia, others are in Moscow, and still others have gone to Tiumen and Apanchin for provisions. We have no extra servitors to send to such Siberian towns as Tara, Berezovo, Surgut and Tomsk.

We have sent provisions to you with the Tomsk servitors who came here. Any Tomsk cossacks who were killed by the Black Kalmyks and the Kirgiz, or who deserted, are to be replaced with reliable new cossacks, not with drifters, so that Tomsk will have a full complement of servitors as stipulated in the ukaz.

Be extremely cautious. Increase your guards and sentries. Keep surveillance over the mobility of the natives. Be vigilant so that the Kalmyks and Kirgiz will not be able to make a surprise attack and harm our farm people and herders. Under no circumstances are you to use peasants as servitors, for this would diminish rather than increase the Sovereign's agricultural production in the future. Take transient volunteers into service, but only those who are worthy, not brigands and drifters.

See: G. F. Müller, *Istoriia Sibiri* (Moscow-Leningrad: 1937), I, 428–430

26

A GRAMOTA FROM TSAR VASILII IVANOVICH TO THE VOEVODAS OF
PELYM, IVAN GODUNOV AND PETR ISLENEV, CONCERNING HIRING
VOLUNTEERS FOR AGRICULTURAL WORK IN THE TABARINSK VOLOST

From the Tsar and Grand Prince Vasilii Ivanovich of all Russia to Siberia, to the town of Pelym, to our voevodas Ivan Mikhailovich Godunov and Petr Danilovich Islenev. On October 8, 1608, you reported to us that in accordance with our ukaz you were to order that between 50 and 100 agricultural workers be brought into the Pelym uezd, to Tabarinsk volost. These were to include fathers, sons, uncles, nephews, brothers and neighboring people who did not have any tax obligations. You were authorized to draw funds from our Treasury to pay them to help with the horses, do field work, and construct outbuildings. You reported that there were no volunteers in the nomadic camps who could be taken to do agricultural work in Pelym, but that you could find them in Perm and Sol Kamskaia; but that unless we issued an ukaz they would not agree to this kind of labor. There was no money in the Treasury to pay them to help construct the outbuildings. Consequently you are requesting that we issue an ukaz concerning this.

When you receive this our gramota, you are to send a reliable *syn boiarskii* with as many streltsy as possible to go from Pelym to Great Perm and Sol Kamskaia. Instruct him that when he reaches Verkhotur'e he is to obtain 150 rubles from the voevodas Stepan Godunov and Ivan Peleshcheev to be used to encourage agricultural workers to enlist in Perm and in Sol Kamskaia. We have sent our ukaz about this money to them. When the syn boiarskii obtains this money and goes to Perm and Sol Kamskaia he is to go to the prikaz people, who are to hire Tabarinsk agricultural workers, but none who have tax obligations, in accordance with our previous ukaz. Between 50 and 100 men are to be hired, fathers, sons, brothers, uncles, nephews and neighbors without tax obligations.

The town crier is to announce this in Perm and in Sol Kamskaia, and in the uezds and in the market places and at small trade fairs, day after day. The crier is to call out, "Anyone who wishes to go as a peasant to Tabarinsk may settle there by our ukaz, cultivate the land as agreed, on any plot of land he chooses!"

Funds for the land and all necessities, as well as financial assistance for buying horses and constructing outbuildings has been authorized from our Treasury. The fields are to be cultivated in the same way as the Tiumen peasants do, on the basis of an agreement, wherever the peasant chooses. Peasants will be granted these privileges for a year or two or more, depending on the area. Only volunteers are to be taken to Tabarinsk to do this agricultural work. The names of such persons are to be registered, as well as an enumeration of how many of them will settle.

Once an agreement with them is reached about privileges and assistance, they are to be given seeds and sets for our fields. They are to sign the agreements and receive money, and then their names and the contracts are to be brought to Pelym. These peasants are to receive one or two rubles per man or per family, either in Perm or in Sol Kamskaia, to enable them to move to Pelym. The money will be sent from Verkhotur'e with the syn boiarskii, and they will receive the rest of their agreed wages in Verkhotur'e.

Our ukaz concerning funds has been sent to Verkhotur'e, and the ukaz concerning peasants has been sent to the *prikashchiks* in Perm and in Sol Kamskaia. When the syn boiarskii from Pelym brings the volunteer agricultural workers to Pelym, you are to set them up in farming in Tabarinsk, and give them the privileges noted in our earlier gramota. Then you are to make a written report indicating how many agricultural workers have been enlisted in Perm and in Sol Kamskaia, setting forth their names, the privileges you are granting them and the number of years, the contractual obligations you have concluded, which person is claiming each portion of land, and how many *desiatinas* [2.7 acres] of land each will cultivate.

Send this written report to us in Moscow, and include a report on other matters pertaining to our affairs. Order a copy to be sent to the Prikaz of the Kazan Dvorets.

See: G. F. Müller, *Istoriia Sibiri* (Moscow-Leningrad: 1937), II, 213–214.

27

1616

A PETITION FROM THE TOMSK SERVITORS, BOGDAN TERSKOI AND HIS MEN, TO BE PAID FOR PAST SERVICE

To the Sovereign Tsar and Grand Prince Mikhail Fedorovich of all Russia, your humble servants petition you, Sovereign, from your distant Sovereign patrimony of Siberia, from the town of Tomsk.

We are mounted streltsy, cossacks, Litva, foot cossacks, gunners and obrok peasants: Bogdan Semen Terskoi, Andrei Ivanov, Vasilii Onanin and Grigorii Iakovlev, writing on behalf of all 234 of our comrades in this place. We, your humble servants, have served you, Sovereign, in your distant Tsarist patrimony in Siberia, in the town of Tomsk, on many assignments, both winter and summer. In summer we use a pair of horses to transport [goods and people] from one station to another. In winter we use skis to go on forays and distant assignments. We are gone for ten to fifteen weeks, and during that time we suffer hunger and every other deprivation. Sovereign, we are dying of hunger and fever on your Tsarist service.

Sire, in the past we, your humble servants, have received rations from your Tsarist provisions that were sent from Russia for our salary. We have received from 5¼ to 6¼ puds of flour per year, and the same amount of groats and oats. But now, Sovereign, the amount of your Sovereign's supplies which reach us is small. We are receiving only 3¼ to 4 puds of flour and the same amount of groats and oats, Sovereign.

Sovereign, we, your humble servants, and our wives and children, have nothing to eat, because your Tsarist rations do not last for the whole year.

On July 8, 1614, many persons betrayed you and attacked the town of Tomsk. These traitors included Kirgiz iasak people and Tatar servitors from the Bagasarsk, Kyzylsk, Chiulymsk, Melesk, Kereksusov and Kuznetsk people. Sire, they ran off our horses and cattle and killed many cossack servitors, and in the fields they trampled the grain that belonged to you, Sovereign, and to the cossacks. Sire, when your Sovereign voevodas, Gavriil Iudich Khripunov and Ivan Borisovich Sekerin, arrived in the town of Tomsk, they sent us, your humble servants, on your Tsarist service to attack these Kuznetsk traitors. Sire, with God's mercy and your Sovereign luck, we defeated the Kuznetsk traitors and brought the rest of the Kuznetsk people under your mighty Tsarist hand to swear allegiance. Now, Sire, these Kuznetsk people serve you, Sovereign, and are loyal and pay iasak. We keep their hostages in town.

After that, Sire, we, your humble servants, were sent on your Tsarist service against the traitorous Chiulymsk and Melesk people, and against the Kereksusov, to bring them under your mighty Tsarist hand. Sire, the Chiulymsk and Melesk and Kereksusov people paid homage to you and took the oath of allegiance and paid iasak to you Sovereign. We also hold their hostages in town.

Then, Sire, on September 30, 1616, your Sovereign's voevodas Gavriil Iudich and Ivan Borisovich, sent us, your humble servants, on your Tsarist service to fight the Kirgiz, Bagasarsk and Kyzylsk people who are disloyal and disobedient to you. Sire, we, your humble servants, with God's mercy and the luck of the Sovereign, brought these Kirgiz, Bagasarsk and Kyzylsk people under your mighty Tsarist hand to take the oath of allegiance. Now, Sovereign, these Kirgiz and Bagasarsk and Kyzylsk people serve you, Sovereign, and are loyal and pay iasak. We took their wives and children into custody and are holding them as hostages in town.

Sovereign, we have also cleared the track to Altyn-tsar and to other lands.

Sovereign, when we, your humble servants, entered your Tsarist service, Sovereign, our pay was agreed on at 20 or 30 rubles per man per year.

Sovereign, when we were out on a campaign we endured a great disgrace in regard to our horses. We were starving, and suffering greatly from the cold, and Sovereign, we ate our horses because we were starving to death.

Sovereign, we, your humble servants, have accumulated great debts in your Tsarist service, and we have no money. Sire, our debts are ruining us. Sire, we cannot free ourselves from debt. Sire, we, your humble servants, are not receiving your Tsarist pay in cash and in provisions in full from the town of Tomsk.

Sire, in the town of Tomsk we, your humble Sovereign servants, have built a new ostrog which is 670½ *sazhens* long. We have also built two new gristmills near the settlement.

Sire, we, your humble servants, were previously given your Tsarist pay in cash in Moscow to buy clothing, as we requested. But now, Sire, we, your humble servants, and our wives and children, are barefoot and naked. Sire, there is nowhere to buy anything. Merchants do not come to this very distant place, and, Sire, the Ob Ostiaks will not let merchants from Surgut and Narym come to the town of Tomsk; they rob and kill them en route. Sire, if we wanted to buy an *arshin* of white cloth in Tomsk for a half-*poltina*, or an arshin of linen for two *grivnas*, we could not do so.

Sire, in summer your Sovereign's voevodas sent us, your humble servants, to serve as convoy guards to transit outposts in groups of 30 or 40 men. Sire, we have to spend ten to fifteen weeks as transport guards and at the transit station. Sire, foot cossacks are sent over the ice to Tobolsk in groups of 40 or 50 men to bring your payroll and provisions. Sire, in Tobolsk we pay from four to five rubles for your Sovereign supplies; and, Sovereign, the journey to Tobolsk takes us 20 or 30 weeks.

Further, Sovereign, they sent 20 or 30 of us, your humble servants, to the murzas of Chat and to the Tom Tatars to defend them against the Black and the White Kalmyks.

Sovereign, we, your humble servants, cannot continue to perform your Sovereign service both winter and summer. In summer, Sovereign, we serve as convoy guards and travel to transit outposts and we also live in the Tatar settlements to protect them.

Sovereign, from spring to fall we travel to Tobolsk to obtain your Sovereign provisions. In winter, Sovereign, your Sovereign voevodas send us, your humble servants, throughout the land and to settlements to collect your Sovereign iasak.

Sovereign, we, your humble servants, are suffering from starvation and deprivation on your Tsarist service. In all these undertakings, Sovereign, we, your humble servants, incur great losses.

Sovereign, there are only a few servitors in the town of Tomsk, just 234 men in all. Sovereign, when they send us, your humble servants, out from Tomsk on your Tsarist service, only the sentries are left in the town and in the ostrog, Sovereign. Sovereign, there are no newcomers in the town of Tomsk. Sovereign, there are many great hordes near the town of Tomsk: the Black and the White Kalmyks, the Kirgiz, Mats, Bratsk, Saiants, Tubints, Kucheguts, Bagasars, Kyzyls and Kuznetsk. All of these people came near Tomsk, Sovereign, and, Sire, they kill us, your humble servants, all through the land and in the fields.

Sire, we cannot hold your Sovereign's town with our present garrison unless we have reinforcements, because, Sovereign, there are so many hordes encamped on all four sides of the town of Tomsk. Sovereign, if you do not have mercy on us, your humble servants, and increase the number of servitors here, Sovereign, then if some disaster befalls your town, Sovereign, we, your humble servants, should not be held in disfavor, nor should we be imprisoned because of this.

Sire, in the year 1607, 100 agricultural peasants were sent from Moscow to Tomsk to cultivate your Tsarist lands. However, Sovereign, some of those peasants were killed by the treacherous Kirgiz, and others died of other causes, so now there is no one to do the work of farming on your Sovereign lands.

Merciful Tsar, Sovereign and Grand Prince Mikhail Fedorovich of all Russia, have mercy on us, your humble servants. Give us additional money and provisions to pay us for our service, and for the blood we have spilled. Consider our desperate need and poverty, Sovereign, and decree, Sovereign, that in Tomsk we be given additional money and provisions from the Tomsk fur revenues and from the Tomsk supplies. Also decree, Sire, that additional servitors and permanent peasant settlers be sent into your distant Tsarist patrimony in Siberia, to the town of Tomsk, so that we, your humble servants, Sovereign, will not perish, but may continue to serve you in the future.

Tsar, Sovereign, be merciful. Grant our request.

See: G. F. Müller, *Istoriia Sibiri* (Moscow-Leningrad: 1937), I, 447–449.

28

MARCH 20, 1616

A GRAMOTA FROM TSAR MIKHAIL FEDOROVICH TO THE VOEVODA OF
MANGAZEIA, IVAN BIRKIN, CONCERNING A RECONNAISSANCE AND
CENSUS OF THE ENISEI RIVER REGION, AND PROHIBITING EUROPEANS
FROM TRAVELING THERE TO TRADE

From the Tsar and Grand Prince Mikhail Fedorovich of all Russia to Siberia, to the town of Mangazeia, to our voevoda Ivan Ivanovich Birkin and to Voin Afanasevich Novokreshchenov.

On March 17, 1616, our boiar and voevoda Prince Ivan Semenovich Kurakin and Prince Grigorii Gagarin and the diak Ivan Bulygin reported to us from Tobolsk that a Dvina merchant named Kondratii Kurkin had told them that he and his men had been in Mangazeia in the year 1610. When they left Mangazeia they went to the Enisei region, to Nikolaev on the Turukhan River. Kondratii took counsel with the Dvina traders, Osip Shipunov and his men, then built *koches* and went to fish on the Pesida River. They spent four weeks going down the Enisei to its mouth, which they reached on the eve of Sv. Petr's day. The mouth of the Enisei was choked with ice from the sea, and the ice was at least 30 sazhens deep. The Enisei empties into the Arctic Ocean. European *nemtsy* [foreigners from western Europe] sail on this ocean to go from their homelands to Arkhangelsk.

They [Kurkin and his men] remained at the mouth of the Enisei for five weeks because there was so much ice it was impossible to move out from the river into the bay of the ocean. At last the wind blew from the south and carried the ice from the mouth of the river out into the ocean. At such times it is possible for larger ships to sail from the sea into the Enisei River.

There are both pine and deciduous forests along the shores of the river, and there are areas of arable land. The river has all the kinds of fish one finds in the Volga. Many of our iasak people and *promyshlenniks* live along the river. A foreigner named Sava Frianchuzhenin told them that seven years before some Dutchmen had come by sea to Mangazeia and tried to enter the Enisei. They returned in summer and reported the summer had been so cold they could not get through the ice into the Enisei. However they continued to wait, and when the wind changed to the south they were at last able to enter the Enisei.

Kondratii Kurochkin and a Tobolsk strelets named Kondratii Korel had told them about the Enisei route, and had said that every year many merchants and promyshlenniks go from Arkhangelsk to Mangazeia with all kinds of European goods and provisions, and that it takes two weeks to reach Karskaia Bay, going by sea from the town. It takes five days to go from Karskaia Bay to the Mutnaia River portage. The portage, where one can carry a koch, is one and a half versts long. From the portage it takes four days to go down the Zelenaia River by koch. One then takes the Zelenaia to the Taz River, then goes along the Taz to Mangazeia. The whole trip from the Mutnaia River to Mangazeia takes two weeks.

Stepan Zabelin told the boiar Prince Ivan Semenovich that he had heard from promyshlenniks in Mangazeia that Europeans were hiring guides in Arkhangelsk to take them to Mangazeia, but that the guides did not dare take them there without an ukaz from us.

On the basis of these reports a Tobolsk strelets named Grigorii Bogdanov was sent to Mangazeia and ordered to go on skis to Surgut, then from Surgut on to Mangazeia. [Kurakin and Gagarin] wrote to you, Voin, that, God willing, when the ice breaks up and the water is flowing again, you are to send as many government servitors and promyshlenniks as you can spare to the mouth of the Enisei. Order them to explore the mouth of the Enisei to determine whether it is closed by ice. If it is, instruct them to wait to see whether a south wind will clear away the ice. They are also to make close inquiries of the promyshlenniks, traders and other persons who often go to the Enisei, to determine whether the wind clears the mouth of the Enisei of ice every year, and if so, when. They are also to determine the best time to reach the Enisei from the ocean, either in sailing vessels or in other kinds of boats.

Merchants and promyshlenniks are to be given strict orders not to reveal the route to Mangazeia to foreigners, and not to guide them there. If foreigners come to the Enisei or to Mangazeia to trade, they are not to be allowed to carry on trade. If it is possible to bring them into the town in some way, you are to order that they be detained in Mangazeia until we have issued an ukaz.

When you receive this our gramota, you are immediately to send as many of our military servitors and promyshlenniks as possible to the mouth of the Enisei. Order them to survey the mouth of the Enisei to determine whether there is some place near the mouth which is suitable for building an ostrog. There should be arable land and meadows and forest nearby for the convenience of settlers. They are also to find out what people inhabit the area, and how near the mouth of the Enisei they live. Instruct them to ascertain precisely which of our Siberian towns are near the mouth of the Enisei, how many versts away those towns are, how long it takes to reach them, traveling by water or overland. If by water, find out what boats are best suited, whether large boats or koches. Where do they think an ostrog should be built? How much arable land is available for the ostrog? How much forest and meadowland is there? How many persons could live in such an ostrog?

Order them to take a census of all the natives who live the following distances in versts from the proposed site: 2, 3, 5, 6, 10, 15, 20, 30, 40, 50, 100, and farther. Note their names and patronymics, their occupations, the town to which they pay iasak, what kind of iasak they pay, or whether they do not pay any iasak. Order them to write down all these details in their books. They are also to inquire of these people whether the Europeans who have previously come to the Enisei by sea to trade have come in sailing vessels or in koches. What manner of trade goods did they bring? How many came? If anyone has information regarding these matters, write down all the details and send the report with the census books to the Prikaz of the Kazan Dvorets to our *dumnyi diaks* Petr Tretiakov and Petr Vikulin and their associates.

You are to issue strict orders to the promyshlenniks and to the iasak Tatars that under no circumstances are they to let any Europeans through to the Enisei and to Mangazeia. They are not to trade with them, nor reveal the route to them. And if any person does trade with Europeans or reveals the route, that person will be in serious disfavor with us and will be liable to imprisonment.

See: G. F. Müller, *Istoriia Sibiri* (Moscow-Leningrad: 1937), II, 232–234.

29

A DECISION BY THE BOIAR DUMA ON THE QUESTION OF RELATIONS WITH CHINA, MONGOLIA AND THE BUKHARA KHANATE.

On December 31 [1616] the boiars heard testimony and reports and decreed that an envoy not be sent to the Altyntsar and to the Chinese Empire now, but that in the future, reconnaissance should provide detailed intelligence for this plan.

In regard to town headquarters, they decreed that after an area examination a town is to be built on the Ishim River.

Concerning the Tiumen voevodas, they decreed that the voevodas of Tiumen have insulted the Kalmyk envoys and have abused and robbed them. An ukaz is to be drawn in the Prikaz of the Kazan Dvorets regarding this.

In regard to the Kalmyk people, envoys are to be sent to them from Tobolsk in the future in order to bring them under Tsarist control. Any envoys or emissaries the Kalmyks may send to the Sovereign Tsar are to be sent on directly from Tobolsk to the Sovereign in Moscow without being detained.

Concerning the gifts, about which the boiar and the diak wrote to the Sovereign: the Kalmyks sent two horses as a gift to the Sovereign, and these were subsequently sold. But the envoys who were sent from the Kalmyks stated when they were questioned in Moscow that they had sent three horses to the Sovereign. The report states that a misdeed has been committed in this matter in selling the gifts. The persons to whom the horses were sold are to be located immediately. The horses are to be retrieved and the gift is to be sent to the Sovereign in Moscow. In the future no gift which is sent to the Sovereign from any land whatsoever is to be sold, but is to be sent intact to the Sovereign.

Concerning relations with the Tsar of Bukhara, they decreed that no letters or gifts be sent from Tobolsk. The title of the Tsar of Bukhara as he himself signs his letters, and his title as he is addressed in correspondence, are to be obtained and sent to Moscow.

Reference: TsGADA, f. Kalmytskie dela, 1616 g., op. 2, d. No. 1, ll. 83–84.

See: *Russko-kitaiskie otnosheniia v XVII veke: Dokumenty i materialy (1608–1691)* (Moscow: 1969), I, 54.

Berezovo, a Russian outpost in the land of the Ostiaks. Early eighteenth-century engraving.

30

DECEMBER 2, 1618

A REPORT FROM THE VOEVODA OF TOBOLSK, PRINCE IVAN KURAKIN,
TO THE VOEVODAS OF PELYM, IVAN VELIAMINOV AND GRIGORII OR-
LOV, CONCERNING A REBELLION AMONG THE SURGUT OSTIAKS

Ivan Kurakin reports to Gospoda Ivan Iakovlevich [Veliaminov] and Grigorii Nikitich [Orlov]. You wrote to Tobolsk that a iasak-paying murza named Artiuk Agaev sent a Vogul named Kulakh to you from Konda. Kulakh had gone to the Berezovo uezd, and on the Irtysh River he met a Berezovo cossack who sent him to Pelym to inform officials that the Surgut iasak Ostiaks, the Kazyms, the Narym prince Dona and all his people have rebelled. On the Ob River above Surgut they killed a voevoda who was en route to Tomsk, and they also killed a number of servitors. At the same time a Vogul from Malaia Konda named Lylei Koromod was in Pelym and reported the same news to you. He said that some 60 Russians have been killed on the Ob River. He also reported that there are now about 1,900 rebels assembled and ready to attack Surgut. They know what has happened on the Ob River. We are writing to ask whether this news is also known in Tobolsk.

Gospoda, in Tobolsk they know about the uprising of Surgut Ostiaks which took place this fall when a few of the Surgut Ostiaks of the Bardakov tribe rebelled and killed some Russians. However, Fedor Boborykin traveled through Tomsk and encountered no trouble. The Ostiaks rebelled because the voevoda mistreated them and subjected them to violent treatment, and also because Surgut servitors were sent to attack them and put down this rebellion. The servitors did not attack them, however, but instead they seized their wives and children from the iurt villages and took them 20 or 30 versts away to Surgut. This is the reason for the rebellion. Actually only a few of the people above Surgut on the Ob have rebelled. The majority of the inhabitants of the volosts on the lower reaches of the river serve the Sovereign, and are loyal to him now as they have been previously. When they come to Tobolsk they report that all of them have been insulted and treated violently by the voevodas, but that they do not plan to join in the rebellion. They promise to bring the rebellious Ostiaks back under the mighty Tsarist hand, through battle if necessary.

Siberian animals. Early eighteenth-century engraving.

Gospoda, we believe that the Ostiaks who rebelled will soon petition the Sovereign. We will send you any news we may obtain in the future. However, gospoda, while these events are fresh in memory, you must be extremely careful while you are living in Pelym. Post a strong guard in the town and in the ostrog, treat the Voguls with courtesy and kindness, and be very cautious. Use every possible means to ascertain whether there is unrest among them, and do not resort to cruelty.

See: G. F. Müller, *Istoriia Sibiri* (Moscow-Leningrad: 1937), II, 247–248.

31

BETWEEN SEPTEMBER 23 AND NOVEMBER 19, 1619

IVAN PETLIN'S REPORT ON HIS EMBASSY TO THE CHINESE EMPIRE

In August of the year 1619 the Sovereign Tsar and Grand Prince Mikhail Fedorovich of all Russia ordered Ivan Petlin, a cossack from the Siberian town of Tomsk, to make a reconnaissance into the Chinese Empire, along the great Ob River, and into other realms. By the God-given grace of the Sovereign Tsar and Grand Prince Mikhail Fedorovich, Autocrat of all Russia, this Siberian cossack Ivan Petlin had the good fortune to make his way into the Chinese Empire, to go along the great Ob River, and into other realms. He visited both settled and nomadic uluses and brought back to Moscow to the Sovereign Tsar and Grand Prince Mikhail Fedorovich of all Russia a map and a report about the Chinese region. His report follows.

From the town of Tomsk it takes twelve days to journey to the Kirgiz River, six days from the Kirgiz to the Abakan, nine days from the Abakan to the Kimchin, and from the Kimchin it takes three days to reach a large lake [Ubsa-nor] where Ivan Petrov reported there are semiprecious stones. To encircle the lake on horseback takes twelve days. Four rivers empty into this lake; a river from the east, one from the south, one from the west, and one from the north. All four of these rivers empty directly into the lake, but the level of the water in the lake neither rises nor falls. Another river, the Nakes [Tes-Kem], empties into the lake from the northeast. It takes fifteen days to go on foot from the lake to the source of that river, where we found the Altyn-tsar's encampment. The route lies wholly through the mountains [Tannu-ula].

It is a five day journey from Altyn-tsar's camp to the next ulus, Algutabus, which is ruled by Prince Tormoshin. From Tormoshin's ulus it takes five days to go to the ulus of Chekurkush, which is governed by Prince Karamula. It takes five days to go from Karamula's ulus to the next, Soldus, which is governed by Tsar Chasaktyi. From there it takes five days to reach the next ulus, Bisut, where Prince Chichen rules. From Chichen's ulus it is a five day journey to reach the next, Ilchigin, ruled by Prince Tazchin-Cherekhtu. From Cherekhtu's ulus it is five days to the next, ruled by Prince Chekur. From Chekur's ulus one must travel without water for four days to reach the next, Giriuk, ruled by Prince

Chichin-noian. From Chichin's ulus it takes four days to reach the next, Tulatumet, where the ruler is Prince Taikudatun. From Taikudatun's ulus the travel time is three days to Iurguchil, governed by Tsar Bushuktui. And from Tsar Bushuktui it takes two more days to reach Yellow Mongolia [Mugal], where the ulus is called Mulgochin and is ruled by Princess Malchikatun and her son Anchulatu.

Two days before one reaches Mongolia it is necessary to travel through a mountain gorge which is so precipitous the traveler recoils in horror! And from that gorge one comes out into the land of the Mongols. At the exit there are two Mongol towns built of stone.* Both are called Baishin. One is governed by the voevoda Prince Tala-tamshcha; the voevoda in the other town is Prince Onba-taisha.

A third town in Mongolia, also built of stone, is called Laba. It is ruled by Princess Malchikatun, who has authority over all the towns in Mongolia. She issues a permit with her seal, to be used as a travel pass, to persons who travel to her land and continue on to China. When you come to the frontier and show the guards this permit with her seal, they will allow you to cross the frontier into China; but no one without such a permit with her seal will be allowed to cross into China.

The land of the Mongols is vast both in length and in breadth. It extends from Bukhara to the sea. The towns in Mongolia are laid out in a rectangular form. Each corner has a great tower with a gun emplacement. The foundation of the walls of these towns is made of grey stone, and the upper portion is constructed of brick. The gates of the towns resemble those of Russian towns. Each gate has a tower and a bell which weighs about 20 puds [720 pounds]. The towers are embellished with ornamental brickwork. The houses in Mongolia are made of brick and are designed in a rectangle. There are high walls around the houses, and inside are low brick sleeping platforms with coverlets beautifully embroidered in various colors. These are so pleasant one does not wish to arise from bed. In Mongolia there are two temples made of Laba brick. In some places the temples have steeples. The doors

---

*In Moscow the basic building material, except for churches, was wood. Thus travelers to foreign lands where stone, masonry or brick construction was common were impressed by this novelty. Petlin constantly refers to *kamen*, stone or masonry construction.—Eds.

of these temples face east and south. There are no crosses on these temples, but there are animals carved of stone atop them. I do not know what the variety of animal is. When one is permitted to enter the temple, there are marvelous wonders inside. Facing the door there are three statues of women which stand about three and a half sazhens [24'6"] high, and are covered with gold leaf from head to toe. They are seated on stone animals one sazhen high. The doors are decorated with all manner of paintings done in various colors.

In their hands the statues hold cups filled with grain, and in front of them are tallow lamps. There are eight statues of male figures on the right side of the temple, and eight of maidens on the left. They are all gilded from head to toe, and their hands are stretched out as if they were worshipping, in the way Mongols worship the idols. Beside these there stand two nude statues which are so lifelike it is difficult to tell whether they are flesh and blood or clay.

In front of these there are slender tapers as thin as a reed, which smoulder without flame. Inside the temples they blow into two great horns that are one and a half sazhens long. When the horns are sounded, the people beat drums and fall to their knees and clap their hands and sway back and forth. Then they prostrate themselves and remain in this position for half an hour. At the moment the horns are sounded one enters the temple, and one is overawed by the indescribable wonders inside. The temples are embellished with brick ornamentation.

All varieties of grain grow in Mongolia: millet, wheat, rye, spring wheat, barley and oats; many other grains also grow and are plentiful, some that are quite unknown to us. They have fine white bread. The gardens in Mongolia yield many kinds of fresh produce such as apples, muskmelons, watermelons, pumpkins, cherries, lemons, cucumbers, onions, garlic and other vegetables.

Mongolian men are dirty, but the women are quite clean. They wear their own styles of clothing made of velvet and silk. Atop their kaftans both men and women wear heavy necklaces over their shoulders. In Mongolia they ferment a beverage from grain without adding hops. They do not have precious stones, pearls or gold, but they do have a good deal of silver which comes from China.

They wear boots of their own design. They do not have good horses, but they do have many mules and donkeys. They cultivate land with plows and *sokhas* [wooden plows], as do the Tatars of Tobolsk. Their harrows are long and narrow.

There are men called *kotukhtas* [living Buddha] who correspond to our Patriarch. There are only two kotukhtas in Mongolia. One is 20 years old and the other is 30. They have neither mustaches or beards. Seats have been built for them in the temples. When they enter the temple, they sit in their places, and according to custom even the rulers bow to these kotukhtas. But Ivan Petrov lied when he said that one kotukhta died and lay in the ground for five years and then came back to life. If a man dies, how can he come back to life?

In their language monks are called *labas*. These persons are tonsured at the age of ten and have no contact with any woman except for their mothers. They either shave off or pluck out the hairs of their beards and mustaches. They go about without breeches, and eat meat every day. Their robes are made of silk of various colors, and are similar to those worn by our monks. They wear yellow cowls. They say that our faith is similar to theirs, but that our monks wear black, whereas theirs wear white. They do not know how our faiths became separated.

There are three lands beyond the land of the Mongols in the direction of Bukhara. The first is Ortursk, and the Tsar is called Inakan. The town is said to be built of stone, and the realm is reputed to be rich. The second land is Tangut, and the ruler is Sulanchin. They say that this town is also built of stone and that the realm abounds in all things. The third is called Zheleznoe [iron]. The town is Shar and the ruler is Temir. This realm is purported to be rich and is not far from Bukhara. From this realm the Zheleznoe Tsar exports diamonds to China. All three realms are in the south.

The Yellow Mongols live on the other side of the Black Mongols, and inhabit the land all the way to the sea. There are both nomadic and settled people.

From the land of the Mongols it takes two days traveling by horse to go from the town of [Princess] Malchikatun to the Chinese wall. The frontier wall extends in a southerly direction toward Bukhara. The travel to the Obdor Tsar takes two months on foot. The town of the Obdor Tsar is built of wood, but the realm is said to be large and rich.

To reach the other end of this realm, lying east toward the sea, takes four months on foot. The wall that surrounds it is built of brick, and on that frontier wall we counted 100 towers on both sides. They say that in the direction toward the sea, and toward Bukhara as well, there are multitudes of towers, and each is one bowshot apart from the next. We asked the Chinese people why they had built this wall to extend all the way from the sea to Bukhara, and why there are so many towers on the wall. The Chinese told us that this wall had been built from the sea to Bukhara because there are two lands, one Mongolian and the other Chinese; this wall is the frontier between the two lands. The towers are spaced close together so that when troops approach the frontier the guards stationed in the towers can kindle fires to alert people to fall into their positions along the wall and in the towers. The Black Mongols live on this side of the wall. Beyond the frontier, the lands and the towns are Chinese.

Five gates below a single tower offer passage through this frontier wall into the Chinese town of Shirokalga [Shira-hoton?]. Within the tower there is a diak of the Chinese Emperor Taibun, who is authorized to examine the travel documents and seals from Princess Malchikatun. The gates that afford passage through the wall are low and narrow, so that anyone on horseback has to lean down in order to ride through. Except for these gates, there is no other entry through the frontier wall. People from all realms pass through these gates into the town of Shirokalga.

Beyond the frontier on the other side of the wall is the stone-built Chinese town, Shirokalga. The voevoda is Prince Shubin [Show-bei, commandant of the fortress], who was sent there by Emperor Taibun for temporary duty. The town is high and fine and ingeniously built. The towers are similar to those in Moscow. They are high and have cannon in embrasures, and there are gates. The cannon are short-barreled, and small arms are plentiful. Guards are posted at the gates, in the towers, and along the walls. As soon as the sun sinks down over the forest, the guards fire three times from their muskets, and the town is locked up and is not unlocked until six o'clock the next morning.

Within the town there are many rows of shops with all kinds of goods. In the market places there are stone shops painted various colors and decorated with dried grasses. There are all manner of goods in these shops; in addition to woolen fabrics there are velvets and silks embroidered with gold, and many silks in all colors. But there are no precious stones. They do have all kinds of garden produce such as various kinds of sugar, cloves, cinnamon, anise, apples, muskmelons, watermelons, cucumbers, onions, garlic, radishes, carrots, cabbage, poppyseed, turnips, nutmeg, violets, almonds, ginger, rhubarb, and many other vegetables about which we know nothing at all, not even their names. They have eating places and taverns. The taverns serve all kinds of things to drink, and there are many drunkards and prostitutes. There are stone prisons along the streets. A person is hanged for theft; for brigandry the punishment is impalement and decapitation; for forgery, the hands are cut off.

From Shirokalga to the Chinese town of Shiro [Siuan-houa-fou] the travel time is one day. This town is built of stone and has tall buildings. They say it takes a full day to encircle it. It has twelve towers, and there are all kinds of weapons on the towers and in the gates. Sentries are posted as they are in the previous town. There are five wide tall gates. The portcullis for each is made of iron, reinforced with iron studs. There are cannon at the gates, and many stone cannon balls. It takes half a day to walk from one gate across the town to another gate. The voevoda in this town is Prince San-chin, who was appointed by the Emperor Taibun. There is more commerce here than in the previous town. Both fresh produce and staples are available. In the morning one must make one's way through great hordes of people.

Quarters for foreigners are located outside the town, and are also built of stone. The town well is made of grey stone, and the roof over the well is sheathed with copper in an attractive manner. This town is more handsome and better built than the previous one, and is tastefully adorned with all manner of statuary. Sentries with pikes and halberds stand before the government building. The tocsin bells there look like Russian barrels. Wherever the voevoda Sanchak [San-Chin] goes, a yellow taffeta sunshade is held over his head.

It takes three days to travel from this town, Shiro, to the Chinese town of Iar. That town is built of stone, is large, and has high buildings. It is said to take a day and a half to encircle it. The town has many towers and four gates. The town gates are tall and wide and the portcullis is of iron. Guards are stationed in the towers and at the gates, and there are cannon, small arms and many different kinds of weapons. The market places in this town are larger than in the previous one, and have all kinds of commodities as well as fresh produce and staples. There are no empty spaces in the city. The houses and shops are all built of stone, and there

87

are numerous streets in the marketplaces. One voevoda in this town is Prince Bimbli [Bim-lei], and the other is Prince Fuchak [Fuchan]. Post stations are established along the road, as in Russia. When one comes into the market place, it smells like manna!

In three days one can travel from this town, Iar, to Taima. The latter is built of stone, is large, and has tall buildings. They say it takes two days to walk around it. There are five gates to the city; these gates are wide, high, and have an iron portcullis. The houses and shops are all constructed of stone. These shops have more goods and fresh produce than shops in the previous towns. Everything here is in great abundance. There are plenty of taverns which serve wine, mead and foreign beverages. Cannon and all kinds of weapons are at the gates and in the towers; guards are stationed here in the same manner as in the previous towns. The voevodas in this town are Prince Toivan [Tavan], Prince Teuda [Yunda] and Prince Zunia. Wherever these voevodas go, they are preceded by twenty whipbearers who run on ahead, and yellow taffeta sunshades are carried over their heads.

This town has a larger population than the others, and there are all manner of commodities and fruits and plenty of rice.

One can travel in two days from the town of Taima to White City [Sin-Pao-ngan]. This city is built of stone which is as white as snow, and hence it is called White City. It is large, and the buildings are high, and they say it takes three days to walk around it. The city has three wide high gates, all located under one tower. The portcullis is reinforced by iron bolts. There are large cannon in the towers and at the gates, and cannonballs which weigh two puds each, and much other weaponry. Guards are stationed in a manner similar to other towns.

Shops in this town run from one gate to the next. Living quarters built of stone are above the shops. Running between the shops are streets paved with grey stone. All the shops and houses are built of stone. In front of each shop are wooden shutters decorated with many colors of paint. Paintings done on heavy paper hang on the walls. These paintings are mounted on velvet or silk. Inside the temples are images and small idols made of clay which have been gilded from head to toe with gold leaf, the way it was done in the land of the Mongols. The effect is quite awe-inspiring!

Everyone is permitted to go inside the temples to look at them. In White City we saw how the ceremony inside the temple is conducted. Three persons proceed abreast; two persons strike a wooden gong with wooden sticks, and the third person carries the idols on his back. These idols are large in both height and width. He also strikes the gong. The idols do not have any inscription on them, but they are carefully painted.

We also saw parrots and peacocks in this city, and falcons being carried by their falconers, and dwarfs. This city has more food, all kinds of art work, more fresh produce and other provisions than previous towns. The voevodas here are Prince Toevan and Prince Sulan.

Whenever these voevodas go to the temple, or go out for a stroll for pleasure, they are preceded by 20 pike bearers and halberdiers, and some 30 whip bearers who shout, "Ok, ok!" In Russian this would be, "Run, run!" Large yellow damask sunshades are carried over the heads of the voevodas. There are four large taverns in the city.

The travel time from White City to Peking, where Emperor Taibun lives, is two days, on foot. This city is large and has high stone buildings which are as white as snow. The city is laid out in a rectangle. It takes about four days to walk around it. There are towers at each corner and also in the middle of the walls. These towers are massive, tall, white as snow, and are decorated in various colors. Large cannon are set in the towers and in embrasures in the wall and at the gates, and there are about 20 guards at each gate.

Inside Peking, within the white city, stands the Forbidden City where Emperor Taibun lives. It is said that there is a stone-paved road from the wall of Peking, from the white city, leading to the Forbidden City. There are shops lining both sides of this road all the way. The shops are built of stone and have all kinds of goods for sale.

The streets are paved with grey stone. Living quarters, also built of stone, are above the shops. The shop fronts have wooden shutters decorated in many colors. The Forbidden City, where Emperor Taibun lives, is adorned with many very fine paintings. The Emperor's living quarters are located inside the Forbidden City, and the roof of his palace has been gilded.

We did not have an audience with Emperor Taibun, nor did we even see him, because we had not brought any gifts to him. The clerk in the embassy told me, "It is our custom not to allow anyone to appear before Emperor Taibun unless he is bearing gifts. If you, as the first emissary of your White Tsar, had brought gifts to our Emperor Taibun, then you would have been permitted to present these gifts to him, and our Emperor would have sent gifts in exchange. Our custom is that your White Tsar should have sent gifts to our Emperor, whereupon our Emperor would have graciously given you an audience and allowed you to go on your return journey, and would have sent his gramota to your Tsar."

The Chinese city is laid out on level ground, and is surrounded by a river called the Iukho, which empties into a bay of the Yellow Sea. They say that it takes seven days to go there on foot from Peking. Large sailing vessels laden with goods do not go to Peking via that river, but small vessels and fishing boats do. Emperor Taibun sends these goods out to all the towns in the Chinese Empire. From the towns and cities of the Chinese Empire, these goods are then sent out to Mongolia, to the Altyn-tsar, to the Black Kalmyks, into many lands, realms and uluses, and to the Zheleznoe Tsar in the town of Shar, below Bukhara. From the frontier these goods are carried from the Ortul realm of the kutukhtas and labas, from the Chinese Empire, from the Yellow Mongols, from the Malchikats, the Chinese and the Manchins. Kutukhtas come with the following goods: velvet, damask, silver, leopard and panther pelts. These goods are then bartered for horses. The horses are brought in to the Chinese Empire, and from there they are shipped abroad, beyond the sea, for foreigners, as we would call them.

Silver is sold in bars. The bars are in denominations of 50, 5, 3, and 2 rubles, as well as in grivna. Their equivalent of a ruble is a *lian*.

The people in the Chinese Empire, both men and women, are clean. They wear clothes cut after their own fashion. The sleeves are wide, similar to our summer wear. As an undergarment they wear a semi-kaftan, in the Russian style.

There are many merchants and military persons in the Chinese Empire. They have firearms, and the Chinese are very skillful in military affairs. They go into battle against the Yellow Mongols who fight with bows and arrows.

They said that their Emperor was not sending our Tsar any gifts because, "Your Tsar has everything he needs, and our Emperor has everything he needs." They said that their Emperor has a very precious jewel which glistens day and night like the sun. In their language it is called a *sara*, and in Russian, a *samotsvet*. There is another stone called an *irdiniat*, to which water will not cling even when the stone is cast into the water.

We asked the ambassadorial secretary about the great River Ob* and he replied, "We have never heard of the great River Ob. We know nothing of it. . . . [paragraph missing] Nor have we heard anything in the Chinese Empire about a pirate ship, nor have we heard that foreign ships have been wrecked at sea. Foreigners come to us from the east and the south by way of the Yellow Sea. I have not heard, nor do I know, what route these foreigners travel."

When we inquired in Kalga, a Buriat Tatar named Kushtuk told us something about the great river Ob. He reported that there is a large river called Karatal. Along the Karatal River there is a nomadic ulus called Kalga, and in the upper reaches of the Karatal River is the camp of Altyn-tsar and his people. The Karatal River empties into the great Ob River, but we do not know the source nor the mouth of this great river. It appears to fall into the Yellow Sea in the northeast. There are two villages built of stone along the Karatal, and in the lower reaches of the river there are Buriat nomadic uluses which are inhabited.

From beyond that great river foreigners with all kinds of goods come to us. They exchange their goods with us and with the Saians for reindeer hides, elkskins, sables and beavers. In return they give us damask, taffeta, velvet and black *zendens*. Then they return beyond that river. That same man also said that he had heard from other Buriats that once a great ship came to the lower part of the river, and that there was something white on the ship, and that the ship ran up on the sand and was wrecked. But we have neither seen nor heard about such a great and fine ship on this river, and we do not know whither this ship was bound, whether to China or to some other land. The distance from our land to China by way of that river is not great.

Reference: ROGPB, F. XVII-15, Sbornik sobraniia Frolova, ll. 364–371
See: N. F. Demidova and V. S. Miasnikov, eds., *Pervye russkie diplomaty v Kitae* (Moscow: 1966), 41–55, second variant.

*Knowledge of the geography of Siberia was incomplete and often inaccurate. Here and in other places in his account Petlin obviously means the Amur River when he refers to the Ob.—Eds.

32

ACCOUNT OF THE AMOUNT OF IASAK COLLECTED BY THE RUSSIANS IN
THE VICINITY OF ENISEISK OSTROG FOR THE YEAR 1620–21, AS RE-
CORDED IN THE "RECEIPT BOOKS FOR IASAK FURS"

On November 16, seven iasak collectors took five sables as pominki for the Sovereign and 50 sables as iasak from prince Tumet in Kuznetsk volost in the Enisei River region. Iasak collectors on the Tumetka River took two sables as pominki for the Sovereign, and 27 as iasak. On May 6 past due assessments were collected from prince Tumet in Kuznetsk volost; these consisted of two sables as pominki for the Sovereign and iasak of 21 sables and 3 beavers in place of 6 sables. In 1621 the iasak people of Kuznetsk volost along the Onkak River gave one sable as pominki for the Sovereign and eleven sables as iasak.

On December 20, 21 iasak collectors took 18 sables as pominki for the Sovereign, and four forties* and 23 sables [183 in all] as iasak from prince Epei of Natsk volost. Epei also gave three sables as pominki for the Sovereign, and 48 as iasak. On April [date missing] the iasak collectors in Natsk volost took past due assessments from prince Epei consisting of three sables as pominki for the Sovereign and 40 sables as iasak, plus four beavers in place of eight sables.

On December 23 collectors took two sables as pominki from prince Iltik and six of his men in Kipansk volost, and 28 sables as iasak. On June 17 the iasak collectors took 15 sables from prince Iltik in Kipansk volost.

On December 30 the collectors took five sables as pominki for the Sovereign from prince Okdon Kymzin and five iasak men on the Kas River, and 35 sables as iasak. An additional 20 sables were collected from prince Okdon and his iasak people. In the same volost they took one sable as pominki for the Sovereign and five sables as iasak from a new man, Olka Oksenov. On May 18, ten beavers were collected as arrears, in place of 20 sables, from prince Okdon Kymzin and his iasak people along the Kas River.

---

*All sables were bundled in groups of 40 for convenience in handling and counting, and unless designated as "immature" or "incomplete," sables were of prime quality.—Eds.

On December 30, ten sables were taken as pominki for the Sovereign and two forties plus eighteen sables as iasak from prince Albepet and seventeen iasak people on the Sym River. The collectors also obtained seven additional sables as pominki for the Sovereign and two forties plus nine sables as iasak from prince Albepet and his iasak people. In the same volost a new iasak man, Kal Nagatebetov, gave one sable as pominki and five as iasak. The new man Onpask Murketov gave one sable for pominki, one sable for iasak, and two black beavers in place of four sables. The new man Nikita Khalianov had one pominki sable taken and five iasak sables. On May 18 prince Albepet and his iasak people on the Sym River had seven sables taken as pominki and 40 as iasak. They also gave 23 beavers in place of 46 sables, and three other beavers in place of three sables.

On January 7 in Pumpokolsk volost collectors took 31 sables as pominki for the Sovereign and seven forties plus four sables as iasak from prince Urnuk and 34 iasak people. They took an additional three pominki sables from prince Urnuk, and 90 iasak sables, and one black beaver as pominki. In the same volost they collected one pominki sable and five iasak sables from a new man, Kam Bobyltsov. From another new man, Pobylchek, they took one sable as pominki and five as iasak. On May 30 in Pumpokolsk volost they collected three sables and one black beaver as arrears for pominki for the Sovereign from prince Urnuk and his people, and iasak of 84 beavers in place of eight sables, plus two beavers in place of two sables.

On May 9 the iasak collectors in the town of Tobolsk brought in the Sovereign's iasak from Tiulkin territory which consisted of 80 sables plus 19 immature sables, 63 sables with tails, 36 prime sables and immature ones without tails, 88 bellies from prime and immature sables, and 11 sables without bellies. The iasak collectors were the cossack Rodion Grigorev, Petr Zhadnaia Braga from Narym ostrog, the strelets Andrei Lisitsin from the town of Verkhotur'e, and Ivan Kazanets, a newly christened [native] from the town of Tiumen. They also brought in the Sovereign's iasak from the new territory of Onpalsk from prince Baiterek, which consisted of 10 sables, 5 sables with bellies and tails, 4 sables with tails but without bellies, and one sable without belly and without tail. They also brought the Sovereign's iasak from Atanzh Chagaev and seven of his men in the upper reaches of Kemsk volost consisting of 20 sables with bellies and tails.

On May 15 the Tungus prince Iulym came to the ostrog and presented 30 sables with bellies and tails for the Sovereign. On May 19 two Tungus men, Irkand and Ilin, came to the ostrog with ten sables with bellies and tails for the Sovereign.

On May 30 Vesel and three of his men from Makutsk volost had two sables taken as pominki and 28 sables as iasak, plus two red beavers in place of two sables. In 1621 Vesel and his men gave an additional sable as pominki and three sables as iasak.

On June 6 prince Irkin came to the ostrog and presented ten sables with bellies and tails for the Sovereign.

On July 23 the cossack Petr Timofeev and his men from the Narym ostrog, who had been sent up the Tunguska River from Eniseisk ostrog, brought in the Sovereign's iasak from the upper reaches of the river from the distant Tungus people, prince Iuchan and his men. The iasak consisted of 73 sables, plus eight immature sables with bellies and tails.

On August 8, the Tiulkin prince Tatysh sent the Sovereign's iasak to Eniseisk ostrog from Vasansk in the new lands. The iasak consisted of three prime sables and seven immature sables with bellies and tails.

See: G. F. Müller, *Istoriia Sibiri* (Moscow-Leningrad: 1937), I, 259–260.

33

APRIL 24, 1620

A GRAMOTA FROM TSAR MIKHAIL FEDOROVICH TO THE ALTYN-KHAN
[ALTYN-TSAR], REGARDING AN EXCHANGE OF EMISSARIES

By the grace of God, from the Great Sovereign Tsar and Grand Prince Mikhail Fedorovich, Autocrat of all Russia, Sovereign and Lord of many realms, to Altyn-tsar, we direct our Tsarist Majesty's gracious word. You have sent our Tsarist Majesty your envoys, Laba Tarkhan and Ketebakhsha, and ten Kirgiz men with them, and you have sent your gramota with them. In your gramota you have written to our Tsarist Majesty that some thirteen years ago our people came to you with our Tsarist Majesty's message and told you that the road from our realm to yours, and from your realm to ours, was to be open. Our envoys who were sent with this communication to you were killed en route by Black Kalmyks so that they never reached you. But after that twelve of our men did reach you, and with these men of ours you sent back your representatives, Kaian and Kichenga and their comrades, to us, the Great Sovereign, with homage and inquiries about our health.

We, the Great Sovereign, as a sign of good will toward you, received your ambassadors graciously and gave our gifts to them, and sent them back to you. With them we sent to you three silver vessels, two muskets, a sword, a bow and two kaftans. Any things you have in your eastern land, Altyn-tsar, which may be useful to us, the Great Sovereign, you may send to us.

We, the Great Sovereign, have your request, Altyn-tsar, that ambassadors and merchants be allowed to travel between us, the Great Sovereign, and your people, and that the road to our realm be kept open so our people can travel to you. This desirable state of affairs between us is impeded by the Karakul [Black] Kalmyk taisha. But since he does not have many followers, you request that we, the Great Sovereign, send our Tsarist order to the voevodas of Tomsk, Tobolsk and Tara, and to all other people, commanding our troops to go into battle with your warriors against the Karakul taisha and against his people, so that the road will be opened. When the road is open, we, the Great Sovereign, and you, will benefit from this.

You also request that ambassadors be allowed to travel freely between our lands, both now and in the future. You report that our men, Ivan and Andrei, came to you, Altyn-tsar, from Siberia and asked you to help them reach China. Out of respect for us, the Great Sovereign, you sent our men on to China, and ordered that Laba Biliktei and Laba Tarkhan and their men guide them to China. They took them to China and brought them back from China in good health to you. You then sent them back to us, the Great Sovereign, and you sent your ambassadors Laba Tarkhan and Ketebakhsha with them to us. They were accompanied by ten Kirgiz men and they carried a gramota.

You sent gifts with them to our Tsarist Majesty consisting of three snow leopard pelts, one Siberian leopard pelt with legs, a lynx, some red silk, yellow silk, and a pair of velvet ceremonial gauntlets. We, the Great Sovereign, have your request that we send you cloth of gold and silver, five lengths of wool in various colors, a suit of mail such as our warriors wear into battle, a helmet, five precious stones of various colors, a sword, a bow, a ewer overlaid with gold, a silver vessel, and a fine spirited saddle horse. You also request that we send a dwarf for you to examine, and master craftsmen who make muskets and powder.

We, the Great Sovereign, will inform you, Altyn-tsar, through an envoy, of anything you may have which we, the Great Sovereign find useful. We will send you an envoy directly from us, not from the Siberian people. We will decree that your ambassadors be released without being detained. Furthermore we, the Great Sovereign, because of our regard for you, Altyn-tsar, will allow your ambassadors Laba Tarkhan and his men to have an audience with us as soon as possible. We will listen graciously to their ambassadorial messages and petitions. And in the future you, Altyn-tsar, and your entire horde, will be in our Tsarist pay, and we will be in a state of friendship with you. We wish to establish relations with you. After we have given your ambassadors, Laba Tarkhan and Ketebakhsha and their men, our Tsarist largesse, we will order that they be sent back to you, Altyn-tsar, without being detained; they will carry this, our Tsarist gramota.

As you have requested, we are sending our Tsarist gifts to you with your ambassadors, Laba Tarkhan and his men. These gifts include cloth of gold, a silver vessel with a cover, five lengths of fine wool, a bow from Iadrinsk [near Kazan], and five precious stones of the sort we have. Accept this, and our ambassador, and be assured of our Tsarist favor in the future. At present we, the Great Sovereign, are not sending you our envoys because of the great distances, and also because at present we are engaged [in battle] with our enemies.

In reference to your request for the saddle horse and a dwarf, we are not sending you the horse because the distance is too great, there is snow on the route, and it would be impossible to deliver a horse to you in such a distant place. We do not at present have a dwarf in our realm. A foreign one was brought here at one time, but he is no longer alive. Such people are not born in our realm.

Concerning the interference which the Karakul Kalmyk taisha is creating between us, the Great Sovereign, and you, Altyn-tsar, about which you have written to us, the Tsarist Majesty, we, the Great Sovereign, have sent our Tsarist order to the voevodas of Tomsk, Tobolsk and Tara, and to all the people there, that our troops are to go into battle with your warriors against the Karakul taisha and his men. Because of our regard for you, Altyn-tsar, we, the Great Sovereign, have sent this Tsarist command to the Siberian voevodas and prikashchiks, instructing them to defend you and your land from the Karakul Kalmyk taisha and from his people. You may expect our Tsarist favor in this regard.

Written in our Sovereign court in the Tsarist city of Moscow on April 24 in the year 1620.*

See: John F. Baddeley, *Russia, Mongolia, China* (New York: 1919), Russian text No. I, ccxxiii–iv. Archival designation: "Mungalskiia dela, 1620, April 24/May 3. . . . Documents in Moscow Foreign Office relating to Mongolia."

*This gramota is written in Tatar. The name of God and the Sovereign's name are lettered in gold. It is signed with the great Tsarist seal in red wax. The diak's countersignature is on the back of the paper. Altyn's name is also lettered in gold throughout.—Eds.

34

A GRAMOTA FROM TSAR MIKHAIL FEDOROVICH TO THE VOEVODA OF TOBOLSK, MATVEI GODUNOV, REGARDING THE INADVISABILITY OF SENDING EMBASSIES TO MONGOLIA AND CHINA

From the Tsar and Grand Prince Mikhail Fedorovich of all Russia, to our boiar and voevoda in Tobolsk, Matvei Mikhailovich Godunov, and to our diak, Ivan Shevyrev.

In January, 1617, we wrote to Tobolsk to the boiar and voevoda, Prince Ivan Semenovich Kurakin, and to the diak, Ivan Bulygin, about establishing contact with the Altyn-tsar and with the Chinese Empire. We stated that we, the Great Sovereign, had agreed with our boiars not to send envoys to the Altyn-tsar and to the Chinese Empire. However [we desire] that all manner of information be collected. How large is the population? How many towns are there? What size are they? Which towns have close relations with other towns? What faith do the people profess? How do they regard our great Empire, compared to other realms, and compared to their own? With which realms are they in a state of war or will be in the future, or are battling at present? What forces do they have? What is their strength? What are their customs? What goods do they have? With which lands do their lands border, in addition to ours and the Kalmyks'?

If it is feasible to send emissaries to the Altyn-tsar and to the Chinese Empire, they should not be sent as ambassadors from us or from you, but rather from the cossacks, or from some other such group, so that their true purpose will be concealed, and they will seem to have come just by chance. They are to go and observe the land, the customs, the towns and inquire about everything as stipulated in our instructions. They are to write down in detail everything they learn about the Altyn-tsar and the Chinese Empire, and send us a detailed report, with a copy to the Posolskii Prikaz. Up to the present time in this year of 1620, the boiar Prince Ivan Semenovich Kurakin and the diak Ivan Bulygin have not reported anything at all to us in the Posolskii Prikaz.

From the Altyn-tsar and the land of the Mongols envoys have come to us, the Great Sovereign. These envoys are Lama [Laba] Tarkhan and his men, and two men as envoys from the land of the

Kirgiz. We have welcomed these men from the Altyn and the envoys from the land of the Kirgiz, and we have allowed them to have an audience with us. Then, having shown them our Tsarist favor, we have allowed them to return to their own lands, and we have sent our Tsarist gifts to the Altyn-tsar with his envoys.

When these envoys come to you in Tobolsk, you are to provide them with food and transport, and allow them to proceed to Tomsk and subsequently back to their own lands without detaining them. You are to order someone to accompany them from Tobolsk to their destinations, just as they were previously accompanied. But in the future you are not to maintain any direct contact with the Altyn-tsar and with the Chinese and Mongol empires without our permission, because these empires are too far distant for their merchants to visit our empire. Furthermore, the Altyn-tsar's hordes are nomadic and warlike, and our empire will receive no benefit from him, only requests for things which we do not presently have nor will have in the future. However, you are to amass all possible information about these empires, in accordance with our previous ukaz, which we sent to our boiar and voevoda, Prince Ivan Semenovich Kurakin, and to our diak Ivan Bulygin. Regarding this we have written the following to Tomsk: in the future you are not to send envoys to the Altyn-tsar and to the Chinese and Mongol empires.

If in the future envoys should come to you in Tobolsk from the Altyn-tsar or from the Chinese and Mongol empires, on their own, you are to house them in the Prikaz office and question them at length. On what business have they come? What request do they bring to us, the Great Sovereign, from their emperors? Do their sovereigns wish to come under our Tsarist mighty rule? What kind of tribute do they intend to pay us? Do they carry letters with them? What oral instructions do they have, and in regard to what matters? You are to question them at length about these and all other matters, and send a written report to us in Moscow by fast courier. You are to house such envoys and couriers in Tobolsk, and post guards over them, and give them food until you have further instructions from us if through questioning you detect some possible advantage and benefit to our empire. But do not send these envoys to us in Moscow without our personal ukaz. If any of the Altyn's and Lama's envoys come to you in Tobolsk in the future, and your questioning does not elicit any benefit or advantage to our empire, and if they have come on their own or to request military assistance, you are to refuse to receive them.

You are to inform us, our Imperial Majesty, about all of this in writing. Do nothing further until you have instructions from us. In the future you will receive our Tsarist instruction about this matter, and you will inform the envoys through your own gramota, using your own courier or anyone who is immediately available. Once you have conveyed this information to them, send them back to their own lands without delay, and without waiting for our order. Do not detain many of them in Tobolsk. Be especially careful that they do not reconnoitre the Siberian lands. Give them just enough food and drink in Tobolsk for their journey so that they will not suffer hunger or thirst. Send a written report on all of this to Moscow, so that we will be fully informed. Send copies to the Posolskii Prikaz, to our dumnyi diak Ivan Gramotin, and to Sava Romanchiukov. We have also written to the voevodas of Tomsk in regard to all of this.

When the envoys of the present Altyn and Lama and the Kirgiz come to you in Tobolsk, you are to send a *poddiak* or syn boiarskii to them, and order this person to make an inspection to determine whether any of them are carrying firearms. If so, they are to be confiscated, so that no persons will take any muskets or other firearms from our empire into their own land. Inform the envoys that these weapons have been confiscated because they were brought into our empire in secret, without being declared in any town.

Reference: TsGADA, f. Mongolskie dela, op. 1, 1619 g., d. No. 1, ll. 65–70.

See: *Russko-kitaiskie otnosheniia v XVII veke: Dokumenty i materialy (1608–1691)* (Moscow: 1969), I, 99–100.

35

JUNE 3, 1620

A GRAMOTA FROM TSAR MIKHAIL FEDOROVICH TO THE VOEVODA OF
TOBOLSK, MATVEI GODUNOV, CONCERNING SALARIES FOR THE LITVA

From the Tsar and Grand Prince Mikhail Fedorovich of all Russia to Siberia, to the town of Tobolsk, to our boiar and voevoda Matvei Mikhailovich Godunov, and to Prince Ivan Fedorovich Volkonskii, and to our diak, Ivan Shevyrev. A Litva from the Siberian town of Tobolsk named Ian Kuch has sent us a petition. He says that in the year 1613 he was sent from Tobolsk with the Cavalry Captain Bartash Stanislavov to explore a salt lake in the upper reaches of the Irtysh River beyond the town of Tara. They explored the salt lake and brought salt to Tobolsk.

In the year 1614 he was sent out from Tobolsk on our service for a year to the town of Tomsk. From Tomsk he was sent against the Bagasarsk and Kirgiz people. He served us and fought the Bagasarsk and Kirgiz people.

In the year 1618 he was sent from Tobolsk with the *striapchii* [scrivener] Aleksei Veleminovich Vorontsov to the steppe against the Tsarevich Ishim and against the Kalmyk taishas. With God's grace and our luck, our servitors defeated the Tsarevich Ishim and the Kalmyk taishas and their ulus people in the steppe. They killed many and took some prisoners. Ian Kuch served us well, fighting against the Kalmyks and killing a man.

In the year 1619 he was sent from Tobolsk to the steppe to the Karakul taisha. He told the taisha to submit to our Tsarist mighty hand, and the Karakul taisha expressed the desire to come under our Tsarist mighty hand, and the Karakul people came with Ian to Tobolsk.

In all, he spent more than 24 weeks with the Karakul taisha, suffering famine and all manner of deprivation. He defiled his soul by eating all kinds of foul matter. He has not received any compensation for all this service on our behalf. Our annual allotment to him has consisted of 9.25 rubles, 6⅛ chetverts of wheat, one of rye, and the same of groats and oats. He petitions us to be recompensed for his services by receiving the belongings of the deceased Tobolsk Litva Semeikin, as well as the money and provisions designated for Semeikin's replacement, Slonskii, who never arrived.

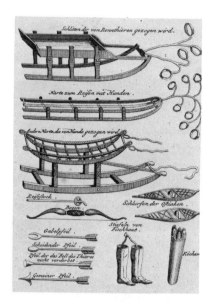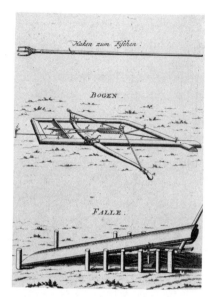

Left: Ostiak equipment for hunting and travel. Early eighteenth-century engraving. Right: Siberian native fishing, hunting and trapping devices. Early eighteenth-century engraving.

So be it, as the Tobolsk Litva Ian Kuch has petitioned. When you receive this our gramota, you are to authorize the Litva Ian Kuch to go to Tobolsk to claim the belongings of Semeikin, and you are also to authorize him to be given the rations set aside for Semeikin's replacement, Slonskii, consisting of 12 rubles, 7⅛ chetverts of wheat, 1⅛ chetverts each of rye, groats and oats. You are to order that this allotment be corrected in the books.

See: G. F. Müller, *Istoriia Sibiri* (Moscow-Leningrad: 1937), II, 252–253.

36

INSTRUCTIONS FROM THE VOEVODA OF TOBOLSK, MATVEI GODUNOV, TO THE TOBOLSK SYN BOIARSKII VASILII TYRKOV, CONCERNING RUMORS OF ABUSES BY THE VOEVODA OF KETSK AGAINST IASAK-PAYING OSTIAK NATIVES

In accordance with the ukaz of the Sovereign Tsar and Grand Prince Mikhail Fedorovich of all Russia, this written instruction dated July 14, 1620, is being sent to the Tobolsk syn boiarskii Vasilii Tyrkov. He is to travel to Ketsk ostrog to make an investigation of the following problem.

On July 6, 1620, the Ketsk uezd iasak-paying Ostiaks of Kirgeev volost, Mancheskum and Airak Sokoticha, petitioned the Sovereign Tsar and Grand Prince Mikhail Fedorovich of all Russia, on behalf of all the iasak people of their region, saying that they have suffered greatly from the violence and oppression inflicted on them by Chebotai Chelishchev. They beg that the Sovereign be merciful and order that a syn boiarskii be sent from Tobolsk to protect them so that they will not die as a result of Chebotai's violence, nor be forced to disperse into all directions. Vasilii Tyrkov, upon arrival at Ketsk ostrog . . . [text missing] is to follow these instructions.

On July 7, 1620, a gramota was sent from the Sovereign Tsar and Grand Prince Mikhail Fedorovich of all Russia, under the signature of the diak Afanasii Istomin, to Tobolsk to the boiar and voevodas Matvei Mikhailovich Godunov and Prince Ivan Fedorovich Volkonskii, and to the diak Ivan Shevyrev. The gramota states that on January 5, 1620, the boiar and voevoda Prince Ivan Semenovich Kurakin and the diak Ivan Bulygin wrote to the Sovereign from Tobolsk, saying that Maksim Trupchaninov had written to them from Enisei. Maksim had been sent from Tobolsk with servitors to guard an outpost on the Enisei. They were to serve as replacements for the former Prikaz people, Petr Albychev and Cherkas Rukin. Maksim had met the Surgut servitors, Vasilii Prokofev and his men, who were in charge of the Ketsk government supply wagons. When Maksim questioned them, the Surgut servitors told him that a newly baptized man, Semen Tumach, had been sent to them from Petr Albychev and from Cherkas Rukin. He had an urgent message that Petr and Cherkas were under siege in Namatsk ostrozhek by Tungus natives. Petr and Cherkas also sent word that Chebotai Chelishchev, deciding not to serve the Sovereign, had turned to lawless and treasonable acts in order to prevent Semen from proceeding to Tobolsk and meeting with Maksim and the people from Ketsk ostrog. Chebotai refused to provide Semen with transport.

In accordance with the Sovereign's ukaz, it is ordered that this be investigated in Ketsk ostrog. When Vasilii reaches Ketsk ostrog, he is to investigate whether Petr Albychev and Cherkas Rukin did write to Chebotai Chelishchev and the Surgut cossack Semen Tumachev that they were under siege in Namatsk ostrozhek by Tungus natives. Did Chebotai Chelishchev, deciding not to serve the Sovereign, refuse to send any servitors to help them in Namatsk ostrozhek? Did he refuse to provide transport for Semen Tumachev? Vasilii is ordered to record the testimony of anyone who speaks in this investigation. He is also to bring with him to Tobolsk the sworn statements of persons he questions. Chebotai Chelischev is to travel together with him to Tobolsk, and when he reaches Tobolsk he is to appear before the boiars and voevodas Matvei Mikhailovich Godunov and Prince Ivan Fedorovich Volkonskii, and the diak Ivan Shevyrev.

The boiars and voevodas Matvei Mikhailovich Godunov and Prince Ivan Fedorovich Volkonskii and the diak Ivan Shevyrev have put the seal of the Siberian Tsardom to this official instruction from the Sovereign Tsar and Grand Prince Mikhail Fedorovich of all Russia.

See: G. F. Müller, *Istoriia Sibiri* (Moscow-Leningrad: 1937), II, 254–255.

37

A GRAMOTA FROM TSAR MIKHAIL FEDOROVICH TO THE VOEVODA OF
VERKHOTUR'E, IVAN PUSHKIN, CONCERNING MONASTERY LANDS

From the Tsar and Grand Prince Mikhail Fedorovich of all Russia to Siberia, to Verkhotur'e, to our voevoda, Ivan Ivanovich Pushkin. Abbot Avram of Sv. Nikolai Monastery in the town of Verkhotur'e in Siberia, and Elder Makarii, a carpenter, and their brethren have sent us a petition. They state that in the year 1621 Archbishop Kiprian of Siberia and Tobolsk came to Siberia and gave them permission to stay at our pilgrim shelter in the monastery. This place is very poor and cannot be sustained without our support. Although some of our agricultural peasants and postal volunteers may be willing to contribute to it, the Verkhotur'e voevodas have not allowed the servitors and agricultural peasants and postal volunteers of those territories to donate anything to the monastery. The place is very poor and they do not have the wherewithal to grow anything. At present they are to receive every fifth sheaf of grain harvested by those who rent fields, with whom they contracted to cultivate the land and provide food for our pilgrim shelter. But it is still very poor, and in the chapel of our pilgrim shelter there are no icons, books or bells, and they have nothing to barter with.

They ask that we issue an ukaz that they be given money and food, and that we make a contribution from the Treasury to construct monastery buildings. We grant the following to Abbot Avram, the carpenter, Elder Makarii, and the brothers of Sv. Nikolai Monastery: servitors, agricultural peasants and postal volunteers who may wish to contribute their agricultural lands, on their own behalf and on behalf of their families, to Sv. Nikolai Monastery in Verkhotur'e will not be forbidden to do so. Rather, we permit them to give those lands to the monastery at will.

When this our gramota reaches you, you are not to prohibit these agricultural peasants and servitors and postal volunteers who wish to give agricultural lands to the Sv. Nikolai Monastery from doing so, either on their own behalf or for their families. You are to permit them to give their lands to the monastery freely, because there is much arable land in Siberia, and the monasteries are poor and have no means with which to build.

However, you are not to grant the request for financial assistance to priests, because they have arable lands and renters will cultivate these lands for them. From the renters you are to collect for us a tax in grain in accordance with our earlier ukaz. The sheave-tax has been imposed on all agricultural workers in accordance with our earlier ukaz except for our servitors. Further, many people in Siberia cultivate land without contributing any part of the harvest. They do not pay quitrent from their fields, and thus provisions for our servitors there have to be sent out from towns in [European] Russia.

In the future you are to collect the tax in grain for us from all persons except from our Siberian servitors. You are to make detailed entries in the register book of all the grain you collect, whether from gunsmiths, town settlers, agricultural peasants, postal volunteers or monastery field renters. Then you are to send the register book to us in Moscow and submit it to the Kazan Dvorets to our boiar Prince Ivan Mikhailovich Vorotynskii and to our diaks Ivan Bolotnikov, Fedor Apraksin and Afanasii Istomin, so that this information will be made known to us.

See: G. F. Müller, *Istoriia Sibiri* (Moscow-Leningrad: 1937), I, 288.

38

NOT BEFORE JANUARY 31, 1623

A REPORT FROM THE VOEVODA OF TOBOLSK, MATVEI GODUNOV, TO
THE VOEVODA OF TURINSK, SEMEN APUKHTIN, CONCERNING LICEN-
TIOUS BEHAVIOR BY THE CLERGY

Matvei Godunov sends this report to Gospodin Semen Dmitrievich [Apukhtin]. Gospodin, on January 31, 1623, in a gramota from the Sovereign Tsar and Grand Prince Mikhail Fedorovich of all Russia, signed by the dumnyi diak Ivan Gramotin and written to us in Tobolsk, it is stated that in the year 1622 Kiprian, Archbishop of Siberia and Tobolsk, wrote to Filaret Nikitich, Holy Sovereign* Patriarch of Moscow and of all Russia. Kiprian reported that while he was traveling to Siberia, he saw en route monasteries in Siberian towns such as Verkhotur'e, Tiumen and Tobolsk where both monks and nuns were living. And the monks and nuns in these monasteries were not living in accordance with their monastic vows, but rather as man and woman, in the same cell. Those who live in such a sinful fashion should be punished in accordance with the rules of the Holy Fathers. People from all walks of life who conceal this lawless behavior so that higher religious authorities will not punish them are supporting this scandalous behavior in all towns.

Many of the servitors such as cossack atamans, *piatidesiatniks*, cossacks, Litva and European converts and peasants also live in this un-Christian manner. They do not wear crosses nor do they observe the fast on Wednesdays and Fridays. They eat every kind of unclean abomination together with heathen Tatars, Ostiaks and Voguls. Russians who are sent out in groups of 20 or 30 as emissaries to the Kalmyks also drink and eat with them, and furthermore they live in illegal liason with Kalmyk, Tatar, Ostiak and Vogul women, and beget children with these heathens. In Siberian towns they live lawlessly with their own blood sisters, with kinfolk, first cousins, mothers-in-law, sisters-in-law and other

---

*This is the only time in Russian history when the spiritual head of the Russian Orthodox Church was officially addressed as "Sovereign" [*Gosudar*]. The reason for this innovation was the fact that Patriarch Filaret was the father of Tsar Mikhail. The practice was discontinued after Filaret's death in 1633.—Eds.

close relatives. Some even live in sinful liason with their own mothers, and in many cases they live with their own daughters who are as young as ten years old. In other cases it may happen that a man begets children by his lawful wife who subsequently dies; he then may marry his daughter and beget children with her and live in a sinful un-Christian alliance.

In all towns both the Black [monastery] and the White [secular] priests willingly or unwillingly give their blessing to these persons and perform illegal marriage ceremonies for them, by order of the voevodas. And if a religious sin is committed by servitors or town officials or priests or monks or nuns or widows or maidens, the voevodas in all of these towns turn a blind eye and do not punish them.

Officials of all ranks disgrace and beat the *desiatilniks* [ecclesiastical court officials] and all manner of evil persons reproach the archbishop himself and spread scandalous gossip about him. Widows and maidens who of their own free will petition against these perpetrators of violence and corruption are seized by force, taken to the men's quarters for lascivious purposes and are held there against their will and without legal process. [These lawless persons] have abducted the wives of many workmen for licentious purposes. Husbands, seeing such violence committed against their wives, abandon them and move far off from town and take up with someone else. Afterward, a week or two later, the man who has abducted the wife brings in some single man and marries off the woman to him. If her former husband comes back to the same town, he will also take a maiden or a married woman, or he will hire a woman for a period of time. Anyone who pays her, exercises his will over her, lives with her and does as he wishes; he can marry her off or sell her or give her without ceremony, as he wills.

In all the towns of Siberia those servitors who have to go to Moscow to convoy the Sovereign's Treasury rent out their wives, whether or not they are legally married, for ten or twenty rubles or more, for the duration of their absence. When a man sets out he takes whatever amount of money he can get and hands over his wife to the buyer, until such time as he reclaims her. The buyer lives with her as his own wife; if the seller does not reclaim her, then the buyer, after the period expires, resells her, either in that town or in another. The voevodas do not punish such immoral behavior in any of the towns. There is great animosity and fighting and commotion over children born to such persons. The archbishop frequently receives petitions concerning such situations, petitions in which accusations are made by husbands against wives, or by wives against husbands; but no one heeds his commands. When the archbishop issues an order on this matter, the guilty party threatens him.

Some Siberian cossacks traveling to Moscow through other towns seduce wives and young girls along the way; then as they travel they have illicit relations with them. They entice them, then hold them by force, and they may bring 50 or more to Tobolsk. When they reach Tobolsk they sell them to the Litva, to foreigners, to Tatars, to the households of the voevodas, and they may even sell them to agricultural peasants to work. When the women realize their fate, some of them run off to the archbishop and submit petitions to him about such servitors and about the violence and seduction. Then the archbishop, because of the violence committed against them, and because of their seduction, and their sale, may order that a particular wife or young girl be set free. But then the servitors conspire with one another and come to the archbishop with a great commotion and announce that they have a gramota from the Sovereign authorizing them to do this. They will also declare that we [the voevoda of Tobolsk] have told the archbishop that we have the gramota from the Sovereign in our office and they are authorized to do this, and that we have been asked to oversee this but that we will not show the archbishop the gramota.

When the archbishop sends monks and priests into towns to build churches so that peasants in those towns will not die without confession and so that young people will be baptized, these towns will not accept these monks and priests, and the voevodas will not issue them any salary or provisions. So then they go back to the archbishop. If we do not send instructions from Tobolsk, they are at a loss and come back to Tobolsk.

The archbishop has learned from various persons in Siberia that priests and laymen come to Moscow and petition the Sovereign to build churches, acquire books, vestments, bells, censors, incense, icons of local saints, the Tsar's Door and other church accoutrements. These priests and laymen manage to acquire these things through deceit, and once they have them, they sell them for drink. Then they say that the matters of church and church construction are lay affairs, and they do not tell the Sovereign anything about it, nor do they submit an inventory of church furnishings; thus they conceal their theft.

When we receive the Sovereign's gramota, we will issue a firm order in Tobolsk and in all the Siberian towns, concerning the fact that cossacks and their wives and other persons of all ranks who have received the tonsure are living in their own homes. Many monks and nuns have discarded their habits altogether and are living in towns with lay persons, as previously, and are conducting themselves in a sinful manner. They are not to behave in this way in the future. They are not to disobey the commandments of the Holy Fathers. They are not to commit such sins; they are not to discard their monks' and nuns' habits; they are not to live with lay persons. Rather, they are to live in monasteries, separately, and not monks and nuns together in sinful fashion.

According to the Sovereign's ukaz, Archbishop Kiprian has been authorized to transfer these monks and nuns from Siberian towns which do not have monasteries into Siberian towns that do have them. In order that old monks and nuns may be fed and clothed, they are to be allowed to live with relatives, but servitors and persons of other ranks are not to have these elderly monks and nuns live in their households, and they are not to commit sins with them. Such persons are to be sent to Siberian towns which have monasteries. Their families are to provide these older monks and nuns with food and clothing, within reason, so that these older monks and nuns will not suffer deprivation in regard to food and clothing, and will not be shamed by having to beg for them.

Archbishop Kiprian has written to the Sovereign that in Siberian towns where monks and nuns live in monasteries, the monks live in the same cells with their women. The archbishop also wrote that he wanted to issue an order based on the rules of the Holy Fathers prohibiting this, but that the men and women who engage in the dissolute conduct are persons of all ranks, and they are causing much evil. In Tobolsk and in all Siberian towns we are to halt the sinful behavior of servitors and persons of all other ranks. We are to issue the proclamation in all towns, repeatedly, that servitors and people from other ranks are not to live together in the same cells with monks and nuns; that all Russians are to wear crosses; that they are not to eat any prohibited foods in company with heathen Tatars, Ostiaks and Voguls; they are not to live with Kalmyk, Tatar, Ostiak and Vogul women; and they are not to live with their own blood sisters, kinfolk, first cousins, mothers-in-law, sisters-in-law, mothers, or any other women who are related to them. They are not to live in sinful fashion nor marry their own children. Neither Black nor White priests are to perform marriages without the approval of the archbishop. Anyone who perpetrates such an evil deed is to be reported. These enemies and violators of the Christian faith are not to be hidden, or God's wrath will fall on all.

Anyone who learns of such religious violation, whether servitor, town official, priest, monk, nun, widow or young girl, is not to involve us in these religious matters, but rather is to report the violation and the persons involved to the archbishop. Any servitors or people from other ranks who do not obey this, who do not report these religious matters to the archbishop, are to be punished by us as their offense merits. If some persons are severely punished in the court of the archbishop, and then brought to us for further admonition, we are to punish those persons according to the recommendation of the archbishop, so that in the future other violators, aware of that punishment, will be deterred from committing crimes prohibited by the commandments of the Holy Fathers.

Any servitors who go into towns and lawlessly seduce women and young girls and carry them off to other Siberian towns are to be punished severely so that servitors and men of other ranks in Moscow and in other towns will not seduce wives, young girls and children, will not do evil to them, will not carry them off to other Siberian towns, will not buy and sell these women and young girls, and will not commit violence against them. If in the future they continue to seduce women, young girls and children, and carry them off to Siberia and buy and sell them, then as punishment for that crime, the Sovereign Tsar and Grand Prince Mikhail Fedorovich of all Russia will punish them severely, including putting them to death.

In all Siberian towns we are to issue a strict prohibition to servitors and to other ranks so that in the future such crimes will not be committed.

When Archbishop Kiprian gives orders for monks and priests to go into Siberian towns to build churches, these monks and priests are to be permitted to give the archbishop's blessing in these churches. We are to order that the religious instructions of the archbishop's desiatilniks be obeyed in all Siberian towns. We are also to order that a census be taken in all the towns of Siberia to determine how many churches there should be in Siberian towns, and in which towns, and how many sextons are needed for each church, to whom monies from the Sovereign are to be given, and in what amount. When the census is completed, the records are to be turned over to Archbishop Kiprian for his information, so that in the future he will know the number of churches, priests, sextons and church outbuildings.

When the archbishop appoints his desiatilniks to Siberian towns, we are to allow them to live in those towns and order that they are to be obeyed in religious matters. In turn, they are not to cause the Sovereign's subjects any unnecessary expense or trouble. And you, Gospodin, are to issue a strict order in Iapanchin that cossacks, their wives, and persons from other ranks who have been tonsured but still continue to live in their own dwellings, as well as monks and nuns who have laid off their habits and live in town with lay persons and cause all manner of evil, are henceforth to desist from this behavior. They are not to violate the commandments of the Holy Father, not engage in sinful acts nor discard their black habits nor live with lay persons. Rather, they are to live apart, in monasteries, and monks and nuns are not to live together. They are not to engage in sinful activity, and servitors and those of other ranks who are related to monks and nuns are not to have them living in their homes, and are not to engage in any sinful activity with them. However, they are to provide these monks and nuns with food and clothing, within reason, depending on what the archbishop orders, so that these monks and nuns will not suffer deprivation of food, clothing or other needs, nor will they be shamed by having to beg for these things.

If monks live in the same cell with their women in the Iapanchin monastery, the archbishop's orders are that they be punished in accordance with the rules of the Holy Fathers. You are to order that the servitors at Iapanchin, and persons of other ranks, are not to support these violators. They are not to bring about any evil, and they are to be restrained from sinful behavior. Further, you are to have a town herald announce in Iapanchin, repeatedly, that servitors and other ranks are forbidden to live in the same cell with monks and nuns, that Russians are to wear crosses at all times; that they are not to eat prohibited foods with heathen

Tatars, Ostiaks and Voguls; and they are not to live with Kalmyk, Tatar, Ostiak and Vogul women, or with their own blood sisters, kinfolk, first cousins, mothers-in-law, sisters-in-law, mothers, sisters or any other women family members. They are not to engage in licentious activity; they are not to marry their own daughters; and neither Black nor White priests may perform marriage ceremonies without permission from the desiatilniks. And you yourself are not to give priests permission to perform marriage ceremonies unless you have authorization.

Anyone who commits an evil crime and is found out is an enemy and a violator of the Christian faith and is not to be succored, lest God's wrath fall upon everyone. If someone informs you that a religious offense has been committed involving a servitor, town official, priest, monk, nun, widow or young girl, do not become involved in these spiritual problems; do not assume this responsibility. Instead, send anyone charged with such a crime to Tobolsk to the archbishop, or to his desiatilnik in Iapanchin. If servitors or others refuse to obey the command to report to the archbishop's desiatilnik, you are to impose whatever punishment their guilt deserves. If some persons are severely punished for religious violations and are then sent to you by the desiatilnik for further punishment, you are to carry this out, in consultation with the archbishop's desiatilnik, so that in the future other potential violators may be dissuaded and prevented from committing sins against the commandments of the Holy Fathers.

In regard to servitors who travel through towns and violate, seduce and abduct women and young girls, you are to issue a strict order that the Iapanchin servitors and others, while they are in Moscow or in other towns, are not to seduce women, young girls and children. They are not to harm them nor carry them off to Siberia; they are not to buy or sell these women and girls, and they are not to become involved in any violence whatsoever in this regard. If in the future they continue to seduce women, girls and children, and carry them off to Siberia, and buy and sell them, then they will be severely punished for this crime, and may even be put to death, by order of the Sovereign Tsar and Grand Prince Mikhail Fedorovich of all Russia. You are to issue this strict order in Iapanchin to servitors and others, forbidding them to commit such criminal acts.

When the archbishop sends monks and priests to you in Iapanchin from Tobolsk to build churches, you are to authorize

Berezovo. In Russian Siberian outposts, churches and monasteries were quickly established. Early eighteenth-century engraving.

them to perform the archbishop's blessing of these churches; also order that the archbishop's desiatilniks be obeyed in all religious matters. In order to ascertain the number of churches in Iapanchina, the number of sextons each church has, and the salary each receives from the government, you are to order that a census be taken, and upon completion of this census, you are to forward this information to the archbishop in Tobolsk for his information, so that in the future he will know the number of churches, the number of priests and sextons, and the number of church buildings.

When the archbishop sends his desiatilnik to Iapanchin, you are to decree that he be obeyed in religious matters, but he is not to subject the Sovereign's people to any violence, nor is he to requisition their property without cause.

See: G. F. Müller, *Istoriia Sibiri* (Moscow-Leningrad: 1937), I, 293–297.

39

OCTOBER 30, 1623

A GRAMOTA FROM TSAR MIKHAIL FEDOROVICH TO THE VOEVODAS
OF TIUMEN, PRINCE MIKHAIL DOLGORUKOV AND IURII REDRIKOV,
PROHIBITING KALMYK AND MONGOL ENVOYS FROM TRAVELING TO
MOSCOW

From the Tsar and Grand Prince Mikhail Fedorovich of all Russia to Tiumen, to our voevodas Prince Mikhail Borisovich Dolgorukov and Iurii Anfinogenovich Redrikov. On October 8, 1623, the voevoda of Ufa, Semen Korobin, wrote to us that on August 1, 1622 an Ufa man named Vasilii Volkov and his interpreter, Fedor Derbysh Aleev, came to him in Ufa from a Kalmyk ulus. They were accompanied by the following envoys of the Kalmyk taisha, Mangit: Egultai Mezinbaev, Karakai Kaderov and Baibol Dabambov. After questioning these Kalmyk envoys [Semen] allowed them to proceed to us in Moscow. We have now written to the voevoda Semen Korobin, directing him to maintain relations with the Kalmyk taishas, depending on local circumstances, because it is impossible not to have dealings with them; but when envoys from Kalmyk taishas or from the Altyn come to him in Ufa, he is to inquire about their journey and the business on which they have come to him, and then he is to send them back and not permit envoys from the Kalmyks or from Altyn-tsar to come to us in Moscow from Ufa or from other Siberian towns.

When you receive this our gramota, if any envoys henceforth come to you in Tiumen from some Kalmyk ulus or from Altyn, you are to order them to stay outside the town, anywhere convenient, either in a tent or in some habitation outside the town, but not inside the town. During that time you are to keep a constant guard over them and be diligent and cautious and permit no negligence. You are to discuss their business with them, and make your inquiries courteously, without any suggestions of threats.

If the Kalmyk or Altyn envoys request permission to come to us in Moscow, you are to tell them that you have no authorization from us to allow them to proceed to Moscow, but that you will write to our Tsarist Majesty about them. Then they are to return home, because they would have to wait too long in Tiumen for our ukaz, since the track to our realm in Moscow is long and the passage is very difficult. You must not permit Kalmyk and Altyn

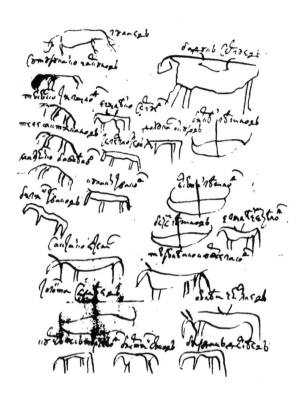

Seventeenth-century Iakut tribal marks used during iasak collection. Russian inscriptions identify names of each tribal leader. From Shvetsova, *Materialy po istorii Iakutii.*

envoys to go to Moscow. You are to refuse them permission to come to us in Moscow because the Kalmyks are very populous, and they are warlike people; they are not to learn the route to Moscow, lest they start coming to our borderlands to pillage, as the Nogais do. There is no benefit in having them come, nor is there any reason to confer with them about anything. They are illiterate, uneducated people, and it would be pointless to send gramotas to them, since they can neither read nor write.

If they come to you in Tiumen to trade, you may barter with them to buy their horses, but you are not to allow them to buy firearms, swords, spears, lances, axes, knives, quivers, arrows, or any kind of weapon or iron implement. If the taishas send gifts to you with their envoys, accept the gifts so you will not turn them away from us. In return you may send these taishas gifts from us such as fabric or long kaftans or some other appropriate item, depending on what gifts they have brought, so that our gifts will be

116

equal in value to theirs, and so that we will not turn them away from our Tsarist grace. If a taisha sends you a horse or two as gifts, accept them, and send him as many gifts from yourself as he sent to you, so that he will not be offended. Do not accept a gift without sending one in return, and do not permit any violence during the negotiation.

You must not allow these Kalmyk and Altyn envoys to proceed individually to Moscow. Refuse by saying that you do not have an ukaz from us about this, and that without an ukaz you dare not permit them to proceed, and furthermore that the road to Moscow is long and the passage is very difficult. Be very careful not to let any Kalmyks or other natives come into the town of Tiumen. When they come to trade you must be very cautious in the town. Do not permit them to inspect the fortifications, and do not allow them to remain in Tiumen very long. Inform us which taishas have sent envoys to Tiumen, and in what year, on what business, what their names are, how you sent them back, what goods they brought, what news they carried with them, and with whom they may be at war.

You are to write this in a report to us and forward it to the Kazan Dvorets, to our boiar Prince Ivan Mikhailovich Vorotynskii, and to our diaks, Ivan Bolotnikov and Fedor Apraksin. I have not asked the Posolskii Prikaz to deal with this because it would be pointless to have diplomatic contact with them since they are illiterate and there is nothing to discuss with them.

See: G. F. Müller, *Istoriia Sibiri* (Moscow-Leningrad: 1937), I, 306–307.

40

INSTRUCTIONS FROM THE VOEVODA OF ENISEISK TO THE SERVITOR
ZHDAN KOZLOV AND HIS MEN CONCERNING BRINGING THE BRATSK
PEOPLE UNDER RUSSIAN SUZERAINTY

On December 11, 1623, in accordance with the ukaz of the Sovereign Tsar and Grand Prince Mikhail Fedorovich of all Russia, the following instructions were issued from Eniseisk ostrog to the servitors Zhdan Kozlov, Vasilii Lodygin and Onan Ivanov.

You are to go from Eniseisk ostrog to the land of the Bratsk. When you reach the land of the Bratsk you are to gather the princes and leaders, and when you have assembled them, you are to tell these princes and leaders that they and all their people are to serve and obey the great Sovereign Tsar and Grand Prince Mikhail Fedorovich of all Russia, that they are to pay iasak to the great Sovereign and be under his mighty Tsarist hand, and that they may come to Eniseisk ostrog to receive the Sovereign's favor without fear.

Zhdan and his comrades are to observe everything carefully and use every possible means to find out what kind of people these are, whether they are settled or nomadic, what the names of the princes or rulers are in these lands, what fortifications they have, how many warriors, whether settled people serve as warriors, how many mounted warriors they have, whether or not they are bellicose people, what their occupations are, what goods they trade, whether they have fine sables or other fur bearing animals, and whether these people might bring some benefit to the Great Sovereign.

When the Bratsk people come to the Kan River, Zhdan and his men are to question the Bratsk princes and leaders and use every possible means to learn why they left their land and came to the Kan River, whether they are at war with some tribe, and whether they plan to come to Eniseisk ostrog with iasak to receive the Sovereign's favor, or whether they plan to resist. Zhdan and his men are to determine precisely how many of them have come to the Kan River, how many forts and warriors they have, for what purpose they have come, how strong they are, whether they have ostrogs or some other fortifications, and if so, where these are located, whether in the steppe or in some stronghold, and what kind of livestock they have.

If, in response to these questions, the Bratsk princes and leaders reply that they are coming to Eniseisk ostrog with iasak, then Zhdan and his men should use every means to persuade these Bratsk princes and leaders to come to receive the Sovereign's gifts so that they will come to Eniseisk ostrog without fear. In Eniseisk ostrog they are to be interrogated in accordance with the Sovereign's ukaz, receive the Sovereign's words of welcome, and upon receiving the Tsar's gifts, they should immediately be allowed to return to their own lands.

Zhdan and his men are personally to represent the Sovereign and summon the Bratsk people to Eniseisk ostrog to receive the Sovereign's gifts, and look for every possible means to bring benefit to the Sovereign. And if Zhdan and his men, when they reach the land of the Bratsks, do not entice the Bratsk princes and leaders to come under the Tsar's sovereignty, or if they fail to use every possible means to learn about the Bratsk lands and do not bring back information about any fortifications, and do not make every effort to bring benefit to the Sovereign, and if subsequently this is discovered, then Zhdan, Vasilii and Onan will be in great disfavor with the Sovereign Tsar and Grand Prince Mikhail Fedorovich of all Russia, and with the officials of the Commerce Treasury [*torgovaia kaznia*]. To this instruction, the voevoda Iakov Ignatevich Khripunov has placed his seal.

Reference: AAN, f. 21, op. 4, No. 22, ll. 18–19, No. 15.
See: G. N. Rumiantsev and S. B. Okun, eds. *Sbornik dokumentov po istorii Buriatii XVII vek* (Ulan-Ude: 1960), vyp. 1, 12–13.

41

A GRAMOTA FROM TSAR MIKHAIL FEDOROVICH TO THE VOEVODA OF
TOBOLSK, PRINCE ANDREI KHOVANSKII, CONCERNING EXPLORATION
FOR IRON ORE

From the Tsar and Grand Prince Mikhail Fedorovich of all Russia to Siberia, to the town of Tobolsk, to our voevodas Prince Andrei Andreevich Khovanskii and Miron Andreevich Veliaminov, and to our diaks Ivan Fedorov and Stepan Ugodtskii.

On October 20, 1624, the voevodas Prince Ivan Shekhovskii and Maksim Radilov wrote to us from the town of Tomsk that they had sent a blacksmith named Fedor Eremeev to make inquiries and prospect for iron ore. The blacksmith, Fedor Eremeev, returned and told them he had found rock containing such ore in the mountains, and that he believed that iron ore could be extracted from this rock.

They sent a cossack named Piatun Kizyl with the blacksmith to take samples of the rock and of the ore. They then ordered Fedor, the blacksmith, to smelt iron from the rock containing ore. Good iron was produced from the ore in this rock, as good as that in Kuznetsk territory. They sent the iron to us in Moscow with the blacksmith Fedor Eremeev.

In Moscow the iron was reprocessed, and is of good enough quality that steel can be made from it. In accordance with our ukaz, this blacksmith Fedor Eremeev who came to us in Moscow with the iron, and who discovered the iron ore, has had his yearly wages increased from 5.25 rubles to 10.25, and we have added a chetvert of groats and of oat flour to his food allowance of five chetverts of flour and one of groats and five of oats, and we have also given him some fine cloth.

We have also given a length of fine cloth to the cossack, Piatun Kizyl from Tomsk, who was sent with Fedor to sample these iron ores. During the interrogation in the Kazan Dvorets in Moscow, the blacksmith Fedor Eremeev stated that if we were to order an ironworks to be built in Tomsk, then iron could be produced there, as well as one-and-one-half calibre regimental muskets, and as much ammunition as these would require, provided capable blacksmiths were available.

In accordance with our ukaz, blacksmiths were sent from Ustiug to live in Tomsk in Siberia. These were Ivan Barshen, with his wife and children, and Vikhor Ivanov. They took a full set of blacksmith tools with them, and a Tobolsk cossack named Terentii Gornostai also went with them. Terentii was instructed to guide the blacksmiths to Tobolsk. In Moscow Ivan and his wife and children received 18 rubles as salary from us, and an extra allowance. Vikhor Ivanov received 12 rubles. Their annual salary was to be seven rubles in cash, and grain in the amount of seven chetverts of rye and four of oats per person. We ordered that these blacksmiths receive their annual salary and food provisions for the year 1625 in full in Tobolsk.

Orders were then issued to send them from Tobolsk to Tomsk. These blacksmiths were ordered to use the Tomsk iron for the continuous production of one-and-one-half calibre regimental muskets, and as much ammunition as each weapon would require. They were also ordered to test fire each weapon in Tomsk by firing at least one shot from each gun, in the presence of the voevodas, to make certain that the weapons are sound enough not to blow up when they are fired. These weapons were to be stored in Tomsk until we decree otherwise.

On August 29, 1625, the voevodas Prince Afanasii Gagarin and Semen Divov wrote to us from the Siberian town of Tomsk, informing us that they had selected a foreman in Tomsk and had given the orders for Fedor to begin smelting the iron. Fedor and his workmen are producing iron by mining rock three versts from town, and they are smelting it. However they are producing very little iron, only one pud per week, and in some weeks they are not even producing that much. Between October 3 and February 28 eleven puds of slab iron have been smelted. Gunsmiths have been ordered to make a *volkopeika* cannon from these slabs, but from the eleven puds of slab iron they have forged only five puds.

They experimented with sending the *guliashchie liudi* [itinerants] who come with the merchants out to cut lumber to make charcoal and kindling to smelt the ore. If we have to pay these people from our Treasury, then the iron will cost five rubles per pud to produce. The guliashchie liudi in Tomsk could be hired for four or five *altyns* per day. In the future these people will cut wood for charcoal and kindling and then go off in various directions. Our order to Tomsk does not specify what kind of people should be used to make charcoal and cut kindling to smelt the ore; we will have to issue a special ukaz about this.

As soon as you receive this gramota from us, you are to send a *pismennaia golova* from Tobolsk to Tomsk to do this. When he reaches Tomsk he is to find the blacksmith Fedor Eremeev and the cossack Kizyl. Instruct him to go with the blacksmith and with the cossack Piatun from Tomsk where they went to take samples of the rock and ore for Prince Ivan Shekhovskii and Maksim Radilov. Have the iron from the place where Fedor is now mining it brought to Tomsk, and in the presence of the pismennaia golova, have the blacksmith smelt iron from the ore, in order to find out precisely how much iron can be produced from the ore.

If the ore produces enough iron to profit our Treasury, then on the basis of our earlier ukaz, when this gramota reaches you, order the blacksmith Fedor Eremeev and his workers to use this Tomsk iron to forge muskets and shot, ploughshares, scythes, sickles and axes for our agricultural peasants in Siberian towns, so that in the future we will not have to send iron tools out from [European] Russia to the peasants, nor will we have to purchase scythes, sickles, ploughshares and axes, nor issue money from our Treasury to assist the peasants in making such purchases themselves.

In regard to firewood, and to the hired workers who make charcoal and mine the ore, you are to issue an ukaz, depending on the situation at the time, so that there will be profit for our Treasury. However, if such a small amount of iron is produced from this ore in the town of Tomsk that our Treasury would suffer a loss from this enterprise, then you are to investigate this matter of the iron in Tomsk, and find out why the voevodas of Tomsk, Prince Ivan Shekhovskii and Maksim Radilov, earlier made a favorable report to us about that iron, as did Prince Afanasii Gagarin and Semen Divov.

You are also to ask the blacksmith Fedor Eremeev why, when he was questioned in Moscow, he stated that it was possible to make one-and-one-half calibre regimental muskets from this iron, as well as shot for them, whereas now Prince Afanasii Gagarin and Semen Divov are reporting to us that very little iron is being produced from the Tomsk deposits.

You are to send a written report to us in Moscow concerning all of this. Send the report to the Prikaz of the Kazan Dvorets, to

Plan of Ilimsk ostrog, north of Irkutsk, established in 1630. From
Makovetskii, *Byt i iskusstvo russkogo naseleniia vostochnoi Sibiri*, Vol. 1.

our boiar Prince Dmitrii Mamitriukovich Cherkaskii and to our
diaks Ivan Bolotnikov and Ivan Griazev. The blacksmith Fedor is
to be kept under strict supervision and is not to leave Tomsk to go
anywhere until we issue further instructions.

See: G. F. Müller, *Istoriia Sibiri* (Moscow-Leningrad: 1937), I, 324–326.

42

NOT AFTER JANUARY 20, 1627

A REPORT FROM THE VOEVODA OF ENISEISK, ANDREI OSHANIN, TO
TSAR MIKHAIL FEDOROVICH AND THE SIBIRSKII PRIKAZ CONCERNING
SUBJUGATING THE BRATSK LANDS

Andrei Oshanin humbly reports to the Sovereign Tsar and
Grand Prince Mikhail Fedorovich of all Russia.

In accordance with your ukaz, Sire, Pozdei Firsov, an ataman
of the streltsy, has been serving as a *sotnik* [commander of 100
men] on your service in Eniseisk ostrog, Sire. However the sotnik
Pozdei Firsov is no longer in your service Sire; he drowned in
the Ob River and now there is no sotnik in Eniseisk ostrog for the
Eniseisk streltsy. The servitors in Eniseisk ostrog are headed by
the piatidesiatnik Piatun Arbenev and the desiatnik Andreev;
they are representing all their comrades in the Eniseisk streltsy,
and they have petitioned you, Sovereign Tsar and Grand Prince
Mikhail Fedorovich of all Russia, that you, Sire, would consent to
poddiak Maksim Perfirev becoming sotnik of the streltsy. They
say that Maksim has been serving you, Sovereign, for a long time.
They brought their petition to me, and I have attached it to this
report and am sending it to you, Great Sovereign Tsar and Grand
Prince Mikhail Fedorovich of all Russia, in Moscow, so that you
may issue an appropriate ukaz, Sovereign Tsar and Grand Prince
Mikhail Fedorovich of all Russia.

On June 11, 1626, Sire, the poddiak Maksim Perfirev was sent
on your service, Sire, up the Upper Tunguska River in a koch to
collect iasak for you, Sovereign, from the Tungus, Oplinsk and
from the shaman people for the year 1626. He was also instructed
to gather information about new lands and particularly about the
Bratsk [Buriat] land. Poddiak Maksim did collect your iasak, Sire,
from the Tungus, Oplinsk and shaman people, and he brought it
to the government warehouse. While he was on your service,
Sire, Maksim brought people back under your Sovereign suzerainty who had previously turned against you: the Tungus prince
Tasei and his brothers, Irkan and Lukash, who had betrayed you
and killed your Sovereign servitors, Sire. He also collected your
iasak from them, Sire. When he was questioned Maksim stated
that he had not been able to approach any closer than three days'
journey away from the Bratsk land because there were great

rapids in the river and the passage through was extremely narrow. It was impossible to go down the rapids because he did not have many men with him and the water in the rapids was very low.

When Maksim questioned the shaman people they told him that the Bratsk land is rich and populous; they are settled people, and they collect iasak from many peoples in smaller regions throughout the Bratsk territory. There are many sables, foxes and beavers, rich Bukhara goods, plain cotton *kindiak* [fabrics], eastern cotton goods [*zenden*], silks and linens. There are rich deposits of silver and multitudes of horses, cattle, sheep and camels. They grow barley and buckwheat. The Bratsk people are awaiting your Sovereign servitors and wish to submit to you, Great Sovereign, and pay iasak to you; and they wish to trade with the servitors.

In accordance with your ukaz, Sovereign, I should like to send 60 men aboard three koches to them in the spring after the ice has broken up so they can make a thorough reconnaissance of the Bratsk land and bring it under your suzerainty, Sovereign, and collect your iasak from the people there.

Sire, when the Bratsk land has been brought under your mighty protection, your state Treasury will receive great profit, Sire, because when the many people of the many settlements of the Bratsk land bow down to you, Great Sovereign, your state Treasury will be much enriched by the iasak collection of sables.

Reference: TsGADA, f. 214—Sibirskii prikaz, stolb. No. 6056/12, ll, 87–89.

See: B. N. Rumiantsev and S. B. Okun, eds. *Sbornik dokumentov po istorii Buriatii XVII vek* (Ulan-Ude: 1960), vyp. 1, 14–15.

43

INSTRUCTIONS FROM THE VOEVODA OF TOBOLSK, PRINCE ANDREI KHOVANSKII, TO ANDREI DUBENSKII TO BUILD AN OSTROG AT KRASNOIARSK

On June 1, 1627, in accordance with the ukaz of the Sovereign Tsar and Grand Prince Mikhail Fedorovich of all Russia, the voevodas Prince Andrei Andreevich Khovanskii and Ivan Vasilievich Volynskii and the diaks Ivan Fedorov and Stepan Ugodtskii ordered Andrei Onufreevich Dubenskii to journey on the service of the Sovereign to the land of the Kachins, up the Enisei River, to Krasnoi Iar. The Sovereign Tsar and Grand Prince Mikhail Fedorovich of all Russia has decreed that in this land of the Kachins, up the Enisei River, at Krasnoi Iar, a new ostrog is to be built; and he has ordered Andrei Dubenskii to build that ostrog. The Sovereign Tsar has ordered that servitors, atamans and cossacks be recruited in Tobolsk and other Siberian towns to go with Andrei, and he has given instructions that they are to receive additional salary and provisions, which are to be issued for a two-year period. Upon receiving the money and provisions, Andrei and his servitors are to take their equipment and proceed to Eniseisk ostrog, and from there go to the Kachin territory. At Krasnoi Iar on the Enisei River Andrei is to build an ostrog, dig a moat, build a palisade, and fortify the ostrog in every possible way. He is to bring the people of the new lands under the Tsarist mighty hand by persuasion, and tell them that they are to serve and be loyal to the Sovereign Tsar and Grand Prince Mikhail Fedorovich of all Russia. They are to collect as much iasak as possible from these lands, without resorting to cruelty, and have the people cultivate the land.

If there are people near Krasnoi Iar where the ostrog is to be built who do not wish to come under the Tsarist mighty hand, and will not consent to pay iasak, and if the newly arrived servitors cannot bring these persons under the Sovereign's mighty hand, then Andrei Dubenskii is authorized to inquire how many people there are in those lands who will not obey and will not pay iasak, and find out how far away from Krasnoi Iar there is another place where an ostrog could be built, and how many people are there in that place, and how many servitors would be needed to bring that land under the Sovereign's mighty hand and collect iasak from the inhabitants.

If there are many natives near Krasnoi Iar who do not want to come under the Sovereign's mighty hand and will not allow the ostrog to be built at Krasnoi Iar, and if Andrei Dubenskii and the newly arrived servitors will not be able to bring these lands under the Sovereign's mighty hand and build an ostrog at Krasnoi Iar without additional servitors then Andrei is to send a report about all of this to Tobolsk, and we will send Andrei leaders and service persons from various towns as reinforcements to carry out this purpose. But the ostrog is to be built at Krasnoi Iar, and the peoples in these lands are to be brought under the Sovereign's mighty hand, as direct slaves, and iasak is to be collected from them.

In accordance with the ukaz of the Sovereign Tsar and Grand Prince Mikhail Fedorovich of all Russia three atamans and 300 cossacks have been selected from Tobolsk and other Siberian towns to build this new ostrog. The following yearly wages have been set for each of them: ataman, 30 rubles; desiatnik, 5½ rubles; line cossacks, 5 rubles. The provision allowance is: ataman, ten chetverts of flour and four of groats and oats; piatidesiatnik and desiatnik and line cossacks, five chetverts of flour and groats and one of oats per man. They are to receive the Sovereign's wages and provisions in full for two years for the period June 1, 1627 to June 1, 1629. Andrei Dubenskii has received the list of names of the servitors who have been ordered to go with him on the Sovereign's service to Krasnoi Iar, and the list has been signed by the diak. Equipment for these persons who are to serve with Andrei has been sent from Tobolsk.

Andrei Onufreevich Dubenskii and the servitors who are to go on the Sovereign's service to the Kachin land to build the new ostrog are to travel on the Ob and Ket rivers to Eniseisk ostrog, with great dispatch, traveling day and night without wasting even an hour anywhere, so that they will reach Makovsk ostrog during this summer with full rations and equipment before the rivers freeze over.

When Andrei reaches Makovsk ostrog, he is to store the Sovereign's equipment, powder and all the supplies and provisions which were sent with him from Tobolsk in the Sovereign's depots and granaries until time for the winter journey. Then, God willing, when the time for winter travel comes, Andrei is to transport the gunpowder, shot, guns and provisions from Makovsk ostrog to Eniseisk ostrog. When the equipment, powder and other supplies have been taken from Makovsk ostrog to Eniseisk ostrog, Andrei is to store the equipment, powder, shot, fabric and the rest of the goods which have been sent with him in the warehouse, and the food supplies are to be stored wherever most convenient. When everything has been moved from Makovsk ostrog to Eniseisk ostrog and has been stored appropriately, Andrei is to order the servitors who have been sent with him to build koches to transport the equipment, powder and other supplies which he has been sent. The boats will also be used to transport Andrei, the servitors, and the food supplies. He is to obtain two or three master boat builders for that purpose from the voevoda of Eniseisk ostrog, Vasilii Argamakov. The voevoda Vasilii Argamakov has received written orders in this regard. When the koches have been built and the ice on the Enisei River has broken, then when the water is first open Andrei is to load onto the koches all the equipment, powder, shot and other supplies which have been sent with him, as well as the food supplies. Then, invoking God's help, he is to go by boat with all the servitors up the Enisei River to the land of the Kachins, to Krasnoi Iar.

While he is sailing up the Enisei River, Andrei is to send out reconnaissance units in light boats ahead of himself to gather all kinds of information and to investigate in detail the movement of any native war parties. Andrei himself and all the rest of the servitors are to proceed with care and caution so that native warriors will not take them by surprise and cause them harm.

When they reach the Kachin territory, God willing, and come to Krasnoi Iar in good health, if the natives have caused them no trouble anywhere, then Andrei and the servitors are to build the ostrog there at Krasnoi Iar. They are to construct towers and dig a moat around the ostrog and build a palisade, and fortify the ostrog in every possible way; then they are to look for arable land. When they have finished building the ostrog, and have given it every possible fortification, Andrei is immediately to send a written report to Tobolsk.

During Andrei's future service to the Sovereign in the new ostrog, he is to conduct himself with great caution so that the inhabitants of the Kachin land and other hordes will not take him by surprise and cause him harm. The local natives who have previously been disobedient to the Sovereign are to be summoned with courtesy to come back under the Sovereign's mighty hand. Andrei is also to inform the natives in the new lands that they are to serve and obey the great Sovereign Tsar and Grand Prince Mikhail Fedorovich of all Russia, that they are to pay iasak, and that the great Sovereign Tsar and Grand Prince Mikhail Fedorovich of all Russia, His Sovereign Majesty, will reward them and keep them in his Tsarist gracious benevolent sight, and will afford them complete protection from people from other parts.

When persons in that land return under the Tsarist mighty hand and pay iasak, Andrei should have them take an oath of allegiance and then collect iasak from them, depending on current conditions, and make certain they are not subjected to insults, so that they will not be alienated again. He is to give them cloth as part of the Sovereign's gifts, depending on their status. He is to offer them food and drink, and show them kindness and welcome. He is to see that servitors do not abuse them.

If, on his way along the Enisei River or in the land of the Kachins at Krasnoi Iar, Andrei and the servitors encounter hostile natives who will not permit him to proceed or to build the ostrog and attack him, then Andrei and his servitors are to invoke God's mercy and engage the natives in battle and conquer them, insofar as merciful God is willing to help him. Andrei is personally responsible for building the ostrog at Krasnoi Iar and seeing that the people in the new lands are brought under the mighty Tsarist hand.

Andrei is to make frequent written reports to Tobolsk, informing them how large the ostrog is to be, what manner of fortifications are to be emplaced there, and what kind of arable lands there are, and how much of these territories he can bring under the mighty Sovereign's hand, how much iasak he can collect, and whether the men who have been sent with him from Tobolsk can maintain themselves in the new ostrog. He is also to report whether people from other lands will harass the Sovereign's men in the ostrog, and what he plans to do in the new ostrog in the future.

If there are people from territories adjacent to Krasnoi Iar where the ostrog is to be built who do not wish to come under the mighty hand of the Sovereign, nor to give iasak, and if they cannot be brought under the mighty hand of the Sovereign by the servitors who have been sent with Andrei, then he is to make inquiries about these lands. How many people live in them? Which persons are disobedient and will not give iasak? How far are such lands from Krasnoi Iar, and how many people live in that land? How many of the Sovereign's servitors will it take to bring these lands under the mighty hand of the Sovereign and collect iasak from them? After he has made detailed inquiries, Andrei is to submit his request for more men to the Eniseisk ostrog, to voevoda Vasilii Argamakov, and to the town of Tomsk, to the voevoda Prince Petr Kozlovskii, and to Griaznii Bartenev. These men have all been instructed by the Sovereign's ukaz about these matters. They have been ordered to send leaders and servitors to reinforce the garrison in the land of the Kachins, as Andrei Dubenskii may request.

On his way to his assignment in the land of the Kachins in the new ostrog, Andrei Dubenskii is to supervise carefully the servitors and keep them under firm control so that they will not fight among themselves, nor pillage, nor start gaming and playing cards, nor gamble away the Sovereign's money and provisions, nor steal, nor cause violence to anyone. When they are sent out to collect the Sovereign's iasak, they are not to rob and kill the iasak-paying people. And if they should steal or gamble or play cards or pillage, a report is to be sent to the Sovereign. Andrei is to keep them from all of this. He is to pass judgment and inflict punishment, depending on the misdeed, so that there will be no stealing, gambling or corruption, and so that no murders will be committed.

Andrei is personally responsible for serving the Sovereign Tsar and Grand Prince Mikhail Fedorovich of all Russia in the Kachin land at Krasnoi Iar by building an ostrog, preparing all the fortifications, searching out arable land, bringing other lands under the mighty hand of the Tsar and collecting iasak. He is to see to it that the servitors are not idle, and that they do not turn anything to their own personal profit. They are not to accept any gifts, and they are not to engage in any violence against any native who might be driven away by cruelty on the part of the servitors.

Andrei is to have full jurisdiction in resolving disputes, in accordance with the oath taken to the Sovereign Tsar and Grand Prince Mikhail Fedorovich of all Russia. Andrei is to conduct the Sovereign's affairs in accordance with this ukaz of the Sovereign, taking into account local circumstances and whatever enlightenment God may give him, so that the Sovereign's business will be more profitable and that the ostrog will be built, and the lands will be brought under the Sovereign's mighty hand, and so that Andrei himself and his servitors on that post as well as en route, will be protected against attack by people from hostile lands.

Andrei has been sent an inventory, signed by a diak, of all equipment, powder, shot, cloth, fresh water pearls, tin goods and spirits for the natives, as well as the mead, food, iron, locks and other things that have been sent with him.

When, God willing, the ostrog is built at Krasnoi Iar in Kachin territory, and all the fortifications have been prepared, and the natives have been brought under the Sovereign's mighty hand, and there is no danger to the ostrog from attack by people of other lands, then Andrei is to select one or two trustworthy natives from among the old iasak-paying people, and instruct them to go to the Kirgiz people and the Kirgiz princes and leading ulus men and inform them, that in accordance with the ukaz of the great Sovereign Tsar and Grand Prince Mikhail Fedorovich of all Russia, many servitors with equipment and with many arms have come to the land of the Kachins, to Krasnoi Iar. They have built a permanent ostrog in that place, with all manner of fortifications, and have brought local people under the Sovereign's mighty hand. They are also to say that many people from other territories, hearing about his Tsarist Majesty's great generosity and concern and protection and intercession, willingly have also come under his Sovereign's mighty hand, and the Tsarist Majesty has ordered that they be held in his merciful and benevolent grace, and that they be protected from attack by other natives.

The Kirgiz people can be confident of the Sovereign's benevolence in all matters; they can live in their own settlements in peace and prosperity and tranquility; they will not have to fear any people from hostile lands, because many of the Sovereign's troops will protect them from these hostile natives of other lands; and they will pay their iasak to the town of Tomsk as previously. If these Kirgiz people will turn to the Sovereign, and repent their misdeeds, and then pay their iasak to Tomsk, and not attack Tomsk, then Andrei Dubenskii is not to insult these Kirgiz people in any way, but to treat them with kindness and courtesy. He is not to cause any disputes with them. But if the Kirgiz people continue to pursue their lawless ways and refuse to ask the Sovereign for forgiveness, and will not pay iasak to Tomsk; and if they attack the ostrog; then Andrei is to do battle against them, as against any other enemy, and pursue them as far as Merciful God enables him to do so.

If the Kirgiz attack the town of Tomsk, and Andrei learns of this, and personally discovers that they have gone to attack the town of Tomsk, then Andrei is to fortify the ostrog and leave a small garrison of as many men as necessary, depending on who is in the ostrog at the time. Then he is to take his servitors and advance on the Kirgiz ulus, fight them, kill the men and take their wives and children prisoners, and use every possible means to subdue them, so that they will thereby be brought in direct slavery under the mighty hand of the Sovereign, as before.

A list is to be prepared of the number of Kirgiz prisoners that Andrei brings into captivity. The prisoners are to be kept in the ostrog, but they are not to be converted [to Christianity] or sold without a new ukaz from the Sovereign. A report about this is to be sent to Tobolsk immediately.

But if Andrei is negligent or careless, and does not reach Makovsk ostrog this summer with all his servitors, equipment and supplies; or if he fails to transfer his equipment and provisions over the portage to Eniseisk ostrog in the winter; or if his travel is so slow that he is unable to build the ostrog at Krasnoi Iar in the Kachin territory; or if he fails to bring the people of those territories under the Sovereign's mighty hand; or if he abuses his servitors or tries to collect bribes and gifts for his own profit from them, then for all of the above, Andrei will be in great disfavor with the Tsar and Grand Prince Mikhail Fedorovich of all Russia.

See: G. F. Müller, *Istoriia Sibiri* (Moscow-Leningrad: 1937), I, 330–333.

44

1633

OATH OF ALLEGIANCE SWORN BY KUNKANCH, THE ALTYN-KHAN
[ALTYN-TSAR], TO TSAR MIKHAIL FEDOROVICH

I, Altyn-tsar, swear my oath of allegiance to my Sovereign, the Tsar and Grand Prince Mikhail Fedorovich, Autocrat of all Russia, of Vladimir, Moscow and Novgorod; Tsar of Kazan; Tsar of Astrakhan; Tsar of Siberia; Sovereign of Pskov; Grand Prince of Smolensk, Tver, Iugra, Perm, Viatka, Bulgaria and more; Sovereign and Grand Prince of Nizhnii Novgorod, Nizovie Territory, Chernigov, Riazan, the land of the Polovtsy, Rostov, Iaroslav, Beloozero, Lifland [the Baltic] . . . [missing], Obdor, Kondinsk and all northern lands; Sovereign and Lord of the Iversk land and of the Kartalinsk and Georgian tsars, and of the Kabardinsk land, and of the Cherkassian and Gorsk princes; and Sovereign and Master of many other realms; and to the Tsarist Majesty's son, the Lord Tsarevich Prince Aleksei Mikhailovich.

I swear that I, Altyn-tsar, and my brothers Dorzei, Kurbai, Belzoi, Katkan and Sarych and my children and my grandchildren and all my relatives and tribesmen and my entire horde will come under the mighty hand of His Tsarist Majesty and his son, the Lord Tsarevich Prince Aleksei Mikhailovich, and in the future, under all of their Sovereign successors, the Great Sovereigns, Tsars and Grand Russian princes, in complete submission, for all eternity, undeviatingly and that we all will live in their Sovereign grace and protection; that we will be obedient and submissive in all ways, and will serve them, the Sovereigns, and be loyal, and in every undertaking will strive for their benefit, and will safeguard their Sovereign honor in all ways. I, Altyn-tsar, and my brothers and sons and grandsons and nephews and all my relatives and tribesmen will pay tribute to the Sovereign, for myself and for all my horde and we will deliver this tribute to the Sovereigns.

I, Altyn-tsar, my brothers, sons, grandsons, nephews, relatives and tribesmen, will camp with all of our people in our horde in our previous campsites, where we have camped with our horde in the past, and we will not encamp near the Sovereign's Siberian lands. We will not harass the Sovereign's iasak-paying Kirgiz, nor iasak-paying people from other lands. We will not take

Saltworks near Iamyshevsk ostrog recall the original holdings of the Stroganovs, early Siberian entrepreneurs. From Shunkov, ed., *Istoriia Sibiri*, Vol. 2.

the iasak from them for ourselves, nor will we steal anything from them, nor will I, Altyn-tsar, or my brothers, sons, grandsons, or any of my relatives or tribesmen attack them or send our warriors against them. We will defend the Sovereign's people from attack by other hordes and warriors.

Wherever the Sovereign Tsar and Grand Prince Mikhail Fedorovich of all Russia may send me, Altyn-tsar, my brothers, sons, grandsons, or relatives and tribesmen and people, on his Sovereign service, against any of his subjects who are disloyal, I, Altyn-tsar, and my brothers, sons, grandsons, nephews, relatives and tribesmen will go, with our people, on his Sovereign service. We will serve him, the Sovereign Tsar and Grand Prince Mikhail Fedorovich of all Russia, and his son, the Lord Tsarevich Prince Aleksei Mikhailovich, loyally in all respects. We will not commit treason. We will battle the Sovereign's traitors and enemies and disobedient subjects, not sparing our lives, and in battle we will defend the Sovereign's Russian people and other [loyal subjects] from the Sovereign's traitors and enemies and disobedient subjects. We will give no succor to the Sovereign's traitors, enemies and disobedient subjects. Further, if I, Altyn-tsar, or my brothers, sons, grandsons, relatives, tribesmen or people in my horde

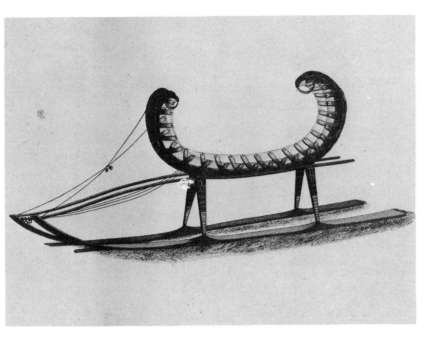

Eastern Siberian dogsled. Eighteenth-century engraving.

hear of any treason being plotted against the Great Sovereign, then I, Altyn-tsar, my brothers, sons, grandsons, relatives and tribesmen will denounce those traitors to the Sovereign, and will report this to the voevodas and diaks in the town of Tomsk.

We will not carry on any relationship or friendship, without the permission of His Tsarist Majesty, with other hordes or other rulers, or Kalmyk taishas, who are disloyal to the Sovereign. Likewise I, Altyn-tsar, my brothers, sons, grandsons, relatives and tribesmen will not battle people of other tribes or realms without the permission of the Sovereign Tsar and Grand Prince Mikhail Fedorovich of all Russia, so that the Sovereign's name will be kept in the highest esteem and honor in all regards.

I, Altyn-tsar, on my own behalf and on that of my brothers, sons, grandsons, relatives and tribesmen and entire horde, do swear allegiance to the Great Sovereign Tsar and Grand Prince Mikhail Fedorovich, Autocrat of all Russia, Sovereign and Lord of many realms, and to his son, the Lord Tsarevich Prince Aleksei Mikhailovich, in every regard herein attested.

See: I. P. Kuznetsov-Krasnoiarskii, ed., *Istoricheskie Akty XVII Stoletiia (1633–1699)* (Tomsk: 1890), 1–4.

45

SEPTEMBER 6, 1633

REPORT TO TSAR MIKHAIL FEDOROVICH FROM THE STRELTSY SOTNIK
PETR BEKETOV CONCERNING HIS EXPEDITION ON THE LENA RIVER

To the Sovereign Tsar and Grand Prince Mikhail Fedorovich of all Russia, a report, Sovereign, from your distant Sovereign patrimony in Eniseisk ostrog, from your humble servants, streltsy sotnik Petr Beketov and his servitors, and from your Sovereign's orphan, the promyshlennik Iakov Zarubeevich Semenov.

On May 30, 1631, Sovereign, in accordance with your ukaz, Sovereign Tsar and Grand Prince Mikhail Fedorovich of all Russia, and in accordance with the instruction of your Sovereign Tsar's voevoda Semen Shekhovskii, I, your humble servant, was sent out from Eniseisk ostrog with servitors on your distant assignment, Sovereign, to the Lena River for one year. Your Sovereign salary and rations were given to me for one year. I, your humble servant, with these servitors and with the promyshlenniks served you, Sovereign Tsar and Grand Prince Mikhail Fedorovich of all Russia, on your distant service on the Lena River, Sire, for two and a half years.

During those two and a half years, while on your distant service, Sovereign, I your humble servant suffered every deprivation. We were starving to death and ate every wretched thing including grass, roots and bark from fir and silver fir trees. I, your humble servant, Petr Beketov, together with the servitors and the promyshlennik, thanks to God's mercy and your luck, Sovereign, brought under your Sovereign Tsarist mighty hand on the Lena River many diverse Tungus and Iakut lands for you, great Sovereign Tsar and Grand Prince Mikhail Fedorovich of all Russia. I, your humble servant, collected iasak from these many diverse Tungus and Iakut lands for you, great Sovereign Tsar and Grand Prince Mikhail Fedorovich of all Russia. And I, your humble servant, collected iasak from many Tungus and Iakut people, using the threat of your Sovereign's might. Sovereign, I, your humble servant, with servitors and the promyshlennik, collected iasak for the year 1632 which consisted of 18 forties of sables.

In the year 1633, from these same Iakuts and Tungus, I, your humble servant, with the servitors and the promyshlennik, added 41 forties and 15 sables to your Sovereign iasak treasury from the Iakuts and the Tungus plus the tithe paid by servitors and by promyshlenniks.

Furthermore, Sovereign, I, your humble servant, collected two forties and 16 sables on the Lena River in your name for your Sovereign Treasury from servitors and the promyshlennik as fees for settling legal disputes. In Eniseisk ostrog these were valued at 130 rubles.

Sovereign, in two and a half years of service on the Lena River I, your humble servant, with the servitors and the promyshlennik, collected a total of 61 forties and 31 sables, 25 Iakut sable shubas, 10 sable *plastinas*, [pelts sewed together] 2 beavers, 7 red fox, and one red fox pup. Sovereign, prior to this no one had collected your Sovereign taxes from legal judgments on the Lena River. Moreover my men and I have brought back under your mighty Tsarist hand many of your previously rebellious subjects who defied your Sovereign Majesty during this two and a half year period. The names of these princes are listed in the official record, and also the names of the hostages I took from them.

I, your humble servant, with the servitors and with the promyshlennik, came to Eniseisk ostrog on September 6, 1634, with your Sovereign iasak and tithe Treasury, from your distant Sovereign service on the Lena River. I submitted my service report in Eniseisk ostrog, in the Prikaz office, to your Sovereign voevoda, Andrei Andreevich Plemiannikov.

Merciful Sovereign Tsar and Grand Prince Mikhail Fedorovich of all Russia, reward us, your humble servants, Sovereign; and grant me personally, your orphan, your Sovereign largesse, as God may enlighten you, Great Sovereign, for our service which we performed on your distant Sovereign assignment on the Lena River. For you, Great Sovereign, we have shed our blood, suffered every privation, starved, eaten every unclean thing, and defiled our souls during those two and a half years. Tsar, Sovereign, have mercy.

This service report also gives details of the service list of the Eniseisk ostrog streltsy sotnik Petr Beketov and his servitors who were sent from Eniseisk ostrog into service on the Lena River for the Sovereign Tsar and Grand Prince Mikhail Fedorovich of all Russia in the year 1631. Details are given on those Eniseisk servitors who served the Sovereign and fought the natives and were wounded, and on the hostile lands they brought under the Sovereign Tsarist mighty hand and in which they established the collection of iasak.

On September 4, 1632, in accordance with the ukaz of the Sovereign Tsar and Grand Prince Mikhail Fedorovich, I, Petr, went with 20 servitors on the Sovereign's service from the mouth of the Idirma River to the portage on the upper Lena River, to collect the Sovereign's iasak and to explore new lands. On September 23 I, Petr, came with the servitors to the Bratsk territory on the upper Lena River to the mouth of the Ona River to collect the Sovereign's iasak from the Bratsk princeling Bukui. These Bratsk people and prince Bukui and his tribesmen had not paid iasak to the Sovereign prior to that, and were not under the Sovereign Tsar's mighty hand. These Bratsk people, led by prince Bukui, gathered their ulus people and surrounded me, Petr, and my servitors and laid siege to us in the forest in order to prevent us from reaching their uluses. I, Petr, and the servitors built a fortified encampment and withstood the siege for three days. Then these Bratsk people came to me, Petr, and to the servitors to ask forgiveness. They said that they, the Bratsk people, had come with iasak for the Sovereign to beg for the Sovereign's mercy.

I, Petr, ordered the servitors to prepare their weapons, and then ordered that the Bratsk people be allowed to enter the fort. These Bratsk people did enter the fort, but they did not bring any iasak for the Sovereign. . . . [missing] Nor did they say anything. They had planned to kill the servitors there and then, and they attacked the servitors. With God's mercy and the good fortune of the Sovereign, God sided with me, Petr, in that struggle, and with the servitors and we overcame the Bratsk people. The rest of the Bratsk, seeing that they could not triumph against the mighty hand of the Sovereign, as well as those who did not want to give iasak to the Sovereign, all ran off. There were also Tungus people from the Naliaska land who had not previously paid iasak to the Sovereign who were living together with the Bratsk people. These Tungus paid iasak to the Bratsk, the same Bratsk people whom, with the mercy of God and the luck of the Sovereign, I, Petr, had defeated.

Seeing how the Sovereign's mighty hand had destroyed the Bratsk people, these Tungus from Naliaska land became frightened by the Sovereign's mighty power and brought to me, Petr, their submission to the Sovereign's Majesty. I, Petr, in accordance with the Sovereign's ukaz, extended to them the greetings and gracious words of his Tsarist Majesty. When these Tungus people agreed to come under the Sovereign's mighty hand, I, Petr, with the servitors brought all of these Naliaska Tungus to take the oath, imposed the Sovereign's iasak obligation on them, which consisted of . . . [missing] sables per man. After imposing the Sovereign's iasak obligation on these Tungus, I left nine of the Sovereign's servitors and an interpreter with these Tungus to collect the Sovereign's iasak. [Names follow.]

I ordered these servitors to build a iasak *zimov'e* to collect the Sovereign's iasak in that Naliaska land. The servitor Andrei Dubin and his men collected Sovereign's iasak for the year 1632 from those Naliaska Tungus and from other new people; the iasak consisted of four forties and 20 sables. At the present time these Naliaska Tungus are firmly under the mighty hand of the Sovereign Tsar for all time.

I, Petr, with God's mercy and the luck of the Sovereign, and with 56 servitors defeated the Bratsk people who had been disobedient to the Sovereign; I defeated them on the upper Lena River. In that battle the Bratsk wounded the servitor Semen Tabunov in the right hand; they cut off two of his fingers, and a native stabbed him. During the struggle the Bratsk also killed two Tungus who had served as guides for the servitors, prince Litsk and the son of a Tungus interpreter who was himself the brother of the shaman. [Names follow.]

On April 6 of that same year, while I was on the Sovereign's service on the Lena River, in accordance with the ukaz of the Sovereign Tsar and Grand Prince Mikhail Fedorovich of all Russia, I, Petr, sent servitors from Eniseisk ostrog into the Sovereign's service from the mouth of the Idirma River to the Kirenga River to new lands to collect the Sovereign's iasak from the Tungus. [Names follow.] These servitors led by Andrei Dubin and his men, collected iasak for the Sovereign from the new Tungus people along the Kirenga River which consisted of three forties and 18 sables. . . . [missing] These Tungus agreed . . . [missing] and became obedient to the Sovereign. I, Petr, with the servitors brought great profit to the Sovereign through this.

That same year I, Petr, sent the servitors Agapit Ivanov, Ivan

Kataev and Fedor Zyrenin on the Sovereign's service on the Lena River. They went from Eniseisk ostrog to the Ust Kirenga River to collect the Sovereign's iasak from the Tungus. They collected iasak for the Great Sovereign consisting of two forties and 22 sables from the Tungus. The total collected from the upper Lena River and the Kirenga and the Ust Kirenga was ten forties and 20 sables for the year 1632. I sent this iasak treasury for the Sovereign from the Lena River to voevoda Zhdan Kondyrev in Eniseisk ostrog under the protection of the servitors of Eniseisk ostrog, led by Ivan Statsov and Bogdan Andreev and their comrades.

On April 8 of that year, in accordance with the ukaz of the Sovereign, the voevoda Zhdan Kondyrev sent 14 additional servitors from Eniseisk ostrog to the Lena River to me, your humble servant, to go on your distant service. They were under the command of the desiatniks Ilia Ermolin and Vasilii Burga. I, Petr, was ordered to proceed with the servitors who had been sent to me; we were to go on the Sovereign's service on the Lena River in the Iakut land to collect the Sovereign's iasak there and to bring new territories under the Sovereign's mighty hand. And so I, Petr, went by way of the Lena portage to the Iakut territory. I, Petr, and the servitors, went by water to the land of the Iakuts. On May 14, 1632, we reached the uluses belonging to the Iakut prince Semen Ulta and his brother, Kamyk. In accordance with the Sovereign's ukaz I, Petr, told these princes and all the ulus people about the Sovereign's majesty, and I summoned them to come under the Sovereign's Tsarist mighty hand, and I conveyed the Sovereign's greetings to them. The princes Semen Ulta and his brother Kamyk and their ulus people tried to repel the servitors and me, Petr, from the bank of the river. They refused to come under the Sovereign's mighty hand, and refused to pay the Sovereign's iasak to me, Petr, and to the servitors. Others started to fight. I, Petr, begging God's mercy, told the servitors to fight on behalf of the Sovereign Majesty. With God's mercy and the luck of the Sovereign, the servitors drove off those Iakuts, and in the struggle they captured Dokai Kamykov, the son of the prince of Butunsk volost.

These princes Semen Ulta and his brother Kamyk, gathered with all their people and submitted to the Great Sovereign Tsar. I, Petr, brought these princes to take the oath, and with the good fortune of the Sovereign, and with threats, I collected iasak from these Iakut princes and their people, Semen Ulta and his brother Kamyk, for the year 1632, consisting of 24 sables and four sable shubas.

From this same Kamyk and his brother Semen Ulta and from Kamyk's son, and from their tribesmen, in the year 1633 I, Petr, collected three forties and nine sables, thus bringing new profit to the Great Sovereign. With the Sovereign's luck, prince Semen Ulta and his brother Kamyk and their tribesmen became obedient to the Sovereign's mighty hand, and came to the new ostrozhek of the Sovereign, at all times without fear, and with their wives and children. There I, Petr, with the servitors and the good fortune of the Sovereign, built an ostrog in the land of the Iakuts.

That same year in accordance with the Sovereign's ukaz, I, Petr, sent the Sovereign's iasak and tithe treasury from the land of the Iakuts to Eniseisk ostrog to voevoda Zhdan Kondyrev consisting of eighteen forties of sables. This was under the guard of servitors from Eniseisk ostrog headed by the desiatnik Ilia Ermolin and his men. The names of the persons from whom the Sovereign's iasak was collected, those Tungus and Iakut people, as well as the names of those from whom the Sovereign's tithe was collected, are all entered in the books in the Sovereign's Treasury office in Eniseisk ostrog. I, Petr, again brought the Great Sovereign profit. Except for me, Petr, no one had ever collected the tithe from the servitors and from the promyshlenniks.

That same year, in accordance with the Sovereign's ukaz, I, Petr, sent servitors on the Sovereign's service to collect iasak for the Sovereign and to urge the Iakut prince Shor, to come under the Sovereign's rule. This Iakut prince Shor and his people had never before paid iasak to the Sovereign, and they were not in good standing with the Sovereign. These servitors traveled for two days to go to prince Shor. When they returned they were questioned, and they told me, Petr, that when they found Prince Shor in his ulus, they urged him and his people to come under the Sovereign's grace and pay iasak to him; but prince Shor and his people did not want to come under the Sovereign's mighty hand, or pay iasak to the Great Sovereign. Instead, they argued, and tried to kill the servitors hoping to receive help from their godless power. The servitors, however, asked God's help, and fell to fighting the Iakuts. With God's mercy and the luck of the Sovereign, they killed prince Shor himself, together with five of his leaders, and they then successfully retreated from those people. [Names follow.]

On July 20 of that same year I, Petr, sent the desiatnik Andrei Dubin and his men down the Lena River to collect iasak for the Sovereign and to explore new lands. Andrei and his men traveled down the Lena for three weeks, and with the good fortune of the Sovereign they collected iasak for the Great Sovereign consisting of 27 sables. They also took a prince hostage. When they returned they reported to me, Petr, that the Tungus who live on the lower Lena had not previously paid iasak to the Sovereign.

On August 1 of that same year I, Petr, in accordance with the ukaz of the Sovereign Tsar and Grand Prince Mikhail Fedorovich of all Russia, sent the Eniseisk ostrog servitors Oleg Arkhipov along with Lev Iakovlev and his men from the land of the Iakuts down the Lena River to collect iasak for the Sovereign from new lands. I instructed the servitors that when they reached new lands they should build a zimov'e at Zhigan and spend the winter in that zimov'e to collect iasak for the Sovereign. The servitor Oleg Arkhipov and his men went down the Lena River from the land of the Iakuts, sailing along past the land of the Dolgans. They came to the Zhigan land, and built a iasak zimov'e there. In that land, with God's mercy and the luck of the Sovereign, they brought the Dolgan and Zhigan regions under your Sovereign mighty hand. They wintered in the zimov'e, and the servitor Oleg Arkhipov and his men collected iasak for the Great Sovereign in that iasak zimov'e from the new Tungus people in those two lands, the Dolgan and Zhigan. With the luck of the Sovereign, the iasak they collected for the year 1633 for the Sovereign consisted of six forties of sables. Thereby they brought profit to the Great Sovereign from the Great Sovereign's distant borderland. And the Tungus princes Chedei and Kaptagai, and all of their people, became obedient and came under the Sovereign's mighty hand for all time.

On August 6 of that same year I, Petr, and the servitors anchored on the shore of the river near the ulus of the Iakut prince Shureniak and urged him and all of his people to come under the Sovereign Tsar's mighty hand and to give iasak to the Sovereign. This prince gathered many of his ulus people together and tried to drive me, Petr, and the servitors away from the river bank, and refused to come under the Sovereign's mighty hand and to give iasak to the Sovereign. He sent his warriors to lure my men into

142

battle so he could kill them. I, Petr, with the servitors, invoked God's help and fell to fighting the Iakuts. With God's mercy and the good fortune of the Sovereign, God helped us defeat the Iakuts.

During the fight we took two prisoners, the Iakut prince Shureniak of Agasilinsk volost and his nephew. When the Iakuts saw how the Sovereign's wrath was visited upon them, they gathered all Shureniak's tribesmen and ulus people and offered the Great Sovereign their submission. I, Petr, collected the Sovereign's iasak from prince Shureniak and his tribesmen and ulus people and his nephew, with the good fortune of the Sovereign. For the year 1632 we took one sable shuba, and for the year 1633 we collected iasak for the Great Sovereign from Shureniak and his tribesmen consisting of two forties and 25 sables and one red fox. To assure future iasak payment for the Sovereign, I took Shureniak's son Byikta hostage, and I left the syn boiarskii Parfenii Khodyrev behind in the new ostrozhek on the Lena River to make certain that these princes would always be submissive to the Sovereign's mighty hand, and pay iasak for all the years to come.

On September 15, 1633, I, Petr, and the servitors went to the uluses of the Iakut princeling Nogui to collect the Sovereign's iasak, and urged him to submit to the Sovereign's authority. This Iakut prince Nogui did not wish to come into the Sovereign's good graces and refused to submit either himself or his people to the Sovereign's authority. On the contrary, he and all his people tried to drive the servitors and me away from the shore, and they called out insults against the Sovereign Majesty. Keeping in mind my oath of allegiance to the Sovereign, I, Petr, ordered the servitors to fight these Iakuts, and with the Sovereign's good fortune, they captured Nogui's brother in the struggle, and after that the other Iakuts ran off.

When he saw how the Sovereign's anger was manifested against his brother, prince Nogui of the Batulinsk volost and his ulus people, through the luck of the Sovereign, resolved to come under the Sovereign's mercy. Nogui humbly submitted himself to the Great Sovereign, and paid iasak for himself and for his people, and swore allegiance in the future to the Great Sovereign, pledging that he and all his people would be loyal for all time to come to the Sovereign. I, Petr, collected iasak from him, with the luck of the Sovereign, which consisted of 30 sables and two sable shubas, thereby once again bringing profit to the Great Sovereign. I took Nogui's brother as a hostage and left him with the syn boiarskii from Eniseisk ostrog, Parfenii Khodyrev, in the new ostrozhek in the Iakut land which has been built for the iasak collection.

On September 25 of that same year, in accordance with the ukaz of the Sovereign Tsar and Grand Prince Mikhail Fedorovich of all Russia, I, Petr, together with the servitors, built an ostrog [Iakutsk] on the Lena River for the Sovereign Majesty in his distant lands for the purpose of collecting the Sovereign's iasak and to receive the Iakut people in submission. There had never before been any of the Sovereign's ostrogs anywhere on the Lena River in the Iakut territory. I, Petr, built the new ostrozhek for the Sovereign near the Iakut prince Mamyk's ulus and very close to many other uluses, in the heart of the whole Iakut territory.

On October 28 of that year, in accordance with the Sovereign's ukaz, I, Petr, sent servitors from the new ostrozhek on the Lena River to the Iakut prince Burukh and to his children, tribesmen and ulus people, instructing them to bring iasak to the new ostrozhek. The servitors spent three days gathering the Sovereign's iasak, and upon their return to the new ostrozhek, they were questioned in the office and they made their report to me, Petr. They said that when they reached Burukh's uluses they urged him and his children to bring the Sovereign's iasak to the new ostrozhek in return for the Sovereign's favor. But the Iakut prince Burukh and his people did not want to submit to the Sovereign and refused to pay the Sovereign's iasak. They wanted to kill the servitors and me, Petr. Thus I, Petr, and the servitors asked God's mercy and fought them, and with God's mercy and the fortune of the Sovereign we killed 20 Iakut men in battle.

The Iakut prince Burukh, seeing that it was impossible to stand against the Sovereign's Majesty, and frightened by the mighty Sovereign's power, sent two of his nephews to the new ostrozhek, Budui and Tantan, sons of Burbui, and also prince Otkon and Durei. They brought their submission to the Great Sovereign, and begged the Sovereign Tsar to have mercy for their previous disobedience, and beseeched that in the future the Sovereign also be merciful and not order his servitors from Eniseisk ostrog to fight them. They pledged on behalf of Burukh that he and all his people would be loyal for all time to the Great Sovereign. In accordance with the Sovereign's ukaz, I, Petr, brought Burukh's nephews to swear allegiance. I collected iasak for the year 1633 from Burukh and his children and nephews and tribesmen; the Sovereign's iasak consisted of three forties and 20 sables, seven Iakut sable shubas and two red foxes. I gave food and drink to his nephews and leaders and sent them back to their land. [Names follow.]

On November 8 of that same year, in accordance with the Sovereign's ukaz, I, Petr, sent servitors on the Sovereign's service from the new ostrozhek on the Lena River to the Iakut prince Ineno-Oiun to collect iasak for the Sovereign. The servitors traveled four days to reach Ineno-Oiun, and when they returned to the ostrozhek they reported in the headquarters that they had gone to the prince and instructed him to give iasak to the Sovereign in the ostrozhek and receive the Sovereign's favor. But this Iakut prince did not want to come under the Sovereign's mighty hand nor go to the ostrozhek, and he and his people began to attack the servitors. The servitors invoked God's mercy and fought them, and with the luck of the Sovereign they killed many Iakuts in that foray and shed their blood for the Sovereign Tsar and Grand Prince Mikhail Fedorovich of all Russia.

In the struggle they captured prince Ineno-Oiun himself, and others . . . . [missing] In this battle the servitor Prokopii Vasilev was wounded by an arrow in his leg. They brought prince Ineno-Oiun to the ostrozhek, and I, Petr, took him into the office and asked him why he had opposed the Sovereign Majesty, and why he had tried to kill the servitors. The Iakut princeling said they had shot arrows at the servitors out of ignorance, that the Sovereign's men had never come to them before, and that they had never even heard about the Sovereign Majesty. He said he hoped the Sovereign would have mercy now and forgive them for their transgressions; he said that in the future they would willingly serve the Sovereign in all ways. I brought prince Ineno-Oiun to take the oath, and he swore that he and all his people would serve loyally under the Sovereign's mighty hand for all time, and that they would pay iasak. For the year 1633 the prince gave iasak to the Great Sovereign, on behalf of himself and his people, which consisted of 20 sables. [Names follow.]

On March 12 of that same year, 1633, I, Petr, in accordance with the Sovereign's ukaz, sent servitors from Eniseisk ostrog out from the new ostrozhek on the Sovereign's service to collect the Sovereign's iasak from the Iakut prince Ospek and other princes. The servitors traveled for three days to reach Ospek. When they returned to the new ostrozhek they reported that they had gone from the new ostrozhek to prince Ospek in Dubsunsk volost. Two men had gone ahead as advance scouts, Ivan Shcherbak and Stepan Markov. They encountered the Iakut scouts, who shot arrows at our scouts, who then began to fight back. With God's mercy and the luck of the Sovereign, our scouts killed one Iakut scout, and the rest of them ran off and carried this news throughout the uluses.

Iakut people from many of the uluses in Dubsunsk volost gathered together in one ulus and built fortifications and took a stand in these fortified places. The servitors came to these fortifications and summoned the Dubsunsk men to come under the Sovereign's mighty hand and told them to obey the Great Sovereign's command to pay iasak. But the Iakut people shot arrows at the servitors who then advanced on the fortification in battle. With God's mercy and the luck of the Sovereign they managed to take one of the fortifications, and killed 20 leaders in it, but they could not take any of the others by assault, and so they set fire to them with all the Iakut people inside.

Because of their insubordination to the Great Sovereign, only three women managed to escape, and the servitors captured them and brought them to the new ostrozhek. I, Petr, took these prisoners from the servitors and brought them into the office and questioned them as to why the Iakuts had been insubordinate to the Sovereign Majesty. The Iakut women said that the Iakuts had not submitted because they had previously killed five of the Sovereign's servitors and a promyshlennik: Vasilii Bystrovo, Ivan Telenov, Orest Kirnai, Andrei Tyzhnov and Polk Onikiev. There were 87 Iakut men in those fortifications, but prince Ospek was not among them, for he had fled to another ulus. In that battle the Iakuts wounded the attacking servitors. Terentii Grigorev was shot in the left eye and was wounded in the right temple; Ivan Shcherbak was wounded in the neck; Vasilii Gorin lost two fingers from his left hand; Oleg Golovo was shot in the left cheek; and the hired cossack Kuzma Gabyshev was shot clear through his right arm and also in the thigh. [Further names follow.]

After that, prince Ospek of the Dubsunsk volost acknowledged his guilt in refusing to submit to the Sovereign Majesty. He gathered other princes of Dubsunsk volost and came with his people to the new ostrozhek to beg the Sovereign's mercy and ask the Great Sovereign's forgiveness for his transgression. Then the

Dubsunsk volost prince Ospek, Manturakh son of Koch, and Sundei, assembled with their people and took the oath of allegiance to the Great Sovereign. They promised that for all time they would be submissive under the Sovereign's mighty hand, and would pay iasak every year without interruption on behalf of themselves and their people. They begged the Sovereign to have mercy on them, and asked that he order that in the future his servitors would not fight them. After taking the oath of allegiance, these Iakut princes gave the Sovereign's iasak for the year 1633 consisting of 20 sables and a Iakut sable shuba. I, your humble servant, again brought profit to you, Great Sovereign, with the servitors.

Then many Iakut people and princes from various uluses saw that your Sovereign mercy was extended to the guilty, and that you spared those who obeyed you. They realized that all those who disobeyed would suffer the Sovereign's wrath in accordance with the Sovereign's ukaz. Thus all these many Iakut princes and all of their ulus people submitted to the Sovereign's mercy and came under the Sovereign's mighty hand, obediently. They came to the new ostrozhek without fear and took the oath for themselves and for their ulus people to serve the Great Sovereign loyally and pay iasak for themselves and for their people without interruption.

I, Petr, and the servitors gave food and drink to the Iakut princes and their ulus people, in the new ostrozhek, in order to show the favor of the Sovereign Majesty. I then sent them back to their own lands. [Names of princes follow.]

I, Petr Beketov, your humble servant, and the servitors brought these Iakut princes from many different uluses and all of their people under your Sovereign mighty hand, and these and other Iakut princes agreed to remain forever under your Sovereign mighty hand.

The total amount of iasak treasure which I collected on the Lena River in the Iakut territory in your Sovereign's new ostrozhek for the year 1633 was 16 forties of sables and 25 Iakut sable shubas, three red fox and one red fox pup. In addition to this, the servitor Aleksei Arkhipov and his men collected six forties of sables from the Zhigansk and Dolgan people as iasak. Aleksei also collected a tithe for the Sovereign from promyshlenniks in the Zhigansk territory which amounted to ten sables. In these matters I again brought profit to the Great Sovereign. I, Petr Beketov, your humble servant, also collected a tithe for the Sovereign from servitors and promyshlenniks which consisted of 19 forties of sables plus five more sables, ten sable plastinas, two beavers and four red fox.

In this manner, I, Petr, and the servitors, while on the Lena River in the land of the Iakuts and the Tungus, brought profit to the Great Sovereign's iasak treasury and tithe treasury. From the Iakuts and Tungus and servitors and promyshlenniks we collected 41 forties and 15 more sables, 25 Iakut sable shubas, 10 sable plastinas, 2 beavers, 7 red fox and one red fox pup.

That same year I, Petr, in accordance with the Sovereign's ukaz, brought the Sovereign new profit on the Lena River when I collected from the servitors and from the promyshlenniks, from court judgments, furs for the Sovereign's Treasury consisting of two forties and 16 more sables, which were valued at 130 rubles in Eniseisk.

I, Petr, and the servitors built the ostrozhek on the Lena River in the Iakut territory with the Sovereign's luck, for the purpose of making the Sovereign's iasak collection from the natives for the year 1633. In accordance with the Sovereign's ukaz I left behind in the ostrozhek the Eniseisk syn boiarskii Parfenii Kodyrev, and I turned over the hostages to him. I, Petr, exchanged written reports with Parfenii, and I received a receipt from him. [Names of servitors follow.]

On June 15, 1633, I, Petr, in an effort to seek out new profit for the Great Sovereign, and to extend the Sovereign's patrimony, selected some of the servitors and sent them down the Lena River on the Sovereign's service to the mouth of the river, to the sea, to collect the Sovereign's iasak and to explore new lands. [Names follow.]

Reference: TsGADA, f. Iakutskaia prikaznaia izba, op. 4, stolb No. 368, ll. 181–161 [in this unit the pages are numbered in reverse order].
See: *Materialy po istorii Iakutii v XVII veka: dokumenty iasachnogo sbora* (Moscow: 1970), III, 1072–1096.

46

NOT BEFORE 1635

A REPORT FROM THE SIBIRSKII PRIKAZ CONCERNING PETR BEKETOV'S
EXPEDITION TO THE BRATSK LANDS AND THE AMOUNT OF IASAK HE
COLLECTED FOR THE YEARS 1629–1633

In the year 1629 the late voevoda Vasilii Argamakov wrote to the Great Sovereign Tsar and Grand Prince Mikhail Fedorovich of all Russia from Eniseisk ostrog in Siberia. In the year 1628 he sent servitors to collect the Sovereign's iasak in Eniseisk uezd, in accordance with the iasak books for that year. In addition to this iasak collection, he sent Petr Beketov and servitors to collect the Sovereign's iasak from distant new lands, in order to bring additional profit to the Sovereign.

Petr Beketov and his men went along the Upper Tunguska River where iasak people fish because these Tungus had not yet been firmly brought under the authority of the Sovereign Tsar. They gave little iasak and pominki and did not fulfill their quota. Others did not give anything, and attacked the servitors. They killed three servitors, including a *tselovalnik*. Petr was ordered to build an ostrozhek there. Petr Beketov built the ostrozhek with the help of the servitors and promyshlenniks, and he summoned the Tungus people to come to the ostrozhek and to bring hostages.

When he had taken the hostages he collected the iasak with great profit, as previously. He made detailed entries in the iasak books as to the amount of iasak he collected for the Sovereign. The voevoda Vasilii Argamakov personally signed the Eniseik iasak books for the year 1629, showing the amount of iasak sent to the Sovereign from Eniseisk ostrog in Siberia.

While Petr Beketov and his servitors were traveling to the Tunguska River to build an ostrozhek near the fishing grounds, they collected iasak from Prince Irkan and his people consisting of two forties of sables and ten sable plastinas and two sable shubas.

In the year 1630 Vasilii Argamakov reported to the Sovereign from Eniseisk ostrog in Siberia that in the year 1629 he sent Petr Beketov and Eniseisk servitors and 19 cossacks from Eniseisk ostrog to the Bratsk rapids to collect the Sovereign's iasak. Petr Beketov and the servitors collected iasak from the Tunguska area, below the Bratsk rapids, and the iasak consisted of 15 forties and two sables. From the Bratsk rapids Petr and the servitors journeyed into the land of the Bratsk for seven weeks to collect the Sovereign's iasak so there would be great profit to the Sovereign from the iasak collection. They summoned the Bratsk people to come under the Tsarist mighty protection and pay iasak. During their travels in the Bratsk land, they starved and had to eat grass and roots, but they were able to bring the princes Kodogon, Kulziz and Aldai and their Bratsk people under the Tsar's mighty protection, with the understanding that these princes and the Bratsk people would henceforth be undeviating subjects of the Sovereign Tsar's authority, and would pay iasak in Eniseisk ostrog. For the year 1629 they collected two forties and three sables from the Bratsk people.

In the Eniseisk iasak record books for the year 1629, the voevoda Vasilii Argamakov personally recorded the amount of iasak sent to the Sovereign from Eniseisk ostrog in Siberia. In the new lands below Bratsk rapids Petr Beketov and his servitors collected the Sovereign's iasak for the year 1629 from the Tungus and Bratsk people, amounting to 17 forties and nine sables, plus fox plastinas and two beaver ski-skins.

It is impossible to ascertain the value, in Siberia and in Moscow, of the furs Petr Beketov collected in 1628 and 1629, because the Eniseisk iasak furs from former and from new iasak-paying people were appraised together, rather than separately.

In the year 1632 the voevoda Zhdan Kondyrev reported to the Sovereign from Eniseisk ostrog that in 1631 Petr Beketov and 30 Eniseisk servitors were sent on government service. They went from Eniseisk ostrog onto the mighty Lena River to collect the Sovereign's iasak and to explore new lands.

In the year 1635 the voevoda Andrei Plemiannikov wrote to the Sovereign from Eniseisk ostrog and included a service report about Petr Beketov and his men, regarding the newly discovered lands, the rebellious iasak people, and the iasak collection. The service report states that Petr Beketov and the servitors went to the Bratsk land in the upper Lena River, to the mouth of the Ona River, to the Bratsk and Tungus people, to collect the Sovereign's iasak. The Bratsk and Tungus were hostile and tried to kill the servitors. Petr and his men were under siege for three days by the Bratsk people, but with God's mercy and the luck of the Sovereign, Petr and his servitors defeated the Bratsk, and in various

Samoed woman and man in stylized winter garments. Early
Dutch engraving.

attacks, killed 90 Bratsk, Iakut and Tungus men. In those same
skirmishes the Bratsk wounded three servitors and two Tungus
who were serving as guides.

After that, these Bratsk and Tungus iasak-paying people were
brought under the Sovereign's Tsarist mighty hand for all time,
undeviatingly. And from these new iasak people, in the years
1632 and 1633, they collected the Sovereign's iasak consisting of
23 forties and 31 sables, and also one red fox. They took a prince
as hostage.

Reference: TsGADA, f. 214—Sibirskii prikaz, stolb. No. 6646/402, ll.
114–120.
See: G. N. Rumiantsev, ed. *Sbornik dokumentov po istorii Buriatii V XVII
VEK* (Ulan-Ude: 1960), vyp. 1, 26–27.

47

MAY 3, 1636

A GRAMOTA FROM TSAR MIKHAIL FEDOROVICH TO THE VOEVODA OF TOMSK, PRINCE IVAN ROMADANOVSKII, CONCERNING MEASURES TO SUBDUE HOSTILE NATIVES IN KRASNOIARSK UEZD

From the Tsar and Grand Prince Mikhail Fedorovich of all Russia to Siberia, to Tomsk, to our voevodas Prince Ivan Ivanovich Romadanovskii and Andrei Andreevich Bunakov, and to our diak Anisim Trofimov. In this year, 1636, the voevoda of Krasnoiarsk, Nikita Karamyshev, has written to us, and enclosed a petition on behalf of the Krasnoiarsk servitors signed by ataman Demian Zlobin. In this petition it is stated that in accordance with our ukaz it was ordered that 300 men be stationed in Krasnoiarsk ostrog. Until 1635 only 200 men served us in Krasnoiarsk ostrog, and presently there are 250 men there.

In accordance with our ukaz of 1635, 100 mounted cossacks were ordered to be stationed in Krasnoiarsk ostrog. Voevoda Nikita Karamyshev selected 100 of the servitors to serve as mounted cossacks, and he paid them from our Treasury the same amount paid to mounted servitors in Tobolsk and Tomsk. However, this amount is insufficient, because it is very expensive for them to buy horses which cost from 15 to 20 rubles each, and in order to buy horses, they have had to spend their entire salary, and they have even had to sell their coats.

In the year 1635 traitorous and disobedient Kirgiz people came to Krasnoiarsk ostrog, together with many other natives, and killed many of the servitors and agricultural peasants, and drove off their horses. This Kirgiz attack caused great losses, so they had to make their way to Tomsk to buy riding horses, and then had to buy draught horses in Tomsk, and those at a dear price. When they drove these horses back to Krasnoiarsk ostrog, half of them died.

On September 14, 1635, the same Kirgiz people, having joined forces with natives disloyal and disobedient to us, the Arinsk and the Kachinsk Tatars and many others again attacked Krasnoiarsk ostrog and drove off all the horses belonging to the servitors and the agricultural peasants. They killed many peasants in the fields and burned all our grain in the fields.

Food provisions which are sent from Tobolsk as salary to the servitors are sent in full, and in Eniseisk ostrog the voevodas issue full rations of provisions to the Eniseisk servitors but in Krasnoiarsk ostrog they send only two or three chetverts per man, and these provisions are spoiled, and are of poor quality. The Kirgiz will not allow our agricultural peasants to cultivate the land at Krasnoi Iar, and the servitors do not have anyone to guard the peasants. Three hundred men are not enough for Krasnoiarsk ostrog. There is no one to pursue natives who are disobedient and disloyal to us. There are many hostile lands near Krasnoiarsk ostrog. In the future the servitors will have no money, and no place to buy horses. Saddle horses belonging to the nearby Tatars have all been driven off to Kirgizia. We are asked to have mercy and send more servitors to Krasnoiarsk ostrog. If no additional servitors are sent to Krasnoiarsk ostrog, then those presently in Kransoi Iar should be withdrawn.

When you receive this our gramota, you are to order that this problem in Krasnoiarsk ostrog be investigated carefully. In the future our servitors are to remain in Krasnoiarsk ostrog and protect the ostrog, the agricultural peasants and the iasak-paying people from hostile and traitorous natives. These warlike people who are disloyal to us must be subdued through battle and brought under our mighty Tsarist hand if possible. Any hostile lands which are near Krasnoiarsk ostrog, however extensive they may be, and the hostile people in them, should also be pacified. If, in your judgment, these Krasnoiarsk servitors cannot remain in Krasnoiarsk ostrog in the future; if the hostile territories and traitorous natives cannot be subdued by force and brought under our mighty Tsarist hand; if there is no one to pursue them; if in the future a large number of servitors cannot survive in Krasnoiarsk ostrog; if Krasnoiarsk ostrog and the agricultural peasants and the iasak-paying people cannot be protected; and if hostile lands cannot be pacified through war, then you must investigate these matters fully.

If in your judgment, and in your assessment of the local situation, there is no one available there, then you are to send as many of our servitors as possible from Tomsk to Krasnoiarsk ostrog. You are to order them and the Krasnoiarsk servitors in accordance with our earlier ukaz as well as this present ukaz, to invoke God's mercy and fight these hostile people. Pursue them, as far as merciful God will help you, so that these hostile lands and their war-like and traitorous inhabitants will be pacified through battle and turned from their evil ways. You are to protect yourself and Krasnoiarsk ostrog and our agricultural peasants and the iasak-paying people from them. Do not permit any interference in the collection of the iasak, as has been the case in the past. Try, inso-far as you are able, to gain the most profit.

Then, God willing, if they bring hostile territories under our mighty Tsarist hand, these are to be fortified and the people brought to take the oath, so that in the future they will be under our mighty Tsarist hand without any disobedience or treason, and they will pay as much iasak as possible, just as their brothers earlier did.

You are to strengthen your position by ordering that hostages be taken. These are to be leaders or their children and brothers and relatives. They are to be held in Krasnoiarsk ostrog, with great care. You are to issue orders to these people, and assure them of our favor, so that they will live in their encampments and pay our iasak, as much as possible, without interruption, as their brothers did previously. They may hunt without interference, and are not to commit any treason. As soon as they come under our mighty Tsarist hand and pay iasak to us and give hostages, we will reward them by not sending our servitors into battle against them. We will instruct our voevodas and servitors not to impose any hardships or unreasonable burdens on them.

You, Prince Ivan, are to write a letter to the voevoda Fedor Miakinin in Krasnoiarsk ostrog concerning this. Instruct him that on the basis of our earlier ukaz as well as the present ukaz, and depending on the local circumstances, he is to go to war against the hostile lands, against the warlike people, and against those who are disloyal to us. Invoking God's mercy, he is to seek them out, and insofar as merciful God may help him, he is to live with great caution in Krasnoiarsk ostrog. And, God willing, he is to pacify the people in hostile territories and bring them under our mighty Tsarist hand; he is to maintain this condition by taking hostages, and both Fedor and the servitors are to treat these people well and with great courtesy so that they will remain under our mighty Tsarist hand and pay iasak.

Prince Ivan, you are to write to Fedor in the strongest possible terms warning him of our disfavor if he and his men inflict any unnecessary hardships or impose burdens on our former iasak-paying people who come back under our mighty Tsarist hand, and thereby drive them away from us. They are to be assured of our favor, so that with this in mind they will persuade their relatives to pay us iasak, and to bring other persons from hostile lands to come under our Tsarist mighty hand and pay as much iasak as possible, as much as their relatives used to pay.

You are to send us a report in Moscow on what you do about this in Krasnoiarsk ostrog on the basis of your investigations. Report whether you are enlisting the aid of servitors already in Krasnoiarsk ostrog without requesting help from additional servitors from Tomsk; or whether your investigation and local circumstances lead you to have servitors from Tomsk sent to make a reconnaissance; or whether you may decide to take some other action on the basis of new information. Send this report with anyone who is available. The report is to be delivered to the Prikaz of the Kazan Dvorets, to our boiar, Prince Boris Mikhailovich Lykov, and to our diaks, Fedor Panov and Nikifor Shipulin. We have already written about this to our voevoda at Krasnoiarsk ostrog, Fedor Miakinin, and we have instructed him to report on this matter to Tomsk in the future. On the basis of his reports, you are to issue an ukaz and communicate with him, according to our ukaz, without delay. Do this as outlined in our gramota and instructions, precisely as you have been ordered, using your judgment in regard to the situation then and there and all available evidence, so that there will be no result detrimental to our affairs.

See: G. F. Müller, *Istoriia Sibiri* (Moscow-Leningrad: 1937), I, 433–435.

48

BETWEEN JULY 14 AND AUGUST 12, 1636

A REPORT FROM THE VOEVODA OF TOMSK, PRINCE IVAN ROMADANOV-
SKII, TO TSAR MIKHAIL FEDOROVICH AND THE PRIKAZ OF THE KAZAN
DVORETS REGARDING SENDING EMISSARIES TO ALTYN-TSAR AND THE
MONGOLS

To the Sovereign Tsar and Grand Prince Mikhail Fedorovich of all Russia, your humble servants Ivan Romadanovskii, Andrei Bunakov and Anisim Trofimov humbly report.

On July 7, 1636, Sire, envoys of the Altyn [-tsar], Torkhan Khonzin, Uran Khonzin and eight other men, in addition to the Tomsk deti boiarskie Vasilii Starkov and Luka Vasilev, and Tomsk servitors, all arrived in Tomsk and delivered, intact according to the inventory, your official gifts and your Sovereign largesse destined for Altyn-tsar. In accordance with your ukaz, Sovereign, your envoys have been ordered to proceed to Altyn-tsar. The men chosen for that assignment are the Tomsk deti boiarskie and servitors, led by Iakov Tukhachevskii and his men. They are to convoy your official gifts from Tomsk to the Altyn-tsar. They are to be accompanied by Altyn's envoys leaving from Tomsk.

When Altyn's envoys left Tomsk to go to you in Moscow, Sire, the Kirgiz attacked your Sovereign towns of Kuznetsk and Krasnoiarsk, as well as the Tomsk iasak-paying volost. Because of this Kirgiz treachery, we, your humble servants, did not allow the shipment of your official provisions and gifts and the envoys to proceed on to Altyn-tsar. Instead, we selected four of the Tomsk servitors and four of Altyn's men and sent them to Altyn-tsar to inform him of the situation regarding your gifts to him, and his envoys and yours. We also instructed the Tomsk servitors and Altyn's men that if any of the Altyn's men were in Kirgizia they should arrange transport and guides for them and send them from Kirgizia back to Tomsk with any news. If there were none of Altyn's people in Kirgizia, then the servitors and Altyn's men were instructed to proceed directly to Altyn-tsar, so that he might send guides and transport to bring your gifts and envoys to him without endangering either the gifts or the envoys.

We have written to Altyn-tsar that he is to send his warriors against those traitorous Kirgiz people, and bring them under your

Equipment for hunting and food gathering reveals primitive means of hauling and carrying. From Makovetskii, *Byt i iskusstvo russkogo naseleniia vostochnoi Sibiri*, Vol. 1.

mighty Sovereign hand in slavery. Their leaders are to be sent to Tomsk as hostages.

Sire, as soon as the Tomsk servitors return from Altyn-tsar with the information that he will provide guides and transport for your Sovereign provisions and envoys, we, your humble servants, will send your official envoys and gifts on to Altyn-tsar from Tomsk, as well as his own envoys. We will send a report to your Sire, on the very day we let them leave Tomsk.

Reference: LOA AN SSSR, F. Portfeli Millera, op. 4, kn. 17, dok No. 169, ll. 289–289 ob.

See: M. I. Golman and G. I. Slesarchuk, eds. *Materialy po istorii russko-mongolskykh otnoshenii 1636–1654* (Moscow: 1974), 30–31.

49

BETWEEN OCTOBER 6, 1636 AND JANUARY 13, 1637

EXCERPT FROM A REPORT COMPILED IN THE SIBIRSKII PRIKAZ CONCERNING AN ATTACK ON TARA BY THE OIRATS, AND THEIR SUBJUGATION BY THE RUSSIANS

The Siberian servitors at Tara report the following to the Sovereign Tsar and Grand Prince Mikhail Fedorovich of all Russia. On January 26, 1635, the voevodas of Tara, Prince Fedor Belskii and Neupokoi Kokishkin, sent a report from the town of Tara in Siberia to the Sovereign Tsar and Grand Prince Mikhail Fedorovich of all Russia. They reported that on September 12, 1635, many Kalmyk warriors belonging to Kuisha-taisha, led by his two sons, Onbo and Konga, and the grandsons of Kuchum, together with insurgents against the Sovereign, and iurt and volost Tatars led by Kochash Tonatarov and his men, attacked Tara. They routed the small garrison and killed some of the men and their horses. Some fled into town and others escaped into the forest. Servitors who were working in the fields were seized by these warriors and killed. Others were captured with their wives and children, and their horses and cattle were driven off. There was no possible way to protect them because the warriors attacked the town of Tara from different directions.

They sent the Bukhara merchant, Konogach Dosmametev, as an emissary to the town and the ostrog. The Tobolsk and Tara servitors, Litva, mounted and foot cossacks and streltsy were sent into battle against these Kalmyks. They battled the Kalmyks from morning until night, and repulsed them from the town and the ostrog. During the Kalmyk attack Konogach turned against the Sovereign and went over to the Kalmyks, and his wife, mother and brother also turned traitor and went with him. It was impossible to pursue the Kalmyks because of our shortage of men. We had very few people in Tara, while they had many. When the Kalmyks came to the ostrog, they demanded that the Bukhara envoy Kazyi be released to them, and said they would release all the Tara people they had taken. Thus this clash was caused by Kazyi, not by any disagreement.

On October 13, 1635, the sons of Kuisha-taisha, Onbo and Ianza, and Kuishin's son-in-law, the *torgout* Onbo, and many other

A hand-hewn storehouse near the Angara River (Bratsk region).
From Saburova, *Kultura i byt russkogo naseleniia Priangaria.*

Kalmyk warriors attacked Tara. They seized and killed all the servitors and agricultural peasants and iurt Tatars who had left the town to gather hay and wood. They took others prisoner, and then attacked the town and the ostrog. Their leader on this Tara expedition was a man from the Ailyn volost who turned against the Sovereign, the iasak-paying Tatar, Saban.

Prince Fedor and Neupokoi sent into battle the following: the Tobolsk syn boiarskii Boris Cherkasov; the Tara Litva Captain Andrei Kropotov; the leader of the mounted cossacks, Nazar Zhadovskii; the Tatar leader, Voin Dementev; the ataman of the volost Tatars, Vlas Kolashnikov; the Tobolsk streltsy sotnik, Volodimir Klepikov; the ataman Gavriil Ilin; the Tara sotnik Malafei Maksheev; the ataman of the foot cossacks, Aleksei Romanov; and also Tobolsk and Tara servitors.

Battle was waged with the Kalmyks near town from morning to night. The Kalmyks withdrew to a distance of ten versts from town. On October 14 the Kalmyks again advanced on the town, and in a meeting with the Russians, said that they wanted the Bukhara envoy, Kazyi, released to them. They said if the envoy were not released, Kuisha-taisha had ordered them not to leave the town, but to continue their attack.

Prince Fedor and Neupokoi, having fortified the settlement, invoked God's mercy and sent all of the following against the Kalmyk warriors: the Tobolsk syn boiarskii Boris Cherkasov; the Tobolsk servitors; the Tatars; the Tara Litva captain Andrei Kropotov and the deti boiarskie, atamans, servitors' Litva, mounted cossacks and agricultural peasants; the leader of the Tatar unit, Voin Dementev, and iurt Tatars; the Tobolsk streltsy captain Volodimir Klepikov with streltsy and foot cossacks; the Tara sotnik, Malafei Maksheev, with streltsy and foot cossacks; and the ataman Vlas Kolashnikov, with volost Tatars.

With God's grace and the fortune of the Sovereign, they killed Kuisha's son-in-law and many Kalmyk warriors, drove off 300 of their horses, and seized their prisoners, both Russian and Tatar. The names of the Russians and Tatars who were killed or taken prisoner during the previous attack have been sent to the Sovereign, and a list has been drawn up with commendations for those persons who have served with particular valor.

The Tara servitors petition the Sovereign Tsar and Grand Prince Mikhail Fedorovich of all Russia, asking that the Sovereign reward them for their service with his Sovereign largesse, as God may inspire him.

Reference: TsGADA, f. Sibirskii prikaz, stolb. 172, ll. 126, 128–130, 137.
See: M. I. Golman and G. I. Slesarchuk, eds. *Materialy po istorii russko-mongolskykh otnoshenii, 1636–1654* (Moscow: 1974), 167–168.

50

A LETTER FROM DAICHIN-NOION, BROTHER OF THE ALTYN-TSAR, TO
TSAR MIKHAIL FEDOROVICH, REQUESTING LARGESSE

To the Sovereign Tsar and Grand Prince Mikhail Fedorovich,
Autocrat of all Russia, Daichin-noion sends greeting.
Greeting to you, Sovereign Tsar and Grand Prince Mikhail
Fedorovich of all Russia. May you have a long life. Sire, our father
served you and was loyal to you and sent envoys to you. Sire,
he serves you still, and is loyal. Recently, Sire, you have given
presents to my brother, Altyn-tsar, and you have allowed him to
live under your mighty Sovereign hand. He rejoices over this,
that the Sovereign has favored him with his Sovereign largesse,
and he is pleased to serve the Sovereign and give him tribute. He
now offers *kuiak* [metal armor], greaves, a helmet, a leopard pelt,
a snow leopard pelt, two wolverines, a lynx with tassels and 90
sables. For the Tsaritsa and Grand Princess Evdokiia Lukianovna,
wife of the Sovereign Tsar and Grand Prince Mikhail Fedorovich
of all Russia, he sends silk. And for the Sovereign Tsarevich,
Prince Aleksei Mikhailovich of all Russia, he sends a belt studded
with silver.

He asks that the Sovereign Tsar and Grand Prince Mikhail
Fedorovich of all Russia give him 1,000 gold coins, 108 large red
beads, 1,000 fresh-water pearls, enough woolen fabric for 1,000
men, a black fox shuba, a fine suit of armor and a sword. He asks
permission to send two envoys, Olzet Tarkhan-baksha and Bokaka,
and a *koshevar*.

Reference: LOA AN SSSR, f. Portfeli Millera, op. 4, dok. No. 179, l. 315.
See: M. I. Golman and G. I. Slesarchuk, eds. *Materialy po istorii russko-
mongolskykh otnoshenii, 1636–1654* (Moscow: 1974), 75.

51

NOT AFTER FEBRUARY 4, 1637

A LETTER FROM ALTYN-TSAR TO TSAR MIKHAIL FEDOROVICH SWEAR-
ING ALLEGIANCE AND PROMISING TO GUIDE RUSSIAN ENVOYS TO
CHINA

To the Great Sovereign White Tsar and Grand Prince Mikhail Fedorovich, Autocrat of all Russia, your subject, Altyn-tsar, humbly reports.

I, Altyn-tsar, will serve you, with all my horde, as I have sworn. I will cause no harm to your state people, as you, Sovereign White Tsar, have instructed me. I am ready to be under your mighty Sovereign protection. In accordance with my counsel, Dural-tabun and Taichin-tabun have also sworn their allegiance to you, Sovereign.

When your Sovereign envoys, Iakov and Druzhina, came here, Druzhina rebuked me and lied to me and insulted me. I sent my envoys to you, Great Sovereign, requesting redress. Now that your Sovereign envoys are here, I have again taken an oath of allegiance, for the second time. I have persuaded my brother, Dural-tabun, to come under your protection with his children and brothers and his entire ulus.

God give the Sovereign Tsar and Grand Prince Mikhail Fedorovich of all Russia good health and long life. I rejoice to serve the Sovereign with my entire ulus; I will go on service wherever the Sovereign orders me; I am ready to proceed with all my horde. Great Sovereign, God is in heaven, and you, Sire, are on earth. You have granted me, your subject, my request. All lands wish to be under your suzerainty. You have granted my request, and I will pay tribute every year.

I have asked my brother, Dural-tabun, to search for the livestock which the Kirgiz people ran off from your state towns. If they are not recovered, then when your envoys come in the future, I will personally battle those Kirgiz and return your iasak-paying people and their livestock to you, and hand over the leaders to you.

In the future, Sovereign White Tsar, favor me, Altyn, and do not send me such envoys as Druzhina Ogarkov.

Your Sovereign envoys, Stepan and Andrei, delivered your Sovereign gifts in full as listed in your Sovereign gramota. I beg you, Sovereign to accept the following from me as tribute: two snow leopards, 250 sables and five lengths of silk. Sovereign, I now humbly offer this to you, but in the future I will give a larger tribute. I beg the Sovereign to grant me a request. In the past when I asked, the Sovereign granted my request. Now it is up to the Sovereign, whatever he may wish to give me. If the Sovereign would give me 8,000 or 10,000 men, I would bring many lands under the Sovereign's authority, and these people would live in Tomsk. When my envoys returned from Moscow these 10,000 would accompany the envoys and be stationed in Tomsk. As soon as these people were available, I would write to Tomsk about them. And may it please the Sovereign to give me pearls, two lengths of *kufter* [Italian gold and silver brocaded silk] and yellow silk and brick red silk.

Sovereign, if you decide to send your envoys to the Chinese lands or the Tungus lands or to the Argan [Noroganchin?], I will be ready to guide them and give them provision. And, Sire, if you should send two or three men to look for towns to be brought under Moscow's control, I will be ready to take my whole ulus to bring those towns and all their lands under your suzerainty. Sire, instruct your envoys to go by horse, not by boat, so they will be able to come more quickly. I will not detain the envoys; they may move about at will.

Reference: TsGADA, f. Sibirskii prikaz, stolb. 74, ll. 46–49.
See: N. F. Demidova and V. S. Miasnikov, eds. *Russko-kitaiskie otnosheniia v XVII veke: Materialy i dokumenty (1608–1691)* (Moscow: 1969), I, 108–109.

52

FEBRUARY 28, 1638

A LETTER PATENT FROM TSAR MIKHAIL FEDOROVICH ACCEPTING
ALTYN-TSAR INTO RUSSIAN SUZERAINTY

By the grace of God, from the Great Sovereign Tsar and
Grand Prince Mikhail Fedorovich, Autocrat of all Russia,
and Sovereign and Possessor of many realms, to Altyn-tsar: our
Tsarist Majesty's gracious greetings.

You have sent your envoys to us, the Great Sovereign, on
many occasions, requesting that we, the Tsarist Majesty, grant
you, Altyn-tsar, the privilege of being received under our Tsarist
Majesty's mighty hand, with your brothers and sons and nephews
and grandsons, and with all your tabuns and your entire horde.
You promise that you, Altyn-tsar, and all your horde, will serve
us, the Great Sovereign, loyally; you will swear allegiance, be
steadfast, pay tribute and be faithful to us, the Great Sovereign.

Further, you, Altyn-tsar, say that on your own behalf and for
your entire horde, in accordance with your faith, you will take an
oath of allegiance, that you and all your brothers, sons, grandsons, nephews, tabuns, and your entire horde will be under our
Tsarist mighty hand, in our Tsarist gracious command, and will
be obedient, forever, undeviatingly. You will pay us, the Great
Sovereign, tribute from yourself and from your entire horde. You
will be in our Tsarist Majesty's service, battle our disobedient
subjects, and go with your whole horde wherever the Sovereign
may send you. You will adhere firmly and steadfastly to this law
and to your oath.

By our ukaz Iakov Tukhachevskii and the poddiak Druzhina
Ogarkov went to you as envoys, with our gifts, from the town of
Tomsk. They had instructions to administer the oath to you in
person. But you, Altyn-tsar, did not take the oath personally. You
authorized your brothers, Dural-tabun and Doichin-tabun, and
your son-in-law, Doiun-tabun, to take the oath for you. You sent
petitions to us, the Great Sovereign, with Iakov and with the
poddiak Druzhina. You sent tribute with your envoys, Dural and
Ural Khonzin. In your petitions, Altyn-tsar, you asked that we,
the Great Sovereign, accept you, Altyn-tsar, under our Tsarist
mighty hand. Therefore we, the Great Sovereign, rewarded your
envoys Dural and Ural Khonzhin, and permitted them to look on

our Tsarist eyes [admitted them into our presence], and having given them our Tsarist largesse, we sent them back to you. We instructed them to take back to you our Tsarist Majesty's letter patent, and ordered that they be accompanied by our envoys from Tomsk.

In our letter to you, Altyn-tsar, we stated that in view of our Tsarist Majesty's largesse and favor, you, Altyn-tsar are to serve us, the Great Sovereign, be loyal to us, obey our commands implicitly, and that you are to personally take the oath of allegiance, according to your own faith, in the presence of our envoys, as you are instructed in writing. This instruction has been sent with them, and you are to adhere to that oath by law, firmly and undeviatingly.

You are to send tribute and additional gifts to us, the Tsarist Majesty. We, the Great Sovereign, will hold you, Altyn-tsar, in our Tsarist mercy and favor, and will defend you against your enemies, depending on your service and loyalty to us, the Great Sovereign.

On April 23, 1637, Stepan Aleksandrov and his men came to Tomsk from you, Altyn-tsar. With them you, Altyn-tsar, sent your envoys, Mergen Deg and his men, with tribute and petitions. Our stolnik and voevoda, Prince Ivan Ivanovich Romadanovskii and his men informed us, the Great Sovereign, and sent your envoys on to us in Moscow. They report, and this is also confirmed by our envoys who visited you, that they gave you our Tsarist letter patent and our Tsarist Majesty's gifts which had been sent with them for you. They informed you about the oath that you, Altyn-tsar, were to take to us, the Great Sovereign, seeing our Tsarist Majesty's great generosity and rewards; you were to swear your loyalty in accordance with your own faith on behalf of yourself and all your brothers, sons, nephews and grandsons; and you were to take an oath in person on behalf of your entire horde.

Further, you, Altyn-tsar, told our envoys that you, Altyn-tsar, and your entire horde would abide by your former oath of loyalty firmly and implicitly, and that in the future you would continue to do so, but that at the present you did not need to swear this again because in your law there has never before been anything like this, and the tsars do not take an oath in person. So you ordered your father and your lama, Dain Mergen-lanza, and your brother Dural-tabun, to take the oath in your place, on the document which was sent with our envoys. However, in order to give greater credence to that document on which they took the oath for you, you, Altyn-tsar, laid your hand on it; you also ordered that the lama and Dural-tabun place their hands on it. Then you sent them to us, the Great Sovereign, with due ceremony.

We, the Great Sovereign, rewarded these envoys of yours, Mergen Deg and his men; we permitted them to look on the eyes of our Tsarist Majesty, and we accepted your petition from them, Altyn-tsar, and ordered that it be translated. We have graciously heard its content.

Your petition repeats the same thing that our envoys reported: that the envoys of our Tsarist Majesty, Stepan and Bazhen and their men, came from us, the Great Sovereign, to you, Altyn-tsar; they brought our Tsarist Majesty's letter and gifts; they informed you of the oath which you were to swear to us, the Great Sovereign; and they further informed you that you are to swear allegiance to us in person, in accordance with your own faith, in their presence, as stipulated, on your own behalf and on behalf of your children, brothers and tabuns, and on behalf of your entire horde.

And you, Altyn-tsar, wishing our Tsarist favor for yourself, took the oath in the presence of our envoys, Stepan and Bazhen and their men, and ordered that your father and your teacher, lama Dain Mergen-lanza and your brother Dural-tabun take the oath, on the oath document. After you took the great oath, in accordance with your faith, you drank from the golden goblet, showing that you, Altyn-tsar, will be under our Tsarist Majesty's mighty hand, and the hands of our Sovereign sons, the Lord Tsarevich Prince Aleksei Mikhailovich and the Lord Tsarevich Prince Ivan Mikhailovich. You will be under their gracious command and obey them for all time, undeviatingly.

You will serve us, the Great Sovereign, loyally, and will wish us good in all things. Wherever our Tsarist Majesty may order you to go, against our disobedient subjects, you will go with your entire horde. You will not commit or contemplate any violence against our Tsarist Majesty's towns and people. You will pay tribute to us, the Great Sovereign, without interruption, in full, as stipulated in the oath document. And for greater affirmation, you, Altyn-tsar personally, and the lama and Dural-tabun, placed your hands on that oath document, signifying that you will be forever loyal and steadfast in all ways.

Furthermore, all the rulers who camp near you, Altyn-tsar, who wish to come under our mighty Tsarist hand, are to give tribute to us, the Great Sovereign; and we will reward them with gifts. You will order your brother, Dural-tabun, to pursue the Kirgiz people who drove off the horses and livestock from our towns and took the iasak-paying people prisoner. If they do not obey your brother, you will march against the Kirgiz yourself, and recover the iasak-paying people and the horses and the live-stock which the Kirgiz took.

Return these to our towns, and behead the Kirgiz leaders. If we, the Great Sovereign, wish to send our envoys to the Chinese Tungus lands, you will provide guides, provisions and transport for those envoys. You will also wish many years of health and good fortune for us, the Great Sovereign. And, Altyn-tsar, you are sending to us, the Great Sovereign, with your envoys Mergen Deg and Arkhan Tarsuk, your tribute which consists of Chinese silk embroidered with gold, four lengths of silk in various colors, two beaver pelts, one Siberian snow leopard, and 250 sables. Your son, Irechin-taisha sends our son, the Lord Tsarevich Prince Aleksei Mikhailovich, two lengths of silk. Your other son, Serenka-taisha, sends our other son, the Lord Tsarevich Prince Ivan Mikhailovich, two lengths of silk.

Now we, the Great Sovereign, will reward you, Altyn-tsar, and order that your tribute be accepted from your envoys. But in the future, Altyn-tsar, you must send us a larger tribute. The items you previously requested from us, the Great Sovereign, have been granted to you. Now you also request that we, the Great Sovereign, in our Tsarist largesse, grant you, Altyn-tsar, your wish and send you a gift of pearls, as many as we may choose to send, two lengths of Italian silk, yellow silk, brick-colored silk, and also that we give presents to your envoys and allow them to return to you, sending our trusted men with them as our envoys.

We, the Great Sovereign Tsar and Grand Prince Mikhail Fedorovich, Autocrat of all Russia, Tsarist Majesty, praise you, Altyn-tsar, for seeking our Tsarist Majesty's favor and gifts, and for wishing to come under our mighty Tsarist hand with your entire horde. You will serve under our gracious Tsarist direction and be obedient for all eternity, undeviatingly. You have taken the oath to us, the Great Sovereign, on your own behalf, according to your faith, and have ordered that your father and your teacher, the lama Dain Mergen-lanza and your brother, Dural-tabun, take the same oath. And in order to even more deeply affirm that oath, you, Altyn-tsar, personally, and the lama and Dural-tabun placed your hands on the oath document.

We will keep you under our Tsarist Majesty's mighty hand, in our Tsarist gracious favor and protection; we will defend you against your enemies. We have sent your envoy Mergen Deg and his men back to you with our Tsarist gifts. In accordance with your request, we, the Great Sovereign, have ordered that the following be sent to you as gifts from us: 28½ *zolotniks* [about ⅓ pound] of fine large pearls, three lengths of Italian silk, one each in black, yellow and green, each length being ten arshins long. We have also sent five arshins of the finest green broadcloth, twelve bales of fine broadcloth in various other colors, measuring four arshins per bale; six strings of large red beads and twelve strings of regular size red beads strung on silver and gold with fine pearl clasps. We also send 188 strings of red beads without clasps and six pounds of fine amber beads, strung.

To your tsaritsa, we send our gifts of fine Italian silk and fine wide Venetian taffeta. To your sons, the tsareviches Irechin and Katach, we send gifts from our sons, the Lord Tsareviches, Prince Aleksei Mikhailovich and Prince Ivan Mikhailovich—a fine steel saber with a silver scabbard.

Now, Altyn-tsar, seeing our Tsarist Majesty's favor and gifts which are sent to you, you are to serve us and be loyal to us, the Great Sovereign, and you are to be trustworthy in accordance with the oath taken on your behalf in the presence of our envoys, Iakov Tukhachevskii and Druzhina Ogarkov, by your brothers, Dural-tabun and Taichin-tabun and your son-in-law Doiun-tabun. In the presence of our envoys, Stepan Grechanin and Bazhen Kortashov and their men, your father and your teacher, lama Dain Mergen-lanza, swore the oath on your behalf, in accordance with your faith, on your soul, Altyn-tsar. Your brother, Dural-tabun also swore the oath with the lama on the document which was sent with the envoys. And you, Altyn-tsar, laid your hand on that document; and the lama and Dural also laid their hands on it. You must remember this oath. Remain steadfast and firm to the law and to the oath. Be forever undeviatingly obedient to our Tsarist command, with your entire horde. Then, in the future, you may expect our Tsarist Majesty's favor and gifts.

You are to send our Tsarist Majesty the currently assessed tribute, as well as additional gifts. You are to allow our envoys to return to Tomsk without being detained; you are not to confine them, nor seize their weapons, nor take their clothes. Order that they be accompanied by guides so they will reach Tomsk in good health.

We, the Great Sovereign, will keep you, Altyn-tsar, in our Tsarist merciful favor and care; we will defend you from your enemies, depending on how well and loyally you serve us, the Great Sovereign.

In your letter, Altyn-tsar, you report that all the rulers who camp near you wish to come under our Tsarist Majesty's mighty hand and pay us, the Great Sovereign, tribute, and hope that we will reward them with our Sovereign gifts. However your letter says nothing about which hordes, what people, and what faith those who camp near you profess. Who are their rulers? How far are they from our various towns? Which towns? How far are they from you? Write to us in detail about this, Altyn-tsar, telling which hordes are nearest to you, what people live there, what their faith is, who their rulers are, what the names of the rulers are, how far from you each horde camps, how many people are in each horde, and what manner of warriors they have. Write to us in detail about all of this. Then, depending on all of this, we will send them gifts.

You also reported in your letter about how the Kirgiz drove off the horses and livestock from our towns and captured iasak-paying people, and how you ordered your brother, Dural-tabun, to deal with this. If these Kirgiz disobey your brother, then because of this disobedience you are to attack them and find the iasak-paying people and the horses and livestock which were driven off. Return the livestock and horses to the towns from which they were stolen. Deliver up the heads of the Kirgiz leaders to our towns. You, Altyn-tsar, serve us well and for this we praise you. You are keeping your oath, you are loyal and you serve us, the Great Sovereign, now, and wish to continue to serve us in the future.

In your letter to us, Altyn-tsar, to us the Great Sovereign, you reported that you took the oath in the presence of our envoys twice, and that when you took the oath you laid your hand on the oath document. Therefore you must remain firm and steadfast, as you have been. If the Kirgiz disobey your brother, Dural-tabun, and refuse to rectify the crime which they have committed against us, the Great Sovereign; if they refuse to give up the captured iasak-paying people, the horses and the livestock, then you, Altyn-tsar, are to perform the following service for us, the Great Sovereign: you are to go in person against the Kirgiz, and conquer them; order that the iasak people, the horses and livestock which they took from our towns be found and returned to the towns from which they were taken. In order to maintain firm control in the future, take hostages from them; take the brothers and sons of the leading men, five or six or as many as necessary, and send them to our towns.

We, the Great Sovereign, will consider your service and will find it pleasing to us. And, Altyn-tsar, you wrote to us in your letter that if we, the Great Sovereign, were to send our envoys to the Chinese and Tungus and Argut lands, you would provide them with guides, provisions and transport. You, Altyn-tsar . . . [several lines missing] will bring many lands under our mighty hand.

In accordance with the ukaz of our Tsarist Majesty, we have our great voevodas and diaks and golovas and many troops stationed in Tomsk, and in all of our Siberian towns we have many troops with firearms and all kinds of weapons, so that wherever our Tsarist Majesty may order them to go, these many troops in our Siberian towns will be ready.

Written on February 28, 1638, in the Sovereign's palace in the Tsarist city of Moscow.*

Reference: LOA AN SSSR, f. Portfeli Millera, op. 4, kn. 11, dok. 41, ll. 24 ob.-25.

See: M. I. Golman and G. I. Slesarchuk, eds. *Materialy po istorii russko-mongolskykh otnoshenii, 1636–1654* (Moscow: 1974), 97–98.

*The letter patent is written on fine paper with the Tsar's great crown. The capital letters are written in gold, as well as the name and title of the Sovereign, and the name of Altyn. The rest is done in black ink. The diak's signature is appended without flourish, as appropriate for writing to a subject of the Tsar. The letter is sealed with a round seal in black wax, imprinted under pressure.—Eds.

53

AUGUST 6, 1638

INSTRUCTIONS FROM TSAR MIKHAIL FEDOROVICH TO THE FIRST
VOEVODA OF IAKUTSK, PETR GOLOVIN, CONCERNING ROUTES TO
EASTERN SIBERIA AND EXPLORATION OF THE IAKUT REGION

On August 6, 1638, the Sovereign Tsar and Grand Prince
Mikhail Fedorovich of all Russia, orders the stolnik and
voevoda, Petr Petrovich Golovin, to go to Tobolsk in Siberia, with
Matvei Bogdanovich Glebov and the diak Efim Filatov. From
Tobolsk they are ordered to proceed to Eniseisk ostrog, and from
thence to the mighty Lena River. In previous years nearby Siberian towns and ostrogs have sent iasak and pominki to the
Sovereign in Moscow which consist of more than the required
number of furs.

At the present time, however, many Siberian towns send
the Sovereign just barely enough furs to make up the iasak and
pominki. The voevodas write to the Sovereign from Siberian
towns that they cannot obtain any more furs. They report that
these Siberian towns and ostrogs are experiencing a depletion of
sables and other furbearing animals because the iasak-paying forest dwelling natives have trapped all the available animals. Many
other iasak-paying natives who used to trap animals have become
Russians.* The number of Russians in Siberia increases every
year. Other iasak-paying natives have turned to agricultural pursuits. All of this results in the deficiency of iasak collection for the
Sovereign in the regions of the nearby Siberian towns.

In the year 1632 Andrei Palitsyn, the voevoda of Mangazeia
in Siberia, came to Moscow from Siberia. In the Prikaz of the
Kazan Dvorets he made his report about the mighty Lena River.
His report states that the Lena River is very great and that the
region is favorable and extensive. The banks of the river are inhabited by various peoples, both nomadic and settled. There are
sables there, as well as many other kinds of animals. He sug-
gested that the Sovereign send a goodly number of Siberian people
to the mighty Lena River and order them to build a town or an

---

*Siberian natives who accepted orthodoxy were freed from iasak obliga-
tion.—Eds.

ostrog in a suitable place along that river so that the natives of these new lands along the mighty Lena and other rivers would be brought under the suzerainty of the Sovereign Tsar and pay iasak to the Sovereign. He believed this would bring great profit to the Sovereign and to the Sovereign's Treasury, and that the Lena River would become another Mangazeia. He prepared a description about the mighty Lena River and about the various people who inhabit the shores of the Lena and other rivers.

In that description he states that to reach the Lena by boat from Mangazeia one proceeds upstream along the Taz and Volo-chanka rivers, thence by lakes and streams in a koch or *kaiuk* to the Enisei portage, a journey which takes ten days. The portage is a little more than half a verst in length. From that portage one goes by boat into the lakes, and from the lakes to the streams, to the Turukhan River, a two-day journey. One then proceeds for ten days down the Turukhan and Shar to Turukhansk zimov'e. From there one goes downriver for two days via the Shar and Turukhan, crosses the Enisei, then goes up the Tunguska River for two days to the mouth of the Titei River; then by portage onto the Chon River.

The winter is spent in this place preparing boats so that in spring one can proceed on the Chon River for ten days to the Viliui, then for three weeks on the Viliui to the mighty Lena.

Many Siniagirs and Nanagirs live along the Chon and Viliui rivers. There is an abundance of sable, fox, ermine, beaver, and all other kinds of animals there, and the rivers abound in fish as well.

Between these rivers and the Lower Tunguska there are many transmontane tributary rivers where various tribes live. There are many fox, beaver and other animals here, also.

If one goes down the mighty Lena River in a boat using oars, it takes two months or more to reach the Northern [Arctic] Ocean; but, weather permitting, one can sail the distance in a week.

Many tribes live along both banks of the mighty Lena, all the way to its mouth, which empties into the Northern Ocean: Iakuts, Tungus, Maiads, Nanagirs, Koiats, Karigils and various others, both settled and nomadic. Below the mouth of the Viliui River many other rivers empty into both banks of the mighty Lena, and along these rivers live the Oseis, Tungus, Shamagirs, Baiakhts and many others. There are many sables and other animals and fish there.

It takes ten days to go up the mighty Lena to the eastern fork of the Aldan River. The Aldan also falls into the Lena. Many tribes of various lands live along the shores of the Aldan, and they also have an abundance of sables and other animals and fish.

If one proceeds from the Aldan up the Lena using a vessel with oars it takes twenty weeks or more to reach the Krasnaia Sea by way of the great Baikal Strait. But if one uses a sail boat and has good weather, the voyage can be made in two weeks.

Many rivers empty into the great Baikal channel of the Mighty Lena above the mouth of the Viliui River: the Ichora, Chaia, Chichiui, Poledui, Olekma, Vitim, Kirenga, Taiura, Kamta and the Branta. Along all of these rivers live the Iakol, Iakut and Bratsk taishas. Some are nomads who travel by horse, while others are nomadic and wander on foot and others are settled. These include the Tungus, Naliakigirs, Kamchiugirs, Suchigirs, Kogirs, Kimzhegirs, Nanagirs, Shamagirs, Sinegirs, Dolgans, and the slave horde and many other peoples. They are subject to no one.

These lands also abound in sable, fox, beaver and ermine, and these people do not know the value of sable and other furs.

The servitors from Mangazeia traveled throughout this region along the mighty Lena River from its mouth upriver for some distance, and from Eniseisk ostrog down to the Lena and up to the mouth of the Viliui. They carried goods with them, and when they stopped at some settlement, they enticed the natives to trade and then took their women and children captive and seized their livestock and domestic animals. They committed many excesses, thereby driving these savage peoples away from the Sovereign's suzerainty, and at the same time, enriching themselves. But very little wealth came to the Sovereign from this activity.

It is possible to procure great wealth for the Sovereign from these distant and inaccessible lands. It would be possible to introduce agriculture in areas up along the Lena, Angara and Oka rivers, and a detachment of troops could bring these settlements into eternal servitude under the mighty hand of the Tsar. No more than 200 armed men, using military force, would be required to accomplish this. An ostrog should be built on the Chon River, and another at the mouth of the Viliui. Fifteen servitors should spend the winter in each of these ostrogs.

A town or a good sized ostrog should be built at the mouth of the east fork of the Aldan. Fifty men should winter there because the tribes who live along that river are stronger and more numerous.

Andrei Palitsyn also stated in his report that there is another water route to the Lena from Eniseisk ostrog, which is shorter than the one from Mangazeia. Using this route, one goes up the Enisei and Lower Tunguska rivers to the Podvoloch and Indim rivers, a journey which takes five weeks or longer using large boats. From the mouth of the Indim one can take a six-day winter trip by dogsled to the Lena portage. Another portage goes from the Indim to the Kup River. A man can cross this portage in one day, but the portage cannot be used in winter because the hills are so steep and rocky that one cannot use dogsleds. One can sail downstream from this portage to the Kup River in one day, and one can also go down the Kup to the great Lena in one day.

The third route from Eniseisk ostrog to the Lena River follows the Enisei to the Lower Tunguska, which takes one downriver for two weeks; then from the mouth of the Tunguska one goes upriver to the mouths of the Titei and Chon rivers, then along the Chon and Viliui rivers. It takes thirteen weeks and a day to reach the mighty Lena.

According to the reports from the Siberian voevodas in Tobolsk, Mangazeia and Eniseisk ostrog who were in Siberia in the winter of 1631–32, they tried to send men to the Lena River to collect iasak for the Sovereign and meet with Siberian servitors who were there from Tobolsk and Mangazeia and from Eniseisk ostrog, but they managed to collect very little iasak.

See: M. N. Tikhomirov, ed., *Khrestomatiia po istorii SSSR XVI–XVII vv.* (Moscow: 1962), II, 550–552.

54

1639

A PETITION FROM THE MERCHANT VASILII GUSELNIKOV TO TSAR
MIKHAIL FEDOROVICH PROTESTING EXCESSIVE REGULATION OF THE
FUR TRADE IN SIBERIA

To Tsar Mikhail Fedorovich, Sovereign and Grand Prince of
all Russia, a petition from Vasilii Fedotov [Guselnikov], a
humble servant in your *gostinnaia sotnia* [merchant guild].

I, your humble servant, send my people Grigorii Ivanov and
Afanasii Andreev and their *prikashchiks* [agents] to the towns of
Siberia, to Eniseisk ostrog, to the mighty Lena River, and to
Mangazeia; they carry all manner of Russian goods and supplies
used to prepare sable pelts.

It is impossible to take any Russian provisions except for fresh
honey to the Lena and Tunguska rivers because of the vast distances involved.

Sovereign, the voevodas and other servitors in the towns in
Siberia stop our rafts and boats and collect taxes on both equipment and vessels from our contract trappers and hired people. On
the winter route from Verkhotur'e they will not issue permits to
go into other Siberian towns to prepare rafts and boats and the
necessary equipment for the sable hunt; rather, they force us to
stay in Verkhotur'e until spring. Neither will they let us travel from
Eniseisk ostrog to the Turukhansk zimov'e with provisions and
equipment, nor from that zimov'e to the sable hunting grounds
and the Lena River. Instead, they keep us here for their own
profit.

Because the voevodas and servitors impose these halts, the
hunters cannot travel the entire distance to the sable hunting
grounds in one season, and the result is that they freeze to death
in barren places. Furthermore, Sovereign, when I, your humble
servant, send my prikashchiks and hired people into Siberia by
way of Kamen and Obdor, the officials there stop them and collect a transit fee of ten percent, in Russian goods or in cash, just as
they do at Verkhotur'e. This is contrary to your ukaz, Sovereign.
Those persons who come to Obdor from Mangazeia with furs
have to pay, in Mangazeia and other towns, an impost of one denga per ruble, based on the customs officials' assessments. These
men issue transit papers with your Sovereign seal. Then in Obdor

there are officials who stop the fur traders and collect another tax of one denga per ruble on the same furs. The officials there re-issue the transit documents, and they stop everyone, causing great losses thereby.

Merciful Sovereign, Tsar Mikhail Fedorovich, Grand Prince of all Russia, have mercy on me, your humble servant. Sovereign, allow my men and my prikashchiks in the sable trade to carry 150 puds of fresh honey with them, free of duty. Allow them to buy provisions in all Siberian towns. Permit them to leave Verkhotur'e by the winter route, so they can procure boats and provisions in any Siberian town. Let them leave Eniseisk ostrog and Turukhansk zimov'e with their rafts, boats and dugouts without hindrance.

Sovereign, decree that in Obdor your officials are to collect your taxes only in accordance with your decree which pertains to collection in Verkhotur'e. Sovereign, do not allow tax collectors to impose a re-issue fee on furs, and do not permit them to re-issue transit documents.

Sovereign, please send your Sovereign decree on this matter to all Siberian towns.

Tsar, Sovereign, have mercy and grant my petition.

See: M. N. Tikhomirov, ed., *Khrestomatiia po istorii SSSR XVI–XVII vv.* (Moscow: 1962), II, 558–559.

55

BETWEEN FEBRUARY 3 AND 16, 1639

A PETITION FROM LAMA DAIN MERGEN-LANZA TO TSAR MIKHAIL
FEDOROVICH, REQUESTING GIFTS AND RUSSIAN ENVOYS FOR A JOUR-
NEY TO THE TUNGUS RULER

To the Great White Tsar, lama Mergan-lanza humbly sends his petition.

Sire, may God have mercy on you on the Muscovite throne, and also on the Tsareviches. I abide here, in good health, with Altyn-tsar and with Mongols beyond counting. Earlier, Iakov and Druzhina came here to strengthen the ties between us, and at that time they had Biunta-taisha and Dural-taisha and Daichin-tabun take the oath of allegiance. All three of them swore the oath. After that, Stepan Grechenin and Andrei, Bazhen and Gerasim were sent to us. They likewise had us swear the oath, to strengthen the ties between us. On behalf of the Altyn-tsar, I, lama Dain Mergen-lanza, his father, took the oath. Dural-taisha also swore the oath on behalf of Altyn-tsar, promising that Altyn-tsar would be in concord with you, Great White Sovereign Tsar. In this regard, there is no dispute on either side. Your envoys, Great White Sovereign Tsar, and those of Altyn-tsar, will have uninterrupted contact.

Great White Sovereign Tsar, all the gifts you sent to me were delivered in good condition. I bow with the honor of having received your Sovereign favor. On bended knee I ask that you, Great White Sovereign Tsar, may have long life and good health. I send these gifts to you, Great White Sovereign Tsar: three Siberian tigers, two boxes with gold locks, seven snow leopards, a cloak of colored silks, some azure Chinese silk, double-faced Chinese silk, some black velvet, and twenty beaver pelts.

With this letter I send my envoy Karchig-baksh and his companion and his koshevar, three men in all. Please favor my envoys, and send them back to me without detaining them. Decree that this winter my envoys be permitted to go to the town of Tomsk so they may hasten back to me. Great White Sovereign Tsar, any envoys you may send to the Tungus tsar should be sent to me with my envoys, so that they may find me before I depart for the Tungus tsar. As soon as they find me, I will guide them to the Tungus tsar.

A Tungus shaman. Early nineteenth-century lithograph.

Great White Sovereign Tsar, have mercy on me, decree that I be sent pearls and fabrics of various colors and red beads.

Great White Sovereign Tsar, send Iakov or Stepan Grechenin as your envoy, and send a trusted Muscovite, and also a Muscovite interpreter.

I, lama Dain Mergen-lanza, have written this with my own hand.

Reference: TsGADA, f. Mongolskie dela, 1639, g., d. No. 1, ll. 60–63.
See: M. I. Golman and G. I. Slesarchuk, eds. *Materialy po istorii russko-mongolskykh otnoshenii (1636–1654)* (Moscow: 1974), 155.

178

56

A PETITION FROM THE TUNGUS INTERPRETER, FEDOR MIKHAILOV, TO
BE RELEASED FROM IMPRISONMENT IN LENA OSTROZHEK

To the Sovereign Tsar and Grand Prince Mikhail Fedorovich
of all Russia, your slave, the Tungus interpreter Fedor
Mikhailov, petitions you from Lena ostrozhek.

On April 3, 1640, Sovereign, I, your slave, made a complaint
in the Prikaz office of Lena ostrozhek against the Eniseisk syn
boiarskii Parfenii Khodyrev. Parfenii had sent me into your Sovereign service with the Eniseisk servitors Kiril Vaniukov and his
men; I was to serve as a Tungus interpreter and go to a new land
where these servitors had asked to go. Sovereign, I, your slave,
was afraid to go on that distant service because the land is far off,
it is unknown, there were no guides, it lacked every necessity, and
we did not have any supplies to take along on your Sovereign's
distant service.

I made the complaint against Parfenii Khodyrev and against
the Sovereign's assignment without knowing what I was doing. In
this I, your slave, am guilty before you, Great Sovereign. Now,
Sovereign, I, your slave, am imprisoned because of what I did.

Merciful Sovereign Tsar and Grand Prince Mikhail Fedorovich
of all Russia, have mercy on me, your slave, and order, Sovereign,
that I be freed from being under guard. Sovereign, forgive my
guilt. I will go on your Sovereign service to the new land with the
Eniseisk servitor Kiril Vaniukov and his men as soon as they are
ready to set out for your Sovereign distant service.

Sovereign Tsar, have mercy, grant my request.

See: Ia. P. Alkor and B. D. Grekov, eds., *Kolonialnaia politika moskovskogo
gosudarstva v Iakutii XVII v.* (Leningrad: 1936), 2.

57

BETWEEN SEPTEMBER 1, 1640 AND DECEMBER 9, 1641

A REPORT TO TSAR MIKHAIL FEDOROVICH FROM THE VOEVODAS OF
IAKUTSK, PETR GOLOVIN AND MATVEI GLEBOV, CONCERNING AN EX-
PEDITION TO THE IANA AND INDIGIRKA RIVERS UNDERTAKEN BY
POSNIK IVANOV AND ANIKA NIKITIN; ALSO CONCERNING THE SEA
VOYAGE OF PROKOPII LAZAREV AND ELESEI BUZA TO EXPLORE A
RIVER EAST OF THE LENA

To the Sovereign Tsar and Grand Prince Mikhail Fedorovich of all Russia, your humble servants Petr Golovin, Matvei Glebov and Eufim Filatov humbly report.

On August 25, 1640, Sire, a Eniseisk servitor named Posnik Ivanov and a servitor from Krasnoiarsk, Anika Nikitin, and their comrades came to us, your humble servants, on the portage of the Lena River, from the new Iukagir lands. Sire, Posnik and his men brought to us, your humble servants, your iasak consisting of four forties and three sables. Sire, we, your humble servants, asked Posnik how far the Iukagir lands are from Iakutsk ostrog, and what people inhabit them, how populous these lands are, whether he thought that they would pay iasak to you in the future, Sire, and how many servitors should be sent there to collect iasak. Sire, during our inquiry Posnik and his men related the following account to us, your humble servants.

On April 25, 1638, Posnik and 30 servitors left Iakutsk ostrog on horseback, crossed the mountains to the Ianga River, and went down the Ianga to the Iakut people, a four-week journey. Sire, the Tungus known as Lamuts live on the upper reaches of the Ianga River and do not pay iasak to you, Sire. Many Iakuts and the Tungus prince Kuturg live on the lower Ianga and along the Ola River, Sire. Posnik collected iasak for you from these Iakuts for the year 1639, Sire. This consisted of six forties of sables. That same year he sent those sables to Iakutsk ostrog with six men.

In order to collect your iasak in the future, Sire, it will be necessary to send six men to these Iakuts on the Ianga and Ola rivers. Sire, your iasak can be collected on the Ianga River without taking hostages. Sire, hostages cannot be kept on the Ianga River because there is no way to feed them, as there are no fish in the river.

In the year 1639, Sire, Posnik and 27 men took horses and went from the Ianga River up along the Tolstak River to the

Indigirka, in the land of the Iukagirs. Sire, he proceeded along the Tolstak and across the mountains to the Upper Indigirka, where there are many non-iasak Lamut Tungus. Then they went down the Indigirka to the land of the Iukagirs, in all, a four-week journey. They took two hostages in the Iukagir territory on the Indigirka River, Sire.

Then, Sire, using these hostages he succeeded in collecting four forties and three sables for the year 1640. Sire, Posnik brought this iasak from the Iukagir land to Iakutsk ostrog with fifteen servitors. He left sixteen men in the land of the Iukagirs to guard the hostages. On his return from the land of the Iukagirs to Iakutsk ostrog, he left three men on the Ianga River to collect your iasak, Sovereign.

Sire, the Iukagir land is well populated, and the Indigirka River abounds in fish. In the future 100 servitors can live on fish and game along the Indigirka River and in the lands of the Iukagirs, and they will not need grain. Furthermore, Sire, the Iukagir land has many sables. Sire, many rivers fall into the Indigirka, and many nomadic reindeer-herding people live along all of these rivers, and there are many sables and other furbearing animals along all these rivers.

The Iukagirs also have silver, Sire, but Posnik could not find out where they obtain it. The Iukagirs told him about many other lands, Sire, but Posnik cannot give details about these because he knew only a little of the Iukagir language. Sire, servitors should be sent to the Iukagirs in the future, and you will profit greatly from the iasak collection, Sire.

Sire, we, your humble servants, sent Posnik out from Iakutsk ostrog, and a Krasnoiarsk cossack with him, Anika Nikitin; we also sent a Eniseisk cossack, Stepan Osipov, four Tobolsk servitors, the Eniseisk desiatnik Fedor Milovanov, and Afanasii Stepanov. We ordered Posnik to give the pismennaia golova Vasilii Poiarkov a detachment of eight volunteer servitors and he was also to give six to Fedor Milovanov and Afanasii. Sire, the reason we ordered that they be given volunteer servitors is that you have no horses in Iakutsk ostrog, Sire, so there is no way to pay servitors for their service, and thus the servitors Posnik and Fedor and their comrades have to buy horses at their own expense.

Sire, we also ordered Posnik to go from Iakutsk ostrog to the land of the Iukagirs to collect your iasak, Sire, and to replace the previous iasak collectors he had left with the Iukagirs to guard the hostages and to search for and learn about new lands and about the silver ore. Sire, we ordered Fedor Milovanov to go to the Iakuts on the Ianga River to collect your iasak. Sire, we sent a pud of fresh water pearls with Posnik to be used as gifts to the natives so they would give your iasak, Sire. We also ordered that he take three *kuiaks* [metal armor] from Iakutsk ostrog, and we sent two hats with Posnik and 12½ grivnas with Fedor Milovanov for helmets. Sire, we, your humble servants, ordered that these boats be dismantled and that each of the natives be given one or two of the boards. Sire, the Iukagirs do not buy any goods other than iron and fresh water pearls.

Sire, the Eniseisk servitor Pronka Lazarev came to us, your humble servants, on the Lena portage, bringing the sable treasury. During the inquiry Pronka told us, your humble servants, the following account of his travels. He went with the Eniseisk desiatnik, Elisei Buza, by sea to explore the Lama River and others which fall into the sea, and to look for new non-iasak-paying lands, and to collect iasak. They collected your iasak, Sire, for the year 1638, from the Iakuts at the mouth of the Ianga River, and this consisted of two forties and 27 sables, four sable shubas, a black-brown fox, eight grey-black foxes, and eleven red foxes. Sire, from the Ianga River, they sailed on the sea for two weeks. While they were along the seacoast they took the Iukagir princeling Bilgei prisoner, and collected iasak from him consisting of a sable shuba which had been made from 15 sable pelts. Sire, the desiatnik Elisei Buza sent Pronka to Eniseisk ostrog with this sable collection and with three promyshlenniks. Elisei remained on the coast with 17 servitors, promyshlenniks, and a hostage.

Sire, Pronka does not know whether you will profit from the iasak collection on the coast where the Eniseisk desiatnik Elisei Buza has remained.

See: *Dopolneniia k aktam istoricheskim* (St. Petersburg: 1846), II, d. No. 88.

58

MAY 30, 1641

INSTRUCTIONS FROM THE PRIKAZ OFFICE IN IAKUTSK TO THE BE-
REZOVO PIATIDESIATNIK MARTYN VASILEV AND TO AKSEN ANIKEEV
TO INVESTIGATE THE ROUTE TO CHINA

In accordance with the ukaz of the Sovereign Tsar and Grand
Prince Mikhail Fedorovich of all Russia, the stolniks and
voevodas, Petr Petrovich Golovin and Matvei Bogdanovich Glebov, and the diak Eufim Filatov, order the Berezovo piatidesiatnik
Martyn Vasilev and the desiatnik Aksen Anikeev to proceed into
the upper reaches of the Lena River, to the Bratsk people and the
non-iasak Tungus. These men are to be accompanied by 50 servitors from Tobolsk, Berezoro and Eniseisk. . . . [missing]

After giving out strong drink, Martyn and Aksen are to question the Bratsk and Tungus people about the Lama and about the
Upper Tunguska River and about the Mongol people who live
along the shores of the Lama. They are to obtain information on
the following questions.

Are these tribes populous? How far does the Mongol prince
live from them? What is his name? What towns does he have?
Has he any ostrogs? What weapons do these people use? What
river does one follow to reach the Chinese Empire? How long
does it take to go there by boat? Overland? How far is the Shilka
River from there? How far away is Prince Lavkai who lives on the
Shilka? Is there any silver ore on the Shilka? How far from Lavkai's
ulus is the copper ore? Which grains grow along the Shilka River?
Where does the mouth of the Shilka empty, into the Lama, or
into the Great Sea? How many days does it take to go by land to
reach the Shilka River and Prince Lavkai from the upper reaches
of the Lena River? Can one go by boat from the Shilka River to
the Lama? How many days does it take by boat to navigate the
length of the Shilka? Is there a salt lake in the upper reaches of
the Tunguska River? How far is the salt lake from the Tunguska,
and from the upper reaches of the Lena, and from the mouth of
the Kulenga River?

Where should an ostrog be built? How does one get to that
lake? Is it possible to cross the mountains from the ostrog to the
Tunguska and to the upper reaches of the Lena? If the lake is not
more than two or three days away, they are to send a servitor

there, accompanied by either a Tungus or a Bratsk, to explore it and bring back some salt. A sample of the salt is to be sent back to Iakutsk ostrog. They are to make careful inquiries into all of these questions, and a servitor is to write down all the answers.

When they have built an ostrog, they are to prepare a map. They are to obtain the following information about the Bratsk and non-iasak-paying Tungus people. How many of these people are there? How many pay iasak? How many do not? How many of the Bratsk can be brought under the Sovereign's mighty hand? They are also to find out about the Lama, about the Mongols, about the route to the Chinese Empire, about other lands, and about the salt lake. They are immediately to send three men with the sketch map, and the answers to these questions, to Iakutsk ostrog, to the stolnik and voevoda Petr Petrovich Golovin and his men.

If they cannot manage to do this immediately, then before the ice breaks up in spring they are to send all this information with the Sovereign's iasak sable treasury, and the sketch map, the answers to the questions and the iasak books. They are to send as many servitors as they can spare to convoy this, and send everything to Iakutsk ostrog.

Reference: TsGADA, f. Iakutskaia prikaznaia izba, op, 3, 1640 g., d. No. 7-a, ll. 347, 354, 355, 359.

See: N. F. Demidova and V. S. Miasnikov, eds. *Russko-kitaiskie otnosheniia v XVII veke: Dokumenty i materialy (1608–1691)* (Moscow: 1969), I, 117–118.

59

BEFORE SEPTEMBER, 1641

A REPORT TO TSAR MIKHAIL FEDOROVICH FROM THE VOEVODAS OF
THE LENA REGION, PETR GOLOVIN AND MATVEI GLEBOV, CONCERN-
ING THE DISCOVERY OF NEW LANDS ALONG THE VITIM, TSYPIR AND
OTHER RIVERS, AND INFORMATION ON NATIVE INHABITANTS OF THE
SHILKA LANDS BORDERING THE CHINESE EMPIRE

To the Sovereign Tsar and Grand Prince Mikhail Fedorovich
of all Russia, your humble servants, Petr Golovin, Matvei
Glebov and Eufim Filatov humbly report. Sire, last year, 1640, as
we, your humble servants were en route from Eniseisk ostrog
to the Lena portage, on July 27 the Eniseisk servitor Maksim
Perfilev and 13 servitors came to us, your humble servants, Sire,
on the Tunguska River. Maksim reported to us, your humble servants, Sire, that in the year 1639 he went from the Olekma ostrog
on the Lena River to search for and to explore new lands of non-
iasak-paying people in the upper reaches of the Vitim River.
Maksim had 36 servitors and promyshlenniks with him, Sire.

Beyond the great falls of the Vitim River, at the mouth of the
Muia River, Sire, Maksim captured a Tungus named Komboiko
from Sheleginsk volost as a hostage. Sire, the Tungus of the
Sheleginsk volost number more than 70, in addition to Komboiko
Pikeev. Maksim collected iasak from them for the year 1640
which consisted of 74 sables with bellies and tails.

Sire, during the interrogation the hostage Komboiko Pikeev
and other Tungus people told Maksim that in the upper reaches of
the Vitim River there is a Daur prince living who is named
Botoga. He lives there with his men, Sire. It takes a month to go
by water from the mouth of the Kotomara River along the Vitim
to reach this prince Botoga who lives on the Vitim River at the
mouth of the Karga River. He and his people live in uluses in one
place, and, Sire, prince Botoga has iurts made of logs. He also
has livestock, Sire, and there are abundant sables there, and
Botoga also has silver. And, Sire, in exchange for the silver, Botoga
buys silk from Prince Lavkai on the Shilka River.

Sire, from Botoga's encampment up the Vitim River to Iaravnia
Lake, along both banks of the Vitim River, there live many
mounted Daur people, Sire, and they use the bow and arrow as
weapon, and, Sire, their language is not like that of the Iakuts and

the Tungus. Sire, from Botoga to the Shilka River portage the travel time is four and a half days on foot. Many settled Daur agricultural people live along the Shilka, and, Sire, they grow the same kinds of grain as the Russians do, and they grow it all the way to the mouth of the Shilka River.

Sire, at the mouth of the Ura River on the Shilka, near Prince Lavkai's ulus, there is silver ore in a mountain, and the Daur prince Lavkai and his men smelt silver from that ore, Sire. There is a great amount of silver ore there, Sire, and the silver is dispersed throughout many volosts and uluses. Sire, they exchange the silver for sables, and, Sire, these sables are purchased by the Chinese on the Shilka River in exchange for silk and other goods. Sire, there are also large amounts of copper and lead ore on the Shilka River. Sire, from the place where the copper ore is found to the mouth of the Shilka River, it takes five or six days to go by boat. Sire, the Shilka River falls into the Lama, and Sire, they call the Lama a sea.*

Sire, the Kolortsy live at the mouth of the Shilka River, and they trade with the Chinese. The Chinese come to them from the Lama by boat, Sire. The people who live at the mouth of the Shilka River have temples and know how to read and write. Sire, the Kilortsy have their own language. The Chinese on the Shilka and Lama do not have firearms. Sire, grain is grown throughout the uluses on the Shilka River in the land of Prince Lavkai and of other princelings. They grow rye, barley and other grains, and sell the grain on the Vitim River to prince Botoga and to other princelings. Sire, the Tungus buy sables from them. Grain grows in abundance there. Sire, the people along the Shilka River are agricultural people, and are not warlike. Sire, the Gil River empties into the left bank of the Shilka, and the Iakuts and Tungus live along that river.

Sire, the same hostage Komboiko told Maksim that the Tsypir River lies beyond the mountain range and that the river rises from a lake, and empties into the Vitim River. The journey to the Tsypir River from the mouth of the Kotomara River, where Maksim wintered, by way of the Vitim River, takes four days. Non-iasak-paying Tungus people such as the Shunilts and Chipchaigilts and

---

*Lama is a Tungus term for a large body of water such as a lake or a sea. Russian explorers appropriated this term for both Lake Baikal and the Sea of Okhotsk.—Eds.

others live along the shores of Tsypir Lake, more than 200 persons in all. They have many sables which they sell for grain and livestock, and they also exchange silver on the Shilka River. They barter on the Shilka, and the Sheleginsk Tungus wear silver ornaments and buttons. Sire, Maksim personally saw the Tungus wear these silver things.

Last year, 1640, this hostage from Sheleginsk volost, the Tungus, Komboiko Pikeev, fell ill in the iasak zimov'e at the mouth of the Kotomara River, Sire. He lay sick for a long time. Maksim and his men were afraid that Komboiko would die before he could be exchanged, so in Komboiko's place Maksim took as hostage his brother, Shipchegin, son of the Tungus, Becherg. Because of his illness, Komboiko was freed.

Sire, in that same year, 1640, Maksim and his comrades went from the mouth of the Kotomara River up the Vitim, with provisions of grain sufficient for themselves. They traveled for eight days up the Vitim River to the Tsypir, then up the Tsypir to the great falls on the Tsypir, which took nine days. Then, Sire, they turned back at the great falls on the Tsypir because they had consumed all their provisions of food. Sire, the falls on the Tsypir are very large where the river falls into the Vitim from the right. Sire, if in the spring we sent 50 or 60 servitors up the Vitim River on your service in small boats, with adequate food supplies, and these servitors went to princeling Botoga and Prince Lavkai on the Shilka, then, Sire, you would realize a substantial profit from the state collection of iasak.

Sire, on January 18, 1641, we, your humble servants, sent a detachment of servitors from Tobolsk, Berezovo and Eniseisk to look for new lands inhabited by non-iasak-paying Tungus. Ivan Osipov and 10 men went on this assignment. They traveled by dogsled in winter, and went from the Lena River up the Chaia River, and, Sire, they traveled on the Chaia for four weeks and in the upper reaches of that river they found non-iasak Tungus named Naederov Kindigirts, Iudka and Albug and their comrades, some 20 men in all. Sire, when they were questioned these people said that Tungus live along the Angara River, which empties into the Lama, and that it takes eight days to travel on foot from the Tungus nomad encampments where these people were found. Sire, the travel time from the Angara to the Lama, going on foot, is two weeks. The Bratsk people live along the shores of the Lama, the Tungus live along the Angara, both Kindigirt

Tungus and other Tungus tribes; and, Sire, the Bratsk people belonging to Prince Lavkai live in the upper reaches of the Vitim, beyond the Shilka portage. These people live in iurts made of logs, and there are ten or more iurts in any one place. They grow all kinds of grain there. The Tungus spend the autumn along the Lama among the Bratsk people.

These people had sables, and sold them to the Bratsk people. These Tungus gave your iasak to the servitors, Sire, for the present year of 1641, and this consisted of two lynx pelts and three sables, including bellies and tails. Sire, they could not give any more because they do not have any more sables.

Sire, the Eniseisk servitors Maksim Kirilov and the Tobolsk man Andrei Pochipugin went to the iurts of these Tungus, where the Tungus man Iudka told them that he had heard from his Tungus relatives that Prince Lavkai on the Shilka River has silver ore which he mines from a mountain, but they did not know how far the portage is from the Shilka to the Vitim. But one goes to the Shilka by way of the Vitim. Sire, the Tungus sold Maksim a circlet worth ten altyns which was made from the silver they get from the Shilka River. This is an ornament which the Tungus wear on their heads. Maksim paid for the silver with two woolen blankets, and brought the silver to us, your humble servants.

When the servitors Ivan Osipov and his comrades were questioned, Sire, they told us, your humble servants, that in the future it will be impossible to go on the Angara River to collect the government iasak, because sleds cannot be used to transport grain, and boats cannot be used on the Chaia River because the water is too low and there are many rapids. Sire, these Tungus come to the Chaia and Chichaia rivers to hunt from time to time.

Sire, we, your humble servants, have sent a pismennaia golova named Enalei Bakhteiarov to the Vitim River to collect iasak and explore new lands, look for silver and copper and lead ores, and locate arable land. He has 51 servitors with him, and four servitors who are acting as Iakut and Tungus interpreters. We also sent a Tungus hostage with Enalei, a man named Bilchaga from Sheleginsk volost. Sire, as a threat to these natives we, your humble servants, also sent a bronze cannon with Enalei. We sent half-pound cannon balls, one and one-half puds of powder, enough for 40 rounds of cannon fire, plus a pud and a half of powder for reserve for the servitors' guns. Sire, the servitors have also been given shot for their service on the Vitim, and half a pud of powder each. Sire, we chose servitors to send with Enalei who had full supplies of their own, and we supplemented these with your gifts of money collected from 100 Eniseisk servitors, ground rye flour from Eniseisk ostrog, and for the next year, 1642, two and one-eighth chetverts of rye flour each, plus one eighth *osmina* each of groats and oats per person.

Sire, we instructed Enalei to go up the Vitim River to Sheleginsk volost, to the Tungus, and upon reaching Sheleginsk volost, we ordered him to take two or three Tungus leaders from that volost as hostages and interrogate them about the Shilka River and about silver, copper and lead ore, and about arable land. We ordered him to send Tungus and servitors to Botoga and prince Lavkai, and to invite these princes to come under your Tsarist mighty hand and pay iasak to you, Sire, from themselves and from their ulus people. Sire, we, your humble servants, instructed Enalei to move about among these princes in such a way that he would not arouse suspicion and could entice them and then take some of the leaders as hostages, and if possible, to erect an ostrog near the location of the silver ore.

Sire, we did not send any more servitors to the Vitim River with Enalei because the servitors do not have enough provisions of their own, Sire, and there is no state grain supply in the government warehouses for the year 1641.

Sire, we, your humble servants, have ordered that the non-iasak Tungus be brought under your Tsarist mighty hand and that iasak be collected from the Bratsk and Tungus who can be brought under your mighty Tsarist hand. And in accordance with your Sovereign ukaz, these people are not to be treated with violence and thus turned away from your Tsarist Majesty.

Sire, we, your humble servants, ordered Enalei to go along the Vitim River and its tributaries to Lake Chibir and to the mouth of the Shilka River to ascertain what people live along these rivers, how many such people there are, where silver and copper and lead ores are to be found, and we instructed him to prepare a map and a description of the road to the Chinese Empire, on the basis of information he obtained from natives.

See: *Dopolneniia k aktam istoricheskim* (St. Petersburg: 1846), II, 258–261.

60

BETWEEN SEPTEMBER 1, 1641 AND JUNE 9, 1642

A REPORT FROM MIKHAIL STADUKHIN AND VTOROI GAVRILOV, FROM
THE OIMIAKON ZIMOV'E, TO THE IAKUTSK PRIKAZ OFFICE, CONCERN-
ING THE COLLECTION OF IASAK AND PREPARATIONS FOR AN EXPEDI-
TION TO THE MOMA RIVER

Sire, the servitors Mikhail Stadukhin and Vtoroi Gavrilov and
their comrades in the Oimiakon zimov'e humbly report to
Petr Petrovich [Golovin] and Matvei Bogdanovich [Glebov], stol-
niks and voevodas of the Sovereign Tsar and Grand Prince Mikhail
Fedorovich of all Russia, and to the diak Eufim Varfolomeevich
[Filatov].

We humbly submit to the Tsar and Grand Prince Mikhail
Fedorovich of all Russia the petition which we submitted at the
Prikaz office in Iakutsk ostrog to the stolniks and voevodas Petr
Petrovich and Matvei Bogdanovich and to the diak Eufim Varfolomeevich, asking that we be recompensed for our service to the
Sovereign on the Oimiakon River, where we replaced Tretiak
Karpov who went to the Iakut prince Bychik, a shaman, and his
children and ulus people. We also went to the Memel Tungus and
to the Lamut Tungus to collect iasak for the Sovereign. For the
year 1642 we collected three forties of sables, and for the year
1641 we collected 30 sables, and so far this year we have collected
four sables with tails from the Iakuts and the Memel Tungus. We
have also collected from the Iakuts and from the Memel Tungus
who live beyond the mountains, and from young adult men,
three forties and 12 sables with tails; two of these have partial
tails, and one has no tail. We sent this treasury of the Sovereign
with the servitors Ivan Ivanovich Kisla, Denis Vasilevich Erilov
and Troika Ivanov to you, stolniks and voevodas Petr Petrovich
and Matvei Bogdanovich, and diak Eufim Varfolomeevich.

We made inquiries of the Memel Tungus people about the
transmontane peoples and others who do not pay iasak. The
Memel told us that people in the transmontane region on the
Tomka River do not pay iasak, so we sent a servitor there, Ivan
Novikov, with Serden Simikanovich as a guide. He was given a
large green copper pan as largesse from the Sovereign. The servitor Ivan Novikov sent Serden from the Tomka on March 25. . . .
[missing]

There is not a single man left on the Oimiakon; there is no way for the servitors to live, nothing for them to eat. The Oimiakon River has its source in the mountains, but along the river banks there are no pastures, no oak groves, meadows or grass fields. It is only flat taiga, full of marshes and rocks. The Oimiakon River has no fish, and there are no animals along its banks. This is the reason servitors cannot live there; there is nothing to eat, and no people live anywhere along that river. The Lama Tungus travel along the river, but do not live there.

According to our reports, a promyshlennik named Ilei Kostentinov was assigned there with the servitors Ivan Kisla and his men, and they caused a great deal of trouble. He has not yet been brought to justice. He merely says that he was sent there on a government assignment. We tried to tell him that God and the Sovereign and you, stolniks and voevodas, will punish him. But he angrily told us not to interfere in the matter, and that he knew more about it than we did.

On April 2, the servitors Grigorii Fofanov and Fedor Mikhailov were sent to make a reconnaissance among the Lamuts. These servitors spent the night in the forest. Fedor approached a Iakut sentry who drew his bow and shot an arrow which struck and killed Fedor. There is no way one can live on the Oimiakon, one would simply die of starvation.

We have learned of a river called the Moma, which is large and has many settled people living along its banks, but not any nomadic people. There is a great deal of fish and game there, many sables and other animals, two varieties of fish [*nelma* and *muksun*]; and there are meadows along this large river, and oak groves and fields of grass. The people have wooden iurts, but they do not keep fire in the iurts. When we heard about this river with fish and game and sables and settled people who hunt sables, we went there to look about among these people and to collect iasak. And, God willing, and with the luck of the Sovereign, we will find out about this Moma River and the people there, and we will collect iasak for the Sovereign from these people. We will send the iasak to the Sovereign's Treasury, and we will send a detailed written report to you, stolniks and voevodas.

There is a promyshlennik named Ivan Pologov who has been on government assignment. We have requisitioned Ivan to repair our weapons and boats and other things. We could not manage without him, because we are going into new territory, and our weapons have suffered damage, and Ivan Pologov is the only one who knows how to repair things. We do not know how to build boats. If we manage to survive, we will bring Ivan Pologov with us, to the Prikaz office in Iakutsk ostrog, to the stolniks and voevodas Petr Petrovich and Matvei Bogdanovich, and the diak Eufim Varfolomeevich. . . . [missing]

A Memel Tungus named Otkon Simikanov told us that he would guide the cossacks and the Sovereign's Treasury on the Aldan by roundabout trails. We trusted Otkon in this matter, because he is loyal to the Sovereign.

The Sovereign's Treasury was sent under my seal and that of the tselovalnik, while the books and inventory were sent under only my seal, Mikhail. This report and the previous records are being sent with Ivan Novikov. The Sovereign's Treasury was sent on May 9 with the servitor Ivan Kisla and his men. With Ivan and his men we sent seven sables with tails, and sables collected as pominki. . . . [the end of the report is missing]

Reference: TsGADA, f. Iakutskaia prikaznaia izba, stolb. No. 14/B, ll. 5–11.

See: N. S. Orlova, ed. *Otkrytiia russkikh zemleprokhodtsev i poliarnykh morekhodov XVII veka* (Moscow: 1951), 119–122.

61

1642

A REPORT ON THE EXPEDITION OF THE DESIATNIK ELISEI BUZA TO THE INDIGIRKA AND NEROGA RIVERS

In this year, 1642, the Eniseisk servitor desiatnik Elisei Buza, brought three Iukagir hostages to Iakutsk ostrog. These were the shaman, Balganch, and the men Imgont and Dalgunt. During questioning in the Prikaz office in Iakutsk ostrog these hostages stated that there is a river called the Neroga which rises near the Indigirka River. The travel time between the two rivers, using reindeer without packloads, is one week.

The headwaters of the Neroga River are also close to the Iana River, and from the source of the Iana to that of the Neroga, the travel time is one month by reindeer. The Neroga empties directly into the [Arctic] Ocean. On the Neroga, not far from where it empties into the sea, there is a hill, and in a cliff overhanging the river there is silver ore. Just above the silver ore, a little farther up the river, people of the Nattyl tribe live in the valley. They build earthen iurts for themselves and have a great deal of silver. They travel on foot, for they have neither reindeer nor horses. The river has abundant fish, and so these people live on fish.

You, Dmitrii, are to demonstrate your zeal in the Sovereign's service and find out about this Neroga River in detail from all the natives. Use every possible means, both direct and indirect, and question them and use force if necessary to find out whether this Neroga River exists. If it does, is there silver ore right there? How many people live along that river? How much ore is there? What kind of people are these? How far is it from that river to the headwaters of the Indigirka River? If there is indeed a Neroga River, and there is silver ore on it, how close is it to the upper reaches of the Indigirka? If there are only a few people there, then with God's mercy and the fortune of the Sovereign, it is to be hoped that we can subdue these people.

See: *Dopolneniia k aktam istoricheskim* (St. Petersburg: 1846), II, 262.

62

AUGUST 24, 1642

INSTRUCTIONS TO THE PIATIDESIATNIK VASILII GOREMYKIN CONCERNING HIRING MEN TO BE SENT TO BRATSK OSTROG AND THEIR CONDUCT TOWARD THE BRATSK NATIVES

On August 24, 1642, in accordance with the ukaz of the Sovereign Tsar and Grand Prince Mikhail Fedorovich of all Russia, the piatidesiatnik Vasilii Goremykin, who has come to the portage to prepare all the government supplies to be transported on horse drawn carts, is instructed that if the estimate of government supplies for horses and for trading are not increased, then these supplies should be acquired, by whatever means possible, before autumn sets in. The money to acquire them is to be taken either from customs revenues or from salt sales, and when he has finished building the carts to transport the government supplies, and when he has collected the Sovereign's iasak in full, he is to summon any merchants and promyshlenniks and other volunteers on the Ilim and Muka rivers who wish to serve the Sovereign and accompany him, Vasilii, to Bratsk ostrog to put down the rebellious Bratsk people.

He is to tell the volunteers that if through God's mercy and the fortune of the Sovereign they defeat the non-iasak-paying Bratsk people and bring them under the mighty protection of the Sovereign Tsar, and if they take hostages, that all of these persons will receive the Tsar's largesse for their service, and whatever booty they take from these non-iasak Bratsk people by force, such as livestock, horses, cows, and furs, they may keep for themselves; and they will not have to pay tax to the government on any of this. All of the booty will belong to the volunteers and servitors. If they take some ulus people prisoner, but not princes or their children or wives, then by virtue of the Sovereign's ukaz these captives can be ransomed. However they may not capture these Bratsk people and keep them as slaves.

If Vasilii is able to assemble fifteen men from among the promyshlenniks and merchants and volunteers, who will bring their own arms, then the names of these promyshlenniks and other volunteers are to be recorded, and he is to take these fifteen men as reinforcements, and proceed to Bratsk ostrog by Stretenets Day, if possible, but no later than a week after Stretenets Day. If there are twenty or more promyshlenniks and others with their own firearms, then Vasilii is to take ten servitors with him, and proceed without delay to Bratsk ostrog. If there are fewer than fifteen merchants and promyshlenniks, then Vasilii is not to go to Bratsk ostrog nor send the servitors there; rather, he is to remain at the Lena portage with all of these people and handle the Sovereign's assignment of transporting provisions in carts and boats; and there is to be no negligence.

But if he can gather fifteen or twenty promyshlenniks and other volunteers, then Vasilii is to go overland to Bratsk ostrog, with great caution. Whenever he halts he is to post sentries, and the servitors and promyshlenniks are to be given strict instructions in this regard. Vasilii is personally to make certain that this is done properly.

While they are en route the servitors and promyshlenniks are not to play cards or gamble. They are not to pillage or inflict any violence or harm on Russian promyshlenniks in the zimov'es or on natives. Anyone who illegally plays cards for money or for grain or tobacco, and in so doing causes some offense or injury to natives, is to be mercilessly whipped for his misconduct.

If Vasilii meets natives en route, he is to tell them that he is on his way to replace servitors in Bratsk ostrog. This exact statement is to be repeated precisely at every portage and every settlement on his way. He is not to tell any of the natives that he is going to fight the Bratsk. When he reaches Bratsk ostrog, he is to ask God's mercy, and then deal with the Bratsk people carefully. He is to consider the local situation in consultation with the piatidesiatnik Kurbatii Ivanov, so that there will be as much benefit to the Sovereign as possible. He is to inquire in detail about any Bratsk people who have not gone to the ostrog or paid iasak to the Sovereign.

When, with the help of the Tungus, he has found those places where the insubordinate Bratsk people live, he is to take the leading princes as hostages. When he takes hostages from them, or from [hostile] Tungus tribes, Vasilii is to take at least two highly regarded leaders. Then, invoking God's mercy, he is to advance against the Bratsk people with great caution, together with Kurbatii and all the servitors going in strong formation. There are to be five men in front as a reconnaissance guard, and five more as a rear guard and there are to be two or three men on each flank as sentries, so that neither the Bratsk nor the Tungus can take them by surprise.

The hostages should be bound very carefully so they cannot escape. In this way Vasilii will be able to tell where a small ulus is and take the Bratsk people there by surprise. Then he is to drive off their livestock. In this way the Bratsk people may be pacified and brought under the mighty protection of the Sovereign Tsar.

Vasilii is not to reveal to the Tungus which day he plans to leave the ostrog to attack the Bratsk, or the direction he plans to take, or which ulus he plans to attack. He is to leave a reliable servitor in the ostrog with the hostages, and leave ten or as many as thirteen other servitors with him to guard the hostages and handle matters there. They are to be instructed to stay on the alert at all times in the ostrog. They are to put up strong barricades and not let any natives into the ostrog. They are not to go out any distance, but hunt only in the immediate vicinity.

If the Bratsk people are there in force, and Vasilii feels he does not have sufficient strength to attack the Bratsk uluses, then he should drive their livestock off and try to subdue them in this way. No matter which Bratsk ulus Vasilii attacks, and takes hostages from, he is then to fall back to the ostrog and send a reliable Tungus messenger to that Bratsk ulus, informing them that their leaders will have to come to the ostrog to ransom the prisoners, and that they will have to swear allegiance to our Sovereign Tsar and Grand Prince Mikhail Fedorovich of all Russia, and that they will be forever under his mighty Tsarist hand, undeviatingly, and in direct servitude and they must pay iasak to the Sovereign from themselves and from their ulus people in full, and without interruption.

If he takes princes or their children or wives as prisoners, these people are not to be ransomed, but held as hostages with great care. If there are no prisoners to keep as hostages, then the Bratsk people should be lured with kindness, and hostages are to be taken from among the common people. At the same time Vasilii and Kurbatii are to be diligent in overseeing the Sovereign's affairs, so that the Bratsk land will be relentlessly brought into servitude. For this service, Vasilii will be rewarded with the Tsar's favor. When he has conquered the Bratsk people, Vasilii is to take the servitors and promyshlenniks, but not all of them, and proceed further. He is to leave some promyshlenniks behind with the livestock, whoever is available.

Then when he reaches the portage, in accordance with his orders and with our present instructions, he is to hunt diligently, and wait for the arrival of the government Treasury from Bratsk ostrog in spring when the rivers thaw. Then he is to go to Iakutsk ostrog. And if, by God's grace and the Sovereign's luck, Vasilii manages to take hostages, then he is to proceed to the mouth of the Kuta River with Kurbatii and write a report. If there are only a few servitors and promyshlenniks and hunters at the portage, Vasilii is not to go in person to Bratsk ostrog, but instead is to choose eight men to send to Bratsk ostrog and he is to send as many volunteers as possible with them. He is to forward the names of the men he is sending to the piatidesiatnik Kurbatii Ivanov in Bratsk ostrog. And when Martyn Vasilev comes from Bratsk ostrog, Vasilii is to give him his written report, which will be presented at Iakutsk ostrog in the spring.

To this instruction the stolnik and voevoda Petr Petrovich Golovin has placed the seal of the Sovereign Tsar and Prince Mikhail Fedorovich of all Russia, which seal bears the new Siberian lands on the great Lena River.

Reference: TsGADA, f. 214—Sibirskii prikaz, stolb. No. 6372/328, ll. 202–206.

See: G. N. Rumiantsev, ed. *Sbornik dokumentov po istorii Buriatii XVII vek* (Ulan-Ude: 1960), Vyp. 1, 38–40.

63

1642-1645

THE OATH OF ALLEGIANCE WHICH RUSSIANS ADMINISTERED TO BRATSK NATIVE LEADERS

I, Bului, a man of the Bratsk tribe, hereby give my firm oath of allegiance to my Sovereign Tsar and Grand Prince Mikhail Fedorovich, Autocrat of all Russia, and to his Sovereign Lordship, the Tsarevich and Grand Prince Aleksei Mikhailovich. I, Bului, and my brother Bura and our other brothers and tribesmen, and all my ulus people, swear on our faith, by the sun, by the earth, by fire, by the Russian sword and by guns, that we will come under His Tsarist Majesty's mighty authority, in eternal servitude, without treason, undeviatingly, for all time. I will serve my Sovereign in every way, loyally and gladly.

I will not commit any treason against his Sovereign servitors or against any other Russians or against his Sovereign people in the Verkholensk ostrozhek, or against agricultural settlers, in any places where the Sovereign's servitors and Russians may be working, nor will I come in war or in secret to kill them or harm them or commit treason against them. Neither I, Bului, personally, nor my brother nor any of my ulus people will incite other hostile Bratsk people to commit treason against the Sovereign's people, nor incite them or guide them to come to kill.

Likewise I, Bului, will encourage other Bratsk leaders and their ulus people to come under His Tsarist Majesty's mighty hand in eternal servitude and to pay iasak and pominki to the Sovereign, in large amounts and in full every year, for themselves and for their brothers, and in every way to be in complete concord with the Sovereign's people.

When the Sovereign's men come to collect iasak in my ulus, I will protect them, and will not allow them to be killed. If any Bratsk leaders and their ulus people become disloyal to the Sovereign, then I, Bului, will report about these disloyal persons to the Sovereign's prikashchiks in Verkholensk ostrog, and I will join the Sovereign's forces in war against these disloyal people, and will try to pacify them by means of war and bring them back under your Sovereign Tsarist mighty hand, and will collect iasak from them for the Sovereign.

If I, Bului, do not carry out all these promises for my Sovereign Tsar, the Grand Prince Mikhail Fedorovich of all Russia, and for the Lord Tsarevich and Grand Prince Aleksei Mikhailovich, as written in this document, and if I do not serve loyally for all time, and gladly, or if I commit any treason against the Sovereign's servitors and go to war against the Russian people near Verkholensk ostrog, or against the agricultural settlers, or in other places where the Sovereign's people may come, or if I commit murder, or do not pay iasak in full for myself and for all my ulus people, or if I commit some foolish act, then, in accordance with my faith, the sun will not shine on me, Bului, I will not walk on the earth, I will not eat bread, the Russian sword will cut me down, the gun will kill me, and fire will destroy all our uluses on our lands.

And if I commit treason, the final punishment will be that the Sovereign's anger will be loosed on me and I will be put to death without mercy and without pity.

See: Ia. P. Alkor and B. D. Grekov, eds., *Kolonialnaia politika moskovskogo gosudarstva v Iakutii XVII v.* (Leningrad: 1936), 10–11.

BETWEEN DECEMBER 15, 1644 AND AUGUST 31, 1645

A REPORT FROM THE VOEVODAS OF IAKUTSK, VASILII PUSHKIN AND KIRIL SUPONEV, TO THE SIBIRSKII PRIKAZ CONCERNING THE REQUEST BY ENISEISK SERVITORS TO EXPLORE NEW LANDS NEAR THE LENA RIVER

To the Sovereign Tsar and Grand Prince Mikhail Fedorovich of all Russia, your humble servants, Vasilii Pushkin, Kiril Suponev and Petr Stenshin humbly report.

On December 14 of this year, 1644, Lena servitors appeared before us, your humble servants, in Eniseisk ostrog, in order to petition you, Sovereign Tsar and Grand Prince Mikhail Fedorovich of all Russia. These men were Osip Semenov, the son of Boiarchin, and Iakun Semenov, the son of Shcherbak. They report, Sire, that they served you on the mighty Lena River for many years prior to the arrival of the stolnik and voevoda Petr Golovin and his men, and that they brought many hostile lands under your authority, Great Tsar.

Sire, when the voevoda and stolnik Petr Golovin and his men arrived on the mighty Lena River in the year 1641, Petr Golovin sent them and some 35 other Lena servitors to Eniseisk ostrog, on his own authority, without orders from you, Sire. These Lena servitors are now in Eniseisk ostrog, Sire, and ask that you grant their request and order that they be sent back to the mighty Lena River on your Sovereign service, as previously.

Sire, we, your humble servants, have interrogated these Lena servitors in Eniseisk ostrog. Sire, in Eniseisk ostrog, in addition to Osip and Iakun, the following Lena servitors are there [18 names follow]. We, your humble servants, asked the Lena servitors about their service, Sovereign, and in the inquiry they told us that in the past, Sire, they were sent from Eniseisk ostrog on various assignments in your Sovereign service on the mighty Lena River, to bring new hostile lands under your great Sovereign authority. In order to collect your iasak, Sire, they went with the Eniseisk deti boiarskie Petr Beketov and Parfenii Khodyrev and the ataman Osip Galkin. When, in accordance with your decree, Sire, the 30 of them came to the great river Lena, to the stolnik and voevoda Petr Golovin and his men, they were transferred by Petr Golovin to the 70 Eniseisk servitors on the Lena as reinforcements, since Petr Golovin and his men, Sire, were authorized to take 100 servitors from Eniseisk ostrog.

Sire, these servitors were with Petr for a short time on the Lena River. Petr Golovin had them serve on the Lena without compensation, Sire. Now they petition you, Sire, and him, Petr Golovin, that they cannot serve you, Sire, on the great Lena River without remuneration in money and provisions. Sire, for no reason at all Petr Golovin beat them with the knout, without your authorization, Sire, and sent them to Eniseisk ostrog. Sire, they insist they are not guilty of anything.

We have carried out the many clauses of your decree, Sire, which has been given to us, your humble servants, about the investigation of Petr Golovin and his companions, concerning these servitors. In accordance with your ukaz, Sovereign, we, your humble servants, have investigated the matter of these twenty persons who are presently in Eniseisk ostrog, including Vasilii Burga and his associates. . . . [the end of the communication is missing].

Reference: TsGADA, f. Sibirskii prikaz, stolb. No. 244, ll. 9–10.
See: N. S. Orlova, ed. *Otkrytiia russkikh zemleprokhodtsev i poliarnykh morekhodov XVII veke* (Moscow: 1951), 199–201.

1645-1646

AN OFFICIAL ADDRESS BY THE VOEVODA OF IAKUTSK, PETR GOLOVIN, TO THE BRATSK HOSTAGES BULUI AND CHEKAR, CONCERNING THE ETERNAL SERVITUDE OF ALL THE BRATSK PEOPLE TO TSAR MIKHAIL FEDOROVICH, UNDER THE THREAT OF ANNIHILATION IF THEY DO NOT COMPLY

Bului, man of the Bratsk people! When the stolnik and voevoda Petr Golovin and his men came here to the Lena portage, by command of the Sovereign's ukaz, and sent the Sovereign's servitors against you disobedient Bratsk people, you fought these servitors of the Sovereign in your uluses. But with God's mercy and the luck of the Sovereign, these people of the Sovereign destroyed your uluses and captured a relative of yours, the leader Kurzhum, and brought him to the mouth of the Kut River to the voevoda Petr Golovin and his men.

In the presence of the voevoda Kurzhum petitioned the Sovereign and took the oath of allegiance to the Great Sovereign that he, Kurzhum, would remain under the Tsarist mighty hand, with all of his Ikirezhsk tribesmen and ulus people, for all time, and pay iasak, and urge other Bratsk princes and ulus people to come under the Sovereign Tsarist mighty hand in eternal servitude and serve the Great Sovereign loyally and gladly in all ways.

After administering the oath the stolnik and voevoda Petr Golovin and his men gave Kurzhum a kaftan as a gift from the Sovereign, and they also gave him food and drink. Kurzhum petitioned the Sovereign Tsar to be allowed to return to his ulus and send his son, you, Chevdok, in his stead as hostage. The stolnik Petr Golovin and his men agreed to Kurzhum's request, and in his place they accepted his son, you, Chevdok, and allowed Kurzhum to return to his ulus. But Kurzhum then violated his oath and abandoned you, his own son, Chevdok. He deceitfully enticed the Sovereign's servitors away from Verkholensk ostrog, Martyn Kislokvas and the newly baptized interpreter Gavriil and six other men, by telling them they might come to his ulus to take down the names of all the Bratsk people who were to pay the Sovereign's iasak. Then when they came to his ulus he killed them.

Later, when the Sovereign's servitors and promyshlenniks, Semen Skorokhodov and 30 men, were sent to the Angara, you also transgressed and killed eighteen of those men. And evidence of that crime is that when the current punishing expedition was sent against you, the Ikirezhsk people, they found government-issue armor in your ulus. Later, two men were sent to you, the interpreter Fedor and Danil; and Kurzhum committed a new offense by plotting to kill the servitors as they came to the iurt. Then two years ago, in 1644, the Sovereign's servitors, piatidesiatnik Kurbat Ivanov and others, were sent to punish Togloi and the Bratsk people who had been disloyal to the Sovereign.

After that you, Bului, and Buchiuk and Daichin, brother of Ongoi, and Torim and his brother Naerai of the Bolgadaisk tribe, you took the oath of allegiance to the Sovereign that all of you Bratsk people would come under the Sovereign Tsarist mighty hand in eternal servitude, without treason, undeviatingly, for all time; you swore you would pay iasak for yourselves and for your tribe and your ulus people, large yearly iasak in full, without interruption. Then, Bului, you and your brother Bora and all your Bratsk people, after taking the oath of allegiance, committed treason against the Sovereign. You gave as little iasak as you pleased, and you came to Bratsk ostrog twice that winter, and you came for a third time in the summer. You stole all the horses and cattle and other livestock the servitors had, and you burned the cut hay. Now the servitors have identified many of the stolen livestock in your uluses. And this is your crime. And you Bratsk people also went to Tutura and destroyed the Overka agricultural settlement and killed five Russian workmen. You stole their horses and livestock and farm equipment and laid waste their provisions and set fire to the hay.

Last year all of your Ikirezhsk Bratsk people rebelled against the Great Sovereign and refused to pay iasak. Because of this, when the voevoda Vasilii Nikitich Pushkin an his men came to Ilimsk portage, they carried out the Sovereign's ukaz and sent the syn boiarskii Aleksei Bedarev and a small number of servitors to punish you without mercy for your rebellion so that in the future you would humbly petition the Sovereign to forgive your treason, and you would confess your guilt and return under his Tsarist Majesty's mighty hand as you were before, in direct servitude for all time, undeviating and submissive, yet not be completely destroyed. But when the syn boiarskii and his servitors reached the Sovereign's territory on the Orlenga River and at the mouth of the Kut River, you and many of your Bratsk people attacked them, on the Sovereign's territory at Botov Creek on the Lena River above the Orlenga.

You attacked them with bows and arrows and killed five of the Sovereign's servitors. Then the syn boiarskii Aleksei and his servitors went out from Verkholensk ostrog and attacked your uluses and mercilessly laid waste the Ikirezhsk uluses, but he did not kill your people. He and his men took some of the women and children as prisoners, including your brother Burins' wife and children, but they let your prisoners be ransomed, and returned your brother Burin's wife and children to you without ransom. When you came to Verkholensk ostrog, Bului, you brought horses to ransom the rest of the prisoners, but then later you and your Bratsk people stole all the horses and livestock from the ostrozhek after you had ransomed the hostage, and this was a new act of treason.

Bului, in accordance with the Sovereign's ukaz, it would be appropriate for you and your brother Burin to be punished by being hanged for your many acts of treason and destruction, because you and your brother induced others to commit this crime and treason. But for the present the Sovereign Tsar and Grand Prince Mikhail Fedorovich of all Russia has ordered that neither you nor your brother be put to death for your guilt or to avenge the death of the Sovereign's servitors. Instead he has ordered that you be under his Tsarist mighty hand in direct and eternal servitude for all time, undeviatingly. He has also granted a reprieve to your brother Burin and to his ulus people and to other Bratsk men who have admitted their guilt in their petition to the Sovereign. He is allowing them to live in their former iurts.

As long as you commit no further treason, the Sovereign will not order any of his Sovereign servitors to destroy you. And in return, Bului, you are to pledge the Sovereign Tsar your firm oath of allegiance that you and your brother Burin and your son Chekar and the rest of your brothers and tribesmen and all your ulus people will be under his Sovereign Tsarist mighty hand in direct servitude, forever, loyally, undeviatingly, and that you will pay iasak to the Sovereign in full, without shortages, every year, both for yourself and for all your ulus people. You are to cooperate with the Sovereign's servitors and join in war parties with his servitors who are sent out to punish other disloyal Bratsk people who may rebel against the Sovereign or oppose him. Furthermore, you are not to attack the government servitors and agricultural settlers in the future, nor incite other hostile Bratsk people to war-

A typical winter settlement on Kamchatka peninsula. Early nineteenth-century print from a Webber drawing.

like action, nor are you to commit any act of treason. You and your brother must alternate annually as hostages in Verkholensk and Bratsk ostrogs. While you are hostages you will receive sufficient amounts of food from the Sovereign's supplies.

But if you rebel against the Sovereign again and do not pay iasak to the Sovereign in full each year, or if you attack agricultural peasants near the ostrozhek, then, in accordance with the Sovereign's ukaz, you will be punished for this treason. The Sovereign's voevoda Vasilii Nikitich Pushkin and his men will send many government troops with guns against you and your ulus. These men will be instructed that not only you and your wives and children and ulus people are to be killed because of your treason, but your livestock are to be destroyed and your iurts are to be burned relentlessly. These men will be ordered not to take any of you prisoner to be held for ransom, and that if they should capture any of you, they are to put you to death by hanging you, just as was done to the Iakut traitors. And you will have brought this destruction upon yourselves.

See: Ia. P. Alkor and B. D. Grekov, eds., *Kolonialnaia politika moskovskogo gosudarstva v Iakutii XVII v.* (Leningrad: 1936), 129–131.

66

A PETITION FROM SERVITORS AT VERKHOLENSK OSTROZHEK REQUEST-
ING REINFORCEMENTS AND BETTER WEAPONS TO ENABLE THEM TO
SUBDUE THE BRATSK PEOPLE

To the Sovereign Tsar and Grand Prince Mikhail Fedorovich of all Russia, your humble servants from the Lena detachment at the Verkholensk ostrozhek, the servitors, the syn boiarskii Aleksei Bedarev, piatidesiatnik Kurbat Ivanov, the desiatnik Pavel Malakhov, and all our other comrades of various ranks, humbly submit this petition.

In accordance with your ukaz, Sire, and the instructions of your Sovereign voevoda, Vasilii Nikitich Pushkin and his men, Sire, we, your humble servants, were sent out with volunteer guliashchie liudi against the rebellious and disobedient Bratsk people. These people were once under your Sovereign Tsarist authority and paid iasak, but subsequently they rebelled against you, Sire, and ceased paying iasak. They enticed our fellow men from the ostrozhek to go to their uluses, and then killed them and others who were sent to collect iasak. In one year they attacked Verkholensk ostrozhek three times. When they attacked they drove off all of the horses and cattle which we the servitors had there.

Sire, with God's grace and thanks to Your Majesty's good fortune, we, your humble servants, when they most recently attacked us, we battled them and subdued two tribes of these rebellious natives, the Ikirezhi and the Sipugae. Sire, we collected iasak for you consisting of thirteen forties of sables, and we also took hostages. Sire, these Bratsk people and their hostages are willing to come under your Sovereign Tsarist mighty hand, and have surrendered their hostages. Then, Sire, we, your humble servants, brought these hostages from Verkholensk ostrozhek to your voevodas at the Ilim portage, Sire.

While we were away, [the natives] attacked the ostrozhek again, Sire, and again drove off our horses and cows. Because of the shortage of men, it is impossible adequately to defend your Verkholensk ostrozhek, Sire. Only with the aid of your regular military forces, through battle, can the Bratsk be pacified.

Merciful Sovereign Tsar and Grand Prince Mikhail Fedorovich of all Russia, have mercy on your humble servants. Decree, Sire, that your government servitors and volunteer guliashchie liudi join with us to battle your rebellious and disobedient natives in order that these traitors be subdued through battle and brought under your mighty Sovereign Tsarist hand, and that they be held in check and prevented from their constant disobedience and treachery. Sire, grant us, your humble servants, this request. Decree that in the future your state servitors in the Verkholensk Bratsk ostrozhek be reinforced. Order that 200 mounted troops from Krasnoiarsk ostrog participate in this. Horses for these men can be taken from the rebellious Bratsk people in battle.

Sire, have mercy on your humble servants. Decree that 200 guns and 200 suits of mesh armor for the servitors and 300 muskets for the volunteer foot troops be sent out from Moscow. Sire, the Bratsk people have many mounted warriors, and they go into battle carrying metal shields and they wear greaves on their forearms, and they have spiked helmets; and we, Sire, your humble servants, are poorly outfitted, we have no armor, and our poor little guns cannot shoot through the shields of the Bratsk warriors. They even kill those of us whose firearms are functional, while with our poor weapons we cannot touch them.

Sire, this Verkholensk ostrozhek could be very profitable to you, the just Sovereign. If 200 servitors were stationed here, they could subdue these disobedient Bratsk men in battle and bring them under your mighty hand, Sovereign.

All of these Bratsk people live near Verkholensk ostrozhek, Sire, just three or four or five days travel away; the most distant is seven days away, near the Lama. Sire, your iasak collection will be large in the future, and the collection of sable for you, Sire, could be carried on from Iakutsk ostrog on the Lena River to the Ilim-Lena portage. Then your state voevodas and servitors and merchants and promyshlenniks will be able to travel on the Lena to carry on their trade in furs to Russian towns. And below this ostrozhek state peasants could be settled on the Kulenga River, and also from the ostrozhek down to the salt deposits and to the mouth of the Kut, following the natural terrain on the Tutur and Orlenga and other small rivers. They could live there in security, protected by your servitors. And in this way, Sire, in your far off patrimonial territory along the Lena, in accordance with your

Bratsk ostrog tower with overlook and gun ports. From Makovet-skii, *Byt i iskusstvo russkogo naseleniia vostochnoi Sibiri*, Vol. 2.

ukaz, we could subdue these Bratsk people through battle and thus extend your boundaries. Other than the Bratsk warriors, there are no other warriors who are inimical toward you, Sire, throughout the entire Lena region and all the way to the great ocean and along other distant rivers. Tsar, Sovereign, have mercy.

Reference: Arkhiv LOII AN SSSR, k. 191, stolb. 13, ll. 1–2.
See: G. N. Rumiantsev, ed. *Sbornik dokumentov po istorii Buriatii XVII vek* (Ulan-Ude: 1960), vyp. 1, 58–60.

67

AFTER JUNE 12, 1646

DOCUMENTS CONCERNING THE EXPEDITION LED BY VASILII POIARKOV
FROM IAKUTSK TO THE SEA OF OKHOTSK

On June 12, 1646, the pismennaia golova Vasilii Poiarkov came to Iakutsk ostrog from the lower reaches of the Lena River. In the prikaz office he reported to the voevodas, Vasilii Nikitich Pushkin and Kiril Osipovich Suponev, and to the diak Petr Stenshin. On July 15, 1643, Vasilii was sent out from Iakutsk ostrog by the stolnik and voevoda Petr Golovin with 112 veteran servitors and newly arrived men and fifteen guliashchie liudi volunteers, plus two tselovalniks, two interpreters and a blacksmith.

In order to strike fear into the people of the hostile lands they carried a cast iron cannon of 1/2 pound calibre and 100 cannon balls. The servitors were provided with eight puds and sixteen *grivenkas* [one grivenka = 205 grams] of powder and the same amount of shot. Vasilii reported that Petr Golovin had sent the piatidesiatnik Iurii Petrov and Patrei Minin and their men to go with him, Vasilii, on the expedition to the Aldan River.

The instructions read that on July 15, 1643, in accordance with the ukaz of the Sovereign Tsar and Grand Prince Mikhail Fedorovich of all Russia, the stolnik and voevoda Petr Golovin ordered the pismennaia golova Vasilii Poiarkov to proceed from Iakutsk ostrog along the Zeia and Shilka rivers to collect the Sovereign's iasak, and to search for new non-iasak-paying people, and also to search for silver, copper and lead ores, and for grain. Maksim Perfilev, a servitor from Eniseisk ostrog, testified that on the Shilka River there are many settled farming people, and that Prince Lavkai also lives there. He has about 30 men in all. Prince Lavkai has silver ore in two places near the mouth of the Ura River: one place is on a steep cliff, and the other is in the water. There are both copper and lead ore down the Shilka, and there is plenty of grain on the Shilka also.

The instruction also mentions collecting information from the Tungus people. A Tungus from the Aldan River region, a Laginsk prince named Shamaev Tonkoni, from Butansk ostrog, was sent with Vasilii as a guide. According to Tonkoni, the Tungus told about the Shilka River and about the settled farming peole who live there. Vasilii was ordered to go to that river as a representative of the Sovereign to look for the silver and copper and lead ore deposits, and to build ostrozheks in those three places, and to fortify them in any way he could.

During questioning the pismennaia golova Vasilii Poiarkov related the following account of his expedition. In the year 1643 the stolnik and voevoda Petr Golovin sent him, Vasilii, on an assignment, and gave him 12 veteran servitors, two interpreters, two tselovalniks, a blacksmith, and 100 newly arrived men, as well as 15 volunteer promyshlenniks. Vasilii went from Iakutsk ostrog down the Lena to the mouth of the Aldan River in two days; then for four weeks he journeyed up the Aldan to the mouth of the Uchur. From the Uchur he spent ten days going to the mouth of the Gonam; then he traveled for five weeks going from the Gonam to the Zamoroza. The Gonam River has many rapids, and as they made their way upriver they were forced to portage their boats. On one of the portages a boat was caught in the rapids and turned over, and they lost eight puds and sixteen grivenkas of lead shot belonging to the government. The shot sank in a deep place in the rapids and could not be salvaged.

By the time the Gonam River froze over, they had encountered 42 rapids on that river, as well as 22 smaller riffles. Six days before they reached the Niuemka River the river froze, and they had to build a zimov'e and live there two weeks. Vasilii left a piatidesiatnik and 40 servitors and two tselovalniks in that zimov'e. He instructed them to follow him in spring before high water, and to proceed along the winter trail, to cross the portage, and bring the government treasury and food supplies. They were to build boats and proceed down the Zeia River without delay. Vasilii took 90 servitors with him in the year 1644, and went from that zimov'e along the Niuemka River. Then from the Niuemka he crossed the portage, which took two weeks, and then, sailing with two winds, the forenoon and the afternoon, they came to the Brianda River.

The Brianda empties into the right bank of the Zeia. There are no people living along it. Then they went down the Brianda to the Zeia, which took two and a half weeks. They proceeded along the Zeia River for two days to reach another river [also] named Brianda, which joins the Zeia, falling into its right bank. The reindeer Tungus people called Ullagirs live along this river. . . . [words missing] and they traveled four days from the Giliaia River to the Ura. The Ura falls into the right bank of the Zeia, and

210

along its banks live livestock-breeding Tungus called Baiagirs. They went on foot for three days to go from the Ura River to the Umlekan, which empties into the right bank of the Zeia. There are no people along the Umlekan. At the mouth of the Umlekan live agricultural people called the Daurs. The Daur prince Dontyul and his tribe number some fifteen men. He lives there together with the agricultural people.

On December 13, 1644, Vasilii took the Daur prince Dontyul Kenchiulae as a hostage and interrogated him about the Zeia and Shilka rivers and the tributaries that join them, and about what manner of people live along those rivers, and whether or not they might pay iasak. Vasilii also inquired about silver and copper and lead ores, and about the blue pigment used to dye calico, and whether the silver and copper and lead ores and the blue pigment are to be found on the Zeia and Shilka rivers. He asked whether they have silk and cotton fabrics. He was told that silver is not to be found along the Zeia, Shilka and tributary rivers, that they do not produce silk and cotton fabrics, that there are no copper or lead ores, nor is there any of the blue pigment used to dye cotton. They receive their silver and silk and cotton and copper and lead from the Khan.

[Dontyul] also said that the Khan lives with his horde and has a town built of logs, and there is an earthen rampart around the town, and the men are armed with bows and arrows, and with guns, and they have many cannon. The Khan's name is Borboi, and he is called the Khan because he is an important person who rules everyone. They all exchange their sables with him for silver and silk and cotton and copper lead. And two or three times a year he sends from two to three thousand of his men to the Zeia and Shilka to battle the Daur people who do not pay iasak to him or trade with him.

The road to the Khan from the Zeia goes from the Umlekan across the mountains, along the Khudynka River. It takes six weeks to reach the Shilka River traveling by horse. Many Daur people and farming Tungus live along the Shilka, and they grow an abundance of food crops. The journey from the Zeia and Umlekan rivers to the Shilka River, to Duva ostrozhek, takes two days if one travels by horse, or four days on foot. Prince Ildega lives in that ostrozhek with his people, some 100 men, and many uluses are under the jurisdiction of that ostrozhek. Prince Lavkai lives near prince Ildega. The former has a small ostrozhek which is mentioned in a report written down during the interrogation of the Enisei servitor Maksim Perfilev. There are about 30 men in his ulus. Prince Dontyul says that Prince Lavkai has 300 men in his ulus and he also says that three Mongol princes live near Lavkai along the Shilka River; they are nomadic stockmen. One has 300 ulus people, and each of the other two has 100 persons. Lavkai has a great deal of grain which he carries in boats to the Mongol princes and sells in exchange for livestock. The Daur prince Dontyul did not go to visit the Khan in person, but his father, Kenchiulai, has visited him many times.

On December 21, 1644, a Shamagir Tungus named Topkun, a Daur prince from the Bokan volost named Bebra, and a Ducher prince named Chinega were questioned. When they brought in their iasak for the Sovereign they told Vasilii Poiarkov that there are no silver, copper, or lead ores, or any of the blue pigment which is used to dye cotton, to be found along the Zeia, Shilka, Shungal or Amur rivers or their tributaries. There is no silver there, nor do they produce silk and cotton fabrics. The silver, silk, cotton, copper and lead come to them from the Khan, from whom they buy it in exchange for sable pelts.

The Khan battles any who do not pay iasak to him or trade with him. Three times a year he sends his troops to attack such people on the Zeia and Shilka rivers. His troops number between 1,000 and 2,000, or even as many as 5,000 men. When he was questioned, the Shamagir Tungus named Topkun further stated that he had personally visited the Daur Prince Lavkai on the Shilka River, but that he did not see nor hear whether or not he had any silver. From the Shilka he portaged to the upper Aldan and to the upper Olekma. He is also familiar with the route from the Shilka along the Nyrcha River to the Karanga and Vitim rivers. During interrogation Bebra gave the following information. "Our tribe numbers more than 100 men, and the Sheleginsk tribe has 300. The leader is Dosiia, who has built an ostrozhek at the mouth of the Selimba River. The name of the ostrozhek is Molydykidich. There are 40 Turks and 30 Ezhegunsk men there also. Along the Selimba River there live 30 men who belong to the Dulantsk settled Tungus tribe."

This same person also said they gather together in Dosiia's ostrozhek. The Biral Tungus, who have many reindeer, live in the uppermost reaches of the Selimba River. Many nomadic Mongols live along the Shilka upriver from Lavkai, so Lavkai takes grain to them in boats and exchanges it for livestock. During the questioning prince Bebra told us that he had not personally visited the Khan, but that his nephew Davar goes there every year, and it takes six weeks by horse to reach the Khan from the mouth of the Selimba. All three, the Shamogirsk Tungus, Topkun; the Daur prince Bebra, and the Ducher prince Chinega, stated during the interrogation that the Khan has a town built of logs, that there is an earthen wall around the town, and that the Khan has firearms and bows and many cannon. They pay iasak to the Khan in sables, and purchase from him silver and silk and cotton and copper and lead ore in exchange for sables. The Khan takes one male hostage from the people who pay him iasak. He has many tribal people as hostages, and when he collects sables as iasak, he sends these sables to the Chinese Empire in exchange for silver, copper and lead. . . . [missing] The Khan does not grow or manufacture the silk and cotton, but rather, receives them from the Chinese Empire.

The Khan's name is Borboi, and he is called this because he is a great man with much power, and exerts control over everyone. The Khan grows a great deal of grain. He battles [the Tungus] because they will not give him hostages. The Khan has his own language, and whenever he takes one of their men prisoner in battle, he has an interpreter for their language. The Khan also has his own system of writing. The Khan has a large amount of silver and silk and many other precious things. The route to the Khan from the Zeia River follows along the small Khudynka River where the Daur and Tungus and many farming Mongols, both settled and nomadic, live.

Bebra's nephew, Davar, told the piatidesiatnik Iurii Petrov and his comrades, during the interrogation, that he had visited the Khan in the summer of 1643, and that the Khan has a log town with an earthen wall around it, and that he has firearms and bows and many cannon, and that his people distill a great deal of spirits from grain, and grow much grain, and that this Khan has many hostages from many different tribes.

Vasilii built a zimov'e on the Umlekan River. The servitors had very little food left, and had nothing to eat until spring. The servitors and the promyshlenniks and the piatidesiatnik Iurii Petrov and the desiatniks and all the servitors petitioned the Sovereign, asking that the Sovereign grant them permission to proceed to the ostrozheks of the Daur princes Dosiia and Kolpa to collect the Sovereign's iasak and to procure food so that they would have enough to last until spring.

Their petition was granted, and Vasilii sent Iurii Petrov and his 70 men to go to the Daur ostrozhek to Dosiia and Kolpa; he instructed them to lure them with kindness to come under the Sovereign's mighty hand, and then when the princes came to them from the ostrozheks, they were to be seized as hostages. Vasilii and his men would hide in the forest beyond the palisade [of the ostrozhek] or in a tower they would build, and not approach the ostrozhek until they had examined the situation to decide what would be most advantageous for the Sovereign. When Iurii and his comrades came to the ostrozhek, the Daur princes Dosiia, Kolpa and Davar met them one verst before they reached the ostrozhek. They kowtowed to the Imperial Majesty and took Dosiia and Kolpa as hostages, but allowed Davar to return to the ostrozhek. They set aside three iurts where Iurii and his comrades could live, and gave him provisions of grain and 40 sacks of groats. They also brought them 10 head of cattle. Iurii and his men spent the night in the iurts. They had their banners with them. Fifty servitors walked around the ostrozhek and examined it for strength and for a possible way to broach it. Iurii told the Daur princes that he would like to be invited to the ostrozhek, but they replied, "Many people live in the ostrozhek and they have never met Russians, so they will fight them, which will cause much trouble." But Iurii and his men were insistent, and took the princes Dosiia and Kolpa to the ostrozhek.

The ulus people belonging to the princes immediately assembled and attacked Iurii and his men from the ostrozhek. Many people came; many came in from the fields on horseback; and there was a great battle in which ten servitors were seriously wounded. They were so badly wounded they could not leave the ostrozhek, so they remained there. Prince Kolpa was killed, but the other prince, Dosiia, killed a servitor who had held him hostage and fled to the ostrozhek. The rest of the servitors were wounded, and those in the iurt near the ostrozhek were besieged. They held out for three days and on the fourth night they returned to Vasilii on the Umlekan. It took them ten days to reach the Umlekan, wearing full armor.

When these men joined Vasilii that winter they divided all the supplies so that each had 30 grivenkas. They lived all winter and spring on pine and on roots. When the service people, led by Iurii

Petrov and his men, went from the ostrozhek to join Vasilii on the Umlekan, the Daur prince Dontyul escaped from his irons and from his captors, the service persons Galka Surinin and Osip Krokha. Subsequently 40 of the service people who had come from the ostrozhek died of starvation.

At last in the spring the piatidesiatnik Patrikii Minin and his men reached Vasilii in their boats. Vasilii gathered the rest of the service people together and they went down the Zeia River. From the Selimba River they went in boats to the Gogulkurga River, which took three days. That river empties into the left bank of the lower reaches of the Zeia. There is a volost called Gogul at the mouth of that river, on the Zeia, and there is a daur ostrozhek in that volost, with two princes in the ostrozhek, Omut and Lombo. There are 200 men from the ulus in the ostrozhek. All of these people farm and raise livestock. They grow a great deal of grain, and they pay iasak to the Khan in sables. Opposite Gogul, across the Zeia, is the volost of Shepka, where there are 100 Daur men; they are also farming people.

From Gogul they sailed to the Toma River in one day. The Toma empties into the left bank of the Zeia. Many settled farming Daurs and Tungus live along that river. From the Toma they sailed for one day to the Daur prince Baldach. Daur farming people live on both banks of the Zeia between Gogul and Baldach, who has an ostrozhek with 100 agricultural men from his ulus who live there with him. From Baldach's ostrozhek they sailed on to the Shilka River in one day. All of Baldach's people are agricultural Daurs. Baldach pays the Khan iasak in sables, and the Khan holds Baldach's wife as a hostage. The Shilka joins the Zeia on the right side, and flows to the Shungal River.

Six grains grow along both the Shilka and the Zeia: barley, oats, millet, buckwheat, pease and flax. Baldach also grows produce such as cucumbers, poppyseed, beans, garlic, apples, pears, walnuts and Russian nuts. Many settled agricultural Duchers live along the Shilka down to the mouth of the Zeia. It takes three weeks to go by boat from the mouth of the Zeia to the Shungal. The Duchers have their own language, and there was no Ducher interpreter.

Vasilii sent the desiatnik Ilia Ermolin and 25 servitors and promyshlenniks to explore and find out how far it is to the sea. They traveled in small boats for three days, and then on their return they stopped to camp overnight half a day's travel from

Vasilii's camp. Many Duchers gathered together and ambushed Ilia and killed nearly all his men. Only two survived, the servitor Pankratii Mitrofanov and the promyshlennik Luka Ivanov.

Many settled farming people called Shungals live along the Shungal River. Nomadic livestock-herding Mongols live in the upper reaches of the river. When the Shungal and the Shilka join, they flow on as the Shungal. From the Shilka River Vasilii sailed down the Amur for six days. Many settled Duchers live on both banks of the Amur. The Amur falls into the right side of the Shungal, and there are farming Duchers living along the Amur there, but the Tungus inhabit the upper reaches. When the Amur and the Shungal join, the Amur flows on to the sea.

Vasilii sailed on the Amur for four days to the Natkas, to prince Chekun and more farming Duchers. From the Natkas he sailed on and reached the Giliaks in two weeks. The Natkas live along both banks of the Amur in uluses, and they do not pay iasak to anyone. From the Giliaks he sailed to the sea in two weeks. The settled Giliaks live on both banks of the Amur in uluses all the way to the sea. They also live along the sea shore, and on islands and in bays. They live on fish. The Giliaks do not pay iasak to the Khan. The Tungus live in the mountains.

Vasilii and his men wintered at the mouth of the Amur, and with God's mercy and the good fortune of the Sovereign, he took three hostages from the Giliaks named Seldiug, Kilem and Kotiug Diskin. When they were questioned they told Vasilii that Seldiug has two uluses and that there are 100 men in one ulus called Mingal and 150 men in the other which is called Gogudin. Kilem has an ulus called Onchin with 200 men. Kotiug Diskin said that his father has five Kalguisk uluses and that there are 250 men in them, and that there are other uluses near them inhabited by Chagodals. A land holder named Chegotot Senburak has four more uluses with 300 men. The ulus of Kultsa belongs to prince Mugottel and has 40 men. Mugottel has another ulus called Rygan, with 30 men. The Taktinsk ulus of prince Uzim has 100 men. From these hostages Vasilii took iasak consisting of twelve forties of sables and six sable shubas, and then took the hostages with him to Iakutsk ostrog.

In the summer Vasilii Poiarkov returned from the mouth of the Amur River to Iakutsk ostrog. He went by sea to the mouth of the Ula River in twelve weeks. He spent the winter on the Ula River, and with God's mercy and the Sovereign's luck he took a hostage and collected from him iasak consisting of seventeen sables, seven immature sables, and seven sable backs. He left the hostage behind on the Ula River with 20 servitors and promyshlenniks who were to collect additional iasak. In the spring Vasilii left the Ula River and continued his journey, using sleds to cross the portage to the upper reaches of the Maia River, which took two weeks. He sailed along the Maia to the Aldan River in six days, then along the Aldan for four days to the Lena, and for six days on the Lena up to Iakutsk ostrog.

When the Sovereign Tsar and Grand Prince Mikhail Fedorovich of all Russia will decree that at least 300 government servitors (that is, more than the number sent with Vasilii to collect iasak and to bring the new lands under his Tsarist suzerainty) be sent to these rivers, the Zeia and the Shilka, and into the lands where Vasilii Poiarkov explored, then the natives in those lands along those rivers can be brought under his Sovereign Tsarist suzerainty, and they can be put into eternal servitude, and solidify the subjugation of those lands through the construction of ostrozheks.

The first ostrozhek should be built where the settled farming Daur people live at the mouth of the Selimba River, where the Daur prince Dosiia rules. For purposes of control there should be a garrison of 50 men in that ostrozhek. Another ostrozhek should be built and fortified on the Zeia River among the agricultural Daur people in a place currently under the control of the Daur prince Baldach. In that ostrozhek there should be a small garrison of fifty men for control. A third ostrozhek should be built among the farming Ducher people on the Zeia, and there should also be a garrison of fifty men there.

The other 150 service people should be sent along the Zeia and Shilka rivers and their tributaries to explore, in order to find ways to bring these settled agricultural people under the Sovereign's mighty hand, and to bring them into eternal servitude to him, and to collect iasak from them. If this is done, then the Sovereign will realize great profit, because these lands are populous and abound in grain and sables and many other animals. Many varieties of grain are grown, and the rivers abound in fish, and the government troops in those lands would not incur any shortage of food supplies.

See: *Dopolneniia k aktam istoricheskim* (St. Petersburg: 1848), III, 50–56.

68

NOT BEFORE JULY 12, 1646

A REPORT FROM THE VOEVODAS OF IAKUTSK, VASILII PUSHKIN AND
KIRIL SUPONEV, TO TSAR MIKHAIL FEDOROVICH CONCERNING THE
NUMBER OF SERVITORS IN IAKUTSK OSTROG AND IN THE ZIMOV'ES,
AND CONCERNING IVAN ERASTOV'S DISCOVERY OF THE ANADYR
(POGYCHA) RIVER

To the Sovereign Tsar and Grand Prince Mikhail Fedorovich of all Russia, your humble servants Vasilii Pushkin, Kiril Suponev and Petr Stenshin humbly report. Sire, in this year of 1646, in accordance with your Sovereign ukaz, we, your humble servants, came on your service on the first of June to Iakutsk ostrog on the great Lena River. Sire, 50 servitors came with us, your humble servants, from Tobolsk, to escort us and to relieve the voevoda. Sire, according to the Tobolsk tax records, the following servitors are in Iakutsk ostrog: five deti boiarskie, 395 servitors, obrok peasants and gunners, two black priests, one white priest, a deacon, two interpreters of the Iakut and Tungus languages, and two blacksmiths. Some of these persons guard your sable treasury, and others collect iasak.

Sire, in 1643 when we, your humble servants, went from Eniseisk ostrog on your service to the great Lena River, Sire, when we had made our way past the first rapids on the Tunguska we sent one man to you in Moscow, Sire, with our report. Sire, when we, your servants, reached the Lena portage in the year 1646, we sent your sable treasury on to you in Moscow, Sire. We had collected these sables upon our arrival at the portage. We also sent our report with three men.

The stolnik and voevoda Petr Golovin had sent your sable treasury for the past four years from Iakutsk ostrog to the Lena portage that winter, and we sent that to you in Moscow, Sire, under the guard of 30 men. While we were at the Lena portage we sent 51 men from the Ilim River on your service, Sire, to Verkholensk and Bratsk ostrozheks. Your sovereign food provisions had been sent to us in 1645, Sire, to the Ilim-Lena portage, but they did not reach us before the river froze over. We left 29 men behind with those provisions with instructions to take the census and collect your iasak, Sire. We left two men at Ust-Kut [portage?] to collect iasak and to keep it under guard at Sol. Also, Sire, when we were in your lands at Ust-Kut we hired five men under an agreement with the former Lena voevodas and stolniks, Petr Golovin and his men. Sire, we sent two men from that roster from Ust-Kut to you in Moscow.

We left five men in the zimov'es to collect your iasak, Sire, and to guard the hostages on the Chichiuisk portage. We left four on the Olekma; three in the zimov'e on the upper reaches of the Viliui; sixteen in the zimov'e on the lower Iana; seven at the zimov'e on the upper Iana; and six on the Olenek.

On July 12 of this present year of 1646, we, your humble servants, Sire, sent men from Iakutsk ostrog to distant rivers on assignments of one year or more to collect your iasak, Sire, and to subdue new hostile lands. We sent 40 men to the new lands on the Lama and on the Ulia and Okhota rivers. Sixteen were sent to the Sobachia and Indigirka, and 20 to the Kolyma. Sire, God willing, your iasak collection for the year 1647 will be as large as the one for 1645 which we sent to Moscow, if you will send eighteen servitors to the Viliui River in addition to the three who are presently there; fifteen to the middle zimov'e on the Viliui River; ten to the mouth of the Viliui; fifteen to the zimov'e on the upper Maia; six to the zimov'e on the middle Maia; six to Butalsk ostrozhek on the Aldan; fifteen to the upper Olekma, with hostages, to subdue the Tungus; eight to the Zhigana; five to the Stolb; and six to the Agma and the Lama. Twenty-three should be sent to the Iana to replace the men presently stationed there in the two zimov'es and fourteen more should go to the Olenek to reinforce the present six men.

We are now sending two men to you in Moscow, Sire, with the reports from us, your humble servants, and with reports on your other affairs, Sire. In this present year, 1646, we have sent a small detachment of fifteen men to Moscow with reports and with your Sovereign iasak and pominki and the sable treasury collected as a tithe. The total number of servitors being sent to you in Moscow this year, 1646, Sire, is the same as it was last year. One man is being sent with the reports, and 400 will soon be sent out to the zimov'es to collect the iasak. Sire, we are sending one of the rifleman, the white priest Vasilii, and one of the obrok blacksmiths, Druzhina Semenov, back from Iakutsk ostrog to the Russian towns in Siberia because they are old and incapacitated, and are much afflicted with blindness so that they cannot see.

Sire, as a result of all these men being sent out, there will only be 50 men left in Iakutsk ostrog for the winter. Sire, we, your humble servants, will have great difficulty holding out all winter in Iakutsk ostrog with only 50 servitors because there are a great many Iakut natives near the ostrog, and during the winter 50 or more Iakut natives will come to the ostrog at a time with the iasak, Sire. Because we have so few men we will be hard put to hold our own. According to the reports of the servitors, who are presently being sent out to collect your iasak, Sire, they are being sent to zimov'es for this purpose in such small numbers, Sire, that it is exceedingly difficult for them to carry out the collection. The Iakuts and Tungus see how few collectors there are, and pay your iasak and pominki, Sire, at their will, and in whatever amount they please. Sire, we, your humble servants, have already written to you from the mouth of the Kuta River about how many servitors are needed at Verkholensk and Bratsk ostrozheks to provide protection against hostile Bratsk natives.

Sire, the servitors have come to us, your humble servants, in Iakutsk ostrog to petition you. These are veteran servitors who were imprisoned by Petr Golovin without instructions from you, Sire, and without the counsel of his associates. He then acquired new men to replace them. Thus there are now more servitors here than you had authorized, Sire.

Ivan Erastov and his 40 men stated during an interrogation that they had found new lands. When they left the mouth of the Lena River they sailed by sea to the east beyond the Lama and beyond the Sobacha and Olozeika and Kovyma [Kolyma] rivers, to a new river, the Pogycha [Anadyr]. There are tributary rivers which empty into the Pogycha. Many natives of various tribes live along the Pogycha and its tributaries, and they do not pay iasak to anyone. Russians have never before been on this river, Sire.

The sables there are very dark and fine. Sire, the servitors ask that you give them money and provisions according to their former pay scale, and that you grant them the right to go for two years to that river, to those people who do not pay iasak, and collect iasak from them and bring them under your Tsarist mighty hand.

Sire, we your humble servants, without instructions from you, have not presumed to give them remuneration on their former scale nor send them to that new river.

Sire, your servitors who are presently being sent to distant tributary rivers have sailed down the Lena to the sea. From the mouth of the Lena they sailed east on the sea, and went to the Sobacha and Indigirka and Kolyma and Pogycha rivers. When they were questioned they reported that there are many Tungus, Iukagir, Kolyma and Shereboi people along these rivers, as well as natives from other tribes, and they talk of countless possible iasak-paying people. Sire, only if you decree that 100 or more servitors be sent to those distant rivers to assist those men already there, can the hostile, non-iasak-paying people be brought under your Sovereign Tsarist authority, Sire, and be forced to pay iasak to you, Sire; and if this is done, there will be great profit for you, Sire.

But this will be true only if you authorize that more servitors be sent to reinforce those already there, and only if you order that weapons be sent out from Moscow for the new people. Only then, Sire, can we recruit volunteer promyshlenniks from the Siberian servitors into your service, Sire, because the promyshlenniks on the Lena River stay for rather long periods of time, for five to six years, and some for as long as ten years or more. We have generally used natives for service on the Lena, because they are accustomed to going out with servitors and taking hostages.

There are no firearms such as muskets and carbines in Iakutsk ostrog on the Lena, Sire. We, your humble servants, have written to you in Moscow about this, Sire, from the Ilim-Lena portage. Sire, unless we have reinforcements, it will not be possible to take the distant lands on the great Lena River for you, because there is such a shortage of servitors in Verkholensk and Bratsk ostrozheks that they have great difficulty defending themselves against the warlike Bratsk people. Sire, servitors are sent out in small groups to collect your iasak in the zimov'es on the Lena River and on the Ianga, Olenek, Sobacha, Indigirka and Kolyma rivers, which empty into the sea; there are too few servitors in these small groups to threaten and subdue the iasak and non-iasak people. Sire, these natives are merciless, and as wild as animals. They will invite servitors and promyshlenniks into their winter quarters and offer them food, and there will be no apparent danger, but then the natives will kill them. Thus the iasak collectors are forced to lock themselves up in their own zimov'es with hostages. . . . [missing]

One iasak collector, a servitor named Maksim Tilitsyn, came to us, your humble servants, Sire, in Iakutsk ostrog, from the Olenek River which lies beyond the mountains. When we questioned him he said that in the winter of this present year of 1646 on St. Philip's Day about 50 Tungus from the Aziansk and Sinegirsk tribes came from Mangazeia uezd, from a river which is a tributary of the Anabar. Sire, these Tungus had been with the Mangazeia servitors who were on the Anabar to collect your iasak, Vasilii Sychov and ten men and twenty promyshlenniks. The Tungus had six hostages who came along with them. When they were on the Olenek River they told other Tungus natives that they had killed the Mangazeia servitor and the promyshlenniks on the Anabar, and had freed their hostages. Sire, on the Olenek River these Tungus killed five promyshlenniks in the zimov'e and in the forest.

Sire, before we came here, when Petr Golovin was stolnik and voevoda here, the Tungus killed many servitors and promyshlenniks.

Sire, there are too few servitors in Iakutsk ostrog to perform your service this winter. In order to carry out your assignment, Sire, and to discover and bring new hostile lands under your mighty authority, Sire, in the future we will need new men with muskets and carbines. Sire, the servitors have been exploring the Pogycha River, but without your ukaz, Sire, people are not at present being sent there.

In regard to other matters such as the white priest and the blacksmith, we, your humble servants, will do as you decree, Sovereign Tsar and Grand Prince of all Russia, Mikhail Fedorovich.

Reference: TsGADA, f. Sibirskii prikaz, stolb. No. 274, ll. 420–426.
See: N. S. Orlova, ed. *Otkrytiia russkikh zemleprokhodtsev i poliarnykh more-khodov XVII veka* (Moscow: 1951), 212–218.

69

A PETITION TO TSAR MIKHAIL FEDOROVICH FROM THE DEACON
SPIRIDON TO BAPTIZE A IAKUT GIRL HE HAS BOUGHT

I, to the Sovereign Tsar and Grand Prince Mikhail Fedorovich of all Russia, your humble pilgrim the deacon Spiridon humbly submits a petition. Merciful Sovereign Tsar and Grand Prince Mikhail Fedorovich of all Russia, grant the request of your pilgrim. Sovereign, permit me to baptize a young Iakut girl captive, whose Iakut name is Tyazal and whose Russian name is Okulina, whom I bought. Sovereign Tsar, be merciful, grant me my request.

[A note added to the petition: July 22, 1646. Inquire as to whether or not she is from iasak people, and from whom she was purchased.]

II. On that same date in the main church of Iakutsk ostrog the deacon Spiridon, in response to these queries, stated the following. In the year 1646, on May 24, a servitor named Oleg Lukianov sold the girl to the monk Semeon, priest of the Iakutsk ostrog church. On June 13 of that same year, 1646, the monk Semeon taught that young woman her prayers and gave her the name of Okulina. On July 13 of that same year 1646 the monk Semeon sold that young girl, Okulina, to me, the deacon.

On November 25, approval was given to Ivan and Panfil to baptize the girl.

See: Ia. P. Alkor and B. D. Grekov, eds., *Kolonialnaia politika moskovskogo gosudarstva v Iakutii XVII v.* (Leningrad: 1936), 161.

70

NOVEMBER 4, 1646

A REPORT FROM THE VOEVODA OF ENISEISK, FEDOR UVAROV, CON-
CERNING THE IMPOSITION OF IASAK ON THE HOSTILE TUNGUS NA-
TIVES, AND THE CONSTRUCTION OF AN OSTROG AT LAKE BAIKAL
NEAR THE HEAD OF THE ANGARA RIVER

To the Sovereign Tsar and Grand Prince Aleksei Mikhailovich of all Russia, your humble servants Fedor Uvarov and Vasilii Shpilkin report. On November 4, 1646, Sire, the ataman Vasilii Kolesnikov wrote to us, your humble servants, in Eniseisk ostrog, from Lake Baikal. He wrote that in the year 1644, in accordance with the ukaz of your late father of blessed memory, the Sovereign Tsar and Grand Prince Mikhail Fedorovich of all Russia, he, Vasilii, was sent from Eniseisk ostrog together with servitors and volunteers from various towns to collect the government iasak and search for new iasak territories and bring these lands under the mighty Tsarist hand of your late father of blessed memory, the Sovereign Tsar and Grand Prince Mikhail Fedorovich of all Russia. He was also sent to explore the Lake Baikal region, and to search for silver and silver ore.

With your good fortune, Sovereign, in the year 1644 Vasilii reached Kultuk on Lake Baikal. One day short of the Upper Angara River he camped for the night in hostile territory at the mouth of the Tikhon River, and managed to capture the Tungus prince Kotega, one of the leading princes in the entire region. He summoned another prince, Mukotei, to the head of the Angara River, and then took both princes hostage. Sire, for the year 1644 the natives paid iasak for these princes, and Sire, in the future they are willing to pay iasak in full. Sire, these princes are appealing to other natives to come under your favor. Vasilii asked these princes about silver and silver ore, but these Tungus princes provide contradictory information, Sire. At first they told Vasilii that they would lead him to the silver ore, but then they said that they did not know anything about any ore. They also said that they knew where a great deal of silver is, and that in the spring they would be willing to procure the silver and the silver ore. These natives wanted to guide the servitors to that ore in the springtime.

Sire, the ataman Vasilii Kolesnikov built an ostrozhek at the head of the Angara River and fortified it well; then because he was short of provisions Vasilii sent 40 servitors and guliashchie liudi out from the ostrozhek to Eniseisk ostrog. They were guided by Petr Golubtsov and his men. We, your humble servants, asked Petr and his men how much iasak these natives gave to ataman Vasilii Kolesnikov, and how many people these princes have, and how many paid your iasak, and whether we could hope to collect iasak from these natives in the future by taking hostages, and whether it would be possible to bring hostile territories under the control of this ostrozhek in order to bring them under your mighty Tsarist hand, Sire.

Sire, this servitor Petr Golubtsov and his men, when they were questioned told us, your humble servants, in the prikaz office, that during the year 1645, Sire, they had wintered with the ataman Vasilii Kolesnikov on Lake Baikal opposite Olkhon Island, and that in the summer, two weeks prior to St. Peter's Sunday, they sailed along the left shore of Lake Baikal, and before they reached the Angara River, a Tungus prince, Kotega, appeared on shore and had ten or more Tungus men with him. Sire, the servitors jumped out of their boats with their guns and started to fight these Tungus. During the battle, Sire, they captured the Tungus and took prince Kotega hostage. Then they sailed to the mouth of the Angara River and built an ostrog. Sire, from that ostrog prince Kotega allowed ataman Vasilii Kolesnikov to send his servitors together with his own ulus people along the Angara River to the ulus of prince Mukotei, in order to bring him under your mighty Tsarist hand, Sire.

Sire, ataman Vasilii Kolesnikov did send servitors to the ulus of prince Mukotei along the upper reaches of the Angara River, and, Sire, with your good fortune these servitors brought prince Mukotei to the ostrog and kept him there as a hostage. Sire, from the princes they collected your iasak consisting of four forties and 35 sables, three red foxes, a Tungus shuba made of sables, and three beavers. Sire, these princes wish to pay iasak in full for 600 archers, at the rate of five sables per man. These princes said, Sire, that along the Angara River there is a prince who has about 300 ulus archers, and, Sire, princes Kotega and Mukotei want to send a messenger to him in order to bring him under your Tsarist mighty hand, Sire. The ataman Vasilii Kolesnikov sent twenty servitors to that prince and he sent others to collect your iasak, Sovereign. Sire, they report that Tungus people live along the Angara all the way to its headwaters.

Princes Kotega and Mukotei told the servitors about the silver, Sire, saying that the silver can be obtained from the Mongols. After Vasilii and his men fortify the place where they are now, they will make appropriate inquiries about the silver and the silver ore. Sire, the ataman Vasilii Kolesnikov and his men have very few provisions left. Sire, on the Angara River they collected four forties and 35 sables, three red foxes, a Tungus sable shuba and three beavers, but they did not send this iasak to us, your humble servants, in Eniseisk ostrog, Sire. The ataman Vasilii Kolesnikov will send this iasak to Eniseisk ostrog in the spring, when he sends the rest of the iasak.

Last year, Sire, in 1645, we, your humble servants, sent the syn boiarskii Ivan Pakhabov and servitors and volunteers from Eniseisk ostrog to Lake Baikal. Ivan's instructions were that if Vasilii's enterprise were profitable, then Ivan was to join him and work with him with all the zeal God's mercy would allow, and he was to give Vasilii the provisions he needed. We sent 200 puds of rye with Ivan to ataman Vasilii Kolesnikov and his men from the government warehouses at Eniseisk.

Sire, in the spring we, your humble servants, will not be able to send any reinforcements or replacements to ataman Vasilii Kolesnikov and syn boiarskii Ivan Pakhabov because we have so few servitors at Eniseisk. However, Sire, there are many guliashchie liudi at Eniseisk who could be recruited. Sire, the servitors who are sent from Tobolsk, Tomsk and other towns in accordance with your ukaz bring no benefit to you, because they are all convicted criminals who steal, kill and gamble all along the way. When they reach Eniseisk ostrog, Sire, they are naked, barefoot and hungry, and before they reach their assigned destination on your Sovereign service, they have run off. In the year 1645, Sire, 46 men were sent from Tomsk to Eniseisk ostrog to convoy the government food supplies to the Lena portage. Every one of them ran off, just as they had done in former years. Only the guliashchie liudi should be recruited, Sire, because they will be more useful to you. In case of theft they guarantee to replace the stolen goods, and they will not run off from government service. Moreover, Sire, the guliashchie liudi are very enterprising, and

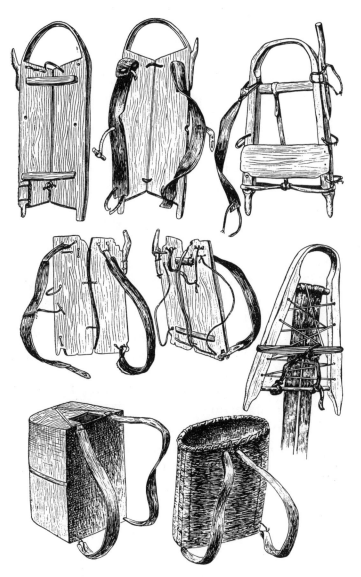

Wood and leather backpacks used for summer and winter transport in eastern Siberia. From Saburova, *Kultura i byt russkogo
naseleniia Priangaria.*

they are not outlaws. There are many of these people at Eniseisk
ostrog, Sire, who have lived there for five, six and even ten years.

Sire, we beg you to instruct us, your humble servants, as to
what to do.

See: *Dopolneniia k aktam istoricheskim* (St. Petersburg: 1848), III, 68–70.

71

FEBRUARY 11–19, 1647

A PETITION TO TSAR ALEKSEI MIKHAILOVICH FROM THE PIATIDESI-
ATNIK MARTIN VASILEV ASKING PERMISSION TO BAPTIZE A IAKUT
GIRL HE HAS BOUGHT

I, to the Sovereign Tsar and Grand Prince Aleksei Mikhailovich of all Russia, a petition from your humble cossack piatidesiatnik, Martin Vasilev, of Iakutsk ostrog. Sovereign, in the
year 1646 I, your humble servant, bought a young woman named
Bakaian from a Iakut to work for me. Merciful Sovereign Tsar
and Grand Prince Aleksei Mikhailovich of all Russia, reward me,
your slave, for my age and disability, and permit me, Sovereign,
to have the young woman whom I bought to do my work for me
baptized into Orthodox Christianity and have the priest teach her
prayers. Sovereign Tsar, be merciful.

II. On that same date in the Prikaz office the Iakut girl was
questioned and said her name was Bakaian and that she was the
daughter of Eiuk. Her father Eiuk lived in Atamaisk volost and
did not pay iasak to the Sovereign, but lived among the Iakut
leaders. When her father died she was still a small child and lived
in Atamaisk volost with a Iakut woman named Otkon Chimchin
who sold her to the piatidesiatnik Martin Vasilev about two years
ago in the spring. She wishes to be baptized into the orthodox Christian faith. Her testimony was interpreted by Ontiush
Odintsov.

II. On February 19, 1647, the voevodas Vasilii Nikitich
Pushkin and Kiril Osipovich Suponev, after hearing this report,
gave instructions that the piatidesiatnik Martin Vasilev be allowed
to have the captive he had bought baptized, but that after that he
must sign an affadavit that he would not use her for prostitution
nor live with her unlawfully nor force her to be his slave [two
words indecipherable], but that he will have her work and will
treat her as cossacks and promyshlenniks treat their wives.

See: Ia. P. Alkor and B. D. Grekov, eds., *Kolonialnaia politika moskovskogo
gosudarstva v Iakutii v XVII v.* (Leningrad: 1936), 163.

72

APRIL 22, 1647

THE REPORT OF THE SERVITOR MIKHAIL STADUKHIN CONCERNING THE KOLYMA, CHIUKHCHA AND ANADYR RIVERS AND THE NATIVE POPULATION IN THOSE VALLEYS

On April 22, 1647, in the Prikaz office in Iakutsk ostrog, the servitor Mikhail Stadukhin appeared before us, the voevodas Vasilii Nikitich Pushkin and Kiril Osipovich Suponev, and the diak Petr Stenshin. On November 23, 1646, prior to the arrival of the voevoda Vasilii Nikitich Pushkin, Mikhail had returned from collecting government iasak on the Kolyma River, and he made the following report.

He spent two years on the Kolyma River collecting the Sovereign's iasak. The Kolyma is a large river, and like the Lena it flows into the sea; also like the Lena, it flows east and north. Along the Kolyma live native Kolyma people. Some are nomadic and herd reindeer, and others are settled. They are populous and have their own language.

Near the Kolyma is another river, the Chiukhcha, which falls into the sea this side of the Kolyma. Along the Chiukhcha live natives of the Chukchi tribe; like the Samoeds they are partly nomadic reindeer-herding people, and partly settled.

Stadukhin's wife was a Kolyma slave captive named Kaliba. She had lived with the Chukchi for three years, and she told him that there is an island in the sea which can be reached by boat, by sailing to the left. It is possible to see the island in the sea from the mainland, on the left, while one is sailing from the Lena, from Sviatyi Nos to the Iana, and from the Iana to the Sobacha, and the Indigirka, and from the Indigirka to the Kolyma. The island is clearly visible; it has snow-covered mountains, waterfalls and small rivers. This mountainous island is surrounded by deep water. Stadukhin's men and the promyshlenniks think it is the same mountainous island called Novaia Zemlia which can be reached from Pomor'e from Mezen, and lies opposite the mouths of the Enisei, Taz and Lena rivers. The Chukchi who live on this side of the Kolyma use reindeer to travel from their settlements to the island in one day in winter. They kill walrus on that island, and bring back the walrus heads with all the tusks and offer prayers to these heads. Stadukhin, however, did not see any walrus tusks. But the promyshlenniks told him that they had seen walrus tusks when they were with the Chukchi, and that the runners on the reindeer-drawn sleds are made from walrus tusks. These Chukchi have no sables because they live in the tundra, near the sea, but sables are very fine and dark all along the Kolyma.

Beyond the Kolyma there is a river called the Pogycha, which can be reached by boats from the Kolyma in about three days if the weather is right. It is a large river, there are sables there, and many natives who have their own language live along its banks.

At present only one servitor Vtoroi Gavrilov. . . . [missing] has been left behind on the Kolyma River. If the Sovereign should decree that a large number of his servitors be sent to these rivers, then his iasak collection from there will be large, and the government Treasury will be greatly enriched. Stadukhin believes that in the future the government iasak collection will be large. The sables there are all fine and dark, the animals are of prime size, and there are also many red and blue foxes. There are no other animals along these rivers, however, because the region is extremely cold. The servitors and promyshlenniks along these rivers live on fish, for these rivers abound in all varieties of fish.

See: *Dopolneniia k aktam istoricheskim* (St. Petersburg: 1848), III, 99–102.

73

REPORTS FROM THE PROMYSHLENNIK GRIGORII VIZHEVTSOV AND THE
PISMENNAIA GOLOVA VASILII POIARKOV CONCERNING THE ROUTE
FROM IAKUTSK TO THE SHILKA RIVER AND THE NATIVES WHO IN-
HABIT THAT REGION

On May 27, 1647, in the prikaz office of Iakutsk ostrog, the
following report was made to the voevodas Vasilii Nikitich
Pushkin and Kiril Osipovich Suponev and the diak Petr Stenshin
by the promyshlennik Grigorii Grigorevich Vizhevtsov, who
is from the town of Zaboria located on the Pinega portage in
Kholmogory uezd, under the jurisdiction of the Church of Sv.
Nikolai the Miracle Worker.

In the year 1646 Grigorii went on his own sable hunting expedition along the Olekma River, taking five reliable men with
him, and a sixth, his own hired man. Grigorii spent two years on
that hunting expedition. His journey from Iakutsk ostrog to the
Olekma River took two and a half weeks. He spent two more
weeks going from the mouth of the Olekma, where it falls into the
Lena, upriver to the mountains, and a further two weeks going
from the mountains up the Olekma. There were ten rapids on the
Olekma in the mountains, but the water is high enough for large
vessels to navigate, provided they are well built and have new anchor, chain and tow ropes.

He went along the Olekma through the mountains to the
mouth of the Tugir River, which took four weeks. There are no
rapids on the Tugir River beyond the mountains, and the water
provides good navigation. Grigorii sailed on the Tugir for four
weeks to reach his zimov'e. The total travel time from Iakutsk
ostrog to his zimov'e was fourteen weeks. The Tugir River falls
into the left bank of the Olekma, from the east, and the mouth is
flat where it empties into the Olekma.

Non-iasak-paying Tungus natives came to him on the Tugir
River, in the summer. They said they belonged to the Uliasint
tribe which had fifteen tents, with two men in each tent, plus
women and children. He saw three Tungus men from another
tribe, the Managir. They said that their tribe is large and has
more than 100 men. When winter approaches these Tungus leave
to go upriver, and they also told Girgorii that in winter they trade

with the Daurs on the Shilka River, which they reach by way of a tributary called the Niuga. The Niuga is a small river about a day's travel from Grigorii's zimov'e.

Grigorii himself sailed to the Niuga, and also sailed on it. From that river the entire mountain range is visible. From the Niuga the Tugir River flows from its source first to the right, then to the west. The Niuga rises in the mountains and falls into the left, or east, bank of the Tugir. The Tungus said that going by way of the Niuga and Shilka Rivers it takes five days to reach the source of the Niuga in the mountains. They go by reindeer, with packs. It takes one day to go from the headwaters of the Niuga across the mountains to the Shilka; they go by way of the small Ui River. Using reindeer with packs, it takes four days to go along the little Ui River, which falls into the Shilka, to the mouth of the Shilka. The total travel time from Grigorii's zimov'e, along the Niuga River, through the mountains, and along the Ui River to the Shilka, is nine or ten days, using reindeer with packs.

The Daurs live at the mouth of the Ui River. They are governed by Prince Lavkai and his ulus people. Lavkai's brother, Shulgan, lives up the Shilka River from him; a third brother, Guldigai, lives along the lower reaches of the Shilka. They do not live far from one another, and come together. The Tungus either did not know or would not tell Grigorii how many ulus people the brothers have. They only said that Lavkai and his brothers have all kinds of grains, wines, arak, and many kinds of livestock. Grigorii observed that these Tungus men and their wives had silver ornaments on their cloaks, and he also noted that they wore silk kaftans. Other Tungus had silk embroidery on their clothing, and silver ornaments a quarter of an arshin and two or three inches in size.

The Tungus said that they buy the silver and clothing and the ornaments and silk decorations from the Daurs in exchange for sables. They did not know whether silver is to be found in Lavkai's land, but they did say that the Daurs travel by horse to another land to obtain silver.

Grigorii traveled on the Olekma and Tugir rivers in a small boat on this hunting expedition. They had 30 puds of provisions with them, in addition to other equipment, in all about 300 puds. Grigorii spent the first winter hunting beyond the Olekma mountains, and the second winter he spent on the Tugir River. He saw these Tungus twice: in the summer of 1646 and in the following fall. They told him that they would like to trade sables in the winter, but they did not come to him. He believes it would be possible to take the Tungus as hostages, because they came to him without fear, and he has also visited them in their hide tents. They came to his zimov'e.

These Tungus had previously encountered the promyshlenniks who were with Shestak Neradovskii, and had traded with them. Shestak Neradovskii and his men were on the Olekma in 1646, beyond the mountains below the Tugir River. They were on a tributary of the Miuga which falls into the Olekma from the same side as the Tugir falls into the Olekma.

In addition to this report by the promyshlennik Grigorii Vizhevtsov, the pismennaia golova Vasilii Poiarkov appeared and was asked whether it is closer to go to the Shilka by way of the Upper Olekma or by the route he traveled? The pismennaia golova Vasilii Poiarkov, having heard the previous report, stated that his journey began with his departure from Iakutsk ostrog on July 13, 1643. He was sent out by Petr Golovin. He traveled along the Aldan to the Uchur, along the Uchur to the Gonam, and along the Gonam to the mountains where they spent the winter, with their provisions, until the Feast of the Intercession of the Holy Virgin in the year 1644. The journey to that place took eleven weeks and three days.

From that zimov'e they used dogsleds to cross the mountains, and came out on the headwaters of the Zeia River, then traveled to the Brianda River, and on that small river. . . . [missing] to the Zeia, then along the Zeia to an ostrozhek where they spent the winter. The dogsled journey took seven weeks. It takes one day to go on foot from the zimov'e to the ostrozhek, across the mountains to the Shilka River. Then from there it takes six days to go by boats to Lavkai and his brothers. Thus Vasilii's route along the Zeia and Shilka rivers is shorter than the Olekma route. If one goes to the headwaters of the Shilka by way of the Olekma and other tributaries, one bypasses the ostrozheks of the Daur prince Boldach and his men; these are beyond the mountains. If one does not wish to winter on the Gonam, one can take dogsleds and in three weeks cross from the Uchur to the mouth of the Gonam, then take a portage across the mountains to the headwaters of the Brianda, which falls into the Zeia.

If one leaves Iakutsk ostrog in the spring soon after the ice breaks up, one can go far along the Gonam River because, although there are many rapids, the water is deep enough to be navigable at that time. The rapids are strong and swift, and they toss the boats about wildly. When the rains fall in the spring it takes a week to navigate the Gonam, although at other times it can be done in two days. Since one can travel only short distances on land, it is necessary to use the rivers.

The promyshlennik Grigorii Grigorevich Vizhevtsov stated that in accordance with the Sovereign's ukaz, the voevodas Vasilii Nikitich Pushkin and Kiril Osipovich Suponev and the diak Petr Stenshin should send the Sovereign's servitors from Iakutsk ostrog up the Olekma River to the mountains to bring new non-iasak Tungus under [Russian] control and collect iasak from them for the Sovereign. They should go up to the N. . . . [missing] River. These servitors should use small boats like the ones Grigorii used earlier and will be using again soon. Each boat should hold no more than six men because the rapids are wild and very fast and the water is very shallow on the upper Olekma in the mountains. Large boats such as doshchaniks which are used to travel to other zimov'es cannot be used on these rapids because their draught is too deep.

Such persons should be sent out from Iakutsk ostrog a week prior to the Feast of St. Peter, because at that time the water will still be high in the great rapids on the Olekma River.

See: Russia. Arkheograficheskaia kommissiia. *Dopolneniia k aktam istoricheskim* (St. Petersburg: 1848), III, 102–104.

74

MARCH 12, 1649

A REPORT TO THE VOEVODAS OF IAKUTSK CONCERNING AN EXPE-
DITION TO THE SHILKA RIVER TO GATHER INFORMATION ON THE
TUNGUS AND DAUR NATIVES

Vasilii Iurev humbly reports to the voevodas of the Sovereign
Tsar and Grand Prince Aleksei Mikhailovich of all Russia,
Vasilii Nikitich [Pushkin] and Kiril Osipovich [Suponev], and to
the diak Petr Grigorevich. On March 12, 1649, I, Vasilii, sent the
servitors Lavrentii Barabanshik, Anastasii Vorobev, Ivan Osetrov
and Martin Vasilev from Tugursk zimov'e to the upper reaches of
the Tugur River, to Ivan Kvashnin in his zimov'e.

I instructed Lavrentii and his men to proceed from Ivan's
zimov'e along the trail where Ivan was hunting sables, beyond
Shilka portage, and then beyond the portage, to investigate
the Tungus people and new Tungus settlements. He also searched
for Daur people to find out where the Daurs live who come from
Prince Lavkai to hunt sables. Iakshakanko reported about these
people in 1648. Lavrentii traveled four and a half weeks looking
for the Tungus and the Daurs, but he did not find them. He
reached the Shilka River where Lavkai and his brothers and relatives and ulus people live. Lavrentii went down two stretches
of the Shilka River, and found a raft along the shore which indicated the Daurs had been there.

He measured the raft and found it was four sazhens long. It
was built in the Russian fashion, the logs were notched as the
Russians notch them and were bound together with ropes made
of flax. The oars and rudder were also similar to Russian design.
From the place where he found the raft Lavrentii sailed down the
Shilka River and found a horse trail, used recently, which led up
the Shilka. At this place Lavrentii measured the Shilka River and
found the width to be about 200 sazhens, not counting the ice.
It would be about 500 sazhens if the ice were included. The
shoreline is very rugged along both banks, and in the mountains
on both sides of the river there are trees suitable for building
rafts.

There are sables and all kinds of animals near the Shilka, including wild boar. Lavrentii and his men turned back from the

Shilka because he had so few men he was afraid the Daurs would capture and kill them. Lavrentii and his men returned along the same trail, and came to the Shilka portage, then went beyond the portage to a forest where he blazed markings indicating the Shilka portage.

From Ivan's zimov'e on the Tugur River, the trail goes to the Shilka portage to a tributary of this river, which river empties into the Ura, and the Ura flows into the Shilka. By using unloaded sleds, they made the trip easily in two days. Large boats can navigate both upriver and downriver.

Lavrentii came to me, Vasilii, and I, Vasilii, ordered him to question a hostage named Archeul about the raft which Lavrentii had seen on the Shilka River. The hostage said that the Leliulsk people use these rafts to carry their horses up the Shilka River, and when the Shilka freezes in the fall, these people buy grain from Lavkai and go back to their settlements on horseback on the ice. These people do not grow any grain, but they have many horses and cows and pigs and sheep. The Leliulsk people hunt sable, fox, lynx and wolverine, and also any other animals. There are many Polish wild boars. The people have their own language. According to the hostage, from the place where Lavrentii was on the Shilka, it takes half a day by horse to reach the mouth of the Ura River, and from there, going down the Shilka River, it takes one day on horse to reach Lavkai. Going upriver from that place where Lavrentii came onto the Shilka, it takes half a day on horse to reach the Leliulsk settlement. Lavkai lives between the Urkoikan and the Oldekon rivers. The Oldekon empties into the Shilka below Lavkai's settlement, and when one sails down the Oldekon River to the Shilka, one can see Lavkai's ulus.

See: *Dopolneniia k aktam istoricheskim* (St. Petersburg: 1848), III, 173–175.

75

INSTRUCTIONS FROM THE VOEVODA OF IAKUTSK, DMITRII FRANTSBE-
KOV, TO THE EXPLORER EROFEI KHABAROV, REGARDING HIS EXPEDI-
TION INTO THE LAND OF THE DAURS

On March 6, 1649, the veteran explorer, Erofei P. Khabarov, reported to the Sovereign Tsar and Grand Prince Aleksei Mikhailovich of all Russia. In his report he stated that in accordance with the Sovereign's ukaz, during the past years he had been sent on government service against [princes] Lavkai and Botogo, under the administration of the stolnik and voevoda Petr Petrovich Golovin, and the pismennaia golova Enalei Bakhteiarov. Seventy servitors were sent with him, but they did not reach these princes. They went along the Vitim, not along the Olekma, because they were not familiar with the direct route. From the government warehouse they received money and provisions of food, powder, shot and firearms.

He now asks that the Sovereign again grant him, Erofei, permission to go, together with volunteer servitors and promyshlenniks, however many may choose to go, and this time without being given government supplies. He wants about 150 men, or as many as possible, and he would provision them himself. He would provide their food and all supplies, including boats and equipment, and, the Sovereign's luck permitting, he would bring Lavkai and Botogo under the Sovereign Tsar's mighty hand, as well as any other transmontane non-iasak people, from whom the Sovereign would receive considerable benefit from the collection of iasak.

In accordance with the ukaz of the Sovereign Tsar and Grand Prince Aleksei Mikhailovich of all Russia, the voevoda Dmitrii Andreevich Frantsbekov and the diak Osip Stepanov have given Erofei permission to proceed, together with volunteer servitors and promyshlenniks numbering about 150 in all, or as many as he can gather, who will be willing to go without receiving government provisions. They will go along the Olekma and Tugur rivers to the Shilka portage and thence along the Shilka; they will put down any indigenous people who are disobedient and disloyal and will not pay iasak either for themselves or on behalf of their

237

ulus inhabitants. They are also to force Lavkai and Botogo and their ulus people and other transmontane non-iasak people to submit, on behalf of the Sovereign Tsar and Grand Prince Aleksei Mikhailovich of all Russia. They will collect iasak and explore new territories. They are instructed to proceed with care, taking due precautions; they are to post sentries wherever they stop so the natives will not harm them in any way.

They are to follow the Olekma River and the Tugur River to the portage, or to the Shilka; they are to ascertain where it would be most advantageous to build an ostrozhek, and then they are to build it and protect it with all possible fortifications so this ostrozhek can provide complete safety and security against attack by hostile non-iasak people for persons who may be sent there in the future to collect the Sovereign's iasak.

Erofei is to go out from this ostrog with the volunteer servitors and promyshlenniks who go with him, against Lavkai and Botogo and other non-iasak transmontane people who are disobedient and insubordinate to His Imperial Majesty. He is to persuade them to submit in eternal iasak servitude under the mighty hand of the Sovereign Tsar and Grand Prince Aleksei Mikhailovich of all Russia, and to pay iasak for themselves, Lavkai and Botogo, and for all their ulus subjects. Erofei is to take guides selected from the Tungus iasak-paying natives and go against those disobedient non-iasak-paying Lavkai and Botogo, and their ulus subjects, and other non-iasak-paying transmontane people. The guides are to be knowledgeable, reliable men, and he is to take as many as he needs, and they are to know where to lead him, and be able to point out to the Russian troops the places where the non-iasak-paying people live, and where their settlements are.

If these newly contacted people, Lavkai and Botogo, and their ulus subjects, and other non-iasak transmontane people are obedient and submissive and willing to come under the mighty hand of the Sovereign Tsar and Grand Prince Aleksei Mikhailovich of all Russia, and pay iasak from themselves and from their ulus subjects, for all eternity, then Lavkai and Botogo and their ulus people can live in their previous nomadic grounds, without fear, and the Sovereign will order that his government troops protect them.

Lavkai and Botogo and other leaders are to be induced to take the oath, according to their religious faith, so that henceforth they and all of their relatives and their ulus subjects will be forever, undeviatingly, in direct iasak servitude, under the mighty hand of the Sovereign Tsar and Grand Prince Aleksei Mikhailovich of all Russia. They are to pay iasak to the Sovereign from themselves and from all of their tribesmen, as much as circumstances allow, forever, without interruption. [Erofei] is to induce the tribesmen of the new non-iasak people to swear allegiance. The names of the leaders are to be written down in the books. And when he persuades them to take the oath of allegiance, he is to take their leaders as hostages, so that in the future these tribes will pay the Sovereign's iasak and pominki for all time to come.

Lavkai and Botogo and their ulus subjects and other transmontane non-iasak-paying people are to be given firm orders and threatened with punishment from the Sovereign, including death, if they steal from the merchants and promyshlenniks or kill them or harm them. If these new non-iasak people become rebellious, and decide not to pay the Sovereign's iasak, or to give hostages, then Erofei and his servitors and the promyshlenniks are to invoke God's mercy and then find them and attack them, using all the servitor and promyshlennik volunteers, so that the hostile non-iasak people, Lavkai and Botogo and their ulus subjects and other transmontane non-iasak people, will be pacified by military means, that is by war, and hostages are to be taken from their leaders, and so that in the future the Sovereign's iasak will be collected from them. Depending on the situation at the time, all measures are to be used to establish complete control over the inhabitants of new territories, Lavkai and Botogo and other non-iasak people, and every effort is to be made, and no mistakes are to be committed, in order to bring substantial profit to the Sovereign's iasak treasury, so that it will be stable and constant in the future. In return for this service they are to receive compensation from the Sovereign.

You, Erofei, are personally entrusted with the government assignment to pacify and bring under the suzerainty of the Sovereign both Lavkai and Botogo as well as non-iasak people who are not paying iasak to the Sovereign. Invoke God's aid, and use force, either war or surprise attacks.

You are to collect iasak for the Sovereign from them, which is to be made up of sables, sable shubas, neck pieces, sable backs, sable bellies, black foxes, black-brown foxes, brown foxes, cross foxes, red foxes, ermine shubas, beavers and otters. Since there are no sables, foxes, beavers or otters in the steppe, then from those non-iasak people who live in the steppe rather than in the forest, you are to collect any other kind of animal pelt, or whatever precious goods the land may offer, such as gold, silver, silk or precious stones, depending on what is available. They must not think that because there is a scarcity of animals for iasak that they will not come under the Sovereign's mighty hand.

They are not to be fearful for themselves because of this, but rather, they should believe that in the future the Sovereign will have firm and solid control and that the new people will not be oppressed or overburdened; otherwise they may be turned away from the mighty Tsarist hand.

If Lavkai and Botogo will not pay iasak from themselves and from their ulus people, and will not willingly come under the mighty hand of the Sovereign Tsar and Grand Prince Aleksei Mikhailovich of all Russia, in eternal servitude, then invoking God's aid, the voevoda Dmitrii Andreevich Frantsbekov and the diak Osip Stepanov will personally assemble and head a large force and will attack Lavkai and Botogo and all the other non-iasak people.

Some will be hanged, and others will be ruined. After they have totally destroyed them, they will take their wives and children into captivity. But if the non-iasak people bow down and are in every way obedient to the Sovereign, then in accordance with their religious practices, these people are to be brought to swear allegiance so that they will be personally under the Sovereign Tsar's mighty hand in eternal iasak servitude, for all time, undeviatingly, and pay iasak for themselves and for their ulus subjects without interruption.

You, Erofei, are to settle any disputes among the servitors and promyshlenniks who go with you as volunteers, depending on what the problem is. Try to avoid trouble. If any of the servitors and promyshlenniks petition you on matters of service, Erofei, or if they seek to bring legal action, accept their petition or the suit regarding service, and record it, but do not give judgment. Record who is the plaintiff and who the defendant. Send these petitions and reports to the Prikaz office in Iakutsk ostrog and make a written report to the voevoda Dmitrii Andreevich Frantsbekov and to the diak Osip Stepanov. Then, God willing, and with God's mercy and the luck of the Tsar, when you cross the Shilka River and go down the Olekma and Tugur rivers you will bring those new people, Lavkai and Botogo and other such non-iasak people, under the Tsar's mighty hand and collect iasak from them for the year 1650, and take hostages.

Erofei, you are to send as many men as possible with the government iasak treasury and the pominki to Iakutsk ostrog, and you are also to enter the names of the iasak people into the iasak books. Prepare a chart of the rivers, noting where there are large numbers of persons living along the rivers and to what tribes they belong. Send this information in writing to the Prikaz office at Iakutsk ostrog, to the voevoda Dmitrii Andreevich Frantsbekov and the diak Osip Stepanov.

Erofei, you are to make a thorough investigation of any merchants or promyshlenniks who are on the Olekma for their own trade and hunting. Look into their belongings, and if you find any furs which they have acquired from the Tungus, make a record of that fact and send those persons under guard to Iakutsk ostrog so that they will not pass through into any other towns. Order them to appear before the voevoda Dmitrii Andreevich Frantsbekov and the diak Osip Stepanov in the Prikaz office in Iakutsk ostrog.

However, if these people do not appear to have acquired any furs from the Tungus, then you are to let them proceed to Iakutsk ostrog without detaining them. Do not bring any false charges. Report on all of this to the Prikaz office in Iakutsk ostrog.

See: *Akty istoricheskie sobrannye i izdannye arkheograficheskoiu kommissieiu* (St. Petersburg: 1842), IV, 67–76.

76

BETWEEN JULY 7 AND AUGUST 31, 1650

A REPORT FROM THE VOEVODA OF IAKUTSK, DMITRII FRANTSBEKOV, TO THE SIBIRSKII PRIKAZ CONCERNING THE LACK OF ENOUGH SERVITORS TO EXPLORE EASTERN SIBERIAN RIVERS: THE OLENEK, IANA, INDIGIRKA, KOLYMA, ANADYR AND AMUR

To the Sovereign Tsar and Grand Prince Aleksei Mikhailovich of all Russia, your humble servants Dmitrii Frantsbekov and Osip Stepanov report.

In accordance with your ukaz and subsequent gramotas, Sovereign Tsar and Grand Prince Aleksei Mikhailovich of all Russia, 350 servitors from Tobolsk, Berezovo and Eniseisk, and *godovalshchiks* [hired itinerant workers] were ordered to be stationed in Iakutsk ostrog on your Sovereign service. However, Sovereign, in accordance with your Sovereign ukaz, no additional servitors were stationed on the Lena River. Sovereign, we need enough men to send out from Iakutsk ostrog on your service to go to nineteen iasak zimov'es to collect your iasak, Sovereign, in addition to going to the new Daur lands.

Sire, before we, your humble servants, came to Iakutsk ostrog, the previous stolnik and voevoda, Petr Golovin, and the voevoda Vasilii Pushkin, and their men in previous years had sent the following numbers of men on your distant Sovereign service to collect your Sovereign iasak: one syn boiarskii and sixteen servitors to the Kovyma River; sixteen men to the Indigirka River; one man to the Alazeia River; ten men to the distant Pogycha River; 22 men to the zimov'e on the Iana River; sixteen to the Olenek River; and 32 to the new Okhota River.

Sire, in 1649, we, your humble servants, in accordance with your previous instructions, sent additional men on your distant Sovereign service, as replacements for other servitors who were to escort your Sovereign sable treasury to Iakutsk ostrog. These included ten men to the Kovyma River, seven to the Indigirka, five men to the Alazeia, fifteen to the Olenek, and Sovereign, we, your humble servants, sent fourteen servitors to the salt lake on the Viliui River and they brought back 1,173 puds of salt to Iakutsk ostrog for you, Sovereign.

Sire, in this present year of 1650 because of the shortage of servitors and the desperate need for them, we, your humble servants, sent twelve men to the zimov'e on the upper Maia River, seven to the middle zimov'e on the Maia, ten to the Butalsk zimov'e on the Aldan, thirty-seven to the new Okhota River, twenty-four to the upper zimov'e on the Viliui, eleven to the middle zimov'e on the Viliui, eight to the mouth of the Viliui, five to Stolbovsk zimov'e, nine to Zhigansk, fourteen to the zimov'e on the lower Iana, eight to the zimov'e on the upper Iana, eight to Olekminsk ostrog on the upper Lena, ten along the upper Olekma River to the Chara River, four up the Lena to Iakutsk uezd below the Chichiui portage, fifteen via the Lena portage to Ilymsk ostrog for food, ten to the new distant Indigirka, Zashiver and Moma rivers, and three men to you in Moscow, Sovereign, with reports; we also sent twenty-one to convoy your Sovereign sable treasury.

At present we have sent two men with the reports and the list of expenditures, and twenty-one to the new Daur land on the great Amur River. Eleven more have been sent as replacements to this same Daur land. But, Sire, we did not send the same number to collect your Sovereign iasak on the Kolyma, Indigirka, Alazeia, Olenek and Viliui rivers as we had sent in 1649; there was such a shortage of servitors we were only able to send fifty-one men. There are only fifty-six servitors left in Iakutsk ostrog, Sire, and these are men who have been exiled and have no weapons, or they are old, and there are some who are blacksmiths and interpreters who are serving as your iasak and pominki collectors and as sentries.

Sire, we, your humble servants, are fearful of the natives because we have such a small number of our own men living in Iakutsk ostrog. Sire, on the basis of a petition and the report of the servitors at Iakutsk ostrog, we need to send three replacements of servitors to the distant rivers near the sea, to collect your iasak in your iasak zimov'es, Sire. We need to send twenty men to the Kolyma River, twenty to the Indigirka, ten to the Alazeia, and thirty to the new Pogycha and Anadyr rivers. We also need to send ten to the Indigirka, Zashiver and Moma rivers, and twenty-five men per year to the lower zimov'e on the Iana River. Consequently, Sire, servitors who were sent to those places as replacements in 1649 cannot be replaced this year; they will have to stay there until the Feast of St. Peter in 1651. Further, Sire, we will not be able to make the two annual replacements of twenty-five men for the Olenek River.

We must send forty-five men for one year's service to the zimov'e on the middle Viliui, twelve to the mouth of the Viliui, twenty to the zimov'e on the upper Maia, eight to the zimov'e on the middle Maia, fifteen to Butalsk zimov'e on the Aldan, seven down the Lena river to the Stolbovsk zimov'e, ten to the Zhigana, ten over the mountains to the zimov'e on the upper Iana, fifteen to Olekminsk zimov'e on the upper Lena, and twelve on the Olekma to the Chara River. Sire, we also need ten men in Iakutsk uezd on the lower Chichiui portage to collect your iasak and pominki, and to staff a tax-collecting station for agricultural peasants so promyshlenniks cannot reach Ilimsk ostrog from Iakutsk uezd without paying a tithe to you, Sovereign, at the Lena portage. There is also a desperate need to send thirty men to the new Okhota River for the third annual replacement because there is such a small garrison there.

At Iakutsk ostrog, Sire, we need eighty men on a seasonal assignment in town because there is a great gathering of Iakut men who live here in the winter, Sire, since that is when they come in to pay your Sovereign iasak and pominki. Also, Sire, other Iakuts come in then to petition against abuses committed against them by their fellow Iakuts. Because of the shortage of servitors in many zimov'es, Sire, the natives have started to pay less than the full amount of your Sovereign iasak. Sire, we need six hundred servitors to live in Iakutsk ostrog, in addition to those needed to go into the Daur lands to collect iasak and pominki and to perform other services both near and far.

On July 7, 1650, Sire, the voevoda Timofei Shusherin wrote to us, your humble servants, from Ilimsk ostrog on the Lena portage; he requested that we, your humble servants, send servitors there to protect them from Bratsk warriors. But Sire, we cannot send any servitors at all from Iakutsk ostrog. We already have such a shortage of servitors that we have had to send inadequate numbers of men on assignments to many places. We are only allotted 350 men, Sire.

Sire, because of the shortage of servitors, collections of your iasak cannot be made along newly discovered rivers and other rivers. Sire, we, your humble servants, cannot send out Tobolsk, Berezovo and Eniseisk servitors who have already been sent out on other distant assignments, in accordance with your ukaz. There are some other men serving nearby, Sire, but without your ukaz I cannot order them to be sent out from Iakutsk ostrog to

Seventeenth-century view of the confluence of Enisei and Angara
rivers. From Semivskii, *Noveishiia povestvovaniia o vostochnoi Sibiri*.

collect your iasak and pominki, Sire, because we are so short of
men it would create even greater shortages of iasak here.

Sovereign, we beg you to instruct us, your humble servants,
as to your decision about the servitors.

[Note on the back of this report from the Sibirskii Prikaz:] Inform the stolnik and voevoda Mikhail Lodyzhenskii and his diak
that they are to make an immediate and careful survey to ascertain the minimum number of men who will be needed on the
Lena in the future to carry out the duties of collecting taxes. Ex-
clude the Daur lands from this estimate. Ascertain how many servitors from Tobolsk, Berezovo and Eniseisk and how many exiles
have been put into service, and how many have not been assigned. They are authorized to use any such persons for service.
The Sovereign is to receive a report about this, sent by special
courier.

Reference: TsGADA, f. Sibirskii prikaz, stolb. No. 360, ll. 434–436.
See: N. S. Orlova, ed. *Otkrytie russkikh zemleprokhodtsev i poliarnykh morekhodov XVII veka* (Moscow: 1951), 289–292.

77

JULY 9, 1650

INSTRUCTIONS FROM THE PRIKAZ OFFICE AT IAKUTSK OSTROG TO
EROFEI KHABAROV CONCERNING HIS EXPEDITION TO THE LAND OF
THE DAURS

In accordance with the ukaz of the Sovereign Tsar and Grand
Prince Aleksei Mikhailovich of all Russia, the voevoda Dmitrii
Andreevich Frantsbekov and the diak Osip Stepanov instruct the
prikashchik Erofei Pavlovich Khabarov to take 21 servitors from
Iakutsk ostrog and 117 volunteer promyshlenniks and go to the
new Daur land. . . . [text missing]

Erofei is to send envoys to Prince Bogdoi. They are to be instructed to say that Prince Bogdoi and his family and tribe and all
his ulus people are to come under the suzerainty of our Tsar and
Grand Prince, Aleksei Mikhailovich, of all Russia, in servitude,
because our Sovereign is awesome and mighty, and he is Sovereign and ruler of many realms and no one can stand in battle
against his Sovereign army.

Our Sovereign has not previously known about their land,
but now he does have information. He has ordered his government troops to advance, not in battle, but to tell [Bogdoi] not to
destroy himself in battle against the Sovereign's men. [They are
also to tell Bogdoi] that many rulers of many realms live under
our Sovereign's protection and are subservient to him; they live in
peace and prosperity and serve the Sovereign and pay tribute to
him. For this reason Bogdoi should give the Sovereign tribute in
gold and silver and precious stones and fine goods, from himself
and from his people.

If Prince Bogdoi and his family and all his ulus people come
under the mighty protection of the Sovereign Tsar and Grand
Prince Aleksei Mikhailovich of all Russia, and if they are loyal
and peaceful and pay iasak and tribute every year from themselves, their tribe and all their ulus people, then Prince Bogdoi
and all his ulus people may live in their previous places without
fear, and the Great Sovereign will order that they be protected by
his own military forces. Prince Bogdoi and his family and tribe
and ulus people are to swear allegiance, according to their faith,
so that he and all his family and ulus people will be under the

mighty protection of the Sovereign Tsar and Grand Prince Aleksei Mikhailovich of all Russia, undeviatingly, for all time, in direct servitude.

However, if Prince Bogdoi and his family and tribe and ulus people are disloyal and uncooperative, and do not give iasak and hostages, then Erofei and his men and the servitors and promyshlenniks are to subdue them in battle, using every possible means. God willing, they will be brought under the Sovereign's mighty hand.

Then [Erofei and his men] are to collect tribute or iasak from Bogdoi consisting of sable shubas, sables, neck pieces, sable backs, sable bellies, black foxes, black-brown foxes, brown foxes, cross foxes, red foxes, ermine shubas, beavers and otters. Any non-iasak people who do not live in the forest but in the steppe, where there are no sable or fox, beaver or otter, are to give whatever goods or precious items they do have. If in their land they have gold or silver or silk or precious stones, then these may be taken. These people should not think that because they do not have enough furs to pay iasak that they are not to come under the Sovereign's mighty hand, nor should they as individuals avoid [the collectors]. In the future the Tsar will be firm and steadfast, and new people will not fall into debt and be burdened. They are not to turn away from the mighty Tsarist hand, for they will be asked to pay [only] what they are able to pay.

If the princes Lavkai, Shilgin, Gildig and Bogdoi and their families and ulus people do not resolve to pay and come in servitude under the mighty protection of the Grand Prince Aleksei Mikhailovich of all Russia, then, asking God's mercy, the voevoda Dmitrii Andreevich Frantsbekov and the diak Osip Stepanov will assemble a large force and go to battle against the princes Lavkai, Shilgin, Gildig and Bogdoi. They will be killed, hanged, ruined; and when they have been completely conquered, their wives and children will be taken into captivity. However if the non-iasak people will be loyal and obedient to the Sovereign in every respect, and then bring others to swear allegiance according to their faith, so that they will all come under the mighty protection of the Sovereign Tsar in eternal iasak servitude, undeviatingly, and pay iasak for themselves and their ulus people without interruption for all years to come. . . . [Khabarov's legal rights and obligations to servitors and promyshlenniks in his detachment are deleted.]

If Erofei sends servitors as envoys to Prince Bogdoi, Erofei is to write down the Sovereign's title, word for word, and instruct the envoys to say that the Tsar and Grand Prince Aleksei Mikhailovich of all Russia has been in good health for many years, and that ever since he has been Tsar there have never been any apprehensions about him, and that the envoys should not reveal any shortcomings in the mission.

The Tsar's titles are to be written as follows: By grace of God and the Holy Trinity, Great Sovereign Tsar and Grand Prince Aleksei Mikhailovich, Autocrat of all Russia, of Vladimir and Moscow and Novgorod, Tsar of Kazan, Tsar of Astrakhan, Tsar of Siberia, Sovereign of Pskov, Grand Prince of Iversk, Iugorsk, Perm, Viatka, Bulgaria and others, Sovereign and Grand Prince of Nizhnii, Novgorod and of Nizovie, of Riazan, Rostov and Iaroslav, Beloozero, Udorsk, Obdorsk, Kondinsk, and Lord of all the Northern Lands, Iversk land, Kartalinsk, Tsar of Georgia, of the Kabardinsk land of the Cherkassian and Mountain Princes, and Sovereign and Lord of many other realms.

In accordance with the ukaz of the Sovereign Tsar and Grand Prince Aleksei Mikhailovich of all Russia, we, the voevoda Dmitrii Andreevich Frantsbekov and the diak Osip Stepanov, tell you, Prince Bogdoi, that you are to come under the mighty protection of our Sovereign Tsar and Grand Prince Aleksei Mikhailovich, autocrat of all Russia. Our Sovereign Tsar and Grand Prince Aleksei Mikhailovich of all Russia is strong, great and awesome. He is master and Sovereign of many tsars and sovereigns and grand princes, who serve him with all their sovereignties, and his titles are written above. None can stand against his armies in battle.

Our Sovereign has previously been unaware of you, Prince Bogdoi. But now our Sovereign has ordered us to send a small number of people to you in order to demonstrate to you our Sovereign's mercy. They are sent not to do battle, but to bring you, Bogdoi, under his Sovereign mighty protection. Bogdoi, if you do not come under his Sovereign mighty protection in eternal servitude, then we will write about you to the Tsar and Grand Prince Aleksei Mikhailovich of all Russia in Moscow, and ask that he, the Sovereign, order his many troops to attack you, Bogdoi, for your disobedience, and order them to ruin you, seize your town for him, and kill all of you and your wives and children, without mercy, so that when other Daur princes who do not live under your jurisdiction see you, Prince Bogdoi, and how the punishments of death and destruction are visited upon you by our Sovereign Tsar and Grand Prince Aleksei Mikhailovich of all Russia, they will become subservient and loyal without a struggle.

Our Sovereign Tsar and Grand Prince Aleksei Mikhailovich of all Russia is merciful. He does not seek bloodshed from those who are humble before him and are willing to become his servants. He does not seek their blood, but rather, he rewards them. You, Prince Bogdoi, know that the voevoda Dmitrii Andreevich Frantsbekov and the diak Osip Stepanov will send the Sovereign's great army of 6,000 men with cannon and firearms against you. They will go into battle against you for your disobedience, Bogdoi.

People have been sent to inquire about Lavkai's princely rule, and now a few people are being sent as envoys to determine whether you will be loyal, Bogdoi. Here, in this one Siberian realm, under the Sovereign Tsar and Grand Prince Aleksei Mikhailovich of all Russia, along both the upper and lower reaches of the Lena and along other rivers in his realm, there are many Iakuts, Tungus and Iukagirs in eternal servitude who are fitted out for war, and in the service of our Sovereign Tsar and Grand Prince Aleksei Mikhailovich of all Russia, they will go into battle against traitors and disloyal peoples.

They will fight, caring nothing for their own death. And you, Prince Bogdoi, are well aware that the iasak Tungus have left Prince Lavkai and his ulus people and live under our Sovereign Tsar and Grand Prince Aleksei Mikhailovich of all Russia, from the Olekma along the upper reaches of the Shilka and Amur rivers.

See: N. F. Demidova and V. S. Miasnikov, eds., *Russko-kitaiskie otnosheniia v XVII: dokumenty i materialy* (Moscow: 1969–1972), I, 126–128.

An ostrog tower of typical design at Belsk. From Makovetskii, *Byt i iskusstvo russkogo naseleniia vostochnoi Sibiri*, Vol. 1.

78

NOT BEFORE DECEMBER, 1650

A REPORT FROM THE VOEVODA OF IAKUTSK, DMITRII FRANTSBEKOV, TO TSAR ALEKSEI MIKHAILOVICH CONCERNING EROFEI KHABAROV'S EXPEDITION TO THE AMUR RIVER

To the Sovereign Tsar and Grand Prince Aleksei Mikhailovich of all Russia, your humble servants Dmitrii Frantsbekov and Osip Stepanov report. Sire, on March 29, 1649 we, your humble servants, reported to you that in accordance with a petition from the veteran explorer Erofei Pavlovich Khabarov we, your humble servants, allowed him to proceed on your government service into the new land along the Olekma River, to go to Prince Lavkai and to Botogo and their ulus people. Seventy servitors and promyshlennik volunteers went with him, and he personally provided the money, grain, supplies, boats, arms, powder and shot for all of them. We, your humble servants, in accordance with our orders, instructed Erofei Khabarov to use kindness to attract these princes, Lavkai and Botogo, and their ulus people to come under your Sovereign Tsarist hand, so that they would be in eternal iasak servitude to you, Sire, and would give you iasak consisting of sables and foxes from themselves and from their ulus people for all time without interruption.

Sire, on May 26 of the present year, 1650, Erofei Khabarov returned to us, your humble servants, in Iakutsk ostrog, and reported that he had gone with his volunteers along the Olekma River, but that he did not reach his destination. He wintered at the mouth of the Tugur River, then from the mouth of the Tugur, they took dogsleds and went up the Tugur. They set out on St. Afanasii's Day in 1650. Using that route they reached the uluses belonging to Prince Lavkai. The town and uluses were all deserted. There were five towers in that town, and large fortifications had been built around the town with deep moats and gun emplacements in each tower and secret approaches to the water. This town was encircled by a river which empties into the Amur. The town had only one gate. There were light towers built of stone, with large window wells about two arshins high, and an arshin and a half wide. The panes were made of paper, and they had made the paper themselves. Sire, 60 or more men live in one such light tower. If the fear of God had not fallen on them, it would not be necessary for these people to have such fortresses. Sire, this happened through God's mercy. Thanks to your good fortune, God revealed a new land and placed it under your mighty Tsarist authority.

Erofei went from Lavkai's town down the Amur in order to take hostages. Then he went to another town, but that town and uluses were also deserted. There were five towers in that town, and great fortifications had also been built around the town, with deep moats and gun emplacements in all the towers, and secret passageways to the water. Sire, this town belongs to a son-in-law of Prince Lavkai.

Erofei went from the second town down the Amur in order to take hostages and reached a third town. This town and uluses were also deserted. The town has four towers, the same fortifications, moats, gun emplacements and secret passageways to the water. Erofei halted in this town with his warriors and volunteers and posted sentries. That same day the sentries noted that five men were approaching on horseback from the town. A sentry informed Erofei, who ordered the interpreter, Loginka, to ask these people who they were. One of them, an older man, announced that he was Prince Lavkai, and that the others were his two brothers, his son-in-law, and their servants. Prince Lavkai then asked the interpreter, Loginka, who these people were, and from whence they had come. Loginka, the interpreter, said, in answer to Lavkai's question, that they were promyshlenniks who had come to trade, and who had brought many gifts for them. Lavkai said to the interpreter, "Why do you attempt to deceive us? We know you are cossacks. There was a cossack here once before, before you came. His name was Ivan Eloimov Kvashnin, and he told us about you. He said there are 500 of you, and that after you come, many more will come, and that you intend to kill us and steal our belongings and take our wives and children into captivity. Because of this I, Lavkai, and my brothers and my son-in-law have left our towns and taken our ulus people with us."

Erofei told the interpreter, Loginka, to ask Prince Lavkai why Ivan had come to him.

Prince Lavkai responded to the question by saying that Ivan had gone along the Amazar River to Lavkai's ulus Tungus people who fish for Lavkai. The cossack, Ivan, came to these Tungus with three other Tungus people who were traveling with him. Prince Lavkai's ulus people gave Ivan gifts of fifty sables, and told him to take these to Erofei. They took Ivan from one ulus to another, on horseback. Ivan gave them gifts of kettles and axes and knives. They had no presents for Ivan, but they did give him one small fresh water pearl. After he had handed out these gifts, they led him off with honor. They do not have any sables now, but some year when they give many sables to Prince Bogdoi, they will send some to the cossack Ivan Kvashin. Lavkai also said that there were three Russians, Ivan Kvashnin's comrades, at the mouth of the Amazar River who collected sables from Lavkai's Tungus people for gifts. Lavkai did not know exactly how many they had.

Erofei instructed the interpreter, Loginka, to tell Lavkai that he was to pay iasak to you, Sovereign Tsar and Grand Prince Aleksei Mikhailovich of all Russia and Sovereign and protector of all Russian lands and of many other realms, and that he would protect Lavkai and his brothers and the princes Shilgin and Gildig, who live in two settlements between the Amur and Shilka rivers. Lavkai is staying with them at the present time because they belong to the same tribe. Lavkai's brothers and son-in-law said that they would not pay iasak. Prince Lavkai said he would have to see what kind of people they were. Then Lavkai and his brothers and his son-in-law left the town. Erofei went after them in order to take them hostage and to find the ulus people.

Erofei left the third town and after a day's travel, he reached a fourth town, which had three towers, and strong fortifications around the town, including a deep moat, gun emplacements, and secret passages to the water.

They left that town at night, and traveled until noon the next day, when they reached the fifth town. That town had four towers, and strong fortifications surrounded the town, with deep moats, gun emplacements under all the towers and secret passages to the water. In the light tower they seized an old woman. Erofei told the interpreter to ask the woman her name. She said her name was Mogolchak, that she belonged to the Daur tribe, and that Prince Lavkai had bought her from captivity from Prince Bogdoi, and that since that time she had called herself Prince Lavkai's sister. They questioned the woman further, and then tortured her by burning in order to learn why Prince Lavkai and his village people had fled from their towns. During both the interrogation and under torture the old woman said the same thing that Prince Lavkai and his brothers and son-in-law had said, which the cossack Ivan Kvashnin had told them, that a great multitude of servitors were coming to kill all the Daur people and steal their belongings and take their wives and children into captivity. This was the reason Prince Lavkai and all his ulus people and their wives and children had taken their belongings and fled from the upriver uluses and settlements three weeks before the arrival of Erofei Khabarov.

Prince Lavkai and his ulus people had taken their 1,500 horses and all their livestock to princes Shilgin and Gildig. They all went in a great group.

From Shilgin's town they went on horseback for two weeks to Bogdoi's town. The old woman had been a prisoner of Bogdoi and said that there was a large town with many towers and earthworks, and that there were shops in town where they had all kinds of goods for sale, and that Prince Bogdoi collects iasak from all the Daur princes. She also said that there are gold, silver, precious stones and other riches in Prince Bogdoi's land. Prince Bogdoi has firearms, cannon, muskets, sabers, crossbows, and all kinds of weapons decorated with gold and silver. In Prince Bogdoi's quarters the tableware is made of silver and gold so that they eat and drink from silver and gold. Furthermore, Sire, there are a great many sables.

Downriver from Bogdoi's town is the great Non River which flows into the right bank of the Amur River. Large boats come along that river carrying goods, but she said she did not know which towns the boats come from, or for whom the goods are destined.

The Khan is even more powerful than this Prince Bogdoi. Near his large town there are a great many agricultural people, and all kinds of livestock. In the upper reaches of the great Amur River, above the towns of Prince Lavkai which Erofei and his companions traveled to, there is the Urak River. It takes three days to go from the Urak to the Amazar River on foot, and two days more to go to the mouth of the Shilka.

Many Tungus live along these rivers, and down the river along the great Amur River live the Daur people who breed livestock and engage in agricultural pursuits. Many Tungus live along the lower tributary. Sturgeon and *kaluga* are found in the Amur, and many more kinds of fish than are found in the Volga. In Prince Lavkai's towns and uluses there are large meadows and cultivated fields. The forests along the great Amur River are huge and dark, and have many sables and other varieties of animals.

If God favors your Imperial good fortune with hostages, then the government Treasury would be greatly enriched. Sire, if Ivan Kvashnin had not given them information about us, Erofei could have taken hostages and collected iasak for you, but now the Daur people have drawn up strong fortifications for themselves, and Erofei could not take Lavkai and his brothers and his son-in-law from his ulus people because these people have run off.

When they left the fifth town they returned to Lavkai's first town because it has strong fortifications and was the first one they came to. Sire, it was impossible to occupy the four other towns, but they found a great deal of grain hidden in pits, Sire, enough for your troops to live on for two or three years. Grains that are grown there include barley, oats, millet, pease, groats and flax. Erofei and his men entrenched themselves in this town at the end of 1650, Sire, and they are waiting for Prince Lavkai to submit himself to your Tsarist Majesty. Sire, if you want us to send your troops against Prince Bogdoi, we will need about 6,000 troops.

Sovereign, we, your humble servants, have sent you a map of Prince Lavkai's towns and lands. Sire, as soon as these Daur princes willingly submit to your will, or are brought by force under your mighty sovereign authority, then agriculture will be undertaken in the Daur lands and you will realize great profit, Sovereign.

Grain can easily be sent to Iakutsk ostrog, Sire, because the distance is only 100 versts from Lavkai's settlements on the Amur River, across the Tugur portage to the new ostrog which Erofei Khabarov has built, and it takes only two weeks to go by water from the Tugur ostrog down the Tugur River and the Olekma and Lena rivers to Iakutsk ostrog. Sire, they believe this Daur land will be more fruitful than the Lena. Erofei has told us, your humble servants, that this area can be as well developed and bountiful as any in all Siberia.

See: *Dopolneniia k aktam istoricheskim* (St. Petersburg: 1848), III, 258–261.

79

JUNE, 1652

A REPORT TO TSAR ALEKSEI MIKHAILOVICH FROM THE VOEVODA OF
IAKUTSK, IVAN AKINFEV, CONCERNING THE HUNT FOR WALRUS AND
THE AVAILABILITY OF WALRUS IVORY ALONG THE COAST OF THE SEA
OF OKHOTSK

To the Sovereign Tsar and Grand Prince Aleksei Mikhailovich of all Russia, your humble servants, Ivan Akinfev and Osip Stepanov, humbly report. Sire, on June 6 of the present year, 1652, a iasak collector, a service man named Semen Epishev, wrote to us, your humble servants, from the new Okhota River, and along with his report he sent an account of his interrogation of hostages. Sire, he writes that on the Motykhla River there are 520 nomadic non-iasak Tungus who belong to various tribes.

Sire, the non-iasak reindeer Tungus are numerous and live beyond the Olekma near the Motykhla River. Sire, Semen Epishev sent 21 servitors from the Okhota River under Ivan Afanasev to Iakutsk ostrog with your Sovereign iasak sable treasury. Sire, when Ivan Afanasev and his fellow servitors were questioned, they told us, your humble servants, that there are more than 5,000 non-iasak Tungus of various tribes beyond the Okhota River near other rivers, and along the seashore, and in the mountains.

Sire, we, your humble servants, also heard from the servitors Oleg Filipov and Ivan Iachmenev and their eight comrades who went from the Okhota River to the new Motykhla River in 1648 that when they went along the coast from the mouth of the Okhota to the Motykhla, they sailed for about a day to a cape where there are walruses. Sire, that cape is two versts or more long, and there are great herds of walrus lying on the shore. Sire, from the mouth of the Motykhla River islands can be seen, and according to the accounts of the Tungus, Sire, it is possible to take many walrus on those islands. Sire, when Oleg and his men were returning from this new Motykhla River to the Okhota River in 1651, they saw many walrus basking both at sea and at this rocky cape. Sire, we, your humble servants at Iakutsk ostrog, asked merchants and promyshlenniks who are accustomed to dealing in the walrus trade whether it would be possible to hunt walrus at these places.

One merchant, Kiril Kotkin Mezenets, told us, your humble servants, that it is possible to hunt walrus there and that he, Kiril, deals in this trade. Sire, there would be a great many tusks and much fish from this trade, and you would have great profit from it. Sire, this Kiril went onto the distant Kolyma River in 1649 and 1650 to collect your Sovereign tithe of sables [from promyshlenniks.] We, your humble servants, have not yet been able to verify Kiril's collection on the basis of the customs books, but, Sire, we, your humble servants, are sending this Kiril to you in Moscow for a lengthy interrogation about the walrus trade and about the tusks. We are also sending the customs books, describing Kiril's collection for the years 1649 and 1650, for verification. With Kiril we are sending the accounts of Ivan Afanasev and his fellow servitors.

Sire, we have instructed Kiril to appear in the Sibirskii Prikaz and to present the reports and the books to your boiar Prince Aleksei Nikitich Trubetskoi, and to the diak Grigorii Protopov.

See: *Dopolneniia k aktam istoricheskim* (St. Petersburg: 1848), III, 348–349.

80

JUNE 16, 1652

A GRAMOTA FROM TSAR ALEKSEI MIKHAILOVICH TO THE VOEVODA OF IAKUTSK, MIKHAIL LODYZHENSKII, CONCERNING THE AVAILABILITY OF WALRUS IVORY

From the Tsar and Grand Prince Aleksei Mikhailovich of all Russia to Siberia, to the Great Lena River, to Iakutsk ostrog, to our stolnik and voevoda, Mikhail Semenovich Lodyzhenskii, and to our diak, Fedor Tonkoi. On January 25 of the present year, 1652, the voevoda Dmitrii Frantsbekov and diak Osip Stepanov wrote to us from the Lena, and sent us ivory tusks weighing 35 puds 2¾ grivenkas [181⅜ pounds]. The value of these tusks on the Lena was 226 rubles. A promyshlennik named Iurii Seliverstov told them about the ivory tusks. When the servitor Mikhail Stadukhin and his men went from the Kolyma River to the new Pogycha River they collected these tusks along the shore, and said that there are great quantities of these tusks lying along the shore, and that it would be possible to load many boats with them, but they had not collected all the tusks because they did not have enough food to winter there.

Iurii Seliverstov also said that in the year 1649 he had been at sea, and many rivers empty into the sea, including the Kovyma, which is in the land of the Chukchi. There are four more rivers beyond the Kolyma, and beyond those are others called the Nakandar and Chandon. Many people live along these rivers, and it would be possible to gain great profit for our Treasury in the iasak collection of sables and of walrus tusks from these new natives.

When you receive this our gramota, and when you send the servitors onto the Kolyma and the new Pogycha River, and onto other rivers to hunt for sables, and when these servitors find these tusks along the shore, both large and small tusks, you are to instruct them to gather them and bring them to you in Iakutsk. Then you are to send them from Iakutsk, along with our sable treasury, to us in Moscow. Make a record of it, and send it with the tusks to the Sibirskii Prikaz, to our boiar Prince Aleksei Nikitich Trubetskoi, and to our diaks Grigorii Protopopov and Tretiak Vasilev. But do not buy these tusks from the promysh-

Dog fur caps were noted for warmth. From Makovetskii, *Byt i iskusstvo russkogo naseleniia vostochnoi Sibiri*, Vol. 1.

lenniks at some inflated price. Instead, instruct the servitors to gather these tusks for us every year, without cost.

Written in Moscow, June 16, 1652.

See: *Dopolneniia k aktam istoricheskim* (St. Petersburg: 1848), III, 349–350.

81

AUGUST, 1652

A REPORT FROM EROFEI KHABAROV TO THE VOEVODA OF IAKUTSK, DMITRII FRANTSBEKOV, CONCERNING HIS EXPEDITION ON THE AMUR RIVER

The humble servant of the Sovereign Tsar and Grand Prince Aleksei Mikhailovich of all Russia, the prikashchik Erofei Pavlovich Khabarov, with the servitors, volunteers and newly recruited Daur servitors, report from the great Amur River and from the mouth of the Zeia River and Kokorei's ulus to the voevoda Dmitrii Andreevich Frantsbekov and the diak Osip Stepanov.

I, the humble servant of the Sovereign, lived with the servitors and volunteers on the great Amur River in the town of Albazin. All the adventures that befell us have been written for the Sovereign in my reports to you, Dmitrii Andreevich and Osip Stepanov.

On June 2, having built both large and small boats, and having asked mercy of God and of the Almighty Merciful Savior, we set out from the town of Albazin. We sailed for two days, and on the second day reached a town which belongs to Prince Dasaul. This town and its iurts had been burned to the ground; only two small iurts remained. We did not find any people there. From that town we sailed until midday, when we came upon iurts, but there were no people in the iurts. The people had fled on horseback. These are Daur people, and they had all run away from us. We were only able to capture an old Daur woman who said that all the Daur people live in uluses. We immediately went aboard the Lena boats and went swiftly downriver and found two iurts. All the Daur people were in those iurts. When they sighted us, they mounted their horses and rode off. We captured only one prisoner. The rest stayed in another ulus and began to deliver iasak to the town. They burned their iurts and raised a cloud of smoke.

That same day we went on to Guigudar's town, using the Lena boats . . . [missing]. Prince Guigudar had two other princes with him as well as the Bogdoi ulus people. These men all stood on the shore in front of us and would not let us land. We fired our guns at them from the boats and killed about twenty Daur people. The princes, Guigudar, Olgemza and Lotodii, and their ulus people, were afraid of the Tsar's wrath and fled from shore. We quickly disembarked from our boats onto the shore and went after them. Princes Guigudar, Olgemza and Lotodii and their ulus people fortified themselves in their towns. They have three new towns which are protected by an earthen wall made of clay on top. The towns are side by side, with only walls separating them. There are tunnels without gates under these walls, and deep excavations have been made in these towns where both live-stock and prisoners are kept. There are two moats one sazhen deep around these towns, and these moats are very close to the walls. Formerly there were uluses around these towns, but they had been burned.

When the princes encamped in the town, the Bodgoi people did not camp together with the Daur people; rather, they went on into the open country. With God's mercy and the luck of the Tsar, and for your pleasure, Dmitrii Andreevich and Osip Stepano-vich, and with my ingenuity, prikashchik Erofei Pavlovich, and with the servitors and volunteers, we immediately laid siege to the town and the Daur people shot arrows at us from the towers. I, the prikashchik, told the interpreters to say that the Tsarist Majesty, our Sovereign Tsar and Grand Prince Aleksei Mikhailo-vich of all Russia, is fearful and awesome, that he possesses many realms, and that no horde can stand up against our Sovereign Tsar and Grand Prince Aleksei Mikhailovich of all Russia in battle. Therefore, I said, princes Guigudar and Olgodii [Olgemza] and Lotodii must be obedient and humble before our Sovereign Tsar and Grand Prince Aleksei Mikhailovich of all Russia. They must surrender without a struggle and give whatever they could in the way of iasak to our Sovereign and allow our Sovereign to protect them from hordes more powerful than theirs.

Guigudar replied, "We pay iasak to the Bogdoi Tsar Shamsha-kan. And as for the iasak which you are asking us to give, it would be like giving up our last child."

Then, asking God's mercy and the Sovereign's luck, we began the Sovereign's service with the usual military action. We ordered large cannon to be fired, and began to fire at the towers from the lower part of town. We fired on the people in the town with our small arms such as muskets and harquebuses. The Daur people fired back at us from the town, and their arrows flew at us from town without cease. The Daurs who were in the town fired so many arrows on us in the field that it looked like grain before the harvest.

We fought with the Daur people all night long until early dawn the next day. We broke through the wall near a tower. Those of us who were wearing armor, and other servitors who were protected with shields, took the wall and entered the town one by one. Thanks to the fortune of the Sovereign, we captured the lower town. The Daurs assembled in the other two towns, and at noon we servitors fought the Daurs of the second town from this town. All of these fierce Daurs then gathered in one town, and we fired at them without cease, from large and small arms, and in these sorties we killed 214 Daur men.

These fierce Daurs could not withstand the Sovereign's wrath and our attack. About fifteen of them managed to break through, but they were the only ones who escaped from the town. The rest of the Daurs were defeated and burned with the city. The battle was fierce and brutal for us cossacks, but with God's mercy and the luck of the Sovereign, we killed all of these Daurs, one after another. In this fearful battle we killed 427 Daur men and boys. The total number of Daurs killed, including the ones who had gathered and those who took part in the attack, was 661 men and boys. Only four of our cossacks were killed by the Daurs. Here in the town, the Daurs wounded 45 of our cossacks, but they all recovered from their wounds.

With the luck of the Sovereign we took this town, with livestock and prisoners. The total number of prisoners taken, partly old women and the rest young girls, was 243. There were 118 young prisoners. We also captured 237 horses, both large and small, from the Daurs; and we also took 113 head of cattle. While the fighting was going on the Bogdoi people circled the field and watched, but did not fire on our cossacks. We asked the prisoners about these Bogdoi people, "Why did these Bogdoi people come to you? How many Bogdoi people are there?" And the prisoners told us, "Fifty of these Bogdoi people live here all the time to collect iasak and other goods, until they are replaced by their own people." Then we asked the old women, "Why did they not come with you into the town? Why did they not join you?" And the prisoners replied, "Our Daur people, our prince Guigudar and his men, took them to the town to help, but the Bogdoi people told him, 'Guigudar! Our tsar Shamshakan has forbidden us to fight with the Russians!'"

The day after the battle these Bogdoi people sent their own Bogdoi man from the fields to us in town. This man came to us in the town and paid proper homage to the Tsarist Majesty, and then began to speak in his own Chinese language. We could not understand his language, for we had no interpreters. The Daur women, who were serving as translators, said, "Our tsar, Shamshakan, did not authorize us to fight with you. Our tsar Shamshakan ordered us to behave honorably toward you cossacks. . . . [missing]." This Bogdoi man wore silk clothing, and had a sable hat, but although he spoke for a long time to us, we did not have an interpreter, and thus could not understand him. I, Erofei, treated this Bogdoi man with honor, gave him gifts from the Tsar, and allowed him to go on his way to his Bogdoi land.

We lived in those towns for six weeks, and sent messages to the Daur princes, Dasaul, Banbulai, Shilginei and Albaz. In the town of Albazin we captured the Daur leaders and sent one man to go with them to tell the Daur princes that they must submit and bow to our Sovereign. We also sent the old women to go with the same message. But not a single man came to us from the Daurs. These people are one day's sail away from us; there are a multitude of people there.

During the battle near Guigudar's town, we fired the three large cannon day and night and used three puds of the Sovereign's powder and a great deal of shot. I, Erofei, lived in those towns with the servitors and the volunteers for seven weeks, but the Daur princes still did not come to [submit to] His Sovereign Majesty. . . . [missing] and I, Erofei, sailed off from this town. We selected horses and put them on the boats and took them with us.

We sailed for two days after leaving this town, and came to Banbulai's town. But when we reached prince Banbulai's town, his ulus and his whole town were empty. There were no people there, for they had all run off. We spent a week looking for them. We, your humble servants, the prikashchik Erofei Pavlovich and the servitors and the volunteer cossacks asked Banbulai to pay iasak, but he said, "What do you mean by asking me for iasak?" After that I, the prikashchik, ordered the servitors and cossack volunteers to go out from Banbulai's town to attack his men downriver. They sailed for a day and came to an ulus where they took two prisoners.

The interpreters questioned the hostages in detail, and they said, "It takes a day and a half to go from there to the mouth of the Zeia River, and on the opposite side of the Zeia, on the right as one sails, there is an ulus belonging to prince Kokorei. Below that ulus, as you sail on, there are three more uluses; below these, there is a strong and well fortified town. This town is fortified by all the inhabitants of our Daur land. Prince Turoncha Bogdoi lives in that same town; he is the brother-in-law of Prince Baldach. And there are also two more princes, Tolga and Omutei, brothers."

Then the humble servants of the Sovereign, servitors and cossack volunteers, brought these prisoners to Banbulai's town, to me, the prikashchik Erofei Pavlovich Khabarov. And I, Erofei, questioned the prisoners using hot irons, and they made the same statements, word for word, as they had before. Then I, Erofei, took counsel with the armed servitors and cossack volunteers. Asking God's blessing on us, we explored downriver from Banbulai's town. We made our way from Banbulai's town to the mouth of the Zeia River, which took two days and a night. There a large river falls into the left side of the Amur, and the name of the river is the Zeia.

The prisoners said that the Daurs live along the Zeia, and that there is a town on the river where the Daur prince Olpel lives with many Daur people. At the mouth of the river, on the right a little below the mouth of the Zeia, there is an ulus of 24 iurts belonging to prince Kokorei, but there are no people there. We immediately sailed down and at midday came upon the iurts, using our small boats. We took prisoners there and rapidly interrogated them. They said that there were two more uluses below the town not far away, and people were living in these. We immediately sailed to these uluses, and rowed to town that evening. We jumped out of the light boats onto shore and ran to the town, which was inhabited by a few people who belong to the Daur princes. All the people were in town, and we took their towers.

Below this town, a bowshot away, there is a large ulus where the Daur princes Turoncha and his brothers, Tolga and Omutei and their people were all drinking. When they saw us, Prince Omutei leaped on his horse, cried out, and galloped off. The servitors and cossack volunteers, seeking God's mercy and the Sovereign's pleasure, attacked that ulus, heedless of their own safety. They surrounded Prince Turoncha and his brothers and wives and children, and Prince Tolga, who had his leaders with him, through God's mercy and the luck of the Sovereign. Other men and prisoners fled from the lower end of the town, but the servitors and cossack volunteers invoked God's mercy and ran after them into the fields and took many of them prisoner and killed others who were escaping.

Just at that moment they heard shots from the large boats, and quickly rowed back. They swiftly mounted the horses from the boats and galloped after the Daurs. They captured the rest of the men in the fields and brought them back to town. Princes Turoncha and Tolga began to fire from their iurts, so I, the prikashchik Erofei, instructed my interpreters to talk with those princes, telling them to submit to the Tsar's mighty hand. I told them that if they would give iasak to our Sovereign, and be obedient and submissive in all ways, that we would not kill them, but would protect them from their mightier enemies.

Prince Turoncha Baldachin . . . [missing] and his brothers and Prince Tolga responded, "We would like to give iasak, provided it is not a permanent arrangement. We will give iasak, but we do not have any sables now. The Bogdoi people were here, and we gave our iasak to them. We have sold everything else, but we will give you any sables we have left." They came out from their iurts to us, and we took them and brought them into town. In all we captured 100 men in the town; we took 170 prisoners, not counting small children. Prince Turoncha and his brothers and Prince Tolga and his ulus leaders told us, "We are Daur people. The people and tribesmen who live under our rule, plus our archers, number more than 1,000 people. Henceforth all of us will serve and obey your ruler and pay iasak for all time to come. Please release our people and the leaders and our wives and children; then we, the princes, will obey you. Believe our words."

Through the interpreter I told them to call all their people together to prove their trustworthiness. Princes Turoncha and Tolga told Prince Omutei and all the leaders to come to us. About 300 did come to us immediately. In accordance with the ukaz of the Sovereign, I, the prikashchik, ordered Turoncha and his brothers and Tolga and Omutei and their brothers, and their princes and the leaders Balun and Anai and Evlogoi and all of their ulus people and their entire tribe to swear allegiance and come under the mighty hand of our Sovereign Tsar and Grand Prince Aleksei Mikhailovich of all Russia in eternal iasak servitude for all time, and to pay their iasak for all time without interruption. . . . [missing] and from their leaders I chose Prince Turoncha's brother-in-

Shuba and shapka enriched with beads, bells and horn. From Okladnikov, *Istoriia Iakutskoi ASSR*, Vol. 2.

law, Baldachin . . . [missing] and his brother, and Prince Tolga and his brother, and Omutei's brother and three ulus leaders as hostages.

They brought in iasak of 60 sables saying, "We do not have any more sables now, but in the fall we will give you iasak in full." I, the prikashchik Erofei, took counsel with the armed servitors and the cossack volunteers, and released all of their ulus men and the leaders, and let them live in their former nomadic encampments without fear. They also wanted to ransom back the prisoners. They offered to pay 40 to 60 rubles for some, and 100 rubles for others. I, the prikashchik Erofei, took counsel with the servitors and the cossack volunteers, and to gratify the Sovereign, we rejected their suggestion and instead, returned the prisoners without ransom. We told them to live without fear, and they did then live near us in their ulus without fear. They brought us food, and frequently came to us in the town, and we went to them.

On September 3, 1652, a cossack desiatnik interpreter, Konstantin Ivanov, originally from Eniseisk, who had come from the syn boiarskii Ivan Galkin in Baikal in 1650, left us and went to them in their iurts, and he lived with them for a time. Then he fled back to us in town and told us, "They tried to sieze me in their iurts, and I barely managed to escape." At that same time when he ran off to us they all mounted horses and galloped off from the ulus with their prisoners. I, Erofei, sent troops into their ulus to dissuade them, but they had all fled, and we were only able to capture two old women. I, Erofei, told these hostages that they had committed treason against our Sovereign, and that they had violated their oath by sending their people away. They replied, "We did not send them away. We are here with you. They made up their own minds." And then prince Tolga said, "We will all die now, we will die together for our land when you capture us."

I, Erofei, tried to dissuade them, but they are fierce unbelievers, these Daurs, and they had broken their oath. They said, "Do whatever you wish with us, now that we have fallen into your hands." I, Erofei, tortured these hostages by burning them, but they only said, "Cut off our heads. The only thing left for us is to die at your hands." And the unbelievers circled in the distance. I, Erofei asked them to submit to the Sovereign's Majesty, but they refused. Then I, Erofei, decided that it would be impossible to spend the winter there because there was no food near the town. I ordered the servitors and the cossack volunteers to gather at the boats.

On September 7, having assembled at the boats, I, Erofei, ordered the cossack volunteer Petr Oksenev to sail down the Amur River to burn Tolga's town. He stayed in that town for three and a half weeks. It took him four days to go by boat from that town to the mountains. The next day Prince Tolga, who was from that town, stole a knife and stabbed himself. There are small iurts in all these uluses, ten iurts per ulus . . . [missing] 120. They sailed for two days and a night to the mountains. All the uluses are small beyond the mountains. The people in the mountains and beyond are known as Goguls, but the people were not there. On the first day of sailing beyond the mountains we came to 21 uluses, and that day we took prisoners in the last uluses and killed

267

some people and captured prisoners. The next day we sailed past uluses, and on the right a river called the Shingal joins [the Amur], and they say that many people live along that river and that they have towns. At the mouth of the Shingal River, on the same side, there are two large uluses, with 60 or more iurts. I, Erofei, ordered the men in this ulus to pay iasak, but they refused to give iasak to the Sovereign. We cossacks took some prisoners and killed many people. We spent the night below that ulus.

We continued down the Amur for two days and a night, laying waste the uluses, all the uluses, and each ulus had 60 or 70 iurts. We killed many people in those uluses, and took others prisoner. Then we sailed for seven days from the Shingal to the land of the Duchers, where all the uluses are large and have 70 to 80 iurts. The Duchers live all along there, and the whole area has arable land under cultivation and has livestock.

We mowed down their men and captured their women, children and the livestock. On the eighth day we sailed . . . [missing]. On the right side there is a very large ulus, but the people, who are called Achans, had left that place. From this point on to the sea the area is not cultivated and has no livestock. They live on fish. From this ulus we sailed for two days, and encountered uluses with as many as 100 iurts. As soon as we approached any ulus in our boats, we would jump out onto the shore, and then they would fight us. With God's mercy and the fortune of the Sovereign, we killed many of these people.

On September 29 we came to a large ulus on the left bank. I, Erofei, took counsel with the servitors and the cossack volunteers and we decided to spend the winter in that ulus. We stopped and disembarked and went into the town, and the men we had captured as we sailed . . . [missing] these Achans brought iasak to us. On October 5 we outfitted two boats and sent 100 men to catch fish for food. We spent five days on that expedition and loaded two boats in those uluses.

At that time about 1,000 Duchers and Achans gathered, and at dawn on October 8 they made a surprise attack on our town from all sides and set fire to it. At the time 106 of our men were in town. With God's mercy and the luck of the Sovereign, we, humble servants of the Sovereign, servitors and cossack volunteers made ready and put on our armor and prayed to the Savior, the Virgin Mary and to Nikolai the Miracle Worker. Then, to gratify the Sovereign we were ready to die for our faith, and without giving thought to our own safety, 70 of us charged the Sovereign's enemies, and 36 men remained in the town. We fought for about two hours, firing cannon and small arms at the Achans and Duchers from the towers, and thanks to God's mercy and the Virgin Mary and the luck of the Sovereign, we defeated these heathens. Then they were seized with the fear of God, those heathen dogs. They could not stand against the Tsar's wrath and our battle. They fled and we pursued them. We killed many and captured many. These heathens jumped into their boats and rowed off on the great Amur River. Their boats are large with stowage, and are painted in colors. Each such boat can accommodate 50 or 60 men.

We, humble servants of the Sovereign, servitors and cossack volunteers, assembled in town. I, Erofei, interrogated the prisoners about the army, and under questioning the prisoners said, "Our entire Ducher and Achan population gathered, and our army numbered 800, but you killed many of our people." We counted the dead heathens around the town, and found 117. In that battle we lost one man, Nikifor Ermolaev, and five of our men were wounded.

The day after the fight the boats returned with fish, and we strongly fortified the town and wintered there. The heathens did not reappear.

On November 28 we, the humble servitors and cossack volunteers of the Sovereign, saw the sled tracks of the heathens. They use dogs, and when my men saw these tracks, they told me, Erofei, about it. I, Erofei, sent 120 servitors and volunteers; then went on foot for a day and reached the tracks, and there, with God's mercy and the luck of the Sovereign, . . . [missing] they took brothers of the Achan prince Kech prisoner, and killed many ulus men. After this foray they returned to town with these men and prisoners on the third day. Kech gave iasak for his brothers, and gave sables as pominki. . . . [missing]. All of this has been entered in the iasak books, both the amount of the iasak collected and the amount of pominki. All will be found with this report.

We, humble servants of the Sovereign, servitors and cossack volunteers lived in this Achan town for the whole winter, fishing. We caught fish with iron hooks and lived on fish.

At dawn on March 24 a strong force made a surprise attack on the Achan town and on us cossacks. This was the Bogdoi army. All the warriors were mounted and wore armor. Our cossack *esaul*, Andrei Ivanov, a servitor, sounded the alarm in town, shouting, "Brother cossacks, rise quickly and protect yourselves with strong armor!" The cossacks rushed to the walls of the town, wearing only their shirts. We cossacks thought it was our cossacks from town who were firing, but it was the Bogdoi army firing their cannon on our cossacks in town. We cossacks fought the Bogdoi army from dawn until dusk for possession of the walls. This Bogdoi army hurled themselves against the cossack iurts, and would not allow us cossacks to move through town. The Bogdoi men covered the town wall with their battle standards, and in our town these Bogdoi people cut out a hole from the top of the wall down to the ground three logs wide.

The leader of the Bogdoi force, Prince Isin, a prince of the Bogdoi tsar, shouted to his men, "Do not burn, and do not kill the cossacks! Take them alive!" Our interpreters heard Prince Isin call and told me, Erofei. Hearing Prince Isin's call, we cossacks put on our armor, and I, Erofei, and the servitors and cossack volunteers prayed to the Savior and the Holy Virgin, the Mother of God, and to the servant of Christ, Nikolai the Miracle Worker. We bade farewell to one another and I, Erofei, and the esaul Andrei Ivanov told our cossack army, "Brother cossacks, we will die for our holy faith. We will defend the house of the Savior and of the Virgin and of Nikolai the Miracle Worker. We cossacks will gratify the Sovereign Tsar and Grand Prince Aleksei Mikhailovich of all Russia! We cossacks will die as one, in battle against the Sovereign's enemy, but we will not fall into the hands of the Bogdoi people alive!"

Bogdoi forces began to charge the shattered wall, and we cossacks brought a large bronze cannon to that shattered town wall and began to fire on the Bogdoi troops. We also fired our small arms from town. And from the cannon we fired on the whole force of Bogdoi. With God's mercy and the luck of the Sovereign, and to our joy, we killed many of those dogs. When the Bogdoi began to fall back as a result of our cannonade, the servitors and volunteer cossacks, 150 strong, in armor, pursued the Bogdoi beyond the town. Fifty remained in the town. When we went outside the town to confront the Bogdoi, they brought two cannon to the edge of town, but with God's mercy and the luck of the Sovereign, we cossacks seized those two cannon from the Bogdoi. We killed them, and took the weapons from the Bogdoi men who had firearms.

The 156 cossacks who were on the sortie . . . [missing]. We rejoiced for the Sovereign and recalled how we had kissed the cross heedless of our own safety and fought the Sovereign's enemies. With God's mercy and the Sovereign's fortune, and for your joy and gratification, Dmitrii Andreevich and Osip Stepanovich, we cossacks killed many of these Bogdoi people with sabers during our attack. The Bogdoi men were seized by great fear, and with God's mercy . . . [missing] and the blessing of the Blessed Virgin Queen Mother, and the Holy follower of Christ, Nikolai the Miracle Worker, we showed our determination, and all the rest of the Bogdoi people ran off and dispersed from town and fled from battle in a group. We cossacks took Bogdoi prisoners, and captured 830 horses from the Bogdoi as well as supplies of food and seventeen rapid firing pieces. These firearms have three or four barrels together, but no flintlocks. We also took two cannon and eight battle standards from the Bogdoi.

I, Erofei, interrogated the prisoners closely, and under questioning they broke. One prisoner, a servitor of the Bogdoi tsar from the town of Niulgutsk named Kabyshei, said, "I will tell you cossacks the whole truth. There is nothing to hide. Last fall we had news about you from the mouth of the Shingal River. The news was brought by the Duchers to the town of Niulgutsk. The Duchers came to us, to Prince Isin and to Ivedakamakh and to Tamfimaf, who are officials in Niulgutsk, having been sent there by officials of the Bogdoi tsar, Uchurv. Then the Ducher men began to cry and said, 'The Russians have come. They have destroyed our whole land they have killed many and have taken our wives and children into captivity. We Duchers have gathered from our whole territory and attacked the town which was being held by only a few Russians, but they killed almost all of us. We cannot stand against them alone, so you will have to defend us. And if you will not defend us, then we will be forced to pay iasak to them.'

"Prince Isin and his councillors reported this to tsar Uchurv in the town of Nadymna, sending a Bogdoi servitor with the report, and he went off within the month. He went from Niulgutsk to Nadymna, to the steppe, and on the way he passed two towns, Labei and Tiumen. These towns are built of stone and have 2,000 or 3,000 dwellings. Tsar Uchurv lives in the town of Nadymna, and his administrator is named Shamshakan. When the servitor came back from Tsar Uchurv, he brought a gramota which authorized Prince Isin and his men to bring a large army together and attack you cossacks, and kill you all. Any cossacks who survived were to be captured and taken with weapons into their territory [China]. Prince Isin and his men quickly assembled an army from the town of Niulgutsk, 600 strong, and set out. They had six cannon, 30 guns and 12 *pinard* [jars] of gunpowder. Each jar held a pud of powder. They took the jars to the town walls and destroyed the walls and the towers as well.

"We had 500 . . . [missing] with us, and there were 420 from Mansan ulus, and more than 500 Duchers from the whole river region. Mansan ulus is about half a day's travel from us, . . . [missing] this ulus has about 1,000 dwellings and is on one side of the river, and opposite that ulus, on the other side of the Shingal River, there is another ulus. We traveled on horseback for about three months after leaving Niulgutsk; every two men shared three horses. . . . [missing] and near there live industrious Daur and Tungus people who raise grain and grow produce for tsar Shamshakan. From the town of Movgen there is a route to the Bogdoi land to tsar Shamshakan.

"I am a man from the Nikan land east of the Bogdoi land. The Buchun River forms a boundary, and that river empties into the sea. There are many people who live along that river, and they are known as the Nikans. They have dark faces and are bearded. Many Nikans also live along another river, the Shungui, which is not far away. There is a town on that river where the Nikan tsar Ziulzei lives. There are also many other towns along that river, all built of stone.

"We fear the Bogdoi tsar, because the Bogdoi tsar Shamshakan makes war on the Nikan people. But he cannot control the entire land because the land of Nikan is very large, and the Nikan tsar does not pay iasak to anyone. In our Nikan land there is gold and silver and freshwater pearls and precious stones. There are several silks produced in our Nikan land, and from the silk, *kamka* and satin and velvet are made. Cotton is grown, and calico is made from it."

I, Erofei, asked this man, "Where are the gold and silver found?" He replied, "Silver and gold are found in a river which rises in the marshes and empties into the sea. That river is not large, and there are mountains along it, and one of the mountains has gold. The gold ore is mined with iron picks, and near the deposit of gold ore there is a town built of stone and many servitors live there. There are many pearls in that same river, below these mountains, and silver is also found along that river. Silver is also found in many other places in the Nikan land, but gold is only found in that one place. Gold, silver, silk, kamka and other precious goods go out to all the hordes from the Nikan land, but I have not heard of any land other than the Nikan land where gold and silver are to be found."

I asked the prisoner how many had been killed near the town of Achan. He replied that 676 men of the Bogdoi force had been killed, and that the Bogdoi had killed ten cossacks, two servitors and eight cossack volunteers. Seventy-eight cossacks were wounded in the battle, but they recovered from their wounds. A list of the names of the cossacks who were killed, as well as of those who were wounded, is appended to this report. After that battle we did not see any of the heathen, not a single man, near the town where we wintered. We are told that it takes ten days to sail from that place to the land of the Giliaks. The Giliaks live all along the sea coast.

On April 22 we outfitted our six doshchanniks and then I, Erofei, and the cossacks took these boats up the river. On the eve of Trinity Sunday I, Erofei, was on the upper reaches of the river and met with the troops that you, Dmitrii Andreevich and Osip Stepanovich, had sent under the command of the servitors Tretiak Ermolin and Artemii Filipov. With them were the new Daur cossack servitors who had been sent to me. I, Erofei, in accordance with the instructions which these servitors brought, received the government supplies of cannon, powder and shot from Tretiak and Artemii. I received their men and gave them a receipt, and I also accepted a hostage named Toencha. All matters concerning Tretiak and Artemii and the newly recruited Daur cossack servitors have been included in Tretiak's report. Each man fulfilled his own obligation in these places.

We camped near the ulus for a week. The native men camped beyond us, and although we talked to them and urged them to come under the suzerainty of the Tsarist Majesty and to give iasak, they would not come close to us.

On June 13 the desiatniks and line servitors and cossack volunteers, indeed the entire armed force, petitioned the Sovereign through me, Erofei, in accordance with the Sovereign's ukaz, to allow them to go after those men who would not obey the Sovereign, using regular military force. I, Erofei, sent 140 men, and with God's mercy and the luck of the Sovereign, the servitors and cossack volunteer troops were pleased and gratified to capture a Ducher leader. The following day the brothers of this man appeared and brought iasak from their tribe amounting to 100 sables. We took those men as hostages.

On June 15 a hostage said that below this place there is an ulus, and that other men live in the mountains opposite the ulus. I, Erofei, sent the 140 servitors and cossack volunteers, and in the course of their expedition they captured five men, all leaders. They also took a Ducher man from the Shingal. They brought them to me, Erofei. I questioned them, and they confessed, "Our people do not wish to give you iasak. They want to fight you." This man also said, "An army of many Bogdoi people will come from the Shingal. More than 6,000 men have gathered from the Shingal and from our Ducher land; they are at the mouth of the Shingal waiting for you. When the cossacks go either downriver or upriver they will come. We will entice them to the shore and kill them there. They did not wait for the cossacks to come from above, they sent me out after you to find out where you are planning to spend the winter, what kind of camp you are going to build. Then we will assemble an army of 10,000 or more and we will crush you."

I, Erofei, tortured him with hot irons, and he still said the same thing, that an army of 10,000 with cannon and large and small arms would attack us.

On April [date missing] the servitors Tretiak Ermolin and Artemii Filipov sent to me, Erofei, six servitors and 21 cossack volunteers from the town of Banbulai, a total of 27 men. They came with news and instructions on serving and benefitting the Sovereign. With God's judgment, I, Erofei, parted company with these troops, and we never saw each other again. I do not know whether they are alive or dead.

The servitors and cossacks who sailed with Tretiak and Artemii submitted a petition to the Sovereign asking permission to go down the river to search for these 27 men. But I, Erofei, did not send them, because I could not send out so small a detachment against the vast army at the mouth of the Shingal River. The whole land was crowded with these warriors. We all had to sail together, or we would not have been able to get up the river this year, and then we could not have sent our reports to the Sovereign about our service, and you, Dmitrii Andreevich and Osip Stepanovich, would have been unaware of our activities.

We stayed near this ulus for two weeks. When we approached Turonchin's and Tolgin's towns, we sent natives to these Daur people with news. The Turonchin children and leaders came out to us and brought 37 sables and 9 bulls as iasak for the Sovereign. The leaders brought these sables and bulls, but the leaders would not come aboard our boats. Through an interpreter I, Erofei, told them to pay iasak in full from their tribe to our Sovereign, and then they could live without apprehension in their former encampments. When we reached Turonchin's and Tolgin's towns we summoned the natives, but they would not come near us. . . . [missing]

From these uluses there is a route to the land of the Bogdoi . . . [missing] to tsar Shamshakan . . . [missing]. Dmitrii Andreevich and Osip Stepanovich, in accordance with the ukaz of the Sovereign and the letter of instruction, you ordered Tretiak Ermolin to select ten men from the troops, any ones he wished, to be under his command. Tretiak chose, and made a list of the names, and on the basis of this list I, Erofei, gave him ten of my troops. Having made his selection, Tretiak was instructed to go to the Bogdoi land as an envoy. I, Erofei, asked the Daur people to provision Tretiak, but they would not come near, but neither did they harass Tretiak and his men. I camped there exactly four weeks, and the heathen did not ever come near.

We had their hostages, so I talked with the hostage Turoncha and his brother and asked them, "Why will your people not lead Tretiak to tsar Shamshakan?" They replied, "How can they take them? They recently fought you, and you killed many Bogdoi people, and now more than 10,000 Bogdoi troops are ready to attack. If our people take Tretiak and his men, they will not let them come back to you, and then you will kill us because of it."

On August 1 we came to Kokor's ulus at the mouth of the Zeia River. I, Erofei, went ashore and began to talk to the troops and servitors and cossack volunteers, and I asked them, "Where should we build our encampment?" The servitors and cossacks, 212 men in all, replied, "Wherever it is most advantageous, and wherever it will bring satisfactory results for the Sovereign, that is where we should place our camp." But some men were outlaws who had violated their oaths and were not well disposed toward the Sovereign. They did not want this land to be permanently Russian. They were only interested in making a personal profit and enriching themselves.

These men were Stepan Poliakov, a free cossack; the cossack desiatnik Konstantin Ivanov, from Eniseisk, who had come from Lake Baikal; Kuzma Fedorov; Andrei Stepanovich Petrov, from Baikal; and with them there were the servitor Ivan Vasilevich Pan, Ivan Artemev, Gavriil, Grigorii and Ivan Shchipunov, Petr Oksenev, Loginko Vasilev, Fedor Petrov, . . . [missing] Ivanov, Antonii Pavlov, Antonii Pankratev and the servitor Semen Sazhin. In all there were 100 men in this conspiracy. Stepan Poliakov set off in a boat, as did Konstantin Ivanov and Loginko Vasilev. They put out in three boats and sailed off.

The Sovereign's cannon, shot, powder and armor were in these boats. Stepan Poliakov, Konstantin Ivanov and Loginko Vasilev hauled one cannon onto the bank of the river and jettisoned another in the water. The servitors and cossacks who had remained with me, Erofei, with Sovereign's treasury, began to cry, seeking the Sovereign's supplies and these outlaws who had broken their solemn vows and abandoned government service, and had run off like thieves. We salvaged the Tsar's supplies from the water and from the bank of the river and took them aboard our boats and set them aright. The outlaws Stepan Poliakov and Konstantin Ivanov and Loginko Vasilev and their comrades took whatever they had aboard their boats, such as the Sovereign's powder, lead, shot and armor, and jettisoned some and took the rest with them. . . . [missing] they hauled anchor and sailed off.

I, Erofei, and the servitors and cossacks went to them, talked to them, and tried to persuade them. We called on them to listen to the Sovereign's ukaz and instructions, and to remember why we were serving on the great Amur River. But they said, "We are not listening to the instructions, and we are not going to come back to you again, now that we have left you."

Stepan Poliakov, Konstantin Ivanov and Loginko Vasilev and their comrades turned outlaw and seized some 30 free cossacks who had gone up the river in their boats. They intercepted them, tied them up, and sailed off with them. The free cossacks, Stepan Vakhromeev and Semen Mikhailov and others who did not want to violate their oath of loyalty and abandon the Tsar's supplies, jumped out of the boat into the water in their shirts, with whatever weapons they had, and powder and shot, but the rebels took

276

the captives and provisions with them. Stepan Poliakov and his men stole military provisions valued at 2,000 rubles, and they also stole the battle standards valued at 50 rubles. And when they sailed off, they plundered the natives.

The total number of those who sailed with Stepan Poliakov and Konstantin Ivanov and Loginko, as well as those they carried off by force, came to 136. 212 men remained with me, Erofei, on government assignment, and of that number four have been sent to you, Dmitrii Andreevich and Osip Stepanovich. These include two servitors, Bogdan Gabyshev and Sergei Andreev, and two free cossacks, Filip Samsonov and Ivan Gavrilov.

The day after Stepan Poliakov and his fellow outlaws deserted, the Daur people of princes Turoncha, Omutei and Kokurei came to us, but they halted at some distance from us in the field and refused to come near. Through their leaders they brought iasak for the Sovereign amounting to 100 sables, [to ensure the safety of] the hostages who are with us, namely, Turoncha and his brother and Baldachin's brother-in-law and Omutei's brother. I, Erofei, instructed the interpreter to persuade them to submit to the Tsarist Majesty, and requested them to guide the envoy Tretiak Ermolin to tsar Shamshakan. But they replied, "We will not come to you, because you deceive us. The interpreter Kost told us that you want to seize us, and he speaks the truth. He told us to flee to the land of the Daurs and the Duchers. Furthermore your other people who went off on the river are pillaging our land. No matter what envoys you send, we will not come to you, nor will we receive your envoys."

I waited there a full six weeks, trying to entice these heathens, but they would not submit to us. We have four male Daur hostages: prince Turoncha and his brother Anai, Mokalei, Prince Shilgin's son, Togochei, and a Ducher hostage, Toencha. The government iasak treasury which I, Erofei, collected from the Daurs and Duchers and other people, consists of fourteen forties of sables, four black-brown foxes, two red foxes, seven fox back cloaks, and two shubas made of 30 sable backs. The Ducher prince Toencha had been taken captive by the servitors and free cossacks, for the benefit of the Tsar, and had been sent from Iakutsk ostrog with the servitors Tretiak Ermolin and Artemii Filipov; and for that hostage Tretiak collected 32 sables as iasak for the Sovereign and brought it to me. And for the safety of that same Ducher hostage, I, Erofei, collected the Sovereign's iasak consisting of 70 sables, and pominki of eight sables, and a shuba made of 17 sable backs. Tretiak collected five sables as pominki from Churoncha for his son, Ikul.

Dmitrii Andreevich and Osip Stepanovich, we do not know where we will spend the winter. We dare not provision ourselves in the land of the Daurs at the mouth of the Zeia or at the mouth of the Shingal, because the Bogdoi land is nearby, and a large military force with firearms and cannon and small arms is advancing against us. We do not wish to endanger the government treasury, nor do we wish to lose the heads of the cossacks in vain. This summer we have sailed along the Amur and have summoned natives to submit to the Sovereign's Majesty, and we have pillaged all natives who have been disobedient and unwilling to submit. We will go downriver to spend the winter.

Dmitrii Andreevich and Osip Stepanovich, the people of this land cannot be conquered, because the land is heavily populated, and they have firearms. We dare not move to go to other rivers beyond this land and this Amur River without the Sovereign's ukaz.

Dmitrii Andreevich and Osip Stepanovich, I have written to you concerning the possibility of establishing a settlement in the upper reaches of the river. I sent twenty men there with food provisions and with seeds, but when Stepan Vasilevich Poliakov, Konstantin Ivanov, and Kozma and Andrei Stepanov, from Baikal and Ivan Parfenov came to me, they did not bring me the number of men necessary to send up the river to establish a settlement there. Moreover, Stepan Poliakov and Konstantin Ivanov and their comrades created discontent among the servitors. They drove off the heathens, laid waste the land, and Stepan and Konstantin have destroyed whatever chances of establishing ties with the natives my plan of sending envoys might have had. But if the heathens should decide to act as guides for Tretiak, I will send him as envoy, whenever it seems appropriate. During these forays 20 men have been killed and 59 have been wounded.

See: *Dopolneniia k aktam istoricheskim* (St. Petersburg: 1848), III, 359–371.

82

A PETITION TO TSAR ALEKSEI MIKHAILOVICH FROM THE MERCHANT
OF THE *GOSTINNAIA SOTNIA*,* VASILII USOV, REQUESTING AID IN AP-
PREHENDING HIS FORMER PRIKASHCHIK WHO HAS ABSCONDED WITH
HIS GOODS AND CASH.

To the Sovereign Tsar and Grand Prince Aleksei Mikhailovich of all Russia, your humble servant Vasilii Usov humbly
submits this petition.

Sovereign, in 1639 I was serving you in Velikii Ustiug as chief
of the customs and liquor tax. I sent my prikashchiks to towns in
Siberia with my goods to carry on trade for me. These men were
Fedot Alekseev, the son of Popov, from Kholmogory; and Luka
Vasilev, son of Siverov, from Ustiug. With them I sent goods and
3,500 rubles in cash. I have the receipt for this, Sire.

At the Lena portage Luka Siverov from Ustiug went into a
monastery because he was ill. Fedot Alekseev Popov from Kholmogory went to the great river Lena with my goods. From the
Lena he went to unknown lands, Sire, and there was no word of
him for more than eight years. But now, Sire, I, your humble servant, have learned that this Fedot is coming back; but I, your
humble servant, do not know if he still has those goods.

Merciful Sovereign Tsar and Grand Prince of all Russia, Aleksei Mikhailovich, have mercy on me, your humble servant.
Sovereign, I beg send your Sovereign instruction to the great river
Lena, to Iakutsk ostrog, to your Sovereign voevoda Mikhail Semenovich Lodyzhenski and to your diak Fedor Vasilev. As soon as
my prikashchik, Fedot, comes to Iakutsk, Sire, decree that they
obtain an account from him, Fedot, of my goods, and that they
make a detailed inventory of everything he has, and this be
sealed, and that he appear in Moscow at the Sibirskii Prikaz with
this property, together with me, your humble servant.

Tsar, Sovereign, have mercy, please.

Reference: TsGADA, f. Sibirskii prikaz, stolb. No. 1056, p. 1, 1. 98.
See: N. S. Orlova, ed. *Otkrytie russkikh zemleprokhodtsev i poliarnykh morekhodov XVII veka na severo-vostoke Azii. Sbornik dokumentov* (Moscow: 1951),
192–193.

Gostinnaia sotnia—Literally, merchant hundred; actually a guild of wealthy
Muscovite merchants.

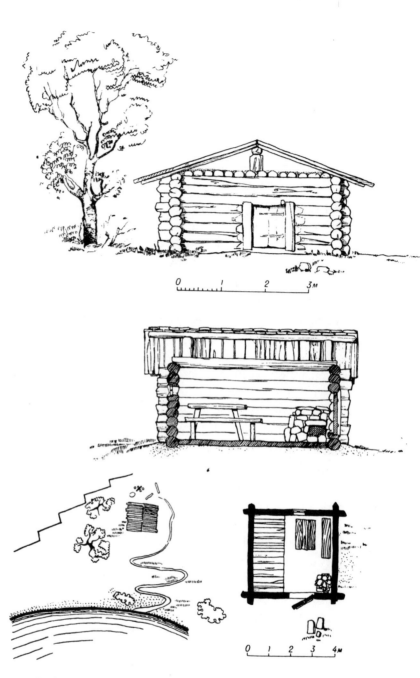

A zimov'e, strategically situated near the rapids of a river, shows a snug winter-resistant construction. From Makovetskii, *Byt i iskusstvo russkogo naseleniia vostochnoi Sibiri*, Vol. 1.

83

1654

INSTRUCTIONS FROM THE PRIKAZ OF THE BOLSHAIA KAZNA TO FEDOR BAIKOV CONCERNING HIS EMBASSY TO THE CHINESE EMPIRE

In February of the year 1654, in accordance with the ukaz of the Sovereign Tsar and Grand Prince Aleksei Mikhailovich of all Russia, the following instruction was given to Fedor Isakovich Baikov.

He is to travel to the Chinese Empire to the Chinese Bugdykhan-tsar, carrying the gramota from the Sovereign Tsar and Grand Prince Aleksei Mikhailovich of all Russia. A gramota from the Sovereign concerning this mission has been sent to Siberia, to Tobolsk, to the stolnik and voevoda Prince Vasilii Khilkov and his associates to enable Fedor to proceed from Tobolsk to the Chinese Empire by way of Siberian towns, and from the Siberian towns to the Kalmyk uluses and nomadic encampments, and to other places which are close to the Chinese Empire and pay tribute to them. The stolnik and voevoda Prince Vasilii Khilkov has been instructed to send word from Tobolsk to the ulus officials and murzas and taishas along the route to the Chinese Empire asking them to provide transport and guides from one place to the next.

When Fedor arrives in Tobolsk in Siberia, he is to give the letter from the Sovereign Tsar and Grand Prince Aleksei Mikhailovich, which was given to him upon his departure, to the stolnik and voevoda Prince Vasilii Khilkov and his associates, and inform Prince Vasilii that in accordance with the Sovereign's ukaz he is to write to the Kalmyk uluses and encampments and to the taishas through whose uluses Fedor will be traveling, instructing them that they are not to obstruct Fedor's journey, and that he is to be allowed to proceed without being detained. When Fedor is sent out from Tobolsk, he is to proceed without delay.

When Fedor leaves Siberian towns to go to the uluses or nomadic encampments, he is to send on ahead to those uluses, to the taishas or murzas or princes, the letters from the stolnik, and voevoda Prince Vasilii Khilkov, which will be given to him upon his departure. He is to tell them that he has been sent by the great Sovereign Tsar and Grand Prince Aleksei Mikhailovich, Autocrat of all Russia, and Sovereign and Lord of many realms, to the Chinese Bugdykhan-tsar, Emperor of all China, his Imperial Majesty, with a letter, and that he has orders to proceed as rapidly as possible. They are not to detain him in their uluses, and they are to provide him with transport and guides to accompany him from one ulus to another, and they are to give him complete protection so that he will safely reach the Chinese Empire.

After the ulus murzas or taishas have allowed Fedor to pass through their uluses, and when he reaches a Chinese town, he is to inform the administrator of that town that he has been sent from the great Sovereign Tsar and Grand Prince Aleksei Mikhailovich, Autocrat of all Russia, and Sovereign and Lord of many realms, to their sovereign, to the Chinese Bugdykhan-tsar, as an envoy, on official government affairs, and that he is carrying a letter of friendship and amity which deals with beneficial affairs of state, which the Great Sovereign, His Tsarist Majesty, has sent to their sovereign, Bugdykhan-tsar. Fedor is also to tell the administrator that he is to be given shelter and food and transport, and he is to be allowed to proceed without hindrance. He is also to be given guides to take him to the city where their ruler, Bugdykhan-tsar, lives, and the [Chinese] sovereign is to be informed of his arrival. As soon as they permit him to leave the first town, he is to travel on without stopping anywhere.

If imperial officials in that town tell him that he is to accompany them to court and hand over the letter from His Tsarist Majesty, Fedor is not to go with them, nor is he to hand over the Sovereign's gramota, nor is he to speak with them at any length. He is to tell them that he has been sent from the Great Sovereign Tsar and Grand Prince Aleksei Mikhailovich, Autocrat of all Russia, and Sovereign and Lord of many realms, to their sovereign, to Bugdykhan-tsar, His Imperial Majesty, with a gramota concerning their friendly official relationship.

He is to say that he is to be taken to their sovereign, Bugdykhan-tsar, that he must proceed to him, and that it would be improper for him to hand over the Tsar's gramota to them because no great sovereign in any realm anywhere follows such a custom, whereby an envoy would hand over an imperial gramota to counsellors without seeing the Sovereign in person. He is to say that when he is brought before their sovereign, Bugdykhan-tsar, he will deliver the gramota from His Tsarist Majesty, and he will tell Bugdykhan-tsar what His Tsarist Majesty has instructed him to say; but it would be improper for him to visit the counsellors without being presented to their sovereign because no such custom exists anywhere. He is to refuse firmly.

If they permit Fedor to proceed on to Chinese towns, and if he reaches the city where Bugdykhan-tsar lives and they send counsellors to him, they may ask him the following questions. From whom does he come? For what purpose has he been sent? Who is on the throne of the Muscovite realm? Does he have a letter with him? Has his Sovereign sent verbal instructions with him? Fedor is to reply as follows. "By the will and mercy of God, on the great and illustrious throne of the Muscovite realm and of all the great and illustrious realms of the Russian Tsardom, sits the Great Sovereign Tsar and Grand Prince and Autocrat of all Russia, descendent of Caesar Augustus, ruler of the entire universe, descendent of the Great Prince Riurik and of other great monarchs who followed him, the great-grandson of our Great Sovereign Tsar and Grand Prince Ivan Vasilevich, of blessed memory, Autocrat of all Russia, and grandson of the Great Sovereign Tsar and Grand Prince Fedor Ivanovich, of blessed memory, Autocrat of all Russia, and son of the Great Sovereign and Merciful, Illustrious and Glorious, most splendid of all Tsars, most esteemed with unsullied praise, the most dignified Great Sovereign Tsar and Grand Prince Mikhail Fedorovich of blessed memory, Autocrat of all Russia.

Our great Sovereign Tsar and Grand Prince Aleksei Mikhailovich, Autocrat of all Russia, was crowned on the throne with the Tsarist crown and the diadems, and he took the scepter of power into his hands. In accordance with the ancient custom of the great Russian Sovereigns, the Great Sovereign sent his envoys and couriers into all the neighboring great realms to announce his ascension onto the Tsarist throne. Now, His Tsarist Majesty, wishing to be in close friendship and amicable relations with Bugdykhan-tsar, has sent Fedor to him, to Bugdykhan-tsar, to inform him of his ascension to power, and to assure him of his imperial health, and to hear news of Bugdykhan-tsar's health, and to discuss good relations which are beneficial to both sovereigns and to the well-being, peace and security of their great empires. Their sovereign, Bugdykhan-tsar, should receive Fedor without undue delay.

If they tell him that Bugdykhan-tsar orders him to appear before him, Fedor is to go to Bugdykhan-tsar and appear before him in accordance with ambassadorial custom. But if Fedor comes to the palace and finds that Bugdykhan-tsar's immediate entourage is present but that Bugdykhan-tsar is not there in person, then when Fedor enters the palace he is to bow to the Bugdykhan-tsar's officials, but he is not to hand over to them the Tsar's gramota, and he is not to make any statements to them.

If the counsellors ask that Fedor give them the Sovereign's letter, and want to discuss his oral instructions with him, or if they say that Bugdykhan-tsar is unavailable because he is somewhere else, then Fedor should respond as follows. "I have been sent from the Sovereign Tsar and Grand Prince Aleksei Mikhailovich, Autocrat of all Russia, Sovereign and Lord of many realms, to their sovereign, Bugdykhan-tsar, carrying His Tsarist Majesty's gramota. I have been instructed by His Tsarist Majesty to give this letter to Bugdykhan-tsar in person, and to speak only with him. I have been told that Bugdykhan-tsar wishes me to appear before him, not before his counsellors. It is therefore improper for me to give His Imperial Majesty's gramota to anyone other than Bugdykhan-tsar, nor may I converse with anyone else. And furthermore, it is you, the counsellors of your sovereign, who have informed me that Bugdykhan-tsar has ordered me to appear before him, and it is he who must accept the letter from His Tsarist Majesty, and personally hear the verbal communication I am to deliver."

If Bugdykhan-tsar's counsellors do not notify him, and if Bugdykhan-tsar indeed is not in the palace, then Fedor is to return to his quarters. He is not to hand over the gramota nor confer with the counsellors. If Bugdykhan-tsar sends his counsellors to Fedor's quarters, and they then request that he hand over the Sovereign's gramota and tell them what business His Tsarist Majesty has sent Fedor on, then Fedor is to make the following response. "If and when Bugdykhan-tsar orders me to appear before him, then when I am actually in his presence I will hand over the gramota from the Great Sovereign Tsar and Grand Prince Aleksei Mikhailovich, Autocrat of all Russia, to Bugdykhan-tsar, and then I will also speak and deliver the verbal message. I have been instructed not to give His Tsarist Majesty's letter to anyone but Bugdykhan-tsar, nor to converse with anyone but Bugdykhan-tsar."

When Bugdykhan-tsar summons him, Fedor is to appear before him. As he approaches the tsarist court and is instructed to kowtow in front of the entrance, in accordance with the custom of their sovereign, which is that envoys and couriers and messengers of all other great sovereigns who appear at the court of Bugdy-khan-tsar must kowtow at the entrance, Fedor is to refuse firmly and tell the officials the following. "I am speaking as an official, and such an action would not be appropriate. Nowhere is there such a custom as to kowtow at the entrance of an imperial palace. I have been sent by the Great Sovereign, His Tsarist Majesty, to your sovereign, Bugdykhan-tsar, with His Tsarist Majesty's gramota about amicable state relations. I will not kowtow before the entrance. This decision is not subject to argument. I will never do this. Such a custom does not exist in the Tsarist Majesty's court, and I would be ashamed even to speak of such a thing." Fedor is to refuse to discuss the matter further.

If the high official or the official greeters tell him that when he comes to the tsar's palace he must kowtow at that palace, and if they say further that Bugdykhan-tsar is present in that palace, Fedor is to reply, "I am indeed most surprised that I have not gazed upon the face of the Emperor."

If they tell him to kowtow to the palace, he is to respond that it would be improper to kowtow to a stone structure.

But if he is taken into the actual presence of Bugdykhan-tsar, then he is to bow to Bugdykhan-tsar, in accordance with the custom observed in all realms, for he knows how honor is accorded depending on the standing of each realm.

When emissaries and envoys of neighboring great sovereigns came to our Great Sovereign Tsar and Grand Prince of all Russia, Mikhail Fedorovich of blessed memory, Autocrat of all Russia, and to our former great Sovereign Tsars and Grand Princes of Russia, of blessed memory, and to our Sovereign Tsar and Grand Prince Aleksei Mikhailovich, Autocrat of all Russia, all of these envoys and ambassadors and couriers were welcomed. The embassy was received ceremoniously, and respect was expressed to all of their sovereigns, from wherever they came, and friendship and amicable relations were extended, according to their status. Consequently, Fedor is not to kowtow in the court of the Bugdykhan-tsar to any palace or to any entrance to it.

If some official tells Fedor that he must kiss the foot of Bugdykhan-tsar, according to their custom, because envoys of other rulers kiss the foot of Bugdykhan-tsar, then Fedor is to make the following response. "From the time of our late Great Sovereign Tsars and Grand Princes of Moscow, and from the time of the great-grandfather of our Sovereign, the Great Sovereign Tsar and Grand Prince Fedor Ivanovich of blessed memory, Autocrat of all Russia, and from the time of the father of our great Sovereign, the Sovereign Tsar and Grand Prince Mikhail Fedorovich of blessed memory, Autocrat of all Russia, who sent envoys and ambassadors to the great sovereigns such as the Sultan of Turkey and the Shah of Persia, and to all the great sovereigns of great neighboring realms, the envoys of our Great Sovereigns, and the emissaries and envoys of the great Christian sovereigns and Muslim sovereigns all kissed the hand, but not the foot.

"Moreover, whenever envoys and ambassadors and couriers of these neighboring great sovereigns came to our late Great Sovereign Tsars and Grand Princes of Russia, to our great Sovereign, His Tsarist Majesty, and to his father, our Great Sovereign Tsar and Grand Prince Mikhail Fedorovich, of blessed memory, Autocrat of all Russia, and to His Tsarist Majesty our Great Sovereign Tsar and Grand Prince Aleksei Mikhailovich, Autocrat of all Russia, all of our great Sovereigns received these envoys, and permitted them to present their respects, and received them and granted them an audience upon their arrival and their departure; each extended his Tsarist hand, and placed his Tsarist hands on them, but never forced them to kiss the foot. Bugdykhan-tsar should not institute a new custom, for this would be an expression of disrespect to our Great Sovereign's Tsarist Majesty. Bugdykhan-tsar should do only what is customary in all realms. If our Great Sovereign, His Imperial Majesty, extends only his Imperial hand, considering the Imperial ukaz and previous customs, it is quite impossible to change customs."

Fedor is to be very insistent, and he is not to kiss the foot of Bugdykhan-tsar.

When Fedor is brought into the palace of Bugdykhan-tsar, he is to bow to Bugdykhan-tsar in the name of the Sovereign Tsar and Grand Prince Aleksei Mikhailovich, Autocrat of all Russia. He is to say this: "By Grace of God and the Holy Trinity, the Great Sovereign Tsar and Grand Prince Aleksei Mikhailovich, Autocrat of all Great and Little Russia; Tsar of Moscow, Kiev, Vladimir and Novgorod; Tsar of Kazan; Tsar of Astrakhan; Tsar of Siberia; Sovereign of Pskov; Grand Prince of Tver, Iugra, Perm, Viatka, Bulgaria and others; Grand Prince of Nizhnii Novgorod, Chernigov, Riazan, Rostov, Iaroslav, Beloozero, Udorsk, Obdorsk, and Kondinsk; Lord of all the Northern Lands; Sovereign of the Iversk lands and of Kartalinsk and Gruzia [Georgia]; Sovereign of the Kabardinsk lands and of Cherkassia and of the Mountain Princes; Hereditary Lord, Heir, Suzerain and possessor of many other realms and territories, east, west and north, has permitted me to bow to you, Bugdykhan-tsar, Lord of the city of Kanbalyk [Peking] and ruler of all the Chinese Empire. He has instructed me to inform you of the health of His Tsarist Majesty, and to observe your tsarist majesty's health." Then Fedor is to bow according to custom, with a normal bow.

When Bugdykhan-tsar inquires about the Sovereign's health, Fedor is to reply that when he left our Great Sovereign, His Tsarist Majesty, by the Grace of God, our Great Sovereign and Grand Prince Aleksei Mikhailovich, Autocrat of all Great and Little Russia and Sovereign and Lord of many realms, was, thanks be to God, in good health, and was governing his great and illustrious realms in the Russian Tsardom.

If Bugdykhan-tsar does not inquire about the health of the Sovereign, then Fedor should state that Bugdykhan-tsar shows lack of respect to our Great Sovereign, His Tsarist Majesty. He should say that by not inquiring about the health of His Tsarist Majesty, as is customary among all great sovereigns, he has shown disrespect to our Great Sovereign. He should say that Bugdykhan-tsar would reveal his friendship and amicability to our Great Sovereign, His Tsarist Majesty, if he were to stand and inquire about the health of His Tsarist Majesty, as is customary among all great sovereigns, and that this would bring about friendship and amicability between our Great Sovereign, His Tsarist Majesty, and Bugdykhan-tsar.

When Bugdykhan-tsar inquires about the health of the Sovereign, Fedor is to tell Bugdykhan-tsar about the Sovereign's health, as explained above. After that he is to state, "The Great Sovereign Tsar and Grand Prince Aleksei Mikhailovich, Autocrat of all Great and Little Russia, and Sovereign and Lord of many realms, has sent you, Bugdykhan-tsar, his Tsarist Majesty's letter of friendship." Then the Sovereign's letter, written in Russian, is to be given to Bugdykhan-tsar, with all due respect.

If the counsellors of Bugdykhan-tsar tell Fedor, during the reception period, that they do not have anyone to translate the letter from His Tsarist Majesty from Russian into Chinese or into Farsi, and that His Tsarist Majesty should have sent their sovereign, Bugdykhan-tsar, a letter of friendship written in Farsi or in Tatar, because they do have persons to translate from those languages, then Fedor should reply, "The Great Sovereign, His Tsarist Majesty, having respect for your sovereign, Bugdykhan-tsar, has sent him this letter of friendship written in the Russian language, to which his great Sovereign seal has been appended, just as His Tsarist Majesty sends his brothers, the Sultan of Turkey and the Shah of Persia and other great sovereigns letters written in Russian. If you do not have anyone to translate the gramota from Russian, then I, Fedor, have brought other letters from His Tsarist Majesty, which also bear the Great Seal of His Tsarist Majesty, written in both Turkish and Tatar languages." Then he is to present the Sovereign's letter written in Tatar.

After that Bugdykan-tsar is to be shown the gifts from the Sovereign, and Fedor is to say, "The Great Sovereign Tsar and Grand Prince Aleksei Mikhailovich, Autocrat of all Great and Little Russia, and Sovereign and Lord of many realms, has sent these small gifts of friendship to you, Bugdykhan-tsar." Then he is to present the beautiful gifts to Bugdykhan-tsar in accordance with the list, and with great care.

The gifts are to be selected and presented to the tsar so that they will please him and give him delight. Of the various gifts which are being sent with Fedor, worth varying amounts of rubles, Fedor is to choose those which he thinks the tsar will prefer, using his judgment in regard to the local situation. If Bugdykhan-tsar should ask whether Fedor has a verbal message, in addition to the written gramota, from His Tsarist Majesty, then Fedor is to reply that he carries no verbal messages in addition to the letter, that everything the Great Sovereign wishes to convey to Bugdykhan-tsar is stated in the gramota. Then Bugdykhan-tsar, having heard the letter from His Tsarist Majesty, should permit Fedor to leave without detaining him. And in return for the gramota from His Tsarist Majesty, he should send with Fedor his own tsarist gramota concerning matters about which he has been written.

If Bugdykhan-tsar tells Fedor anything about this or about other matters, then Fedor is to write everything down secretly in his notebook.

If Bugdykhan-tsar extends his hand to Fedor during the reception, then Fedor is to go to his hand.

If Bugdykhan-tsar's counsellors tell Fedor that in the letter from His Tsarist Majesty which Fedor brought, the name of the

[Russian] Tsar and his titles were written, but that Bugdykhan-tsar's titles were not used properly, as he himself uses them in writing letters, than Fedor is to reply, "You yourselves know very well that there have never before been any embassies between our Great Sovereign Tsars and Great Russian Princes and your sovereign Chinese tsars, and therefore our Great Sovereign's Tsarist Majesty does not know what titles your Bugdykhan-tsar uses in correspondence.

"For this reason your sovereign, Bugdykhan-tsar, should not be surprised, because only now has the first contact been made between our Great Sovereign Tsarist Majesty and your Bugdykhan-tsar. There have never before been contacts between the former great Sovereign Tsars and Grand Russian Princes, our Great Sovereign Tsarist Majesty's father, the Great Sovereign Tsar and Grand Prince Mikhail Fedorovich of blessed memory, Autocrat of all Russia, and the ancestor of your Chinese sovereign; because of this, the names and titles of Bugdykhan-tsar were not known to our Great Sovereign, His Tsarist Majesty."

When Bugdykhan-tsar permits Fedor to return to our Great Sovereign, His Tsarist Majesty, and writes down the names and titles for our Great Sovereign, His Tsarist Majesty, and when Bugdykhan-tsar sends his envoys and ambassadors, then our Great Sovereign, His Tsarist Majesty, will in the future in His Tsarist Majesty's letters, use Bugdykhan-tsar's name and titles just as he himself writes them.

If, after the official reception, the counsellors invite Fedor to come to them, or if they go to his quarters and ask him the same questions they asked when he was in the presence of their ruler, Fedor is not to discuss any matters except for those which His Tsarist Majesty has addressed in his letter to their sovereign. His Tsarist Majesty, the Great Sovereign, wishes to be in friendly and amicable relations with their sovereign, and Fedor is not authorized to discuss anything else.

[. . . Since His Tsarist Majesty] has learned that Bugdykhan-tsar has also sent envoys and emissaries with messages of friendship and amicability to his neighbors who are close to the Chinese Empire, Fedor has been sent by His Tsarist Majesty to Bugdykhan-tsar with His Tsarist Majesty's letter of amity, openly expressing the friendship and amicability of His Tsarist Majesty, and declaring that the Great Sovereign, His Tsarist Majesty, wishes to be in a state of friendship and amity with Bugdykhan-tsar now and in the future, as he is with other great neighboring sovereigns.

Our Great Sovereign, His Tsarist Majesty, has written all of this to their sovereign, Bugdykhan-tsar, in His Tsarist Majesty's gramota. Their sovereign, Bugdykhan, should allow Fedor to leave without detaining him, so he may return to the Great Sovereign, His Tsarist Majesty; he should also send with Fedor his own gramota of friendship.

And in the future their sovereign, Bugdykhan-tsar should also send his envoys to His Tsarist Majesty, with news of their mutual good relations and friendship and amicability, and they should be instructed in detail how to establish and maintain the friendship and amicability between our Great Sovereign, His Tsarist Majesty, and Bugdykhan-tsar.

When their tsar's envoys are sent to His Tsarist Majesty, His Tsarist Majesty will welcome them and allow them to be received in His Tsarist Majesty's patrimony in Siberia. He will decree that they be allowed to proceed from Siberia to him in the capital city of Moscow. He will provide them with an official escort, and with food, drink and transport. They will be given everything by His Tsarist Majesty, and will not be in need of anything. And if Bugdykhan-tsar wishes to send his merchants and trade goods with these envoys into the Muscovite state, then His Tsarist Majesty will decree that these merchants be received in Siberia, and he will order that officials give them shelter, food and adequate transport, and he will also decree that out of friendship and respect for Bugdykhan-tsar, they will not have to pay any state taxes.

When the envoys come to the capital city of Moscow, our Great Sovereign, His Tsarist Majesty, will agree to receive them with honor, and will permit both the envoys and the merchants to have a personal audience with him, and he will hear their ambassadorial message and accept their gramota. He will listen to them with friendship, will give the ambassadors and merchants his Sovereign largesse, will allow their merchants to trade freely in the Muscovite state, and will exempt them from government taxes on their goods all through the whole Muscovite state.

Our Great Sovereign, His Tsarist Majesty, will also allow the envoys of the sovereign Bugdykhan-tsar to meet with His Tsarist Majesty's boiars and other distinguished persons, and he will permit the envoys to converse with these persons on matters regarding how the two sovereigns can maintain their firm friendship and amicability in the future, and be in contact with one another, so that merchants from both realms can travel and trade freely, and through that trade profit their respective states. Our Great Sovereign, His Tsarist Majesty, and their sovereign, Bugdykhan-tsar, should maintain firm friendship and amicability for all time. Then, whatever Bugdykhan-tsar's counsellors discuss with Fedor should be written down.

If Bugdykhan-tsar invites Fedor to dine with him, he is to inform the counsellors and officials of the tsar that he will come to dine with Bugdykhan-tsar only if envoys and ambassadors of other realms are not present at Bugdykhan-tsar's table at the same time. But if Bugdykhan-tsar is not to be present at the table, or if other envoys and ambassadors will be there, Fedor is not to accept the invitation. However if they tell him that no envoys or emissaries of other sovereigns will be at Bugdykhan-tsar's table at the same time, then Fedor is to proceed to Bugdykhan-tsar, and conduct himself at the table in a dignified manner, being careful not to become drunk nor to speak in an unmannerly fashion.

If the tsar or his counsellors should ask him about anything at the table, he is to respond, after listening carefully to their questions, in such a manner that the name of the [Russian] Sovereign will be held in the proper honor and prestige, and so that his reply will bring benefit to the Muscovite state. If they speak about highly important matters, then he is to reply that he has not had the opportunity to be privy to these matters. He is to make a written account of everything they discuss with him, when he returns to his quarters.

If Bugdykhan-tsar or his counsellors inquire about the birth date of the Great Sovereign Tsar and Grand Prince Aleksei Mikhailovich of all Russia, and about his appearance, then Fedor is to reply, "Our Great Sovereign Tsar and Grand Prince, Aleksei Mikhailovich, Autocrat of all Russia, His Tsarist Majesty, is 26 years old. God has endowed our Great Sovereign Tsarist Majesty with handsome features, bravery, intelligence, good fortune and generosity toward all of his people. His conduct is exemplary and he has all the best attributes, more than any other person."

If the counsellors or the administrators and officials of the various towns where Fedor stops should ask how the Great Sovereign Tsar and Grand Prince Aleksei Mikhailovich, Autocrat of all Russia, gets along with the neighboring sovereigns whose lands are adjacent to the Muscovite state, or if they should ask Fedor about some specific sovereign, then he is to reply that our Great Sovereign Tsar, Mikhail Fedorovich of blessed memory, Autocrat of all Russia, and Sovereign and Lord of many realms, maintained friendship and amicability with His Tsarist Majesty, the Sultan of Turkey, and with the Shah of Persia, and with the kings of Denmark, France and England, and with other nearby sovereigns and with the Dutch estates, and that at the present time the son of that Sovereign, our Great Sovereign Tsar and Grand Prince Aleksei Mikhailovich, Autocrat of all Russia, and Sovereign and Lord of many realms, maintains the same friendship and amicability and contact with all of these sovereigns as his father did. They frequently exchange envoys and ambassadors on friendly missions. And our Great Sovereign Tsar and Grand Prince Aleksei Mikhailovich, Autocrat of all Russia, is also in friendship and in contact with the Crimean tsar.

If they should ask about the Great and Little Nogai hordes, and about other lands under the Sovereign's mighty hand, inquiring whether or not these people obey the Tsar, Fedor is to respond that the murzas of the Great and Little Nogai uluses have from time immemorial been subject to the Great Muscovite Sovereign Tsars, and that they are now obedient to the will of His Tsarist Majesty as they were previously during the reign of the father of our Sovereign, our Great Sovereign Tsar and Grand Prince Mikhail Fedorovich of blessed memory, Autocrat of all Russia.

If they ask about Siberia and the present state of the Siberian Tsardom, Fedor is to state that many towns have been built in Siberia, and that all the servitors and settlers have received many benefits from the Sovereign. Agriculture has been introduced, and the servitors and the settlers live in peace and tranquillity. They serve and pay taxes to our Great Sovereign Tsar and Grand Prince Aleksei Mikhailovich, Autocrat of all Russia, just as they served and paid taxes to his father, the Great Sovereign Tsar and Grand Prince Mikhail Fedorovich of blessed memory, Autocrat of all Russia. The tribute from the Siberian people is large, and consists of sables, martens, foxes, squirrels and other furs.

If they should inquire about other matters which are not included in the Sovereign's written instructions, Fedor is to make a reply depending on what the question is. He is to be very cautious so he will not compromise the name, the dignity and the standing of the Sovereign. If he does not know the answer, or even if he does know, he should refuse to make a response on important matters, saying that he is not informed on that particular question because he has been on special assignment in remote areas. But he is to make notes of everything they discuss with him, entering these in his journal.

While Fedor is in the Chinese land, he is to use every possible means to secure secret information by gaining the confidence of officials or of other local people through offering them food and drink. He is to discover who is the most trustworthy, and who speaks most truthfully. He is to profer whatever gifts he has available. He is to learn whether the sovereign Bugdykhan-tsar is pleased that the [Russian] Sovereign has sent Fedor with his Sovereign gramota; whether he wishes to maintain friendship, amicability and contact [with Russia] in the future; whether he will send his own envoys and ambassadors to the Russian Sovereign; whether he will send these soon after Fedor leaves, or with Fedor; whether he will send merchants with these envoys; what goods he will send with them; and whether he will permit his merchants to trade in the Muscovite state in the future.

Fedor is to make inquiries of all kinds of officials, and he is to converse with Chinese merchants about China to ascertain whether they are happy with their sovereign, Bugdykhan-tsar. Would they be favorably disposed to the idea of sending envoys to Moscow? Would merchants like to travel to the Muscovite state to trade? He is to tell Chinese people of all ranks, and merchants, about the [Russian] Sovereign's generosity and kindness to all foreigners who come from neighboring realms, and about the Sovereign's generosity to all foreign merchants who come to Moscow, how they will receive his Sovereign largesse and will be able to trade their goods freely. He is to tell Chinese merchants that His Tsarist Majesty's land abounds in all manner of fine goods which are very scarce in neighboring lands, and that merchants from India and Persia and other neighboring lands come to the Muscovite land to purchase goods.

Fedor is also to learn with whom Bugdykhan-tsar has friendly relations and maintains contacts at the present time; with whom he is in hostility; which lands send envoys to Bugdykhan-tsar, and on what business; whether merchants come with them, and if so, what goods they bring; what goods there are in the Chinese Empire, and the price at which they are sold; what gifts envoys bring to Bugdykhan-tsar, and what gifts he sends back with them; what protocol is observed when envoys are with Bugdykhan-tsar; how strong the military force in the Chinese Empire is; how large the treasury is; what equipment the troops have; how many cavalry troops there are, and how many infantry, and what their battle equipment is; how they wage war; with whom they are presently at war, and what was its cause; and who is stronger in that war at this time?

While Fedor is in China he is also to make inquiries about what kinds of precious goods and precious stones there are in China; whether the goods are made there; whether the precious stones are mined there or imported from elsewhere; whether velvet and satin and finely woven silk and taffeta are made in China or imported; how much they pay for these goods; which velvet and satin and silk and taffeta and other such goods are indigenous to China; from which states they are imported if they are not indigenous, and by what route, and whether by land or by sea; and how near or far the lands are from whence these precious goods are imported. What kind of goods would it be profitable to purchase from them for the Muscovite state? Which goods from Muscovy should be sent in to the Chinese Empire? What would be the price of goods sent in to them? Would such trade be steady in the future? Would there be a good profit in that trade? What kind of people are there in China? What kind of towns? What weapons do they have? What faith do Bugdykhan-tsar and the Chinese profess?

All of this information is to be gathered in detail in the capital city of Kanbalyk, as well as in other towns through which Fedor travels. If he is unable to secure this information secretly, then he is to tell his official escort that he wishes to go through shops to see and purchase samples of goods the Chinese Empire has. While he is in the shops examining these goods, he is to obtain the details of prices, and discover which goods the Chinese buy for themselves and how much they pay. He is to buy a few examples of all kinds of goods for informational purposes. He is either to sell or barter the goods he takes with him, depending on the situation, but he should be careful with this.

He is to inquire whether merchants from foreign [European] countries and other remote lands come to the Chinese Empire, and if so, what goods they bring, what route they use, whether they come by sea or by land, through which lands and towns they travel, how much their shipping costs are, what the distance is between one town and another, and how much duty per pud they pay, or how much duty per packload. If Fedor finds goods that have been imported from European or other lands, and these same goods are available in Moscow, or have come from Muscovy, he is to make every effort to learn the prices of these goods. He is to ascertain which goods that are imported into China these merchants buy and then resell; how much it costs the Chinese state to acquire these imported goods; which European and Russian goods the Chinese prefer; how much duty they collect on these goods; and whether it is collected in goods or *efimka**; whether grain is grown in the Chinese Empire, and if so, which varieties, how abundant is it, how much does it sell for; which fibers are grown; what produce is grown and which is imported, and how much the imported produce sells for.

Fedor is to use every possible means to ascertain whether in the future there will be friendship, amicability and contact between His Tsarist Majesty and Bugdykhan-tsar, and how it would be best to communicate with the Chinese Empire from the Tsarist patrimony of Siberia, that is, through which lands, uluses and nomadic settlements, and whether in the future people in these places will do harm to Tsarist envoys; whether the journey should be made overland or by water or over the mountains; what the distance is from one town to another, or from one ulus to another, in versts or miles or days of travel; and what is the preferred manner of overland travel, by horse or by camel. How much does it cost to cart a packload of goods from one town to another? To which Chinese border town is it unwise to come from the uluses? How many days or weeks does it take to travel from a Chinese border town to the capital city of Kanbalyk? How many versts or miles or days does it take to go from one town or place to another in the Chinese Empire? Is there only one road in China which links these towns, or are there others? Which route is closest and safest? What kind of people live along the way between Siberia and the Chinese Empire? Which princes live there? Are they subject to the [Russian] Sovereign? What are the names of these princes? What are the uluses called? Do these people harm traveling

---

*Joachimsthaler. A silver coin used in the Holy Roman Empire and in other European countries.—Eds.

servitors and merchants? Are there any of these princes who are not loyal to the [Chinese] Tsar, and if so, do they owe allegiance to someone else?

Fedor is to gather information about all of this, in detail, using every means at his disposal, and from as many reliable sources as possible. He is to be very careful not to be misled by a lie that might subsequently be damaging. And once he has satisfactorily answered these questions, he is to write all the information down in detail in his journal, using appropriate headings.

If Fedor should be detained in China in any way, he is to find out precisely why he was detained and who was responsible. He is to make the inquiry secretly, and not ask anyone directly, so that no one will become aware of his questions. He is primarily to ask officials and merchants who are known to be reliable. Once he has learned the details of why he was detained, he is to record it carefully in his journal. He is to keep this very secretly, and protect it carefully so that no one will find it. He is personally to find the answers to all the questions the Sovereign has expressed an interest in. Each problem is to receive a detailed analysis so that not one question written in the Sovereign's instructions will go unanswered.

While Fedor is en route to the Chinese Empire, and while he is traveling there, he is to bear in mind all the interests of the Tsar and of his country. He is to gather all the information which the Sovereign has instructed him to obtain. And he is to use his judgment, depending on the situation at the time and how God may direct him, to protect the Sovereign's name and honor. Everywhere he is to glorify the Sovereign's name and honor, and elevate the Sovereign's name in all cities and other places. He is to say only those things that will magnify the Sovereign's name and honor. He must be on guard not to harm the Sovereign's interest by using uncouth speech.

When Fedor is ready to return, and he has been given a gramota for the [Russian] Sovereign at the court of the [Chinese] emperor, or if such is brought to him in his quarters, but Bugdykhan-tsar has not granted him an audience, then Fedor is not to accept the gramota. He is to tell the counsellors or their subordinates that such an ambassadorial custom has never existed among our Great Sovereign Tsars and Grand Princes of Russia. Envoys, ambassadors and couriers who come from other great sovereigns to our Great Sovereign are welcomed upon their arrival, and are received in person upon their departure. His Tsarist Majesty personally gives them leave and personally gives them gramotas for their sovereigns. This same custom prevails among neighboring great sovereigns as well as at His Tsarist Majesty's court. There the envoys, ambassadors and couriers are bade farewell by the great sovereigns in person, and these sovereigns give gramotas to them in person. If their sovereign, Bugdykhan-tsar, wishes to be in a state of friendship, amicability and contact with our Great Sovereign, His Tsarist Majesty, then he must give Fedor an audience on the eve of his departure, personally give him a gramota to the Great Sovereign, His Tsarist Majesty, and personally give him leave to return to the Great Sovereign, His Tsarist Majesty, directly from that audience. This would indicate the inception of a fine relationship and of friendship between the two great sovereigns. And if, God willing, our Great Sovereign, His Tsarist Majesty, receives ambassadors, envoys or couriers from their sovereign, Bugdykhan-tsar, then our Great Sovereign, His Tsarist Majesty, will reciprocate this same courtesy to their sovereign envoys, ambassadors and couriers. Fedor is to insist that this be arranged, and he is to stand firm on this.

If the [Chinese] tsar's counsellors reply that their sovereign's custom is to have ambassadors, envoys and couriers from other sovereigns brought to him upon their arrival, but that they are not granted an audience upon their departure, and that gramotas are sent to them in their quarters, and that this custom has been observed for many years and that this is how it has been done since the beginning of their Empire; and if Fedor cannot persuade him to change this custom so that he would receive the gramota to the [Russian] Sovereign from their sovereign in person; and if they inform him of this directly; and if Bugdykhan-tsar will not grant him an audience prior to his departure; and if Fedor learns in advance that this truly is customary there, that gramotas from their sovereign are sent to all ambassadors, envoys and couriers in their quarters rather than being handed to them personally by the tsar in his court prior to their departure, then Fedor is to accept the gramota to the Sovereign, but he is to tell the person who brings it to him that the counsellors must give him a summary of the contents of the gramota so that he will know the manner of message their sovereign is sending to his Tsarist Majesty.

If the [Russian] Tsar's name and titles in that gramota are written just as they appear in the gramota from the Sovereign which

Fedor brought with him, that is, using his full Sovereign name and titles, then Fedor is to accept the [Chinese] Tsar's gramota and return with it. But if the Sovereign's name and titles are not correctly written, then Fedor is to return the gramota and insist that it be rewritten so that the Sovereign's name and titles are properly written as they appear in the gramota from His Tsarist Majesty which Fedor delivered to their sovereign, Bugdykhan-tsar.

If the counsellors tell him that he must accept the gramota as originally written because in the gramota from His Tsarist Majesty the name and titles of their sovereign are only partially correct, then Fedor is to respond as follows: "Our Great Sovereign, His Tsarist Majesty, did not know how your sovereign, Bugdykhan-tsar, writes his name and titles. But in the future in his Tsarist correspondence His Tsarist Majesty will write the name and titles of Bugdykhan-tsar precisely as your sovereign has written them in his gramota. Therefore the counsellors should inform your sovereign of this, so that he might prove his regard for our Great Sovereign by ordering that in his gramota the name and titles of our Great Sovereign be written precisely as they were in the gramota from His Tsarist Majesty, because our Great Sovereign Tsarist Majesty is addressed in this way by all great sovereigns." It is important to insist on this, and to present firm arguments, so that in Bugdykhan-tsar's gramota he will write the Sovereign's name and titles precisely as they are written in the Tsarist letter to Bugdykhan-tsar.

If Fedor receives the gramota in person [from Bugdykhan-tsar], then he is to insist that they bow together to our Great Sovereign, as is customary in relations with all great sovereigns. When Bugdykhan-tsar gives him leave to be on his way, and personally hands him the gramota for the Tsar, or instructs his counsellors to do so, and when he orders them to bow to the Sovereign, then Fedor is to make a written record of this in his quarters.

If Fedor is summoned to Bugdykhan-tsar's hand during the departure ceremonies, he is to go to the hand courteously.

If Bugdykhan-tsar receives him, and dismisses him with full honor, then during the departure ceremonies Fedor is to bow to Bugdykhan-tsar for his kindness, and he is to say, "Bugdykhan-tsar, Lord of the city of Kanbalyk and of the entire Chinese Empire, our Great Sovereign and Grand Prince Aleksei Mikhailovich, Autocrat of all Great and Little Russia, Sovereign and

Ruler of many realms, has sent me, his humble servant, to you, Bugdykhan-tsar, with His Tsarist Majesty's gramota of friendship. You, Bugdykhan-tsar, have received me with honor, and are dismissing me with honor, on behalf of the Great Sovereign, and out of friendship for his Tsarist Majesty. I thank you for your tsarist generosity. God willing, when I reach our Great Sovereign, His Tsarist Majesty, I will convey to him, my Great Sovereign, your sovereign friendship and amicability."

However if it should happen that the Chinese Bugdykhan-tsar is no longer there, or if for some reason the tsardom does not exist, or another tsar has come to power in his place, then Fedor is to state to the officials and counsellors that the Great Sovereign Tsar and Grand Prince, Aleksei Mikhailovich, Autocrat of all Great and Little Russia, has sent him to their former sovereign, Bugdykhan-tsar, with His Tsarist Majesty's gramota of friendship; since Bugdykhan-tsar is no longer in power, or for some reason the Empire does not exist (Fedor should investigate the situation to ascertain what has happened), and a new tsar has been chosen (find out his name and how he is addressed), our Sovereign, His Tsarist Majesty, was unaware of the fact that this sovereign, their new tsar, had become tsar of the Chinese Empire.

Consequently he, Fedor, has the following instruction from His Tsarist Majesty: "If Bugdykhan-tsar is no longer living, and his place has been taken by a new tsar, then our Great Sovereign Tsar and Grand Prince Aleksei Mikhailovich, Autocrat of all Russia, instructs Fedor to go to this new tsar and present him with the gramota from His Tsarist Majesty, and deliver the gifts of friendship. The counsellors should so inform their sovereign, that he might invite Fedor [for an audience]." When the new tsar invites Fedor to an ambassadorial reception, then when Fedor arrives, he is to bow to the new tsar in the name of the Sovereign Tsar and Grand Prince Aleksei Mikhailovich of all Russia, since the new tsar has replaced Bugdykhan-tsar, and give him the gramota, and display the gifts, and carry out the above instructions.

While Fedor is in the Chinese Empire on the Sovereign's business, for which reason he has been sent to Bugdykhan-tsar, he is to behave in all respects toward the new tsar as indicated in the Sovereign's instructions.

This *nakaz* from the Sovereign is to be kept on Fedor's person, secretly, so that no person will learn its contents. He is not to re-

Means of conveyance: ice sled with sail; sled with dogs suggest
more wishful thinking than reality. From Shunkov, ed., *Istoriia
Sibiri*, Vol. 2.

veal his mission to anyone while he is in China or en route to
China. He is to memorize these instructions, so that he knows
every word, and that all the articles written in the Sovereign's
nakaz are familiar to him, and so that he will be able to make satisfactory inquiries into each item.

When Fedor has completed the Sovereign's business and is dismissed from the Chinese Empire, he is to proceed to the Sovereign Tsar and Grand Prince Aleksei Mikhailovich of all Russia
post haste, but with great caution. When he reaches Moscow, he
is to appear with Bugdykhan-tsar's letter and his detailed written
account in the Prikaz of the Bolshaia Kazna, and submit the report to boiar Ilia Danilovich Miloslavskii and to the *dumnyi
dvorianin* [influential courtier] Ivan Pavlovich Matiushkin and to
the diak Anika. . . . [the rest is missing]

Reference: TsGADA, f. Snosheniia Rossii s Kitaem, op. 2, 1654, g., d. No.
4, 11. 25–97.
See: N. F. Demidova and V. S. Miasnikov, eds. *Russko-kitaiskie otnosheniia
v XVII veke: Dokumenty i materialy (1608–1691)* (Moscow: 1969), I,
152–165.

84

AUGUST, 1654

To the stolnik and voevoda Mikhail Semenovich [Lodyzhen-skii] and the diak Fedor Vasilevich, of the Sovereign Tsar and Grand Prince Aleksei Mikhailovich of all Russia, the pri-kashchik Onufrii Stepanov humbly reports from the great Amur River and from the new Daur lands.

In the year 1654, in accordance with the ukaz of the Sovereign Tsar and Grand Prince Aleksei Mikhailovich of all Russia, the *dvorianin* [courtier] Dmitrii Ivanovich Zinovev came to the great Amur River with the Sovereign's largesse of gold coins, and he gave these gifts of gold coins from the Sovereign to the prikash-chik Erofei Pavlovich Khabarov and to all 320 of us, humble ser-vants of the Sovereign, in accordance with the Sovereign's ukaz. When Dmitrii Zinovev left from the mouth of the Zeia River with the Sovereign's iasak sable treasury to go to the Sovereign in Moscow, he took the prikashchik Erofei Pavlovich Khabarov with him, and in Erofei Khabarov's place he appointed me, Onufrii, to attend to the Sovereign's affairs on the great Amur River.

He charged me with preventing violence among the servitors, and gave me the necessary document of instructions. The pri-kashchik Erofei Khabarov left no inventory of the Sovereign's sup-plies of powder, shot and provisions, nor did he leave a list with the servitors. The servitors from various lower Siberian towns who had accompanied Dmitrii Ivanovich were left behind by him on the great Amur River, but he did not put me, Onufrii, in charge of them. Dmitrii Ivanovich also took with him the iasak collection books, both white and black, as well as the hostages and the interpreters. Now it is impossible to collect the Sovereign's iasak from the iasak-paying people on the great Amur River with-out these books.

The Daur and Ducher princes ask for interpreters, but we do not have any. I, Onufrii, took counsel with the troops and then I went by boat with the entire force from the mouth of the Zeia River down the great Amur River to the mouth of the Shingal to secure food and supplies for the boats. There is little food on the mighty Amur River, and no timber, so that we cannot built boats. The voyage was late in the season; we went downriver on September 18. I, Onufrii, was with the entire force on the Shingal River. We loaded the provisions onto the boats and then I, Onufrii, went down the river with all the troops. We wintered on the great Amur River in the land of the Duchers, before reaching the land of the Giliaks. We took hostages, and for [the safety of] these hostages we again collected the Sovereign's iasak. We also collected iasak from other non-iasak Duchers, but we could not collect the Sovereign's iasak from the iasak people Erofei Pavlovich Khabarov collected from in past years, since we did not have the iasak books.

I, Onufrii, spent the winter with all the troops, and then in the spring we built large sailing vessels and rowboats. In this present year of 1654 I sailed with these vessels up the great Amur River, and other Ducher people brought us the Sovereign's iasak along the way. When we came to the mouth of the Shingal, there were cossacks there who had come along the Amur, and 50 servitors headed by Mikhail Artemev Kashinets.

According to their accounts and our conversations with them, they had spent the winter on the great Amur River at the mouth of the Tura River. They had taken a hostage, and for that hostage they had collected eighteen sables for the Sovereign's iasak. In accordance with their request, I, Onufrii, took the servitors and the hostage from Mikhail Kashinets, as well as the Sovereign's iasak collection. In return, Mikhail Kashinets transferred two servitors from his small ostrozhek who had been on the great Amur River, Vtoroi Telenka and Ivan Iurev. These servitors were questioned, and Vtoroi Telenka said that in the spring of 1654 the dvorianin Dmitrii Ivanovich Zinovev sent eight servitors with Semen Overkeev and his men from the Tugur portage. Dmitrii Ivanovich Zinovev sent instructions with them, but he did not send any government supplies of powder or shot, or the Sovereign's treasury, from Tugur portage to the great Amur River. Through God's judgment [most of] the servitors with Semen Kosoi drowned; only two survived, Vtoroi Telenka and his comrade. Mikhail Kashinets and his men took them aboard their small boat.

That same day, May 20, after meeting with the servitors with Mikhail Kashinets, following the counsel of the troops and the esauls, I, Onufrii, went up the great Shingal River to bring the non-iasak-paying Duchers under the Sovereign's mighty hand,

and to secure food. We were on the Shingal River three days. On June 6 we were confronted by a large Bogdoi military force armed with cannon and firearms. We fought the Bogdoi troops. The mounted Bogdoi fought from horseback, and the infantry from row boats. The Bogdoi fought fiercely using their cannon and guns. They fired the cannon on our boats, and fought us from behind revetments and earthen walls.

I took counsel with my entire force, and then sent cossacks in row boats to attack. With God's mercy and the luck of the Sovereign, they defeated the Bogdoi troops on shore from their small boats. The Bogdoi took a stand in a fortified place on the bank of the river and fired a barrage. In the attack many servitors were wounded, and it was impossible to fight the Bogdoi any longer because our supplies of powder and shot were exhausted, and Dmitrii Ivanovich Zinovev had not sent any supplies from the government warehouses from the Tugur portage.

Before the Bogdoi army met us, we sent servitors against the Duchers, and in that foray the cossacks took Ducher prisoners. When the prisoners were interrogated they said that the Bogdoi tsar had hurriedly sent the army from three lands, the Bogdoi, the Daur and the Ducher. When we fought the Bogdoi they had bright battle standards in white, black, red and yellow. Each unit had its own standard. Wherever there was a white standard, all the men under it wore white silk insignia. Those who wore black or red or yellow were grouped under standards of the same color, and special insignia were sewed onto their silks. Their battle order was well planned. We fired our cannon on the Bogdoi army, but they did not let us take food along the Shingal. We moved out of the Shingal and used sails to go up the great Amur River on the advice of our troops.

In the present year, 1654, 34 servitors came down the great Amur River from the syn boiarskii Petr Beketov on Lake Baikal; they reported that they had left because of the shortage of food and other necessities. I, Onufrii, accepted these servitors, at their request. Then I, Onufrii, took the servitors and went on an expedition on the great Amur River on July 4, by boat. During that expedition I, Onufrii, captured a Nikan man who said during questioning that he was an unimportant prisoner from the Nikan tsardom, that he had been captured by the Bogdoi tsar and had subsequently been sold to the Duchers as a slave. That same day we captured a Ducher woman on our way, and found she was the wife of Toenchin. When she was questioned she said that Dmitrii Ivanovich Zinovev had sent five servitors as envoys to the Bogdoi tsar: Tretiak Ermolaev Chechigin, Vasilii Panfilov, Ivan Shchipunov, Vladimir Ivanov and Tomas Vasilev. She also said that these envoys had been killed by the Duchers, by Toenchin's brothers Ortoko and Esiun and their tribesmen and ulus people. In this, they were abetted by the Kilan tribesmen and ulus people. The cossacks were killed inside the iurts, and their belongings divided, but the Bogdoi tsar was not informed about this. In the past Toenchin and his brothers had sworn allegiance to our Sovereign Tsar and Grand Prince Aleksei Mikhailovich of all Russia, and had paid iasak. One of Toenchin's brothers is being held as a hostage, but now they have turned against the Sovereign Tsar and have murdered his envoys.

Then I, Onufrii, after taking counsel with the servitors, went out after these traitors, but I could not find Toenchin's brothers. The envoys had been entrusted into the care of Toenchin and his wife and brothers. Many of the belongings of these murdered servitors were found in a number of the iurts, remnants of coats, breeches, shirts, leggings, boots and fishing gear; we also found kettles and axes and skillets and knives which had belonged to the dead men, as well as a cartridge belt, shreds of cloth, belt buckles, laces and bindings, bedding, gun barrels—and all had been cut into bits.

That same day I, Onufrii, met . . . [missing] the syn boiarskii Petr Beketov from Baikal and 20 of his men on the great Amur River. In our conversation he said that they had come from up the river because they were short of food and other supplies. These servitors submitted a petition to me, Onufrii, and in acordance with their request I accepted these servitors, pending the Sovereign's ukaz. But Petr Beketov, when he sailed up with the rest of the men, asked to be allowed to remain on the great Amur River until the Sovereign's ukaz. Then Petr Beketov's armed unit, nine men, sailed on the great Amur River, and upon their request, I accepted them into my group.

In the present year, 1654, after Dmitrii Ivanovich Zinovev went to Moscow to the Sovereign, he left me, Onufrii, written instructions to build an ostrog in a suitable place belonging to Lavkai, and we are to remain there until we have an ukaz from the Sovereign, and we are to prepare food supplies of all kinds for the new servitors, numbering some 5,000 or 6,000, for at least one year's time. He also gave me another document in which we are ordered to build an ostrog within a bowshot of the mouth of the Urak River, and another at the mouth of the Zeia River, between the Amur and Zeia rivers. We have not been able to build these ostrogs because of the heavy fighting with the Bogdoi people. Moreover, there is very little food along the great Amur River now, because the natives who live along the Amur have been ordered by the Bogdoi tsar not to plant any grain. He has ordered these natives to remove themselves to his lands. Many Daurs have left because of this, and we are now in desperate need of grain. We have learned about all of this from prisoners whom we have captured in our forays; they have told us during interrogation that the Bogdoi people are building a fort at the mouth of the Shingal River and will not let us obtain grain, although there is plenty of grain along the Shingal River.

Dmitrii Zinovev also ordered the servitors to collect the tithe, and I, Onufrii, have requested the servitors to pay a tenth of the pillaged loot they have taken. However the servitors will not pay the tithe. They swear that they have sent petitions to the Sovereign in Moscow about this, and that they will not pay until the Sovereign issues an ukaz regarding this.

If the Sovereign Tsar and Grand Prince Aleksei Mikhailovich of all Russia should send his Sovereign voevodas and servitors onto the great Amur River in the future, they must be very careful that the Bogdoi people do not intercept them on the way.

There is very little food on the Amur River. When the Bogdoi people fire their cannon, the range of the balls is two versts or more. We have only one cannon for our unit, and two small iron pieces.

In the present year, 1654, the servitors whom Dmitrii Ivanovich Zinovev left behind submitted a petition asking the Sovereign to permit them to return to Russian towns in Siberia. I did not grant the request of these servitors to leave the great Amur River without the Sovereign's ukaz, because we are very short of men and there are frequent clashes.

Dmitrii Zinovev released a hostage, a leading Daur prince named Laptai, to go back into the land of the Daurs. This prince had been captured by the armed troops during an expedition, and we had held him for five years. Dmitrii Zinovev also wrote in a document that there were hops in the government warehouse, and he instructed that the hops be kept for the natives. I, Onufrii, did not find any hops in the government warehouse, and when I asked the tselovalniks whom Dmitrii Zinovev had left, they stated that there were no hops in the government warehouse.

In the present year, 1654, after Dmitrii Zinovev's departure, prior to August 2, we collected the Sovereign's iasak from the natives, which amounted to 28 forties and 36 sables, six sable shubas, 74 sable backs, a caftan of sable tails lined with bright silk, two black-brown foxes, and . . . [missing] foxes. However it has become impossible to send this government iasak treasury on, because the whole region is in a state of siege. There are frequent battles, and we cannot send it with only a few men because the natives would seize the Sovereign's treasury. Only a strong force of servitors could convoy it, and we have too few men in our force as it is.

On August 2, I, Onufrii, interrogated the Nikan about the Nikan tsardom, but he replied that his is just a simple prisoner and does not know anything, although he did say, during the interrogation, that in regard to the Bogdoi army it had been sent to the mouth of the Shingal River for three years now, and that the Bogdoi tsar had given them orders to stay at the mouth of the Shingal, and to fight us, and not let us move into the Shingal. He has sent an army of 3,000 and wants to send 2,000 more, in addition to the Duchers and Daurs.

That same day, August 2, the syn boiarskii Petr Beketov handed over his iasak collection of ten sables which he had collected as he made his way down the Amur River from the iasak-paying Daur people who had paid in previous years. I, Onufrii, accepted this iasak collection.

On June 6 of this present year, 1654, and on other occasions, the armed force refused to obey the esauls Trofim Nikitin and Semen Zakharov. They stripped the esauls of their authority, and Dmitrii listed the names of these esauls in his report.

This year, 1654, a servitor named Hanka Ivanov Bezottsov petitioned the Sovereign and presented the petition to me, asking that I allow him to return to Russian towns in Siberia, because of his age and his needs. He came here from Baikal from the syn boiarskii Petr Beketov. In accordance with his petition, I, Onufrii, permitted Hanka to leave, because he could no longer perform adequately in government service.

View of Irkutsk. Arrow indicates flow of Angara River from Lake
Baikal. City's wolverine seal hovers over the myriad churches.
From Semivskii, *Noveishiia povestvovaniia o vostochnoi Sibiri.*

At present I, Onufrii, and all of my men are sailing up the
great Amur River. We will spend the winter wherever we find
grain along the Amur.

I am sending the servitors Gerasim Maksimov, Pronka Grigorev and nine of their comrades with these dispatches, and also
Ivan Litvinov, one of syn boiarskii Petr Beketov's men, with his
reports.

In this year, 1654, the Amur servitors and free cossack volunteers whom Dmitrii Zinovev left behind, and also the free cossack
volunteers from Bratsk ostrozhek on the upper Lena River, have
submitted a petition to me, Onufrii. I have accepted their petitions and am attaching them to this report, and sending all of this
to you, voevodas of the Sovereign.

See: *Dopolneniia k aktam istoricheskim* (St. Petersburg: 1848), III, 523–528.

85

NOT BEFORE APRIL 4, 1655

A REPORT TO THE VOEVODA OF IAKUTSK, MIKHAIL LODYZHENSKII, FROM THE PRIKASHCHIK ONUFRII STEPANOV, CONCERNING THE SIEGE OF KUMARSK OSTROG BY MANCHU ARMIES

The prikashchik Onufrii Stepanov humbly reports to the stolnik and voevoda Mikhail Semenovich [Lodyzhenskii] and to the diak Fedor Tonkoi, of the Sovereign Tsar and Grand Prince Aleksei Mikhailovich of all Russia, from the new Daur lands along the mighty Amur River.

In the present year, 1655, the following servitors have been sent to Iakutsk ostrog: Osip Olenev, Evsei Gurylev, Sergei Kiprianov, Petr Savin, Nikolai Iurev, Iakov Surgutskoi, Ivan Onisimov and Artemii Sazhin. They were accompanied by the tselovalniks Anton Evsevev and Ivan Ivanov. They were transporting sables belonging to the church and money belonging to the government because here on the mighty Amur River the government storehouse does not have any gunpowder or lead, and the church office has no church books, wax, candles or incense.

When these servitors come to you, voevoda of the Sovereign, you, voevoda of the Sovereign, should pay them according to the decree of the Sovereign, and send as much powder and shot as possible from the government warehouse, because here on the mighty Amur River in this government supply depot there is no powder or shot; and without powder and shot we cannot carry out government assignments on the mighty Amur River. A few servitors should also be sent to this government outpost because the state interest must be protected here and state service must be performed. Each year servitors are sent with the government supplies and with reports, but new people are not sent out to the mighty Amur River from towns. Servitors on the mighty Amur River who are to be sent to Iakutsk ostrog should be sent back with the [other] servitors because here along the mighty Amur River there are fierce clashes with the Bogdoi troops, for the Bogdoi tsar has sent armed forces here.

In the year 1654 the dvorianin Dmitrii Ivanov, son of Zinovev, wrote instructions ordering me, Onufrii Stepanov, to collect the government iasak sable treasury, and when it had been collected, to sent it to the Sovereign Tsar and Grand Prince Aleksei

Mikhailovich of all Russia in Moscow. I, Onufrii, signed the Sovereign's sable collection in the year 1654 and in the current year, 1655, with my seal, and sent it with a report to the Sovereign Tsar and Grand Prince Aleksei Mikhailovich of all Russia in Moscow, with reliable servitors, Trofim Nikitin and Bogdan Gabyshev and their comrades. When the tselovalniks Anton and Ivan come to you with the church supplies, voevoda of the Sovereign, you should pay them and give them what you think necessary for the needs of the church, but send them back this same year to the Amur River, so they will reach the Amur River in this year, 1655. Also, voevoda of the Sovereign, please send official paper to the Amur River for official records, because there is nowhere to buy it on the great Amur River.

In the past year, 1654, the servitors Gerasim Maksimov and Prokofei Grigorev and their comrades were sent from the mighty Amur River with reports to Iakutsk ostrog to you, voevoda of the Sovereign, because these few servitors cannot be sent along the great Lena River to Iakutsk ostrog.

In the present year, 1655, two newly christened natives from the Nikan realm, captives, were sent to the Sovereign Tsar and Grand Prince Aleksei Mikhailovich of all Russia in Moscow, along with the government iasak sable treasury and the servitors. They had been captured by the Bogdoi tsar in his Bogdoi land, and from that Bogdoi land these prisoners were sold as slaves on the great Amur River in Daur land. These Nikan people petitioned the Sovereign Tsar and Grand Prince Aleksei Mikhailovich of all Russia, and submitted their petitions to me, Onufrii, in the court office on the great Amur River. They wished to be christened, and asked that the Sovereign grant them their wish and bring them into the Orthodox Christian faith in accordance with the faith of the Holy Apostles and Holy Fathers. These Nikan people were brought into the Orthodox Christian faith in this year, 1655, in accordance with their petition, and with the rules of the Holy Apostles and the Holy Church Fathers.

On March 13, in the present year of 1655 the Bogdoi armies gathered from various lands and came to the Ust Kumarsk ostrozhek. At three o'clock in the afternoon they laid siege to us, government servitors, servants and Amur cossack volunteers, who had gone out from the ostrog to cut lumber for boats. They captured twenty men, Ivan Teliatev and his comrades from various towns, and they killed these servitors in their encampments.

I, Onufrii, sent other servitors from Kumarsk ostrozhek on an expedition of reconnaissance, and these servitors and the Amur cossack volunteers went on reconnaissance and the servitors drove off the natives and the Bogdoi men and defeated the Bogdoi troops. The Bogdoi came with all manner of firearms such as cannon and muskets, and they had battle standards in all colors. This Bogdoi army is grouped into companies, but there are no interpreters, so we do not know how many men are in each company.

On March 20 they advanced to the Ust Kumarsk ostrozhek from the mighty Amur River, around the rock, and the rock is 40 sazhens high, and the distance from the rock to the ostrozhek is 150 sazhens. Using heavy guns, the Bogdoi fired them from three o'clock until seven that day, and at six o'clock in the evening these Bodgoi troops shot flaming arrows into the ostrozhek from a distance of 70 sazhens. There were inscriptions on the arrows. From the lower side, the Bogdoi troops fired cannon from a distance of 150 sazhens.

On March 24 these Bogdoi people attacked the ostrozhek from all four sides, carrying battle standards, and they had gun shields fastened to carts on wheels. The shields were made of wood covered with leather and thick felt, and the carts had siege ladders with wheels at one end and iron hooks at the other. The carts had wood and tar and straw fastened to them for the purpose of starting fires, and these contraptions were to be set up against the ostrozhek. Every Bogdoi warrior had iron spears and they also had many other kinds of ingenious equipment.

By the grace of God and the luck of the Sovereign, the government servitors and Amur cossack volunteers from various towns and from the upper and lower ostrozheks fought a valiant battle from the ramparts using cannon and muskets, and they defeated the Bogdoi army. During the attack against the walls, they killed many Bogdoi warriors. From Kumarsk ostrozhek the state servitors and the Amur cossack volunteers went on reconnaissance, and killed many Bogdoi people and took two fortress cannon from them, as well as gunpowder and cannon balls and some of the ingenious equipment. They took the wounded men prisoner.

I questioned the prisoners, and during the interrogation they said that the Bogdoi tsar had sent out this Bogdoi army. The prince of the army is named Tagudai, familiarly known as Ezher; and the army was made up of men from various lands such as the Bogdoi, Mungut, Nikan, Ducher, Daur and other territories whose natives are under the jurisdiction of the Bogdoi. They had fifteen cannon and many small arms, and the Bogdoi army attacked us, your Sovereign's humble servants. The Daur princes and ulus people asked the Bogdoi tsar to protect them because they did not want to pay their iasak to the Sovereign, nor to be under the protection of the mighty Tsarist hand. At the present time these Daur princes and their ulus people along the mighty Amur River who previously paid iasak to the Sovereign have turned against the Sovereign.

The total number of men in the Bogdoi force was 10,000. In their attack they found our sacks of powder and cannon balls, and they cut loose our sailboats and rowboats. From March 13 to April 4 this Bogdoi army fired their cannon on Kumarsk ostrozhek day and night, and then these Bogdoi people fell back from the ostrog.

Our ostrog was built on a rampart, with piers at the corners. The ostrog was constructed during the snow season. On November 2, an extremely cold day, we dug a moat around the ostrozhek. The ground was frozen, and the moat is one sazhen deep and two sazhens wide. We built a wooden palisade around the moat, with a ring of iron spikes around the palisade.

By God's mercy and the luck of the Sovereign, when the Bogdoi advanced with their shields, they attacked against the wooden palisade and then many were pinned on the spiked iron fence and could not advance on to the ostrog walls from these iron spikes. In the ostrog there was fighting going on both above and below. They fought with stones at the lower level and with cannon fire from the upper part. Within the ostrog we dug a well five sazhens deep, and from the well we filled water containers in all four corners, six sazhens tall, in case of fire. On top of the ostrog we set iron containers filled with oil, and we ignited the oil to create enough light to see the movement of the Bogdoi troops at night beyond the walls. They set up siege ladders and shields made of long wooden ship's planks against the ostrog. We placed tubs on the ostrog in case of Bogdoi assault, and inside we built an earthen platform from which we fired our cannon against the Bogdoi. They prevented us from going out from the ostrog on the river side to have access to water and our boats. The Bogdoi camped around the ostrog in groups.

During the Bogdoi siege on the ostrog, the cossacks fasted and prayed, and at that time there appeared to many a vision of the

Icon of the Merciful Savior and the Icon of the Holy Mother of God, the Virgin Mary, Queen of all the saints. At the time of the siege of Kumarsk ostrog there were servitors and Amur cossack volunteers within the ostrozhek who had come with Dmitrii Ivanovich Zinovev who were from various towns such as Tobolsk, Tiumen, Surgut, Verkhotur'e and from Turinsk ostrozhek and Verkholensk, Bratsk ostrozhek; there were also cossack volunteers who had come from the upper Shilka River and from Lake Baikal with the Eniseisk syn boiarskii, Petr Beketov.

After the Bogdoi troops fell back, the servitors and the Amur cossack volunteers went to the Bogdoi encampments and saw that the bodies of some of the Bogdoi men who had been killed at the foot of the wall had been dragged off under cover of night, and that in accordance with their dreadful heathen faith, the Bogdoi people had burned these bodies in their encampments; but there were other dead Bogdoi warriors whom they had not managed to drag away from the ostrog.

When these Bogdoi people saw God's miracle, they were seized with fear and terror. They threw the gunpowder from their camps into the water, as well as their fire-making devices, and then they burned their battle garb. Eventually we gathered about 350 cannon balls from inside and around the ostrog.

The Bogdoi next attacked the ostrozhek at one o'clock in the morning. They used their shields, and the attack lasted until they withdrew from the ostrog at one o'clock in the afternoon. We captured two muskets in that attack, as well as a fire-making device. These guns and devices, with certain inscriptions and markings, have been sent to the Sovereign Tsar and Grand Prince in Moscow. No one here on the Amur River can decipher the markings which these Bogdoi people made on their arrows and on the fire-making devices. Two of these devices with inscriptions have been sent to you, voevoda of the Sovereign, in Iakutsk ostrog.

Voevoda of the Sovereign, you should reward those servitors who have been sent from the great Amur River with the iasak sable treasury, and with petitions and reports to the Sovereign in Moscow; and when these servitors come to you at Iakutsk ostrog requesting the necessary transport so they can proceed along the mighty Lena River from the mouth of the Olekma upriver, if they do not have any boats or provisions, you, voevoda of the Sovereign, should give them these. Do not detain these servitors, but allow them to proceed to the Sovereign in Moscow so that the

Рис. 7. Летний караван.

In summer the clan and tribal wealth, including the reindeer herd, was moved to richer grazing. From Potapov, ed., *Sibirskii etnograficheskii sbornik.*

Sovereign Tsar will be informed as soon as possible that we are expecting a large Bogdoi force again, and that we have no powder or shot in the government warehouse, nor do we have food, and that we are in a desperate situation and do not know whether we will be able to hold the Sovereign's ostrog.

The Bogdoi troops had great long sacks of powder, fifteen or twenty sazhens long, and very thick like a shaft. We now have 730 Bogdoi cannon balls in the government storehouse. Each of these balls weighs at least a pound and a half. We also have their fire-making devices, and arrows with the inscriptions on them. We have a great many of these.

In this present year of 1655 we have sent to you, voevoda of the Sovereign, to Iakutsk ostrog, the following servitors: the Amur cossack volunteers, the petitioner Andrei Stepanov Potapov, and the Eniseisk servitor Liubimir Pavlov. These servitors have been sent because Liubimir Pavlov was exiled by an ukaz of the Sovereign, and last year, 1654, he tried to escape by going down the Amur River, but he had difficulty finding anything to eat and he fell ill.

Reference: LOA AN SSSR, f. Portfeli Millera, op. 4, kn. 31, No. 75, 11. 136–142.

See: N. F. Demidova and V. S. Miasnikov, eds. *Russko-kitaiskie otnosheniia v XVII veke: Dokumenty i materialy (1608–1691)* (Moscow: 1969), I, 205–208.

86

MARCH 15, 1655

A GRAMOTA FROM THE SIBIRSKII PRIKAZ TO THE DAUR SERVITORS
ONUFRII STEPANOV AND HIS MEN, CONCERNING THE ADMINISTRA-
TION OF THE AMUR TRIBES AND INQUIRING INTO THE FATE OF THE
EMBASSY OF TERENTII CHECHIGIN, SENT TO THE DAURS

March 15, 1655. From the Tsar and Grand Prince Aleksei Mikhailovich, Autocrat of all Great and Little Russia, to Siberia, to the Daur, Ducher and Giliak lands, to the servitors Onufrii Stepanov and his men.

In accordance with our ukaz from the year 1652, we sent Dmitrii Zinovev to the Daur land on our affairs, and in this present year, 1655, Dmitrii Zinovev has returned to Moscow from the Daur land with our sable treasury which you collected. He also brought several Daur, Ducher and Giliak people with him to be questioned; these were Anai and seven men, a woman and a girl. In accordance with our ukaz, these Daur, Ducher and Giliak people, Anai and his comrades and the woman and the girl, were rewarded with our Tsarist largesse and were sent back from Moscow to their land with the Enisei servitor Kost Ivanov and the Daur cossack, Gavriil Shipunov.

When you receive this our gramota, and Kost and Gavriil and the natives reach you, you are to keep the native interpreter Moldeg with you to translate, but let Anai and his six men and the woman and the girl go back to the lands from which they were taken, without detaining them further. Instruct them that when they are in their own lands again, they are to tell their people about our Tsarist largesse, how Anai and his people were rewarded with our Tsarist largesse and were sent back to their own land. Thus the natives of those lands, hoping for our Tsarist largesse in the future, will serve us, the Great Sovereign, and be loyal too, along with their Daur, Ducher and Giliak relatives. They will also encourage people under the jurisdiction of the Bogdoi tsar to come to our Tsarist Majesty and pay iasak and be under our Tsarist Majesty's mighty hand in eternal servitude. When natives from these lands come to you with iasak you are to keep some of them with you as replacements for hostages you are presently holding. Whenever possible replace the hostages with native leaders who are free and powerful in their lands.

When you and your servitors are in the land of the Daurs, Duchers and Giliaks, unless you receive a new ukaz from us you are not to make war against iasak peoples of those lands, nor pillage nor kill nor take them into captivity. Any of the prisoners who were captured prior to the receipt of this our gramota, and who have not been baptized, are to be freed and allowed to return to their own lands without being detained.

You are to collect our iasak from these Daur, Ducher and Giliak people with kindness and friendliness, not through harshness, war or torture. Iasak [when possible] is to be paid in sables or foxes [but] other furs [may be accepted] so that the Daurs, Duchers and Giliaks will be attracted to our Tsarist mercy and into eternal servitude, and will not be driven away.

If Bogdoi people or others threaten you with war, you are to beg God's mercy, and then pursue these persons and ascertain if you are able why they are threatening you, whether it is to avenge some wrong, or for their own personal gain. You are to protect our iasak-paying Daur, Ducher and Giliak people from them while you are making your inquiry into the intentions of these armed intruders. In the future you will receive our Tsarist generosity commensurate with your service.

You are to report to us concerning events that are now transpiring, and those which may occur in the future. When the Daurs and the Duchers from the Turunchin and Tanchin uluses bring Terentii Chechigin back to you from the Bogdoi tsar, release Terentii and his associates, and send him and his servitors to us in Moscow, along with the iasak you have collected for us, the iasak books, and an inventory. Instruct Terentii Chechigin and the servitors to bring the report and our sable treasury to the Sibirskii Prikaz, and report to our boiar Prince Aleksei Nikitich Trubetskoi and to our diak Grigorii Protopopov.

If the Daurs and the Duchers have not brought Terentii Chechigin and his men to you by the time you receive this gramota, you are to ask the Daurs and Duchers of the Turunchin and Tanchin uluses why [Terentii and his men] are being held by the Bogdoi tsar in the Bogdoi land. When you have looked into this matter, send a report to us.

The Daur, Ducher and Giliak people who have come under our Tsarist Majesty's mighty hand in eternal servitude and pay iasak to us are not to be ruined through war; you are not to pillage nor kill them, nor take their wives and children prisoner, nor bap-

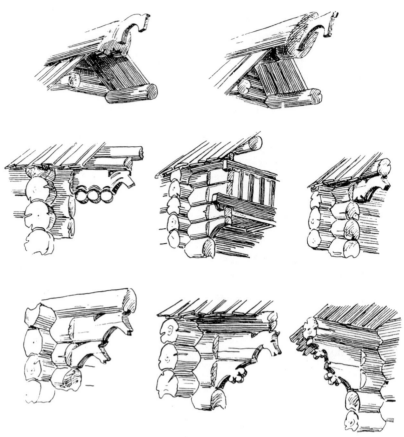

Eave details. From Makovetskii, *Byt i iskusstvo russkogo naseleniia vostochnoi Sibiri*, Vol. 1.

tize them. You are to collect our iasak from them with kindness and courtesy, not through harsh means; thus seeing our Tsarist grace, they will attract people from other hostile lands to come to us, the Great Sovereign, in eternal servitude, and they will pay iasak to us.

See: N. F. Demidova and V. S. Miasnikov, eds. *Russko-kitaiskie otnosheniia v XVII veke: Dokumenty i materialy (1608–1691)* (Moscow: 1969), I, 203–204.

87

APRIL, 1655

REPORTS TO THE VOEVODA OF IAKUTSK, IVAN AKINFEV, FROM THE
SERVITORS SEMEN DEZHNEV AND NIKITA SEMENOV CONCERNING
THEIR EXPLORATIONS ALONG THE ANADYR RIVER

I. To the stolnik and voevoda Ivan Pavlovich Akinfev and the diak
Osip Stepanov, of the Sovereign Tsar and Grand Prince Aleksei
Mikhailovich of all Russia, the servitors and promyshlenniks Se-
men Dezhnev and Nikita Semenov humbly report from the new
Anadyr River.

In 1649 the syn boiarskii Vasilii Vlasov and the tselovalnik Kiril
Kotkin sent me, Nikita, and my comrades from the Kolyma
River up the Aniui River to fight the non-iasak-paying people.
With the luck of the Sovereign, we found non-iasak-paying people
of the Khondynsk tribes whom we looted, and during the fight
we took their leader hostage in order to obtain the Sovereign's
iasak collection. This man was called Angara, and on the Kolyma
River we turned him over to the syn boiarskii Vasilii Vlasov and
the tselovalnik Kiril Kotkin. When he was interrogated this man
told about his defeat and his captivity, and said that beyond the
mountain range there is a new river called the Anadyr which is
near the headwaters of the Aniui River. On the basis of this information, promyshlennik volunteers gathered and petitioned the
Sovereign Tsar and Grand Prince Aleksei Mikhailovich of all
Russia, and submitted their petition to the syn boiarskii Vasilii
Vlasov and the tselovalnik Kiril Kotkin, on the Kolyma River, and
in the petition they asked that the Sovereign allow them to move
on to the new areas along the Anadyr River beyond the mountains in order to search for new iasak-paying people, and to bring
them under the Tsarist mighty hand. . . . [missing]. Other promyshlenniks submitted petitions in 1650 to Semen Motora, asking that they and certain servitors be allowed . . . [missing] to go
with Semen, and so the servitors went with Semen.

In 1649 Mikhail Stadukhin, a servitor from the Lena ostrog,
went from the Kolyma River by sea to the Pogycha River. Then
on September 7, 1650, he went by sea back to the Kolyma River,
and from there Mikhail wrote to the voevoda Vasilii Nikitich
Pushkin and his comrades at Lena ostrog that he, Mikhail, and his

men had made a seven-day voyage by sea, with runaway servitors, and that they had come across a small group of people called Koriaks whose language they could understand. When they were questioned they said that there are more people beyond that, but that there is no river beyond that they know of.

When Mikhail learned this, he bought the prisoners from us whom we had taken and began to make plans to go to those new places along the Anadyr River where we, the servitors and promyshlenniks, had been sent. Mikhail and his men and the runaway servitors, Iarofei Kiselev and his comrades, pursued and threatened everyone on the way along the Aniui and Anadyr rivers. He stole our food and weapons and all our hunting equipment, as well as our dogs and sleds, and he caused all kinds of discord among us in order to hinder our government service. He did this because he was jealous and did not want us to be in the Tsar's favor.

On the Kolyma River Mikhail abused our comrades, the promyshlenniks Matvei Kalinin and Kiril Proklov, and together with the runaway servitors he took Kiril's prisoners by force. We submitted a petition about Mikhail's crimes to the servitors Mok Ignatev and Ivan Ivanovich Permiak in the iasak zimov'e on the Kolyma River. When we went from the Kolyma River up the Aniui River to the mountains we took Argishinsk natives and went after them . . . [missing], and with the Sovereign's luck, we took a hostage, a Khondynsk man named Chekchoi. He has four blood brothers and many relatives. It was on March 24 that we took this hostage. We sent Chekchoi to his relatives to urge them to bring the Sovereign's iasak to our boat on the fourth day.

On March 26 Mikhail Stadukhin returned from the Kolyma River and came up the Aniui River and camped near us. When the natives brought us their iasak, which consisted of nine sables, in exchange for the [safety of] the hostage, Mikhail and his men fired their guns just as we were collecting the iasak. We do not know why they did this, but they drove the natives away. We pleaded with Mikhail but he would not listen to us. We felt it would have been possible to collect more iasak from these natives, since there were a considerable number of them, 50 or more. When we went on to the Anadyr River Mikhail boasted along the way and terrified one of our prikashchiks, the servitor Semen Motora, by seizing him and holding him for nine days. Semen rejoined us on the tenth day and reported, "Mikhail Stadukhin put me in stocks and tortured me and forced me to write a letter saying that I, Semen Motora, and my comrades should not go on a separate government assignment on the Anadyr River, but that we should be under Mikhail's command."

On April 23 Semen Motora and his comrades reached the iasak zimov'e of Semen Dezhnev on the Anadyr River, and from that day on I, Semen Dezhnev, and my men, joined together in government service with Semen Motora and his men, and together we provided food for the hostages. I, Semen, and my men have two hostages. They are recently captured Anauls; one is named Kolupai and the other is Negov. Mikhail Stadukhin bypassed this iasak zimov'e, looted the Anauls and killed many of them in battle, including the fathers and relatives of the iasak-paying men, Kolupai and Negov.

I, Semen, and my men, came to the Anaul ostrozhek and tried to tell Mikhail that he was doing a very bad thing by killing natives indiscriminately. Mikhail replied that they were non-iasak-paying people, and that only if they were iasak-paying people should we go to them and summon them from the ostrog and collect the Sovereign's iasak from them.

I, Semen, told the natives that they could go to give the Sovereign's iasak without fear, and a relative of the Anaul hostages did begin to bring in the iasak for the Sovereign from his iurt, which consisted of *opolniki* [sable pieces]. Mikhail snatched the furs from my hands and hit me in the face because I had joined forces with Semen Motora and his men for our government service, because we were so few in number. Mikhail shouted and cursed us over and over again. We, the servitors and promyshlenniks, Semen Motora and I, Semen Dezhnev, and our comrades, servitors and promyshlenniks, ran and hid from Mikhail. In the fall we used dog sleds to go on to the Pianzhina River and across the mountains to search for new non-iasak-paying people and to bring them under the mighty Tsarist hand. We did not have any experienced guides to lead us to that river, so we walked for three weeks and did not find the river. Thus with the prospect of starving to death in the cold, we returned to the Anadyr.

In the year 1641, in the fall when the water was at half depth, Mikhail sent nine servitors and promyshlenniks down the Anadyr to the Anauls. The Anaul natives killed all the servitors and promyshlenniks, and then fled far off down the Anadyr with the Sovereign's iasak and would not come to the iasak zimov'e. We went down the Anadyr River to where the Anauls had built an ostrozhek and we went to them in that ostrozhek so that they might repent their transgression against the Sovereign and pay the Sovereign's iasak. The Anauls harried us, but God helped us to take the nearest iurt, and then we entered their ostrozhek and fought them with our bare hands. In the ostrozhek the Anauls had assembled many weapons including spears, axes, long poles and knives, because since they had killed Russians, they expected that the Russians would come after them.

They killed our servitor Sukhan Prokofev and three promyshlenniks, Putil Afanasev, Evgenii Materik, and Kiril Proklov. In this same attack a servitor named Pavel Kokoulin was wounded by an axe and a spear in his head and his arm, which incapacitated him for the whole winter. The soldier Artemii was wounded by an arrow in the forehead, and the promyshlennik Terentii Nikitin was wounded by an arrow in the bridge of his nose. Foma Semenov and Nikita Semenov were wounded by spears in a skirmish but God helped us to capture their ostrozhek and to pacify the Anauls in battle.

In order to assure the collection of the Sovereign's iasak we took their leader Kogiun hostage. He and his family said that they had not previously paid iasak to the Sovereign. The fathers of these Anaul hostages, whose names are Kallik and Obyi, and their tribesmen, went back to their settlements to carry on.

During the summer a man named Mekerk and his tribesmen came secretly to the Anaul and killed the fathers of these hostages and all of their tribesmen. Then in November, 1652, Mekerk and his tribesmen, also secretly, went to Kogiun and killed him and his tribesmen . . . [missing]. On December 7 the Anaul hostage Kolupai and his tribesman, Lok, petitioned the Sovereign, asking that the Sovereign favor them by sending servitors and promyshlenniks after Mekerk to subdue him by force, because he had killed their fathers and relatives. He also stated that Mekerk was planning to kill servitors and promyshlenniks in the same way in the future. Semen Motora and I, Semen Dezhnev, and our comrades, went after Mekerk and his tribesmen and told him to come under the Sovereign Tsar's mighty hand. He and his relatives were rebellious and shot at us and killed the servitor Semen Motora. Another servitor, Pavel Kokoulin, was wounded in the shoulder and thigh by an arrow. Fedor Vetoshka was wounded by an arrow in the knee, and Stepan Sidorov, a promyshlennik, was wounded by an arrow in his arm. We captured all their wives and children, but Mekerk and his tribesmen escaped, although some were wounded.

The merchant Onufrii Kostromin and a promyshlennik, Vasilii Bugor, and their comrades, petitioned the Sovereign Tsar and Grand Prince Aleksei Mikhailovich of all Russia and submitted their petition to us, Semen and Nikita, asking that we continue to be on your Sovereign's service and that we assume responsibility for the hostages and for all government affairs, in accordance with the instructions which had been given to Semen Motora on the Kolyma River by the syn boiarskii Vasilii Vlasov and the tselovalnik Kiril Kotkin.

On January 12, 1651, the following persons went up the Anadyr River to the iasak zimov'e to take food and clothing and supplies to the Sovereign's hostage, Chekchoi and to our comrade Semen Motora and his men: our comrades, the promyshlennik Mikhail Zakharov, the prikashchiks, Beson Astafev and Afanasii Andreev, who worked for Vasilii Guselnikov, a member of the gostinnaia sotnia and their agent, Efim Merkurev Mezen, and also Petr Mikhailov and Foma Semenov. These comrades of ours were starving to death while they were at the government outpost with the hostage. They had been living on cedar bark because there were almost no fresh fish; and they gave the government hostage just enough food so he would not die of scurvy, and so that we would not be held responsible by the Sovereign and by the Treasury if he died.

Mikhail Stadukhin heard that our comrades were going to the iasak zimov'e and he intercepted them on the way and stole their goods, weapons, clothing, dogs, sleds and all their personal belongings. He beat our comrades nigh unto death, but before they died they submitted petitions about their struggle and about the pillage.

In the year 1652 we collected the Sovereign's iasak and the hostage Chekchoi . . . [missing]. Also during 1652 we sailed in boats on the sea in order to acquire additional profit for the Sovereign. We discovered a spit at the mouth of the Anadyr River behind the bay which opens into the sea. There were many walruses basking on that spit and we, the servitors and promyshlenniks, hunted these animals and took the tusks. There are a great many of these animals on the spit, on the cape itself along the sea side, for half a verst or more and up the slope for 30 or 40 sazhens, but not all the animals come out of the water to bask. There are also a great many of these animals in the sea close to shore. We did not wait for all the animals to come up on land, for the iasak zimov'e is up the Anadyr River and the fish were moving up the river and we had no food, and if we did not catch enough fish in time we would face starvation. . . . [missing]

On July 17, 1652, on the eve of the Feast of Saints Peter and Paul, the Holy Apostles, we left the spit to go up the Anadyr. We had spent four days hunting these animals and their carcasses covered the ground. In the year 1654 the animals appeared later, so that the first hunt was on St. Elias day. The reason the animals appeared later was that the ice had not been carried out from shore. Promyshlenniks from the Pomor'e region [near Arkhangelsk] say that there are not many of these animals in Russian Pomor'e. We servitors and promyshlenniks put the tusks we had taken in the Sovereign's Treasury warehouse; there were fourteen of them and they weighed three puds.

In 1653 we, Semen and Nikita and comrades, cut lumber and planned to sail by sea to take the Sovereign's treasury to Iakutsk ostrog; however I, Semen, realized that the sea was very rough and that there was a great offshore surf, so that we did not dare proceed without a good knowledge of navigation and without good sails and anchors. The natives told us that the ice does not break up and go out to sea every year. We did not dare send the Sovereign's treasury with only a small detachment of men by the overland route across the mountains and through the lands of the many non-iasak tribes, because servitors and promyshlenniks who had been in government service had been killed and other promyshlenniks had gone off to join Mikhail Stadukhin. These latter included Matvei Kalinin, Kalin Kuropot, Ivan Vakhov, Ivan Suvorov, Semen Zaiko and Bogdan Anisimov. The late Semen Motora noted the names of those who left for any reason in his book and appended his signature.

In the year 1653 we attacked the non-iasak Chuvansk who are reindeer herding people. They ran off and took their wives and [most of] their children with them, but a few children [were captured]; later many of them returned and recaptured these children and killed the servitor Ivan Puliaev and four promyshlenniks, Mikhail Zakharov, Efim Merkurev Mezen, Ivan Nesterov and Foma Kuzmin. They wounded Filip Danilov in the shoulder and Vasilii Markov in the thigh and Platon Ivanov in the arm.

These men were agents of the gostinnaia sotnia merchant Vasilii Guselnikov. This was the reason the government treasury was not sent on: so that no loss would thus come to the government [iasak] treasury collected from the natives, and so that the servitors and promyshlenniks would not be killed.

In the winter and spring of 1654 the iasak Khondynsk people, brothers and tribesmen of the hostage Chekchoi, said that in 1655 they would transport the government treasury over the mountains, using reindeer, to the Aniui River, provided that we gave their tribesmen the necessary iron equipment. On April 27, 1654, the volunteer servitor Iurii Seliverstov came from the Kolyma River and brought volunteer servitors and promyshlenniks with him. Every day Iurii went out to the iasak natives, Chekchoi's tribesmen, or a number of the natives came to him in the iasak zimov'e. Then Iurii left the iasak zimov'e and attacked the natives and took their food and hunting equipment. He wounded many of them, and killed others and took hostages, the iasak-paying Lulan and his brother Keot.

That same year, 1654, Iurii secretly put out to sea and sent a promyshlennik named Averkii Martemianov with a report to Iakutsk ostrog. Iurii was envious and did not want us, humble servants and orphans of the Sovereign, to receive favorable consideration from His Tsarist Majesty. Iurii plotted to gain the Sovereign's favor for himself by using our service and our discoveries. Iurii wrote to Iakutsk ostrog that he had discovered the spit and the sea animals and the tusks during his service with Mikhail Stadukhin and that it was not us, the servitors and promyshlenniks who had done this. We know he wrote this deceitful report because in the year 1646 Mikhail Stadukhin wrote from the Kolyma River that he and his men had gone from the Kolyma River by sea to the Pogycha River and that he, Mikhail, had sailed by sea for some seven days but did not find any river. Mikhail did find a few Koriak people, and took a few prisoners. When he interrogated these people they told him that they did not know of any river in that direction. Mikhail and his men and the fugitive servitors returned to the Kolyma River and Iurii was with Mikhail.

Iurii therefore made a deceitful report, because Mikhail did not go all the way to the great mountain promontory where the cape projects far out into the sea and where the Chukchi people live. Opposite that cape, on islands, there are people living who are known as the Tooth People, because they wear two large ivory teeth [ornaments] protruding through their lips. I, Semen, and my men know that this Holy Cape is not the first beyond the Kolyma, but that the Great Cape is. On that cape the vessel of the servitor Erasim Onkudinov and his men was wrecked. I, Semen, and my men rescued the survivors of that shipwreck, taking them into our boats. We also saw the Tooth People on the island, and from that cape it is a long distance to the Anadyr River and the spit.

We, Semen and Nikita and our men, servitors and promyshlenniks, gave Iurii and his men two koches fully equipped . . . [missing] and a large fishing boat so that they would not be prevented from carrying out their government service for a whole year because they had no boats or equipment, and so that they would not be prevented from hunting in the sea, and so that the government Treasury might be greatly enriched thereby. When Iurii took the boats he personally supervised his people and sent them in those boats on their sea voyage . . . [missing]. Iurii gave us a written receipt for these boats and for the equipment and for the fishing boat. Iurii lost one boat through carelessness, and he lost a great deal of time thereby. He had put a few men aboard that boat but when the boat began to ship water they could not handle it so Iurii abandoned it. We took Iurii's men who had been on that boat and distributed them among our other boats and Iurii went with us on the sea hunt.

On April 10, 1654 we took non-iasak Chuvansk men hostage in order to secure the Sovereign's iasak. One was named Legonta and the other Pondonzia. We took iasak for the Sovereign from them which consisted of one sable and one sable back. Their tribesmen, who were with the Khondynsk iasak people whom Iurii had pillaged, wanted to come to bring their iasak to the iasak zimov'e. They wanted to redeem their children but fearing that Iurii would kill them, they went far off to other tribesmen. Iurii took over their iurts and lived there for three weeks.

This year, 1655, when the iasak hostage Chekchoi and his brothers and tribesmen came to the iasak zimov'e, we asked them about the Chuvanzei. Why had they not come to the iasak zimov'e with the Sovereign's iasak? Chekchoi and his brothers replied that they had seen some of their tribesmen in two iurts and that they were going to search for others because they wanted to present the Sovereign's iasak together.

On November 16, Chekchoi was sent to his tribesmen to instruct them to procure iasak for the Sovereign and bring it to the iasak zimov'e. Chekchoi left his wife and two young sons as hostages. Chekchoi came to the iasak zimov'e with his brothers and relatives on March 19.

Through us, Semen and Nikita and our comrades, he reported to the Sovereign Tsar and Grand Prince Aleksei Mikhailovich of all Russia that in this present year, 1655, in the fall, many hostile Koriak people came from beyond the mountains from the Pianzhina River and killed many of their relatives and seized their wives and children and drove off their reindeer. These people always cause them much hardship through killing and pillage and they cannot defend themselves. They pleaded that the Sovereign help them by sending his government servitors against their enemies, together with these iasak people, in order to subdue the Koriaks. For this reason they had not been able to hunt during 1655 to procure the Sovereign's iasak for the Sovereign's Treasury; they had not been able to go beyond the mountains to the Aniui River because they had suffered two defeats this year, one at the hands of the Russians under Iurii and his men and the other at the hands of the Koriaks. They want to provide transport for the Sovereign's Treasury and to pay the Sovereign's iasak for the year 1654 and for the two subsequent years with an extra amount added.

In 1654 they fought the Koriaks on the spit. They live not far from this spit and they try to approach undetected and kill the Koriaks. They kill walrus for food. I, Semen and my men, attacked these [Koriak] people. We attacked fourteen of their iurts in a fortified ostrozhek and God helped us defeat all of these men. We took their wives and children. The others fled and the leaders took their wives and children with them. They are populous and have large iurts. Up to ten families live in one iurt. We were very few; there were only twelve of us in all. In that attack Pavel was wounded by an arrow but he shot a man in the head with his gun.

The Anadyr River is not forested so there are few sables there. In the upper reaches of the river, a journey of six or seven days, there are a few small deciduous trees, but no coniferous trees at all, only birch and aspen. Beyond the Little Maen there are no trees at all except for the rose willow. These grow only along the river banks. Everything else is tundra and rock. We have prepared a chart of the Anadyr River from the Aniui and beyond the mountains to the upper reaches of the Anadyr. We have included all the tributaries, both large and small, all the way to the sea to the spit where the animals bask.

It takes two weeks or more to take loaded sleds from the mountains of the upper Anadyr to the iasak zimov'e. We could not make written reports about government service because we had no paper to write on. . . . [missing]. We ask that the Sovereign grant us hostages to catch fish, new nets for fishing and guns, because there is good hunting if one has guns. The river is rocky and deep, especially when the fall rains come. Since the water has been high this fall the sea urchin is not here. There are salmon in abundance. This fish comes up the Anadyr from the sea. When it first enters the river it is good but after it goes upriver it is poor because the fish dies in the upper reaches of the Anadyr River and does not go back to sea. We get very little white fish because we do not have good nets. New nets cost fifteen rubles or more. We do not dare feed salmon to the Sovereign's hostages for fear they will get scurvy and die and then we would be in disgrace with the Sovereign and the Treasury. We feed them as well as we can with white fish. There are very few craftsmen here. No one knows how to make nets and work with lumber and the like.

In the year 1650 the total amount of the Sovereign's iasak collection was as reported above. That year we took nine sables from the hostage Chekchoi for the Sovereign's iasak. In 1651 Chekchoi's brothers and tribesmen did not come to the iasak zimov'e because there was no food and they had gone far away to hunt. But in 1652 we took six sables and five sable backs for the Sovereign's iasak. In 1653 we took seven sables and five backs and 1654 fourteen sables and twelve backs. In 1655 we took seven sables. In 1652 we took two sables from the Anaul. In 1653 the tithe from the promyshlenniks amounted to eight sables with bellies, two sables and sable backs and thirteen sable bellies; and for 1655 three sables with tails. In payment of duties and taxes we collected five sables and three sable bellies. The total amount of money collected by us is two rubles fourteen altyns and two dengi. The late Semen Motora collected two rubles twenty-nine altyns and two dengas. In the year 1654 one sable was collected instead of cash.

We have recorded all of these matters in the record books in the iasak zimov'e on the Anadyr River—iasak, from whom it was taken, the kind of pelt, the year, the tithe collection, sables purchased, petitions submitted and duties collected, both in cash and in sables.

The servitor, Ivan Puliaev, who was killed while on government service, dictated an oral report in the iasak zimov'e and after it had been taken down he signed it. The report stated that when he died he wanted his property to go to the Sovereign's Treasury, and we carried out this wish. The inventory of his will, which he dictated, is being sent with this report.

The promyshlennik Sidor Emelianov paid 30 sables to settle a debt owed to Ivan; Terentii Kursov paid four sables to buy a woman's fur coat; Pavel Kokoulin paid three sables for some old canvas, three spools of thread, a small fur hat, a small bag and a net; Stepan Kakanin paid five sables for candles, berries and a bag; Grigorii Burka gave one sable back for berries and a flint; Sidor Emelianov gave two grivnas in cash for a boat; Vasilii Burga paid two grivnas for a fishing net; Vasilii Markov paid four small sables for caviar and meat; Sidor gave one sable back for some tanned leather breeches and for a cloak and for some bits of net; the servitor Ivan Iakovlev gave one pud of tusks, seven, and three sables to settle his debt; [name missing] paid 33 pounds of tusks to settle a debt of 8 rubles and 10 altyns and he also paid three rubles for a shuba and five rubles and ten altyns for a kettle and ten pots. Semen Dezhnev, to whom Ivan had owed six rubles, took an axe, a dog and a net made of hair [as settlement for the debt]. The merchant Onisim Kostromin took a net, a tanned hide, two pounds of shot, a metal dish, a pistol, a piece of canvas, a pipe, plus seven rubles and a half-grivna. The soldier Andrei, who was owed three rubles twenty altyns, took a cross, ten [word missing], a net and a plate. Semen Dezhnev paid four rubles for a pound of shot, two spools of thread, needles, a piece of cloth and a dog. Fedor Vetoshka and his cohorts gave eight rubles 29 altyns for twenty fish, a pound of lead, an amulet, canvas, a hat with a red top, a pipe, and a bowstring. Six puds of Ivan's ivory tusks remained, 43 in number, and a list has been drawn up of some other small goods and is being forwarded.

On February 1, 1651, the promyshlenniks Platon Ivanov and Pavel Semenov came to Semen Motora and his men in the iasak zimov'e and informed Semen that Mikhail Stadukhin was planning to take his men to Semen's zimov'e and sack it and kill the servitors. Since Platon and Pavel wanted no part of this, they had left Mikhail. The promyshlennik Ivan Fedorov from Kazan wrote down their reports, and the servitor Evsei Pavlov swore to their testimony, and that report has also been forwarded. And with that report, still another has also been sent. Ivan from Kazan and Evsei Pavlov came to us from Mikhail and petitioned us to allow them to perform government service with us. In the year 1654 we went to sea, and Evsei left his position as sentry for the Sovereign's Treasury and guard over the hostages and instead joined government service as a volunteer assistant to the servitor Iurii Seliverstov. The servitor Vasilii Bugor came to us from Mikhail and performed government service with us, without petitioning. He came to the Anadyr on February [date missing], 1651, and performed all manner of duties, took hostages, provided food and served on sentry duty.

When we went on an expedition up the Aniui River, we took a hostage for the Sovereign named Chekchoi, and in the struggle the piatidesiatnik Shalam Ivanov was mortally wounded and died on July 5 of that same year on the Anadyr River. Nikita Semenov was wounded in the thigh by an arrow. In that foray the servitor Vetoshka killed one of the enemy and the promyshlennik Vasilii Bugor also killed one. When we attacked the Anaul iurts Pavel Kokoulin, the servitor, was wounded in the head and the arm but he wounded one of the enemy with his spear. Terentii Kursov was wounded in the arm by an arrow.

In the year 1654 we attacked the Koriaks from the sea spit and during the battle I, Semen, shot one man. In that same battle Pavel Kokoulin was wounded in the side by an arrow but he shot one man with his gun.

On May 3, 1653, in the iasak zimov'e on the Anadyr River, we servitors, Semen Dezhnev and Nikita Semenov, asked the merchant Onisim Kostromin and the promyshlenniks Vasilii Burga and his men to join in collecting the Sovereign's iasak and the tithe for the sable Treasury, to replace the dead servitor Ivan Puliaev, who had been the tselovalnik there, but they refused and would not assist.

In the presence of other persons we examined the belongings of the late Efim Merkurev Mezen, the prikashchik of the gostinnaia sotnia merchant Vasilii Guselnikov, and we made a list. No one made any claim to his belongings, and we did not want to put them into the government Treasury without an ukaz from the Sovereign, so we put them in the government storehouse under guard until we should receive an ukaz from the Sovereign regarding their disposition. The description of his belongings was forwarded.

On March 25, 1655, we sent servitors and promyshlenniks from the iasak zimov'e to Iakutsk ostrog with the Sovereign's Treasury, but they could not continue "because we were starving, we were in need of food and we only had spoiled whalemeat to eat." They submitted a petition to us about this.

On March 26, 1655, a volunteer servitor, Iurii Seliverstov, in the iasak zimov'e read the instructions which had been sent to Mikhail Stadukhin ordering him to send the servitors Semen Motora and his men and the merchant Anisim Kostromin and the promyshlennik Ivan Burga and his men from the Anadyr River. But I, Semen, did not send these men from the Sovereign's service, because we serve the Sovereign together, and furthermore the Sovereign's [iasak] treasury had been collected and we had to transport that treasury together.

A description of the men who procured tusks and how many, in the years 1652 and 1654, is being sent with this report, as well as a petition from the servitors and promyshlenniks, Fedor Vetoshka and Onisim Kostromin and their men, concerning their needs. Another petition from Nikita Vasilev has been sent, as well as a petition from the servitor Nikita Semenov and a petition from the servitors Pavel Kokoulin and Nikita Vasilev about their needs. There has also been sent a petition from the promyshlennik volunteer, Danilo Filipov, who came to the Anadyr with the volunteer servitor Iurii Seliverstov. He reported on certain government matters to Iurii and his report has also been sent.

On February 10, 1655, I, Semen, and Nikita instructed the servitors and promyshlenniks to go on with the Sovereign's Treasury, and they replied, "Give us until March 25 to think about it." We, Semen and Nikita, told the servitors and promyshlenniks for the second time that they must be off two weeks before Holy Easter. The servitor Vetoshka Emelianov said, "If you are going to force me, then I am going to go off to join Iurii Seliverstov. I will not haul the treasury." The servitor Saldat and the promyshlenniks Onisim Kostromin and Vasilii Bugor and their men said, "We are going to submit a petition about our needs and about the lack of food." Nikita replied, "I, [missing]." And from that time on, we began to write reports. They said, "You are writing these reports to Iakutsk ostrog, and we are going to hand in our petition. Go with these reports now and send our petition along with the report to Iakutsk ostrog." When the servitors and promyshlenniks wrote their petition, Nikita learned that our reports had been written and that there had been just enough paper for them, so he, Nikita, with Evsev's cleverness and his own wit, said, "I did not order you into service. I have to take the Sovereign's Treasury. Time is short. We no longer have any iron to give to the natives as presents. And furthermore we do not have any paper for writing."

On November 21, 1654, we took the Sovereign's iasak from a Khodynsk man named Keot and from his brother Lulan; we were aided by the volunteer servitor Iurii Seliverstov. In all we took five sable backs, and this service for the Sovereign was carried out together with Iurii.

On March 22, 1655, together with Iurii Seliverstov, we took a Khodynsk man named Meniagin and his son as hostages, to obtain the Sovereign's iasak. We did not collect any iasak in 1655 because it was late in the year when we took these hostages, but these hostages say that the father is well-to-do. The hostage Chekchoi went with us as a guide, with Sidor Emelianov and Panfil Lavrentev. Chekchoi remained and Sidor and Panfil were sent with the reports to the Kolyma River. On the Kolyma they were told to hand these reports to the servitors or to the merchants or promyshlenniks, whoever might be there. These reports were sent on April 4, [1655].

II. The Lena servitor Semen Ivanovich Dezhnev reports to the voevoda of the Lena ostrog, Ivan Pavlovich [Ankifev] and to the diak Osip Stepanovich of the Sovereign Tsar and Grand Prince Aleksei Mikhailovich of all Russia.

On June 20, 1648, I, Semen, was sent from the Kolyma River to a new river, the Anadyr, in search of new non-iasak people. The next year, 1649, on September 20 I was on a boat which belonged to the merchant Fedot Alekseev; I was going from the Kolyma River out to sea. The Chukchi attacked us and wounded Fedot. We became separated and I lost sight of him.

I, Semen, drifted at sea until after the feast of the Shroud of the Holy Virgin, October 1. The boat drifted here and there. At last the sea tossed us on shore beyond the mouth of the Anadyr

River. There were 25 men on our koch. We all took to the hills. We knew not where we went. We were hungry, cold, naked, barefoot. I, poor Semen and my comrades walked ten whole weeks to reach the Anadyr River; we came out onto the lower Anadyr near the sea. We could not catch any fish. There were no trees. We, poor starving creatures, decided to separate. Twelve men went up the Anadyr. They walked for twenty days but did not find any people or trails so they started back. But three days before they reached camp they made an overnight stop and dug holes in the snow. The promyshlennik Foma Semenov was with them and told them there was no good place to make an overnight camp and that they should move on to the campsite where the rest of their comrades were. Only the promyshlenniks Sidor Emelianov and Ivan Zyrianin went with Foma. The rest of the men remained there because they were starving and could not walk. They told Foma to tell me, Semen, to send blankets to sleep under and old parkas to wear and some food to eat, so that they could reach camp. Foma and Sidor did reach the camp and told me, Semen about this.

I, Semen, gave my last sleeping roll and blanket to them, sending these through the mountains with Foma. But he did not find the other men [where he had left them] and we do not know whether the natives took them off . . . [missing] with the rest of the goods belonging to the prikashchiks Beson Astafev and Afanasii Andreev. Their agent, Efim Merkurev was left behind and instructed . . . [missing]. We did not have any poddiaks at that time and there was no one there who could write. There were only twelve of our group of twenty-five, so we twelve went by boat up the Anadyr River. We went all the way to the Anaul people where we captured two men in a foray. I was badly wounded there. We took iasak from them and noted the names of the people who gave iasak and the amount in the iasak books. I, Semen, wanted to take additional iasak for the Sovereign from the Anaul people but they replied that since they did not live in forest land they had no sables, but that when the reindeer people came to them they would buy sables and then bring more iasak for the Sovereign.

Mikhail Stadukhin came to the iasak zimov'e and without any provocation he sacked the Anaul people. After that the Anauls Lok and Kolupai . . . [missing] could not give anything for the years 1651 and 1652 because Kolupai's father . . . [missing]. On April 15, 1655, Kolupai and Lok went to the reindeer Khondynsk tribe in the mountains in order to obtain sables for the Sovereign's iasak. The Khondynsk people took Kolupai and Lok to the mountains and did not come to the iasak zimov'e. Lok lives along a tributary river and has not appeared at the iasak zimov'e and the Khondynsk people killed Kolupai. During the time Lok and Kolupai went to the mountains the Anaul prince Mikera killed all their tribesmen.

When one goes by sea from the Kolyma River to the Anadyr River, one passes a cape which juts far out into the sea, but this is not the same cape which is located near the Chukhota River. Mikhail Stadukhin did not go to this cape. Opposite this cape there are two islands inhabited by Chukchi. They wear tooth ornaments made of ivory which protrude through holes which they pierce through their lips. This cape lies north to northeast. On the Russian side of the cape there is a small river where the Chukchi have built a tower made of whalebone. The cape bends around toward the Anadyr River. If there is a favorable wind it takes no more than three days to sail to the Anadyr River from the cape. It is not far from the coast to the river because the Anadyr River empties into a bay.

In the year 1654 I, Semen, took part in a foray near the sea. I, Semen, raided the Koriaks and took Fedot Alekseev's Iakut woman who told me that Fedot and a servitor named Gerasim had died of scurvy and that some of their other comrades had been killed. Only a few men survived and they fled together in boats. She did not know where they had gone. The government iasak in sables which I, Semen, collected is not on the Anadyr River.

The servitor Nikita Semenov took the belongings of the dead servitor Semen Motora. The servitor Evsei Pavlov, who deserted from the Lena ostrog, served with Mikhail Stadukhin and then ran off from Mikhail and served with me, Semen. Evsei abused the promyshlenniks greatly and because of this, the promyshlenniks have submitted a petition against Evsei, but he has not submitted to the court for judgment. In the year 1653, during a battle, Terentii Nikitin, a promyshlennik, submitted a petition against Evsei for abuse. Evsei was brought to trial where he was very rude and behaved like a criminal. Because of this rude behavior I, Semen, wanted to whip Evsei, but he fled from the

Giliak shaman's girdle (upper left) showing bone, horn and prized bells to embellish the sound of his tambour of membrane or hide. Amur region. From Von Schrenck, *Reisen und Forschungen im Amur-Lande*, Vol. 3.

camp to the esaul Vetoshka Emelianov and his promyshlenniks, where Evsei said that he had come on the Sovereign's business. When Iurii Seliverstov appeared, then Evsei ran off to join him. This Evsei Pavlov has caused much trouble for the servitors and promyshlenniks.

See: *Dopolneniia k aktam istoricheskim* (St. Petersburg: 1848), IV, 16–27.

88

AFTER MAY 17, 1657

A PETITION TO TSAR ALEKSEI MIKHAILOVICH FROM THE SERVITOR
FEDOR MAKSIMOV TO BE COMPENSATED FOR HIS SERVICE AND TRIBU-
LATIONS ON THE AMUR RIVER

To the Sovereign Tsar and Grand Prince Aleksei Mikhailovich, Autocrat of all Great, Little and White Russia, a petition from your humble slave, the volunteer servitor on the great
Amur River, Fedor Maksimov, son of Korkin.

Sovereign, in the year 1650 I, your slave, was on the Olekma
River hunting sables. A servitor from Iakutsk ostrog, Mikhail Artemev, son of Kashinets, and 40 of his men came onto the Amur
River from the Amur prikashchik Erofei Khabarov. They took
me, your slave, and my twelve promyshlennik comrades, and all
our hunting equipment, from the zimov'e on the Olekma River to
the land of the Daurs on your Sovereign service. I, your slave,
Sovereign, with nine of my comrades, hauled your Sovereign
supplies which we had left on the Olekma River when we went to
the Daur lands to join Erofei Khabarov. These consisted of weapons and powder and shot and food and all kinds of boat equipment and anchors. We hauled this during winter, using skis and
sleds and took it to the Tugursk ostrozhek and over the Tugur portage to the Amazar River. This journey carrying your Sovereign
supplies took seven weeks to reach the Amazar River.

When we reached the Amazar River we built a boat nine
sazhens long to carry your Sovereign supplies, but we could not
use this boat on the Amazar River at that time, Sovereign, to
reach the Amur, because the water was too low. Sovereign, since
we did not want to hold up the delivery of your Sovereign supplies, we built a small bark five sazhens long and with that little
craft we took your Sovereign supplies down to the Amur River.
When we came to rapids and fast water we had to unpack your
supplies and carry them on our backs. We took your Sovereign
supplies which had been left on the Olekma River to the great
Amur River to the fortress of Albazin. We took them to the prikashchik Erofei Khabarov and handed them over to him.

When he accepted your Sovereign supplies, Erofei ordered
me, your humble slave, to serve you, Sovereign, on the Amur

River, on a number of your assignments. I, your humble slave, did serve you, Sovereign, for six years on your Sovereign service on the Amur River, with the prikashchiks Erofei Khabarov and Onufrii Stepanov. Sovereign, I performed all your service without any pay from you, Sovereign, going at my own expense on forays against subjects hostile to you, Sovereign, the Bogdois and the Daurs and the Duchers and the Giliaks. I fought them in battle, took many prisoners and hostages, and collected iasak from them for you, Sovereign. Sovereign, I, your slave, was wounded four times on your service.

Sovereign, in the year 1655 while I was on your Sovereign service in Kumarsk ostrog, the Bogdoi people killed two of my brothers, Ilia Maksimov and Obrosim Fedoseev. My brothers had served you, Sovereign, on the Amur River for four years without receiving any pay from you, Sovereign. They had provisioned themselves at their own expense and had accumulated many debts. After their death I, your slave, paid their debts which amounted to 60 rubles. There are receipts for some of these but not for others.

Sovereign, in the year 1656 the prikashchik Onufrii Stepanov sent me, your slave, from the mouth of the Shingal River with 100 men onto a tributary to search for non-iasak people to bring them under your mighty Tsarist Sovereign hand. I, your slave, went along that tributary river and searched out the non-iasak Duchers. We fought these Duchers and killed many, and took one of their leaders hostage. After taking this hostage we took him to the prikashchik Onufrii Stepanov. Sovereign, the Duchers brought 30 sables as iasak for this hostage. On July 20 Onufrii appointed me, your slave, as tselovalnik to take your Sovereign sable treasury from the Amur River.

So with your Sovereign . . . [missing] 50 servitors under Mikhail Kashinets were sent to convoy the sable treasury to you in Moscow, Sovereign. While en route with your Sovereign treasury, 27 of the servitors died from privation and starvation on the Tugur portage and on the Olekma River. I, your slave, Sovereign, abandoned all of my own belongings while I was transporting your Sovereign sable treasury. I carried your Sovereign treasury on my back and suffered great privation and starvation. We bought provisions for two or three rubles per pud and incurred enormous debts, but we brought your Sovereign treasury to Iakutsk intact.

A 1690 document identifies this whimsical design as the coat of arms of Siberia. From Shunkov, ed., *Istoriia Sibiri*, Vol. 2.

Merciful Sovereign Tsar and Grand Prince Aleksei Mikhailovich, Autocrat of all Great, Little and White Russia! Reward me, your slave and decree, Sovereign, that your Sovereign's stolnik and voevoda Mikhail Semenovich Lodyzhenskii and the diak Fedor Tonkovo accept my petition in the Prikaz office in Iakutsk ostrog, attach it to their report and send it to you, Sovereign, in Moscow. Sovereign Tsar, have mercy!

See: *Dopolneniia k aktam istoricheskim* (St. Petersburg: 1848), IV, 94–95.

89

AN UKAZ FROM TSAR ALEKSEI MIKHAILOVICH TO THE TARA SYN BOI-
ARSKII IVAN PERFILEV AND TO THE TOBOLSK SERVITOR, THE BU-
KHARA MAN, SEITKUL ABLIN, CONVEYING INSTRUCTIONS FOR THEIR
EMBASSY TO THE CHINESE EMPIRE AND TO THE KALMYK TAISHA

An ukaz from the Sovereign Tsar and Grand Prince Aleksei Mikhailovich, Autocrat of all Great, Little and White Russia, to the Siberian town of Tara, to the syn boiarskii Ivan Perfilev and to the Bukhara man, Seitkul Ablin, resident of the town of Tobolsk.

The Great Sovereign Tsar and Grand Prince Aleksei Mikhailovich, Autocrat of all Great, Little and White Russia has ordered that they be sent to the Chinese Empire to the Emperor Bugdykhan and to the Kalmyks, to Ablai-taisha, with gifts, to establish commercial relations. They have received 493 rubles from the Prikaz of the Bolshaia Kazna in Moscow to be used for purchases and they have also been authorized to receive 257 rubles from the government Treasury in Tobolsk in Siberia. A gramota from the Sovereign has been sent to Tobolsk with Seitkul, addressed to the stolnik and voevoda concerning this money and their mission. The Bukhara man, Seitkul, is to use that money to purchase gifts for the [Chinese] tsar in Moscow and in other towns, gifts such as fine quality fabrics and other goods which will be in demand in the Chinese Empire and among the Kalmyks and which can be sold to bring profit to the Sovereign's Treasury.

When [Seitkul] arrives in Tobolsk he is to hand over the gramota of the Sovereign Tsar and Grand Prince Aleksei Mikhailovich, Autocrat of all Great, Little and White Russia, which is being sent with him from the Prikaz of the Bolshaia Kazna to the stolnik and voevoda Prince Aleksei Buinosov-Rostovskii and the diak Grigorii Uglev. When Ivan Perfilev comes to Tobolsk from Tara, then Ivan and Seitkul, after collecting the designated 257 rubles in Tobolsk, are to use that money to purchase sables, blackbrown foxes and ermine shubas and other items which will be desirable in the Chinese Empire. After they purchase these goods, then Ivan and Seitkul are to pick up a document in Tobolsk from the stolnik and voevoda and from the diak.

This document concerns their mission to the Kalmyk uluses and the nomadic taishas and murzas and princes. Then they are to proceed to the Kalmyks and to China without delay. When they reach the Kalmyks, they are to go to Ablai-taisha and deliver the gifts of the Sovereign Tsar and Grand Prince Aleksei Mikhailovich, Autocrat of all Great, Little and White Russia, which gifts are valued at 50 rubles. While they are among the Kalmyks they are to trade and sell their goods and exchange them with the greatest possible profit for the Sovereign's Treasury.

From the Kalmyks they are to proceed to the Chinese Empire, to the city where Tsar Bugdykhan lives. When they reach that city they are to appear before the councillors of Tsar Bugdykhan who are in charge of foreign ambassadors so that these men will inform Tsar Bugdykhan of their arrival. When the councillors instruct them to go to the tsar, Seitkul is to go to the tsar and list His Tsarist Majesty's titles and present the Sovereign's letter as instructed, which letter was given to him from the Posolskii Prikaz [in Moscow]. After this he is to display and present the 40 sables, 15 black-brown foxes, the four bolts of fine fabric in various colors: vermillion, red, cherry and green, in five-arshin lengths, the three ermine and white fox shubas and the mirrors, all of which are worth a total of 200 rubles.

When Tsar Bugdykhan accepts the gramota and the gifts from His Tsarist Majesty and permits trade, then Ivan and Seitkul, while they are in the Chinese Empire, are without any delay to engage in trade and exchange Russian goods for rubies, lapis lazuli, sapphires, emeralds and pearls, which they are to obtain as cheaply as possible, so as to bring great profit to the Sovereign's Treasury. Each purchase and each sale is to be recorded in the books, with the price given in Chinese and Kalmyk currency and opposite these figures, the equivalent in Russian currency, so the difference can be noted. At the same time Ivan and Seitkul are to examine all the various goods in the Kalmyk and Chinese Empire and purchase precious stones, large pearls and goods which will bring a large profit. They are not to try to deceive, nor to enrich their own purses, nor are they to sell their own personal goods before the government trade goods are sold.

The Prikaz of the Bolshaia Kazna in Moscow has given Seitkul three and a half puds of dry tobacco to be used for gifts to the Kalmyks.

Ivan and Seitkul have further been instructed by the Great Sovereign to recruit master craftsmen from the Chinese Empire who know how to make beautiful items of silver and gold, intricate ornaments, enamel ware and black lacquer goods; also diamond cutters, persons who know how to gild, those who can work with silver, iron and copper, persons who know how to work with wire and experts who can refine gold, silver and copper ore and make lead from ore. They are personally to conduct these hired master craftsmen to the Sovereign in Moscow and they are to promise to pay them the following yearly wages: 40, 50 or 60 rubles for a goldsmith, the same for a diamond cutter, 30 rubles for other master craftsmen, or if necessary, up to 40 or 50 rubles.

After they have purchased these goods and hired the master craftsmen, they are to proceed to Moscow to the Sovereign Tsar and Grand Prince Aleksei Mikhailovich, Autocrat of all Great, Little and White Russia. There they are to present the goods they have purchased for the Sovereign and bring the master craftsmen. They are to submit the revenue and expense books to boiar Ilia Danilovich Miloslavskii and dumnyi dvorianin Ivan Pavlovich Matiushkin and diaks Anika Chistoi and Afanasii Tashlykov at the Prikaz of the Bolshaia Kazna. The master craftsmen are to be well fed en route to Moscow so they will suffer no hunger and the cost for that is to be recorded in the expense book.

Reference: TsGADA, f. Sibirskii prikaz, stolb. 535, 11. 153–158.
See: N. F. Semidova and V. S. Miasnikov, eds. *Russko-kitaiskie otnosheniia v XVII veke: Dokumenty i materialy (1608–1691)* (Moscow: 1969), I, 218–219.

90

1657-1658

A PETITION FROM THE KOLYMA IUKAGIR NATIVE PRINCES, EGUPK, KILTIG AND CHEK KALIAMIN, AND THEIR ULUS PEOPLE TO THE VOEVODA OF IAKUTSK, MIKHAIL LODYZHENSKII, COMPLAINING OF EXTORTION AND ABUSES BY THE SERVITOR GRIGORII TATARINOV

To the Sovereign Tsar and Grand Prince Aleksei Mikhailovich, your Sovereign's orphans on the Kolyma River, the iasak Iukagir princes Egupk and Kiltig and Chek Kaliamin and their ulus people [names follow] humbly petition you.

Sovereign, our petition concerns the servitor Grigorii Ivanov Tatarinov. Sovereign, in the year 1657 Grigorii, who was a Prikaz official in the iasak zimov'e on the middle part of the Kolyma River, beat us many times and ordered us your orphans to bring swans, geese and berries, in addition to our iasak, to the iasak collector at the zimov'e. Sovereign, in the fall of 1658 in addition to your Sovereign's iasak collection, Grigorii and his men took six sables with bellies and tails from me, prince Cherm, because we had failed to go to the iasak zimov'e with the swans, geese and berries.

After I, your orphan, prince Kiltig, brought in your Sovereign's iasak collection, he put me into prison and tortured me in order to obtain two sables. He ordered my brothers to ransom me with sables, and he beat me mercilessly.

He took four fine sables from me, prince Chek, and my brothers, and he took two sables from Cherm Alivin. And when we, your orphans, came to your Sovereign iasak zimov'e with your Sovereign iasak collection, when he took your Sovereign's iasak, Grigorii hit the tselovalnik Ivan Dorofeev in the face and sent him away from your iasak collection; then with the tselovalnik gone, he set aside the best sables we your orphans had brought and kept them for himself. They pay us one arrow per sable or one *agniv*, but they do not give us anything for others, and they make us accept inferior goods such as axes and arrows and steel for making fires, and saws and knives and poor dogs. They take sables from us for these things while they are collecting your Sovereign iasak. They select the best sables and set aside what they call damaged and spoiled and torn pelts, so this creates a shortage in our iasak. We have to make up this shortage by hunting in the winter without food and with great hardship. For these sables of ours which they take, in addition to your Sovereign iasak, they give us from their goods one arrow for a sable, one fire-making steel for a sable, one saw for a sable and a half or two, one knife for a sable, one axe for two or three or even more sables, and they exact a very high price for dogs.

They summon us to come to the iasak zimov'e very frequently in summer and in winter. At these times we are gathering food for ourselves such as fish, wild game and birds. They order us to come to the zimov'e every week to bring sables, and if we do not bring any in some week, they beat us and lock us up and torture us to get sables. They also take our children for our debts. They take our young girls for sables, for a very small price, and then sell them to Russian men. Because of all the travel we cannot procure enough food, and so we have often suffered great famine. And because of Grigorii's violence we, your orphans, have become improverished and have accumulated great unendurable debts.

Merciful Sovereign Tsar and Grand Prince Aleksei Mikhailovich, have mercy on us, your orphans, your iasak-paying natives. Sovereign, permit that our petition be accepted on the Kolyma River in the Prikaz office by the piatidesiatnik cossack Ivan Kozhin and the tselovalnik customs collector Ivan Dorofeev, and that it be sent under his signature to Iakutsk ostrog to the Prikaz office to the stolnik and voevoda Mikhail Semenovich Lodyzhenskii and the diak Fedor Tonkovo. Tsar, Sovereign, have mercy. Grant our request.

See: Ia. P. Alkor and B. D. Grekov, eds. *Kolonialnaia politika moskovskogo gosudarstva v Iakutii v XVII v.* (Leningrad: 1936), 98–99.

91

JANUARY 30, 1658

A GRAMOTA FROM TSAR ALEKSEI MIKHAILOVICH TO THE VOEVODA OF IAKUTSK, MIKHAIL LODYZHENSKII, CONCERNING THE COLLECTION OF WALRUS TUSKS ALONG THE SHORES OF THE PACIFIC OCEAN

From the Tsar and Grand Prince, Aleksei Mikhailovich, Autocrat of all Great, Little and White Russia, to Siberia, to the Lena River, to Iakutsk ostrog, to our stolnik and voevoda, Mikhail Semenovich Lodyzhenskii, and to our diak, Fedor Tonkovo.

You have written to us, the Great Sovereign, that in the year 1656 the volunteer servitors Semen Dezhnev and Iurii Seliverstov reported to you from the newly discovered Anadyr River that they had gathered walrus tusks along that river and along the [Pacific] ocean shore. Semen Dezhnev and his men gathered 239 puds of tusks, and Iurii gathered 50 puds. The weight of the tusks varies from 3,4,5,6,7,8,10,12,13 or 16 tusks per pud. For example, Semen Dezhnev sent you a pud of ivory which consisted of six tusks. You appraised this ivory in Iakutsk and sent it to us, the Great Sovereign, in Moscow, with the Iakutsk streltsy stolnik Trofim Eveseev and his men. The Iakutsk appraised price of that ivory was 60 rubles. You sent the Iakutsk servitors, 30 men, led by the stolnik Amrosii Mikhailov and the cossack Fedor Kaigorov, to the new Anadyr River to collect walrus tusks. You gave them iron harpoons and all other equipment needed for this walrus-ivory expedition. You ordered the servitors to cooperate on this expedition; they were to have half the catch for themselves, but pay a tithe of it into our Treasury in ivory. You ordered the sotnik Amrosii Mikhailov to collect 100 puds of ivory for us from the volunteers and servitors under Semen Dezhnev and Iurii Seliverstov; this was to be collected at the rate of 50 puds per *vataga* [group of hunters]. In addition to this, they were to collect a tithe of the rest of the ivory for us, and send it to you at Iakutsk ostrog.

When this our gramota reaches you, you are to instruct the servitors and all volunteers who may be gathering walrus ivory along the Lena River and other rivers, that they are to set aside half of the take for us, the Great Sovereign; and you are to collect a tithe of the other half for us. Then you are to instruct them that we will purchase whatever is left for ourselves. You are to pay, out

Eastern Siberian natives clung fast to their sleds, for their dogs ran
on until exhausted with or without a driver. From Von Schrenck,
Reisen und Forschungen im Amur-Lande, Vol. 3.

of our Treasury, between 15 and 20 rubles per pud for large tusks,
and 12 rubles per pud for small tusks. You are to have the ivory
appraised in the Iakutsk ostrog by merchants. After the ivory has
been appraised, you are to prepare an inventory of it and send it
to Moscow to us, the Great Sovereign. Send it every year, without interruption, with the Lena servitors. Order that an inventory be submitted to the Sibirskii Prikaz to our boiar Prince Aleksei Nikitich Trubetskoi, and to our diaks Grigorii Protopopov
and Fedor Ivanov. You are not to purchase these tusks for yourself, nor are you to realize any profit from them.

See: *Dopolneniia k aktam istoricheskim* (St. Petersburg: 1848), IV, 99–100.

92

NOT BEFORE JUNE 18, 1658

A REPORT TO TSAR ALEKSEI MIKHAILOVICH AND TO THE SIBIRSKII PRI-
KAZ FROM THE VOEVODA OF THE DAUR TERRITORY, AFANASII PASH-
KOV, CONCERNING THE ATTACK BY A MANCHU WARSHIP AGAINST
SERVITORS ON THE SHILKA RIVER

To the Sovereign Tsar and Grand Prince Aleksei Mikhailovich, of all Great, Little and White Russia, and to the Heir
Apparent, the Tsarevich and Grand Prince Aleksei Alekseevich,
of all Great, Little and White Russia, your humble servant Afanasii Pashkov reports.

Sovereigns, on June 18 of this year, 1658, in accordance with
your ukaz, Sovereign Tsar and Grand Prince Aleksei Mikhailovich, Autocrat of all Great, Little and White Russia, and Heir
Apparent, Tsarevich and Grand Prince Aleksei Alekseevich of all
Great, Little and White Russia, I, your humble servant, sent servitors from your Sovereign ostrog on the great Shilka River. These
were 30 men headed by the cossack piatidesiatnik Andrei Potapov, who carried your Sovereign gramota, and were sent to the
Daur land and to the sea [of Okhotsk] in search of the Daur servitors under Onufrii Stepanov. Sovereigns, I instructed them to
work together to build your Sovereign ostrog in the Daur land.
Sovereigns, I, your humble servant, wrote to you in Moscow concerning this on July 29, 1657, and I sent this report with the cossack piatidesiatnik Ignatii Suvorov and his comrades.

Sovereigns, on August 18, 1657, the cossack piatidesiatnik
Andrei Potapov whom I, your humble servant, had sent to the
Daur land with your Sovereign gramota, returned to me, your
humble servant, in your Sovereign ostrog on the upper Shilka
River. Twenty men, servitors and new recruits, headed by Iakim
Iakovlev, came with him from Daur service. When the piatide-
siatnik Andrei Potapov was questioned, he told me, your humble
servant, the following information.

When Andrei left me, your humble servant, he sailed on the
great Shilka River with his comrades. When he reached the great
mountains near the Shingal [Sungari] River in the land of the
Duchers, he met Daur servitors there, 160 men led by Klim
Ivanov, who related the following account. They had left the
Daur prikashchik Onufrii Stepanov and the rest of the servitors

Of necessity travel by dogsled was developed into a basic skill.
From Shunkov, ed., *Istoriia Sibiri*, Vol. 2.

below the Shingal River so as to go on to the land of the Duchers,
up along the Shilka River to inquire as to the whereabouts of your
Sovereign Russian people, and to collect your Sovereign iasak.

They defeated the Kyshtyms in the land of the Duchers, and
then sailed back down the Shilka River to join the Daur servitors
headed by Onufrii Stepanov. As they sailed along the Shingal
River there were many Bogdoi people aboard large boats with
sails. They realized that some of their comrades whom they had
left behind were on these Bogdoi boats. [The Bogdoi] had destroyed the barges of the prikashchik Onufrii Stepanov and his
men. Before they had reached the Shingal River [Klim and his
men] had seen Bogdoi spears which had been thrust into a tree on
the bank of the river, and these spears were covered with blood.
Sovereigns, we know that the Daur servitors under the command
of the prikashchik Onufrii Stepanov were killed right there. And
Sovereigns, there were 300 men with Onufrii.

Reference: TsGADA, f. Sibirskii prikaz, stolb. 508, 11. 68–69.
See: N. F. Demidova and V. S. Miasnikov, eds. *Russko-kitaiskie otnosheniia v
XVII veke: Dokumenty i materialy (1608–1691)* (Moscow: 1969), I,
234–235.

93

OCTOBER 3, 1659

THE REPORT OF THE MILITARY ATAMAN ARTEMII FILIPOV CONCERN-
ING A CHINESE ATTACK AGAINST A RUSSIAN DETACHMENT ON THE
AMUR RIVER

On October 3, 1659, a group of Amur servitors appeared before the voevoda Ivan Ivanovich Rzhevskii and the poddiak Vikul Panov in the Eniseisk Prikaz office. These men were the elected military ataman Artemii Filipov, the line servitor Ivan Garasimov son of Chebychakov, Sidor Timofeev, Sidor Dementev, Isak Kirilov and Ivan Grigorev. They made an oral report concerning the fact that on June 30, 1657, when they were on the great Amur River below the Shingal [Sunguri] River, they were attacked by a large Bogdoi force aboard 47 vessels carrying great firepower in both cannon and small arms.

The Bogdoi force attacked the Amur servitors using the cannon on their ships, defeated them, and sacked the Sovereign's iasak sable treasury which the prikashchik Onufrii Stepanov and his men had collected for the previous year. The Sovereign's iasak treasury consisted of 87 forties [of sables made up] in shubas, and red foxes; and only four black fox pelts of all this which Onufrii had collected were saved on the ship *Spaskii*, which the servitors used to escape to the sea. The Bogdoi also took the Sovereign's equipment, including cannon, gunpowder, shot, supplies of food and clothing for the cossacks and all their possessions. In the battle the Bogdoi killed the prikashchik Onufrii Stepanov and 270 of his men. The servitors who survived that massacre escaped on the *Spaskii* and fled up river on the vessel to join the 227 other servitors who had started out on the expedition with them. After this rout, the servitors joined together, and in the year 1658 their total was 180 men.

These men collected the Sovereign's iasak from the Duchers and Giliaks; this consisted of 18 forties of sables, shubas made of sable backs and of sable with fox, and the four black fox pelts that had been saved after the battle. They moved in from the sea and collected the Sovereign's iasak from the Giliaks; they collected three black foxes. With that state treasury they went up the Amur River on their way to the voevoda Afanasii Pashkov. When they reached Kumarsk ostrog they found there was a food shortage and they had to endure hunger. At that time there were 227 men, so they divided into two groups; one remained at Kumarsk ostrog so they could go up the Zeia River to search for food; the other group, 107 servitors, continued on their way up the Amur River to go to the voevoda Afanasii Pashkov, expecting to find him at Albazin in the old town. They reached Albazin, but Afanasii Pashkov was not there.

On the upper part of the Amur River they found logs floating in the river, logs which had been used for building dwellings, ostrogs and towers; some of these logs were floating singly, and some were tied into rafts; and the rafts carried boat equipment and hides.

From Albazin they went via the Tugursk portage to the Urak River, but they still did not find Afanasii Pashkov, nor did they see any sign of him. There was a shortage of food there, and famine, so they did not go beyond the Tugursk portage to the Shilka River, but instead they took the Tugursk portage to reach the Olekma River. They carried the Sovereign's iasak sable treasury on their backs over the Tugursk portage. While they were crossing the portage they lived on mushrooms, grass, berries and roots. Then they learned from natives and from prisoners who had been taken in battle that the Bogdoi force which had attacked the servitors in 1657 had divided, and that a third of them had gone up the Amur River to find Afanasii Pashkov and the sovereign's troops. However Artemii Filipov and his Amur servitors were unable to find out if Afanasii Pashkov and his men were still alive on the upper reaches of the Shilka River.

From the Tugursk portage [Artemii Filipov and the servitors] carried the Sovereign's iasak sable treasury to Ilimsk ostrog. At Ilimsk ostrog the scrivener and voevoda Petr Bunakov ordered that the Sovereign's sable treasury be spread out and appraised by merchants; once they had appraised it, he ordered that it be sent to Moscow to the Great Sovereign and Grand prince Aleksei Mikhailovich, Autocrat of all Great, Little and White Russia, and that Artemii Filipov and six of his servitors transport it there. It was late when they set out for Eniseisk, the river was already beginning to freeze over, and they could not go on by sled that fall and winter to carry the Sovereign's sable treasury.

See: *Dopolneniia k aktam istoricheskim* (St. Petersburg: 1848), IV, 176–177.

94

THREE PETITIONS TO TSAR ALEKSEI MIKHAILOVICH FROM IAKUT NA-
TIVES PROTESTING INEQUITABLE AND RUINOUS IASAK IMPOSITIONS

[A petition from the Iakuts of Bordonsk volost.]

To the Sovereign Tsar and Grand Prince Aleksei Mikhailovich, Autocrat of all Great, Little and White Russia, we,
your orphans of the Bordonsk volost, the iasak-paying Iakuts Ke-
tyrei and Ochei, sons of Mygiev, submit this petition.

Sovereign, ever since 1652 we, your orphans, have had great
difficulty in paying iasak for you, Great Sovereign, and pominki
for the voevoda and the diak. We are assessed both for ourselves
and for our dead father. This added burdensome iasak obligation
for our dead father's past years' arrears has been imposed on us,
your orphans. But, Sovereign, our father was poor. There is no
livestock left. Our father lived on the lake and ate fish. When he
died he had a cow, but Iakuts stole that cow. Our father was assigned to pay your Great Sovereign's iasak of eighteen sable pelts
per year, but he could not pay all of that because he was so poor.
Now we, your orphans, have no way to pay this enormous extra
iasak for you, Great Sovereign, because, Sovereign, we, your orphans, do not have any livestock. All the livestock we had, Sovereign, we have already sold in order to pay your iasak, Great Sovereign. And now, Sovereign, we, your orphans are ruined, and
poor right down to the bone. Now, Sovereign, if you order that
this extra iasak be collected from us, your orphans, for you, Sovereign, for our father's past years' arrears, we, your orphans, will
certainly perish.

Merciful Sovereign Tsar and Grand Prince Aleksei Mikhailovich, Autocrat of all Great, Little and White Russia, have mercy
on us your orphans; Sovereign, do not order that your Great Sovereign's extra iasak for our father for the past years be collected
from us, lest we, your orphans, perish. Tsar, Sovereign, have
mercy, we beg you.*

---

*Reference: TsGADA, f. Iakutskoi prikaznoi izby, op. 4, stolb. No. 588,
l. 6.

The light and shadows of the Giliak bear festival intensify the clamor of the people, snarling dogs and the tormented bear. From Von Schrenck, *Reisen und Forschungen im Amur-Lande*, Vol. 3.

[A petition from the Iakuts of the Baturrusk volost.]

To the Sovereign Tsar and Grand Prince Aleksei Mikhailovich, Autocrat of all Great, Little and White Russia, your orphans, your iasak-paying Iakuts . . . [17 names follow] submit this petition.

Sovereign, for the past years, since 1642, we your orphans have had great difficulty in paying iasak and pominki to you, Great Sovereign, and pominki for the voevoda and diaks. We pay both current assessments and past arrears for ourselves and for our dead fathers and brothers. And your additional heavy iasak for years past is now also due for those who are dead, Great Sovereign. Great Sovereign, we your orphans cannot pay this enormous extra iasak for our dead fathers and brothers, and in the future, Sovereign, we your orphans will not be able to pay iasak and pominki to you and pominki to the voevoda and diaks because we do not have any livestock, Sovereign. Sovereign, we sold all the livestock we had to the Tungus in exchange for sables in order to pay your Sovereign's iasak. We sold one cow for two sables, and a mare for three or four, so that now, Sovereign, we, your orphans, are ruined, and impoverished right down to the bone.

Now, Sovereign, if you order your great additional iasak for our dead fathers and brothers for the past years to be collected from us your orphans for you, Great Sovereign, we will perish. Sovereign, how can we pay your Great Sovereign's iasak for ourselves and also for our dead fathers and brothers, especially since they have been dead for twenty years?

Merciful Sovereign Tsar and Grand Prince Aleksei Mikhailovich, Autocrat of all Great, Little and White Russia, have mercy on us, your orphans. Sovereign, do not order that his huge additional iasak for past years for our fathers and brothers be collected, lest we, your orphans, perish, and not be able to pay our current assessment of iasak and pominki, as well as pominki for the voevoda and diaks.

Sovereign Tsar, be merciful.*

[A petition from Iakuts of various volosts.]

To the Sovereign Tsar and Grand Prince Aleksei Mikhailovich, Autocrat of all Great, Little and White Russia, your orphans, iasak-paying natives from various volosts, submit this petition. . . . [Names of 36 petitioners from 11 volosts and other uluses follow.]

For the past years, Great Sovereign, they have been collecting iasak for your Great Sovereign's Treasury from us, your orphans and slaves, who do not hunt foxes. Instead of each fox pelt they have collected money from us, 20 altyns. But now, in this year of 1664, Great Sovereign, your Great Sovereign's stolnik and voevoda Ivan Fedorovich Bolshoi Golenishchev-Kutuzov wants to collect iasak from us, your slaves, who do not hunt [foxes], in the amount of one ruble for each fox pelt not presented. Great Sovereign, we your orphans will surely be ruined from this burdensome imposition, and then we will not be able to obtain any furs for iasak. We travel to faroff places now, in every direction, be-

---

*Reference: TsGADA, f. Iakutskoi prikaznoi izby, op. 4, stolb. No. 588, l. 8-8 ob.

cause all the animals have been killed or driven away, and it is only with great difficulty and great hardship that we can trap.

Merciful Sovereign Tsar and Grand Prince Aleksei Mikhailovich, Autocrat of all Great, Little and White Russia, have mercy on us your orphans, and decree, Great Sovereign, that your Sovereign's stolnik and voevoda Ivan Fedorovich Bolshoi Golenishchev-Kutuzov collect only as much iasak from us, your orphans and slaves, for your Great Sovereign's Treasury, as was collected in previous years, that is, 20 altyns in place of each fox pelt. Otherwise we your orphans and slaves will suffer ruin and eventual death as a result of the heavy impositions of iasak, and from the additional payments of money in place of fox pelts.

Sovereign Tsar, be merciful.*

---

*Reference: TsGADA, f. Iakutskaia prikaznaia izba, op. 4, stolb. No. 361, ch. 1, ll. 5–6.

See: *Materialy po istorii Iakutii XVII veka. (Dokumenty iasachnogo sbora)* (Moscow: 1970), III, 909–912; 951–953.

95

AFTER JULY 17, 1662

A REPORT TO TSAR ALEKSEI MIKHAILOVICH FROM THE VOEVODA OF
IAKUTSK, IVAN GOLENISHCHEV-KUTUZOV, CONCERNING THE NEED
FOR MORE SERVITORS IN IAKUTSK AND OKHOTSK OSTROGS FOR DE-
FENSE AGAINST NATIVES AND THE CHINESE

To the Sovereign Tsar and Grand Prince Aleksei Mikhailovich, Autocrat of all Great, Little and White Russia, your
humble servant Ivan Bolshoi Golenishchev-Kutuzov reports. On
June 7 of the present year, 1662, Sovereign, I your humble servant received a communication from Leontii Iurev, son of Kutuzov, on the Okhota River. On June 27, 1662, Leontii sent servitors out from Okhotsk ostrozhek; these were an interpreter named
Andrei, Bogdan Polomoshnov, Ivan Stepanov, Fedor Shtipnikov
and Aleksei Osipov. He sent them to Ostrovna, to the Kilarsk
tribe, to Zelemei and his tribesmen and to Guliugir, who have in
the past rebelled against you, Great Sovereign.

On the Ostrovna, Zelemei's only relative is a brother who
came down from the hills to hunt with the Ozians. These Ozians
attacked Andrei using bows and arrows, but Zelemei's brother
would not let them kill the cossacks because they were on their
way to Okhotsk ostrozhek with your iasak, Great Sovereign. He
guided Andrei and would not let him be killed. Andrei brought
back a hostage named Oekan, a member of the reindeer herding
Guliugir tribe, who had in the past been disloyal to you, Great
Sovereign.

The Ozians told Andrei and his men that in the fall of 1661
Bogdoi warriors had come to the Tugur River on nine vessels, and
there were 70 vessels anchored at the mouth of the Amur River in
the land of the Giliaks. They were collecting iasak from the Tu-
gurs and the Tungus, and they gave them many gifts such as silks
and calico and bows. The Bogdoi inquired about the Russians,
asking where they live, and they wanted the Tungus to guide
them. The Tungus said that they did not know anything about
your Great Sovereign's Russian people. They went aboard the
Bogdoi vessels and were asked about the Russians and about
where they live, but did not give any detailed information.

Great Sovereign, there are only 60 of your Great Sovereign's
servitors in Okhotsk ostrozhek; they are under the command of

Leontii Kutuzov. And in Iakutsk ostrog, according to the tax records, there are only 610 servitors. I, your humble servant, sent an additional 30 men under the piatidesiatnik cossack Vasilii Burlak to the Okhota River to Leontii to help in the defense against the Bogdoi. But, Great Sovereign, I, your humble servant, cannot send any more servitors than that to the Okhota River, and furthermore, Sovereign, when these Bogdoi discover the route via the Shilka River to the Tugur portage and onto the Olekma River, and then along the Olekma to the Lena and along the Lena to Iakutsk ostrog . . . [missing] I will personally inform you about this, Great Sovereign, to let you know what Iakutsk ostrog needs. In order to defend it against the Bogdoi people and to collect iasak for you, Great Sovereign, we need a thousand men at the very least. We must prevent the Bogdoi people from attacking Okhotsk ostrozhek with their many vessels and multitudes of men, Sire, and prevent them from killing your servitors and iasak-paying people.

Sire, we have a report from the ataman Artemii Petrilovskii in Iakutsk ostrog who was sent to the land of the Daurs on your service in the year 1651, Sire, with servitors and volunteers and promyshlenniks. Envoys were sent with him also, to go to the Bogdoi tsar; these were Terentii Chechigin, Frantsbekov's trusted man Dmitriev and a Tatar named Osip Ruslanov. Osip betrayed you, Great Sovereign, and in the year 1653 he left the mouth of the Shingal River and deserted to the Bogdoi people. According to Daur natives, Osip was given the status of nobility by the Bogdoi tsar. Great Sovereign, because of Osip Ruslanov's treason there were many problems.

Great Sovereign, in good weather it is possible to go by boat to Okhotsk ostrozhek. A koch can sail the distance in ten days. Because of this, Great Sovereign, it would be well to have a garrison of 1,000 men in Iakutsk ostrog so that, with God's mercy and your luck, Great Sovereign Tsar and Grand Prince Aleksei Mikhailovich, Autocrat of all Great, Little and White Russia, new lands will be discovered and their iasak will be of great profit to you, Great Sovereign.

Great Sovereign, in order to bring non-subject lands under your great Tsarist authority and to take hostages, it will be necessary for me, your humble servant, to build ostrozheks and zimov'es in those places, Sovereign, where hostages from those lands can be held to ensure the collection of iasak. Great Sover-

Bratsk ostrog, here sketched in its basic form in the Remezov manuscript, was described by Archpriest Avvakum (document 98), and later by Nikolai G. Spafarii (document 109) during his embassy to China. From Makovetskii, *Byt i iskusstvo russkogo naseleniia vostochnoi Sibiri*, Vol. 1.

eign Tsar and Grand Prince Aleksei Mikhailovich, Autocrat of all Great, Little and White Russia, I beg you, instruct me, your humble servant, about these matters.

See: *Dopolneniia k aktam istoricheskim* (St. Petersburg: 1848), IV, 122–123.

BETWEEN JULY 24 AND AUGUST 31, 1662

A REPORT TO TSAR ALEKSEI MIKHAILOVICH AND TO THE SIBIRSKII PRI-
KAZ FROM THE VOEVODA OF IAKUTSK, IVAN GOLENISHCHEV-KUTUZOV,
CONCERNING THE DISCOVERY OF COPPER ON THE OLENEK RIVER

To the Sovereign Tsar and Grand Prince Aleksei Mikhailovich, Autocrat of all Great, Little and White Russia, Ivan
Bolshoi Golenishchev-Kutuzov, your humble servant, reports.

On July 24 of the present year, 1662, Great Sovereign, the servitor Mikhail Shchavr returned from assignment on the Olenek
River. Mikhail had been sent to the Olenek River to collect your
tithe, Great Sovereign. Mikhail reported to me, your humble servant, that he learned from a promyshlennik named Timofei Usha-
rov, who has sent a sample of copper ore valued at 26 zolotniks 4
dengas, that there is a mountain of that ore along the river. The
ore is visible even in high water, and when the water is low, the
strata of ore can be seen.

I, your humble servant, am sending this ore to you in Moscow, Great Sovereign, for your information. I assigned six servitors to Mikhail and ordered him to go back to the Olenek River
post haste, traveling day and night; and, Great Sovereign, I instructed Mikhail to take with him the promyshlennik who gave
him this information and the sample of copper ore. I instructed
them to reach that mountain of ore this autumn, Great Sovereign,
and upon reaching it, to build a zimov'e. Then, Great Sovereign,
they are to smelt the copper ore and bring the copper back to the
zimov'e and keep it there under guard until you issue instructions, Great Sovereign. I also told Mikhail that if he was not able
to smelt the ore, to take three or four puds of the copper ore, depending on the situation, and transport it by sled.

Great Sovereign, there is also good iron ore in the Iakutsk region; however, Great Sovereign, there are no smelters for either
copper or iron ore. Great Sovereign, if you should issue an ukaz
to provide us with copper and iron ore smelters, you would receive great profit from this.

Reference: TsGADA, f. Iakutskaia prikaznaia izba, op. 1, stolb. No. 174,
ll. 121–122.
See: N. S. Orlova, ed. *Otkrytiia russkikh zemleprokhodtsev i poliarnykh morekhodov XVII veka na severo-vostoke Azii.* (Moscow: 1951), 452–453.

JUNE 3, 1663

INSTRUCTIONS FROM VOEVODA OF IAKUTSK, IVAN GOLENISHCHEV-KUTUZOV, TO PRISON TSELOVALNIK SEMEN BRUSENKIN AND FOMA KONDRATEV, ABOUT PROCEDURES FOR GUARDING PRISONERS

You are to be present in the prison compound, and exercise extreme caution and vigilance with the prisoners day and night, so they cannot tunnel out from prison and escape. When you go outside the prison grounds, out of kindness you may take prisoners with you who are there for minor offenses; however any prisoners who have committed serious offenses are not to be allowed out of the prison without permission from the voevoda and stolnik Ivan Fedorovich Bolshoi Golenishchev-Kutuzov. If they are let out, they are either to be in chains or to have their legs shackled. Guards are to walk behind them. No one is to be allowed to enter the prison secretly either day or night. If anyone brings a gift to the prison as a kindness, or if someone wants to bring food into the prison for one of the prisoners, then such persons are to appear before the tselovalnik and the guards when they enter the prison.

If any persons try to enter the prison secretly, without appearing before the tselovalnik and the guards, such persons are to be seized and brought to the Prikaz office. In accordance with this instruction, prisoners are to be guarded very cautiously and with great vigilance. If anyone escapes from prison because of your inattention and lack of vigilance, you tselovalniks and guards will be severely punished by order of the Great Sovereign, and may be put to death.

You are also to be very careful that no prisoner sends any written message out of prison. No letters, ink or paper are to be brought into the prison. You tselovalniks are to keep paper and ink in your quarters. If anyone wishes to write a petition, then it is to be written in your presence. No petition is to be written unless you are present. If any unauthorized communications come out of prison, or if ink and paper are found inside the prison, then you will be severely punished by order of the Great Sovereign.

See: Ia. P. Alkor and B. D. Grekov, eds. *Kolonialnaia politika moskovskogo gosudarstva v Iakutii v XVII v.* (Leningrad: 1936), 65–66.

1664

EXCERPTS FROM ARCHPRIEST AVVAKUM'S ACCOUNT OF HIS EXILE IN
SIBERIA AND OF THE PERSECUTIONS HE ENDURED, AND HIS FORMAL
COMPLAINT AGAINST THE BRUTALITY OF THE VOEVODA OF THE DAUR
TERRITORY, AFANASII PASHKOV

I was exiled to Siberia with my wife and children. The journey was full of misery, but of all the things I could relate, I will tell only a small part here.

My wife gave birth to a child, and while she was still recovering we took her by cart [from Moscow] to Tobolsk. It took us thirteen weeks to make the journey of 3,000 versts. We made half of the journey by cart and by water, and the other half by sleigh.

The Archbishop assigned me to a church in Tobolsk. In that church I was besieged by bad luck. In a year and a half I was five times accused of conspiracy against the Tsar, and a certain diak from the Archbishop's court, Ivan Struna, shook me to my very soul. The Archbishop had left to go to Moscow, and while he was away Ivan, possessed by the devil, assaulted me and unjustly tried to torment my deacon, Antonii. Antonii eluded him and ran to me in the church.

Ivan Struna gathered some people together and later that day he came into the church while I was singing vespers. He rushed into the church and grabbed Antonii by his beard as he stood in the choir stalls. I immediately closed the church doors and locked them and would not let anyone else in. Struna whirled about the church like one possessed. I stopped singing vespers and sat him down on the floor in the middle of the church and strapped him for causing a disturbance in church. The others, some twenty, all fled, persecuted by the Holy Spirit. I extracted Struna's repentance before I would let him come to me. Then Struna's relatives and the priests and monks all roused the townspeople to kill me. At midnight they brought sleds to my house, broke into the place and tried to seize me to take me off to drown me. But they were stricken with the fear of God and finally ran off.

For about a month I was tormented and would try to secretely elude them. Sometimes I would spend the night in the church, and other times I would go to the voevoda [Prince Vasilii Ivanovich Khilkov] and ask to be put in the prison but they would not let me in. On many occasions I was accompanied by Matvei Lomkov, whose monastic name is Mitrofan, who later became steward to Metropolitan Pavel in Moscow. He and the deacon, Afanasii, tonsured me in the cathedral. At that time he was a good man, but now the devil has possessed him. Then the Archbishop returned from Moscow and rightly put Struna in chains because Struna had accepted a bribe from a man who had committed incest with his daughter. Struna had not punished the man, and had let him go. The prelate ordered that Struna be put in chains and at the same time he made note of my situation. But Struna went to the voevodas in their office and spoke out "the word and deed of the Sovereign" against me.

The voevodas turned him over to the well known syn boiarskii Petr Beketov to be under guard. Alas, disaster befell the house of Petr! My soul still grieves. The Archbishop consulted me and then in accordance with the laws regarding incest he condemned Struna on *Nedelia Pravoslavia* [first Sunday of Great Lent]. Petr Beketov came to the church and began to swear at the Archbishop and me. Then as he left the church he suddenly went mad on his way home, and he died a wretched death. The Archbishop and I ordered that his body be thrown to the dogs in the street so the citizens could grieve over his sin. For three days we ourselves prayed devoutly that even Beketov would be forgiven on the Day of Judgment. He brought this demise on himself because he took pity on Struna. After three days the Archbishop and I buried his remains with dignity. Well, enough of this sorry affair.

Then [1655] an ukaz came [from Moscow] ordering that I be transferred from Tobolsk to the Lena River because of my condemnation of Nikon and my charge that he was a heretic * . . . [omitted]

So once again I climbed into a boat and set off toward the Lena. When I reached Eniseisk there was another ukaz awaiting me ordering me to go to the Daur land, over 20,000 or more versts from Moscow [actually 5,500 versts]. They assigned me to the regiment of Afanasii Pashkov who had some 600 men under

---

*Nikon was Patriarch of Moscow from 1652 to 1666. In that capacity he introduced a series of far-reaching church reforms which caused a great schism among the believers. Avvakum was one of the strongest critics of Nikon's reforms, for which reason he was exiled to Siberia and ultimately burned at the stake.—Eds.

him. Because of my sins [I came under] this harsh man. He constantly burned, tortured and beat his men; I had many times tried to persuade him to stop this, and then I myself fell into his hands. Orders came from Nikon in Moscow to torture me.

We left Eniseisk, and on the great Tunguska River a storm completely swamped my barge. The barge was in the middle of the river, and full of water, the sail was torn, and only the steering platform was above water, everything else was under water. My wife somehow managed to drag the children out of the water up on the deck. I looked up to Heaven and cried out, "Lord, save us! Lord, help us!" It was God's will that we reach the shore. I could go on at great length about this. Two men on another barge were swept off and drowned. We made the necessary repairs on the river bank and then set out again.

When we reached Shaman Rapids people came out to meet us, and among them were two widows, one about sixty and the other one older. Both were on their way to a convent. Pashkov tried to stop them because he wanted to give them in marriage. I told him, "It is against canon law to give such women in marriage." But instead of listening to me and letting the widows alone, he became angry and began to devise ways to torment me. On another rapids called Long Rapids he tried to knock me off the barge. "It's your fault the barge is badly handled! You heretic! Go off into the mountains, don't come along with cossacks!" Oh, but I was miserable! The mountains there were high and the ravines impassable. There was a rock crag like a wall. You would break your neck if you tried to see the top of it! The mountains were full of huge snakes, and there were geese, ducks with red feathers, black crows, grey jackdaws, hawks and falcons and gerfalcons and pelicans and swans and other wild birds. Many beasts roam through these mountains such as goats, deer, elk, boar, wolf, and wild sheep. They were easy to see but impossible to catch! And Pashkov wanted me to wander in these mountains, with the wild beasts and the snakes and the birds.

I wrote him a brief letter which began, "My good man, fear God, sitting amidst the Cherubim and regarding the universe. Before Him all the heavenly powers tremble and all living creatures, including man. You alone disdain Him and reveal discontent, etc. etc." I wrote a great deal and sent it to him. Then some fifty men rushed up and grabbed my barge and dragged it off about three versts to him. I made kasha and gave it to the cossacks. The poor creatures, they ate and shivered, and others who were looking on cried and felt pity for me. The barge was brought up, and the hangmen took me before him.

He stood with his sword and quivered with rage. Then he began to speak to me. "Are you, or are you not, a priest?" I replied, "I am Avvakum the Archpriest. Tell me what your business is with me." He roared like a wild beast and struck me first on one cheek and then on the other and then on my head. Then he knocked me off my feet and hit me three times on the back with a hammer. and knouted me 72 times on my naked back. I kept saying, "Lord Jesus Christ, Son of God, help me!" I repeated this over and over. He was very annoyed that I did not cry out for mercy. At each blow I said a prayer, but finally in the middle of the flogging I shouted at him, "You have beaten me enough!" He ordered them to stop and I asked him, "Why are you beating me? Do you know?" Then he ordered them to beat me again on my sides. Then they let me go. I was trembling all over and I fell down. He ordered them to drag me back to the government barge. They shackled my hands and feet and threw me on the deck.

It was autumn, the rain was falling on me, and all night I lay under the drip. When they were beating me it had not been so painful because I was praying, but lying there I began to wonder, "Son of God, why did You let him beat me so fiercely? I was defending your widows! Who will pass judgment between myself and You? When I stole, You never inflicted such outrages on me. And now I don't even know what sin I have committed." . . . [omitted]

In the morning they threw me into a small boat and we continued on our way. Later we came to the greatest rapids of all, Padun Rapids, where the river is about one verst wide, with three reefs stretching across. If you miss the passage between them, you will be shattered to pieces! They brought me up to the rapids. Both rain and snow were falling on me, so they put a plain little kaftan over my shoulders. Water dripped over my belly and my back and I felt wretched. They took me out of the boat and dragged me, fettered, over the rocks near the rapids. It was quite wretched for my body but good for my soul. I didn't complain to God . . . [omitted].

Then they took me to Bratsk ostrog where they threw me into prison and gave me some straw. I was there in the freezing tower until the fast-day of St. Philip. It is still winter there at that time, but God kept me warm even without clothing. I lay on the straw like some poor mongrel. Sometimes they gave me food, sometimes not. They were many mice and I would hit them with my cap because the fools would not give me a stick! And all this time I was lying on my belly because my back was putrefying. There were many fleas and lice. I wanted to shout out to Pashkov, "Forgive me!" But God's strength forbade this. He willed me to suffer.

Then Pashkov moved me into a warm hut where I remained through the winter, shackled, with native hostages and dogs. My wife and children were exiled to a place some twenty versts away. Her woman servant, Xenia, kept after her all winter long with complaints and whining. My son Ivan, still a boy, came to visit me after Christmas, and Pashkov ordered that he be thrown in the freezing prison where I was, and the poor little fellow almost froze to death. In the morning he was ordered back to his mother, and I never saw him again. He went back to his mother with frostbitten hands and feet.

In the spring we moved on. We had few provisions left, because everything had been ransacked. Someone had stolen the books and clothing, but there were other things left.

I nearly drowned in Lake Baikal. I was ordered to pull a tow-rope on the Khilok River. It was bitterly hard work, and there was nothing to eat, no time to sleep. I suffered all summer. People died from working so hard in the water. My legs and stomach turned blue. For two summers we made our way through the waters, and in the winters we crossed over portages.

It was on the Khilok that I almost drowned for the third time. The current pulled me and my barge out into the water. People who were standing on shore tried to grab us and drag us back. My wife and children were still on the bank, and only the helmsman and I were on the barge. The water was fast, and it turned the barge upside down. I crawled up on it and cried, "Blessed Virgin, help us! Our Hope, don't let us drown!" Sometimes my legs were in the water, and at other times I crawled on top. The barge was carried off for a verst or more, and then the people managed to catch it. Everything was shattered to bits! But how can one complain, when Christ and the Immaculate Virgin have ordained it? When I came out of the water I was laughing, but the people were aghast. My clothes were draped over the bushes, satin and taffeta coats and some other trifles, of which plenty were still left in the trunks and bags. Everything fell to pieces there, and we had nothing to wear.

Pashkov wanted to beat me again, and said, "You are making a fool of yourself!" I again pleaded with the Holy Mother of God, "Queen of Heaven, save me from this idiot!" And She, Our Hope, answered my prayer, and he began to feel compassion for me.

Then we moved on to Lake Irgen. There is a portage there and during the winter we portaged our belongings over it. Pashkov took my workmen away and would not let me hire others. The children were little, and there were many mouths to feed, but no one to do the work. This one poor miserable Archpriest built a sledge and hauled things over the portage all winter long.

In the spring we went down the Ingoda River. It was my fourth year of travel since leaving Tobolsk. They were cutting lumber there for dwellings and for the town. Food was scarce and people died of hunger and from constantly working in the water. The river was shallow, the rafts heavy, the guards merciless, the sticks big, the cudgels gnarled, the knouts cruel, and the suffering was terrible. Fire and the rack! People were starving and as soon as anyone began to torture them they died. Oh, what a time! I do not know what caused Pashkov to behave so irrationally. My wife had one gown left from Moscow which had not yet rotted away. It had originally cost about 25 Russian rubles, but it was worth much more here. He gave us four sacks of rye for it, and we managed, with this and with eating grass, to live along the Nercha River for another year.

Everyone was dying of starvation but he would not let anyone hunt, and he allocated a very small amount of space to them. They roamed over the steppe and the fields to gather grass and roots, and we went with them, and in the winter, pine. Sometimes God would give us a dead mare, and sometimes we would find the bones of a wild beast which had been killed by a wolf. Any bit the wolves had not devoured, we did. Some people ate wolves and foxes that had frozen to death, and any kind of offal. A mare foaled, and the starving people secretly ate both the foal and the placenta. When Pashkov learned of this he had them beaten to death with the knout. Then another mare died because people were so desperate they pulled the foal from her body. The moment they saw the head appear they pulled it out and even ate the blood that issued forth. Oh, what a time!

Two of my small sons died during these sufferings. With the others, naked and barefoot I roamed over the hills and the sharp rocks, living on grass and roots. And what I did not endure! Even I, like it or not, shared in the devouring of the mare and the dead animals and birds. . . . [omitted]

We were helped in Christ by the boiarina Evdokiia Kirilovna, the daughter-in-law of the voevoda, and by the wife of Afanasii [Pashkov], Fedla Semenovna. They saved us from starvation by secretly giving us food without his knowledge. Sometimes they would send us a piece of meat, sometimes a loaf of bread, sometimes flour and oats, however much they could, a quarter of a pud or a grivenka, or sometimes they would manage to gather half a pud. They would give that to us, and sometimes they would scrape up feed from the cattle's trough. Agrofena, my poor little daughter, would sneak over to her window. Alas, what a sad thing! Sometimes they would chase the youngster away from the window without the boiarina knowing, but other times she would bring back large amounts of food. She was very tiny then, but now she is 27 and still unmarried, my poor child. She lives with her younger sisters on the Mezena River, mourning. Her mother and brothers are buried. . . . [omitted]

We suffered great privation in the Daur land for six or seven years, but there were some good times in these years, too. But Afanasii kept slandering me and was forever seeking my death. During that time of privation he sent me two widows who had been his concubines, Maria and Sofia, who were tormented by the evil spirit. . . . The devil tortured them so cruelly that they were fighting and screaming. Pashkov summoned me and bowed to me and said, "Please, take them and care for them and pray to God. God listens to you." I replied, "Sire, your request is greater than my powers, but in response to the prayers of our Holy Fathers, God makes everything possible." So I took them in, poor souls. . . . They also brought me women who were possessed. As customary, I fasted, and did not give them anything to eat. I prayed and anointed them with oil and did everything I knew how to do. The women became aware of Christ's presence and recovered their sanity. I heard their confessions and gave them Communion. They lived with me and prayed to God. They loved me and would not go home. Pashkov learned that they had become my spiritual daughters and became angry with me again and wanted to burn me. "You have been worming out my secrets!" he said. But how can one give Communion without first hearing confession? And without Communion, it is impossible to exorcise the devil. . . .

Pashkov took the poor widows away from me and cursed me rather than thank me. He assumed, "Christ will resolve this simply," but they went mad again and were worse than before. He locked them in an empty hut and no one was allowed to go near them. He sent for a monk but they threw sticks at him so he went away. I was at home weeping and did not know what to do. I did not dare approach his household and I was sick at heart. I secretly sent them holy water and told them to wash themselves and to drink, and the poor creatures became better. They came to me secretly, and I anointed them with oil in the name of Christ, and as before, God gave them their sanity and they again went home, but at night they came to me secretly to pray to God. . . .

Then from the Nercha River we returned to [European] Russia. For five weeks we traveled over the ice in sleds. Pashkov gave us two small ponies for our children and our belongings, so my wife and I had to go on foot, stumbling on the ice. The country was barbarous and the natives were hostile. We did not dare to become separated from the horses, but neither could we keep up with them because we were so hungry and tired. My poor wife would drag along and then collapse. One time when she fell another weary soul fell on top of her. They both cried out and could not get up. The man exclaimed, "Forgive me, Lady, Matiushka*!" And she cried, "Are you trying to crush me?" Then I came, and the poor soul began to complain to me, asking, "Archpriest, how long are these sufferings going to continue?" I replied, "Markovna, until our very death." So with a sigh she said, "Very well, Petrovich, let us be on our way then." . . .

Soon after that Pashkov wanted to torture me again. Listen to the reason. He had sent his son Eremei off into the Mongol Empire to fight. He had sent 72 cossacks and 20 natives with him, and he made a native shaman foretell whether or not they would return home victorious. The sorcerer was close to my zimov'e. In the evening he brought a live ram and began to work his magic by twisting it way around, and then he twisted its head off and threw

---

*Literally, "little mother"; affectionate term used to refer to the wife of the priest.—Eds.

364

it aside. He began to leap and to dance and to call up the evil spirits; then, shrieking loudly, he fell down on the ground and foamed at the mouth. Devils weighed heavy on him and he asked, "Will the expedition be successful?" The evil spirits replied, "You will return with a great victory and with enormous wealth." The voevodas were pleased, and all the people rejoiced, saying, "We will come back rich." . . .

Then Pashkov sent his son off with the army. They marched at night by the light of the stars. I was very sorry for them, for my spirit foresaw that they would be killed, and I prayed for them for their death. Some of them came to bid me farewell and I told them, "You will perish there." As they galloped off their horses neighed in unison, the cows lowed, the sheep and goats bleated, the dogs barked, and even the natives howled like dogs. All were struck with dread. Eremei, with tears in his eyes, sent me a message asking that I, his spiritual father, pray for him. I felt very sorry for him. He had been my friend in secret, and he had suffered for me. When his father had beaten me with the knout he had tried to intervene on my behalf and his father had gone after him with a sword. . . .

Then Pashkov's replacement came and I received a gramota. We were both ordered to travel to Russia. He left but did not take me with him. He thought, "If he travels alone perhaps the natives will kill him." He set out on a boat with weapons and with men, but I heard from the natives as I traveled that they were trembling and fearful. A month after he left I gathered together the old and the sick and the wounded. Those who were no longer useful, some ten persons, and my wife and children and I, seventeen of us in all, placed our trust in Christ and set off in a boat. We set up a cross on the prow and sailed as God directed, fearing nothing. I gave the *Kormchaia Kniga* [the *Nomocanon*, a Collection of Church Laws, but literally *Pilot Book*] to the prikashchik, and he in turn assigned a pilot to me. I also ransomed back my friend Vasilii who during Pashkov's tenure had spread malicious lies about people and had shed blood and had also sought my head. When he beat me he wanted to impale me, but God saved me! After Pashkov left the cossacks wanted to beat him to death. But pleading with them for Christ's sake, I ransomed him from the official and took him to Russia and saved him from death. . . .

After we left the Daur land our food was scarce. We all prayed to God, and Christ gave us a stag, a huge beast, which provided us with food until we reached Lake Baikal. Near the lake we came across a sable-hunting camp where some Russians were fishing. These good folk were glad to see us, and Terentii and his comrades took us from our boat and led us from the lake up onto the bank. These kind people wept to see us, and vice versa. They gave us as much food as we could use, bringing about forty fresh sturgeon to me and saying, "Here, Father, God sent them into our nets for you. Take them all!" I thanked them and blessed the fish and then told them to take them back, saying, "What will I do with so many?" We stayed with them and they gave me all the provisions we needed. After we had repaired our boat, we unfurled the sail and set out across the lake. . . .

I spent the winter in Eniseisk, and after a summer of sailing, I spent the next winter in Tobolsk. On my way to Moscow I preached the word of God and taught in all the towns and village and in the churches and at the trade fairs, and I exposed Godless flattery. Thus I reached Moscow. I had journeyed for three years from the Daur land, and it had taken me five years to get there, sailing against the current, to travel east through all the hordes and settlements. I could say a great deal about that! And I had fallen into the hands of the natives. On the great Ob River they killed twenty Christians right in front of me and they wanted to kill me, too, but for some reason they let me go. Then again, on the Irtysh River, a group of natives was waiting to ambush our men from Berezovo and kill them in their boats. I did not realize this and went right up to them on the bank. They surrounded us, armed with bows. I went up and embraced them as if they were monks and said, "Christ is with me and also with you." They treated me kindly and brought their wives to meet my wife. My wife used flattery to deal with them. Their women were kind, and we know that when women are good, everything under Christ is well. The men put away their bows and arrows and began to trade with me. I bartered with them for some bear meat and they let me go. When I reached Tobolsk I told my story, but people would not believe it, because at that time the Bashkirs were fighting with the Tatars all through Siberia. . . .

[The formal complaint against the brutality of the voevoda of the Daur land, Afanasii Pashkov, which Avvakum submitted to Tsar Aleksei Mikhailovich upon his return from exile, 1664.]

In 1661 Afanasii Pashkov sent out two natives named Danilo and Vasilii from the Daur Nikan land, and these men went out in the name of the Sovereign into the Daur lands into a regiment of cossacks. Two other interpreters, a Ducher named Ivan Timofeev and a Tungus named Ilia, lived among the Daur cossacks for many years. With the assistance of the interpreters Ivan and Ilia and the cossacks collected tribute for the Sovereign's treasury for many years.

After the defeat of the Bogdoi armies the rest of the cossacks came to Afanasii Pashkov on Lake Irgen. These four men, Danilo, Vasilii, Ivan and Ilia, came with the cossacks to serve the Great Sovereign. But the voevoda Afanasii forcefully took them from the cossacks for his own use in his quarters, and right up to the very present day they weep and live and suffer there and cannot help themselves. They petition the Great Sovereign to free them from slavery and ask that they be assigned to the rank of the Sovereign's servitors. This same Afanasii took three hostages named Gavriil, Aleksei and Andrei from the ostrozhek under the command of Larion Tolbuzin. He also took nineteen prisoners from the cossacks: Bakulai and his two daughters whose names I do not recall, Maria, Anna, two women named Evdokiia, four named Marina, two named Paraskeviia, three more named Evdokiia, three named Anna, and Efrosiniia and her brother Ivan. All of these people lived with him.

Without the hostages this land has become a wasteland. Government servitors have nothing to do. Even the government Treasury has no function. This same Afanasii forced two servitors, Oleg Bratskov and Iurii Ivanov, to go to his own quarters. None of these people has anyone to turn to for aid but the Sovereign.

When Afanasii was living in the Daur land, he would not send any of the government servitors out to hunt so these poor people would have something to eat. As a result more than 500 people starved to death. Some refused to endure starvation and went out to hunt for food. Afanasii tortured these people, beat them with the knout and broke their ribs and burned them. When because of the famine Ivan Svatenysh and Klim Shamandrukhin and their comrades, eight men in all, ate one of the cossack horses, he tortured them in prison and killed them. Iakov Krasnoiarskii observed, "If only the voevoda would follow the Sovereign's ukaz properly, we would never suffer such privations." For that, Afanasii beat Iakov with the knout and burned him to death. He threw Iakov's body under the window of my zimov'e saying that while Iakov was being tortured he had prayed to Jesus.

Afanasii Pashkov also knouted two other men, Galakhtion and Mikhail, just because one of them had begged him for food and the other had said, "Death would be better than this existence!" For that he knouted them and sent them naked to the river to be eaten up by flies. Then after he had left them there for a day he had them brought back. Mikhail died after that, and Pashkov ordered Matvei Zarian to cane Galakhtion in the empty bathhouse. Prior to that he also knouted Galakhtion, Stefan Podkholiug and Kharpeg and many others who were so starved that they ate unclean horse guts and snatched up the snow into which the horse's blood had spilled and ate that too, because they were so desperately hungry.

He knouted the Berezovo cossack Akisha because he had split three of Afanasii's fish improperly, through lack of skill. Such was Afanasii's kindness toward the Sovereign's servitors. He gave the cossacks only the hides and legs and heads of game to eat, saving the meat for his own household. And he hanged two other men, although they had committed no offense.

A year would not be long enough for me to tell about his other abuses and tortures which he inflicted on the Sovereign's servitors. It is strange and terrible for me to relate some of Afanasii's other crimes. He would not let me give dying men Communion, and he took the Communion bread away from me and kept it in a box in his room. Then when the piatidesiatnik Ivan Eliseev and his fellow servitors came from Eniseisk to Nerchinsk ostrog with the Sovereign's gramota announcing that God had given the Sovereign a daughter, the Tsarevna and Grand Princess Sofiia Alekseevna, Afanasii, in order to make sure that no one in Russia would learn about his misdeeds, would not let these men return. He killed two of them on their boat, the prikashchik Ivan and the interpreter Konstantin.

See: Protopop Avvakum, *Zhitie Protopopa Avvakuma im samim napisanoe i drugie ego sochineniia* (Moscow: 1960), 67–88 [excerpts].

1664

A STATEMENT FROM TSAR ALEKSEI MIKHAILOVICH RECOGNIZING LOZAN, SON OF ALTYN-TSAR, AS THE NEW MONGOL RULER, AND AC-CEPTING HIS SUBMISSION TO THE RUSSIAN EMPIRE

Lozan, son of the Mongol tsar Altyn, has sent his envoys Achik Baksha and Tuma and their entourage to the Great Sovereign Tsar and Grand Prince Aleksei Mikhailovich, Autocrat of all Great, Little and White Russia, to petition the Great Sovereign Tsar and Grand Prince Aleksei Mikhailovich, Autocrat of all Great, Little and White Russia, to keep Lozan in his gracious favor under his mighty Tsarist hand in eternal servitude, and that the Great Sovereign decree that in his gramotas Lozan may be referred to as a subject tsar, since Lozan has succeeded his father Altyn tsar as tsar of the Mongol lands.

The Great Sovereign Tsar and Grand Prince Aleksei Mikhailovich, Autocrat of all Great, Little and White Russia, in accordance with his Tsarist favorable disposition, has granted Lozan his request, because of his father, Altyn-tsar's service, and because of his own submission. He has graciously consented to look favorably on him and to refer to him as the Mongol tsar in his own gramotas, and the Great Sovereign will allow Lozan to remain in the Tsarist Majesty's favor and grace.

See: *Polnoe sobranie zakonov rossiiskoi imperii*, Series I, 603–604.

FEBRUARY 17, 1665

A GRAMOTA FROM TSAR ALEKSEI MIKHAILOVICH TO THE VOEVODAS
OF TOMSK, IVAN VASILEVICH BUTURLIN AND PROKOPII POVODOV,
CONCERNING PERMISSION FOR A NEWLY BAPTIZED KALMYK TO ENLIST
INTO COSSACK SERVICE

From the Tsar and Grand Prince Aleksei Mikhailovich, Autocrat of all Great, Little and White Russia, to Siberia, to Tomsk, to our voevodas Ivan Vasilevich Buturlin and Prokopii Prokopevich Povodov. In this present year, 1665, a newly baptized Kalmyk named Ivan Vasilev has petitioned us, the Great Sovereign. He states that Nikifor Nashchokin brought him, Ivan, from Tomsk to Moscow and baptized him into the Holy Orthodox Christian faith. Ivan's relatives are murzas of the Chat tribe and serve in Tomsk, and his brother, Timek and Malot, are serving as mounted cossacks. Ivan requests that we, the Great Sovereign, allow him to serve as a mounted cossack in our Sovereign service in Tomsk, to replace Ivan Shchitov, who is to be taken to the Posolskii Prikaz in Moscow to serve as an interpreter.

When you receive this gramota from us, the Great Sovereign, you are to enlist the Kalmyk, Ivan Vasilev, into our Sovereign service in Tomsk as a mounted cossack, to replace Ivan Shchitov, at his rate of pay. No one else in Tomsk is to be chosen to fill Ivan [Shchitov's] place. Ivan [Vasilev] is to take the oath in Tomsk and he is to put his mark on a statement that he will serve us, the Great Sovereign and that he will never commit treason. He is not to leave Tomsk to go to any heathen land, nor is he to act in concert with traitors in such a manner as to injure or kill any of our Sovereign's loyal subject, of any rank. Ivan's uncles and brothers who serve in Tomsk are to be instructed to watch over Ivan carefully and supervise him to make certain that he will not commit treason or leave to go anywhere without notice.

If Ivan's guarantors uncover any treason or violation of his oath, they are to inform on Ivan. They will then receive a reward from us, the Great Sovereign and Ivan will be put to death. But if they learn of any plotted treason and do not report it, and then Ivan commits that treason and disappears without a trace, and subsequent investigation reveals that they knew of his plotted

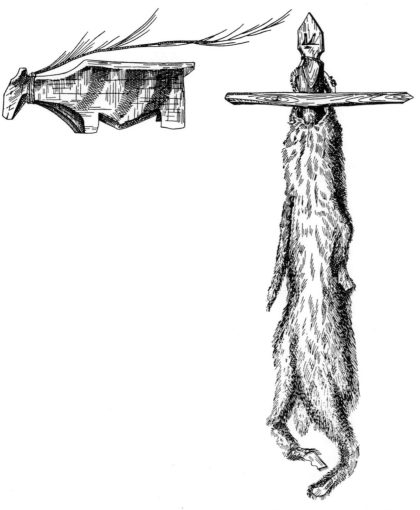

Wooden carvings and family totems abound in the records of all the tribes associated with the Siberian forest. From Shunkov, ed., *Istoriia Sibiri*, Vol. 2.

treachery and did not report it, then we, the Great Sovereign, will sentence them also to death.

See: I. P. Kuznetsov-Krasnoiarskii, ed., *Istoricheskie akty XVII stoletiia (1633– 1699)* (Tomsk: 1890), I, 22–23.

101

NOT AFTER JULY 21, 1665

A PETITION TO TSAR ALEKSEI MIKHAILOVICH FROM THE SYN BOIARS-KII VTOROI KATAEV REQUESTING COMPENSATION FOR HIS SERVICE ON THE KOLYMA RIVER

A petition to the Sovereign Tsar and Grand Prince Aleksei Mikhailovich from your humble servant in Iakutsk ostrog, syn boiarskii Vtoroi Kataev.

Great Sovereign, in the year 1660 I, your humble servant, was sent from Iakutsk ostrog to go on your service, Great Sovereign, to the Kolyma River by the sea. I was sent by your stolnik and voevoda Ivan Fedorovich Bolshoi Golenishchev-Kutuzov, Great Sovereign, to replace the syn boiarskii Ivan Iarastov, to collect your iasak, Great Sovereign, and to search for new non-iasak-paying people.

When I, your humble servant, was carrying our your assignment on the Kolyma River, Great Sovereign, I collected your iasak, Great Sovereign, for the years 1662 and 1663. I also collected iasak for previous years, Great Sovereign, with profit. Further, I, your humble servant, explored the lands of new non-iasak-paying Lamut people in company with the servitors and promyshlenniks headed by Ivan Ermolin and his comrades. We found these Lamut people in the upper reaches of the Kolyma River. By the grace of God and with the luck of the Great Sovereign, the servitors Ivan Ermolin and his men, having discovered these Lamut people, took hostages from them after a battle. The two hostages were named Nirkan and Nirich. Great Sovereign, we used these hostages to assure your Great Sovereign's iasak collection, and in the year 1663 we collected 11 sables; 22 in 1664; and 36 in this present year of 1665. Great Sovereign, these hostages have agreed to pay great amounts of iasak to you in the future, and they wish to come under your Tsarist mighty hand and to be slaves for all time, Great Sovereign, and to pay iasak for their Lamut relatives who have moved away.

In the future, Great Sovereign, these Lamut people, their tribesmen and members of other tribes all wish to come under your protection and pay iasak every year.

I, your humble servant, spent five years in this service, Great

Siberian natives: representations of Iakut, Kalmyk, Ostiak and Tangut tribes. Though hardy, these groups were subdued eventually. From Shunkov, *Istoriia Sibiri*, Vol. 2.

Sovereign, and I suffered deprivation and poverty and cold and hunger.

Merciful Sovereign Tsar and Grand Prince Aleksei Mikhailovich, . . . [missing] reward me, your humble servant, for my service to you, and for the suffering, hunger and cold which I have endured in your service, Great Sovereign. Merciful God will bless you, Great Sovereign.

Tsar, Sovereign, have mercy, reward me.

Reference: TsGADA, f. Sibirskii prikaz, stolb. No. 361, ch. II, ll. 324–325.
See: N. S. Orlova, ed. *Otkrytiia russkikh zemleprokhodtsev i poliarnykh morekhodov XVII veka na severo-vostoke Azii* (Moscow: 1951), 339–340.

102

JULY 21, 1665

INSTRUCTIONS FROM THE VOEVODA OF IAKUTSK, IVAN GOLENISH-
CHEV-KUTUZOV, TO THE SYN BOIARSKII KUZMA LOSHAKOV, CON-
CERNING HIS ASSIGNMENT TO REPLACE ANDREI BULYGIN AT THE
ZASHIVERSK OSTROG AND TO INVESTIGATE HIS MISCONDUCT AND
ABUSES THERE

On July 21, 1665, in accordance with the ukaz of the Great Sovereign Tsar and Grand Prince Aleksei Mikhailovich, and the Sovereign Lord Tsarevich and Grand Prince Aleksei Alekseevich, and the Sovereign Lord Tsarevich and Grand Prince Fedor Alekseevich, and upon the instructions of the stolnik and voevoda Ivan Bolshoi Golenishchev-Kutuzov, the syn boiarskii Kuzma Loshakov of Iakutsk ostrog is given the following orders.

He is to proceed on the service of the Great Sovereigns to the Indigirka River because in this year of 1665 the Great Sovereign Tsar and Grand Prince Aleksei Mikhailovich and the Sovereign Lord Tsarevich and Grand Prince Aleksei Alekseevich and the Sovereign Lord Tsarevich and Grand Prince Fedor Alekseevich have received a written petition against the syn boiarskii Andrei Bulygin signed by Nikita Vorypaev and 24 merchants and promyshlenniks. The petition was sent from the Indigirka River to Iakutsk ostrog with the cossack sotnik Amos Mikhailov. The petition states that in the years 1664 and 1665 Andrei drove off these merchants and promyshlenniks and wronged them in every possible way. He forced them to accept useless goods in trade, killed them with his own hands, beat them mercilessly with canes to gain his own unearned profit, forced them to become his slaves, distilled spirits and beer, and sold spirits by the cup and beer by the pail. The Indigirka Iukagirs reported to the merchants and promyshlenniks that Andrei has committed abuses against them as well. He has forced them to accept useless goods in trade and has stolen every single head of livestock and reindeer from the Iukagirs so that they can no longer hunt to procure iasak, and they can no longer survive. The petition asks that the Great Sovereigns grant the request of the merchants and promyshlenniks and natives and order that all of Andrei's impositions and abuses and forced trading of valueless articles on the Indigirka River be investigated on behalf of the merchants, promyshlenniks and the iasak-paying Iukagirs.

Consequently, in accordance with the ukaz of the Great Sovereign Tsar Aleksei Mikhailovich and the Sovereign Lord Tsarevich and Grand Prince Aleksei Alekseevich and the Sovereign Lord Tsarevich and Grand Prince Fedor Alekseevich, when you reach the Indigirka River you are to find and bring in the servitors and merchants and promyshlenniks to give sworn testimony on the Holy Immaculate Gospel of the Lord. The iasak Iukagirs are to swear in accordance with their faith. Did Andrei Bulygin, while he was on the Indigirka River, drive away merchants, promyshlenniks and the iasak Iukagirs? Did he abuse them in various ways? Did he force them to accept useless goods for barter? Did he personally beat them? Did he kill anyone, and if so, whom? Did he knout them mercilessly for his own profit? Did he force any of them into slavery? Did he distill spirits? Did he brew beer? Did he sell spirits by the cup and beer by the pail? Did he forcefully confiscate reindeer from the iasak Iukagirs?

You are to take down the statements of everyone who testifies during this investigation. You are to write down their testimony in the official reports in detail, and take down their names. The Russians who know how to read and write are to sign their names personally, and those who are illiterate are to have their names written by witnesses. The iasak Iukagirs are to have their names written by witnesses. The iasak Iukagirs are to append their tribal marks. The report with the signatures and witnesses and native tribal marks and your own signature is to be sent to Iakutsk ostrog with any available courier, and you are to order that this report and the results of the investigation be sent to the Prikaz office to the stolnik and voevoda Ivan Fedorovich Bolshoi Golenishchev-Kutuzov.

You, Kuzma, are also to interrogate the Iansk and Khromovsk Iukagirs who rebelled against the Great Sovereign on the Iana River in 1663, and who in this present year of 1665 came to the Indigirka and confessed their guilt to the Great Sovereign and brought in their iasak and paid it to Timiuk and his men. Ascertain how much iasak they brought for their own obligation and for their relatives' assessments for the Great Sovereign for the year 1665, and then gave to the syn boiarskii Andrei Bulygin. When you have inquired into this, you are to write down their replies in a report and have them append their tribal marks and send their testimony with their tribal marks to Iakutsk.

You, Kuzma, are personally to go from the Indigirka River to Zashiversk ostrozhek. When you have come to the ostrozhek, you are to take command of Zashiversk ostrozhek from the syn boiarskii Andrei Bulygin. You are to question the servitors and hostages in the iasak zimov'e of that ostrozhek. Check the iasak collection books and the other official records, as well as the Great Sovereign's goods in the warehouse and the court records and judgments. You are to question Andrei in regard to all the information you obtain. You are to take the previous instructions from Andrei, and collect the iasak for the Great Sovereigns, and carry out those instructions. The names of the servitors who are to go with you to Zashiversk ostrozhek are being given to you with this present instruction.

Likewise in this year of 1665 the Great Sovereign Tsar and Grand Prince Aleksei Mikhailovich and the Sovereign Lord Tsarevich and Grand Prince Aleksei Alekseevich and the Sovereign Lord Tsarevich and Grand Prince Fedor Alekseevich have received a petition from the Podshiversk iasak zimov'e from the iasak-paying Iukagir Shcherbachko Volotomanov and from his brother's son, Shelyga Shamanov. They sent their petition with their tribal marks to Iakutsk ostrog, complaining against the promyshlennik Piatun Mironov. Their petition states that Shcherbachko and his brother owed Piatun four sables, a debt which they had incurred through a iasak-paying Iukagir named Kruchink. Because they were afraid of Piatun, they gave him a particularly fine sable, which he took in place of four sables. They had paid a good reindeer to a iasak-paying Iukagir for that sable. But then Piatun threatened to make them pay three sables more, and he continues to harass them. Because they are afraid of his threats they do not dare to bring in the iasak for the Great Sovereign to the iasak zimov'e. Piatun also took Shelyga's sister for himself, and he did not pay Shelyga anything for her. He kept the sister for a time and then sold her to the promyshlennik Sidor Grigorev for 40 sables.

In accordance with the ukaz of the Great Sovereign, you are to confiscate the sable which Piatun took from Shcherbachko in place of the four sables, and send it to Iakutsk ostrog with anyone available. You are to return Shelyga's sister to him, the girl for whom Piatun paid nothing and sold for 40 sables; let this be an example not to take women by force without paying for them. If she has not been baptized, after you take her from Sidor you are to return her to Shelyga.

You are immediately to send Piatun under guard to Iakutsk to the office of the Great Sovereign. Instruct the guard to manacle him so that he will not be able to make an escape on the way or attack the guard. When the guard reaches Iakutsk, he is to deliver Piatun to the Prikaz office, to the stolnik and voevoda Ivan Fedorovich Bolshoi Golenishchev-Kutuzov.

Then, Kuzma, on April 4, 1666, you are to receive from the Indigirka customs tselovalnik Terentii Cherepanov all the customs goods for the Great Sovereign's Treasury, the official instructions to the previous tselovalnik which were sent from Iakutsk, Terentii's books and customs collection reports, and the sables collected as the tithe and the financial accounts signed by Terentii. You are to keep these records in the Great Sovereign's Treasury as a guide for future customs collections. You are also to accept from Terentii the sealed instructions from the Great Sovereigns, signed by the stolnik and voevoda Ivan Fedorovich Bolshoi Golenishchev-Kutuzov concerning how the Great Sovereign's customs duties are to be collected and how to handle customs matters in accordance with this ukaz, until a new tselovalnik is sent out. When the new tselovalnik arrives, you are to write down in the record books the amount you personally collected from Terentii and sign it, and send it to Iakutsk ostrog immediately with the first available person.

Once you have resolved all of these matters with Terentii, you are to send him with the collected sables and monies for the Great Sovereign. Send him over the mountains to Iakutsk ostrog with his books, and also send your own report with instructions. Terentii is to hand it over to the stolnik and voevoda Ivan Fedorovich Bolshoi Golenishchev-Kutuzov when Terentii appears in the Prikaz office.

See: Ia. P. Alkor and B. D. Grekov, eds., *Kolonialnaia politika moskovskogo gosudarstva v Iakutii XVII v.* (Leningrad: 1936), 66–68.

103

MARCH 6, 1666

A GRAMOTA FROM TSAR ALEKSEI MIKHAILOVICH TO THE VOEVODAS
OF TOMSK, IVAN LAVRENTII SALTYKOV AND PRINCE FEDOR MESH-
CHERSKII, CONCERNING THE ALLEGIANCE OF KALMYK TAISHAS

From the Sovereign Tsar and Grand Prince Aleksei Mikhailovich, Autocrat of all Great, Little and White Russia, to
Tomsk, to our stolniks and voevodas, Ivan Lavrentii Saltykov and
Prince Fedor Nikitich Meshcherskii, and diak Vasilii Shpilkin. In
this present year of 1666, the Black Kalmyk taishas, Senga and
Chekur, and Chekur's son Bakhan-Ubash, sent us, the Great Sovereign, their envoys, Chinka and his men. In discussion with us,
the Great Sovereign, and with our privy councillors, the envoys
humbly requested in the name of their taishas that we, the Great
Sovereign, allow the taishas and all their ulus people to come
under our Tsarist Majesty's mighty hand in allegiance and order
that our mighty Sovereign forces not attack them, and that we
permit their ulus people to come to Tomsk to trade.

We, the Great Sovereign, order the taishas to enter our Great
Sovereign's service. The taishas and their ulus people will serve
us, the Great Sovereign, and will stand ready to join us in making
war against any of our rebellious subjects. In accordance with our
Great Sovereign's ukaz, these taishas have been notified through
our Great Sovereign's gramotas that we, the Great Sovereign, have
granted the taishas' request, and will permit them to come in servitude under our Tsarist Majesty's mighty hand; that we will allow them to send their ulus people into Tobolsk and Tomsk to
trade; that we will give their envoys our Great Sovereign's largesse;
and that we will order that they be allowed to leave Moscow to
return to their taishas. The syn boiarskii Vasilii Litosov, from the
town of Tomsk, and an eleven-man cossack escort have been assigned to accompany them. We, the Great Sovereign, have sent
gifts to these taishas: ten arshins of green wool, ten of silk and ten
of satin to Senga taisha, and ten arshins of English wool and silk
and plain satin to the taishas Chekur and his son Bakhan.

When you receive this gramota from us, the Great Sovereign,
and the Tomsk syn boiarskii Vasilii Litosov comes to Tomsk with
the Kalmyk envoys, you are to give these envoys the gifts from us,

Valuable dogs are sacrificed with stone and bone weapons when the Giliak toion is cremated. Amur region. From Von Schrenck, *Reisen und Forschungen im Amur-Lande*, Vol. 3.

the Great Sovereign, and provide them with food, drink and transport for their journey from Tomsk, and then send them back to their taishas in the uluses without detaining them, by whatever route is most convenient. Along with our Great Sovereign gramotas you are to send with them our Tsarist Majesty's gifts, and a reliable syn boiarskii and servitors from Tomsk, and instruct them to present the gramotas and gifts from us, the Great Sovereign, in their entirety, to these taishas. Instruct them to remind the taishas that in accordance with their petition they are now in servitude under our Tsarist Majesty's mighty hand and that they are to serve us, the Great Sovereign, loyally. They are to make war against any of our rebellious subjects and search for runaways. They may send only a few of their ulus people to Tomsk and Tobolsk to trade, so that by sending only a few, there will be no arguments or disputes with the Russians.

Whenever our Great Sovereign's servitors or Bukharans travel from Tobolsk and Tomsk to China, in accordance with our Great Sovereign's ukaz, carrying our Tsarist Majesty's gramota, or whenever they are sent there with goods to trade, the taishas are to protect our Great Sovereign's people from hostile uluses and provide them with guides both to China and back to Tomsk by way of whatever is the most convenient route. Whenever any of our Great Sovereign's servitors and merchants come to them in their uluses to trade, they are to allow them to trade freely and not take their goods from them by force, nor are they to attempt to force their own Kalmyk goods on them.

You are to prepare a written report listing the names and the number of persons you are going to send to the taishas with our Great Sovereign's gramotas and gifts. State what food and drink the Kalmyk envoys are being given for their journey, the date upon which your couriers will return to Tomsk from the taishas, any information you may receive from the taishas, and the report which your couriers make to you in conference when they return. You are to send this written report to us, the Great Sovereign, and have a copy sent to the Posolskii Prikaz to our dumnyi diak Almazii Ivanov and his men. When these ulus people come from the taishas to Tomsk to trade you are to be firm and see to it that only a few come. Watch them very carefully. Permit them to trade only at some distance out of town. Allow no Kalmyks except the envoys to enter the town, and issue a firm order that there are to be no discords or arguments between Russians and the Kalmyks.

See: I. P. Kuznetsov-Krasnoiarskii, ed., *Istoricheskie akty XVII stoletiia (1633–1699)* (Tomsk: 1890), I, 25–27.

104

A GRAMOTA FROM TSAR ALEKSEI MIKHAILOVICH TO THE VOEVODA OF TOMSK, NIKITA VELIAMINOV, CONCERNING PURSUIT OF RUNAWAY EXILES

From the Tsar and Grand Prince Aleksei Mikhailovich, Autocrat of Great, Little and White Russia, to Siberia, to Tomsk, to our stolnik and voevoda Nikita Andreevich Veliaminov and to our diak Vasilii Shpilkin. We, the Great Sovereign, have ordered that any persons who were sent into exile from Moscow to Siberian towns, but who have been left in Tomsk without our Sovereign ukaz, are now to be sent on to their assigned towns and into their stipulated positions. If such exiles run away from these designated places to other Siberian towns, then they are to be apprehended and punished, and then sent to the specified Siberian towns.

When you receive this, our Great Sovereign gramota, you are to see to it that any exiles who have been left in Tomsk contrary to our Sovereign ukaz are to be sent from there to the Siberian towns designated for them, and assigned there to the specified positions. Any runaways in Tomsk are to be interrogated at length and punished and then sent to their specified towns. You are to record the number of persons sent to the various Siberian towns, and report their names to us, the Great Sovereign. Forward a copy to the Siberian Prikaz to our okolnichi Rodion Matveeivich Streshnev and to our diaks Grigorii Poroshin and Lev Ermolaev.

See: I. P. Kuznetsov-Krasnoiarskii, ed., *Istoricheskie akty XVII stoletiia (1633– 1699)* (Tomsk: 1890), I, 35–36.

105

FEBRUARY 3-AUGUST 28, 1666

A REPORT FROM FEDOR PUSHKIN CONCERNING A TUNGUS UPRISING NEAR OKHOTSK

Fedor Pushkin humbly reports to Ivan Fedorovich, stolnik and voevoda of the Sovereign Tsar and Grand Prince Aleksei Mikhailovich, Autocrat of all Great, Little and White Russia, and of the Sovereign Lord Tsarevich and Grand Prince Aleksei Alekseevich, of all Great, Little and White Russia, and of the Sovereign Lord Tsarevich and Grand Prince Fedor Alekseevich, of all Great, Little and White Russia, and of the Sovereign Lord Tsarevich and Grand Prince Simeon Alekseevich, of all Great, Little and White Russia.

Sire, on December 3 of the year 1665 the iasak-paying headman Zelemei and his men came to Okhotsk ostrog and reported that non-iasak-paying Tungus of the Kukugir tribe had come to the Okhota and urged the iasak-paying people to rebel. Previously, in the year 1664, these same Kukugirs had come to the Okhota River at approximately the same time and had likewise urged the iasak-paying people to rebel. That spring the servitors who had been sent to Iakutsk ostrog with your treasury, Sire, Ivan Ignatev and his men, were pursued by the Kukugirs and members of the Gotnikan tribe and by iasak-paying Tungus. [The natives] wanted to kill them, but they could not catch up with them. We reported this to the previous prikashchik Evdokii Kozitsyn. At this time the Kukugirs are living just two days travel away from Okhotsk ostrog and are waiting for the Sovereign's treasury to reach Iakutsk ostrog, and they plan to kill the servitors. We have summoned them to come to Okhotsk ostrog but they will not heed us, and they have not appeared.

Sire, on the basis of the report to Evdokii and of native information, and of past and present Kukugir lawlessness and conspiracy, I took leaders from the iasak-paying people as hostages. Then I took 50 servitors and promyshlenniks headed by Potap Mukhoplev from Okhotsk ostrog to deal with any danger from the native multitude. I ordered them to summon the Kukugirs to Okhotsk ostrog, using kindness, not brutality. But [the natives] killed all of those servitors and promyshlenniks, and we do not have any first hand information here in Okhotsk ostrog as to how they were killed, because not one Russian from that expedition has been left alive. We heard about the massacre from [native] guides who went with them and who are now under confinement in the stockade, as well as from other iasak-paying natives who have come to Okhotsk ostrog.

They report that Potap and his men went to the Okhota and took five of the Kukugir leaders and left them on the Okhota in the iurt of a man named Kulik, and they left six servitors to guard them. Potap took the rest of his men and went further into the Kukugir camp and took many Kukugirs prisoner, and was on his way back to Okhotsk ostrog. We do not know how Zelemei persuaded the iasak-paying people of the various tribes to ambush Potap and his servitors on the road, but all were killed, as well as those who were on guard in Kulik's iurt. The natives tell us that the rebels are planning to kill the rest of us and are trying to deceive us.

Zelemei is the leader of all these people. He tells them, "You are ignorant. You do not know the Russians' trails. You too could live the way I live. You know how many Russians I kill when some offense is committed against me.

"You seem to think that the Russians are the best of all people. But the Russians deceive us. They tell us that they will be reinforced every year with more people at Okhotsk ostrog. But so far there have only been a few men at Okhotsk ostrog. As long as the big reinforcement has not come we can kill the men who are there and free our hostages. Then when the Russians come to the Okhota we will ambush them and will not let the reinforcements arrive. We can trick the Russians on the Okhota and on the Maia and other rivers. We will trick them all. And in the future we will invite the Bogdoi people to help protect us, because they are not far from us. We will begin to pay iasak to them, in small amounts, not the excessive amounts we have had to pay these past years, a matter on which we have sent many petitions to the Great Sovereign, and about which we receive no satisfaction, and about which no ukaz has been issued."

This Zelemei brought many natives from various tribes to the ostrog and asked that the hostages be released. He tricked us in every way he could. Up to the present time, many iasak-paying people have come and paid a small bit of iasak to the Great Sovereign so they could look over the ostrog. At present, as of February 3, the Sovereign's Treasury in Okhotsk ostrog consists of 40 forties of sables.

Sire, it is impossible to send any cossacks with a report from Okhotsk ostrog to Iakutsk ostrog. I have sent reports with natives on two occasions, in order to alert Iakutsk ostrog as quickly as possible.

Sire, at present in Okhotsk ostrog, counting old and young, sick and scurvied, there are thirty men and sixty hostages. In addition to deaths from wounds, many servitors in Okhotsk ostrog have died of disease. The ostrog is very run down, and because of the small number of men, no one dares to go out into the forest to get wood to repair the ostrog. It is impossible to procure food for ourselves and for the hostages, because the natives will not let us go out. We have our guns ready both day and night.

Sire, in view of the present conditions, in order to maintain control over the Lama lands for the Great Sovereign along the Maia and other rivers which fall into the sea, it will be necessary to send at the very least 150 men to Okhotsk ostrog. Of course more would be better. At least half of the servitors should come to the Lama to prepare fish to prevent the rest from starving. At the present time, Sire, we thank God for His mercy, remember His great miracles, and hope and await God's help. We await replacement and reinforcement from the Great Sovereign. And we place our trust in you, stolnik and voevoda of the Sovereign.

See: *Dopolneniia k aktam istoricheskim* (St. Petersburg: 1853), V, 68.

106

NOT BEFORE FEBRUARY 13, 1671

A REPORT FROM THE VOEVODA OF IAKUTSK, IVAN BARIATINSKII, TO
THE SIBIRSKII PRIKAZ CONCERNING THE SIEGE OF ALBAZIN OSTROG
BY MANCHU TROOPS

To the Sovereign Tsar and Grand Prince Aleksei Mikhailovich, Autocrat of all Great, Little and White Russia, your humble servants, Ivan Bariatinskii and Stepan Elchiukov report.

Great Sovereign, on February 13 of this year, 1671, the syn boiarskii Matvei Iarygin came to Iakutsk ostrog from Olekminsk ostrozhek and brought with him your iasak treasure, Sovereign, which he had collected at Olekminsk ostrozhek from your Tungus and Iakut iasak-paying people, Great Sovereign, for the current year of 1671.

In the Prikaz office Matvei gave us, your humble servants, a report which the natives had signed with their tribal marks. That report states that on January 17, 1671 a iasak-paying Tungus named Iupchaneik Dachigin, of the Nanagir tribe, had made a report at the time he was making his iasak payment. He said that he had been out hunting sables and had seen a runaway Tungus named Onkoul Seglenkin on the upper reaches of the Olekma River. Onkoul told him that in the summer of 1670 he had been in the land of the Daurs. Onkoul further told Iupchaneik that Nikifor Chernigovskii and his men who had killed the voevoda of Ilimsk, Lavrentii Obukhov, had run off to live on the Amur in Lavkai's ostrozhek. This man Nikifor Chernigovskii was under heavy siege in that ostrozhek by the Bogdoi people, and there were many boats with people on the Amur River near that ostrozhek. Later mounted troops came and dug a moat around the ostrozhek. Onkoul said that he thought Chernigovskii and his comrades had been killed.

Sire, the Bogdoi have built a settlement at the Tugur portage, and they have brought in substantial supplies of food there. Sire, it takes two days to sail from that settlement on the Tugur River to the Olekma. One can sail in three days from the Tugur settlement via the Olekma to the Lena River where Olekminsk ostrozhek is located. Then it takes five days to go by boat from Olekminsk ostrozhek down the Lena River to Iakutsk ostrozhek. Sire, these Bogdoi people have said that they are going to cross over onto the

Olekma River and follow that river to your towns, Great Sovereign. They would go among the people who pay iasak to you, Great Sovereign, with the intention of collecting that iasak from them for the Bogdoi ruler. . . .

That same day, Sire, Matvei Iarygin told us, your humble servants, that in the fall iasak-paying Iakuts from Borogoisk volost named Sykrachk Oniukiev and Devedgach Nesidin, and their men, came to him, Matvei, at Olekminsk ostrozhek. They had been sable hunting, and they were bringing their iasak payment in from the iasak collection zimov'es to Matvei. Another man came with them, Sire, a iasak-paying Tungus named Kildyg from the Kindigirsk settlement; he had also come to pay his iasak. Sykrachk told Matvei that he had gone sable hunting up the Chara River beyond the mountains from Olekminsk ostrozhek, and that he had discovered a place there beyond the mountains where it is possible for the Iakuts to camp. There are meadows and a large lake there. In the Iakut language the lake is called Kuskenda. Sovereign, it takes fifteen days travel by horse to go from Olekminsk ostrozhek to that place.

Great Sovereign, in the past years 1668 and 1669 we, your humble servants of Iakutsk ostrog, together with the cossack piatidesiatnik Iustin Panfilov and the cossack desiatnik Danilo Mikhailov, reported to you, Great Sovereign, that the Bogdoi people are trading with your iasak-paying people, and that in exchange for sables they give them presents of silver rings, bows [weapons], kaftans, silks and other goods. They are inviting these people to come to their own Daur land along the Zeia tributaries and beyond the Zeia River. The Iakuts are going out searching for lands where they can encamp.

Great Sovereign, in the year 1669 the Tugirsk iasak-paying Tungus named Pargaul and Iziak and their men, who had been hostages of the Inkagul tribe petitioned you, Great Sovereign, before us your humble servants in the Prikaz office, and they told us that they live on the Uda River with their families and pay iasak to you, Great Sovereign, in Verkhomansk zimov'e but that subjects of the Bogdoi tsar come to them and abuse them in all sorts of ways and take the iasak away from them. Great Sovereign, they petition that you grant them their request and defend them from the Bogdoi people. An official report submitted by various ranks of servitors in Iakutsk ostrog about this intrusion by the

Iakuts in insect-resistant summer festival costumes. From Oklad-nikov, *Istoriia Iakutskoi ASSR*, Vol. 2.

Daurs upon your Great Sovereign's iasak-paying people has been forwarded to you, Great Sovereign, in a report for 1668, with this same man, Iustin.

Sire, there are very few people left in your service in Iakutsk ostrog. There were two regimental artillery pieces, and two in-operative ones, prior to our arrival. Thirty puds of powder and lead have been sent from Tobolsk over the past three years. They have also sent fifteen puds of lead and powder per year in barrels, as well as bast matting and rope, with the persons who are sent on your service, Great Sovereign. At present, Great Sovereign, there are 29 puds of powder and 38 puds of lead in Iakutsk ostrog, but we have no food. The cossacks who winter in Iakutsk ostrog have each received a yearly ration of six puds of rye, oats and barley, as part of their pay from you, Great Sovereign. From Ilimsk ostrog they have sent a very little supply of food here.

See: *Dopolneniia k aktam istoricheskim* (St. Petersburg: 1857), VI, 153–154.

107

OCTOBER 11, 1671

<small>A REPORT TO THE TOBOLSK PRIKAZ OFFICE FROM THE TOBOLSK SER-
VITOR, SEITKUL ABLIN OF BUKHARA, AND THE COSSACK IVAN TAR-
UTIN, CONCERNING THEIR JOURNEY TO THE CHINESE EMPIRE</small>

On October 11, 1671, the Tobolsk [merchant, Bukhara-born] Seitkul Ablin, and the mounted cossack Ivan Tarutin, came to Tobolsk from the Chinese Empire with the Emperor's treasury. In the Prikaz office they reported to the boiarin and voevoda, Prince Ivan Borisovich Repnin and his associates.

In July, 1667, in accordance with the gramota of the Sovereign, they were sent from Tobolsk with the Sovereign's treasury to trade in the Chinese Empire. They had with them the Sovereign's goods and furs valued at 4,539 rubles, 27 altyns, 4 dengi. Three *posada tselovalniks* [sworn townsmen] from Tobolsk were sent with them, and one Bukhara man; and to guard the Sovereign's treasury, there were sent sixteen mounted cossacks and members of the Tobolsk Litva, and ten Tatar servitors.

They spent seven weeks traveling from Tobolsk to Lake Iamysh near Tara, and at Lake Iamysh they met a golova of the Tiumen streltsy, Samoilo Bludov, and government servitors who had been sent with him to procure salt. At that time Ablai-taisha's son Chagan heard that Seitkul and his men were on their way to the Chinese Empire with government goods, and he sent a caravan of 47 camels to the salt lake, Iamysh. Samoilo Bludov packed the Sovereign's goods on the camels himself. They remained at the salt lake for three days. Bukhara merchants from Ablai's ulus supplied carts for the servitors, and using these carts they proceeded from the salt lake to Ablai's ulus, which took three weeks. For their protection on the journey from the salt lake to Ablai's ulus, they were accompanied by Ablai's ulus Kalmyks and by Bukhara men. They remained in Ablai's ulus for seven weeks and purchased camels there. Ablai could give them only small quantities of food because he had been pillaged by armed bands, but he gave them good protection and treated them with respect, and they were not in any way abused or oppressed there.

From Ablai's ulus they packed the Sovereign's treasury on the camels they had purchased, and the tselovalnik and the servitors bought camels for their own goods. Ablai-taisha sent his own envoy, Biliukt, with them to the Chinese Empire, and 200 Bukhara merchants went along as well. They went to the Chinese Empire with these Bukhara people, but Ablai's envoy and a *koshevar* [camp official] were fed by the Tsar's supplies all the way to the Chinese Empire and back. The envoy received the Tsar's goods in exchange for food, which has been recorded in the books.

From Ablai's ulus they followed natural trails to the Akbazar River where Ablai-taisha spends the winter. This journey took three days. From that river they went on to the Temin-Chergor [Cherga] River, to the ulus of Chokur-abasha, a journey of four days, and they spent three days in that ulus. Chokur wanted to give them food and transport, but they did not accept this offer in order to prevent Ablai-taisha's people from arguing about it, and also because they already had a goodly number of Ablai's escorts.

They traveled for three days from Chokur's ulus to the Eseta [Espe] River, and from there to the Alatai [Taizhuzgen] River, also in three days. From that river they proceeded to the upper Irtysh and to the Iuriunga River, which took a week. Along all of these rivers Chokur-abasha-taisha's settled agricultural people live. From the Iuriunga River they moved along the other side of the Irtysh River, the same side on which Tobolsk stands, to the Bulugan River, in three weeks. The ulus of Senga-taisha and of his uncles Agai-taisha and Danzhin-taisha is located on the Bulugan River. They went around this ulus because there are many lawless persons who live there. From that ulus they went across the mountains for one day to the land of the Mongols. And from those mountains to the ulus of Elden-taisha, they traveled in three weeks. They stayed for three days in Elden's ulus to trade. Elden-taisha gave them two rams for food for three people, but he did not give anything for the rest.

From that ulus they traveled to the ulus of the Mongol taisha, Katan-batyr, which took three weeks. They stayed in that ulus for four days to trade, but Katan only gave them enough food for three people.

From that ulus they traveled through Mongol territory to the Selenga River for a week and a half to an ulus belonging to a lama, but they by-passed the ulus itself because it was out of their way.

From there they traveled for two weeks to the ulus of Sain-khan, where they lived for five weeks, until spring. Seitkul gave Sain-khan a letter bearing the seal of the Sovereign Tsar and Grand Prince Aleksei Mikhailovich, Autocrat of all Great, Little

389

and White Russia. It was written in Tatar, and Seitkul, using an interpreter, translated the Sovereign's letter into the Kalmyk language. The Sovereign's letter requested that Sain-khan allow the Sovereign's envoys and the other merchants to pass through all of his territories without detaining them, and that he supply food and guides for the travellers. Sain-khan gave them five guides and provided food for a few persons, but not for all of them.

From this ulus they traveled with the khan's men to the border of the Chinese Empire of Budgykhan, a journey of four weeks. At the border of the Chinese Bugdykhan's land, his officials took down the names of Seitkul and his companions and allowed them to enter the Chinese Empire, and sent ten guides with them for their protection against bandits.

They traveled for a week and a half from the border to the Chinese wall. When they came to the gates there was an office in which officials and clerks examined them. After they had looked them over they sent word of their arrival into the city, but ordered them to remain at the gate. It took two weeks to carry this message, and during that time they [Seitkul and his men] waited at the wall. An official came to them with ten men and inquired from whom had they come? From what people? For what purpose? They replied that they were envoys and merchants of the Great Sovereign. They were then sent into the inner part of the city where they waited five days. Then another official with twenty men came and took down all their names and confiscated their weapons and then brought them into the city. From the gates they traveled for two days with the men to the town of Baiansum [Siuankhuafu]. It took two days more to go from that town to Chegankerem, and two more days to go to the capital city [Peking]. Between these towns they traveled through several small towns ten or fifteen versts apart.

In all, it took them 48 weeks and three days to travel from Tobolsk to the Chinese Empire, including their stopovers.

When they came to the Chinese capital, they were met at the gates by a nobleman of the Chinese tsar, who was accompanied by 30 or more men. Tents were then set up and they were taken inside the tents before the noblemen, who inquired abut their health, about the lands they had traveled through, and whether they had incurred any losses. They replied that thanks to God they had traveled in good health and had arrived safely. After that they were given wine and tea, and Seitkul and his companions were taken into the city and lodged in quarters for foreign envoys, built of stone. This building is about 150 sazhens in circumference; it has three gates; and inside the courtyard are two large stone structures and some 30 smaller buildings also of stone. The Bukhara merchants who traveled with him from Ablai were kept outside the city and were lodged in the Bukhara compound which is larger than the ambassadorial court and is also built of stone, but does not have the main building or smaller dwellings.

That same day Seitkul Ablin and his companions were ordered to appear before the Chinese tsar in the summer palace. Seitkul and his five companions presented the gifts from the Sovereign consisting of two bolts of woolen broadcloth and other goods. All were noted in the book of expenditures. The Tsar's gifts to the Chinese tsar were accepted from them by his councillors at the gate of the summer palace, and these same men brought them before the tsar who instructed the councillors to place the gifts in his Treasury. But neither Seitkul nor his companions witnessed this because they were standing at the gate. Then at about three o'clock the Chinese tsar had them brought before him into the summer palace. When they approached the tsar, he was sitting on his throne which had been placed on carpets and pillows. He did not rise. He is young, about twenty years old. He inquired about the health of the [Russian] Sovereign while he was still sitting, and he allowed his councillors to interrogate them. Seitkul and his companions spoke about the Sovereign's health, but remained standing. After this the Chinese tsar thanked the Great Sovereign for his gifts and his largesse. Then he asked Seitkul and his companions about their own health, and offered them wine and invited them to dine with him. The tsar dined while sitting on the throne in the summer palace and presented them with some gifts. After the meal he told them they could trade their goods at will for food and drink, and he sent them back to the ambassadorial court, and soon afterward sent them food and drink.

They lived in the Chinese Empire for three and a half months. They received quite adequate amounts of food and drink, and were allowed to trade freely. There were an official and poddiaks and ten servitors in the ambassadorial court who wrote down every commercial transaction, recording who bought and who sold each item. But they did not impose duty payments. The official assigned an interpreter to Seitkul and his companions, who was to make certain that Chinese people did not bring any adulterated silver or other goods of poor quality to sell, and to see that they were not deceived. They dined at the Chinese tsar's invitation three times in the garden during their stay there, and Ablai's Bukhara people and other Kalmyk taishas were also with them at the meals, about 500 in all. Seitkul and his companions were always seated higher than the others, but the tsar was never present at these feasts.

After these meals, before they left, Seitkul and his companions were all taken to the Mongol office, where a nobleman presented them with gifts for the Great Sovereign consisting of silver and silk and beaver pelts and snow leopard pelts. Everything that was presented was recorded in the books. In making the presentation, [the noble] said that their Bogdoi was honored to receive the gifts from the Great [Russian] Sovereign and asked that the Great Sovereign accept his gifts. He also informed them that in the future when the Great Sovereign sends envoys for commercial purposes they will be given food and good protection and will have free trade privileges. He said that 170 of their own iasak-paying people had defected from the Bodgoi tsar and now pay their iasak to the [Russian] Great Sovereign, and asked that the Great Sovereign order that these people be returned to him. But he did not put his request in writing.

About a week later, just before Seitkul's departure, he and his companions were brought back to the same Mongol Prikaz, and the same noble gave them gifts from his tsar. Seitkul Ablin received 60 silver coins called *lan*, three bolts of silk and 27 bolts of cotton. Ivan Tarutin received 40 silver lans, three bolts of silk and seventeen of cotton. The servitors and the tselovalniks and the Tatar servitors, 30 persons in all, and the sixteen porters, each received one bolt of silk and eight of cotton.

Three days later Seitkul and his companions set out from the Chinese Empire. There were no officials present at the time of their departure, but they were given enough food for two months, and guides were assigned to take them to the walls where they had been met; but they were not furnished with transport. During their stay in the Chinese Empire their horses and camels had been fed by the order of the Chinese tsar.

When they were a half-day's journey beyond the frontier, they received news that caused them to halt for a whole year. They heard that Ablai-taisha and his ulus people had been routed to the last man by the Kalmyks, and that many had been killed. Sengin-taisha sent his men to Seitkul and his companions, and he sent a letter with his seal. The letter informed them that they could travel with the Sovereign's treasury through Sengin's ulus without fear on their way back to Tobolsk. Seitkul and his companions followed Sengin-taisha's instructions and proceeded with the Sovereign's treasury; but while they were in Mongol territory, in Cheon-kontaisha's land, they received the news that Sengin-taisha had been killed. Seitkul and his companions did not dare to travel farther with the Sovereign's treasury. They sent word to Sengin's ulus with the Tobolsk servitor Vasilii Sosnin and the Tatar Elok Shchakhmametev, and Kotech, one of Sengin-taisha's men who had been serving them as a guide, and a Bukhara man named Tav-khoz. [Seitkul and his companions] remained in Mongol territory, in Cheon-kontaisha's land, for three and a half months until Vasilii Sosnin and the others returned. Sengin's brother Gagan had sent his own son, Araptar-taisha, back with Vasilii Sosnin. He also sent his men under the leadership of Irkegents, who told Seitkul and his companions that even though Sengin-taisha was dead that they could continue their journey with him, with the Sovereign's treasury, into the ulus without fear. So Seitkul and his companions went with these Mongol envoys with the Sovereign's treasury. As they traveled they ran short of supplies and left three camels with Gagan-taisha's ulus people to be cared for.

When they reached Gagan-taisha's and Araptar-taisha's ulus, they presented gifts from the Great Sovereign, and recorded in their books any presents that they received. When Seitkul and his men presented the Sovereign's gifts to Gagan-taisha and to Arap-tar-taisha, the taishas accepted the Sovereign's gifts and told them to remain in that ulus, which they did for four months. The tai-shas took six *portishches* [about four arshins per portishche] of the Sovereign's very best green broadcloth. Seitkul and his men told Gagan and Araptar that they were to proceed to Tobolsk with the Sovereign's treasury without being detained, and so Gagan-taisha and Araptar-taisha allowed them to travel onward to Tobolsk without further delay.

From Sengin's ulus they went to Sol [Lake Iamysh], a journey of five weeks. The [Mongol] envoys Mametelup and Chadyr were sent with them to help convoy the Sovereign's treasury to Tobolsk and on to Moscow. When they set out, Seitkul and his men were given only two camels and nine horses. They had been given short rations of food and drink while they were in the ulus, and they were given none for their journey. They were told the reason for this was that they had been sent through Ablai's ulus. Except for this they met with no rebukes or hardships. However in the ulus thieves stole two of the Sovereign's camels and one horse, seven bolts of silk, two lengths of silk (which had cost six lans and two gold zolotniks), and they also stole four camels and twenty horses which belonged to Seitkul and the cossacks. Seitkul told the taishas Gagan and Araptar about these thefts, and asked that the horses and camels and the silk be searched for. Gagan and Araptar ordered a *zaisan* to carry out the search, but whether he actually did so they do not know; they only know that these were not returned.

Five days after they left Sengin's ulus, they reached a settlement on the great Chara River. From there Seitkul sent a Tobolsk mounted cossack named Fedor Zaev and a Kalmyk to Lake Ia-mysh, requesting that the pismennaia golova Lev Poskochin and his servitors not leave Lake Iamysh, but wait until Seitkul and his men reached them with the Sovereign's treasury. In the course of the round trip Fedor lost two of his horses.

When they reached Lake Iamysh they gave 24 camels from the Sovereign's treasury to the traveling Bukhara men as payment of their debt in Ablai's ulus. The reason for doing this was that the camels could not travel all the way to Tobolsk, and they would be useful to the Bokhara men. The names of the persons to whom the camels were given, the number, and value of the camels were all recorded in the books.

At the lake the pismennaia golova Lev Poskochin put Seitkul and his men aboard government doshchanniks, and aboard these boats they brought the Sovereign's treasury to Tobolsk on October 11 of the present year, 1671.

Reference: TsGADA, f. Sibirskii prikaz, stolb. 535, ll. 187–203.
See: N. F. Demidova and V. S. Miasnikov, eds. *Russko-kitaiskie otnosheniia v XVII veke: Dokumenty i materialy (1608–1691)* (Moscow: 1969), I, 288–293.

108

NOT AFTER 1675

A REPORT PREPARED IN THE PRIKAZ OF SECRET AFFAIRS CONCERNING
ROUTES TO INDIA AND CHINA *

A statement as to why it is impossible to go by sea from the town of Arkhangelsk to the Chinese Empire, and from there to East India.

In past years at various times the English and the Dutch have sent two or three ships to find a passage past Novaia Zemlia to the Chinese Empire and from there to East India. They undertook these voyages because by using such a route they could reach their destinations more quickly. However, they have been unable to accomplish this end.

They have not been able to proceed beyond Novaia Zemlia because of the great ice packs, the intense cold, the darkness and fog. Some returned but others died because the ice there reaches a depth of 20 or 30 sazhens or more, and it floats out to sea like great islands and breaks up ships because all of the sea freezes. There are polar bears on the ice, and foxes and other animals which attack the ships. The sun is barely visible for only three months, from June to September, and even then only a slight warmth prevails. For three months there is total darkness, when only the moon illumines day and night. There is a sea strait called Aipan which might be used, if it were navigable, to sail to China and India. However, as is true with the Arctic Ocean and with Novaia Zemlia, no one has enough information to ascertain whether it is indeed a strait, or the sea. We do not know whether Novaia Zemlia is an island, or a promontory of the mainland, or whether it is joined to America, that is, part of the New World; this latter is an opinion held by many writers about these parts, who believe that Novaia Zemlia is joined to North America.

For these reasons no one has been able to explore the shores of that ocean, even near the Ob River. Geographers write that if one did not sail close to shore, but went far out into the ocean, one could sail to China. But the darkness makes it difficult to find a

---

* This report was probably prepared as part of the briefing for the embassy of Mohammad Iussof Kasimov to Bokhara and India.—Eds.

direct route. No one has yet discovered whether such a voyage would be possible, using the Ob or Irtysh or other Siberian rivers.

One can travel overland to India and China through Astrakhan from Iaik, a town built of stone, as is evident from the following report.*

A description of the horse trail from the town built of stone [Iaik] to the land of India.

From the town of Iaik [Gurev], one travels by way of the steppe across the Enba, the Dar [Amu-Dar] and other rivers.

It takes two weeks to reach the Bukhara town of Khiva; one week from Khiva to the Bukhara town of Balkh; half a week from Balkh to the Indian border town of Kabul; less than a week from Kabul to another Indian town, Maltan [Multan]; from Maltan to the town of Zhenabat [Delhi], one week; half a week from Zhenabat to the town of Lagur [Lahore] where an Indian tsar** lives. From Lagur to the great imperial city of Agra, the journey takes five days. The great Indian tsar Mogul lives in this city of Agra. This tsar rules over many Indian tsars. It takes three weeks and two days to go from the imperial city of Agra to the Indian town of Narabad [Hyderabad], where a third Indian tsar lives. In all, to go from the town of Iaik to the third Indian tsar in the town of Narabad, it takes ten weeks if one travels by horse, but twice that time if one travels with packloads on camels.

Great quantities of precious stones are mined in Narabad in India. It takes one week to go from Narabad to the seaport in an ocean bay where the town of Abasbenderuk [Bender-Abbas] is located.

[European] foreigners say that it takes about four years to sail from foreign lands to the lands from which they come to Arkhangelsk to trade, and then from Arkhangelsk on to the harbor at Narabad. It is quite necessary to go by sea.

The journey from Abasbenderuk to Bender-Suret [Surat] takes eight days. This town is also located on an ocean bay. It takes seven days to go from Bender-Suret to the shah's town of

---

*Reference: TsGADA, f. Gosarkhiv, Razriad XXVII, d. No. 333, 11. 1–1a.
**Aurangzeb, son of Shah Jahan, ruled 1658–1707 and was the last of the great Mogul emperors of India.—Eds.

Bender-Abas, which is located in that same ocean bay. Near the bay is a shah's town named Khurmys [Ormuz], and it takes four days to go there from Bender-Abas. Pearls are obtained in that bay near these towns, and foreigners often buy all that are taken. The total travel time from Iaik to Khurmys is fourteen weeks with horses. The route takes one constantly through towns and inhabited places.

If one travels by horse it takes two and a half weeks to go from Iaik to the Bukhara town of Samarkand. And it takes three months, traveling quickly, to go from Samarkand to the Chinese Empire.

The total travel time from Iaik to the Chinese Empire is fourteen weeks traveling quickly. If one travels with packloads, it takes twice as long. The route takes one through all the towns and inhabited places.

There is a shorter route from Iaik to the Chinese Empire by way of the steppe, but this route cannot be used because Kalmyks and Tatars and many other nomadic people live there. There is also a route from Astrakhan along the shore of the [Caspian] sea across the Terek River and across the Kumyk [Kumytskaia] lands, then across the shah's territory to that same ocean bay and the towns of Bender-Abas and Khurmys.

Travel time by that route is: overland from Astrakhan to Terek, seven days; to the village of Andreev [northern Dagestan], one day; to Tarki [Tarkov], two days; to Buinak, two days; to Usmei, one day; to Derbent, one day; to Shamakh [in Persia], five days; from Shamakh across the mountains to Ardevil, eight days; to Kabzin, six days; to Sava, three days; to Qum, one day; and to Kashan, two days.

Reference: TsGADA, f. Gosarkhiv, Razriad XXVII, d. No. 485, 11. 1–3.
See: N. F. Demidova and V. S. Miasnikov, eds. *Russko-kitaiskie otnosheniia v XVII veke: Dokumenty i materialy (1608–1691)* (Moscow: 1969), I, 488–490.

109

FEBRUARY 28, 1675

INSTRUCTIONS FROM THE POSOLOSKII PRIKAZ TO NIKOLAI G. SPAFARII [MILESCU] FOR HIS EMBASSY TO THE CHINESE EMPIRE

The Great Sovereign Tsar and Grand Prince Aleksei Mikhailovich, Autocrat of all Great, Little and White Russia, commands Nikolai Gavrilovich Spafarii* to travel on the Great Sovereign's affairs to the Chinese Bugdykhan as an ambassador. Two persons from the court are to be sent with him: the newly baptized natives Fedor Pavlov and Kostiatin Grechanin. The poddiaks Nikifor Veniukov and Ivan Favorov are to accompany him to keep written records for the Posolskii Prikaz. The physician and alchemist Jan Han is to go with them to learn about local medications and herbs from apothecaries. Since Nikolai has so few persons in his party, he may personally choose six of the very best young deti boiarskie from Tobolsk to go with him.

Two gramotas written in Russian are being sent to the Chinese khan from the Great Sovereign. In one, Nikolai is identified as an ambassador, and in the other, he is referred to as an envoy. Four exact copies of these gramotas, in Latin and Tatar, have been drawn up and given to Nikolai to hold in reserve. If no one in the Chinese Empire can translate from Russian into their own language, he is to present these gramotas for their correct understanding at such time and under such circumstances as will be explained below. He is also to take with him gifts from the Great Sovereign to the Chinese khan: strings of pearls, sables, ermines, broadcloth, mirrors, watches and amber; the whole is to be valued at 800 rubles. Six gerfalcons are to be sent with him from Tobolsk.

In addition he is to be given 1,500 rubles worth of sable pelts which he is to use to purchase all kinds of local goods there such as precious stones, silver, velvet, satin, silk and other things, whatever he may find. If he is asked to pay duty into the khan's treasury on goods he purchases, he is to pay such duties from these funds.

---

*A Moldavian noble in Russian service. His family name was Milescu, but he was generally referred to as "Spafarii", his rank in his Guards unit.— Eds.

Gifts are to be sent with Nikolai from the Great Sovereign to the Mongol taishas Galdan and Araptar; these goods are to be worth 100 rubles. Further, 200 rubles worth of sable pelts and 20 puds of tobacco are to be given to him to hand out in the name of the Great Sovereign.

Nikolai is to travel from Moscow to the Siberian town of Tobolsk, and from Tobolsk to the Chinese Empire through the Kalmyk uluses, having ascertained carefully which routes are the most direct and the most suitable.

Gramotas are being sent with him from the Great Sovereign concerning his journey from Tobolsk to the Chinese Empire, instructing the boiar and voevoda Petr Mikhailovich Saltykov and his men to give him as many deti boiarskie, interpreters and guides as necessary for safe travel. These are to be men who know a safe route to the Chinese Empire and to the Mongol taishas Galdan and Araptar. Nikolai is also to receive from the Posolskii Prikaz a description of the route to the Chinese Empire which was previously used [1653–57] by Fedor Baikov and the Bukhara man, Seitkul Ablin.

When Nikolai reaches the uluses of the Mongol rulers, he is to meet with the Mongol taishas Galdan and Araptar and present the Great Sovereign's gramota and the gifts which are being sent with him from the Great Sovereign to reward them for their service [to Seitkul Ablin's trade mission] and for the assistance which they will be rendering to His Tsarist Majesty's men on this present journey to the Chinese Empire. He is to reach a firm understanding with them about a future safe travel route across their uluses to the Chinese Empire, and learn in detail the shortest route to the Chinese Empire.

When Nikolai comes to a town on the frontier of the Chinese Empire, he is to contact the administrator of that town and tell him that he has been sent from the Great Sovereign Tsar and Grand Prince Aleksei Mikhailovich, Autocrat of all Great, Little and White Russia, Heir through Father and Grandfather, and Lord and Master of many realms and lands in the East, West and North, that he has come to the Chinese Bugdykhan as an envoy on His Great Sovereign's affairs of state, and thus should be received and given escort, food, transport and guides without delay to the capital city of the Chinese Empire, Kanbalyk [Peking].

When this frontier official sends him on from the frontier town to Kanbalyk he is to travel post haste to the capital city, and while he is traveling he is to make certain inquiries. What other countries send ambassadors and envoys to the Chinese khan? Are they allowed to have a personal audience with the khan during their mission? Do they present their ambassadorial credentials to him in person? If Nikolai ascertains that ambassadors and envoys from all realms who visit him conduct their ambassadorial affairs before the khan in person, and deliver their gramotas and gifts to him personally, as is customary in other neighboring realms, then when the time comes that Nikolai is admitted into the presence of the khan bearing the gramota from the Great Sovereign and the khan's councillors come to Nikolai to accept it, Nikolai is to inform them that he wishes to present the gramota to the khan in person and is ready to do so that very day, provided that no other ambassadors or envoys or couriers from other realms are present at the same time. If the councillors reply that on that particular day the khan will not be receiving any other ambassadors or envoys or couriers from other realms, then Nikolai is to make himself ready and take all the other persons of the Great Sovereign's embassy and go to the khan in accordance with ambassadorial custom.

Upon reaching the khan's court he is to proceed to the palace where the khan is in residence. Upon entering Nikolai is to bow to the khan on behalf of the Great Sovereign Tsar. He is then to say, "By the Grace of God, the Great Sovereign Tsar and Grand Prince Aleksei Mikhailovich, Autocrat of all Great, Little and White Russia, Tsar of Moscow, Kiev, Vladimir and Novgorod, Tsar of Kazan, Tsar of Astrakhan, Tsar of Siberia, Sovereign of Pskov, Grand Prince of Smolensk, Tver, Iugra, Perm, Viatka, Bulgaria and Sovereign of others, Grand Prince of Nizhnii Novgorod, Chernigov, Riazan, Rostov, Iaroslav, Beloozero, Udorsk, Obdorsk, Kondinsk, Master of all northern lands, Sovereign of the Iversk lands of the Kartalin and Gruzin tsars, Sovereign of the Kabardinsk lands of the Cherkass and mountain princes, Heir through Father and Grandfather and Lord and Master of many other realms and lands in the East, West and North, has commanded me to bow to you, Greatly Esteemed Bugdykhan, Master of the city of Kanbalyk and of the entire Chinese Empire, and he has commanded me to inform you of His Tsarist Majesty's health, and to inquire about your health, the khan." He is then to bow in the usual manner.

While Nikolai is on his way to, and in, Kanbalyk, he is to learn the correct names and titles of the khan as he personally uses them, and he is to ascertain this information accurately so that in the speech above described he can use the khan's names and titles in full as he himself uses them, provided that the khan does not refer to himself as the Sovereign of the entire world, and provided that he does not use name and titles of other neighboring lands which belong to the Great Sovereign.

When Bugdykhan inquires about the health of the Great Sovereign, His Tsarist Majesty, Nikolai is to rise and reply, "When we left our Great Sovereign, His Tsarist Majesty, by the Grace of God, our Great Sovereign Tsar and Grand Prince Aleksei Mikhailovich, Autocrat of all Great, Little and White Russia, and Heir through Father and Grandfather and Lord and Master of many realms and lands East, West and North, was in good health, thanks to God's Grace, and was reigning over his great and illustrious lands of the great and reknowned Russian Tsardom."

After that Nikolai is to say, "The Great Sovereign Tsar and Grand Prince Aleksei Mikhailovich, Autocrat of all Great and Little and White Russia, and Heir through Grandfather and Father and Lord and Master of many realms and lands, East, West and North, has sent His Tsarist Majesty's gramota of friendship to you, Bugdykhan." Then he is to hand over the gramota to the khan written in Russian, the one wherein he is referred to as an ambassador. This is to be done with proper ceremony. This gramota from the Great Sovereign is being sent with him.

After presenting the khan with the Great Sovereign's gramota written in Russian, he is to announce that he has two additional gramotas from the Great Sovereign written in Latin and Tatar in which he is also referred to as an ambassador. He is to say that according to the ukaz of His Great Sovereign Tsarist Majesty, these two gramotas were sent to the khan from His Tsarist Majesty, under the Great Sovereign's seal, written in Latin and Tatar, so that he might more readily comprehend their import. If no one is able to translate readily from Russian into Chinese, then his highly esteemed khanship may accept the other two gramotas from His Tsarist Majesty, and so that they may be properly understood, command the gramota to be translated from whichever language he prefers into whatever language will be best comprehended.

Then Nikolai is to present the gifts from the Great Sovereign to Bugdykhan, saying, "The Great Sovereign Tsar and Grand Prince Aleksei Mikhailovich, Autocrat of all Great and Little and White Russia, and Heir through Grandfather and Father, and Lord and Master of many realms and lands East, West and North has sent you, the Chinese Bugdykhan, these small tokens of friendship." Then he is to give the presents to the khan, as specified, with due observation of ceremony.

If the Chinese khan does not receive Nikolai in person, does not give him a personal audience [literally "allow him to see his eyes"], but insists on conducting the ambassadorial business in accordance with his previous customs, and orders that Nikolai give the gramota and the tokens of friendship from the Great Sovereign to the councillors, and instructs Nikolai to conduct his official business with his councillors, then Nikolai is to tell the khan's councillors that he has been sent from the Great Sovereign Tsar and Grand Prince Aleksei Mikhailovich, Autocrat of all Great and Little and White Russia, and Heir through Grandfather and Father, and Lord and Master of many realms and lands East, West and North to their sovereign, Bugdykhan, with His Tsarist Majesty's gramota of friendship to discuss matters of state of vital concern to both sovereigns and empires, and that he has been instructed to present His Tsarist Majesty's gramota to Bugdykhan in person, and not to them, and that he is not permitted to do otherwise. To do so would indicate that their sovereign Bugdykhan is offending His Tsarist Majesty.

They must inform their sovereign Bugdykhan that Nikolai is to present His Tsarist Majesty's gramota to Bugdykhan in person, and conduct the ambassadorial business with him in person, not with the councillors. Nikolai is also to tell the khan's councillors that if their sovereign Bugdykhan were to send his ambassadors with Nikolai to the Great Sovereign, His Tsarist Majesty, at some later date, then the Great Sovereign, His Tsarist Majesty, would order that the khan's ambassadors be received in His Tsarist Majesty's hereditary territory, in Siberian towns; and from Siberia he would command that they be sent on to the capital city of Moscow, and that they be given an official escort, food and drink and transport guides with proper ceremony, so that everything would be done to the fullest satisfaction of their sovereign, Bugdykhan. His Tsarist Majesty would give them a personal audience and would be pleased to listen attentively to Bugdykhan's embassy. And when he had granted them His Great Majesty's largesse, he would decree that they be allowed to return to their sovereign without delay, and with every satisfaction and honor.

But if their sovereign Bugdykhan does not allow Nikolai into his personal presence to conduct his ambassadorial business, and will not accept His Tsarist Majesty's gifts in person, although His Tsarist Majesty promises to do everything for the khan's ambassadors, . . . [missing] and if the khan's councillors are obdurate and will not allow Nikolai to appear before the khan in person, then Nikolai should be very resolute and inform the khan's councillors that it is imperative that he be allowed to present the Great Sovereign's gramota and his gifts to the khan in person, and conduct his ambassadorial business in person with him also. If after many arguments about this the khan's councillors reject Nikolai's request and will not permit him an audience with the khan, then he is to tell the councillors that he has been sent from the Great Sovereign, His Tsarist Majesty, to their sovereign Bugdykhan with His Tsarist Majesty's gramota of amity for the purpose of discussing matters urgent and vital to both sovereigns and that he must obey the will and instructions of his own sovereign, His Tsarist Majesty, but that in this matter he will conduct himself in accordance with the will of Bugdykhan, and whatever he decrees will be done.

Then he is to show the councillors the three gramotas from the Great Sovereign to Bugdykhan wherein he is referred to as an envoy, one written in Russian, one in Latin and a third in Tatar, explaining that the content of all three gramotas from the Great Sovereign is the same, so that they may accept whichever gramota can most easily be translated into their own language for their comprehension. If they ask for all three gramotas, Nikolai is to hand all three to the khan's councillors, as well as the gifts from the Great Sovereign; and in handing them over he is to say that the Great Sovereign, His Tsarist Majesty, has directed that these three gramotas sealed with his Great Sovereign seal be sent to their sovereign, Bugdykhan, his tsarist majesty, for the following purpose. The gramota written in Russian expresses friendship for his khanist majesty, because all great neighboring sovereigns who have relations with their neighbors write their gramotas in the language of their own countries, and then for greater clarity they write in some other language which can be understood in the country to which the letters are addressed. The gramotas written in Latin and Turkish have been prepared so that in the empire of their sovereign Bugdykhan they may perhaps be more readily translated into Chinese, since not many persons in the Chinese Empire are familiar with the Russian language. [Nikolai] is not to bow nor conduct His Tsarist Majesty's ambassadorial business with the khan's councillors.

Then Nikolai is to state to the khan's councillors that the Great Sovereign, His Tsarist Majesty, received written communications about certain matters from the predecessors of their sovereign Bugdykhan, from former Chinese khans, and also from Bugdykhan himself; but because the Great Sovereign is not familiar with the Chinese language, these communications have been sent back with Nikolai so that these earlier gramotas from their khan may be properly understood. In order to be certain of the meaning, the khan's councillors are asked to take them to their sovereign, Bugdykhan, so that he may order that the Chinese gramotas be translated into Latin and be returned to Nikolai. They are requested to inform Nikolai in detail as to what is written in those gramotas, and what it is that their sovereign Bugdykhan is requesting from His Tsarist Majesty in the gramotas. Then Nikolai will report all of this to the Great Sovereign, His Tsarist Majesty, upon his return from China to the capital city of Moscow.

When the khan's councillors translate these Chinese gramotas, or make some request in a special letter and then insist on a response to their request, Nikolai is to reply, depending on the circumstances at the time, but making certain that there will be no injury to the name and honor and dignity of the Great Sovereign, or loss to his Treasury. If it is not possible to give an immediate reply, nor to discuss such matters with them, he is to state that he will report to the Great Sovereign, His Tsarist Majesty, upon his return to Moscow.

If Nikolai manages, while he is on his way to Kanbalyk or in Kanbalyk, to have these Chinese gramotas translated into Latin without the assistance of the khan's councillors, for some small sum of money, then he is not to return these gramotas to the khan's councillors, but rather he is to insist that for his own proper understanding they be translated in his own quarters. If the gramotas appear to contain something derogatory to the honor of His Tsarist Majesty, he is to instruct the khan's councillors to correct everything, so that the Tsarist Majesty's name will be held in honor and dignity.

Nikolai is to come to an understanding with the khan's councillors as to what language will be used in future correspondence between the Great Sovereign, His Tsarist Majesty, and their sovereign, Bugdykhan, so that both parties will be able to understand clearly, and so that they will send their gramotas to our Great Sovereign written either in Latin or in Turkish.

They are to have in writing the full name and titles of the Great Sovereign as they are to be used in the future in writing to His Tsarist Majesty. Likewise the name and titles of the khan are to be received from them in writing, and Nikolai is to be on guard lest the khan refer to himself in his titles and names as the sovereign of other neighboring great realms so that in the future he will not use such titles and thereby cause trouble for our Great Sovereign, His Tsarist Majesty, by incurring the ill will of other rulers.

If the Chinese khan sends a letter with Nikolai to His Tsarist Majesty in which he writes the titles and names of the Great Sovereign in such a manner as to impugn his Imperial dignity, and not as the Great Sovereign himself has written the titles to the khan in the gramota he has sent with Nikolai; or if he has omitted certain titles, then Nikolai is to insist firmly that the Chinese khan decree that in his gramota the Tsarist Majesty's name and titles be written in full precisely as the Great Sovereign has written them.

Nikolai is also to tell the councillors of the khan that in regard to His Tsarist Majesty, all neighboring Christian and Muslim great sovereigns write to our Great Sovereign using his exact Tsarist Majesty's names and titles, and that therefore their sovereign Bugdykhan, in order to indicate his friendship and amity toward His Tsarist Majesty, must decree that the names and titles of His Tsarist Majesty be written precisely as he himself, the Great Sovereign, writes them. Nikolai is to make a firm request at the time of his visit to the Chinese khan that the khan in his gramota to His Tsarist Majesty use his name and titles in full to preserve the highest honor and dignity of His Tsarist Majesty.

Nikolai is to obtain from the councillors the khan's exact name and titles, which His Tsarist Majesty will use in the future in his Tsarist gramotas. However only those titles are to be used in which he is not referred to as the ruler of the entire world or of other neighboring great sovereigns. Nikolai has been given a full statement of the names and titles of His Tsarist Majesty which neighboring Christian and Muslim great sovereigns use in their correspondence with the Great Sovereign.

If there are Russian prisoners in the Chinese Empire, Nikolai is to negotiate about them, so that their sovereign Bugdykhan will express his friendship and amity toward the Great Sovereign, His Tsarist Majesty, by releasing all Russian prisoners without ransom, and sending them from his empire to the Russian empire. In the future he should not force Russians to adopt his faith against their will. The Great Sovereign on his part will likewise release any subjects of their sovereign Bugdykhan, without ransom, who are being held in the Russian Empire, and he will forbid that they be harassed. If the [Chinese] tsar's councillors refuse to agree to this and maintain that they will not release Russians from captivity without ransom, because they had to pay a high price for them, and if they demand a ransom of 5 or 10 or 15 or 20 or 30 rubles apiece for those captives, Nikolai may negotiate, but he is not to agree to anything more than this.

He is to inform the khan's councillors, and be very firm, that their sovereign should send his Chinese ambassadors to the Great Sovereign, His Tsarist Majesty, as an expression of friendship and amity. They should bring rich gifts, and not be citizens of any other realm. The khan should send the Great Sovereign gifts of precious stones, silver, velvet, Chinese silk and textiles and local herbs with this ambassador. Nikolai may promise that this ambassador will be received in His Tsarist Majesty's Siberian towns, and will be accompanied to the capital city of Moscow and be given ample food and transport and all the appropriate appurtenances of rank. If, acting upon this request, the khan appoints an ambassador or an envoy to go with Nikolai, he [Nikolai] is to write to the boiars and voevodas in Tobolsk and other Siberian towns so that they will prepare food and transport for this ambassador or envoy in the towns of the Great Sovereign. Nikolai should accompany this person from the Chinese Empire to the towns of His Tsarist Majesty, and see that he is protected in every possible way.

Nikolai is to use every means to reach a firm agreement with the khan's councillors in regard to silver. He is to have previously ascertained the price in Kanbalyk from various persons, so that their sovereign Bugdykhan will agree to send 1,000 or 2,000 or 3,000 or more puds of silver to the capital city of Moscow with his ambassadors or envoys or merchants. In Moscow, His Tsarist Majesty will reciprocate with whatever goods may be useful for them from his Treasury, in exchange for the silver. The details of this matter are to be agreed upon, such as the local price of silver.

Likewise Nikolai is to have a written agreement on what goods they wish to obtain from His Tsarist Majesty's Treasury in exchange for their silver. If they write that in exchange for the silver they wish to have woolens, sables, ermines, other furs, elk hides or other goods which are abundant in the Russian Empire, then Nikolai is to conclude a written agreement with the khan's counsellors so they will commit themselves to export a certain number of puds of silver each year without interruption and without change. Prices of His Tsarist Majesty's goods which they may request in exchange for the silver will be established in Moscow at the time when the khan's ambassadors visit His Tsarist Majesty in Moscow, and Nikolai is not to set the prices for these goods. Nikolai is to purchase a Chinese grammar and bring it to the Great Sovereign in Moscow.

If he should learn that the Chinese Bugdykhan has precious stones and other such things in his Treasury, which hitherto have not been readily available in the Russian Empire, Nikolai is to discuss this with the counsellors, suggesting that their sovereign Bugdykhan order these stones and other goods to be sent to His Tsarist Majesty with his ambassador or envoy, and that in return for those precious stones and other goods, the khan should inform His Tsarist Majesty, in writing, of whatever items he would like to have. Then His Tsarist Majesty will issue an ukaz to arrange matters.

While Nikolai is in China he is to use every possible means to ascertain whether there is a water route from the Chinese Empire to His Tsarist Majesty's towns, so that such a water route might become a safe and advantageous route for the Russians to use, going via the Ob, Ianysher [Enisei?], Selenga and Irtysh rivers.

While Nikolai is in China he is also to find out whether white and yellow silks are produced in the Chinese Empire, and if so, in what quantity. Having ascertained this, he is to reach some agreement on price, so that the Chinese could export large amounts of silk to the Russian Empire every year in exchange for Russian goods they might want. The price for silk should be established. In Moscow the current price is 40 rubles per pud for white and 20 rubles per pud for yellow silk.

Also while Nikolai is in China he is to find out what faith the East Indian shah professes, what his name is, how he is addressed in writing by his distant neighbors, and with which sovereigns he shares frontiers. He is also to learn what faith the Chinese khan and all the other Chinese people profess, which of all faiths they prefer, and with which realms they share frontiers.

If he encounters medications and herbs which do not exist in the Muscovite state, which can cure certain illnesses, he is to buy such medications and herbs in whatever quantities may be needed for experimentation.

Nikolai does not have specific written instructions about poultry and plants, as described below, because he has already had oral instructions to purchase these.

If he finds garden seeds, or small gamebirds or animals which could be raised in the Russian Empire, he should buy as many of these as possible in China, and bring them out. He is also to buy all kinds of seeds for fiber plants, and for garden vegetables. If he can bring back fresh samples he should do so, but if not, he is still to buy samples and preserve them to bring back.

The instructions from the Great Sovereign also state that Nikolai is to suggest that the khan's councillors levy a tax for the khan on Nikolai's purchases, so that in the future we can levy such a purchase tax on any Chinese who come to the Russian Empire.

If there are expert stone bridge builders in the Chinese Empire, Nikolai is to invite these craftsmen to come into the service of the Great Sovereign for a period of time. If the khan allows them to come, they should be brought to Moscow with Nikolai.

If the councillors ask with which distant sovereigns the Great Sovereign, His Tsarist Majesty, shares frontiers, and with whom he is not presently at war, Nikolai is to reply that the Great Sovereign, His Tsarist Majesty, shares frontiers with the following great sovereigns: Jan III [Sobieski, 1674–1696], by Grace of God King of Poland and Grand Prince of Lithuania; the illustrious sovereign, Charles [XI, 1660–1692], King of Sweden; and His Royal Highness, the Shah of Persia [Suleiman, 1667–1694]. Friendship, amity and good relations prevail among them. The empire of His Tsarist Majesty reaches to the borders of the empire of the Sultan of Turkey and the Khan of Crimea. His Tsarist Majesty also has relations with other great sovereigns such as the Holy Roman Emperor and the kings of France, Spain, England and Denmark. There are no wars or disagreements among them, except that the Turkish Sultan Mohamed [IV, 1648–1687] and the Crimean Khan have abandoned the brotherly friendship and amity that have long existed between them and the Great Sovereign, His Tsarist Majesty, and have gone to war against the brother of the Great Sovereign, His Tsarist Majesty, King Jan of Poland. The Great Sovereign, His Tsarist Majesty, in accordance with ancient friendship and amity, has agreed with all of the abovementioned neighboring sovereigns and with the Shah of Persia to punish these two enemies, and there have been many victories over them, resulting in constant major defeats. Further, it has been unanimously agreed to provide assistance in the future to King Jan of Poland.

If the khan's councillors inquire about Siberia, how the Siberian land is governed, Nikolai is to reply that many towns have been built in Siberia and all manner of servitors and permanent settlers have received favors from the Great Sovereign there. Large agricultural settlements have been established, and the servitors and settlers live in peace and tranquillity. They serve and pay tribute to the Great Sovereign Tsar and Grand Prince, Aleksei Mikhailovich, Autocrat of all Great, Little and White Russia, as they did previously to his Father, the Sovereign of blessed memory, the Great Sovereign Tsar and Grand Prince Mikhail Fedorovich, Autocrat of all Russia.

He is to tell the khan's councillors that their sovereign Bugdykhan should send his subjects from China to trade in the Russian Empire of His Tsarist Majesty, where they would be warmly welcomed in his Tsarist Majesty's Siberian towns. After they had been given food and drink and transport they would be sent from Tobolsk to the capital city of Moscow without delay, and His Tsarist Majesty would order that no taxes on their goods be collected either in Siberian towns or in Moscow, until an agreement had been reached with the ambassadors of the Chinese emperor on the matter of taxes. If Bugdykhan's subjects were to come regularly to the Russian Empire of His Tsarist Majesty to trade, then at that time His Tsarist Majesty would reach an agreement with their sovereign Bugdykhan in regard to imposing an appropriate tax on the subjects of His Tsarist Majesty and on the subjects of the khan, similar to that paid by foreign merchants from all realms who come to the Russian Empire.

While Nikolai is in China he is to use every means at his disposal to discover secretly, by offering drink and food to the official escort or to other similar persons, which people are the most reliable, and which are most truthful and should be given additional

409

gifts in order to find out the attitude of the khan toward the Great Sovereign, that is, whether he is favorably disposed toward him, whether he is pleased that the Great Sovereign has sent his Great Sovereign gramota to him with Nikolai, whether in the future he wishes to be in a state of friendship and amity and contact with the Great Sovereign, whether he plans to send ambassadors or envoys to the Great Sovereign, whether he will send merchants with these ambassadors or perhaps with Nikolai, and if so what kind of goods he will send with them, and whether he will allow his merchants to trade in the Muscovite Empire in the future.

Likewise he is to discuss with persons of all ranks, and with Chinese merchants, whether they are pleased that the Sovereign's embassy has been sent to their sovereign, Bugdykhan, and whether his merchants may wish to travel to the Muscovite state to trade.

Chinese of various ranks, and merchants, are to be told about the generosity and largesse which the Great Sovereign offers all foreigners of neighboring states. They should also be told about the Great Sovereign's exceptional generosity to all incoming foreign merchants, the manner in which they live, thanks to his generosity, and how they trade freely in all goods. In regard to Russian trade goods, the Chinese merchants are to be told that there are all kinds of precious goods in His Tsarist Majesty's Empire which are not to be found in any neighboring states, and that merchants come from India, Persia and other distant great realms to buy these goods.

Nikolai is also to find out with which realms Bugdykhan is presently in a state of friendship and contact, and those with which he is having hostile relations. Which realms send ambassadors to Bugdykhan, and what business do they conduct? Do they bring merchants with them? If so, what kind of goods do they bring? What goods do they buy in the Chinese Empire? What prices do they pay? What goods of their own do they sell? What gifts do the ambassadors bring to Bugdykhan? What manner of gifts does he present in return? What ceremony takes place when ambassadors come? What is the military strength of the Chinese Empire in manpower? How sound is the Treasury? What weapons do the troops have? How many mounted troops are there? How many infantry? How do troops perform in battle? What kind of battle do they wage? With whom are they at war?

What were the causes of the war? How did it develop? Who presently has the upper hand?

While in China Nikolai is also to ascertain to his satisfaction what precious goods and stones there are in the Chinese Empire, whether the goods are produced there, whether the stones are mined there and, if not, from where they are imported. Are velvets and satins and silks and taffetas produced in China or imported? If imported, how much do they cost? What kinds of velvets and satins and silks and taffetas and other precious goods are there in China? From which lands are these imported? By what route? Overland, or by sea? How near or far are the lands from which these goods are imported? How near or far are lands from which these goods were previously imported? Which goods would it be most profitable for the Muscovite state to purchase? What goods should be sent to the Chinese Empire from the Muscovite state? What price should be set on these goods? Will trade be stable in the future? Will there be significant profits in such trade? What manner of people and towns are there in China? What kind of weapons do they have? What faith do Bugdykhan and all in the Chinese Empire profess? Nikolai is to find answers to all of these questions, in detail, in the capital city of Kanbalyk and in other towns he may travel through.

If he is unable to learn these things in secret, he is to ask the escort assigned to him to allow him to go strolling in shops to buy and to look around at all the goods which are available in their Chinese Empire. Then while he is in the shops examining goods, he is to ascertain in detail the prices Chinese people themselves pay for goods, and the prices they charge when they resell them. He is also to obtain precise information about whether European merchants or others come to the Chinese Empire, and if so, what goods they bring, by what route they come (water or overland), through which realms and towns they come, how much it costs per verst per pud or pack to transport goods from one town to another. If the Chinese receive certain goods from European and from other lands which are the same as are available in the Muscovite state, or as goods which are produced in towns in the Muscovite state, then the prices for such goods should be ascertained at all costs.

Nikolai should find out how much it costs to import goods into the Chinese Empire, and how much they cost at resale. How many imported goods are distributed through the Chinese Empire? Which of the goods imported into China are better, those that come from Europe or other foreign lands, or those which come from the Russians? How much duty do they collect on imported goods? Is the duty collected in goods or in efimkas? Is grain grown in the Chinese Empire, and if so, what variety? Is it plentiful? How much does it cost? What kinds of fibers and vegetables are available in China? Are they grown locally or imported? If the latter, how much do they cost?

Nikolai is also to use every means to find out whether there will be friendship, amity and contact between His Tsarist Majesty and the Chinese Bugdykhan in the future. He is also to discover which route is best for travel to the Chinese Empire from the Sovereign's patrimony in Siberia, and through which lands and uluses or encampments this route lies. In the future can the Sovereign's people travel by that route without fear of being harmed? Is the route overland or by water or through the mountains? What is the distance in versts or miles or days from one town to another or between uluses? How is overland travel accomplished? By horse or by camel? What is the charge per packload between one town and another? Into which Chinese border towns should one not travel, from uluses or other places? How many days or weeks does it take to travel through the Chinese territory from the border town to the capital city of Kanbalyk? Is there only one road to China, or are there others? If there are others, which route is closest and safest? What people live along the route between Siberia and the Chinese Empire? Which princes live there? Are they loyal to the Great Sovereign? What are their names? Which uluses do they rule? Have they harmed traveling servitors and merchants? Are any of the princes disloyal to the Sovereign? If so, do they serve someone else? What is their basic occupation? Nikolai is to use every possible means to find the answers to these questions, and make inquiries of as many informed persons as possible.

After he has made proper inquiries about all these things, he is to write down the answers in his official report, in detail, by item, under proper headings for each category. He is to make a chart of the entire Chinese Empire from Tobolsk along the route to the Chinese border town, listing all the territories and towns, and his route, on the chart. Enroute to China and during his stay in the Chinese Empire, Nikolai is to attend always to the affairs of the Great Sovereign, and gather all pertinent information in accordance with this instruction from the Great Sovereign, depending on circumstances at the time and how God may enlighten him. He is to protect the name and honor of the Great Sovereign, and strive everywhere to augment the name, honor and dignity of the Great Sovereign. He is to praise the name of the Great Sovereign in all towns and places, and speak only those things that will accrue to the benefit of the name and honor and dignity of the Sovereign.

When Nikolai is dismissed from China, he is to travel from the Chinese frontiers and find the most direct route to Moscow through Astrakhan, from whichever places are best. He is to select two trusted men from among the Tobolsk deti boiarskie and assign a reliable poddiak to them and instruct them to find a route to Astrakhan, so that in the future it will be possible to travel from Moscow through Astrakhan to trade in the Chinese Empire. When they find such a route, and reach Astrakhan, then they are to proceed to the Great Sovereign in Moscow from Astrakhan. Nikolai himself is to travel with the khan's ambassadors, if he sends any, to Moscow, using the same route by which he traveled to the Chinese Empire.

In Moscow he is to report to the Posolskii Prikaz with his official report and the description of the Chinese Empire, including the routes, and the places to which he traveled en route from Moscow to China, and from China to Moscow. He is to submit this report and chart to the boiar Artemii Sergeevich Matveev and to the dumnyi diaks Grigorii Bogdanov, Ivan Evstafev, Vasilii Bobinin, Stepan Polkov and Emelian Ukraintsov.

Reference: TsGADA, f. Snosheniia Rossii s Kitaem, op. 2, 1674 g., d. No. 1, ch. 1, 11. 75–134.

See: N. F. Demidova and V. S. Miasnikov, eds. *Russko-kitaiskie otnosheniia v XVII veke: Dokumenty i materialy (1608–1691)* (Moscow: 1969), I, 335–349.

110

1675

A LETTER FROM TSAR ALEKSEI MIKHAILOVICH TO THE EMPEROR OF CHINA CARRIED BY NIKOLAI G. SPAFARII

By the Grace of God, We, the Great Sovereign Tsar and Grand Prince Aleksei Mikhailovich, Autocrat of all Great, Little and White Russia, Tsar of Moscow, Kiev, Vladimir and Novgorod, Tsar of Kazan, Tsar of Astrakhan, Tsar of Siberia, Sovereign of Pskov, Grand Prince of Smolensk, Tver, Iugra, Perm, Viatka, Bulgaria, Sovereign of other realms, Grand Prince of Nizhnii Novgorod, Chernigov, Riazan, Rostov, Iaroslav, Beloozero, Udorsk, Obdorsk and Kandinsk, Lord of all the Northern Lands, Sovereign of the Iversk Lands, Tsar of Kartalin and Gruzin and of the Kabardinsk territory, Prince of Cherkassia and the Mountains, Heir through Father and Grandfather Lord and Master of Lands in the East and West and North, We, the Lord and Master of all these lands send greetings to the Supreme Bugdykhan, Ruler of the city of Kanbalyk [Peking] and Master of the entire Chinese Tsardom.

As is known, mighty Bugdykhan, from ancient times the Great Sovereigns, our distinguished forebears have reigned on the throne of the great and illustrious Tsardom of Russia. They were of the line of Caesar Augustus, ruler of the entire world, and of the line of Great Prince Riurik, and of the Great Sovereign and Grand Prince Vladimir Vsevolodovich Monomakh, who received his most deserved title from the Greeks. We are also descended from our most praiseworthy Great-Grandfather, the Great Sovereign of blessed memory, Great Sovereign Tsar and Grand Prince Ivan Vasilevich, Autocrat of all Russia; and of his son the Great Sovereign, our Grandfather of blessed memory, the Great Sovereign Tsar and Grand Prince Fedor Ivanovich, Autocrat of all Russia; and from our Father, the Great Sovereign of blessed memory, the just and merciful and most illustrious, most revered and glorious Tsar and Grand Prince Mikhail Fedorovich, Autocrat of all Russia, and the Sovereign and Ruler of many realms. The names of these Great Sovereigns, our forebears, have been heralded in all great realms. Their great Russian possessions have increased year after year, and many neighboring great sovereigns, both Christian and Muslim, have maintained relations with our Great Sovereigns, and others have received assistance from our Great Sovereigns.

Because of the vast travel distances, our great ancestors and our Father, the Great Sovereign of blessed memory, did not have any contacts with your ancestors, Khan of the Chinese Empire, nor with you, Bugdykhan, nor did they send ambassadors or envoys to you. Because of our unfamiliarity with the Chinese language, the content of your gramotas, Bugdykhan, which have come to our Great Tsarist Majesty, to us, the Great Sovereign, is unknown to us, and we, the Tsarist Majesty, do not know what you, Bugdykhan, desire of us.

Because of this we, the Great Sovereign, our Tsarist Majesty, have now decided to send our Tsarist Majesty's envoy, the highborn nobleman Nikolai Gavrilovich Spafarii, to you, Bugdykhan, on official matters, to learn what your wishes are, Khan. We have instructed him to deliver our Great Sovereign Tsarist Majesty's gramota to you, Bugdykhan, and to inform you of our Great Sovereign Tsarist Majesty's health and to inquire about your health, khan and to discuss friendship and amity.

We, the Great Sovereign, our Tsarist Majesty, wish to be in a desirable state of friendship and amity and uninterrupted relations with you, most illustrious khan and most esteemed neighbor, just as we, the Great Sovereign, our Tsarist Majesty, maintain friendship and amity with illustrious sovereigns such as the Holy Roman Emperor and other neighboring great sovereigns, and with the Shah of Persia.

So that there may be beneficial relations between you, Bugdykhan, and us, the Great Sovereign Tsarist Majesty and our Tsarist Majesty's illustrious lands of the Russian Tsardom, ambassadors or envoys should be exchanged. Everything should be agreed upon in writing, and we, the Great Sovereign, our Tsarist Majesty, will do everything possible to fulfill your wishes, Bugdykhan. Because we, the Great Sovereign, our Tsarist Majesty, in our Tsarist Majesty's gramota to you, Bugdykhan, may not have written your name and titles precisely as your dignity as the khan requires and as you yourself write them, you should not be offended, Bugdykhan, for you well know that between our forebears, the Great Sovereign Russian tsars and your ancestors, the khans of the Chinese Empire, no contacts existed. Because of that, we, the Great Sovereign Tsarist Majesty, do not know how

Many principalities and kingdoms celebrated the legend of St. George destroying the evil dragon; here it forms part of the Russian double-headed eagle. From Baddeley, *Russia, Mongolia, China.*

you, Bugdykhan, write your name and titles in your gramotas. Therefore, Bugdykhan we beg of you to send back to us, the Great Sovereign, our Tsarist Majesty, our Tsarist Majesty's above-mentioned envoy, without detaining him, and give him all assistance, and also send your envoys to us, the Great Sovereign, our Tsarist Majesty.

God willing, when you send back our Tsarist Majesty's envoy to us, the Great Sovereign and Tsarist Majesty, and also send your envoys to us, the Great Sovereign, our Tsarist Majesty, and in your gramotas of friendship inform us of your name and titles, then we, the Great Sovereign, our Tsarist Majesty, will instruct our frontier towns to receive your envoys with honor, and we will order them to accompany your envoys to our great city of Moscow and to render them all assistance.

When we have heard the contents of your gramota of friendship and have considered the content, we will order that your envoys be sent back to you without delay, and in the future, Bugdykhan, we will use your name and titles in our Tsarist Majesty's gramotas to you in accordance with your dignity and position, using your full names and titles just as you yourself write these in your gramotas, according to your position.

We pray to Almighty Lord God to protect you, most noble Khan, and we wish you a reign of good fortune and many years.

Written at our Sovereign court in the great capital city of Moscow on February 28, in the 7183 after the creation of the world [1675].*

Reference: TsGADA, f. Snosheniia Rossii s Kitaem, op. 2, 1674 g., d. No. 1, ch. 1, 11. 135–142.

See: N. F. Demidova and V. S. Miasnikov, eds. *Russko-kitaiskie otnosheniia v XVII veke: Dokumenty i materialy (1608–1691)* (Moscow: 1969), I, 332–334.

*The gramota was written on a large sheet of Alexandria paper. The capital letters were written in gold, as were all references to God and the Great Sovereign, Moscow and Bugdykhan; the rest was in black ink. A similar letter, also written in Russian, was sent with Spafarii; but in that letter he was referred to as an ambassador [*posol*], while in this one, he is called an envoy [*poslannik*]. The Muscovite government did not designate the precise rank of its representative, preferring to permit Spafarii to act as circumstances dictated while in the Chinese court. Translations of both letters in Latin and in Tatar were also sent. These were likewise written on large Alexandria sheets, but were not so elaborately decorated. All were sealed with the great State Seal in red sealing wax with the intaglio. Nikolai was given a length of gold watered silk in which he was to wrap whichever letter he presented to the Chinese Emperor.—Eds.

111

AUGUST 13, 1676

INSTRUCTIONS FROM THE VOEVODA OF IAKUTSK, ANDREI BARNESH-LEV, TO THE COSSACK VASILII TARASOV TO COLLECT IASAK ON THE PENZHINA RIVER

On August 13, 1676, in accordance with the ukaz of the Sovereign Tsar and Grand Prince Fedor Alekseevich, Autocrat of all Great, Little and White Russia, and by order of the voevoda Andrei Afonasevich Barneshlev, the following instructions were given to Vasilii Tarasov, a cossack from Iakutsk ostrog.

Vasilii is to proceed with the Great Sovereign's servitors onto the Omolon and Penzhina River for the purpose to be explained below. In the year 1672 the cossack piatidesiatnik Vasilii Burlak was sent to these rivers from Iakutsk ostrog with servitors to collect the Grat Sovereign's iasak. He was instructed, upon reaching these rivers, to take command of the Great Sovereign's iasak zimov'es, the servitors and the hostages which were under the command of the cossack Andrei Shchupunov.

Vasilii Burlak was to give Andrei a receipt for all of this, and to collect the Great Sovereign's iasak in exchange for the safety of these hostages. But in this present year, 1676, Vasilii came to Iakutsk as a monk, and he is now called by his monk's name, Benedikt. And he did not bring the Great Sovereign's iasak treasure with him. He said that he did go to the Omolon and Penzhina rivers in the service of the Great Sovereign, and that he took servitors, and that he had accepted command of the iasak zimov'e and of the two hostages from Andrei Shchupunov, and that he, Benedikt, had lived in that zimov'e for three years. But he said that the iasak natives had not come to the zimov'e at all during those years with the Great Sovereign's iasak. They had abandoned their hostages, who starved to death in the zimov'e. Benedikt nearly starved to death as well.

[Now Vasilii] is to go to the Kolyma River to Ruzhnikov zimov'e. When he reaches the Indigirka and Alazeia and Kolyma rivers, he is to take as many of the promyshlennik volunteers as possible and go with them into the Great Sovereign's service on the Penzhina and Omolon rivers. When he reaches those rivers he is to build a iasak zimov'e and fortify it strongly. Then, having fortified it, he is to invoke God's mercy and find the natives and take as many hostages as Merciful God permits. Subsequently he is to collect iasak for the Great Sovereign in exchange for the safety of the hostages. But he is not to harm them.

When the natives come to the Omolon and Penzhina rivers to bring the Great Sovereign's iasak, he and the servitors are to collect the Great Sovereign's iasak from these iasak-paying Iukagirs. The Great Sovereign's iasak will consist of valuable sable pelts with bellies and tails, sable shubas, sable backs, ermine shubas, beavers, black and black-brown beaver pups, brown, chestnut and black foxes, black-brown, brown and cross foxes, grey and red foxes, lynx, river otters, black and blue polar foxes with paws and tails, and wolves. The iasak is to be collected in full, with additional amounts to compensate for deficiencies in past years, however much remains to be paid from past years. This is to be collected in full, in accordance with the iasak books. *Zakhrebetnik* [a category of dependent] iasak people and their sons and brothers and nephews are to be assiduously searched for and found. When they are located, iasak for the Great Sovereign is to be collected from them in the same manner as from their relatives, with kindness rather than brutality, and depending on their ability to pay, so that there will be better profit in the Great Sovereign's iasak collection than in previous years, but also so that this increase for the Great Sovereign will be stable and constant in future years. Vasilii is to accept as iasak for the Great Sovereign only fine whole sable pelts, with bellies and tails. He is not to accept incomplete or imperfect pelts, or pelts that have been damaged or torn, or any that are from immature animals.

If any iasak people try to hand in iasak for the Great Sovereign which includes sables of poor quality, or those that are imperfect, spoiled, in summer pelt or immature, these are not to be accepted. They are to be returned to the natives with orders to replace them with prime sables for the iasak of the Great Sovereign. The natives should, however, be encouraged to sell the poor quality rejected sables at any price they choose, to any [Russian] person they wish.

Vasilii is to collect iasak for the Great Sovereign from these former Iukagir princes and their ulus people and from non-iasak people from newly discovered lands. Iasak is to be collected on the basis of the current levy, plus any which is past due. The iasak is to be recorded in the iasak books with Vasilii's name and seal. The iasak people are to be given a receipt for the iasak which is to be handed to them personally, with a stamp on it, so that in the future there will be no disagreement with other iasak collectors and these iasak people will not be burdened with future impositions [for the same year] by servitors. When the Iukagir natives bring in the Great Sovereign's iasak, they are to receive gifts from the Great Sovereign consisting of the same amounts of copper and iron as they have been given in the past.

Either during the designated time for collection of iasak, or before or after, the natives are to bring additional sable, fox, beaver and other pelts to Vasilii and the servitors on the Omolon and Penzhina rivers as pominki for the Great Sovereign. When Vasilii accepts these furs into the Treasury of the Great Sovereign, he is to record in the books the name of each iasak person and what kind of pelt he has brought as pominki for the Great Sovereign. He is not to appropriate these pominki furs for himself, nor exchange the best sables and other furs for his own furs, nor is he to use any deceit to cheat the Great Sovereign's sable treasury. Neither is he to buy any young girls or children or women from the iasak people, nor persuade any such females to go to Iakutsk with him.

If it appears that the iasak people have sables and other furs above and beyond the government iasak which they have paid in full, Vasilii is to purchase the sables from these natives in exchange for goods from the Great Sovereign which have been set aside for this purpose. Purchased sables and other furs which are paid for with the Great Sovereign's goods are to be recorded in the same iasak books, by name and by article.

Vasilii is also to take strict precautions to prevent servitors, merchants and promyshlenniks from trading with the natives or purchasing furs from them before the Sovereign's iasak has been collected. Furthermore, Vasilii and the servitors are not to bring any Russian trade goods such as alcohol and tobacco into the iasak volosts to be used to buy furs from the natives. And if any servitors or merchants or promyshlenniks barter their own goods with the natives for furs before the Great Sovereign's iasak has been collected in full for the current year and for any past years, Vasilii is to confiscate such purchased sables and other furs from the servitors, merchants and promyshlenniks, and keep them for the Great Sovereign, and record the names and itemize the furs in the books.

Vasilii is to make it very clear to all the present iasak people, as well as to Iukagirs who are now being brought under the mighty hand of the Great Sovereign Tsar, that after they have paid their iasak for the Great Sovereign if they have any other sables or other furs left over, they are not to trade these with people from hostile lands who have not yet been brought under the mighty hand of the Great Sovereign Tsar. They are not to take these fine furs from the Sovereign's lands into alien lands, which might be of disadvantage to the Sovereign's treasury and cause a deficit in the tithe collection.

When the Iukagir princes and their ulus people come to Vasilii with the Sovereign's iasak, he is to order that these Iukagirs be provisioned adequately with the Great Sovereign's supplies, and inform them that this is the Great Sovereign's largesse for them. When they have been sent back to their encampments he is to give them strict orders to pay the Great Sovereign's iasak in full in future years, both for themselves and for the ulus people and for their sons and brothers and nephews, for the zakhrebetnik people, and for minors, with no deficiencies. He is also to tell them they they are to bring other tribesmen under the mighty hand of the Great Sovereign Tsar, and serve the Great Sovereign in every possible way, promptly and cheerfully, and cooperate as one with the servitors.

If any of the iasak people plot treason, rebellion or murder, the Iukagirs are to inform Vasilii and the servitors, and in return for this information, the Great Sovereign will reward them by giving them all the belongings of the traitors, and the servitors will protect the Iukagirs from people who have not yet been conquered. The iasak Iukagirs will live under the mighty hand of the Great Sovereign Tsar in security, fearing nothing. But they are to bring in the Great Sovereign's iasak on time, early in the fall, so that the Sovereign's iasak will be paid in full each year without any deficiency.

If any of the natives disobey the Great Sovereign and fight with the servitors, Vasilii, the servitors, the traders and promyshlenniks are to fight back, but they are not to fight those who are obedient to the Great Sovereign Tsar and pay iasak for themselves, or those who confess their transgressions and start to pay iasak. Hostile peoples are to be pacified through war and brought under the mighty hand of the Great Sovereign Tsar. Iasak and hostages are to be taken from them and they are to be brought in to take the oath so that they will be brought under the mighty hand of the Great Sovereign Tsar and Grand Prince Fedor Alekseevich, Autocrat of all Great, Little and White Russia, and will be in eternal servitude and pay iasak as other iasak natives do. Their names and their tribe are to be registered in the books. The manner in which you search for disobedient natives and hostages is to be reported in writing to Iakutsk ostrog to the voevoda Andrei Afonasevich Barneshlev.

Vasilii is to go in person with the servitors to collect the sable pelts and other furs for the Great Sovereign's iasak, and he is to make certain that the Great Sovereign's iasak is collected in full for this year and previous years on the Omolon and Penzhina rivers and their tributaries, so that this service will be profitable for the Great Sovereign, and that the profit will be firm and constant in the future. Once the iasak has been collected for the sable treasury, trail conditions permitting, it should be sent to Iakutsk with servitors without delay. The sable treasury is to be convoyed by as many servitors as advisable so that the Great Sovereign's iasak collection will not be endangered by a shortage of men. The servitors who accompany the Great Sovereign's sable treasury are to be rigidly instructed to guard it and take it to Iakutsk ostrog with great care. They are to bring it to Iakutsk ostrog intact, in good condition, with lists identifying the sables which are to be bound in forties according to quality, and identifying other kinds of pelts. There is to be an inventory of the pelts in addition to the iasak books, including the names of the persons who accompanied the Great Sovereign's sable treasury for verification, and with the signatures of Vasilii and the others.

When they reach Iakutsk ostrog they are to appear with this Great Sovereign's sable treasury in the Prikaz office of voevoda Andrei Afonasevich Barneshlev. While Vasilii is on the Omolon and Penzhina rivers, he is not to send any servitors out to hunt sables or other animals, nor is he personally to leave the zimov'e for any reason whatsoever. He is to hold the hostages with great care, posting sentries day and night without fail. The hostages are not to be moved from one zimov'e to another, nor are they to be released, lest there thus be created a deficiency in the collection of the Sovereign's iasak.

Vasilii, if you do allow servitors to go hunting along the Omolon, and if you do hold hostages with inadequate guard and not in close confinement, or if you move them from one zimov'e to another and any of this is subsequently discovered, then you will be in serious disfavor with the Great Sovereign because of this, and you will be subject to punishment including the death penalty, without mercy, and all of your possessions will be immediately confiscated for the Sovereign.

You, Vasilii, are to collect the Great Sovereign's iasak from the iasak people in a kind and friendly manner. While you are on the Omolon and Penzhina rivers, if servitors, traders and promyshlenniks fall into arguments with one another or become indebted to each other and then petition the Great Sovereign for a judgment, you are to settle the matter yourself without complications if the case involves only two, three, five or ten rubles. You are to collect fees for such disputes from the guilty parties for the Great Sovereign at the rate of one grivna per ruble. For a pre-trial investigation the fee is to be two grivnas per ruble, and for a judgment, four dengas. In cases which involve less than one ruble the fees are to be collected from the guilty party as stipulated, but pre-trial costs and judgment fees are not to be collected from such petty cases.

Concerning cases of slavery because of indebtedness, if the debt involves ten rubles or more, the fee will be ½ poltina, and if it is less than ten rubles, one grivna. Servitors or others who petition for a judgment, but who settle their own dispute prior to an official judgment, are to pay one grivna. But you are to collect double the amount of the fee if deceit is involved. These sums are to be registered in the books, giving the names of the persons involved and the money is to be kept carefully until it is sent to Iakutsk to the Great Sovereign's Treasury.

You are also to collect a fee for paper from petitioners. If there is a shortage of official paper for the affairs of the Great Sovereign, or if there is a shortage of copper with which to pay natives, or a shortage of nets or of twine, Vasilii, you are to make an immediate report about this and send servitors after these supplies.

Vasilii is not to purchase any goods on the Omolon and Penzhina rivers, such as nets, twine, boats or boat equipment, nor is he to keep any money there to be used to pay the Great Sovereign's servitors, or for any other purpose. Any cash he may have should be sent to Iakutsk together with the sables. During his stay on the Omolon and Penzhina rivers, Vasilii is not to distill any liquor or make beer, ale or mead, or set up a drinking place or a whore house or a gambling place, so there will not be thievery and so the servitors will not gamble away their wages from the Great Sovereign, or their arms and clothing. Any person who does distill hard liquor or who brews mead, beer or ale, or who sells any kind of hard drink, will be fined, and his alcoholic drink will be confiscated, as well as his kettles and other equipment. Anyone who set up a drinking house or serves hard liquor is to be arrested. Such persons are to be fined, the fines are to be registered, and they are to be ordered to appear with witnesses in the Iakutsk ostrog office before voevoda Andrei Afonasevich Barneshlev. Their belongings are to be inventoried for the Great Sovereign and sent with them to Iakutsk ostrog. The Iakutsk office will have an ukaz from the Sovereign regarding these drink sellers.

You, Vasilii, are to see to it with firm resolution that while servitors are traveling on the trails and along the Omolon and Penzhina and other rivers that they never abuse or pillage traders, promyshlenniks or natives. They are not to try to buy or abduct the iasak natives' wives, daughters and children; they are not to keep such women; they are not to fight among themselves; they are not to abuse anyone.

If anyone starts a fight or commits some other offense or forcibly detains wives, daughters or children of iasak natives, you are to halt any such infractions and punish the perpetrator, depending on his guilt.

Likewise you yourself are to refrain from doing any of these things. You are not to gamble, nor take wives, daughters or children from iasak people. If any servitors, traders or promyshlenniks do take slaves, and this is proven through an inquiry, you are to take the names of the persons enslaved and question them at length to ascertain to which tribe they belong, whether or not they are iasak natives, how they were captured, whether they were taken during a battle or were bought. You are to forward written reports on any such matters to Iakutsk ostrog.

If any servitors or traders or promyshlenniks take slaves to Iakutsk, you are to prepare a list, and send the list with your report to Iakutsk ostrog. You are also to register the names of servitors, traders and promyshlenniks, and any other persons who have lived there for a long time who have slaves. Those who do not have slaves are also to be identified and their names forwarded to Iakutsk ostrog. Servitors, traders and promyshlenniks are not to be taxed unjustly, and you are not to do this for your own personal profit.

You are not to allow any conspiratorial groups to develop, or bands of plotters, or antagonistic individuals, any of whom might create disharmony and have an adverse effect on the interests of the Great Sovereign. Any time persons are found gambling they are to be whipped mercilessly. If anyone lawlessly engages in some reckless activity which might be detrimental to the Great Sovereign's interests, the matter is to be investigated in detail, and the troublemaker is to be sent to Iakutsk ostrog under guard and a report about it is to be sent to the voevoda, Andrei Afonasevich Barneshlev.

Using both Russians and natives on the Omolon and Penzhina rivers, Vasilii is to discover the whereabouts of the piatidesiatnik Vasilii Burlak and the servitors who were with him. He is to ascertain whether these servitors inflicted injury and abuse on the natives while they were on the Omolon and Penzhina rivers. Did these servitors and other persons acquire native women and young girls and children through pawning or purchase, or by force? Did they sell them? If so, to whom? Vasilii, you are to give instructions that any testimony taken during the investigation is to be written down, with names. Each person must testify under oath and sign his name; any who are illiterate are to make their marks; natives should use their tribal mark. If your investigation reveals that certain servitors, traders or promyshlenniks have taken women, girls and children, and that these women and girls have been taken from iasak people who have paid their iasak to the Great Sovereign, such persons are to be punished by being beaten mercilessly for their crime, and they are to be fined, and the money from the fines is to go to the Great Sovereign. The women and girls and children of the iasak people are to be returned to the native iasak people from whom they were abducted.

If any have been baptized into the Orthodox faith, such women and girls and children are to be taken from their abductors and sent to Iakutsk ostrog. The names of native women and girls and children of iasak natives of the Great Sovereign who have been abducted by Russians but who have not been baptized should be noted, as well as the names of those to whom they are being returned. These names are to be sent to Iakutsk. Baptized females are to be sent to Iakutsk. A list of these females is to be prepared and sent to Iakutsk over your signature, as well as a list of the [Russian] men from whom they were taken, and the marks of those persons to whom they are to be returned. All this is to be written down in detail.

Furthermore, you are to issue a strict prohibition, informing Russians of all ranks that they are not to purchase the wives and children of iasak people, nor hold them, because the Great Sovereign strictly forbids the purchase, sale or detention of iasak people in Siberia.

Vasilii is also to make an inquiry and an investigation to determine whether any of the servitors, traders and promyshlenniks along the Omolon and Penzhina rivers or elsewhere may have died through God's justice or have been killed by natives; and if so, whether they may have left property, clothing, sables or other furs; whether there are written wills; whether they had slaves. The property of such persons is to be inventoried listing the name and items of property. After the inventory has been made, the property and slaves are to be sent to Iakutsk ostrog with servitors, and a report is to be sent to Iakutsk ostrog as soon as possible with any available person. The servitors who deliver such reports and inventories from the Omolon and Penzhina rivers are to be instructed to appear in the Prikaz office before the voevoda Andrei Afonasevich Barneshlev.

Vasilii and the servitors, traders and promyshlenniks who are on the Omolon and Penzhina rivers guarding the Great Sovereign's sable treasury are not to burn anything or light cooking fires [in the zimov'e] in either spring or summer or at any time during the year. If they wish to cook something, they are to go well out from the zimov'e so there will be no danger of the warehouses and the sable treasury of the Great Sovereign catching fire. If anyone wishes to bake bread, it is to be done on rainy days, never on hot days, and water should be at hand.

Sentries are to be posted in the zimov'e day and night without fail, and hostages are to be held in special quarters with great caution. They are to be in irons behind bars, with strong guard protection, so that in case their tribesmen and hostile non-iasak Iukagirs come by stealth to the Omolon and Penzhina rivers, they will not be able to cause harm or free the hostages. Vasilii is to inspect the sentries in person from time to time to make certain they are standing guard attentively and that they are armed. While en route, he is not to accept any runaways, transient servitors, traders or merchants into his group of men. If he encounters runaways en route, he is to send them to Iakutsk ostrog under guard as soon as possible, and order them to appear in the Iakutsk office before the voevoda Andrei Afonasevich Barneshlev. Vasilii, if you accept any runaways and come back with them you will be severely punished without mercy. Furthermore, Vasilii, you will personally have to make restitution to any persons from whom the runaways may have stolen goods.

While you are on the service of the Great Sovereign, you are to consider yourself personally responsible for the affairs of the Great Sovereign and for the collection of iasak. You are to conduct yourself according to the instructions of the Great Sovereign. And, Vasilii, if you and the servitors, while you are in the service of the Great Sovereign, do not concern yourself with the interests of the Great Sovereign, and with his service, and with the collection of iasak and the search for new unpacified lands, and with bringing these under the mighty hand of the Great Sovereign; and if instead, you conduct yourself carelessly in regard to hostile people and rebellions among iasak people; and if you do not hold your hostages securely under close guard; or if you accept poor furs to fulfill the obligations for iasak and pominki for the Great Sovereign, furs that are rotted, torn, damaged or immature; and if thereby you obtain rewards and gifts for yourself; or if you use the Great Sovereign's sable treasury for your personal advantage; or if you resolve disputes between persons of various ranks not in accordance with proper procedure but for your personal gain; or if you conspire with them in some way; or if you and the servitors distill liquor or brew beer, ale or mead and sell it; or if you gamble or form exclusive little groups or engage in conspiratorial activity; or if you take wives, girls and children from iasak people, and detain them; or if you do not send all former servitors to Iakutsk but rather allow them to remain with you in return for a bribe—then as punishment for these things you will be imprisoned and all your goods confiscated and the voevoda Andrei Afonasevich Barneshlev will collect from you and from the servitors involved, mercilessly, all the uncollected iasak for the present year and for past years, plus an additional assessment.

Vasilii, while you are on the service of the Great Sovereign, any government boats, koches, barges, boat tackle, anchors, chain and other equipment which is sent to you is to be cared for and guarded. Never leave these things in the tundra. Do not use them

427

Ox-powered plows made an indifferent impression on the half-frozen, permafrost soils of the Siberian sub-arctic. From Oklad-nikov, *Istoriia Iakutskoi ASSR*, Vol. 2.

for your personal needs. Bring or send them back to Iakutsk ostrog. If you are careless and these boats and barges and anchors and equipment are left in the tundra or elsewhere, or if you use these things for your own personal gain and do not return them to Iakutsk, then the voevoda Andrei Afonasevich Barneshlev will order you to pay for these boats and anchors and pieces of equipment and he will also have you punished mercilessly.

Finally, Vasilii, when you reach the Omolon and Penzhina rivers, you are to bring the iasak Iukagir natives to take the oath, so that they will be brought under the mighty hand of the Great Sovereign Tsar and Grand Prince Fedor Alekseevich of all Great, Little and White Russia in eternal iasak servitude, for all time, without fail, and will pay the Great Sovereign's iasak for the year 1678 and for past years in full, without deficiency, and so that these Iukagirs in all other regards will serve the Great Sovereign loyally and without conniving.

See: *Dopolneniia k aktam istoricheskim* (St. Petersburg: 1859), VII, 139–145.

APRIL 17, 1679

TESTIMONY REGARDING THE SALE OF NATIVE WOMEN INTO SLAVERY

On April 17, 1679, an unbaptized young Tungus woman named Lavruk came to the Prikaz office. She belonged to the Shcholgansk tribe, and she had been the purchased slave of a cossack named Aleksei Konstantinov, who had died. During the questioning she said, "My master, Aleksei Konstantinov, left me behind in Okhotsk ostrozhek with his children when he was sent from Okhotsk to Iakutsk with the government treasury. Aleksei died during that journey. After his death a prikashchik, the syn boiarskii Petr Iaryzhkin, took me, Lavruk, to the Okhotsk ostrozhek and gave me to the interpreter Ignatii Olferev. He told Ignatii to sell me to the Tungus. Ignatii sold me, Lavruk, to a Tungus named Kevani who belonged to the Shcholgansk tribe. But the prikashchik syn boiarskii Petr Iaryzhkin kept the furs which Kevani had paid for me for himself. There were ten sables and ten red fox pelts. Then Kevani sold me, Lavruk, to a man named Inkan who was a Tungus of the Shcholgansk tribe."

That same day Kevani, a Tungus of the Shcholgansk tribe, came to the Prikaz office and inquired about the woman Lavruk. During the questioning Kevani said, "Last year, in 1678, the prikashchik syn boiarskii Petr Iaryzhkin sold his woman named Lavruk to me, Kevani. She had been bought by the cossack Aleksei Konstantinov who is now dead. For that woman I paid him seven sables, four sable backs and ten red foxes. Ignatii Olferev served as interpreter for Petr and me, Kevani, for the sale of this woman, and I, Kevani, gave Ignatii two sables for his services as interpreter."

See: *Dopolneniia k aktam istoricheskim* (St. Petersburg: 1859), VII, 285–286.

1680

EXCERPTS FROM "A HISTORY OF SIBERIA, OR, INFORMATION ABOUT
THE TSARDOMS OF SIBERIA; THE COAST OF THE ARCTIC AND EASTERN
OCEANS; THE NOMADIC KALMYKS; AND ACCOUNTS OF CERTAIN DECEP-
TIONS PRACTICED BY JEWELERS, SMELTERS AND ALCHEMISTS . . ." BY
THE CROATIAN JESUIT, IURII KRIZHANICH*

Siberia is the easternmost region of Scythia and of the Muscovite Tsardom. Its terminus is the Eastern [Pacific] Ocean,
and it borders on the Chinese Empire.

Persons leaving Moscow, after traveling 500 *levk* [1562 miles],
reach the Kama River and the town of Sol Kamskaia, where salt
water is obtained from very deep wells. This is poured into cast
iron vessels and evaporated into salt by using earth-covered fur-
naces. This place marks the end of Russia and the beginning of
Siberia. From here mountains stretch out to the south; they are
long but not overly high. They divide Russia from Siberia and
the Astrakhan territory from the land of the Kalmyks.

The first of the Siberian towns, Verkhotur'e, is located on the
eastern slopes of these mountains. It is named from the source of
the nearby Tura River. This river serves as a water route to another more important river, the Tobol. From the second one can
reach the Irtysh River, the largest of the three, and the town of
Tobolsk which is built across from the mouth of the Tobol River

---

*Iurii Krizhanich [1618–1683] was a Croatian Jesuit priest who traveled to
Russia twice. In 1648 he was part of a Polish delegation to Moscow and remained in Russia for six weeks. In 1659 he had an unexpectedly prolonged
stay. His real purpose for traveling there is not known; some feel he went to
promote Slavic unity, while others believe his mission was to promote closer
cooperation between Orthodox Russia and the Papacy. Soon after his second arrival in Moscow he was arrested and exiled to Tobolsk in Siberia
where he lived for fifteen years until 1676. In Siberia Krizhanich wrote a
major analysis of politics, economics, justice and society, *Politika: ili besedy o
pravleni* (Politics, or a discourse on government), 1663–1666. When he returned from exile to Moscow, the Danish ambassador to Russia, Hildebrand
von Horn, intervened on his behalf and he was allowed to leave Moscow. At
Hildebrand von Horn's request Krizhanich wrote this account of Siberia in
1680.—Eds.

on the east bank of the Irtysh. It is nearly 100 levk from Ver-khotur'e to this place.

I cannot say precisely how many levk there are between To-bolsk and the end of Siberia, but I believe that the distance is tre-mendous. Travelers going from Tobolsk to Moscow in winter can return home in twelve weeks, although the distance is about 3,000 Russian versts, or 600 levk. However, travelers going from To-bolsk to the Daur land, to the farthest outpost called Nerchinsk, usually cannot make the return journey in the same winter.

Siberia came under the authority of the Muscovite tsars in the following manner. Among the many who fled from the tyranny of Tsar Ivan Vasilevich [the Terrible] were persons who were roaming brigands. One of these was a bandit by the name of Er-mak, who was engaged in robbing travelers along the Volga River. When Ermak learned that a strong unit of warriors was coming to apprehend him, he and his comrades abandoned their boats, left the river and set out for lands to the east.

When they reached the town of Vychegda, where salt is ob-tained as it is on the Kama, they met a salt merchant, a wealthy man by the name of Stroganov. His descendants still live in that place to the present day; they have extensive property holdings there and carry on a significant trade. They have no military or civil service obligations. They live in comfort from their busi-nesses and enjoy privileges unlike any other entrepreneurs. The Stroganovs have the special title of *imenitye liudie* [distinguished persons]. In their petitions to the Tsar they do not sign their names as nobles do, *kholop tvoi* [your humble servant], but rather as merchants and peasants do, *sirota tvoia* [your orphan]. In mean-ing and etymology this term is synonymous with the word "vas-sal", that is, an orphan or ward. In the German tribe known as Goths everyone, high and low, used this same term in commu-nicating with their kings. Thus it is not surprising that Muscovite nobles call themselves "humble servants" of the Tsar, because by this they imply something higher than "orphan" or "vassal".

But let us return to the Stroganovs. Every year they pay the Tsar a sizable assessment, and in the tsarist *Sobornoe Ulozhenie* [Code of Laws of 1649], they are granted important privileges. They are referred to by name repeatedly, and they are exempt from certain obligations. These privileges were granted to them because they contributed so much to the conquest of Siberia. . . .

The town of Sibir [the first to be captured by Ermak and his cossacks] was destroyed by the Muscovites and the cossacks. From this town, the first conquered, the Russians took the name "Siberia" for all the regions both near and far, although each region does have a name of its own derived either from the river which washes it or the tribe which inhabits it. Subsequently the Muscovites gradually moved eastward and brought the rest of the regions under their control. They built ostrogs in various locations along the banks of rivers and stationed garrisons there. The easternmost river in Siberia is the Lena, from which are derived the names of a town and an oblast. The finest pelts of sable and black-brown fox come from this oblast. I personally met the man who built the fort on the banks of the Lena and imposed tribute on the region in the name of his Tsar [i.e., Peter Beretov].

Siberia has three climate zones which extend from west to east. The first is northerly and is washed by the Arctic Ocean. Neither fruits nor vegetables will grow here, but the area does supply sable and black-brown fox furs. The rivers of this region flow from south to north into the sea and abound in fish. The closer one is to the sea, the more fish one finds. The indigenous peoples live on fish and reindeer meat, and for this reason they only inhabit river banks.

Dogs are the only domesticated animals. They are harnessed to very light sleds and are used to transport packloads. Reindeer abound and the natives use their hides for clothing. Few Muscovites live in this region, except in the towns of Berezovo, Turukhansk, Lensk and others; however streltsy are sent out from towns in the next climate zone to collect the Tsar's tribute here. The collectors hand out trivial gifts to poor natives, and for these, in addition to the tribute, they are given sable pelts. They also give the natives needles, fishhooks, knives, axes, etc. The elders in these settlements, who are referred to as princes, receive groats, a food which they consider sybaritic.

In this zone there is a peninsula called Mangazeia. A Muscovite garrison was formerly stationed there, and every year eight or nine round-bottomed boats called koches sailed out from Tobolsk along the Irtysh and Ob rivers to bring food supplies and weapons. However since these boats frequently ran aground, it was very difficult to deliver the supplies and cargo to the town, and so the fort was recently [1671] dismantled and the garrison was transferred to another place.

This northern zone is inhabited by various tribes, each with its own dialect, such as the Voguls, Ostiaks, Zyrians, Bratsk, Daurs and others. All are heathens and worship wooden idols which the Dutch saw when they attempted to penetrate to China by way of the Arctic Ocean between Novaia Zemlia and these parts of Siberia. The idols are wooden carvings which have been placed along the trails. The tops of the carvings look somewhat like heads. The carved blocks are decorated with sable furs, and the Muscovites are not punished when they steal them. The Tatars call the priests of these natives *shaitans*, which is the same as *shamans*. Most of them are seers and servants of the devil. . . .

The second climate zone, the middle, is adjacent to the previous one and is inhabited by Russians and Tatars. The following towns are located there: Verkhotur'e, Tiumen (formerly the abode of the Tatar tsars), Tara, Tobolsk (the capital, with the residence of the Metropolitan and the headquarters of the chief voevoda who supervises other Siberian voevodas), Tomsk, Krasnoiarsk, Kuznets, Eniseisk and others in which one or two superiors or namestniks live, who are appointed for a period of three years and have a well equipped army (the Muscovites call these officials voevodas). They are well armed. The heads of garrisons are stationed in other forts.

This zone is rich in vegetation, and it is considerably easier to cultivate the land here. The soil does not need to be fertilized with manure. A settler guides his horse in front of himself; the horse is harnessed to a light plow which turns the furrow. He does this almost at a running pace, so the earth is not plowed more than three fingers deep. They cut hay in a special way here. The natives use shorter and lighter scythes than our settlers do, with a curved haft, so that the scythe cuts on both sides. The scythe is thus never swung without cutting; every stroke, either to the left or the right, cuts the grass.

A certain variety of tree grows in places between the northern and middle climate zones. It is coniferous, unusually straight and tall, and is up to four feet in diameter at the lower part of the trunk. It is called a cedar. Cedar is also found in our Rus near the Carpathian Mountains. It has cones similar to those in Siberia, but grows taller. Possibly it could be used for building, but not without a foundation. It bears nuts similar to the ones which the Italians call *pignoli* although these nuts are not oblong. Oil can be pressed from them.

There are very few sables in this middle zone. However there are quantities of ermine, fox and elk. In the western part of this region on the Astrakhan border there is a special kind of falcon called a gerfalcon, which is rarely found in our land. This is larger than the usual falcon and is distinguished by its very sharp sight. It is magnificent for use in hunting birds. Especially appointed Tatars hunt with them. In the winter the voevoda divides the summer's bag among the hunters and gives each one a special carriage in which the hunter sits with his bird and sets out for Moscow. The Tsar keeps some of the birds for himself and sends others as gifts to the Shah of Persia, the Sultan of Turkey, the Khan of the Crimea, and sometimes to the King of Poland, all of whom accept the birds with expressions of gratitude.

There are two means of transport here. In the winter one travels by sleighs harnessed to dogs, but because of the difficulties involved this is only used by the voevodas or by tsarist couriers. Other travelers use water routes in summer. From Verkhotur'e one can go along the Tura, Tobol and Irtysh rivers, then enter the Ob River near where it falls into the sea. On the upper reaches of this river one can enter the Tom River, and when he reaches a particular portage, that is, a narrow strip of land between the Tom and Enisei rivers, he can unload his goods, beach his boat on the bank of the river, and then portage overland to the Enisei. One can sail on the Enisei to the town of Eniseisk and beyond. Although this route is inconvenient because of the necessary portaging of the boats, it nevertheless has important advantages. It is free from the dangers associated with the sea and overland travel such as storms, pirates, wars and bandits.

The third climate zone is the vast steppe where nomadic Kalmyks roam with their herds. These tribes comprise a people different from the Tatars. The two groups differ in language, outward appearance and religion. The Tatars are Mohammedans; the Kalmyks are by all indications heathens. They call an ordinary priest a *mandza*. An elder priest is called a *laba* or *lama*, and the highest priest is called a *kutukhta*. . . .

The Kalmyk steppe stretches from the borders of the Astrakhan oblast all the way to China. The distance can only be traveled over a period of several weeks. All of this steppe region is barren since the soil is sandy and salty. The land abounds in lakes whose waters usually leave a salty deposit along the shore in summer, similar to lakes in the Crimea. Grass grows there, but it is low, and no trees are to be found anywhere except along the river banks. The natives' sheep are larger than ours. They have huge tails that contain two or three pounds of fat, and the wool of their hides is exceptionally coarse. The Kalmyks do not use salt, which is abundant there, nor do they use it in food, except to preserve such as would spoil otherwise.

Many rivers flow out from this region to Siberia, but they are not so filled with fish as here. Furthermore, the Kalmyks do not grow flax, and so they do not have nets and do not engage in much fishing. This lack of flax also means they cannot make clothing like ours for themselves. Instead, the Kalmyks felt cows' hair, transforming it into a solid mass similar to the thick woolen which the Italians call *feltrum*. They wind this around sticks placed in the ground, and make a tent for themselves which they call a *kibitka*. The Kalmyks remain in one place as long as their herds have enough forage. Then when all the grass is gone they drive their herds to another place. In summer they camp in the southern part of the region near the borders of the Bukharans, the Mongols and the Chinese. In the fall they move to an area nearer Siberia because of the abundance of fuel there. Therefore some of the taishas (two, while I was there) pay tribute to the Sovereign Muscovite Tsar in order to enjoy peaceful grazing in these frontiers and disputed territories. The Kalmyks do not prepare any hay, but in winter they force their livestock to live on shrubs, even in the northern regions of Tatary. Pack animals break the ice with their hooves, push the snow aside here and there and search out the scanty grass.

In regard to military affairs, the Kalmyks go into battle wonderfully armed with helmets, spears and hauberks. They fight with bow and arrow and with sabers that are shorter than ours and not curved. These are similar to the Roman weapons called *siccae*, but these are called *sulimams*.

These people are extraordinarily populous, no less so than the Scythians or the Tatars. Yet the Muscovites reported that when they conquered Siberia the Kalmyks were not numerous. Perhaps there was inadequate information about them. At that time they had only one taisha or prince, but since then they have multiplied so much that it is impossible to make a real count of them, and therefore many have tried to estimate. . . .

Boris Morozov, a very influential statesman and one of the principal nobles of Muscovy, once asked me whether I had heard

435

or read about Altyn-tsar, Kon-taisha, Ablai-taisha, Vezurt-taisha or other Kalmyk taishas or princes who formerly lived or live in that region. I replied that I had never heard of these persons. Morozov was astonished that such a populous and warlike nation as the Kalmyks had been passed over in silence by European historians with whose works he assumed I was familiar.

Formerly the Kalmyks had only one prince; now they have many and call them taishas. Each has a large army, and from time to time they go into battle against one another. These taishas try to live as peaceful neighbors with the Muscovites, providing their ambassadors are favorably received. The Muscovites generally adhere faithfully to this protocol because it does not cost them much. When a Kalmyk ambassador arrives in Tobolsk he is not permitted to have a personal audience with the voevoda unless he represents the great or supreme taisha. An ordinary ambassador is given accommodations in the outlying area and a poddiak is sent out to inquire as to the purpose of his visit.

Generally the purpose of an embassy is the desire to inquire about the health of the illustrious Sovereign Muscovite Tsar and to report the good health of their sovereign, the taisha, and his readiness to be of service to His Tsarist Majesty at all times and in all places, with all his forces, wherever he may be ordered to go. The ambassador is provided with diverse food and drink every day. When he leaves he is given two or three lengths of ordinary fabric, and cloth of a finer quality for his taisha. Because of this generous treatment these ambassadors often stay for an entire year, although they have nothing to do. However, some of them, if they ask and if it is deemed appropriate, are escorted to Moscow, from whence they return with more expensive gifts.

I personally witnessed an extraordinary example of the loyalty of the Kalmyks. One time the voevoda Petr Godunov, in an effort to demonstrate his special dedication and zeal to the Tsar, outfitted several merchants and soldiers with Siberian goods to be traded in China. When these men had completed their transactions, they left the Chinese wall and then learned that internecine war had broken out among the Kalmyks. Consequently they decided to remain near the wall and wait for a safe time to return. They stayed there some two months.

Then a Selenginsk taisha, that is, a taisha who camps along the Selenga River, heard about this situation. He immediately took his troops to these merchants, who were in a state of great trepidation. The taisha took them under his protection, delivered them to the town of Eniseisk which was then under the jurisdiction of the Tsar of Moscow, and provided them with horses and camels to transport their baggage. He sent his own ambassador with them with the declaration that he was ready at all times to serve Muscovite ambassadors or merchants on their way to China, and to provide them with his pack animals and armed men for protection. In the same manner all the taishas maintain friendly relations with the Muscovites. However there are bandits among the Kalmyks who do not obey any taisha. These men sometimes create difficulties for the Muscovites, especially near the towns of Tara and Krasnoiarsk. During harvest time they pillage and take farming people into captivity.

Every year the voevoda of Tobolsk sends a flotilla of 40 or more sailing vessels up the Irtysh River into Kalmyk territory to a salt lake not far from the river. The journey lasts about four months. A particular taisha, most recently Antsian, rules over his ulus there, that is, a tribe subject to his authority. The Kalmyks use the word *ulus* to refer to what the Tatars call *orda*, an Arabic word which means "camp". As soon as the Muscovites reach this place they fire a volley from their cannon and then reload the cannon and fire their muskets. When they have saluted the local taisha in this fashion the Muscovites give hostages and take some from the Kalmyks. That very day they are to build a fortification on the lake shore, and emplace cannon for protection in case of rebellion.

After they have procured salt from the lake they load it on their boats and then barter their goods. Money is not used at such market places. The Muscovites bring all kinds of goods with them and in exchange the Kalmyks offer livestock and draft animals, their sweetmeats, and Chinese tobacco. They also sell male and female slaves, their own relatives, and their own children. If those who have been sold into slavery begin to weep, the Kalmyks tell them, "Be on your way, poor creature, and don't grieve. You will be better off there! You will not go hungry as you have here." And so there is not a single [Muscovite] person in Siberia, regardless of his means, who does not have at least one male or female Kalmyk slave. After the salt has been loaded on the vessels and trading has been completed, both sides return the hostages. The Muscovites give the taisha small presents, remove their cannon, and sail away.

The Bukhara merchants are always present during these trading sessions. They do not trade here, but take their goods to Tobolsk on Muscovite ships. The Bukharans are not barbarians like the Scythians and the Tatars, although they use the Scythian language and adhere to the Mohammedan heresy. They are tall and have handsome features. They do not engage in warring, pillage or banditry, but live by trade and farming. They live in walled towns and have their own tsar, Uzbek; but since the Bukharans are peaceful, they are forced to pay tribute to the Kalmyks to avoid being attacked. The Bukharans maintain frequent contact with the Chinese. In the winter they travel from China by camel, and in summer by boat, along the route noted above. They bring their trade goods to Tobolsk: raw cotton, cotton textiles dyed various colors which the Muscovites call *kitaikas*, cinnamon, although this latter is coarse and poor in quality, and a particular kind of fragrant herb called *badian* [star anise], which has only become known in Siberia in recent years. The only way the Muscovites use this herb is to flavor vodka, which then tastes as sweet as if sugar had been added to it. One curious person tried to discover the precise characteristics of star anise. He believed the herb was useful for preparing a beverage for invalids instead of the usual barley water. He felt it had the ability to increase alertness, and could be compared to Turkish coffee and Chinese tea.

The Bukhara merchants also import tea, which is used like coffee, but is a different type of plant. They bring in Chinese tobacco, too, cut so fine it is like human hair. It is so fine, in fact, that at first many people do not believe it really is tobacco; but Russian merchants maintain they have seen with their own eyes how the Chinese cut tobacco leaves like this. This tobacco is available in a dark color, or a light shade, or green. The dark tobacco has a very pleasant aroma and produces a greater headiness than the other varieties, so persons who have weak heads should avoid using it. They say that this tobacco is cured in a sugar solution. The Chinese and Russians who use it revel in the smoke. They fall into a swoon and are subject to convulsions, and some even breathe their last. However, since the Chinese have had more experience with it, they know how to avoid this danger. They have small copper pipes with an opening the size of half a filbert nutshell. Apparently there is no danger in putting a tiny amount of tobacco in such a pipe and then smoking it.

The Bukharans also bring in precious stones, and they know amazing ways to deceive the inexperienced or unwary buyer. They offer glass decorated in various colors. It is in various shapes and looks like precious stones that are still in the rough, not polished, as if they had just been mined in the hills, with roots and dirt still clinging to them. Each stone has its own form and shape, so that in a hundred stones there are no two alike. When a buyer sees such diversity he is easily deceived. . . .

About thirty years ago the Muscovites built an ostrog near the Eastern Ocean on the Shingal River. From there they attacked the subjects of the Chinese Emperor and forced them to pay tribute. But then the Chinese tsar sent a fleet which sailed from the ocean into the mouth of that river and attacked the ostrog. The troops laid siege, using cannon as well as volley guns. The Muscovites held out behind walls, but many fell dead from shots fired from these weapons. When they had spent all their gunpowder they had to abandon the ostrog and retreat.

The Chinese did not pursue them, but destroyed the fort and returned to their land. However, after that the Muscovites built another ostrog, Nerchinsk, from which they harassed the same Chinese subjects, the Daurs and the Nikans. Because of this, some ten years later the Chinese Emperor sent his ambassador to the voevoda of Nerchinsk. The ambassador asked that the voevoda accept Chinese hostages and give him two or three Muscovite soldiers for the Chinese Emperor to interview. He said that the subjects of his tsar were refusing to pay him tribute because they were burdened by extra levies which the Muscovites had imposed. His tsar could not believe this and wanted to be convinced personally. He said, "If all this is really true, then the [Chinese] tsar will send your soldiers back with peaceful terms for delineating the frontier."

The voevoda sent three soldiers, who later reported that it took them four weeks to go from Nerchinsk to the wall and the Chinese gates, and six weeks to travel from the gates to the capital city of Kanbalyk. They were brought before the tsar who examined them with curiosity, gave them presents, and told them to tell their Tsar to send an ambassador with the authority to delineate frontiers between the two empires and to conclude a treaty for the purpose of peaceful neighborly relations. The ambassadors returned and carried the gramota to Moscow, but because it was written in Chinese, no one could be found who was able to read it.

Three years later the Muscovite Tsar sent an ambassador there, a Greek by the name of Spafarii, with power to conclude an agreement concerning frontiers with China and future trade. When he traveled through Tobolsk, Spafarii said there were two members of the Society of Jesus in Moscow who had been sent there by the Papal Throne. They had pleaded with the Tsar to be allowed to travel with the embassy to Peking, but because it was uncertain what the outcome of this embassy might be, since up to that time the route was still not well known, the priests' request was refused. They were sent through Astrakhan to Persia. Spafarii once told me, "The Sovereign gave me orders that if any priests of the Society of Jesus wanted to return to Europe with me, I should take them, no matter how many there might be." Spafarii reached China, went across the wall, and reported back to Moscow. But what happened to him subsequently, I do not know.*

Twenty years or so prior to that, there was an officer in the town of Eniseisk, a Pole by birth. His young sister was deprived of her innocence by his commanding officer. The Pole was outraged and persuaded his comrades to rebel. They killed the officer, pillaged the merchants' stores, fled from the town and headed south. After many days' journey they built a fort on the river and called it Albazin. For ten years they held their fortified position, sent gifts to Moscow and petitioned His Tsarist Majesty to pardon them for the crime they had committed. They also promised to collect tribute from the natives on a yearly basis and send it to the Tsar. The Tsar pardoned them, granted the Pole the position of voevoda, and ordered the voevoda of Eniseisk to give him and his men all the supplies they needed.

A few years later a strelets in the town of Krasnoiarsk followed their example. He gathered a group of companions and without committing any crimes they moved far south of the Selenga River. They found that the river was teeming with fish, and discovered that the land was rich and fertile. They built a fort, and after several years sent couriers to the Tsar with gifts. I met

---

*Spafarii remained in Russian diplomatic service until his death in 1708.— Eds.

440

and talked with one of the couriers who was the leader of the group. They asked that they be accepted under the Tsar's authority and promised to pay him tribute. The Tsar graciously granted their request.

According to reports the Chinese Empire is surrounded by a wall. The Portuguese call the country China, or Sina; and they call the capital city Kanbalyk. Earlier there was some doubt as to whether the two were the same or different empires, but recently it became apparent that Kitai is Sina and Kanbalyk, Peking.

There was another puzzling question. Is the Arctic Ocean connected with the Eastern Ocean which washes the east coast of Siberia as well as the southern regions of the Daur and Nikan lands and the Chinese Empire? Or are those oceans, that is, the Arctic and the Eastern or Chinese, separated from one another by land which extends east from Siberia? This question was very recently resolved by soldiers from the Lena and Nerchinsk oblasts. As they collected tribute from the natives, they traveled the length of the entire country to the ocean itself. They declare that there is no land to the east, and that these seas are not divided by land, and that Siberia, the Daur and Nikan lands, and Kitai or Sina are washed on the east by one continuous ocean.

In response to those who ask whether ships can reach Kitai from the harbor of Arkhangelsk or from the mouth of the Ob River or from the town of Berezovo, by sailing constantly near the shores of Siberia and the Daur and Nikan lands, these soldiers reply that the ice in the Arctic Ocean never completely melts, and that in summer huge icebergs float there and collide with one another. These icebergs could easily crush a ship, especially during a heavy wind.

In regard to this one may ask, how did the above mentioned ships from China enter the mouth of the Shingal River in order to penetrate into the Nikan land? It is generally known that the Shingal lies far south of the Arctic Ocean and is in the same climate zone as the land of the Kalmyks, where the heat of the sun in summer is enough to evaporate standing water into salt. Therefore it is not surprising that in this climate icebergs either melt, or simply never form at all. Consequently, while it seems quite unlikely that ships could sail from any point of Siberia or Russia to India, it does appear that it is possible to make such a voyage along the shores of the Daur or Nikan lands near the mouth of the

Coats of arms of Siberian towns. From Shunkov, ed., *Istoriia Sibiri*, Vol. 2.

Shingal, Albazin, Amur, Selenga and other rivers which empty into the Eastern Ocean.

A. A. Titov, ed., *Sibir v XVII v.: Sbornik starinnykh russkikh statei* (Moscow: 1890), 163 ff.

1680

A GRAMOTA FROM TSAR FEDOR ALEKSEEVICH TO THE VOEVODA OF
TURINSK, IVAN POGOZHEV, CONCERNING AGRICULTURAL LANDS

From the Tsar and Grand Prince Fedor Alekseevich, Autocrat
of all Great, Little and White Russia, to Siberia, to Turinsk,
to our voevoda Ivan Fedorovich Pogozhev. It has come to our
Great Sovereign attention that in Turinsk in the slobodas and volosts which belong to us, the Great Sovereign, the agricultural
peasants plow the tithe lands which belong to us, the Great Sovereign, but many of them do not plow in accordance with our
Great Sovereign ukaz. Others do not plow at all, but live like
privileged Prikaz officials. Instead of performing their obligatory
service, they send the newly arrived people out to do it. Furthermore, the deti boiarskie of the Metropolitan, prikashchiks, [local]
authorities, the Arkhimandrit, abbots, deti boiarskie, Russian
servitors of all ranks, dragoons, postal drivers and [some] natives
have taken over many lands, built villages and settlements, and
have settled newly arrived people on those lands as farmers.

This has caused disputes with the natives in many parts of the
country and has resulted in hardships for our iasak people. The
deti boiarskie who were previously sent from Tobolsk and other
towns to survey these lands and to register peasant households
and others, have registered these contrary to our Sovereign ukaz
and orders. They have concealed many lands and peasants and
have personally profited from this, and they have treated other
persons on the basis of their personal friendship with them. Now
we, the Great Sovereign, have ordered that in Siberia, in Tobolsk
and in the towns of the Tobolsk *razriad*, in Verkhotur'e, Pelym,
Turinsk, Tiumen, Tara and the uezds of those towns, and in the
settlements which belong to us, the Great Sovereign, and in the
slobodas and villages, and in all the estates belonging to our pilgrim the Reverend Pavel, Metropolitan of Siberia and Tobolsk—
all the monastery peasants and church lands, all the lands belonging to deti boiarskie and all ranks of servitors, dragoons, postal
volunteers, agricultural and obrok peasants, posada people and all
other persons, and the agricultural and non-agricultural lands and
meadows and other properties are to be re-registered, in order to

determine the ownership of these villages, lands and other properties, by our Great Sovereign ukaz.

Our *striapchii* Lev Mironov, son of Poskochin, has been sent from Moscow to those towns to carry out the re-registration. Lev has been authorized to obtain from you when he reaches Turinsk a register of the servitors who have farmlands and villages and who have obligations to provide food. The list is also to contain the names of agricultural and obrok peasants in Turinsk and in the Turinsk uezd, indicating who is working our Sovereign fields, how much land each has under cultivation, and how much grain he delivers as obrok. The list is also to detail agricultural peasants belonging to the Metropolitan and to the monasteries, as well as all other lands and properties. These statistical records and register books for 1659 will be used to prepare the poddiak's records and to make assignments for the servitors, and to determine how much official paper, ink, wax and other supplies will be needed for this business.

When Lev has obtained this list, in accordance with our Great Sovereign ukaz, he has been authorized to review the lands in the settlements, villages and slobodas of the Turinsk region to ascertain and register the name of each person: how many of our Great Sovereign peasants cultivate the tithe lands, and which ones; how much obrok grain they pay; how much land they cultivate for themselves; who have fishing rights and what fish they catch; where the hay meadows, forests and other properties are located; which lands are disputed, and who is involved in the disputes.

He is also to delineate property lines between the Russians and the iasak people. Taking both individual persons and families into consideration, he is to increase the obrok grain obligation from agricultural and obrok peasants on their personal land holdings, and to increase the size of their tithe obligation on their tithe lands. Peasants who have carried on some small enterprise and have settled guliashchie people and their wives and children in slobodas, and have assigned tax obligations to them instead of paying them personally, and have returned to their former privileged enterprises and have been living in comfort for many years—such persons, elder peasants who have been enjoying privileges and have settled peasants in the slobodas, or who cultivate small fields and do not pay tax, are to be re-settled on agricultural land. Peasants who cultivate small fields should receive more of our Great Sovereign tithe land, depending on individual situations.

Any *zakhrebetnik* [dependent] people who so desire are also to be settled on farmlands.

If there are any peasants who have left our Great Sovereign slobodas, and have settled on monastery lands, and who appear on the Metropolitan and monastery register books beyond the year 1659, they are to be taken from the Metropolitan and monastery lands and sent to voevodas in towns, and then be re-assigned to the towns and uezds where they belong. If there are any arguments over lands between peasants from our Great Sovereign slobodas, and Metropolitan and monastery peasants and iasak people, then a petition is to be sent to us, the Great Sovereign.

Lev is to delineate correctly the boundaries between slobodas, mark property lines, and establish lines and boundaries. Peasants who have re-settled close to iasak people and who travel to the iasak settlements on personal matters are to have their lands which are adjacent to iasak lands delineated. They are not to be permitted to go onto the lands of the iasak people.

And if there are any persons who are distilling spirits, in slobodas and in villages, either for themselves or for someone else, or for sale, the spirits are to be seized, with witnesses present, and the distillation equipment and piping are to be appropriated for us, the Great Sovereign, and the tubs and other equipment are to be turned over to the town voevodas.

See: *Dopolneniia k aktam istoricheskim* (St. Petersburg: 1862), VIII, 228–229.

115

MARCH 8, 1680

A GRAMOTA FROM TSAR FEDOR ALEKSEEVICH TO THE MONGOL LOD-
ZHAN KHAN, EXPRESSING APPRECIATION FOR SENDING HIS AMBAS-
SADOR TARKHAN BAKSHA WITH DECLARATIONS OF LOYALTY AND
SUBMISSION TO THE RUSSIAN EMPIRE

By Grace of God, the Great Sovereign Tsar and Grand Prince Fedor Alekseevich, Autocrat of all Great, Little and White Russia, Heir through Father and Grandfather, and Lord and Master of many realms and lands, East, West and North, Our Tsarist Majesty sends greetings to the Mongol Khan Lodzhan, and to his brothers and sons and nephews. In this present year of 1680 you, Lodzhan Khan, have sent to us, the Great Sovereign, our Tsarist Majesty, your ambassador, Tarkhan Baksha and his companions; and in your gramota to us, the Great Sovereign, you have written that your father Altyn, and you, Lodzhan khan, both faithfully and loyally served our Sovereign Grandfather of blessed memory, the Great Sovereign Tsar and Grand Prince Aleksei Mikhailovich, Autocrat of all Great, Little and White Russia, and now you wish to serve us, the Great Sovereign, our Tsarist Majesty. You promise to defend us against our Tsarist Majesty's enemies, wherever our Tsarist Majesty may order you to go.

Now we, the Great Sovereign, our Tsarist Majesty, for your service and loyalty to us, the Great Sovereign, our Tsarist Majesty, and for the fact that you now seek our Sovereign favor and have become subject to us, the Great Sovereign, our Tsarist Majesty, as your father was subject to our Imperial predecessors, we now extend our favor to you and graciously praise you and send you our Great Sovereign largesse. This consists of two lengths of fine English wool, four of silk and one of fine satin. We, the Great Sovereign, have also given orders that our Tsarist Majesty's earlier largesse, which was to be sent to you with your envoys but was detained in Tomsk, be sent on to you in your ulus.

In regard to the matters about which you, Lodzhan khan, have written and forwarded to us, the Great Sovereign, our Tsarist Majesty, with your envoys, our Tsarist Majesty's ukaz has already been sent to Siberia, to Tobolsk, to our stolnik and voevoda Aleksei Semenovich Shein and his men. You, Lodzhan khan, in view of our Tsarist Majesty's favor and largesse, are to serve us,

A bear's pelt and head are suspended over a carved fish offering while Giliaks feast from the common pots. Amur region. From Von Schrenck, *Reisen und Forschungen im Amur-Lande*, Vol. 3.

the Great Sovereign, our Tsarist Majesty, and our Tsarist Majesty's descendants, in accordance with your faithful oath of loyalty.

You are to act in our best interest and if necessary stand firm against our enemies and seek them out, wherever our Tsarist Majesty may direct you, just as your father Altyn khan served our Tsarist Majesty's ancestor. We, the Great Sovereign, our Tsarist Majesty, will keep you, Lodzhan khan and all the Mongol lands in our Tsarist Majesty's gracious favor and view, and your service to us, the Great Sovereign, will never be forgotten. We, the Great Sovereign, our Tsarist Majesty, have rewarded your ambassadors with our Tsarist Majesty's largesse, and we have ordered that they be sent back to you, Lodzhan khan, without being detained.

See: *Polnoe sobranie zakonov rossiiskoi imperii* . . . , First series, II, 236–237.

116

1681

A REPORT FROM THE SYN BOIARSKII ZAKHAR SHIKEEV TO THE VOE-
VODA OF IAKUTSK, IVAN PRIKLONSKII, CONCERNING FAMINE ON THE
OLENEK RIVER, EXTINCTION OF FUR-BEARING ANIMALS, AND THE
DIFFICULTY OF COLLECTING IASAK

The syn boiarskii Zakhar Shikeev reports to Ivan Vasilievich Priklonskii, stolnik and voevoda of the Sovereign Tsar and Grand Prince Fedor Alekseevich. In the year 1681, in accordance with the ukaz of the Great Sovereign, I was ordered to go to Zhigansk zimov'e to collect iasak for the Great Sovereign from the Iakuts and the Tungus. On November 4, 1681, I began to collect the Great Sovereign's iasak, but the Iakuts had great difficulty in paying the iasak. Many Iakuts have left the Olenek River to go to the middle zimov'e on the Viliui, and others have gone to the Anabar River or to Zhigansk and Krasnoi zimov'es. Many have simply left and there is no information on their whereabouts. The descendents of cossacks and the posada people also have gone to the Anabor River.

A list of the names of the cossack descendents, posada people and Iakuts who went to the middle zimov'e on the Viliui and to the Anabar River is appended to this report. Many Iakuts left the Olenek River for Zhigansk and Krasnoi zimov'es after the first snowfall, and took their wives and children with them. Many nearly starved to death. One posada man, Isaak, did die of hunger. The reason that the Iakuts have left the Olenek River is that there is great famine on that river. Last spring and fall the Iakut hunters were unable to kill a single animal. Because of this the Iakuts are naked and starving. In Zhigansk and Krasnoi zimov'es the reindeer Iakuts supply the other Iakuts, but when spring comes there will be famine again. The iasak collection has received a severe setback because there are no animals to be hunted. The Zhigansk Iakuts found themselves in this predicament about a year ago, because the animals will not cross the Olenek. The animals come in from the sea near the banks of the Olenek, by God's direction, and then go to the Kheta River, whose source is near the Enisei River.

Recently the cossack Kiprian reported to me about Kunnechka, the runaway daughter of the Iakut Somogochk Tolkonov.

Carrying out the Great Sovereign's ukaz and your instructions, voevoda, on September 23 I sent three cossacks after that runaway Iakut girl, to the Olensk zimov'e to the syn boiarskii Artemii Kurpetskii. The cossacks brought the girl to the Zhigansk zimov'e on October 5, and she now lives under guard at the dwelling of the cossack Kiprian. God willing, in the spring I will be ready to interrogate her in the Iakutsk Prikaz office, in accordance with the ukaz of the Great Sovereign and your instructions, voevoda.

I sent the cossack Kiprian to the Anabar River, with great hardship, to collect iasak from the runaway iasak people; and he was to go to the posada people to collect the obrok money. I sent him because there has been no replacement for the convoy people along the Olenek River, and it takes three months for a round trip to that desolate area, using the convoy people and the dogs without replacements. May God guide Kiprian. He was the only one who could be sent there because he had been there before, in the previous year. In accordance with the ukaz of the Great Sovereign I instructed Kiprian either that the iasak people and the posada people from the Anabor River were to be sent to Zhigansk to live, or that they should send their iasak and obrok payments from the Anabar River every year in the fall, because the long journey is difficult for them and transport is hard to come by.

The Iakuts of Betunsk volost, Kurzhega Riuliakov, Bakchigir Dedeev and Cheko Andreev, who were visiting their relatives here, are being released at the time of this report. Iasak was not collected from them here because they had already paid it in town. Their wives and children live in Betunsk volost.

See: Ia. P. Alkor and B. D. Grekov, eds., *Kolonialnaia politika moskovskogo gosudarstva v Iakutii XVII v.* (Leningrad: 1936), 120–121.

117

AFTER MARCH 16, 1682

A REPORT TO TSAR FEDOR ALEKSEEVICH FROM THE VOEVODA OF
NERCHINSK, FEDOR VOEIKOV, CONCERNING PETITIONS FROM NA-
TIVES WHO WISH TO BE ACCEPTED INTO RUSSIAN SUZERAINTY, AND
PREPARATIONS BY THE CHINESE TO ATTACK NERCHINSK AND ALBAZIN

To the Sovereign Tsar and Grand Prince Fedor Alekseevich, Autocrat of all Great, Little and White Russia, your humble servant Fedor Voeikov reports. Sire, on December 20, 1681 a Targachinsk man named Daralna, a member of the Boiagir tribe under prince Dydokir Dimetsev, petitioned you, Great Sovereign Tsar and Grand Prince Fedor Alekseevich, Autocrat of all Great, Little and White Russia. He appeared before me, your humble servant, in the Prikaz office at Nerchinsk ostrog and made an oral petition.

He said that he had been sent to Nerchinsk ostrog from the Naun River by prince Aius of the Tuldulsk tribe and by prince Loskiudoi of the Daur tribe and prince Kaiald of the Targachinsk tribe to present their petition. He said their total tribal population is more than 400, and he asked, Great Sire, that you grant them your favor and permit me, your humble servant to receive them under your mighty Sovereign Tsarist Autocratic hand in eternal iasak servitude, and that you send your Great Sovereign troops from Nerchinsk ostrog so that Aius and his men may go from the Naun River to Nerchinsk ostrog without fear of attack by the Bogdoi people. These princes and their tribesmen can not live under the Bogdoi people because the Bogdoi drive them out and plan to take them from their encampments to their Bogdoi empire, together with their wives and children.

Prince Aius and his men instructed Daralna to inform me, your humble servant, in Nerchinsk ostrog, that Bugdykhan has prepared large supplies of provisions and is assembling a great force which he plans to send to Zeia ostrog to kill your servitors there, Great Sovereign. They plan to destroy Zeia ostrog and settle many of their own people there, and for this reason, Great Sovereign, your servitors there are in great danger from the Bogdoi people. The smooth words of the Bogdoi people should not be trusted because they plan to kill the servitors through deceit and destroy Zeia ostrog.

Great Sovereign, Aius and his men wish to serve you in eternal iasak servitude, with their tribal people. They sent Daralna to petition you, Great Sovereign, with absolute truth, not through devious flattery. The iasak natives have to live with caution, for they are in danger; they have to be in fortified places. In accordance with the petition, I your humble servant, accepted them under your Great Sovereign mighty Tsarist hand. But I could not send Nerchinsk cossacks to bring Aius and his men to Nerchinsk ostrog without an ukaz from you, Great Sovereign, because Aius and his men and their tribesmen pay iasak to the Chinese Bugdykhan. Furthermore, in your Great Sovereign ukazes and gramotas to me, your humble servant, you have written that it is not permissible to initiate quarrels with the Chinese people.

Sire, on March 16, of the present year, 1682, my son Andrei Voeikov wrote to me, your humble servant, in Nerchinsk ostrog, from Albazin ostrog, saying that on March 5, sixteen men under the cossack Vasilii Terentev came to Albazin ostrog from your Great Sovereign's service on the Zeia River at the Upper Zeia iasak zimov'e; they brought with them hostages and your Great Sovereign's iasak sable collection consisting of four forties and 27 sables with bellies and tails.

Vasilii and his men told my son Andrei the following news in the Albazin Prikaz office. While Vasilii and his men were in the upper Zeia iasak zimov'e, they went out to collect iasak and came to a trading place where they found both Daur and Bogdoi men. At that trading place a Daur named Altin told Vasilii and his comrade Vitai, not deceitfully but under oath according to his own faith, swearing on the sun and the moon, that their Bogdoi Bugdykhan is planning to assemble a great force to send to attack Nerchinsk and Albazin ostrogs. He has summoned his Black Mongols who are of the same faith, and he has given them handsome presents of silk, satin, velvet, silver coins, silver and enough food for two years. Bugdykhan has also sent an influential nobleman to the Daur people to order them to build barges to carry the food provisions. These supplies are ready, as well as horses to be slaughtered for meat, and grain. All these supplies are being made ready for war.

In the spring of 1682 an advance scouting unit consisting of great numbers of Mongol light cavalry will attack these ostrogs, supported by the rest of the Bogdoi force arriving by water and bringing provisions, firearms, cannon and all other battle equipment. The Daur man, Altin, told Vasilii this in secret, in great fear, and begged him not to tell the other Bogdoi and Daur men who were with him at the trading place. After Altin finished speaking, he asked Vasilii to go to Albazin ostrog to report this at the Prikaz office so that the servitors and other persons in Albazin ostrog would know about the hostile preparations of the Bogdoi and would be prepared to meet the Bogdoi force at the ostrog.

Vasilii also said that at the trading post and in the zimov'e there was talk about war, which was reported by a iasak Zeia Tungus named Davoshcha. Davoshcha heard these rumors at the trading post and from Bogdoi men that the Bogdoi force is very large and that it will be ready to go to war this spring. On February 20, 1682, Logchodoi, the son of a Daur sotnik and brother of Ivan Iakovlevich Vyezzheii's wife, came to Albazin ostrog to visit Ivan and to do some small trading. He told Ivan that he had been sent by his father, who instructed him to say that a large Bogdoi force will attack Nerchinsk and Albazin ostrogs in waves in the spring. He was to inform the Albazin cossacks, but try to stay away from the Bogdoi and Mongol troops. He was to go to the ostrog, but not live far off from the ostrog in the village, lest the Bogdoi troops abduct him. Ivan Vyezzheii reported this conversation in the office of Albazin ostrog.

Sire, there are very few of your Great Sovereign's servitors in Nerchinsk, Telenbinsk, Irgensk, Eravinsk and Itantsonsk ostrogs, only 200 men in all; and these servitors are divided among the various ostrogs. Sire, because of the shortage of men, it will be impossible for me, your humble servant, to defend Nerchinsk ostrog against the great strength of the Chinese forces. Sire, the Nerchinsk cossacks are foot soldiers, not mounted men. Sire, what order do you give me, your humble servant? Sire, it is impossible to make any defense in Nerchinsk ostrog without mounted cossacks. I, your humble servant, am now living in Nerchinsk and Albazin ostrogs in great danger from the approach of the Chinese troops.

Sire, those few promyshlenniks who are in Nerchinsk ostrog do not have any weapons. All the weapons that were left in your Great Sovereign's warehouse in Nerchinsk ostrog by the voevoda Afonasii Pashkov have rusted and have suffered other damage so that they cannot be fired. Some weapons that might perhaps be repaired cannot be repaired because there is no gunsmith at Nerchinsk ostrog.

A leader of the Giliak tribe is prepared for cremation with his hunting and war equipment. Amur region. From Von Schrenck, *Reisen und Forschungen im Amur-Lande*, Vol. 3.

The gunsmith who was earlier sent to Nerchinsk ostrog, Kozma Fedorov, became old and senile and blind, and he can no longer repair weapons. There are no battle-axes, regular axes, pikes or sabers in the government warehouse, nor do the Nerchinsk cossacks have any. Some Nerchinsk cossacks have their own weapons, but not all of these are good. In case of an enemy siege we have nothing but knives to defend ourselves in hand to hand combat.

Great Sovereign, what instructions have you for me, your humble servant?

See: *Dopolneniia k aktam istoricheskim* (St. Petersburg: 1875), IX, 208–210.

JUNE 20, 1683

A REPORT TO TSARS IVAN ALEKSEEVICH AND PETR ALEKSEEVICH (THE
GREAT) FROM THE VOEVODA OF IAKUTSK, IVAN PRIKLONSKII, CONCERN-
ING A PETITION FROM ESEISK IASAK-PAYING TUNGUS NATIVES AGAINST
BRUTAL TREATMENT AT THE HANDS OF RUSSIAN PRIKASHCHIKS

To the Sovereign Tsars and Grand Princes Ivan Alekseevich
and Petr Alekseevich, Autocrats of all Great, Little and
White Russia, your humble servant Ivan Priklonskii reports. Great
Sovereigns, on June 20 of the present year, 1683, iasak Tungus
natives came to me, your humble servant, at the Iakutsk prikaz
office. They were from the Turukhansk uezd of Eseisk zimov'e,
and belonged to the Banandyrsk tribe; their names are Gigalei,
Boldrigach, Tonkoich and Kitanich, the latter being from Muansk
uezd. They petitioned you, Great Sovereigns, through me, your
humble servant, and presented me with an account to which they
appended their tribal mark.

In their account they state that in previous years the prikashchik of the town of Turukhansk, in Eseisk zimov'e, a man named
Timofei Petukhov, hanged one of their tribesmen, a leader of the
Muansk tribe named Mudir, alleging that Mudir had tried to
commit treason against you, Great Sovereigns, by killing servitors. Timofei and the servitors obtained that information from
their slave Uriia, of the Ochinsk tribe; the latter hoped to receive
many things from the Tungus for giving this information.

On another occasion a Eseisk prikashchik named Tomas Pan-
teleev whipped one of their tribesmen to death, a nephew of
Kitakin named Diubgun. Tomas killed Diubgun because when he
paid your Great Sovereigns' iasak he brought very few extra sables to sell to the servitors. Then, a Turukhansk cossack named
Piatun Sukholom forcefully took for himself the wife of one of the
Tungus tribesmen, Albug. The Eseisk prikashchiks and servitors
ordered the natives to bring 20 or 30 sables in addition to your
Great Sovereigns' iasak, and the prikashchiks and servitors threatened Gigalei and his tribesmen by saying that if any of the natives
did not bring in the required number of sables they would be
beaten to death. [The Russians] also put them in irons and held
them in solitary confinement.

These Tungus suffered great hardships and harassment and were ruined by these Eseisk prikashchiks operating for their own profit. In this present year of 1683 the Eseisk prikashchik Ilia Stepanov and his servitors have also brought hardship and harassment and ruin to the Tungus, and as a result they have not been able to collect your Great Sovereigns' iasak from Gigalei and his tribesmen during the winter. They collected furs for themselves instead of collecting your Great Sovereigns' iasak. They have taken elk hides and the pelts of wolverine, lynx, mink, reindeer and fox, and they have even had the children work for them. The natives did not give them any sables beyond those for your Great Sovereigns' iasak because there were no more available.

A cossack from the Eseisk zimov'e, Terentii Ivanov, told Gigalei and his tribesmen that the prikashchik Ivan Stepanov and his men were planning to hang their leaders. For this reason, because Gigalei and his tribesmen had already been burdened and harassed and ruined through the Eseisk cossacks, and now learned that the latter planned to kill their leaders, the natives killed Ivan Stepanov and his men, eleven cossacks in all, and freed eight of their own people being held as hostages. For this they are guilty before you, Great Sovereigns. After the killing Gigalei and his tribesmen pillaged your warehouse of a musket, armor, a copper kettle, two sets of leg irons, sixteen axes, sixteen Russian knives without handgrips, sixteen lengths of iron rod and a bag of small pearls, the weight of which is not known. They also took a musket which had belonged to one of the cossacks. They did not take anything other than these things from your Great Sovereigns' warehouse and from the cossacks.

Gigalei and his tribesmen did not kill the cossack Terentii Ivanov, who had told them of the planned hanging. They took him with them so he could testify to that claim, and Terentii is presently alive, with the natives. More than 150 tribesmen and young natives took part in this rebellion and killing in the Eseisk zimov'e, and all had been paying iasak to you, Great Sovereigns. A number of Banandyrsk tribal leaders also took part in the killing: Gigalei, Kylmanich, Charkygach, Sintach, Siuiagach, Diukach, Dedaliach, Bokangach, Odech, Albugach and Nanbach. They submitted a list of the names of all those who had paid their iasak to you, Great Sovereigns, with the amounts paid, and they signed it with their tribal mark. The natives sent Gigalei and his men to Iakutsk as hostages to petition you, Great Sovereigns, to pardon them for their transgressions, and to be merciful to them. Gigalei and his tribesmen have promised to pay your Great Sovereigns' iasak on the basis of the amounts previously assessed at the Olensk zimov'e in Iakutsk uezd.

Pending such time as I receive an ukaz from you, Great Sovereigns, I your humble servant am holding these Eseisk Tungus natives as hostages, that is, Gigalei, Tokach and Kitanich; but I am allowing Boldrigach to return to his tribesmen and I have instructed him to announce that they are to pay your Great Sovereigns' iasak on the basis of the previous assessment at the Olensk zimov'e.

According to the list Gigalei signed with his mark and submitted to me, your humble servant, I collected five forties and 36 sables from the Eseisk Tungus as the iasak for you, Great Sovereigns. I have ordered them to return everything they took from your warehouse, Great Sovereigns, and from the cossacks; they are to hand it in at the Olensk zimov'e, to the prikashchik there. I also ordered that they are to return the cossack Terentii Ivanov, whom they took during the killing, to the zimov'e; he is to be given over to the prikashchik.

After their fellow tribesman Boldrigach left, Gigalei and his two companions died of the plague. In August of this year, 1683, I your humble servant wrote to the voevoda of Turukhansk, Mikhail Beklemishev, about the treachery committed by these Tungus.

See: *Dopolneniia k aktam istoricheskim* (St. Petersburg: 1867), X, 344–346.

119

AFTER FEBRUARY, 1684

A REPORT FROM THE VOEVODA OF IRKUTSK, IVAN VLASOV, TO THE
VOEVODA OF ENISEISK, PRINCE KONSTANTIN SHCHERBATOV, CON-
CERNING THE CHINESE AND THE MONGOLS, AND THE INTENTION OF
THE BRATSK NATIVES TO MOVE INTO MONGOLIA

Ivan Vlasov humbly reports to Gospodin Prince Konstantin
Osipovich [Shcherbatov]. In February of the present year, 1684,
the prikashchik syn boiarskii Ivan Perfirev wrote to me in Irkutsk
from Selenginsk. He reported that in January, 1684, the Selenginsk servitors Taras Afonasev, the interpreter, and his comrades
journeyed from Selenginsk into Mongolia to buy livestock. When
they returned to Selenginsk ostrog they went to the Prikaz office to make their report. They had heard from the Mongols
about the Chinese military plans; Taras and his comrades gave
their sworn statement to Ivan, who sent this statement to me in
Irkutsk, Sire.

The statement says that when Taras was in the uluses belonging to a Mongol taisha named Tsynben, he was told by one of
Tsynben's subjects, a man named Kianar Kyts, that Kyts had
been in the Chinese Empire and that many troops had been sent
in boats to defend their land. Now these troops are being reinforced by new men from China. The Chinese Bugdykhan has
asked the Mongols to come to his assistance in order to drive out
the Russians from their lands, and to ensure that in the future
there will be no Russians anywhere in their lands.

All the Mongol khans and taishas have sent their sons and
leaders to China to consult on this matter. When Taras and his
comrades left the Mongol lands for Selenginsk, the khans' sons
and the taishas' sons had not yet returned from China. Kianar
Kyts also told Taras that the Mongol khans and taishas do not
wish to become involved with the Chinese Bugdykhan, nor to become embroiled in a controversy with the Great Sovereigns' [Rus-
sian] people. Other Mongol people secretly expressed this same
opinion, but Taras does not know whether or not they were being
truthful.

Taras also said that the Mongol khan Kutukhta, from Ochiro,
told him that he wanted to send his envoys to the Great Sover-

457

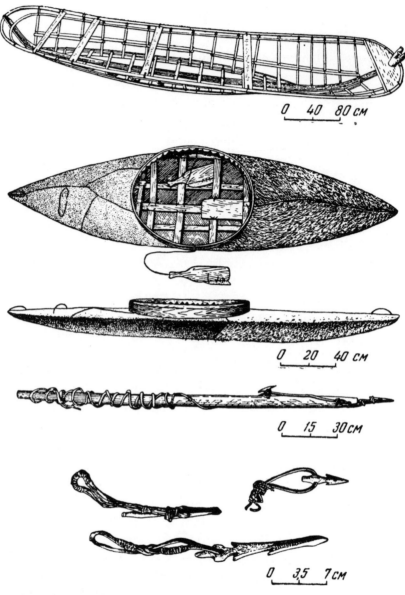

Boats and equipment for hunting at sea. Light wood, bone and hide were combined for maximum efficiency. From Kurvich, *Koriakskii natsionalnyi okrug*.

eigns in Moscow and wondered if they would be allowed to go to Moscow. He asked Taras to send him information about this. Taras replied that he was not informed on this matter, nor were the leading officials [in Siberia], but that he would submit the question to the appropriate authorities.

On that same day in February the prikashchik, cossack piati-desiatnik Kozma Fedorov, reported to me in Irkutsk from Bargu-zinsk that on January 8, 1684, he had received a young Bratsk in Barguzinsk ostrog. This young man was from the area along the great Bugyldeikh River beyond Lake Baikal. He reported that certain Bratsk people who had been in the Barguzinsk ostrog in the year 1683 were planning to rebel against the Great Sovereigns and escape beyond Lake Baikal to the Selenginsk area. As soon as Lake Baikal froze over they intended to flee into Mongolia, and for that purpose all the Bratsk people, right down to the last man, had moved from Olkhon Island to the mainland, to the great Bugyldeikh River, to discuss this.

Sire, these Bratsk people from Nerchinsk are newcomers, and have come to camp in the steppe near Barguzinsk ostrog.

Acceding to the petition of the Barguzinsk iasak people whom the newcomers have harassed and insulted, and who were afraid of not being able to meet their iasak obligations, I ordered that these Bratsk people be removed from the Barguzinsk steppe, Sire. About 150 iurts belonging to these Bratsk people were resettled onto Olkhon Island in Lake Baikal so that they would not create trouble, and so that from now on the servitors will be able to live safely in the ostrogs and zimov'es, and the peasants cultivating the land and the nomadic iasak people will also be allowed to live in peace in their volosts and nomadic encampments.

All of this has happened because the Bratsk have not been forced to pay iasak and no hostages have been taken from them in Nerchinsk. They came to Nerchinsk in the year 1680, together with other Bratsk people. This was reported to the Great Sover-eigns by the Ilimsk stolnik and voevoda Prince Ivan Gagarin, with the report of the prikashchik Ivan Shelkovnik of Verkholensk ostrog. Sire, once we have details in the Prikaz office in Nerchinsk ostrog on how many Nerchinsk Bratsk people are camping in iurts near Verkholensk ostrog and how much iasak is collected from them each year, I will send this information to you. Because of the shortage of servitors, it is impossible to prevent these Ner-chinsk Bratsk people from carrying out their lawless intention of settling beyond Lake Baikal.

See: *Dopolneniia k aktam istoricheskim* (St. Petersburg: 1869), XI, 71–73.

120

AFTER FEBRUARY, 1684

A REPORT FROM THE VOEVODA OF IRKUTSK, IVAN VLASOV, TO THE
VOEVODA OF ENISEISK, PRINCE KONSTANTIN SHCHERBATOV, CON-
CERNING ARABLE LANDS ALONG THE SHILKA AND NERCHA RIVERS

Ivan Vlasov humbly reports to Prince Konstantin Osipovich
[Shcherbatov]. In an ukaz of the Great Sovereigns, which was
sent to me from the Sibirskii Prikaz and signed by the diak Pavel
Simanov, the following information is given. In the year 1683 the
stolnik and voevoda Fedor Voeikov reported from Nerchinsk in
the land of the Daurs to the Great Sovereign Tsars and Grand
Princes Ivan Alekseevich and Petr Alekseevich, Autocrats of all
Great, Little and White Russia. He reported that prior to his arrival and during his administration, lands had been cultivated
along the Shilka River in Nerchinsk uezd and in other places; in
areas which had been ploughed a good harvest of grain was taken.
Peasants have settled there, and there are other such lands in the
Nerchinsk and Novoargunsk uezds which are suitable for agriculture. Sire, I have been instructed to send a reliable syn boiarskii
from Nerchinsk to those places, with an adequate number of servitors, to survey the arable lands to determine whether these
lands belong to iasak people, whether there are forests nearby and
if so whether they have sables in them which could be trapped,
and whether such lands are near to the Chinese and Mongol territories, and whether these people are considering sending troops
there, and whether they contemplate moving in troops for defense. Sire, I have been instructed to report on all of this to the
Great Sovereigns in Moscow [Peter I and Ivan V].

In accordance with an ukaz from the Great Sovereign Tsars
and Grand Princes Ivan Alekseevich and Petr Alekseevich, Autocrats of all Great, Little and White Russia, I sent men into the
Nerchinsk uezd, up and down the Shilka, Nercha and Uiurga
rivers, and to other places, to survey the arable lands. The men I
sent were a syn boiarskii from Nerchinsk named Ignatii Milovanov and the servitors Semen Gavrilov and Semen Tomskov. When
Ignatii and his men had finished their survey of these lands they
reported to me. They said that they had gone from Nerchinsk up
and down the Shilka and Nercha and Uiurga rivers, and to other
areas, looking over arable lands. Sire, there is a very great deal of

arable land in Nerchinsk uezd, but there are no likely sable hunting lands near by, and no possibility for iasak profit. Sire, although sable were once trapped there, it has now been many years since the sable hunting has ceased. Sire, these people live in settlements behind walls with towers, and in ostrogs. They are in constant danger from Chinese and Mongol warriors. Further, Sire, the men I sent out visited those places and all the native encampments in the arable lands where the Daur ostrogs are located. Sire, the iasak people are not experiencing any hardships because of the introduction of agriculture, since they do not camp near these agricultural settlements.

Sire, the 23 agricultural peasants who were sent from Moscow to the Daur ostrogs in the year 1682 during the administration of the stolnik and voevoda Fedor Voeikov have begun to build their peasant settlements in this year, 1684. This year they planted 18½ puds of winter rye on half of the Great Sovereigns' desiatinas of arable land, and they also planted spring rye on twelve desiatinas.

If the Great Tsars were to order that 500 peasant families be resettled from certain Siberian towns onto the Daur land, not simply as a support to the servitors of the Daur ostrogs, then it would be possible to have these agricultural peasants produce grain, Sire, if the Great Sovereigns would send large numbers of troops to defend the Daur land from the Chinese armies. There are many lands suitable for agriculture along the great Shilka River and its tributaries and in the meadows and forests. Further, Sire, according to the report of the syn boiarskii Grigorii Lonshakov there are abundant lands suitable for agriculture near the Argun ostrog. Sire, I have not previously reported either to the Great Sovereigns in Moscow or to you, Sire, in Eniseisk, about the Argun agricultural lands.

See: *Dopolneniia k aktam istoricheskim* (St. Petersburg: 1869), XI, 73–74.

121

JUNE 3, 1684

A REPORT TO TSARS IVAN ALEKSEEVICH AND PETR ALEKSEEVICH FROM THE VOEVODA OF IAKUTSK, MATVEI KROVKOV, ON MEASURES TAKEN TO PACIFY REBELLIOUS IAKUT NATIVES

To the Sovereign Tsars and Grand Princes Ivan Alekseevich and Petr Alekseevich, Autocrats of all Great, Little and White Russia, your humble servant Matvei Krovkov reports. Great Sovereigns, on April 14, 1684, prior to the time that I, your humble servant arrived in Iakutsk, a petition was presented in the Prikaz office to the stolnik and voevoda Ivan Priklonskii for you, Great Sovereign Tsars and Grand Princes, Ivan Alekseevich and Petr Alekseevich, Autocrats of all Great, Little and White Russia, from the Iakuts Tokach Meltekin and Tegach Sednev, of the Idigei volost.

The petition states that in this year, 1684, Tokach and Tegach were attacked by Iakuts from Batulinsk volost, Dachigach Sekuev and ten of his tribesmen who beat and injured Tokach and his tribesmen and drove off their livestock. Dachigach and his tribesmen planned to rebel against you, Great Sovereigns, and run off to the Omokon River into the Tungus settlements. Tokach and Tegach request that you, Great Sovereigns, decree that in response to their petition, servitors be sent out against those Iakuts, and that justice be administered in battle to avenge their injuries and the loss of their livestock. On the basis of their petition the stolnik and voevoda Ivan Priklonskii sent the syn boiarskii Sarzin Krupetskii and five servitors after these Iakuts, instructing them to search for Dachigach and his Iakut tribesmen and to bring them to Iakutsk to trial. On April 27 Sarzin wrote to the stolnik and voevoda Ivan Priklonskii from Tata that these Iakuts, Dachigach and his brother Oriukan and their sons and tribesmen, did not come to Iakutsk. Rather, they grew stronger and became rebellious and threatened to kill them and plotted to kill the Iakuts and drive off their livestock and then flee to the Omokon River.

On the basis of Sarzin's report, the stolnik and voevoda Ivan Priklonskii sent ten more servitors to Sarzin, and instructed him to seize the Iakut tribesmen from the Batulinsk volost, Kunkei Tymkin and his tribal leaders; he also instructed Sarzin to persuade Oriukan and his tribesmen that they must not run off to the

Omokon River, and they must stop killing and pillaging and causing other harm to the servitors and to the Iakuts.

On May 16, in accordance with your ukaz, Great Sovereign Tsars and Grand Princes Ivan Alekseevich and Petr Alekseevich, Autocrats of all Great, Little and White Russia, I, your humble servant, went to Iakutsk. That same day the Iakuts from the Batulinsk volost, Letiach Tymkin and Kunzhegach Kachalin, made an oral report in the Prikaz office. They stated that on May 11 Oriukan and his brothers and sons and tribesmen, 30 men in all, killed Letiach's brother Kunkei Tymkin, and nine other men and five women, in the dead of night. Oriukan and his tribesmen stole sixteen iasak sables which were to go to the Great Sovereigns, and took six women into captivity. They stole clothing and anything else they could carry off. They drove off 300 horses and mares and 110 cows and bulls. The prince of the Batur volost, Setei Nemiakov, told me, your humble servant, that these traitors Oriukan and his tribesmen killed four Iakut men from the Batur volost, Andrei Delgev and his comrades, and took two men into captivity. They stole livestock from others of Andrei's tribesmen, and fled to the Tungus settlements on the Omokon River.

In accordance with your ukaz, Great Sovereigns, I your humble servant, sent 15 more cossacks to the syn boiarskii Sarzin Krupetskii to help put down the Iakuts. I ordered Sarzin to take at least 50 iasak-paying Iakuts whom he could trust, and go to meet with the rebels Oriukan and his tribesmen to persuade them to return to their previous condition of eternal servitude under your mighty Tsarist Sovereign hands and humbly petition you, Great Sovereigns, to pardon their transgressions so they could come to Iakutsk without misgivings and fears.

No matter what the reasons were for their uprising and killing, I told them to petition you, Great Sovereigns, and that an investigation would be made. But if they will not heed your ukaz, Great Sovereigns, and submit to an investigation and offer a petition for their guilt, then I, your humble servant, asking mercy from the Savior and from the Holy Mother of God, and begging your just holy prayer, Sovereigns, ordered Sarzin to punish these thieves and rebels however Merciful God might direct him. Sarzin did punish these traitors, and sent me, your humble servant, a written report, on June 3.

I, your humble servant, will report the final outcome, whatever it may be. I will send the report to you in Moscow, Great

463

The city seal of Irkutsk depicts the savage wolverine clutching a sable. From Baddeley, *Russia, Mongolia, China*.

Sovereigns, along with other official business. Great Sovereigns, there are very few servitors in Iakutsk. We do not have anyone to send out on two-year assignments to collect your iasak, Sovereigns, and pursue rebels. We are using cossacks' young children as sentries, and we have no replacements. We have no firearms in your Great Sovereigns' warehouses. We have no servitors to send out to put down native rebellions.

    . . . [Remainder is omitted because of extensive damage to the manuscript.]

See: *Dopolneniia k aktam istoricheskim* (St. Petersburg: 1869), XI, 155–156.

122

AFTER SEPTEMBER 17, 1684

A REPORT FROM THE VOEVODA OF IRKUTSK, LEONTII KISLIANSKII, TO
THE VOEVODA OF ENISEISK, PRINCE KONSTANTIN SHCHERBATOV,
CONCERNING A TUNGUS REBELLION AND A FORAY BETWEEN ALBAZIN
COSSACKS AND CHINESE FRONTIER TROOPS

Leontii Kislianskii humbly reports to Prince Konstantin Osipovich [Shcherbatov], boiar and voevoda of the Sovereign
Tsars and Grand Princes Ivan Alekseevich and Petr Alekseevich,
autocrats of all Great, Little and White Russia.

On September 17, 1684, the Albazin cossacks Stepan Nikiforovich Kolobov, Ivan Prokhorovich Golko and Fedor Iakovlevich
Sovianykh appeared before me in the Prikaz office at Irkutsk
ostrog. When I questioned them Stepan, Ivan and Fedor stated
that in June of 1683 Stepan and Ivan had been sent out from
Albazin ostrog by the prikashchik Ivan Semenov on the Great
Sovereigns' service to Selenginsk ostrog to collect iasak with the
Albazin cossack Andrei Mokrushubov. There were 21 men in the
group.

Stepan and his comrades came to Selenginsk ostrozhek on St.
Semen's Day early in the summer of 1684. They sailed down the
Amur for eight days to the mouth of the Zeia, and then walked
eight more days up the Zeia to the mouth of the Selenga River.
From there they walked for more than five weeks up the Selenga
to Selenginsk ostrozhek, and this was in addition to a two-week
stopover. They remained at the Selenginsk ostrozhek until the
Feast of St. Philip. During the time they stayed there five or six
hundred Bogdoi troops kept coming to the ostrozhek and menac-
ing the Albazin cossacks, threatening to attack the ostrozhek. The
only fortifications in the Selenginsk ostrozhek were two zimov'es,
but the stockade around them had fallen into disrepair.

The Albazin cossacks feared that the Bogdoi troops would attack, and so on the Feast of St. Philip the cossacks escaped from
the ostrozhek and crossed the mountains to the Ud River to join
the Iakutsk cossacks at Udsk ostrozhek. They took their hostages
with them so that the Bogdoi troops would not capture the hostages at Selenginsk ostrozhek and harm them. There were four
hostages. When they left Selenginsk ostrozhek they traveled by

dogsled for five days. When they crossed the mountains to the Usikan River they encountered some Selenginsk iasak Tungus natives.

Stepan and his men collected the Great Sovereigns' iasak from these Tungus, and it amounted to three forties of sables. However, as they went on along the Usikan River, the iasak Selenginsk Tungus natives attacked Stepan and his comrades. They forced them to separate and then killed fifteen of the Albazin cossacks and freed the hostages. Stepan's ten remaining men abandoned their sleds with the Great Sovereigns' sables, and other goods which had been given to them from the Treasury to distribute as gifts to the iasak people. They could not take these things with them as they fled from the river up over the mountains. The person who taught the Tungus how to kill and ordered them to kill the Albazin cossacks was Liubomir Ivanovich Vyezzhii, an interpreter for the Albazin cossacks who had been sent from Albazin ostrog with them. Liubomir had turned traitor against the Great Sovereigns. The Tungus and the traitor-interpreter Liubomir stole the iasak sables belonging to the Great Sovereigns, and everything else they could carry off from the sleds, and they took the hostages with them.

From this place on the Usikan River, Stepan and his men traveled for six days on foot to the zimov'e at the mouth of the Shivlei River, and they endured much hunger. On the seventh day before they reached the zimov'e they found a cache of fish belonging to some promyshlenniks, so they ate the fish. From there they walked for two days to the mouth of the Shivlei and the zimov'e. They remained there until the eve of Lent, when the Udst prikashchik, piatidesiatnik cossack Gerasim Ivanovich Tsypandin, ordered the Albazin cossacks Stepan and his comrades to move on from Shivleisk zimov'e to Udsk ostrozhek. Stepan and his men spent eight days going from the Shivleisk zimov'e to the Udsk ostrozhek. Two weeks before Easter the prikashchik Gerasim Tsypandin sent Stepan from Udsk ostrozhek to the Maia iasak zimov'e, which is located on the Maia River. It took them four weeks to reach that zimov'e.

From the Maia zimov'e Stepan traveled by boat for the two weeks prior to the springtime Sv. Nikolai's Day. He sailed along the Maia and Aldan rivers, and then from the Aldan up the Lena to Iakutsk. Stepan and his men came to Iakutsk to be with the

Iakutsk cossacks on the eve of Sv. Petr's Day, and stayed there during the fast of Sv. Petr, then after that, he left Iakutsk with the stolnik and voevoda Ivan Priklonskii.

Ivan Golko left Udsk ostrozhek one week before the spring-time Sv. Nikolai's Day and reached Iakutsk a week before St. Petr's Day with the Great Sovereigns' sable treasury. The prikash-chik Ivan Semenov sent Fedor from Albazin ostrog on the Great Sovereigns' service on the Bystraia and Amgun rivers to collect iasak together with the Albazin cossack Grigorii Mylnikov and his 73 men. They sailed from the mouth of the Zeia River for a day and a half and encountered Chinese Bogdoi people. The Bog-doi leaders invited Grigorii Mylnikov to break bread with them. Grigorii took ten or more cossacks and the priest Maksim with him when he went to feast with the Bogdoi troops. But the Bog-doi troops would not permit Grigorii Mylnikov and his men to leave. The rest of the 50 Albazin cossacks and promyshlenniks who had been under Grigorii Mylnikov's command remained in their camp. Grigorii Mylnikov sent an Albazin cossack, accom-panied by Chinese guards, to Fedor and his comrades in the camp, and secretly instructed them to pretend to hunt as close as pos-sible to the place where Grigorii was being held by the Bogdoi people.

That same day Fedor and 23 men fled hurriedly up into the hills, into densely wooded forest without trails. They walked through the hills and came out on the Zeia River, then went along the Zeia to Selenbinsk ostrozhek. All this time they lived on ber-ries. They remained in the Selenbinsk ostrozhek for six days. The rest of the 50 men stayed in camp near their boats, but no one knows what became of them. From the Selenbinsk ostrozhek [Fedor and his men] went over the mountains to the zimov'e at the mouth of the Shivlei River. They did not stay at the Selenbinsk ostrozhek because previous cossacks had left no supplies there. Then in the winter, just before Lent, they met Stepan and his men at Udsk ostrozhek.

Their reports have not been sent to any town or ostrog. I sent the Albazin cossacks, Ivan Prokhorov and Fedor Iakovlevich, from Irkutsk to the Eniseisk merchant quarters with their report so they could be questioned in greater detail. They went by boat with Aleksei Ushkov on September [date missing], but Aleksei stayed on in Irkutsk because of a shortage of money. I have sent

A rough sketch of Nerchinsk in 1693 suggests that the founders of this settlement followed the basic plan for most Siberian settlements. From Demidova, *Russko-kitaiskie otnosheniia*, Vol. 2.

this report with him and instructed him to go to Eniseisk to give it to you, boiar and voevoda Prince Konstantin Osipovich, and your men.

I sent the third Albazin cossack, Stepan Nikiforov, from Irkutsk across Baikal to Udinsk and to Nerchinsk ostrog, to the stolnik and voevoda Ivan Vlasov, with a copy of this same report, so that this information would also be made known in the Albazin ostrog. Because they were poor and destitute Stepan and Ivan each received one ruble from government funds in Irkutsk to cover their expenses to Eniseisk. This was done in response to their petition, in accordance with the ukaz of the Great Sovereigns. The Nerchinsk stolnik and voevoda Ivan Vlasov has been informed in writing about this payment.

See: *Dopolneniia k aktam istoricheskim* (St. Petersburg: 1869), XI, 217–219.

123

AFTER JUNE 20, 1685

A REPORT FROM THE VOEVODA OF NERCHINSK, IVAN VLASOV, TO
PRINCE KONSTANTIN SHCHERBATOV CONCERNING THE CHINESE SIEGE
OF ALBAZIN

Ivan Vlasov reports to Prince Konstantin Osipovich [Shcher-batov].

On June 20 of the present year, 1685, a promyshlennik named Grigorii Olkhon appeared in Nerchinsk with his comrades. He came to me in the Prikaz office and made his report. He had been sent from Albazin to Nerchinsk post haste to inform me that Chinese enemy troops had come to Albazin ostrog in boats and by horse. He gave me a report from Aleksei Tolbuzin which said that on June 10, 1685, hostile Chinese troops came by boat and by horse and encamped around the lower part of Albazin ostrog, and made ready to attack the ostrog.

The garrison at Albazin ostrog is small, and there are very few cannon and small arms, and an inadequate supply of powder and shot. The troops which you, boiar and voevoda Prince Konstantin Osipovich, sent from Eniseisk to the Daur ostrogs have not yet arrived. He has asked me to send troops to him at Albazin, as well as powder and shot and cannon and small arms, to enable him to withstand the siege, for he and his servitors there are now under siege. Sire, as of June 20 the troops, cannon, firearms, powder and shot which you sent from Eniseisk with Afanasii Baiton had not reached Nerchinsk. [Aleksei] asks me to send men from Nerchinsk to reinforce him because he has so few men there.

On June 14 I received a dispatch from the Argun ostrog, from the cossack desiatnik Vasilii Zapisin. He says that a native named Boiar, who is headman of the iasak Tokon tribe, told him that his ulus people had gone after their runaway horses to the Naun River. On the Naun they have massed an army of about 8,900 men who say that they are on service but do not know any details of where they are being sent.

In the year 1684 a fairly good trail was cleared through the forest from the Naun settlements to Argun ostrog. Sire, as soon as Afanasii Baiton and his men reach Nerchinsk, I will send those troops along with weapons, powder and shot to Albazin, and I

Ermak Timofeev, first conqueror of Siberia. Nineteenth-century engraving.

will send some of my men with them. I have sent word to Afanasii more than once that he was to come with his troops as quickly as possible without any delay. I will also send a reconnaissance unit to Albazin immediately, and I will report to you, Sire, immediately on what they discover. I will send the report by reliable couriers. Now, Sire, I am sending Grigorii Olkhon and his men from Nerchinsk to go to you in Eniseisk. He is the messenger from Aleksei Tolbuzin whom I have provisioned.

See: *Dopolneniia k aktam istoricheskim* (St. Petersburg: 1872), XII, 108.

124

A REPORT FROM THE VOEVODA OF NERCHINSK, IVAN VLASOV, TO THE VOEVODA OF ENISEISK, PRINCE KONSTANTIN SHCHERBATOV, CONCERNING THE CHINESE ATTACK ON ALBAZIN OSTROG, ITS DESTRUCTION AND REBUILDING

Ivan Vlasov humbly reports to Prince Konstantin Osipovich. On July 28, 1685, I sent you a report, Sire, with the Moscow piatidesiatnik strelets Luka Stepanov, and with Liubim Sergeev and the desiatnik Iakov Alekseev. The report stated that the Chinese troops had taken Albazin ostrog and that the voevoda Aleksei Tolbuzin and all his servitors had come to Nerchinsk on July 10. The Chinese would not let Aleksei take any cannon or hostages with him. The Chinese troops pursued Aleksei in boats, with cannon and all manner of firearms, all the way to the mouth of the Argun River; but they did not follow him to the Shilka River.

A Chinese interpreter, a former rebel named Stepan Verkhotur, told Aleksei that the Chinese enemy troops would come to Nerchinsk ostrog in boats and over the mountains by horse, with all the requisite firearms. The Albazin servitors and the promyshlenniks and agricultural peasants all petitioned the Great Sovereigns in my presence, Sire, asking repeatedly that they be allowed to leave Nerchinsk for some place suitable for agriculture because they had lost everything. I feared the anger of the Great Sovereigns and did not wish to bring disgrace on myself by losing the Sovereigns' Daur territories and being run off from Nerchinsk, so I tried to reassure the Albazin servitors, promyshlenniks and other people by telling them that we were expecting help momentarily from the Sovereigns and that they must not abandon the frontier lands of our country simply because the Daur ostrogs are so desperately undermanned.

On July 15, Sire, I sent the Nerchinsk mounted cossacks out from Nerchinsk; these included the cossack desiatnik Iakov Telitsyn and 70 others, including twenty Nerchinsk cossacks, 40 men who had just come from Tobolsk, Tiumen, Turinsk and Verkhotur'e, and ten Albazin men. I sent them in five light boats and ordered them to go from Nerchinsk down the Shilka River. I gave orders that if they did not encounter Chinese enemy troops by the time they reached the mouth of the Argun River, Iakov and his men were to proceed with great caution to the Albazin uezd to areas where they might find the Chinese enemy, so they could take prisoners and obtain details from them about the intentions of the enemy. Iakov, the Albazin servitors, other ranks and the agricultural peasants will all wait in Nerchinsk ostrog for news of this expedition.

On August 7 Iakov Telitsyn and his men reported that they had been sent out from Nerchinsk to capture Chinese prisoners and that he and his men had sailed down the Shilka and Amur rivers as far as Albazin ostrog, but did not encounter enemy troops anywhere. In Albazin ostrog and the settlements all throughout Albazin uezd everything had been burned right down to the ground [by the Chinese] but the grain in the fields was still standing. In the place where Albazin ostrog had formerly stood, the servitors did manage to capture a Chinese man, as well as an 18-pound bronze cannon and two iron cannon balls, one weighing eight pounds and the other, two pounds.

I interrogated the Chinese prisoner. He stated that he belongs to the Nikan people and that his name is Uontsysia. In regard to the Chinese troops he said that the Chinese had come in a war party to Albazin ostrog and that he had come with them. After they destroyed the ostrog and burned all the dwellings they sailed down the Amur to a new military outpost at the mouth of the Zeia River, traveling as fast as they could, day and night. He said he had heard from the Chinese troops that 500 men would be stationed in that new outpost on the Zeia River. These men will be selected from among the iasak people; they will have four cannon and will be commanded by a low-ranking officer. The higher ranking officers and the rest of the servitors will take their equipment and go by boat to Naun. The entire Chinese force that came to Albazin ostrog by water sailed on 100 boats. Each boat carried between 40 and 50 men armed with bows and arrows. This number included 1,200 workers who were unarmed, and there were also 100 men with muskets which they had captured from Russian servitors on the Zeia, Silimba, Khamun and Uda rivers. There were also 1,000 men on horseback who rode along the banks of the river, armed with bows, and they had 30 large cannon and 15 smaller ones.

The Chinese emperor had assembled this army over a period of three years for the purpose of attacking Albazin ostrog. In addition to Chinese troops the army included Nikans, Daurs, Duchers, Tungus and Mongols. Uontsysia had sailed from Albazin ostrog for six days under the following circumstances. His father, Uongechi, was a pilot on one of the boats. His boat ran onto submerged rocks and damaged the bottom, so that the boat sank. There were 50 men aboard, as well as a large bronze cannon and a cargo of official uniforms, silk kaftans, satin, hats and Chinese boots, all of which were to have been given out as enticements to Russians who would be willing to defect. All of this was lost, and many of the men drowned.

But Uontsysia and his father managed to swim to shore, whereupon the Chinese officials arrested the father for having damaged the ship on the submerged rock. They sentenced him to death, accusing him of treason. Uontsysia was alarmed at this and fled from the Chinese and came to the site of Albazin ostrog where there was an abundance of Russian supplies. He waited there until the Russians returned, because the Chinese could not remain at Albazin for very long. The officers commanding the Albazin campaign had to return to China because the Nikan people have gone to war against the Chinese tsar.

During this interrogation the interpreter was Fedor Mikhailov, an Albazin cossack who was also a member of the Nikan tribe.

According to the reports of the Albazin people, more than 50 desiatinas of government land had been put into spring grain. Cossacks and peasants and other persons had planted more than 1,000 desiatinas of grain in addition to this. Sire, I did not want to lose this grain which could be used to feed the Great Sovereigns' military personnel, nor did I want to let it be spoiled and thus lose the Great Sovereigns' share of the harvest, as well as that which was to go to the servitors, the peasants, and others. Neither did I wish to let the servitors, peasants and other people and their wives and children disperse. Therefore, since the Great Sovereigns have decreed that troops will be sent to defend the Daur lands to protect the harvest, I sent 198 foot soldiers to the Albazin uezd from Nerchinsk. They are under the command of Afanasii Baiton, the Eniseisk syn boiarskii whom you, Sire, sent from Eniseisk with the troops. With him I also sent a bronze one-pound cannon, 20 cannon balls, five puds and 16½ pounds of powder without wood, and 5¼ puds of powder with wood, for a total of 10 puds, 26½ pounds; and cannon powder totaling 3½ puds; and 10 puds and 16½ pounds of shot. I ordered Afanasii and the foot soldiers to sail down the Shilka and Amur from

Nerchinsk to Albazin uezd as quickly as possible so that neither the Chinese nor the Mongols could burn the harvest in the field.

In August of the present year, 1685, praying for Almighty God's assistance and hoping for the Sovereign's efficacious prayers, I sent out Albazin servitors, persons of other ranks and agricultural peasants to help harvest the grain and settle there. Sire, at the request of the Albazin servitors I sent a former Albazin voevoda with them, Aleksei Tolbuzin, whom I instructed to remain with them until directed otherwise by an ukaz from the Great Sovereigns or by your instructions, Sire. I sent 193 newly recruited foot soldiers with Aleksei, in addition to 123 Albazin men and four bronze cannon. One cannon weighed 19¼ puds; one was 8½ puds; and there were two that weighed 5¼ puds each. I also sent 160 cannon balls, two small calibre artillery pieces with 500 rounds of ammunition, and 40 puds of gun and cannon powder and 40 puds of shot. I also sent supplies with the Albazin cossacks under Ivan Belokopytov and Ivan Martynov; this was government equipment which consisted of small calibre cannon, 100 volley guns with wooden stocks and iron barrels, ramrods, broadaxes and battle standards.

Sire, I ordered Aleksei to travel as quickly as possible with his troops to the place where the Albazin ostrog formerly stood, and to the dwellings still standing in the lower part of the Albazin uezd. I instructed him to build a small fort as quickly as possible when he reached the Albazin uezd. He is to build it in the most suitable place, and keep sentries constantly on patrol so that in case the enemy should come in force they will not harm the servitors and the workers. I told Aleksei to tell the servitors whom I had sent with Afanasii Baiton to protect the harvest, that they were all to be under Aleksei's command. Sire, Aleksei has a total of 514 troops, as well as 155 promyshlenniks and peasants and two Muscovite cannoneers.

I ordered that the newly arrived servitors be given, both for food and for future planting, the share of the harvest designated for those Albazin servitors and others who betrayed the Great Tsars and defected to the Chinese Empire, or who crossed the Olekma to the Lena. Sire, I further ordered that the names of the people who receive that grain are to be recorded. I instructed Aleksei to explore the left bank of the Amur for a likely location near water and forest where an ostrog could be built. He is to dig a well in the ostrog for use in case of a siege because there was no well in the former Albazin ostrog and it was impossible to obtain water. I gave orders that this ostrog is to be built below the old one, with all defense fortifications, so the enemy will not have any access to it. If Merciful God is willing, a new ostrog will be built there, not far from the old one, and it will have additional fortifications. Sire, I have instructed Aleksei to prepare a wooden model or a drawing, and send it to the Sibirskii Prikaz in Moscow for the Great Sovereigns. He is to send a written report to you in Eniseisk, Sire.

I ordered Aleksei to do everything in accordance with the ukaz of the Great Sovereigns, and the instructions which were given to him in Moscow from the Sibirskii Prikaz, signed by the diak, and in accordance with your oral instructions to him, Sire.

Sire, I instructed Aleksei to send out servitors and other persons of all ranks to find the natives of various tribes who had formerly been under the Sovereigns' autocratic suzerainty in eternal submission, and who had paid iasak, and whose hostages were held in Albazin. When he finds them, he is to bring them again under the Sovereigns' autocratic protection, in eternal servitude, and they are to pay iasak again. They are to be assured of the Great Sovereigns' mercy. He is to take hostages from those tribes as was done previously, and iasak is to be collected from them.

I have sent certain persons to the Great Sovereigns in Moscow with the Nerchinsk desiatnik cossack Iakov Telitsyn and the cossack Nikita Poletaev; these are the Nikan men whom Iakov Telitsyn and his comrades brought in, and the Albazin cossack who had been a refugee from the Chinese, Fedor Mikhailov. He was brought as an interpreter and is the only one who speaks Nikan. I also sent the cannon and the Chinese cannon balls, and the petition which the Albazin cossacks submitted asking that Aleksei Tolbuzin be sent with them. I told Iakov and Nikita that they must petition you, Sire, in Eniseisk in regard to having left Eniseisk.

Sire, after having sent out all the servitors, I now have in Nerchinsk ostrog 140 mounted cossacks and 33 men who recently arrived. As of August 26 the 126 men who remained on board small government boats in the Eniseisk uezd because of the freeze have not yet arrived in Nerchinsk.

See: *Dopolneniia k aktam istoricheskim* (St. Petersburg: 1872), XII, 111–114.

DECEMBER 31, 1685

A PETITION TO TSARS IVAN ALEKSEEVICH AND PETR ALEKSEEVICH FROM MERCHANTS SEEKING PROTECTION FROM VOEVODAS WHO IMPOSE UNAUTHORIZED FEES ON THEM IN SIBERIA

To the Sovereign Tsars and Grand Princes Ivan Alekseevich and Petr Alekseevich, Autocrats of all Great, Little and White Russia.

We, your humble gosti from the gostinnaia sotnia and your orphans from various towns, your merchants from Velikii Ustiug and Vychegodskaia Sol and the *lalecha* from Erensk and from many other towns, humbly submit this petition. We, your humble servants . . . send out our prikashchiks and we travel in person. We, your orphans, travel to towns in Siberia with Russian goods by way of Kai-gorodok, but there is no profit in our trade there because the voevodas of Kai-gorodok detain us, your humble servants and orphans, and our prikashchiks, our servants and our wagons of goods; they do this for their own personal profit. They force our drivers to pay one and a half rubles per wagon, and the local customs poddiaks collect a grivna or more per wagon. Likewise in Sol Kamskaia the voevodas collect from our drivers between ten and sixteen altyns and four dengas per wagon.

When we, your humble servants and orphans, go to Verkhotur'e with those goods and stop at the *gostinnyi dvor*, our goods are examined by the customs officials and by the golova of the inspection post and by his men. In the towns en route to Verkhotur'e these detentions by the voevodas are not for the purpose of imposing taxes, but for the purpose of appraising our goods in Verkhotur'e—not on the basis of Your Sovereigns' ukaz or the regulations of the Novyi Torgovyi Ustav [1667], which would be on the true value of the goods, but on the basis of previous prices of 30 or 40 years ago when currency was based on copper [as opposed to silver now]. Thus all our goods are appraised at twice or four or even ten or more times their present real value. According to your ukaz, Great Sovereigns, and the Novyi Torgovyi Ustav, goods are to be appraised on the basis of actual price, not previous price. In the Great Customs House in Moscow, in Astrakhan and Arkhangelsk and in all other towns there are no extra impositions above and beyond the current price either on Russian or on foreign merchants.

Thus when we travel from Verkhotur'e with these Russian goods, because of the high appraisal, we pay the transit fee in Verkhotur'e and proceed from there to Tobolsk by way of Epanchin and Tiumen, where the voevodas and golovas of these towns also cause us hardship by collecting from us, your humble servants and orphans, one and a half rubles per 100 rubles of goods, for their own personal profit.

When we reach Tobolsk with these goods the customs official and his men rewrite the Verkhotur'e gramotas; they closely examine the Verkhotur'e appraisals and compare them with those from Tobolsk and then increase the appraisal of our goods by a third or more.

In like manner in all Siberian towns they appraise our goods on the basis of the previous higher prices, so that the goods which were in our possession before reaching Verkhotur'e and Tobolsk are overvalued. Then in addition, they levy transit fees on our goods, based on the higher appraisals.

When we travel through the Siberian towns the voevodas collect two or three rubles per hundred, based on the high appraisals. They use violence and threats, and anyone who refuses to pay these impositions is imprisoned and subjected to all kinds of torture, including branding.

When we travel with furs back toward Russia, in all the towns along the way the voevodas collect from us the same amount per 100 rubles of goods based on the high appraisal, and they also subject us to violence and abuse.

When we, your slaves and orphans, travel from Tobolsk, there is an inspection point at Nostsy, not far from Tobolsk. That inspection point has only recently been established; there has never been one there before now. And because of that point, and because of the Demiansk and Samarovsk points, we, your humble servants and orphans, suffer loss and ruin. When we, your orphans, and our prikashchiks travel by way of Surgut, the voevodas and golovas there collect from our prikashchiks and from us, your orphans, one or two rubles for each 100 rubles of goods, for themselves. And when our prikashchiks and we, your orphans, travel by way of Narym and Ketsk, the voevodas there also collect a ruble or two for themselves for each 100 rubles of goods.

When our prikashchiks and we, your orphans, go to Eniseisk, to the Lena and to the Daur region and sell our goods and purchase sable pelts and bellies and other small goods, we pay a tithe to you, Great Sovereigns, and all the transit fees along the way. Then when we take these sables and other furs and travel from Eniseisk through the [Ural] mountains to Russia by way of Ketsk and Narym, the voevodas again collect fees per 100 rubles of goods. In Surgut the voevoda again collects his share from our prikashchiks and from us, your orphans. They all collect huge fees and add further impositions.

Great Sovereigns, you and your Treasury do not receive any benefit from these inspections and we, your humble servants and orphans, suffer great ruin in regard to our goods and many abuses from those voevodas.

When we, your humble servants, and our prikashchiks travel by way of Berezovo, the voevoda of Berezovo, Sergei Iazykov, causes our prikashchiks and us, your orphans, great ruin, and he detains us. He collects three to four rubles for each 100 rubles of goods.

When our prikashchiks and we, your orphans, reach the Sobsk inspection point, a pismennaia golova from Tobolsk is sent to the Sobsk inspection point, and a customs golova from Berezovo; 30 servitors are sent with the pismennaia golova and another 30 from Berezovo. Our prikashchiks and we, your orphans, are detained there for a long time. That inspection point has been established in a place that is unpopulated, unlike the previous Taz and Mangazeia locations. In previous years in accordance with the ukaz of your Father of Blessed Memory, the Great Sovereign Tsar and Grand Prince Aleksei Mikhailovich, Autocrat of all Great, Little and White Russia, neither your treasury agents nor merchants nor promyshlenniks traveled by sea in koches from Taz and Mangazeia.

At the Sobsk inspection point the sables belonging to our prikashchiks and to us, your orphans, are reappraised and our gramotas are rewritten. When our prikashchiks and we, your orphans, journey across the mountains and reach Vyzhemskaia slobodka, they will not let our prikashchiks nor us, your orphans, anchor on shore; instead they make us tie up to a pole in the river. They will not let us out of the boats until they have carried out their intentions. As a result neither you, Great Sovereigns, nor your Treasury receive payment. In Vyzhemskaia slobodka our prikashchiks and we, your orphans, suffer great losses and delays.

Merciful Sovereign Tsars and Grand Princes Ivan Aleksee-vich and Petr Alekseevich, Autocrats of all Great, Little and White Russia, have mercy on us, your humble servants and orphans, and decree, Sovereigns, that the Russian goods which we transport to Verkhotur'e and Tobolsk and to all Siberian towns be appraised in accordance with your Sovereigns' ukaz and the provisions of the Novyi Torgovyi Ustav, based on the actual sale price, and that no previous prices be added to them; that they be appraised just as they are in Moscow in the Great Customs House, in Astrakhan and in Arkhangelsk and in all of your towns, on actual price, and that when trade goods are sold, no previous high appraisal is added.

Sovereigns, decree that the Sobsk inspection point be relocated in some inhabited place where you order, not in an unpopulated place. Likewise, Great Sovereigns, decree that the Izhemsk inspection point be abolished, because that inspection point does not bring any profit to your Great Sovereigns' Treasury. That inspection point causes delays and great losses to our prikashchiks and to us, your orphans.

And, Sovereigns, decree that our prikashchiks and we, your orphans, be assessed only a head tax for you, Great Sovereigns, when we travel beyond Epanchin and Tiumen and Somarov Iam and Surgut and Narym and Ketsk, and that the duty from our boats be collected in the custom house in Tobolsk so that our poor prikashchiks and we, your orphans, will not be arbitrarily detained by the golovas and voevodas in those towns and they will not collect unfair fees from us for every 100 rubles of goods. Further decree that the inspection point in Nostsy be abolished because it has only recently been established there.

And, Sovereigns, decree that our goods which are sent to Verkhotur'e and Tobolsk and other towns be appraised by local customs officials on the basis of their actual price, in the same year that our goods reach that town. Likewise in Kai-gorodok and in Sol Kamskaia, Sovereigns, decree that no taxes will be collected from our prikashchiks and from us, your orphans, for our wagons and our goods, so that such impositions of extra duties on our goods and furs will not prevent us, your humble servants and orphans, from fulfilling our obligations to you, Great Sovereigns.

See: *Arkheograficheskii ezhegodnik za 1964 god* (Moscow: 1965), 354–356.

126

MARCH 4, 1686

AN UKAZ FROM TSARS IVAN ALEKSEEVICH AND PETR ALEKSEEVICH
INSTRUCTING THE VOEVODA OF IAKUTSK, MATVEI KROVKOV, TO PRE-
VENT FURTHER ABUSES BY RUSSIAN OFFICIALS AGAINST NATIVES,
PROHIBITING SIBERIAN VOEVODAS FROM ISSUING DEATH SENTENCES
FOR TUNGUS NATIVES, AND PREVENTING IASAK COLLECTORS FROM
INFLICTING PUNISHMENT ON NATIVES

From the Tsars and Grand Princes Ivan Alekseevich and Petr
Alekseevich, Autocrats of all Great, Little and White Russia,
to Siberia, to Iakutsk, to our general and voevoda Matvei Osipovich Krovkov.

In the year 1683 our stolnik and voevoda Mikhail Beklemishev
wrote to us, the Great Sovereigns, from Mangazeia. He reported
that in that year the Mangazeia Eseisk iasak Tungus had rebelled.
They killed thirteen iasak collectors, Ilia Riabov and his Mangazeia servitors, and took one man into captivity.

On February 3, 1685 our stolnik and voevoda Ivan Priklonskii
wrote to us, the Great Sovereigns, from Iakutsk. He reported that
Gagilei, an Eseisk Tungus from the Turukhansk uezd, and his
tribesmen had come to him in Iakutsk and submitted a confession
to which they set their tribal mark. They said that because of oppression and impositions by the Eseisk prikashchiks and servitors
they had killed Ilia Riabov and his iasak collectors and freed eight
of their own men who had been taken as hostages. Gigalei and his
tribesmen confessed their guilt to us, the Great Sovereigns, but
promised to pay their iasak for us, the Great Sovereigns, in Iakutsk, as they had done previously.

Further, the Mangazeia strelets, Terentii Krylov, who had
been taken prisoner by the iasak Tungus rebels in that battle in
the Eseisk zimov'e, stated during an interrogation in Iakutsk that
in the year 1683 he and his men had been sent from Mangazeia to
the Eseisk zimov'e to collect iasak. Their group included the prikashchik Ilia Riabov and the servitors Timofei Perelomov, Osip
Shcherbakov, Petr Kobylnikov and fourteen others. Ilia and the
servitors harrassed and abused the Eseisk iasak Tungus. They
beat them mercilessly and threatened to hang them all if they did
not bring extra pelts of fine sables in addition to their iasak, for
the personal profit of the iasak collectors. When Ilia Riabov was

collecting iasak in the Eseisk zimov'e he ordered Terentii to build a gallows, and then he beat him because Terentii would not do this. Ilia wanted to hang the Eseisk Tungus. When Gigalei and his Eseisk Tungus tribesmen learned that Ilia Riabov and his men had been killed they took Terentii prisoner.

Now, on January 3 of this year, 1686, our stolnik and voevoda Ivan Poltev has written to us, the Great Sovereigns, from Mangazeia. He says that if these Eseisk Tungus are not sent from Iakutsk to Mangazeia in the future, and if because of this other iasak collectors are killed in other zimov'es in the Mangazeia uezd, he will need an ukaz from us, the Great Sovereigns, on how to handle this situation.

We, the Great Sovereigns, order these Eseisk iasak Tungus who have been transferred to Iakutsk to remain there but to pay the same iasak as they paid in Mangazeia. And in the future no one, including voevodas, is to execute or hang these Tungus unless we, the Great Sovereigns, issue an ukaz to that effect. Likewise, iasak collectors are forbidden to inflict punishment on these Tungus. Only the voevodas may punish them, depending on their guilt, after an investigation has been made. When this our Great Sovereigns' gramota reaches you, you are to act in accordance with this ukaz of ours, the Great Sovereigns.

See: Ia. P. Alkor and B. D. Grekov, eds., *Kolonialnaia politika moskovskogo gosudarstva v Iakutii XVII v.* (Leningrad: 1936), 245–246.

127

1687

A REPORT TO TSARS IVAN ALEKSEEVICH AND PETR ALEKSEEVICH
FROM THE BOIAR FEDOR GOLOVIN CONCERNING THE SIEGE OF AL-
BAZIN BY THE MANCHU ARMY IN 1686

To the Sovereign Tsars and Grand Princes Ivan Alekseevich and Petr Alekseevich, Autocrats of all Great, Little and White Russia, your humble servant Fedor Golovin reports.

Sovereigns, on January 14 of this year, 1687, the stolnik and voevoda Ivan Vlasov wrote to me, your humble servant, from Nerchinsk that on November 9 three Albazin cossacks, Ivan Busunov, Vasilii Baksheev and Iakov Martynov, appeared before him in the Prikaz office at Nerchinsk. They brought him a report from the cossack golova Afanasii Baiton at Albazin, which bore your Great Sovereigns' seal of Albazin.

In the inquiry which I, your humble servant, conducted, these men from besieged Albazin recounted that on July 7 of last year, 1686, Chinese troops laid siege to the town of Albazin and fired their cannon onto the town unceasingly. On the fifth day after the Chinese arrived the voevoda Aleksei Tolbuzin was killed. A cannon ball tore off his right leg at the knee and Aleksei died from that wound on the fourth day. The cannon ball had penetrated an embrasure in the tower where Aleksei was standing at that very moment. While Aleksei Tolbuzin was still alive, and likewise after his death, the besieged inhabitants formed a five-man reconnaissance party. During their sorties out from Albazin they killed about 150 enemy men. They killed two Chinese sotniks with explosive grenades. On the third sortie they captured three men who spoke a language similar to Nikan, but no one can actually understand them, since none of the Albazin servitors speaks Nikan. They do not speak either Chinese or Mongol.

The enemy killed 21 men from the besieged garrison at Albazin; these men were out on reconnaissance. They killed 40 in town, and 50 more died of scurvy. Ivan says he does not remember the names of the servitors who were killed outright or who died later. The [Manchu] Chinese enemy have stationed themselves around the town in a circle about 200 sazhens in circumference. Albazin itself is surrounded by a wall. There are embrasures in the wall, and in four places, platforms with two cannon; around one platform there are fifteen mobile cannon. Earthworks have been thrown up on the other side of the Amur River opposite the town. Sovereigns, there are about 800 people of all ranks in the besieged settlement of Albazin. They have 8 bronze cannon, 3 volley guns, 60 puds of shot and gunpowder, a horse-drawn cannon, 5 light cannon balls, 33 heavy ones and 70 grenades. Ivan believes that their food will last until the first of April, 1687. Sovereigns, there are about 5,000 Chinese troops stationed around the town, including many laborers for the army. They have 40 cannon, 6 barges of powder and shot and 2 barge-loads of arrows.

Sovereigns, the Chinese have repeatedly sent beautifully worded letters from their camp to the town asking for the surrender of the town. In these guileful letters they say that Bugdy-khan has sent them two men who are assigned to receive the surrender of the town from the besieged people, and that if anyone wishes to go to your towns, Great Sovereigns, they will be given food and provisions and safe conduct to the Daur ostrogs, and that anyone who wishes to serve Bugdykhan will be received in his name with honor and privilege. The enemy have built three settlements near Albazin, with many iurts in them. The people under siege have agreed together that they will hold out as long as their food lasts. When the food is gone, they will collect all their firearms and melt them down, then they will set fire to the powder and explosives depot. They will take their light weapons and go to the town of Nerchinsk.

Ivan came from Albazin traveling by boat on the Amur River at night, sailing between floes of ice. From Albazin he sailed for some four versts, but then his boat was crushed by ice. Ivan and his comrades stayed on an island for eight days waiting for the Amur to freeze over. When the Amur was frozen they walked on the ice and then went through the forest to Nerchinsk. They walked day and night for three weeks, living on wild berries. Sometimes they found scorched grain in fields which had been burned by the Chinese. These fields had been farmed by the Albazin agricultural peasants [who had been sent out from European Russia].

See: A. A. Zimin, ed., *Khrestomatiia po istorii SSSR, XVI–XVII vv.* (Moscow: 1962), II, 534–536.

A TREATY CONCLUDED BETWEEN THE MONGOL TAISHAS AND THE RUSSIAN AMBASSADORS ON THE CHINESE FRONTIER

The okolnichi and namestnik of Briansk, Fedor Alekseevich Golovin, and his companions, great plenipotentiary ambassadors of Their Tsarist Majesties, glorious in the grace of Almighty God and the Holy Trinity, the Great Sovereign Tsars and Grand Princes Ivan Alekseevich and Petr Alekseevich, Tsars of Tsars, Lords of realms, conquerors of empires, Autocrats of lands from East to West, Possessors of lands from North to South, Emperors of their realms of Moscow, Kiev, Vladimir, Novgorod, Kazan, Astrakhan, Siberia, Pskov, Smolensk, Tver, Iugra, Perm, Viatka, Bulgaria and others, Sovereigns and Grand Princes of the lands of Nizhnii Novgorod, Chernigov, Riazan, Rostov, Iaroslav, Beloozero, Udorsk, Obdorsk and Kondinsk; Sovereigns of the lands of Iversk which belong to the Kartalin and Gruzin tsars, and of the Kabardin lands of the Cherkassian and Mountain princes; and Sovereigns of many other realms which they have conquered and brought under their authority and mighty hand, Mighty Autocrats who extend peace and tranquillity to those who seek it, Administrators of peaceful affairs for betterment and progress, Christian Monarchs, endowed with every grace of the Highest Tsar, God the Tsar—[these ambassadors] have concluded this treaty and concord, eternally inviolable, with the Mongol Irka Kantazi and other taishas who have appended their names below, and who will continue to be the rulers over their Mongol ulus peoples.

On November 10 these taishas sent their envoy Uizaisan to the great plenipoteniary ambassadors of the Great Sovereigns, their Tsarist Majesties, to the okolnichi and namestnik of Briansk, Fedor Alekseevich Golovin and his associates, with letters wherein they requested that the Great Sovereigns, Their Tsarist Majesties, grant their request and give orders that they be accepted under Their Tsarist Majesties' mighty autocratic hand with all of their present and future ulus people.

The taishas promise to serve Their Tsarist Majesties loyally, never betraying them. The taishas request that they and their ulus people be permitted to camp near the town of Selenginsk which belongs to Their Tsarist Majesties, along both banks of the Selenga River, and that they not suffer oppression at the hands of Their Tsarist Majesties' subjects.

In accordance with the ukaz of the Great Sovereigns, Their Tsarist Majesties, the great and plenipotentiary ambassadors, the okolnichi and namestnik of Briansk, Fedor Alekseevich Golovin and his associates, have granted the request of Irka Kantazi and the other taishas that they and all of the *zaisans* and ulus people be brought into eternal servitude under the mighty hand of the Autocrats, Their Tsarist Majesties, under the terms of the following articles.

I. These taishas Irka Kantazi, Erden Batur, Serenzab Bantukhai, Chin Erden Dorzh, Irka Akhai and Elden Akhai, and all the zaisans and their ulus people and all of their descendents are to be in eternal servitude to the mighty autocratic hand of Their Tsarist Majesties, firm and steadfast, never betraying; and they are to serve the Great Sovereigns, Their Tsarist Majesties, in complete loyalty. Whenever an order of Their Tsarist Majesties is issued, directing them to go into battle against peoples who may attack subjects of Their Tsarist Majesties, these taishas are to send their ulus people with the armies of Their Tsarist Majesties in accordance with the instructions of the Great Sovereigns, Their Tsarist Majesties, or in accordance with the instructions written to them by the voevodas of Their Tsarist Majesties from border towns.

The Great Sovereigns, Their Tsarist Majesties, will never withdraw their favor from these taishas for their loyal service, and they will order that they be protected from attacking forces of other powers.

II. If for some urgent reason there is a need for troops of the Great Sovereigns, Their Tsarist Majesties, to proceed to the Daur ostrogs or to other places, then the taishas are to take part in this undertaking to the extent of their ability, and send as many horses and camels as possible for purposes of transport. All transport animals which return from the expedition alive will be returned to the taishas.

III. Subjects of Their Tsarist Majesties who may camp near the taishas' nomadic people are not to be subjected to any oppression or injuries, nor are their livestock and horses to be driven off. The taishas are to issue firm orders regarding this in their uluses. If any of the ulus people breaks this rule and drives off the horses or livestock belonging to Russian people or to iasak natives, when such a criminal is apprehended he is to be punished by the taishas in accordance with their own laws. For every horse driven off, the criminal must repay three horses to the owner of the horse he drove off. The Great Sovereigns, Their Tsarist Majesties, will issue like orders to their ulus people.

IV. If any of the [Mongol] ulus people kill a Russian subject of Their Tsarist Majesties or a iasak native, then this outlaw and his accomplices are to be punished by death. Their Tsarist Majesties will invoke the same punishment for their own people.

V. Neither taishas, zaisans or their ulus people are to be converted or forced to accept Orthodox Christianity. Further, neither taishas nor their ulus people will have to pay iasak to the Great Sovereigns.

If any ulus people flee to Their Tsarist Majesties' border towns, the runaways are to be remanded to their taishas. The taishas are to issue strict orders in their uluses that if any iasak or non-iasak native subject to Their Tsarist Majesties commits a crime and flees to ulus people, they are to be apprehended; and the taishas are to remand them to Their Tsarist Majesties' border towns without delay. If anyone secretly harbors such runaways he is to be severely punished in accordance with the prevailing custom.

VI. The Mongol Batur Kontaisha caused the present war without any provocation on the part of the Great Sovereigns, Their Tsarist Majesties. The taishas are henceforth never to request any special favor from the Great Sovereigns, Their Tsarist Majesties, in regard to conquered Mongol ulus people who have voluntarily sought the protection of the Great Sovereigns or people who have been brought under the Mighty Autocratic Hand of Their Tsarist Majesties and who have been paying iasak up to the present time, such as the Bratsk or the Tungus people. The taishas have many times in the past petitioned in regard to these peoples, but they are not to do so in the future, nor are they to oppress them, impose payments on them, or try to annex them in servitude into their uluses at any future time.

VII. The taishas are not to follow the commands of their previous kutukhta, or their khan Ocharai, or other Mongol rulers, or rulers of other realms; nor are they to maintain contact with such persons without the knowledge of Their Tsarist Majesties, whose authority is vested by ukaz in the voevodas of Nerchinsk and Selenginsk. They are not to conclude an agreement on any matter, nor make any commitment to provide assistance. If they wish to contact their kutukhta Chechen, or their khan or any other Mongol ruler on any matter, they are to send a request for permission to the voevoda of Selenginsk or the voevodas of other frontier towns belonging to Their Tsarist Majesties. Likewise, if the khan or kutukhta or other rulers send their envoys to the taishas on any matters, they are to make a detailed report about their business to the great and plenipotentiary ambassadors of Their Tsarist Majesties; in the absence of the ambassadors they are to report to the voevodas of the above mentioned towns.

VIII. As subjects of the Great Sovereigns, Their Tsarist Majesties, the taishas are to summon other Mongol rulers to come under the mighty hand of the Great Sovereign Autocrats, Their Tsarist Majesties. If the plenipotentiary ambassadors or voevodas of border towns send servitors to the taishas on official matters, the taishas are to provide these persons with transport, provisions and an adequate number of guides. They are to answer all their questions and then send them on their way with due respect.

IX. Upon the request of the above mentioned taishas, their envoys are to be allowed to proceed to Moscow to the Great Sovereigns in the spring.

Irka Kantazi and the other taishas have sworn on their own faith to uphold these articles personally, and have committed future taishas to do the same, and they have personally signed this treaty.

In addition to these articles which were sent to the Mongol taishas from the Great Plenipotentiary Ambassador, okolnichi and namestnik of Briansk Fedor Alekseevich Golovin and his associates, the taishas have negotiated with Ivan Kachanov and have agreed to the following terms of the nakaz from the Great Plenipotentiary Ambassador, the okolnichi and the namestnik of Briansk, Fedor Alekseevich Golovin; and they have affirmed this by oath, by signature, and by imprinting with the seal.

1. Irka Kantazi, Erden Batur, Serenzab Bantukhai, Chin Erden Dorzh, Irka Akhai and Elden Akhai are to make an annual gift to the Treasury of the Great Sovereigns in the town of Selenginsk, from five of their encampments. The gift will be fifty fine horses, fifty fine head of cattle and fifty fine sheep. If any of their brothers or tribesmen does not contribute in a certain year, or does not give his full share, then he must [later] give threefold.

Personal iasak is not to be collected from their ulus people. The taishas are to continue to give orders to their own ulus people in accordance with their laws.

2. If envoys are sent to taishas in the Mongol uluses on the Great Sovereigns' business and anyone abuses these envoys in any way, the persons who commit such offenses are to compensate the envoys with five camels, ten horses, ten head of cattle and twenty sheep.

3. An interpreter is to be compensated for an abuse with two camels, five horses, five head of cattle and ten sheep.

4. If a servitor is abused the compensation is to be three horses, three head of cattle and five sheep. And if anyone harms the envoy, or hits him with his fist or with a wooden club, then the guilty party must pay double the fine indicated above.

5. If murder is committed without cause, a full investigation is to be conducted, and then the murderer and any accomplices are to be punished by death in the presence of observers appointed by both sides specifically for that purpose.

6. If any of the taishas or zaisans plots an evil act, or if their ulus people plan to commit treason and rebel against the mighty autocratic hand of Their Great Majesties, and another taisha or Their Tsarist Majesties' iasak natives or some Bratsk people or people from other tribes should discover this contemplated evil action and intent, the taishas, upon being informed of this, are to seize the guilty person and confiscate all of his belongings; they are to take his wife and children from him, and turn him over to Their Tsarist Majesties' voevoda in the nearest border town, where the person will be punished in accordance with Russian law.

7. If any iasak natives from any place run off to another ulus, these runaways are to be remanded without delay. If that same person attempts to run off again, he is to be apprehended, his arm and his leg are to be broken, and he is to be remanded to the place from where he fled.

See: *Polnoe sobranie zakonov rossiiskoi imperii. . . .* First Series, III, 3–7.

MARCH 12, 1689

TREATY ARTICLES AND OATH SWORN BY THE TABUN SAITS* PLEDG-
ING ETERNAL SUBMISSION TO THE RUSSIAN EMPIRE

In the name of Almighty God, Glorious in the Holy Trinity, and before the Great Sovereign Tsars and Grand Princes Ivan Alekseevich and Petr Alekseevich, Autocrats of all Great, Little and White Russia; and before the great plenipotentiary ambassadors of their Illustrious Tsarist Majesties, the okolnichi and namestnik of Briansk, Fedor Alekseevich Golovin and his associates; and in the presence of an official of the Posolskii Prikaz, the dvorianin Fedor Prokhorovich Ushakov; and in the presence of the syn boiarskii Petr Mnogogreshnyi; and in the presence of the poddiak Fedor Udashin; we, the Tabun Saits—Sain Okin, Narmo Tarkhan, Batur Sotui, Nachin Mosogo, Sainkia Sotulai, Kartsagai, Nesk zaisan, Irkinia, Inkibei, Bashk Darkhan, Shiretui Udzin, Kaska Unen, Guin zaisan, and the *shulengas*** Temdekei Darkhan, Kosiuchi Mongotei, Koton Serchi, Chelonka, Temdei, Buda, Mergenkia, Sorchi Dalaikia, Zitugei, Nachin, Naptagar, Buda, Mergen, Sadziski, Sotku, Shiretui, Gonbo Darkhan, Darzia Menzei, Kultsadai Guriushki, Dalai Tseren and Tsebul, and all their children and ulus people pledge to serve loyally and swear to uphold the following articles.

1. Sain Okin, Narmo Tarkhan, Batur Tokui, Nachin Mosoga, Sain Sotulai, Kartsagai, Nesk zaisan, Inkin, Irkibei, Bashka Dakhhan, Shiretui Udzin, Kashka Unen, Guin zaisan, and the above mentioned shulengas and their children and ulus people are to be subjects in eternal servitude under the Mighty Autocratic Hand of the Great Sovereigns, Their Illustrious Tsarist Majesties. They are to serve the Great Sovereigns loyally and steadfastly and to act for their good, without cunning. The Tabun Saits, Sain Okin and his companions, are to safeguard the long life and health of Their Illustrious Tsarist Majesties and not plot evil against the Great Sovereigns nor abuse or injure Their Illustrious Tsarist Majesties'

---

* *Tabun*, a title conferred on the sons-in-law of ruling Mongol princes; *Sait*, a representative of Mongol military aristocracy.—Eds.

** *Shulenga*, Buriat or Evenk prince, head of a tribe or family.—eds.

Russian people and iasak natives. The Saits and Shulengas and their children and ulus people are to go to war against hostile forces or any other people, together with the Great Sovereigns' troops. They are not to spare their lives, but fight to the death. For this, the Great Sovereigns will instruct their troops to defend the Saits and the Shulengas and their ulus people from attack by enemy forces.

2. As subjects of, and in eternal servitude to the Mighty Hand of Their Illustrious Autocratic Tsarist Majesties, the Tabun Sait, Sain Okin, and his companions are not to transfer their allegiance to their previous rulers, the Chinese and Mongol khans and Gegen [Chechen] Kutukhta, nor are the Tabun Saits to conspire with them, nor incite the Chinese, Mongols, or hostile natives to make war against the frontier towns of Their Illustrious Tsarist Majesties along the Selenga River near Udinsk or near Nerchinsk ostrog, nor are they to take part in such attacks. Likewise they are not to kill nor pillage nor are they to hold secretly captive Russians of various ranks who are subjects of Their Illustrious Tsarist Majesties, nor iasak natives who are hunting sables or other animals near towns and ostrogs or who are out on the trail. They are not to send captives as gifts to people of other realms.

3. If the Saits and Shulengas and ulus people learn of any conspiracy being plotted by subject people of Their Illustrious Tsarist Majesties, they are to seize the treacherous plotters and deliver them under guard to the great plenipotentiary ambassadors, the okolnichi and namestnik of Briansk, Fedor Alekseevich Golovin and his associates, or to the voevodas of the Sovereigns' frontier towns. When they hand over the prisoners they are to make a full report, and as a reward for their loyal service, they will never lack the favor of the Great Sovereigns.

4. The Saits and the Shulengas are to make absolutely certain that the ulus people do not harm one another, do not inflict hardships on one another, nor drive off horses and livestock. If anyone drives off livestock belonging to a subject of the Sovereigns, and investigation leads to the iurt of the thief and he is apprehended, the Saits and Shulengas are to order an investigation and the livestock is to be returned to the owner. Further, in addition to returning the livestock, the thief is to pay a double penalty to the owner.

If anyone is killed and the Saits and Shulengas learn the identity of the killer, he is to be apprehended and taken to the great plenipotentiary ambassador, the okolnichi and namestnik of Briansk, Fedor Alekseevich Golovin, and his associates, or to the Great Sovereign's frontier towns. Upon delivery of the prisoners a full report is to be made. Guilty persons are not to be concealed, nor are the Saits and Shulengas to make a personal profit from this. The Saits and Shulengas and ulus people are not to engage in any unprovoked quarrels nor impose fines without cause.

5. They are to pay iasak from themselves into the Treasury of the Great Sovereigns every year. This is to consist of prime sable, lynx and fox pelts. They are not to make excuses for not fulfilling their iasak obligations. In extreme cases if there is a shortage of furs for iasak, they may give good livestock, and deliver it to whatever town the Great Sovereigns decree.

6. If, in accordance with an ukaz of the Great Sovereigns, Their Illustrious Tsarist Majesties, or orders of the great plenipotentiary ambassador, the okolnichi and namestnik of Briansk, Fedor Alekseevich Golovin, and his associates, or orders of the voevodas of frontier towns, someone is sent to the Saits on business, or to arrange for transport, then the Saits, in accordance with that ukaz, are to provide the transport. They are to respond to the request and provide adequate provisions, and send the officials back without detaining them. Likewise, when someone is sent through their uluses on the business of the Great Sovereigns, the Saits are to provide the envoys with transport and guides and send them on without detaining them, to wherever their assignment directs.

After they had heard these articles, the Saits took the oath in accordance with their own law, and swore to uphold these articles in the future with all their might.

The Saits and Shulengas also took this oath on behalf of their children and all their ulus people. They kissed the barrel of a musket, slashed dogs with swords and licked the bloodied blades, drank a cup of cold water and affirmed thereby that they would uphold these articles in the future with all their might.

After the Saits had agreed to these articles in full, the document was sent to the headquarters of the okolnichi Fedor Alekseevich Golovin and his associates.

See: *Polnoe sobranie zakonov rossiiskoi imperii. . . .* First Series, III, 15.–17.

THE SENTENCES IMPOSED BY THE VOEVODA OF IAKUTSK, PETR ZINO-
VEV, ON THE PARTICIPANTS IN A COSSACK REBELLION

In accordance with the ukaz of the Great Sovereigns, the stolnik
and voevoda Petr Petrovich Zinovev questioned all of the rebels in great detail, and then interrogated them under torture. This
was done in accordance with the instructions of the Great Sovereigns, the articles of the *Sobornoe Ulozhenie* [1649 Code of Laws],
the letters of the Great Sovereigns and the articles of the New
Code. He sentenced the outlaw rebels Filip Shcherbakov and
Ivan Palamoshnoi who admitted and confessed under torture that
they had plotted to pillage the Great Sovereigns' supplies of gunpowder and shot in Iakutsk, and had plotted to kill the stolnik and
voevoda Petr Petrovich Zinovev and the townsmen and make off
with their possessions, and to steal goods from the merchants and
promyshlenniks at the *gostinnyi dvor*,* and then flee beyond the
cape to the Anadyr and Kamchatka rivers.

Zinovev ordered that the syn boiarskii Mikhail Ontipin be
executed along with his comrade, the desiatnik Ivan Golygin.
The cossacks Sofronii Ilin, Ivan Ondronov, Nikita Grebenshchikov, Ignatii Shishev, and the townsman Onufrii Balushkin, all of
whom had taken part in the banditry and rebellion, and who had
confessed their guilt under torture, were not put to death but
were knouted and then exiled with their wives and children to
Nerchinsk ostrog. The townsman Onufrii Balushkin and his wife
and children were permanently exiled to the Omolonsk zimov'e
beyond the rivers that flow to the sea. The accomplices, ataman
Stepan Poluekhtov and the cossacks Nikita Karmolin and Nikita
Popov were exiled with their wives and children to Irkutsk ostrog. The cossack Sergei Mukhoplev was sent into permanent
exile with his wife and children to the sea at the mouth of the Iana
River.

The wives and children of the dead outlaws Filip Shcherbakov, and those of Mikhail Ontipin and Ivan Palomoshnoi were

---

*The *gostinnyi dvor* was a large covered structure that housed numerous re-
tail shops in some Russian towns that enabled authorities to keep a close eye
on all transactions.—Eds.

exiled to Nerchinsk ostrog in order to teach them not to steal in the future or plot rebellion or kill townsmen or rob anyone else.

The stolnik and voevoda Petr Petrovich Zinovev authorized these sentences to be carried out in accordance with the ukaz of the Great Sovereigns. The sentences were read to the thieves and rebels Mikhail Ontipin and his comrades. A decree of the Great Sovereigns was issued authorizing the sentences ordered by the stolnik and voevoda Petr Petrovich Zinovev to be carried out.

The syn boiarskii Mikhail Ontipin was sentenced to death, and his wife and children and his unmarried brother Ivan were exiled; but his wife remained in Iakutsk with her young children because she is ill and near death.

The piatidesiatnik Filip Shcherbakov and Ivan Palamoshnoi, in accordance with the ukaz of the Great Sovereigns, died under torture in prison. Filip's wife and children were exiled, but Ivan Palamoshnoi's wife was not exiled because she is very ill, close to death, and has no children.

The desiatnik Ivan Golygin and the line cossacks Ivan Ondronov, Sofronii Ilin, Nikita Grebenshchikov, Ignatii Shishev, and the townsman Onufrii Balushkin were manacled and knouted without mercy and then sent into exile.

The other outlaws and rebels, and their wives and children, are listed below, with their places of exile.

Exiled to Irkutsk ostrog:
The cossack ataman Stepan Poluekhtov and his wife Irena, and their children Anfilofeva, Ivan, Onufrei, Petr and Oleg.
The cossack Nikita Karmalin and his son Petr.
The cossack Nikita Spiridonov Popov and his sons Fedor, Ivan and Vasilii and his daughter Evdokiia.

Exiled to Nerchinsk ostrog:
The desiatnik Ivan Golygin and his wife Irena and their daughters Efimiia, Marta and Anastasiia.
The unmarried line cossack Sofronii Ilin, Ivan Ondronov, Nikita Grebenshchikov and Ignatii Shishev.
The outlaw and rebel Mikhail Ontipin's son Filip, his wife Mariia, and Ivan's three brothers.
The outlaw and rebel Filip Shcherbakov's wife Evdokiia Vasileva and their sons Stepan and Ivar and their daughters Anna and Paraskeviia.

A seemingly fanciful Chinese drawing of the siege of Albazin (1685) is rich in realistic tactical and topographical details that support the written accounts. From Demidova, *Russko-kitaiskie otnosheniia*, Vol. 2.

The cossack Sergei Mukhoplev and his wife Marina Osipova and their son Ivan and daughter Anna were sent into permanent exile to the sea at the mouth of the Iana River.

The townsman Onufrii Balushkin and his wife Dariia Ofanaseva and their daughter Anna were sent into permanent exile to Omolonsk zimov'e beyond the rivers which flow to the sea.

Reference: TsGADA, f. Iakutskaia prikaznaia izba, stolb. No. 2330, 11. 1–3.

See: N. S. Orlova, ed. *Otkrytiia russkikh zemleprokhodtsev i poliarnykh morekhodov XVII veka na severo-vostoke Azii* (Moscow: 1951), 477–478.

131

AN UKAZ CONCERNING THE RECEPTION OF CHINESE AMBASSADORS IN SIBERIAN TOWNS

Chinese ambassadors and envoys who are sent to the Great Sovereigns in Moscow with official papers are to be received in all Siberian towns to which they may be sent. They are to be given food and transport and allowed to proceed to Moscow. Depending on their rank, they are to be billeted with other ambassadors and envoys. Before they continue to Moscow, the Great Sovereigns in Moscow are to be notified in writing by means of special express messengers.

Persons who are sent to Siberian frontier towns from China for the purpose of negotiation, but who do not carry any official papers for the Great Sovereigns in Moscow, as well as those who do have such papers, are to hand over their documents in the frontier towns. These documents are to be accepted and forwarded to those towns where the envoys wish to go. They are to be allowed to proceed without delay to those towns. No person, however, is to be permitted to go to Moscow. All official papers, ambassadorial reports and written accounts on matters to be discussed are to be sent by express messenger to the Sibirskii Prikaz in Moscow.

See: *Polnoe sobranie zakonov rossiiskoi imperii.* . . . First series, III, No. 1422, 117.

132

FEBRUARY 25, 1695

A GRAMOTA FROM TSARS IVAN ALEKSEEVICH AND PETR ALEKSEEVICH
TO THE VOEVODA OF TOMSK, VASILII RZHEVSKII, CONCERNING EXILES

From the Great Sovereign Tsars and Grand Princes Ivan Alekseevich and Petr Alekseevich, Autocrats of all Great, Little and White Russia, to Siberia, to Tomsk, to our stolnik and voevoda Vasilii Andreevich Rzhevskii. In the present year, 1695, in accordance with our Great Sovereigns' ukaz, prisoners from Vologda have been sent to Tobolsk to be exiled in Siberia. The prisoners are being escorted by Siberian servitors. These prisoners have been ordered to be sent from Tobolsk to Tomsk under special escort. The names of these prisoners and their assigned destinations have been written in a separate document enclosed with this, our Great Sovereigns' gramota.

When this our Great Sovereigns' gramota reaches you, and the prisoners from Tobolsk have arrived in Tomsk, you are to receive the guards from Tobolsk and carry out all the provisions of this, our Great Sovereigns' ukaz, and prepare a list indicating the date on which the prisoners were sent from Tobolsk to Tomsk, the names of their escorts, the names of those to be assigned to cossack infantry service in Tomsk without salary, and the names of those who are to be settled on our agricultural lands. You are to send this written report to us, the Great Sovereigns, with a copy to the Sibirskii Prikaz, to our boiar Prince Ivan Borisovich Repnin and his associates.

See: I. P. Kuznetsov-Krasnoiarskii, ed., *Istoricheskie akty XVII stoletiia (1633–1699)* (Tomsk: 1890), II, 26–27.

133

THE TREATY OF NERCHINSK*

By the Divine Grace of God, the great plenipotentiary ambassadors of Their Tsarist Majesties, the Great Sovereign Tsars and Grand Princes Ivan Alekseevich and Petr Alekseevich, Autocrats of all Great, Little and White Russia, Heirs through Father and Grandfather, and Lords and Masters of many realms and lands, East, West and North, have appointed the Most Honorable Okolnichi and Namestnik of Briansk, Fedor Alekseevich Golovin; the Stolnik and Namestnik of Elatomsk, Ivan Ostafevich Vlasov; and the diak, Semen Kornitskii, who have taken part in an ambassadorial meeting near Nerchinsk, and have met with the great ambassador of the Ruler of the Great Asian lands, the most Autocratic Monarch of the enlightened Bogdoi nobles, the upholder of the law, and protector of the affairs and glory of the Chinese people, the true Bogdoi Chinese Majesty, Bugdykhan; with his great ambassador, Samgut, Commander of the Palace Guard and Voevoda of the Court; and with the Imperial Councillor Timki-Kam, Voevoda of the Court, and Prince and Lord of the Khan's standard, and Ilamt, uncle of the Khan and Lord of the Banner; and with others; and the following articles have been affirmed.

ARTICLE I

The river named Gorbitsa which on its downward course empties into the left bank of the Shilka River near the Black [Amur] River, shall form the boundary between the two Empires. This boundary shall then proceed from the headwaters of that river along the crest of the Kamennyi Mountains which commence at the headwaters of the said river and extend all the way to the sea [of Okhotsk]. All rivers, great and small, which flow

---

See: *To Siberia and Russian America*, Vols. 2 and 3.

*This important first Russo-Chinese treaty was twice amended in the following century (1727 and 1768), but the territorial agreements remained in force until the middle of the 19th century. Consequently Russia's expansionist energies were redirected toward northeastern Asia, Kamchatka, the North Pacific and eventually the northwest coast of North America—Eds.

Manchurian text, Treaty of Nerchinsk, 1689. This treaty temporarily ended bloody border clashes between Russia and China over the rich river bottoms of the Amur. From Demidova, *Russkokitaiskie otnosheniia*, Vol. 2.

Russian text, Treaty of Nerchinsk, 1689. Although this treaty provided a long compromise to the border disputes between Russia and China, the basic tensions still exist today. From Demidova, *Russko-kitaiskie otnosheniia*, Vol. 2.

south from these mountains and empty into the Amur River shall be under the suzerainty of the Chinese Empire. Likewise, all rivers which flow from these mountains in the other direction shall be under the authority of His Tsarist Majesty's Russian Empire. All other rivers which lie between the Ud River and the said Mountains, shall be under the suzerainty of the Russian Empire, while those rivers which are close to the Amur and flow to the sea are to be under the suzerainty of the Chinese Empire.

All other territories which lie between the said Ud River and the mountains, which are not part of the frontier and which have not yet been delineated, shall remain unresolved because the great plenipotentiary ambassadors do not have His Tsarist Majesty's authorization to settle their disposition. This will wait until an appropriate time when, upon the return of the ambassadors of both parties, the Tsarist Majesty will permit and the Bugdykhan Majesty will agree to the appointment of ambassadors or envoys; then either through official correspondence or through ambassadorial meetings, the disposition of these undelineated territories will be resolved in a peaceful and dignified manner.

ARTICLE II

Likewise the river Argun, which empties into the Amur, shall form the boundary. All lands which are on its left bank [looking upriver] proceeding all the way to the mountains shall be under the suzerainty of the Chinese Khan, while the right bank and all of its territories shall belong to the Russian Empire of His Tsarist Majesty. [The Russians] are to relocate all of their buildings from the southern bank of the Argun River onto its northern bank.

ARTICLE III

The town of Albazin, which was built by His Tsarist Majesty's subjects, is to be completely razed and all persons who dwell there, and all military equipment and other provisions, are to be moved to His Tsarist Majesty's side of the river. Neither property nor small goods are to be left behind.

ARTICLE IV

Deserters, whether from His Tsarist Majesty or from the Bugdykhan Majesty, who run off prior to this peaceful settlement, shall remain where they are. Persons who desert after this treaty has been signed shall be promptly returned to the frontier officials.

ARTICLE V

In accordance with the terms of this treaty of friendship, all persons, regardless of their station, may come and go in full freedom to both Empires, and buy and sell whatever they wish, provided they have appropriate travel documents.

ARTICLE VI

All previous discords which may have occurred between frontier inhabitants prior to the signing of this concord shall be forgotten and shall not be avenged. However, if subsequent to the conclusion of this concord promyshlenniks of either Empire should pillage or commit murder, such persons, when apprehended, will be remanded to border officials of their respective countries, and will be punished severely. If such brigandage is committed by a group of persons, then when these lawless persons are apprehended they will be remanded to border officials and will be executed for their crimes. Neither side will declare war or shed blood because of the actions of its frontier population. Each side will make reports about any such discords to its respective Sovereign, and such disagreements will be resolved peacefully through diplomatic channels. In accordance with the articles negotiated by the ambassadors pertaining to the frontier, the Bugdykhan Majesty reserves for himself the right to install markers of his choice along the frontiers in order to know the exact location of the frontier.

See: Russia. *Polnoe sobranie zakonov rossiiskoi imperri.* . . . First Series, III, 31–2.

SELECTED BIBLIOGRAPHY

Bibliographies

Kerner, Robert J. *Northeast Asia: A Selected Bibliography. Contributions to the Bibliography of the Relations of China, Russia and Japan, with Special Reference to Korea, Manchuria, Mongolia and Eastern Siberia in Oriental and European Languages.* 2 vols. Berkeley, 1939.

Mezhov, V. I. *Sibirskaia bibliografiia. Ukazatel knig i statei o Sibiri na russkom iazyke i odnikh tolko knig na inostrannykh iazykakh za ves period knigopechataniia* [Siberian Bibliography. Guide to the Books and Articles about Siberia in Russian, and to Books in Foreign Languages for the Entire Period of Book Printing]. 3 vols. in 2. St. Petersburg, 1903.

Polansky, Patricia and Robert Valliant. *Siberia: a Bibliographic Introduction to Sources.* Honolulu, 1980.

Tomashevskii, V. V. *Materialy k bibliografii Sibiri i Dalnego Vostoka (XV–pervaia polovina XIX veka)* [Sources for a Bibliography of Siberia and the Far East (Fifteenth to the First Half of the Nineteenth Century)]. Vladivostok, 1957.

Sources

Alekseev, M. P. *Sibir v izvestiiakh inostrannykh puteshestvinnikov i pisatelei* [Siberia in the Reports of Foreign Travelers and Writers]. Irkutsk, 1936.

Armstrong, Terence, ed. *Yermak's Campaign in Siberia.* A Selection of Documents translated from the Russian by Tatiana Minorsky and David Wileman. London, 1975.

Arsenev, Iu. V., ed. "Puteshestvie chrez Sibir ot Tobolska do Nerchinska i granits Kitaia russkogo poslannika Nikolaia Spafariia v 1675 godu" [Journey across Siberia from Tobolsk to Nerchinsk and the Borders of China by the Russian Ambassador Nikolai Spafarii in 1675], *Zapiski imperatorskogo russkogo geograficheskogo obshchestva po otdeleniiu etnografii.* vol. 10, pp. 1–214. St. Petersburg, 1882.

Bakhrushin, S. V. and S. A. Tokarev, eds. *Materialy po istorii Iakutii XVII veke (Dokumenty iasachnogo sbora)* [Sources on the History of Iakutiia in the Seventeenth Century (Documents Concerning the Iasak Collection)]. 3 vols. Moscow, 1970.

Bantysh-Kamenskii, N. N., ed. *Diplomaticheskoe sobranie del mezhdu Rossiiskim i Kitaiskim gosudarstvami s 1619 po 1792 god: sostavlennoe po dokumentam khraniashchimsia v Moskovskom Arkhive Gosudarstvennoi Kollegii Inostrannykh del v 1792–1803 godu* [Diplomatic Collection of Materials between Russia and China from 1619 to 1792: Compiled from Documents Preserved in the Moscow Archive of the Government College of Foreign Affairs from 1792–1803]. Kazan, 1882.

Belov, M. I., ed. *Russkie morekhody v Ledovitom i Tikhom okeanakh. Sbornik dokumentov.* [Russian Seafarers in the Arctic and Pacific oceans. A Collection of Documents.]. Leningrad-Moscow, 1952.

Demidova, N. F. and V. S. Miasnikov. *Pervye russkie diplomaty v Kitae. ("Rospis" I. Petlina i Stateinyi Spisok F. I. Baikova).* [The First Russian Diplomats in China. (The "Account" of I. Petlin and a Detailed Report by F. I. Baikov)]. Moscow, 1966.

Demidova, N. F. and V. S. Miasnikov, eds. *Russko-kitaiskie otnosheniia v XVII veke: Dokumenty i materialy (1609–1691)* [Russo-Chinese Relations in the Seventeenth Century: Documents and Sources (1609–1691)]. 2 vols. Moscow, 1969–1972.

Divin, V. A., ed. *Russkaia tikhookeanskaia epoceia* [The Russian Epic in the Pacific Ocean]. Khabarovks, 1979.

Duman, L. I., ed. *Russko-kitaiskie otnosheniia v XVII veke: Materialy i dokumenty, 1608–1683* [Russo-Chinese Relations in the Seventeenth Century: Sources and Documents, 1608–1683]. Moscow, 1969.

Golman, M. I. and G. I. Slesarchuk, eds. *Materialy po istorii russko-mongolskikh otnoshenii, 1636–1654* [Materials for the History of Russo-Mongolian Relations, 1636–1654]. Moscow, 1974.

Iakor, Ia. P., and B. D. Grekov, eds. *Kolonialnaia politika Moskovskogo gosudarstva v Iakutii XVII v.* [Colonial Policy of the Muscovite State in Iakutiia in the Seventeenth Century]. Leningrad, 1936.

"Istoricheskie akty o podvigakh Erofeia Khabarova na Amure v 1649–1651 gg." [Historical Acts Concerning the Exploits of Erofei Khabarov on the Amur in 1649–1651]. *Zhurnal dlia chteniia vospitannikam voenno-uchebnykh zavedenii*, No. 105. St. Petersburg, 1840.

Kuleshov, V. A., ed. *Nakazy sibirskim voevodam v XVII veke. Istoricheskii ocherk* [Instructions to Siberian voevodas in the Seventeenth Century. A Historical Essay]. Tashkent, 1888.

Kuznetsov-Krasnoiarskii, I. P., ed. *Istoricheskie akty XVII stoletiia, 1633–1699. Materialy dlia istorii Sibiri* [Historical Acts of the Seventeenth Century, 1633–1699. Sources for the History of Siberia]. 2 vols. Tomsk, 1890–1897.

Müller, G. F. *Istoriia Sibiri* [The History of Siberia]. 2 vols. Moscow-Leningrad, 1937–1941.

N. A. N., ed. *Sibirskie goroda. Materialy dlia ikh istorii v XVII stoletii. Nerchinsk, Selenginsk, Iakutsk* [Siberian towns. Materials for their History in the Seventeenth Century. Nerchinsk, Selenginsk, Iakutsk]. Moscow, 1886.

Potanin, G. N. "Materialy dlia istorii Sibiri" [Materials for the History of Siberia], *Chteniia v imperatorskom obshchestve istorii i drevnostei rossiiskikh pri Moskovskom universitete*, No. 4 (October–December, 1866), pp. 1–128; No. 1 (Janaury–March, 1867), pp. 129–230; and No. 2 (April–June, 1867), pp. 231–324.

Orlova, N. S., ed. *Otkrytiia russkikh zemleprokhodtsev i poliarnykh morekhodov XVII veka na severo-vostoke Azii: Sbornik dokumentov* [Discoveries of Russian Overland Travelers and Polar Seafarers of the Seventeenth Century in the North-East of Asia. A Collection of Documents]. Moscow, 1951.

Rumiantsev, G. N. and S. B. Okun, eds. *Sbornik dokumentov po istorii Buriati: XVII vek* [A Collection of Documents on the History of the Buriat Region: The Seventeenth Century]. Ulan Ude, 1960.

Russia. Arkheograficheskaia kommissiia. *Akty istoricheskie* [Historical Acts]. 5 vols. St. Petersburg, 1841–1842.

———. *Dopolneniia k aktam istoricheskim* [Supplements to the Historical Acts]. 12 vols. St. Petersburg, 1846–1872.

———. *Sibirskiia letopisi* [Siberian Chronicles]. St. Petersburg, 1907.

Russia. *Polnoe sobranie zakonov rossiiskoi imperii s 1649 goda* [Complete Collection of Laws of the Russian Empire since 1649]. 1st Series. 44 vols. St. Petersburg, 1830.

Shvetsova, T. M., ed. *Materialy po istorii Iakutii XVII veka: Dokumenty iasachnogo sbora* [Materials on the History of Iakutiia in the Seventeenth Century: Documents on the Collection of Iasak]. Moscow, 1970.

"Stateinii spisok posolstva N. Spafariia v Kitai" [Detailed Account of the Embassy of N. Spafarii to China], *Vestnik Arkheologii i Istorii*, 17, No. 2 (1906), pp. 162–339.

Titov, A. A., ed. *Sibir v XVII veke. Sbornik starinnykh russkikh statei o Sibiri i prilezhashchikh k nei zemliakh* [Siberia in the Seventeenth Century. A Collection of Ancient Russian Accounts about Siberia and the Lands Bordering It]. Moscow, 1890.

Trotskii, I. M., ed. *Kolonialnaia politika moskovskogo gosudarstva v Iakutii v XVII v.* [Colonial Policy of the Muscovite State in Iakutiia in the Seventeenth Century]. Leningrad, 1936.

Monographic Literature

Aleksandrov, V. A. *Rossiia na dalnovostochnykh rubezhakh (vtoraia polovina XVII v.)* [Russia on the Far Eastern Frontiers (the Second Half of the Seventeenth Century)]. Moscow, 1969.

———. *Russkoe naselenie Sibiri XVII–nachala XVIII v.* [Russian Population of Siberia, Seventeenth–Early Eighteenth Century]. Moscow, 1964.

Andreev, A. I. *Ocherki po istochnikovedeniiu Sibiri. XVII vek* [Essays on the Source Studies of Siberia. The Seventeenth Century]. 2nd ed. Moscow, 1960.

Andreevich, V. K. *Istoricheskii ocherk Sibiri po dannym predstavliaemym polnym sobraniem zakonov* [Historical Essay on Siberia based on Materials Contained in the Complete Collection of Laws]. 6 vols. St. Petersburg, 1886–1889.

———. *Istoriia Sibiri* [History of Siberia]. 5 vols. in 2. St. Petersburg, 1887–1889.

Baddeley, John F. *Russia, Mongolia and China, Being Some Record of the Relations between Them from the Beginning of the XVIIth Century to the Death of the Tsar Alexei Mikhailovich A.D. 1602–1672*. 2 vols. London, 1919.

Bakhrushin, S. V. *Kazaki na Amure* [The Cossacks on the Amur]. Leningrad, 1925.

———. *Ocherki po istorii kolonizatsii Sibiri v XVI i XVII vekakh*. [Essays on the History of the Colonization of Siberia in the Sixteenth and Seventeenth Centuries]. Moscow, 1927.

———. "Ostiakskie i vogulskie kniazhestva v XVI–XVII vv." [Ostiak and Vogul Principalities in the Sixteenth and Seventeenth Centuries]. Leningrad, 1935.

Bannikov, A. G. *Pervye russkie puteshestvenniki v Mongoliiu i Severnyi Kitai* [The First Russian Travelers to Mongolia and Northern China]. Moscow, 1954.

Bazilevich, K. V. *V gostiakh u bogdykhana (Puteshestviia russkikh v Kitai v XVII veke)* [Visits to the Bogdykhan (Russian Journeys to China in the Seventeenth Century)]. Moscow, 1927.

Belov, M. I. *Mangazeia*. Leningrad, 1969.

———. *Podvig Semena Dezhneva* [The Exploits of Semen Dezhnev]. 3rd ed. Moscow, 1973.

———. *Raskopki "Zlatokipiashchei" Mangazei* [Excavations in "Gold-Effervescent" Mangazeia]. Leningrad, 1970.

———. et al. *Mangazeia. Mangazeiskii morskoi khod* [Mangazeia. Mangazeia Sea Passage]. Leningrad, 1980.

Burney, James. *A Chronological History of the North-eastern Voyages of Discovery; and of the Early Navigations of the Russians*. London, 1819. [Reprinted in Amsterdam in 1969].

Butsinskii, P. N. *Istoriia Sibiri: Surgut, Narym i Ketsk do 1645* [A History of Siberia: Surgut, Narym and Ketsk before 1645]. Kharkov, 1893.

———. *Mangazeia i mangazeiskii uezd, 1601–1645* [Mangazeia and the Mangazeia Uezd, 1601–1645]. Kharkov, 1889.

———. *Zaselenie Sibiri i byt pervykh eia naselnikov* [The Settlement of Siberia and the Life of Its First Settlers]. Kharkov, 1889.

Chen, Vincent. *Sino-Russian Relations in the Seventeenth Century*. The Hague, 1968.

Dolgikh, B. D. *Rodovoi i plemennoi sostav narodov Sibiri v XVII veke* [Clan and Tribal Composition of the Peoples of Siberia in the Seventeenth Century]. Moscow, 1960.

Donnelly, Alton S. *The Russian Conquest of Bashkiriia, 1552–1740: A Case Study of Imperialism*. New Haven, Conn. 1968.

Efimov, A. V., ed. *Atlas geograficheskikh otkrytii v Sibiri i v Severo-zapadnoi*

505

Amerike XVII–XVIII vv. [Atlas of Geographical Discoveries in Siberia and Northwestern America in the Seventeenth and Eighteenth Centuries]. Moscow, 1964.

———. *Iz istorii velikikh russkikh geograficheskikh otkrytii v severnom ledovitom i tikhom okeanakh, XVII-pervaia polovina XVIII v.* [A history of Great Russian Geographical Discoveries in the Northern Arctic and Pacific Oceans, Seventeenth Century to the First Half of the Eighteenth Century]. Moscow; 1971.

Fischer, J. E. *Sibirische Geschichte von der Entdeckung Sibiriens bis auf die Eroberung dieses Landes durch die russischen Waffen* . . . [Siberian History from the Discovery of Siberia to Its Conquest of this Land by Russian Forces]. 2 vols. St. Petersburg, 1768.

Fisher, Raymond H. *The Russian Fur Trade, 1550–1700.* Berkeley, 1943.

———. *The Voyages of Semen Dezhnev in 1648.* London, 1981.

Firsov, N. N. *Chteniia po istorii Sibiri* [Lectures on the History of Siberia]. 2 vols. in 1. Moscow, 1920–1921.

Frolev, Nikolai, ed. *Magazin zemlevladeniia i puteshestvii. Geograficheskii sbornik* [A Journal of Landownership and Travel. A Geographical Anthology]. Vol. 4, pp. 465–570. Moscow, 1855.

Gibson, James R. *Feeding the Russian Fur Trade. Provisionment of the Okhotsk Seaboard and the Kamchatka Peninsula, 1639–1856.* Madison, 1969.

Glinka, G. V., ed. *Aziatskaia Rossiia* [Asiatic Russia]. St. Petersburg, 1914.

Goldenberg, L. A. *Semen Ulianovich Remezov sibirskii kartograf i geograf, 1642—posle 1720 gg.* [Semen Ulianovich Remezov, Siberian Cartographer and Geographer, 1642—after 1720]. Moscow, 1965.

Golder, Frank A. *Russian Expansion on the Pacific, 1641–1850: An Account of the Earliest and Later Expeditions Made by the Russians along the Pacific Coast of Asia and North America; Including Some Related Expeditions to the Arctic Regions.* Cleveland, 1914.

Golitsyn, N. N. *Portfeli G. F. Millera* [The G. F. Müller Portfolios]. Moscow, 1899.

Gurvich, I. S. *Russkie na severo-vostoke Sibiri v XVII v.* [Russians in Northeast Siberia in the Seventeenth Century]. Moscow, 1963.

Iakovleva, P. T. *Pervyi russko-kitaiskie dogovor 1689 goda* [The First Russo-Chinese Treaty of 1689]. Moscow, 1958.

Ionina, A. A. *Novaia danniia k istorii vostochnoi Sibiri XVII veka* [New Information on the History of Eastern Siberia in the Seventeenth Century]. Irkutsk, 1895.

Ionova, O. V. *Iz istorii iakutskogo naroda (pervaia polovina XVII veka)* [A History of the Iakut People (the First Half of the Seventeenth Century)]. Irkutsk, 1945.

Katanaev, G. E. *Kratkii istoricheskii obzor sluzhby sibirskago kazachego voiska s 1582 po 1908* [A Brief Historical Survey of the Service of the Siberian Cossack Army, 1582–1908]. St. Petersburg, 1908.

Kerner, Robert J. *The Urge to the Sea. The Course of Russian History. The Role of Rivers, Portages, Ostrogs, Monasteries and Furs.* Berkeley, 1946.

Korsak, A. *Istoriko-statisticheskoe obozrenie torgovykh snoshenii Rossii s Kitaem* [A

Historical-Statistical Review of Commercial Relations between Russia and China]. Kazan, 1857.

Kudriatsev, F. A. *Vosstaniia krestian, posadskikh i kazakov Vostochnoi Sibiri v kontse XVII v.* [Uprisings by Peasants, Townsmen and Cossacks of Eastern Siberia at the End of the Seventeenth Century]. Irkutsk, 1939.

Kurts, B. G. *Russko-kitaiskie snosheniia v XVI, XVII i XVIII stoletiiakh* [Russo-Chinese Relations in the Sixteenth, Seventeenth and Eighteenth Centuries]. Kharkov, 1929.

Lantzeff, George V. *Siberia in the Seventeenth Century: A Study of the Colonial Administration.* Berkeley, 1943.

————. and Richard A. Pierce. *Eastward to Empire: Exploration and Conquest on the Russian Open Frontier to 1750.* Montreal—London, 1973.

Lebedev, D. M. *Geografiia v Rossii XVII veka* [Geography in Russia in the Seventeenth Century]. Moscow-Leningrad, 1949.

————. and Vasilii A. Esakov. *Russkie geograficheskie otkrytiia i issledovaniia s drevnykh vremen do 1917 goda* [Russian Geographical Discoveries and Explorations from Ancient Times to 1917]. Moscow, 1971.

Lensen, George A. *The Russian Push Toward Japan: Russo-Japanese Relations 1697–1875.* Princeton, 1959.

————. *Russia's Eastward Expansion.* Englewood Cliffs, 1964.

Mancall, Mark. *Russia and China: Their Diplomatic Relations to 1728.* Cambridge: 1971.

Müller, G. F. *Opisanie sibirskogo tsarstva i vsekh proisshedshikh v nem del ot nachala a osoblivo ot pokoreniia ego rossiiskoi derzhave po sie vremena* [A Description of the Siberian Tsardom and All Events Occuring There since the Beginning, but Especially since Its Subjugation to the Russian State, to the Present Time]. 2nd ed. St. Petersburg, 1787.

————. *Sammlung russischer Geschichte* [A Collection of Russian History]. Vol. 3, parts 5–6; vol. 6, parts 2–6; and vol. 8, parts 1–6. St. Petersburg, 1732–1764.

————. and P. S. Pallas. *Conquest of Siberia and the History of the Transactions, Wars, Commerce, etc. Carried on between Russia and China from the Earliest Period.* London: 1842.

Mirzoev, V. G. *Istoriografiia Sibiri* [The Historiography of Siberia]. Moscow, 1970.

————. *Prisoedinenie i osvoenie Sibiri v istoricheskoi literature XVII veka* [Annexation and Assimilation of Siberia in the Historical Literature of the Seventeenth Century]. Moscow, 1960.

Nebolsin, P. I. *Pokorenie Sibiri* [The Conquest of Siberia]. St. Petersburg, 1949.

Novoselskii, A. A. and N. V. Ustiugov, eds. *Ocherki istorii SSSR. Period feodalizma XVII v.* [Essays on the History of the USSR. Feudal Period in the Seventeenth Century]. pp. 815–869, Moscow, 1955.

Ogloblin, N. N. *Obozrenie stolbtsov i knig sibirskogo prikaza, 1592–1768* [A Survey of the Rolls and Books of the Siberian Prikaz 1592–1768]. 4 vols. Moscow, 1896–1900.

Ogorodnikov, V. I. *Iz istorii pokoreniia Sibiri. Pokorenie iukagirskoi zemli.* [The

History of the Conquest of Siberia. The Conquest of the Iukagir Land]. Chita, 1922.

————. *Ocherki istorii Sibiri do nachala XIX st. Zavoevanie russkimi Sibiri* [Essays on the History of Siberia to the Beginning of the Nineteenth Century. The Conquest of Siberia by the Russians]. Vladivostok, 1924.

————. *Russkaia gosudarstvennaia vlast i sibirskie inorodtsy v XVI–XVIII vv.* [Russian Administration and the Siberian Natives from the Sixteenth to the Eighteenth Century]. Irkutsk, 1920.

————. *Tuzemnoe i russkoe zemledelie na Amure v XVII v.* [Native and Russian Agriculture on the Amur in the Seventeenth Century]. Vladivostok, 1924.

Okladnikov, A. P. *Ocherki iz istorii zapadnykh buriat-mongolov XVII–XVIII vv.* [Essays on the History of the Western Buriat-Mongols in the Seventeenth and Eighteenth Centuries]. Leningrad, 1937.

Pelensky, Jaroslaw. *Russia and Kazan: Conquest and Imperial Ideology.* The Hague, 1974.

Platonov, S. F. *Proshloe russkogo severa: Ocherki po istorii kolonizatsii Pomoriia* [The Past of the Russian North: Essays on the History of the Colonization of Pomor'e]. Petrograd, 1923.

Porokhova, O. G. *Leksika sibirskikh letopisei XVII veka* [A Dictionary of Siberian Chronicles of the Seventeenth Century]. Leningrad, 1969.

Pypin, A. N. *Istoriia russkoi etnografii: Belorussiia i Sibir* [History of Russian Ethnography: White Russia and Siberia]. St. Petersburg, 1892.

Pokrovskii, F. I. *Puteshestvie v Mongoliiu i Kitai sibirskago kazaka Ivana Petlina* [A Journey to Mongolia and China of the Siberian Cossack Ivan Petlin]. St. Petersburg, 1914.

Preobrazhenskii, L. A. *Ocherki kolonizatsii zapadnogo Urala v XVII–nachale XVIII v.* [Essays on the Colonization of the Western Urals in the Seventeenth and Early Eighteenth Centuries]. Moscow, 1956.

Sadovnikov, D. N. *Nashi zemleprokhodtsy (razskazy o zaselenii Sibiri, 1581–1712 gg)* [Our Overland Explorers (Tales of the Settlement of Siberia, 1581–1712)]. 2nd ed. Moscow, 1898.

Samoilov, V. A. *Semen Dezhnev i ego vremia. S prilozheniem otpisok i chelobitnykh Semena Dezhneva o ego prokhodakh i otkrytiiakh* [Semen Dezhnev and His Times. With an Appendix of the Dispatches and Petitions of Semen Dezhnev about His Journeys and Discoveries]. Moscow, 1945.

Sebes, Joseph. *The Jesuits and the Sino-Russian Treaty of Nerchinsk (1689). The Diary of Thomas Pereira.* Rome, 1961.

Semyonov, Yuri. *The Conquest of Siberia.* London, 1944.

Serebrennikov, I. N. *Pokorenie i pervonachalnoe zaselenie Irkutskoi guberni* [The Conquest and First Settlement of the Irkutsk Gubernia]. Irkutsk, 1915.

Shastina, N. P. *Russko-mongolskie posolskie otnosheniia XVII veka* [Russo-Mongol Ambassadorial Relations in the Seventeenth Century]. Moscow, 1958.

Shchebenkov, V. G. *Russko-kitaiskie otnosheniia v XVII v* [Russo-Chinese Relations in the Seventeenth Century]. Moscow, 1960.

Shcheglov, I. V. *Khronologicheskie perechen vazhneishikh dannykh iz istorii Sibiri, 1032–1882* [Chronological Summary of the Most Important Facts from the History of Siberia, 1032–1882]. Irkutsk, 1883.

Shunkov, V. I., ed. *Istoriia Sibiri* [History of Siberia]. Vol. 2: *Sibir v sostave feodalnoi Rossii* [Siberia in the Structure of Feudal Russia]. Leningrad, 1968.

———. *Ocherki po istorii kolonizatsii Sibiri v XVII–nachale XVIII v.* [Essays on the History of the Colonization of Siberia, Seventeenth–Early Eighteenth Century]. Moscow, 1946.

———. *Ocherki po istorii zemlevladeniia v Sibiri, XVII v.* [Essays on the History of Landownership in Siberia in the Seventeenth Century]. Moscow, 1956.

———. *Osvoenie Sibiri v epokhu feodalizma (XVII–XIX vv).* [The Assimilation of Siberia during the Period of Feudalism (Seventeenth to Nineteenth Centuries)]. Novosibirsk, 1968.

Sibirskaia sovetskaia entsiklopediia [Siberian Soviet Encyclopedia], 3 vols. [to "N"] Novosibirsk, 1929–1932.

Skalon, V. N. *Russkie zemleprokhodtsy—issledovateli Sibiri XVII veka* [Russian Overland Travelers—Explorers of Siberia in the Seventeenth Century]. Moscow, 1951.

Slovtsov, P. A. *Istoricheskoe obozrenie Sibiri s 1585 do 1742* [Historical Survey of Siberia from 1585 to 1742]. Moscow, 1838.

Stepanov, N. N *Iakutiia v XVII veke* [Iakutiia in the Seventeenth Century]. Iakutsk, 1953.

Svatikov, S. G. *Rossiia i Sibir* [Russia and Siberia]. Prague, 1929.

Tokarev, S. A. *Ocherki istorii iaktuskogo naroda* [Essays on the History of the Iakut People]. Moscow, 1940.

Trusevich, Kh. *Posolskie i torgovye snosheniia Rossii s Kitaem do XIX v.* [Ambassadorial and Commercial Relations between Russia and China before the Nineteenth Century]. Moscow, 1882.

Vilkov, O. N. *Remeslo i torgovlia zapadnoi Sibiri v XVII veke* [Crafts and Trade of Western Siberia in the Seventeenth Century]. Moscow, 1967.

Vize, V. Iu. *Russkie poliarnye morekhody iz promyshlennykh, torgovykh i sluzhilykh liudei XVII–XIX vv. Biograficheskii slovar* [Russian Promyshlenniks, Merchants and Servitors as Polar Seafarers in the Seventeenth to Nineteenth Centuries. A Biographical Dictionary]. Moscow, 1948.

Vladimirtsov, B. *Obshchestvennyi stroi Mongolov* [Social Structure of the Mongols]. Leningrad, 1934.

Vvedenskii, A. A. *Dom Stroganovykh v XVI–XVII vekakh* [The House of Stroganov in the Sixteenth and Seventeenth Centuries]. Moscow, 1962.

Witsen, N. C. *Noord en Oost Tartarye.* [North and East Tartary]. 2 vols. 2nd. ed. Amsterdam, 1785.

Zamechatelnye russkie liudi. Erofei Khabarov i Semen Dezhnev [Outstanding Russians: Erofei Khabarov and Semen Dezhnev]. St. Petersburg, 1897.

Zlatkin, I. Ia. *Istoriia Dzhungarskogo khanstva* [A History of the Dzhungar Khanate], Moscow, 1964.

Periodical Literature

Andreev, A. I. "Trudy G. F. Millera o Sibiri" [The Works of G. F. Müller on Siberia] in G. F. Müller, *Istoriia Sibiri*. Vol. 1, pp. 57–144. Leningrad, 1937.

Andrianov, S. A. "K voprosu o pokorenii Sibiri" [The Question of the Subjugation of Siberia], *Zhurnal Ministerstva Narodnogo Proveshcheniia*, Vol. 286, Pt. 4 (1893), pp. 522–50.

Bakhrushin, S. V. "G. F. Miller kak istorik Sibiri" [G. F. Müller as a Historian of Siberia], in G. F. Müller, *Istoriia Sibiri*, Vol. 1, pp. 3–55. Leningrad, 1937.

———. "Iasak v Sibiri v XVII veke" [Iasak in Siberia in the Seventeenth Century]. *Sibirskie ogni*, No. 3 (May–June, 1927), pp. 95–129.

———. "Izbrannye raboty po istorii Sibiri XVI–XVII vv." [Selected Studies of the History of Siberia in the Sixteenth and Seventeenth Centuries], in *Nauchnye trudy*. Vol. 3. Moscow, 1953.

———. "Ocherki po istorii krasnoiarskogo uezda v XVII v." [Essays on the History of the Krasnoiarsk uezd in the Seventeenth Century], in *Nauchnye trudy*. Vol. 4. Moscow, 1953.

———. "Sibirskie sluzhilye Tatary v XVII v." [Siberian Tatar Servitors in the Seventeenth Century], in *Istoricheskie Zapiski*, Vol. 1 (1937), pp. 55–80.

———. "Torgi gostia Nikitina v Sibiri i Kitae" [The Trade of *Gost* Nikitin in Siberia and China]. in *Nauchnye Trudy*. Vol. 3. Moscow, 1955.

Bartenev, Iu. P. "Geroi Albazina i Daurskoi zemli" [The Heroes of Albazin and of the Daur Lands], in *Russkii Arkhiv*, Bk. 1, No. 2 (1899), pp. 304–36.

Bagrow, Leo. "The First Russian Maps of Siberia and Their Influence on the West European Cartography of N.E. Asia," in *Imago Mundi*, (Leiden), Vol. 9, pp. 83–93.

Beazley, C. Raymond. "The Russian Expansion toward Asia and the Arctic in the Middle Ages (to 1500)," in *American Historical Review*, Vol. 13, No. 4 (July, 1908), pp. 731–41.

Belov, M. I. "Istoricheskoe plavanie Semena Dezhneva" [The Historic Voyage of Semen Dezhnev], in *Izvestiia Vsesoiuznogo Geograficheskogo Obshchestva*, Vol. 81, No. 5 (September–October, 1949), pp. 459–72.

Chen, Agnes Fang-chih. "Chinese Frontier Diplomacy: The Coming of the Russians and the Treaty of Nertchinsk," in *The Yengching Journal of Social Studies*, Vol. 4, No. 2 (February, 1949), pp. 99–149.

Chulkov, N. P. "Erofei Pavlov Khabarov: dobytchik i pribylnik XVII veke," [Erofei Pavlov Khabarov: Freebooter and Profiteer of the Seventeenth Century], in *Russkii Arkhiv*, No. 2 (1898), pp. 177–90.

Dmitriev, A. A. "Rol Stroganovykh v pokorenii Sibiri" [The Role of the Stroganovs in the Subjugation of Siberia], in *Zhurnal Ministerstva Narodnogo Prosvesheniia*, Vol. 291, Part 2 (1894), pp. 1–45.

Dmytryshyn, Basil. "Russian Expansion to the Pacific, 1580–1700: A Historiographical Review," in *Slavic Studies* (Hokkaido University), No. 25 (1980), pp. 1–25.

Dolgikh, B. O. "Proishozhdenie nganasanov" [The Origin of the Nganasan People], in *Sibirskii Etnograficheskii Sbornik*. Vol. XVIII, pp. 5–87. Moscow, 1952.

Fisher, Raymond H. "Dezhnev's Voyages of 1648 in the Light of Soviet Scholarship" in *Terrae Incognitae*, Vol. 5 (1973), pp. 7–26.

———. "Kerner, Bering and the Amur: A Refutation," in *Jahrbücher für Geschichte Osteuropas*, Vol. 17, No. 3 (September, 1969), pp. 397–407.

———. "Mangazeia: A Boomtown of Seventeenth Century Siberia," in *Russian Review*, Vol. 4 (Autumn, 1944), pp. 89–99.

———. "Semen Dezhnev and Professor Golder," in *The Pacific Historical Review*, Vol. 25, No. 3 (August, 1956), pp. 281–92.

Fuchs, Walter. "Die russisch-chinesische Vertrag von Nertschinsk von Jahre 1689, Eine textkritische Betrachtung" [The Russo-Chinese Treaty of Nerchinsk in 1689. A Critical View of the Text], in *Monumenta Serica, Journal of Oriental Studies of the Catholic University of Peking*, Vol. 4, No. 2 (1939–1940), pp. 546–93.

Golovachev, D. M. "Chastnoe zemlevladenie v Sibiri" [Private Landownership in Siberia], in *Sibirskie Voprosy*, No. 1 (1905), pp. 122–70.

Iadrintsev, N. M. "Trekhsotletie Sibiri, 26 Oktiabria 1881" [Tercentenary of Siberia, October 26, 1881], in *Vestnik Evropy* (December 1881), pp. 834–50.

Ilovaiskii, D. "Ermak i pokorenie Sibiri" [Ermak and the Subjugation of Siberia], in *Russkii Vestnik*, No. 9 (1889), pp. 3–39.

Katanev, G. E. "Eshche ob Ermake i ego sibirskom pokhode (Novyia variatsii na staruiu temu)" [More about Ermak and His Siberian Campaign (New Variations on an Old Theme)], in *Zapiski zapadnosibirskogo otdela Imperatorskogo Russkogo geograficheskogo obshchestva*, Vol. 15, Pt. 2 (1893), pp. 1–36.

Kerner, Robert J. "The Russian Eastward Movement: Some Observations on Its Historical Significance," in *Pacific Historical Review*, Vol. 17, No. 5 (May, 1948), pp. 135–48.

———. "Russian Expansion to America: Its Bibliographical Foundations," in *The Papers of the Bibliographical Society of America*, Vol. 25 (1931), pp. 111–29.

Kirby, E. Stuart. "The Trail of the Sable: New Evidence of the Fur Hunters of Siberia in the Seventeenth Century," in *Slavic Studies* (Hokkaido University), No. 27 (Winter, 1981), pp. 105–18.

Lantzeff, George V. "Russian Expansion Eastward before the Mongol Invasion," in *The American Slavic and East European Review*, Vol. 6, Nos. 18–19 (December, 1947), pp. 1–10.

Maikov, L. N. "Khronologicheskie spravki po povodu 300-letnei godovshchiny prisoedineniia Sibiri k Russkoi derzhave" [Chronological Information Commemorating the Tercentenery of the Annexation of Siberia by the Russian State], in *Zhurnal Ministerstva Narodnogo Prosveshcheniia*, Vol. 217, No. 9 (1881), pp. 21–36.

Mikahilov, K. P. "Krepostnichestvo v Sibiri" [Serfdom in Siberia], in *Sibiriskii Sbornik*, Bk. 1 (1886), pp. 93–137.

Müller, G. F. "Istoriia o stranakh pri reke Amure lezhashchikh, kogda onye sostoiali pod rossiiskim vladeniem" [A History of the Countries along the Amur River, when They Became Subject to Russian Authority], in *Ezhemesiachnye sochineniia k polze i uveseleniiu sluzhashchie*, (July, 1757), pp. 3–39; (August, 1757), pp. 99–130; (September, 1757), pp. 194–227; and (October, 1757), pp. 291–328.

——. "O pervykh rossiiskikh puteshestviiakh i posolstvakh v Kitai" [Concerning the First Russian Journeys and Embassies to China], in *Ezhemesiachnye sochineniia k polze i uveseleniiu sluzhashchie*, (July, 1755), pp. 17–62.

Ogoblin, N. N. "Semen Dezhnev, 1638–1671. Novye dannye i peresmotr starykh" o Semene Dezhnve, 1638–1671. [New Information and a Review of the Old], in *Zhurnal Ministerstva Narodnogo Prosveshcheniia*, Vol. 272, (November–December, 1890), pp. 249–306.

——. "Sibirskie diplomaty XVII veka" [Siberian Diplomats of the Seventeenth Century], in *Istoricheskii Vestnik*, Vol. 46, No. 10 (1891), pp. 158–71.

——. "Tomskii bunt 1637–1638" [The Tomsk Conspiracy, 1637–1638], in *Istoricheskii Vestnik*, Vol. 85 (1901), pp. 229–50.

——. "Vostochno-sibirskie poliarnye morekhody XVII v." [East-Siberian Polar Seafarers of the Seventeenth Century], in *Zhurnal Ministerstva Narodnogo Prosveshcheniia*, No. 347 (May, 1903), pp. 38–62.

Ogryzko, I. I. "Ekspeditsiia Semena Dezhneva i otkrytie Kamchatki" [The Expedition of Semen Dezhnev and the Discovery of Kamchatka], in *Vestnik Leningradskogo universiteta*, Vol. 3, No. 12 (December, 1948), pp. 36–47.

Okun, S. B. "K istorii Buriatii v XVII v." [Concerning the History of the Buriat Region in the Seventeenth Century], in *Krasnyi Arkhiv*, No. 3 (1936), pp. 153–91.

Peizen, G. "Istoricheskii ocherk kolonizatsii Sibiri" [Historical Essay on the Colonization of Siberia], in *Sovremennik*, Vol. 77, No. 9 (1859), pp. 9–46.

Pypin, A. N. "Pervaia izvestiia o Sibiri i russkoe eia zaselenie" [First Information about Siberia and Its Settlement by Russians], in *Vestnik Evropy*, Vol. 26, No. 8 (August, 1891), pp. 742–89.

Safronov, S. A. "Materialy o vozniknovenii zemledeliia sredi iakutov" [Materials on the Emergence of Agriculture among the Iakuts], in *Istoricheskii Arkhiv*, Vol. 5 (1950), pp. 50–73.

Sbignev, A. "Okhotskii port s 1649 po 1852 g." [The Port of Okhotsk from 1649 to 1852], in *Morskoi Sbornik*, Vol. 105, No. 11 (November, 1869), pp. 1–92; Vol. 105, No. 12 (December, 1869), pp. 1–63.

Shashkov, S. S. "Rabstvo v Sibiri" [Slavery in Siberia], in *Sobranie Sochinenii*. St. Petersburg, 1898. Vol. 2, pp. 503–48.

Shumakher, P. V. "Pervyia russkiia poseleniia na sibirskom vostoke" [First

Russian Settlements in Eastern Siberia], in *Russkii Arkhiv*, No. 5 (1879), pp. 5–36.

Shunkov, V. I. "Geografiia khlebnykh tsen v Sibiri v XVII v." [Geography of the Grain Prices in Siberia in the Seventeenth Century], in *Voprosy Geografii*, No. 31 (1953), pp. 169–205.

———. "Iasachnye liudi v zapadnoi Sibiri XVII v." [The Iasak-Paying People of Western Siberia in the Seventeenth Century], in *Sovetskaia Aziia*, No. 3 (1930).

Spasskii, G. V. "Svedeniia russkikh o Amure v XVII stoleti." [Information of the Russians Concerning the Amur River in the Seventeenth Century], in *Vestnik imperatorskogo russkogo geograficheskogo obshchestva*, Vol. 7, Pt. 2 (1853), pp. 15–42.

Tokarev, S. A. "Kolonialnaia politika moskovskogo gosudarstva v Sibiri v XVII veke" [Colonial Policy of the Muscovite State in Siberia in the Seventeenth Century], in *Istoriia v shkole*, Vol. 4 (July–August, 1936), pp. 73–99.

Ustiugov, N. V. "Bashkirskoe vosstanie 1662–1664 gg.," [Bashkir Uprising in 1662–1664], in *Istoricheskie Zapiski*, No. 24 (1947), pp. 30–110.

Vernadsky, George. "The Expansion of Russia," *Transactions of the Connecticut Academy of Sciences*, Vol. 31 (July, 1933), pp. 393–425.

———. "Gosudarevye sluzhilye i promyshlennye liudi vostochnoi Sibiri XVII veka" [The State Servitors and Promyshlenniks of Eastern Siberia in the Seventeenth Century], in *Zhurnal Ministerstva Narodnogo Prosveshcheniia*, Vol. 16 (March–April, 1915), pp. 332–54.

Zamyslovskii, E. D. "Zaniatie russkimi Sibiri" [The Seizure of Siberia by the Russians], in *Zhurnal Ministerstva Narodnogo Prosveshcheniia*, Vol. 223, Pt. 2 (1882), pp. 223–50.

INDEX

Baiterek (Tungus prince), 93
Baiton, Afanasii, 469–70, 473–74, 482
Bakaian (Iakut girl), 228
Bakhan-Ubash (Black Kalmyk), 378
Bakhrushin, Sergei V., lxiv–lxvi
Bakhteiarov, Enalei, 188–89, 237
Baksha, Achik, 369
Baksheev, Vasilii, 482
Baldach (Baldachin, Boldach) (Daur prince), 215, 217, 233, 264, 266
Balganch (Iukagir shaman), 193
Balkh, 396
Balun (Daur), 265
Balushkin, Onufrii, 492–94
Banandyrsk people, 454, 455
Banbulai (Daur prince), 263, 264, 274
Bantukhai, Serenzab (Mongol taisha), 485, 487
Barabanshchik, Lavrentii, 235–36
Bardakov people, 80
Barguzinsk, 459
Bariatinskii, Ivan, 385
Bariatinskii, Ivan Mikhailovich, 43
Barneshlev, Andrei Afonasevich, 418, 422, 424–27
Barshen, Ivan, 121
Bartenev, Griaznii, 130
Basandai (Tomsk prince), 51, 52
Basarak (Kuznetsk), 60
Bashkir people, 7, 366
Batulinsk, 143, 462
Batur, 463
Batur, Erden (Mongol prince), 485–87
Baturrusk volost, 349
Bazaiak (Kuznetsk prince), 60
Bebra (Daur prince), 212–13
Becherg (Tungus), 187
Bedarev, Aleksei, 203, 204, 206
Beketov, Petr, xli, 136, 137, 303, 304, 306, 307, 312, 358, 432; Expedition 1629–33 report,

149–50; Lena River expedition report, 138–48
Beklemishev, Mikhail, 456, 480
Belogolov, Ivan, 62, 63
Belogorsk, 56, 57
Belokopytov, Ivan, 474
Belov, M. I., lxviii
Belskii, Fedor, 158, 159
Belskii, Postnik, 51
Belzoi (Mongol), 133
Bender-Abbas, 396–97
Benedikt (monk), see Burlak, Vasilii
Berezovo, xl, 43, 50, 55–57, 68, 80, 183, 187, 242, 244, 245, 366, 432, 441, 478
Betunsk, 449
Bezobrazov, Aleksei Ivanovich, 50
Bezottsov, Hanka Ivanov, 306
Bilchaga (Tungus), 188
Bilgei (Iukagir prince), 187
Biliktei (Mongol), 96
Biliukt (Kalmyk), 389
Bim-lei (Bimbli) (prince of Iar), 88
Biral people, 212
Birkin, Ivan Ivanovich, 75
Bisut, 82
Biunta-taisha (Mongol), 177
Black Kalmyk people [Karakul], lix, 63, 66–68, 73–74, 90, 95, 97, 378
Black Mongol people, 85, 86, 451
Bludov, Samoilo, 388
Bobinin, Vasilii, 413
Boborykin, Fedor, 80
Bobyltsor, Kam, 93
Bogasar people, 74
Bogdanov, Grigorii, 76, 413
Bogdoi, see Bugdykhan
Bogolsk, 50
Boiagir people, 450
Boiar (Tokon), 469
Boiarov, Okseit (Ostiak prince), 53
Bokaka (Mongol), 161
Bokan, 212
Bokangach (Tungus), 455
Bokhara, (Bukhara), 11, 78–79,

391, 398, 417, 436, 446;
Bokhara, 438; Bratsk, 125;
Chinese, 86–91 *passim*, 177,
213, 352, 386, 392, 407, 411;
Daur, 211; Kalmyk, 435;
Mongol, 83, 84, 85, 161, 163,
167–68; Nikan, 272
Copper, 355

Dabambov, Baibol, 115
Dachigin, Iupchaneik (Tungus),
385
Daichin (Bratsk), 203
Dalai Lama, lix
Dalaikia, Sorchi (Mongol), 489
Dalgunt (Iukagir), 193
Danilov, Filip, 322
Danul (Tungus prince), 64
Danzhin-taisha (Mongol), 389
Daralna (Boiagir), 450, 451
Darkhan, Bashk (Mongol), 489
Darkhan, Gonbo (Mongol), 489
Darkhan, Temdekei (Mongol), 489
Dasaul (Daur prince), 260, 263
Daur, 213, 214
Daur people, liv, 185–86, 232,
235–36, 242–46 *passim*, 334,
335, 344, 353, 385, 387, 433,
439, 450–52, 460–61, 472,
483, 485; Khabarov expedi-
tion, 237–41, 251–55, 260–
78; Poiarkov report, 211–15,
217; Stepanov report, 303–10,
314–15
Davar (Daur), 213
Davoshcha (Tungus), 452
Dedaliach (Tungus), 455
Dedeev, Bakchigir, 449
Delgev, Andrei (Iakut), 463
Delhi, 396
Dementev, Sidor, 346
Dementev, Voin, 159, 160
Demiansk, 477
Derbent, 397
Deruik, 55

Derun (Ostiak prince), 56
Dezhnev, Semen Ivanovich, xli,
342; Anadyr River report,
317–33
Diakov, Fedor, xli
Dimetsev, Dydokir (Boiagir
prince), 450
Disease and illness, l, lii, 36–37,
71, 187, 219, 321, 326, 332,
384, 407, 456, 482
Diskin, Kotiug (Giliak), 216
Diubgun (Tungus), 454
Diukach (Tungus), 455
Divov, Semen, 121, 122
Dmitriev, (envoy to Daurs), 353
Dmitrii (Tsar Dmitrii Ivanovich,
the False Dmitrii), 54
Doichin-tabun (Daichin, Taichin)
(Mongol), 777, 161, 162, 164,
168
Doiun-tabun (Mongol), 164, 168
Dolgan people, 142, 147, 173
Dolgikh, B. O., lxviii
Dolgorukov, Mikhail Borisovich,
115
Domozhirov, Boris, 28
Dona (Ostiak prince), 80
Dontyul (Daur prince), 211–12,
215
Dorofeev, Ivan, 340, 341
Dorzei (Mongol), 133
Dorzh, Chin Erden (Mongol tai-
sha), 485
Dosiia (Daur prince), 212, 213,
217
Dosmametev, Konogach, 158
Dubenskii, Andrei Onufreevich,
126–29
Dubin, Andrei, 139, 142
Dubsunsk, 146–47
Ducher people, liv, 212, 215–17,
268–69, 271–72, 274, 277,
302–304, 306, 310, 314–15,
335, 345, 346, 472–73 ·
Dulantsk people, 212

Dural-tabun (Mongol), 162, 164, 166–70, 177
Durei (Iakut), 144
Dutch people: Arctic exploration, 75, 395, 433
Duva, 211
Dvina, 75
Dzhungaria, lviii–lix

Egultai, Mezinbaev, 115
Egupk (Iukagir prince), 340
Eiuk (Iakut), 228
Elatomsk, 497
Elchiukov, Stepan, 385
Elden-taisha (Mongol), 389
Eletskii, Andrei, 27, 28
Eletskii, Fedor Borisovich, 27
Eliseev, Ivan, 368
Elizarov, Grigorii, 64
Elgoz (Ostiak), 55
Emelianov, Sidor, 327, 330, 331
Emelianov, Vetoshka, 329, 333
Enba River, 396
English people: Arctic exploration, 395
Enisei River, xl, liv, lviii, 66, 75–77, 126, 128, 129, 172, 174, 229, 407, 434
Eniseisk, xl, 103, 118–19, 124, 126–32 *passim*, 153, 171–76 *passim*, 182, 183, 185, 187, 200–201, 224–27 *passim*, 242–46 *passim*, 346, 347, 368, 433, 434, 440, 457, 460, 461, 467–68, 470, 475, 478; Avvakum account, 358–59, 366; Beketov report, 136–50 *passim*; furs collected, 1620–21, 92–94
Enochk (Ostiak), 56
Enok (Ostiak), 56
Epanchin, 477, 479
Epei (Tungus prince), 92
Epishev, Semen, 256
Eran (Ostiak), 57
Erastov, Ivan, 220
Eravinsk, 452

Eremeev, Fedor, 120–23
Erensk, 476
Erilov, Denis Vasilevich, 190
Ermolaev, Lev, 381
Ermolaev, Nikifor, 269
Ermolin, Ilia, 140, 141, 215
Ermolin, Ivan, 372
Ermolin, Tretiak, 273–75, 277
Eseisk, 454–56, 480–81
Eseta River (Espe), 389
Esiun (Ducher), 304
Eveseev, Trofim, 342
Evlogoi (Daur), 265
Evsevev, Anton, 308, 309
Evstafev, Ivan, 413
Exiles, xl, liv, 11, 243, 245, 313, 381, 492–93, 496; Avvakum's account, 357–68
Ezhegunsk people, 212

Favorov, Ivan, 398
Fedorov, Ivan, 120, 126, 328
Fedorov, Kozma (gunsmith at Nerchinsk), 453
Fedorov, Kozma (cossack), 459
Fedorov, Kuzma, 276
Fedorov, Nechai, 41, 50
Fedorovich, Nechai, 64
Feodor I (Tsar Fedor Ivanovich), 22, 23, 27, 30, 33
Feodor II (Tsar Fedor Alekseevich), 418–453 *passim*
Filatov, Eufim Varfolomeevich, 171, 180, 183, 185, 190, 192
Filipov, Artemii, 273, 274, 277, 346, 347
Filipov, Danilo, 329
Filipov, Oleg, 256
Firsov, Pozdei, 124
Fischer, Johann E., lxiii–lxiv
Fisher, Raymond H., lxix
Fofanov, Fedor Konstantinovich, 42, 44
Fofanov, Fedor Osipovich, 40
Fofanov, Grigorii, 191
Food, 65, 71, 102, 127, 152–53,

520

Griazev, Ivan, 123
Grigorev, Amalyk, 53
Grigorev, Ivan, 346
Grigorev, Prokofei, 309
Grigorev, Pronka, 307
Grigorev, Rodion, 93
Grigorev, Sidor, 376
Grigorev, Terentii, 146
Gudunov, Matvei Mikhailovich, 98, 101–102, 103, 104, 107
Guin Zaisan (Mongol), 489
Guliugir (Iakut?), 352
Gurev, *see* Iaik
Guriushki, Kultsadai (Mongol), 489
Gurylev, Evsei, 308
Guselnikov, Vasilii Fedotov, 175, 321, 323, 328

Han, Jan, 398
Historiography, Russia, xxxvi, lxiii–lxx; Excerpts from Krizhanich, *A History of Siberia . . .* , 430–42
Hyderabad, 396

Iabolak, 19
Iachmenev, Ivan, 256
Iadrinsk, 96
Iaik [Gurev], 396, 397
Iaiva River, 23
Iakol people, 173
Iakovlev, Grigorii, 71
Iakovlev, Iakim, 344
Iakovlev, Ivan, 327
Iakovlev, Lev, 142
Iakut people, xli, liv, lv, 172, 173, 190, 205, 220, 223, 244, 249, 385, 386, 448–49, 462; Beketov expedition, 136, 137, 140–51; Golovin report, 180–185; petition to Tsar, 348–51
Iakutsk, xl, xli, 180–84 *passim*, 193, 197, 200, 207, 210, 216, 217, 228, 229, 231, 235, 241, 244, 255, 256, 258, 279, 308,

313, 342, 343, 355, 372, 377, 382, 384, 385–86, 418–28 *passim*, 448, 454, 456, 457, 460, 462–64, 466–67, 480, 492; Beketov report, 144–48; servitors, 218–22 *passim*, 242–45, 352–54
Iakutsk Prikaz office, 190, 209
Ialym, 27, 28
Iana River, 180, 193, 219, 229, 243, 244, 492
Ianga River, 180–82, 221
Ianza (Kalmyk), 158–59
Iapanchin, 40, 68, 112, 113–14
Iar, 87
Iarastov, Ivan, 372
Iaravnia Lake, 185
Iarygin, Matvei, 385, 386
Iaryzhkin, Petr, 429
Iasyr, Grigorii, 27
Iazykov, Sergei, 478
Ichora River, 173
Idigei, 462
Idirma River, 138, 139
Ignatev, Ivan, 382
Ignatev, Mok, 318
Ignatevich, Mikhail, 66
Ikirezhsk people, 202, 203, 206
Ikul (Daur), 278
Ilamt (Manchu), 497
Ilchigin, 82
Ildega (prince), 211–12
Ilgulai (Tatar prince), 27, 28
Ilia (Tungus), 367
Ilim River, 194, 206, 218
Ilimsk, 203, 243, 244, 347, 385, 387, 459
Ilin (Tungus), 94
Ilin, Gavriil, 159
Ilin, Sofronii, 492, 493
Iltik (Tungus prince), 92
Imgont (Iukagir), 193
Inakan (Ortusk tsar), 85
India, 395, 396
Indigirka River, xl, xli, 180–81, 193, 219, 221, 229, 242, 243,

Khilkov, Vasilii Ivanovich, 281, 357
Khilok River, 361
Khiva, 396
Khodekin, Fedor, 62
Khodyrev, Parfenii, 143, 144, 148, 179, 200
Kholmogory, 231, 279
Khondynsk people, 317, 323, 324–25, 332
Khonzin, Dural (Mongol), 164–66
Khonzin, Torkhan (Mongol), 156
Khonzin, Ural (Uran) (Mongol), 156, 164–65
Khoranskeii Andrei Andreevich, 120, 126
Khripunov, Gavriil Iudich, 71–72
Khripunov, Iakov Ignatevich, 119
Khudynka River, 211, 213
Kicheg (Mongol), 51, 52
Kichenga (Mongol), 95
Kilan people, 304
Kilarsk people, 352
Kildyg (Tungus), 386
Kilem (Giliak), 216
Kiltig (Iukagir prince), 340
Kimchin River, 82
Kimzhegir people, 173
Kindigirsk, 386
Kindigirts, Naederov (Tungus), 187
Kinotu (Mogulin woman), 51
Kipansk, 92
Kiprian, Archbishop, 105–14
Kiprianov, Petr Savin, 308
Kireev, Ivan, 26
Kirenga River, 139, 140, 173; see also Ust Kirenga River
Kirgeev, 103
Kirgei (Ostiak prince), 64
Kirgizia, 153
Kirgiz people, lvii–lix, 51, 62, 63, 66–68, 71–72, 74, 95, 96, 99, 101, 131–34, 152–53, 156–57, 162, 167, 169–70
Kirgiz River, 82

Kirilov, Isak, 346
Kirilov, Maksim, 188
Kirilovna, Evdokiia, 363
Kirnai, Orest, 146
Kiselev, Iarofei, 318
Kisla, Ivan Ivanovich, 190–92
Kislianskii, Leontii, 465
Kislokvas, Martyn, 202
Kitakin (Tungus), 454
Kitanich (Tungus), 454, 456
Kizyl, Piatun, 120, 123
Klementev, Ivan, 31
Klepikov, Volodimir, 159, 160
Kobylnikov, Petr, 480
Kobyt (Tungus prince), 64
Koch (Iakut), 147
Kochebai (Kirgiz prince), 62, 63, 66
Kochurentevich, Bagai, 33
Kodaul, (resident of Perm), 3–4
Kodogon (Bratsk prince), 150
Kogir people, 173
Kogiun (Anaul), 320
Koiat people, 172
Kokhrom (Ostiak), 56
Kokishkin, Neupokoi, 158, 159
Kokorei (Kokurei) (Daur prince), 260, 263–64, 275, 277
Kokoulin, Pavel, 320, 325, 328, 329
Kolashnikov, Vlas, 159, 160
Kolesnikov, Vasilii, 224, 225–26
Kolkildeev, Temsen, 28
Kolobov, Stepan Nikiforovich, 465–66, 468
Kolortsy people, 186
Kolpa (Daur prince), 213, 214
Kolupai (Anaul), 319, 331–32
Kolyma (Kovyma) people, 221, 229, 340
Kolyma (Kovyma) River, xl, xli, 220, 221, 229–30, 242, 243, 257, 258, 317, 323, 330, 340, 372, 419
Konda, 80
Kondinsk, 53, 54

COLOPHON

Designed and produced by Western Imprints, The Press of the Oregon Historical Society, this volume is the ninth in the Oregon Historical Society's North Pacific Studies Series and first in a three volume set entitled *To Siberian and Russian America: Three Centuries of Russian Eastward Expansion, 1558–1867.*

The text typeface is called Janson. This face, often confused with Jensen and mistakenly attributed to a Dutchman, Anton Janson, in actuality was cut during the last decade of the seventeenth century by Nicholas Kis, a Hungarian who worked in Amsterdam. Janson is part of the Geralde family of typefaces, with an oblique incline in all its letters, and a strong contrast between thick and thin strokes. The curved ear of the lower case g and rounded style of the italic *v* and *w* are earmarks of Janson.

Deepdene is used for all display typography. Created in 1927 by the legendary American type designer, Frederick W. Goudy, Deepdene was one of the first classical faces designed with mechanized typesetting in mind—a merging of beauty and form with modern functions and needs.

The text was set by G&S Typesetters of Austin, Texas; MacKenzie-Harris Corporation of San Francisco, California set the display. McNaughton & Gunn Lithographers of Ann Arbor, Michigan printed this volume on 701b Warren Olde Style, an alkaline paper. A three-piece combination of Roxite cloth and Papan paper was used in the binding.